THE
NEW BOOK
OF
KNOWLEDGE

THE
NEW BOOK
OF
KNOWLEDGE

Grolier Incorporated, Danbury, Connecticut

VOLUME 7

G

G, the seventh letter in the English alphabet, is one of the youngest of our 26 letters. It did not become a separate letter until the time of the Romans. Before that it was the same as the letter C.

The ancient Greeks called their C *gamma* and pronounced it like a G. Another ancient people, the Etruscans, gave their C the sound of K, as in *cat.* When the Romans adapted the Greek alphabet to their own language, they were very much influenced by the Etruscans; they gave their letter C both the Greek G sound and the Etruscan K sound. This proved to be very confusing, so later they introduced a new letter, G, for words with the G sound, and kept the old letter, C, for words with the K sound. The Roman G is used in English today.

In English the sound of G is usually "hard," as in the word *goat.* It has this sound before A, O, and U, before consonants, and when it appears at the end of a word, as in *wag.*

In some English words that are of French origin, such as *rouge* and *beige,* G is pronounced "zh." When followed by N, in words such as *sign, gnat,* or *gnarl,* the G is silent. It is also silent in a number of words with the combination GH, such as *though* or *sight.* In some other words, however, GH has the sound of F, as in *rough.* Quite often too, the letter G is pronounced like a J, as in the word *giraffe.* This G is called the "soft" G.

In music G is the fifth note in the scale of C major. In slang "one G" means the sum of $1,000, and on a report card a G shows that a student's work is good. G is also found in some abbreviations. On a map, G. stands for gulf. In measurement, small g is the symbol for gram, a very small unit of mass. GI is an abbreviation for Government Issue, the name for various kinds of government supplies given to U.S. soldiers during World War II. The popular World War II name for an enlisted man was GI Joe.

Reviewed by MARIO PEI
Author, *The Story of Language*

See also ALPHABET.

GABLE, CLARK. See MOTION PICTURES (Profiles: Movie Stars).

SOME WAYS TO REPRESENT G:

The **manuscript** or printed forms of the letter (left) are highly readable. The **cursive** letters (right) are formed from slanted flowing strokes joining one letter to the next.

The **Manual Alphabet** (left) enables a deaf person to communicate by forming letters with the fingers of one hand. **Braille** (right) is a system by which a blind person can use fingertips to "read" raised dots that stand for letters.

The **International Code of Signals** is a special group of flags used to send and receive messages at sea. Each letter is represented by a different flag.

International Morse Code is used to send messages by radio signals. Each letter is expressed as a combination of dots (•) and dashes (−−).

GABON

Gabon, a former French colony, became an independent nation on August 17, 1960. The republic lies astride the equator on the Atlantic coast of Africa.

▶ THE PEOPLE

Most of Gabon's people live in the large coastal towns of Libreville and Port-Gentil or in settlements along the rivers and in the hills of the north.

The people of Gabon belong to many different ethnic groups. The Fang, who make up the largest group, live mainly in the north but are scattered throughout the country. The Fang were once fierce warriors. Today they are prosperous, settled cacao growers. The Eshira and Bapounou live in the south and east. The Omiéné, a group of small tribes, were the first to come into contact with Europeans. They live along the coast and in the upper Ogooué River region around Franceville and are centered at Lambaréné, Libreville, and Port-Gentil. The Bakota of the northeast are well known for their wood carvings—especially those made of ebony. A few groups of

Libreville, the capital and largest city of Gabon, is a port on the Atlantic coast, north of the equator.

Pygmies dwell in the southern forests. They live by gathering leaves, berries, and wild honey and by hunting and trapping.

Most people in the interior of the country live in villages ruled by a local chief. Authority over a group of villages is held by a religious or clan leader.

The Fang live in houses with corncob walls and thatched roofs. Woven mats of reeds serve as window shutters. Most villages have a few shelters by the roadside that serve as social gathering places.

Gabon has one of the best educational systems in equatorial Africa. Almost all children go to school. French is the official language.

▶ THE LAND

Gabon is bounded on the north by Cameroon and Equatorial Guinea, on the east and south by the People's Republic of the Congo, and on the west by the Atlantic Ocean. Much of Gabon is low and marshy. A broad plateau and several low mountain ranges rise in the north, southeast, and center of the country. There are two rainy seasons—from March to May and from October to December. The two dry seasons are from January to March and from June to September.

Gorillas, hippopotamuses, monkeys, lions, panthers, buffaloes, and pygmy elephants are among the many wild animals in Gabon. But there are few domestic animals because the disease-bearing tsetse fly attacks cattle and horses as well as human beings.

▶ THE ECONOMY

Gabon is sparsely settled and must import much of its food. Manioc, bananas, and yams —the main foods of the people—are grown in the forest clearings around the villages. Other food crops include avocados, pineapples, and mangoes. Some cacao, coffee, peanuts, and palm products such as copra are grown for export.

Wild animals are hunted for meat. Children often go along on trapping expeditions and catch small game with their nets. Fish are caught for food in Gabon's many rivers and along the coast.

Gabon has rich deposits of several minerals. These resources have been greatly developed since the mid-1960's. Gabon has become one of the wealthiest nations in black Africa, with prospects for further growth. Petroleum, found along the coast, is by far the country's most important export. There is an oil refinery at Port-Gentil. Natural gas is also exported. Manganese, uranium, iron, and gold are mined in the interior. Gabon's manganese deposits are among the richest in the world.

Another Gabonese export is the timber of the rare okoume tree. It is made into plywood at Port-Gentil.

In the past the Ogooué River and its tributaries have been the major transportation route for bringing minerals and timber from the interior to the coast. Today many new roads that will not wash away in the heavy rains are being built. The Trans-Gabon Railroad, opened in the late 1970's, links Libreville with the mineral deposits of the interior.

▶ CITIES

Libreville is the capital, chief port, and largest city of Gabon. It is located just north of the equator. Libreville is a modern city much like European cities. Port-Gentil, the nation's second-largest city and port, lies on an island near the mouth of the Ogooué River. The city of Lambaréné is located farther inland on the Ogooué River. There Albert Schweitzer—physician, scholar, and musician—operated a hospital for more than 50 years.

FACTS
and figures

GABONESE REPUBLIC is the official name of the country.

LOCATION: West central Africa.

AREA: 103,346 sq mi (267,667 km²).

POPULATION: 1,250,000 (estimate).

CAPITAL AND LARGEST CITY: Libreville.

MAJOR LANGUAGE(S): French, (official), local languages.

MAJOR RELIGIOUS GROUP(S): Muslim.

GOVERNMENT: Republic. **Head of state**—president. **Head of government**—prime minister (appointed by the president). **Legislature**—National Assembly.

CHIEF PRODUCTS: Agricultural—cacao (cocoa beans), coffee, manioc, bananas, yams, copra (dried coconut), peanuts. **Manufactured**—refined petroleum, timber products, processed agricultural products. **Mineral**—petroleum, natural gas, manganese.

MONETARY UNIT: African Financial Community (CFA) franc (1 franc = 100 centimes).

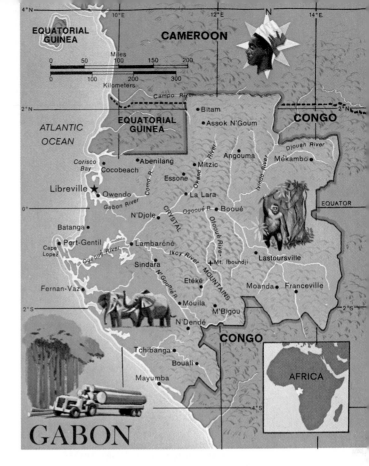

GABON

▶ HISTORY AND GOVERNMENT

The first Europeans to reach Gabon were the Portuguese sailors Lopes Gonsalvo and Fernan-Vaz, who landed there at the end of the 1300's. Little is known about Gabon before this date. This is because the people of this region of Africa had no way of writing down their history, and their tribal legends do not go back very far. It was not until the 1800's that the Fang and many of the other tribes came to the area. The Pygmies are the only people who claim to be the original inhabitants of the Gabonese forests.

European slave traders dealt with the tribes along the coast for several centuries. The French established a permanent naval and trading post in 1839, after signing a treaty with local chiefs. In 1849 a group of freed slaves were landed at the place that later became Gabon's capital, with the name of Libreville (meaning "free town").

During the late 1880's the French gained control first over the coastal tribes and then over the tribes of the interior. French explorers made their way up the Ogooué River into the heart of Africa. Gabon came under French rule in 1903, and in 1910 it became a part of French Equatorial Africa. It remained a French colony until 1958, when it became a self-governing republic within the French Community. Since gaining complete independence in 1960, Gabon has generally maintained close relations with France.

Gabon is headed by a president, elected for five years, who appoints a prime minister to lead the everyday operations of the government. The legislative body is the National Assembly, which is also elected for five years. Since 1967, Gabon has been governed by President Omar Bongo, head of the Gabonese Democratic Party, formerly the country's only legal political party. Popular protests forced the adoption of a new constitution in 1991, allowing opposition parties to compete. In the first elections under the new constitution, in 1993, Bongo was declared the winner despite charges of fraud by his opponents.

JOHN A. BALLARD
University of Ife (Nigeria)

GAINSBOROUGH, THOMAS (1727–1788)

Thomas Gainsborough was an intelligent, lively, and generous man. He loved music, and could play several instruments. But his first love, even when he was very young, was drawing.

At 14 Gainsborough left the town of Sudbury, England, where he was born, to study art in London. After completing his studies he remained in London and tried to earn a living by painting. He was unsuccessful, and in 1746 he returned to Sudbury, where he married Margaret Burr.

No one is completely certain who the subject was for *The Blue Boy*, painted by Gainsborough in 1770.

Although Gainsborough was most interested in landscapes, his earliest success was achieved with his portraits. About 1760 he moved to the resort town of Bath. Before long he was a very popular portraitist there, and his reputation spread to London.

Gainsborough disagreed with Sir Joshua Reynolds, the famous English artist and critic, who wrote that blue could not be used successfully except as a minor color in a picture. To prove his point, Gainsborough painted a picture called *The Blue Boy*, in which he used many shades of blue and almost no other color. A great many people must have agreed with Gainsborough, for *The Blue Boy* has become one of the most popular paintings in the world.

In 1768 Gainsborough was made one of the first members of the Royal Academy, an exhibiting society for artists that still exists. Well-known people in London asked him to paint their portraits. He painted King George III eight times. In 1774 he settled in London, where his popularity grew, and his services continued to be in great demand until his death on August 2, 1788.

HERBERT B. GRIMSDITCH
Former Executive Editor
Fleetway Publications (London)

GALÁPAGOS ISLANDS. See ECUADOR.
GALAXY. See UNIVERSE.

GALILEO (1564–1642)

For most of his life as a scientist, Galileo was engaged in a struggle with a man who had been dead for almost 2,000 years. The man was Aristotle—the greatest scientist of the ancient world.

In Galileo's day Aristotle's writings on science were accepted as absolute truth. Yet, in fact, Aristotle had made many errors. Many of his views would not stand up under questioning—and questioning was Galileo's approach to science. It was an approach that Aristotle himself would have approved. But Galileo had to deal with men who objected to any questioning of the ancient authorities. Fortunately for modern science, Galileo was not easily discouraged.

Galileo Galilei was born in Pisa, Italy, on February 15, 1564. His father, Vincenzo Galilei, was a composer and theorist. Vincenzo had high ambitions for his son—he wanted Galileo to be a doctor. When Galileo was a young boy, the family moved from Pisa to Florence. He received his early education in a nearby monastery.

Then, in 1581, he was sent to the University of Pisa to study medicine. Galileo had little interest in medicine and found his classes boring. But his active and curious mind led him to the world of science.

One day, while sitting in the cathedral of Pisa, Galileo noticed the oil lamps swinging overhead. Some were swinging in higher arcs than others. Galileo expected the lamps with wider arcs to take longer to complete their swings than those with smaller arcs. When he timed the swings against the beats of his pulse, he found that they all took the same amount of time. After experimenting at home, he worked out the laws that govern a pendulum. Galileo used his findings about pendulums to invent a timing device. More important, however, he had set the pattern of his life—a simple observation led to questions and experiments, which led to new knowledge and applications.

Galileo left medical school without becoming a doctor and returned to Florence. By this time he was deep in serious studies of mathematics and science. His writings on physics

Galileo was famous for his studies of the laws of falling bodies and the laws of motion. He was the first person to use a telescope to make important discoveries about the planets and the stars in the Milky Way.

made him known, and he became professor of mathematics at the University of Pisa.

Aristotle had stated that heavy objects fall faster than light ones. This seems true if you drop a coin and a sheet of paper at the same time. The heavier coin reaches the ground first. But this happens because the paper has a large surface, so the paper is held back more by the air. In a vacuum, without air resistance, the coin and the paper would fall together.

In working out the laws governing falling bodies, Galileo is said to have dropped balls of various weights together from the same height. All reached the ground together, proving Aristotle wrong. To measure the speed at which the balls fell, Galileo used a tilted board (an inclined plane) so that the balls would roll slowly enough to be timed. There were no clocks then, so Galileo let water from a bucket run into a measuring cup. Thus he measured time by the height of the water in the cup. His questioning of Aristotle's ideas made Galileo unpopular, and he left Pisa. He moved to the University of Padua, where he was free to teach and to do his research.

Using his knowledge of light and lenses, Galileo constructed the first of his many telescopes in 1609. When he used the telescope to look at the heavens, he saw what no one had ever seen before. The Milky Way was actually composed of many stars. The moon was not, as people had thought, perfectly smooth. It had mountains and craters. Night after night Galileo used his telescope to look at the wonders he had discovered.

In January 1610, Galileo made one of his most important discoveries: The planet Jupiter had moons that revolved around it. According to Aristotle and other ancient people all things revolved around the earth. People still believed this, although some sixty years earlier Copernicus had shown that the earth and planets circle the sun. Galileo's discovery showed that moons revolved around Jupiter, just as Copernicus had described our moon as circling the earth. This was the first evidence that supported Copernicus. And Galileo's description of his discovery gave the first public hint that he believed in the Copernican system.

A short time later, Galileo discovered that Venus, like the moon, went through phases. This could be explained only if Venus was revolving around the sun.

The church, as the chief supporter of Aristotle, opposed the Copernican system. In 1611, however, Galileo visited Rome, where he was given a warm welcome by the pope and other church officials. They were particularly impressed by his telescope.

Galileo was now at the height of his fame, but he was soon to fall from favor. Everything he published seemed to support the Copernican system. His last such work was on sunspots—which he and a handful of other men had discovered. Then, in 1616, the Copernican system was condemned by the church as an attack on its teachings. The pope ordered Galileo to stop supporting it. Galileo promised to obey.

In the meantime Galileo had left Padua for Florence, where he continued his other work. He studied magnetism. He worked on some of his inventions. He perfected the compound microscope. Finally, he turned back to the Copernican system. He could not leave it alone. As a Catholic he had no desire to quarrel with his church. But at issue was the right of a scientist to seek the truth.

In 1632, Galileo published *Dialogue on the Two Chief Systems of the World,* a clever book that consisted of a conversation among three men with different ideas about the universe. Galileo pretended not to take sides, but there was no doubt that the winner of the argument was the man who supported the Copernican system. Galileo was called to Rome, imprisoned, and forced to deny his belief. He was allowed to return home, but only when he promised to stop writing on astronomy.

Galileo spent his last years confined to his villa near Florence by order of the church. But he was allowed to teach. He carried on his research. He invented new instruments. He also wrote his great book on motion and mechanics, summing up his work in this field.

Through all these years, Galileo kept up his varied and lively interests. He had always been talented in many fields. He was an artist; he played the lute and the organ; he wrote songs, poems, and literary criticism. These and even his scientific writings were lively and witty in style, designed for a large audience. It is no wonder that he was one of the few people to become known to all by his first name. There was only one Galileo.

Indeed, it was Galileo's way of writing that probably caused the most trouble between him and the authorities. Galileo was the first scientist to write in language that ordinary people could understand. In an age when most scholars still wrote in Latin, Galileo chose to write his books in Italian.

Galileo's many discoveries, theories, inventions, and books are all important. But his main achievement is that he established for all time the need and the right of scientists to question. Above all, he insisted on searching for the truth. He was still searching when he died on January 8, 1642. As we now know, he had laid the groundwork for modern physics. And his search would be carried on by scientists like Isaac Newton, born the same year Galileo died.

PATRICIA G. LAUBER
Author, *The Quest of Galileo*

GALL. See INDIANS, AMERICAN (Profiles).

GALTON, SIR FRANCIS (1822–1911)

Sir Francis Galton was an English scientist who made important contributions to many fields—statistics, meteorology, heredity, and genetics—and who originated the study of eugenics, a science concerned with controlling human traits through selective breeding.

Francis Galton was born near Birmingham, England, on February 16, 1822. He studied at Cambridge University but was much more interested in travel than in a formal education. He divided his university years between study and travel until the death of his father in 1844. He then used his inheritance to travel full-time. Galton became famous for his explorations through little-known parts of southwestern Africa and the Middle East from 1850 to 1852, for which he received a gold medal from the Royal Geographical Society (a famous society of explorers). He was elected to the Society in 1860.

Galton did little traveling after this period but he had the curious and inventive mind of a scientist and spent most of his life investigating fields that caught his interest. Galton believed that all things could be measured. He developed several statistical formulas and techniques to measure and study the role of hereditary characteristics in human biology and intelligence. He was also the developer of the idea to use fingerprints to identify people and of the idea to chart the weather.

Galton's major interest in the latter part of his life was heredity. Ever since his cousin Charles Darwin had proposed that human beings had evolved from other species, Galton had been fascinated by the notion that human beings could affect their own evolution and improve the human race. Galton proposed that if intelligent people married each other, their children would be of "superior" quality. This controversial theory was criticized by scientists who believed that intelligence is the result of culture and the environment as well as genetics. Galton's research developed into the eugenics movement in the late 1800's. In 1909, Galton was knighted for his life's work. He died in Surrey, England, on January 17, 1911.

RACHEL KRANZ
Editor, Biographies
The Young Adult Reader's Adviser

GAMA, VASCO DA (1460?–1524)

Vasco da Gama, a Portuguese sailor, was the first European to find a sea route to India. His discoveries helped open trade between western Europe and Asia and made Portugal a great power in the 1500's.

Da Gama was born in Sines, Portugal, about 1460. By that time, Portuguese sailors had already begun to explore the west coast of Africa. Then in 1487, Bartholomeu Dias (1450?–1500) sailed around the Cape of Good Hope, at the southern tip of Africa.

In 1497, King Manuel I of Portugal asked Da Gama to continue Dias' explorations. Da Gama sailed from Lisbon on July 8, 1497, with four ships and about 170 men. Instead of following the African coast, as earlier explorers had done, he sailed boldly into the South Atlantic. After three months out of sight of land, Da Gama reached the Cape of Good Hope. Fierce winds and high seas hammered the ships. Finally they fought their way around the Cape to the point Dias had reached. Da Gama sailed up the east coast of Africa, stopping at Mozambique and the ports of Mombasa and Malindi in what is now Kenya. At Malindi, Da Gama obtained the services of an experienced Arab seaman to guide him across the Indian Ocean. In May 1498, after a voyage of ten months, Da Gama landed in Calicut (Kozhikode) on the southwest coast of India. Here Da Gama was able to acquire samples of valuable spices and precious stones before sailing for home. In September 1499, over two years after setting out, Da Gama returned to Portugal. He had sailed over 24,000 miles (38,600 kilometers).

King Manuel rewarded Da Gama with the title Admiral of India and sent him on a second voyage to India in 1502. Other Portuguese adventurers established colonies in southwest India, and in 1524, Da Gama was sent there as viceroy (royal governor). He died in India on December 24, 1524.

Reviewed by HELEN DELPAR
Editor, *The Discoverers: An Encyclopedia of Explorers and Exploration*

GAMBIA, THE

The Gambia, a small nation of West Africa, is one of the most oddly shaped countries on the African continent. It consists of a narrow strip of land, ranging from about 15 to 30 miles (24 to 48 kilometers) wide, situated on both sides of the Gambia River. Except for a small coastline on the Atlantic Ocean, The Gambia is completely surrounded by the territory of the nation of Senegal. The Gambia was formerly a British territory, before gaining its independence in 1965.

▶THE PEOPLE

Most Gambians belong to one of the country's five major ethnic groups. These include the Mandingo (the largest group), Fula (or Fulani), Wolof, Jola, and Serahuli. The Gambians are mainly settled farmers, except for the Fula, who are nomadic herders of cattle.

Language and Religion. English is the country's official language, but various African languages are spoken. The great majority of the people are Muslims. Christians make up about 5 to 10 percent of the population.

▶THE LAND

The Gambia extends inland about 200 miles (320 kilometers) from the Atlantic Ocean. It is a low-lying country, rising no more than 240 feet (73 meters) above sea level. The Gambia River, which runs the length of the country, is the dominant geographic feature. Thick mangrove swamps line both sides of the lower half of the river. Farther inland the country is more open. The mangrove trees give way to a flat area, which floods during the wet season. Farther from the river, the land rises to a grassy plateau, which extends into Senegal. Much of the soil is poor, and The Gambia has almost no mineral resources.

Climate. The climate is subtropical with two distinct seasons—wet and hot, and dry and cool. Temperatures range from about 60 to 110°F (16 to 43°C), depending on the season and location. The Gambia receives about 35 to 45 inches (900 to more than 1,000 millimeters) of rainfall a year, mainly between June and October.

Banjul. Banjul (formerly called Bathurst) is The Gambia's capital and largest city, with a population of about 50,000 in the city proper and more than 100,000 in its metropolitan area. Located on St. Mary's Island at the mouth of the Gambia River, it is the country's seaport and the center of the important peanut processing industry.

Peanuts, The Gambia's chief crop, are loaded on board a small steamer on the Gambia River. Running the entire length of the country, the river is The Gambia's dominant geographic feature and the main source of transportation to the interior.

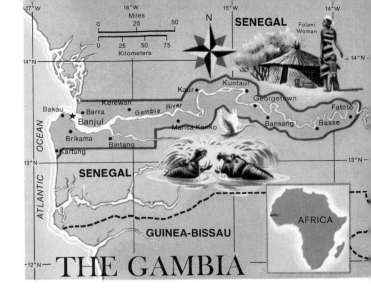

THE GAMBIA

▶**THE ECONOMY**

The Gambia's economy is based almost entirely on agriculture. Peanuts are the most important crop and the country's chief export. Rice is grown along the riverbanks, and millet, manioc, corn, and beans are cultivated farther inland. Cattle are raised on the grassy plateau. Industry involves the processing of peanuts and animal hides and the manufacture of clothing and handicrafts.

Schoolgirls in Banjul, capital of The Gambia, enjoy a brief recess from class. Primary school for Gambian children begins at age 8 and lasts for six years.

▶**HISTORY AND GOVERNMENT**

Early History. The inhabitants of what is now The Gambia probably migrated to the region from present-day Senegal. The first Europeans, the Portuguese, arrived in the area in 1455. During the late 1600's and 1700's, Britain and France competed for trade in the region. The Treaty of Versailles in 1783 granted the territory around the Gambia River to Britain. The country's unusual borders came about as a result of Britain's 1889 treaty with France, which controlled Senegal.

Independence and After. The Gambia gradually moved toward independence in the years following World War II. It gained self-government in 1963 and complete independence in 1965. A constitution adopted in 1970 proclaimed The Gambia a republic with a president, elected for five years, as head of state and government. The elected legislative body is the House of Representatives.

In 1982, The Gambia joined with Senegal to form the Confederation of Senegambia. The armed forces of the two countries were merged and an economic union was planned, but the confederation was dissolved in 1989.

The Gambia's longtime president, Sir Dawda K. Jawara, governed the country from independence until 1994, when he was overthrown in a military coup led by then Lieutenant Yahya Jammeh, who took control of the government. Jammeh was elected president in 1996, but the voting was considered flawed.

R. J. HARRISON-CHURCH
London School of Economics
and Political Science
Author, *West Africa*

GAMES

Do you have a favorite game that you enjoy playing with your friends or family? Do you like to play chess or checkers, or do you prefer playing video games? Did you know that many of the games we play today are similar to games that were played thousands of years ago?

Games are played throughout the world by people in all cultures and in all walks of life. Some games reflect the particular history or traditions of the people who play them. Others are remarkably similar from one culture to another. While this may seem surprising, it actually reflects the fact that some games have ancient origins and have been passed down from one culture to another throughout history.

▶ ORIGINS OF GAMES

Games have been played since the beginning of civilization. The most popular game of ancient Egypt was Senat, a game in which

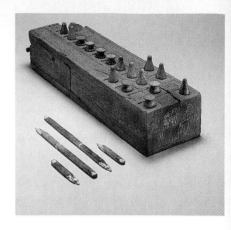

Examples of games found in ancient Egyptian cities and tombs include the popular Senat (*right*) and the slate game board (*opposite page*) probably used to play Mancala or Wari.

counters, or markers, were moved around a game board. Moves were determined by the way thrown sticks landed on the ground. For the ancient Egyptians, Senat symbolized the struggle between good and evil. The games known as Mancala or Wari are among the oldest games, dating as far back as 5000 B.C. In these games, beans, seeds, or other small objects were moved around a playing board with

Card games first became popular in Europe during the late 1300's. This painting of a playing card factory in France in the 1600's shows enthusiasts how their favorite decks of cards were produced during that period.

hollowed out cups. A player tried to capture as many objects as possible. Variations of Mancala or Wari are still played throughout much of Africa and in other places, including India, Java, and the Philippines.

Sources of Information on Early Games

It is often very difficult to identify the origins of games because many games evolved over centuries and modern versions often bear little resemblance to their predecessors. Important sources of information on early games are archaeological artifacts, (objects that were made and used by a culture at a certain stage in its development), ancient writings, and early laws.

Archaeologists have learned about early games through artifacts discovered in ancient tombs and temples. When the tomb of Tutankhamen, an Egyptian king who reigned from about 1348 to 1339 B.C., was discovered in 1922, Senat game boards were found inside. Mancala game boards, which are more than 3,500 years old, have also been found at ancient sites in Egypt. Archaeologists have also learned about games through pictures on ancient buildings and objects. A mural painted on the wall of an ancient Egyptian tomb shows two people playing the finger game of "odds and evens." A painting on an ancient Greek vase shows the heroes Achilles and Ajax playing *tablé*, a game similar to backgammon. Such pictures help clarify how early games were played and how game artifacts were used.

Information about games has also come from various ancient writings. The Greek poet Homer (700's B.C.) wrote about the playing of games and referred to a game similar to backgammon. Some early manuscripts from China and the Middle East also discuss games, including chess and games using dice.

Other historical sources of information about games are written laws. Ancient Roman laws of more than 2,000 years ago outlawed gambling. This showed that gambling games existed. In Europe in the 1500's, laws were written that restricted where people could play marbles!

Beginning as early as the 1200's, books about games were written. These books made it easier to trace the origins of games. From the late 1600's to the mid-1700's, Edmond Hoyle (1672–1769), an English lawyer, compiled the rules of many adult games. His book, *Hoyle's Games*, became the foundation for many of the reference books that have been written about games since then.

The Role of Early Games

Some ancient games originated for reasons other than enjoyment. For example, some were associated with myths or religious beliefs and served to teach or reinforce these ideas. Ancient card and dice games probably began as ways of predicting the future. Some ancient writings mention the "casting of lots," or the throwing of arrows or stocks, to foretell future events. Cards are still used today as a fortune-telling device.

Other games probably originated as a way of training young people in skills—such as hunting and fighting—that were necessary for their survival. Native American children, for example, learned accuracy and dexterity (mental and physical quickness) by throwing darts through rolling hoops. In addition to teaching physical skills, some games helped to sharpen mental skills. The game of chess, involving strategy and planning, is a good example of an early game that helped to develop a player's mental abilities.

The painting on this Greek vase from the 500's B.C. shows the warriors Achilles and Ajax playing *tablé*, an early version of backgammon.

This illustration of Arabs playing chess (*left*) was painted for a page in a collection of books commissioned by Philip II of Spain (1165–1223). The knight, queen, and bishop (*right*), carved out of walrus ivory during the 1100's, are part of a collection of chess pieces found on the Isle of Lewis, off the coast of Scotland.

Although most games today are played for enjoyment, the connection to learning and to the sharpening of skills still exists. Many games require players to use imagination, reasoning, quick thinking, coordination, speed, and other mental or physical abilities.

▶TYPES OF GAMES

Games can be classified into several groups according to the method of play or the format of the materials. Such classifications are very general, however, because many games use elements from more than one group.

Board Games

A board game is a game played on a flat surface called a game board, which may be decorated. Board games have been played for more than 4,000 years. The earliest game boards that have been discovered are more than 3,500 years old. In Asia, board games seem to have developed at a later date, perhaps not until about 400 B.C. Board games were very popular in ancient Greece and Rome, and from there they spread to other parts of Europe. It is thought that some early games may have had a religious purpose.

Board games generally involve two basic types of play—strategy and racing, and many board games are a combination of both. The objectives of games of strategy are to capture or block opposing pieces, to gain control of larger portions of the game board, to enter pieces on the board so that a number of them form a row, or to trap or eliminate a prey. In racing games, the primary objective is to begin at one point on the game board and race along one or more paths to a finishing point.

Strategy Games. Many strategy games have been played in one form or another for centuries. Checkers, which is called draughts in England, was played in Europe in medieval times. The game probably derived from much older games played in the Middle East and Egypt. For example, the British Museum in London has an ancient Egyptian game board and primitive "checkers" dating from about 3,000 years ago. Other variations of checkers include halma, which was invented toward the end of the 1800's, and Chinese checkers, which derived from halma. The objective of both halma and Chinese checkers is for players to move their pieces into the area of the game board opposite their own. In both games, unlike checkers, pieces that are jumped are not removed from the game board.

A copy of a wall painting from the tomb of Nofretari, wife of Ramses II (1304–1237 B.C.). The Egyptian queen is shown playing Senat.

Another strategy game with a long history is chess. It is believed that chess developed in India sometime around the 500's A.D. From there it spread to Persia and Arabia and entered Europe through Italy and Spain. The form of the game as it is now played probably developed about 400 years ago.

Although it is uncertain how or where backgammon originated, it is thought to be much older than chess. The ancient Romans played a game very similar to it. The game probably developed from the rolling of dice and keeping score of rolls by moving a counter along a track. Called trictrac in some countries, backgammon was called tables in early Europe.

Another strategy game with ancient origins is Nine Men's Morris, also known as Mill, Morelles, or Merels. Game boards for a "Morris" type game have been found carved in the roofing slabs of an ancient Egyptian temple dating from between 1400 and 1300 B.C. During the Middle Ages the game was very popular in Europe, and it is one of the oldest games played there. Nine Men's Morris is played on a game board marked with three squares, one inside the other, and with points in the centers of the squares' sides connected by lines. At the beginning of the game, each player has nine "men" (counters or playing pieces). The object of the game is for each player to try to capture an opponent's piece and to prevent the opponent from moving any pieces. There are different versions of the game, including Three Men's Morris, Five (or Six) Men's Morris, Eleven Men's Morris, and Twelve Men's Morris. A related game is Noughts and Crosses, a version of tic-tac-toe.

The game of Go is an ancient Asian strategy game that probably originated in China about 4,000 years ago. Known in China as Wei-ch'i, the game spread from China to Korea and then to Japan, where, known as I-Go, or Go, it became very popular. Go is a type of war game. While the object of many war games (including chess and checkers) is to capture enemy forces, the objective of Go is to enclose areas of your opponent's territory through the movement of playing pieces. It was introduced to Europe in the 1880's.

Fox and Geese originated in northern Europe during the Viking period. Early references to the game have been found in Icelandic writings from the 1100's and ancient game boards have been found carved in English castles and Roman churches. Over the centuries, there have been many versions of the game. The design of the game board, the number of pieces, and the procedures for making moves have differed from country to country as well. Generally, the game is played with one piece representing the fox and several other pieces representing the geese. The aim of the fox is to eliminate geese by jumping over them. The aim of the geese is to trap the fox so it cannot move or capture more geese.

A Japanese wood-block print from the 1600's shows a man and a woman playing the ancient strategy game of Go.

Racing Games. One of the oldest racing games is the Game of India, also known as Pachisi. This game, which is thought to have originated in Asia more than a thousand years ago, is the forerunner of many modern race games. The objective of the game is for players to try to be the first to get all their playing pieces around the game board from start to finish. The playing area of the game board is

This game board was produced around 1890. It was used in the Game of Four Nines, a version of the Game of India, or Pachisi, which originated in Asia. If you own a Parcheesi game, notice how similar your game board is to this one.

in the shape of a cross and is divided into small squares. The number of squares a piece can be moved is determined by throwing dice or substitute objects, such as small seashells. If a player's piece lands on a square occupied by an opponent's piece, the opponent must return to the starting point. A version of the game called Ludo was played in England in the late 1800's. Parcheesi, a version of the game first produced in the United States around 1870, remains one of the most popular racing games.

Game of Goose, invented in Italy in the 1500's, was very popular in Europe until the end of the 1800's. In this racing game, players threw a die to determine moves and then raced their counters around a spiral route on an illustrated game board. Certain spaces on the route were marked with symbols (including a goose) and printed instructions that told the player to either throw again, lose a turn, or advance or retreat a certain number of spaces. Game of Goose was a forerunner of racing games in which the progress of the players could be advanced or hindered by landing on certain squares.

In the 1700's and 1800's, many racing games were designed to be educational and to teach morals or useful facts. For example, in a game about geography, a player might advance after discovering a foreign land. In a game that stressed morals, the game board might show everyday scenes with an emphasis on the triumph of good over evil.

Both Snakes and Ladders and Chutes and Ladders developed from earlier racing games.

The Game of Monopoly

Monopoly, one of today's most popular board games, had its origins in the early 1900's with a game called The Landlord's Game. This game, patented in 1904 by Elizabeth Magie, was based on economic principles and sought to teach the foolishness of a property ownership system in which all players attempted to become "monarch of the world." After 1910, The Landlord's Game became known as Monopoly and became very fashionable, especially on college campuses. In time, the game lost its teaching aspect and became only a race for financial dominance.

Monopoly was played in many areas of the United States, and properties on the game board were given regional street names. One version appeared in Atlantic City, New Jersey. In 1933 the game was copyrighted by Charles Darrow, who was once credited with being the game's inventor. Darrow used the Atlantic City street names in his version of the game. These names were kept when Parker Brothers bought the rights to Monopoly in 1935. Rich Uncle Pennybags—the mustached character on the Monopoly box, game board, and cards—was created by Parker Brothers in 1936.

Monopoly is a very popular game. It has been produced in at least 15 languages, and more than 100 million sets have been sold worldwide. Special editions of the game have been made using everything from chocolate to solid gold.

In 1974 a game called Anti-Monopoly was the subject of a lawsuit filed by Parker Brothers, which claimed that the name of the game infringed on their trademark. The suit was successful and thousands of Anti-Monopoly games were destroyed. Several years later, however, an appeal overturned the earlier decision and Anti-Monopoly got its name back.

A modern version of Monopoly.

Upon landing on a square with a snake's head, in Snakes and Ladders, or the top of a chute, in Chutes and Ladders, a player must slide down to a lower square. Upon landing on a square with the base of a ladder, the player climbs up to a higher square.

Dice Games

Games in which objects are thrown to see how they land have a long history. In fact, the objects used in these games are probably the oldest forms of gaming devices. Even before they were used for games, such objects were used as magical devices to foretell the future.

Modern-looking dice have been found in ancient Egyptian tombs dating from 1500 B.C. Such dice no doubt evolved from common objects such as stones, shells, and bones. Stones and shells were scored according to the positions in which they landed. In time, these stones and shells were replaced by bones such as the knucklebones of animals. Because they tended to land in four different ways, these bones were used as four-sided dice. In Asia, sticks used in predicting the future led to the "long dice" still used in some Asian games. These "long dice" have from two to six sides and are rolled rather than thrown. Another variation of dice used in Asia is the teetotum —a device similar to a spinning top with numbers printed on the sides. Today most people are familiar with dice that are six-sided cubes marked on each side with one to six dots.

Over the centuries, one of the most common uses of dice was in gambling. The Roman emperor Nero played dice games and gambled money on each throw. And King Henry VIII of England gambled away the bells of St. Paul's Church in London during a game of dice. In addition to their use in gambling games, dice are also used frequently in a number of board games to determine how far a player will move on the game board.

Tile Games

A tile game is played with pieces called tiles, which may be made of ceramic, wood, ivory, bone, plastic, or some other material. These tiles contain pictures, numbers, or symbols representing numbers. Tile games often do not require game boards.

One of the best-known tile games is dominoes. Although no one knows exactly how the game of dominoes came about, domino tiles,

Backgammon tournaments like this one are popular in the United States. This strategy game has very old origins—early versions were played by the ancient Greeks and Romans.

or blocks, are probably derived from six-sided dice. It is believed that dominoes may have been brought to Europe from China in the 1300's. What is certain is that domino games were being played in Italy by the 1700's. Early sets of dominoes had one to six pips, or spots, per half block that represented the numbers 1 to 6. Some sets included blocks that were blanks. Modern domino sets are similar, although some sets contain as many as nine, or even twelve, pips per half block. A standard domino set has 28 tiles.

There are many ways to play dominoes. The objective of one type of domino game is for players to add tiles to a layout on a playing surface by matching the pips on their tiles with those on tiles already laid down. In another type of game, players do not need to match pips. Instead they add pips to reach a predetermined number.

Mah-jongg, which became a craze in the United States in the 1920's, has been one of the most popular games in China for hundreds of years. The word "mah" means "a flax or hemp plant" and supposedly refers to the sound of the plant's leaves rustling in the wind. The word "jongg" means "sparrow" and is said to recall the chattering of that bird

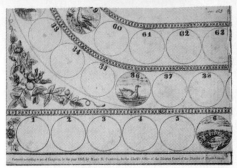

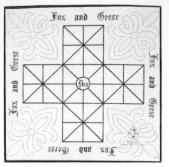

Game of Goose game board, printed around 1855.

Box for the Authors card game, printed in the 1880's.

Fox and Geese game board, printed in the 1940's.

(and perhaps the sound of the tiles clicking together during a game). Mah-jongg can be played with three or four players. A standard mah-jongg set has 144 tiles (136 playing tiles and 8 flower or season tiles). These tiles are grouped into three different suits: circles (or dots), bamboos (or bams); and characters (or craks). The object of the game is to collect sets of tiles and try to complete a hand in a prescribed manner. Scores are calculated, and the player with the most points at the end of the game is the winner.

Card Games

The exact origins of playing cards are unknown. Cards probably first developed in China from painted sticks used in fortune-telling. Over time the symbols painted on these fortune-telling sticks were copied onto gambling sticks, then onto thin strips of oiled paper. The oldest-known playing card was found in Asia and dates from the 1000's.

Early cards may have reached Europe through trade with Asia as early as the 900's. They did not become popular, however, until the 1300's and 1400's. Playing cards began to appear in the present form around the year 1370. The four suits in a card deck represented the four classes of medieval society: Spades represented the nobility; hearts, the clergy; diamonds, the merchants; and clubs, the peasants. These four suits are still used in certain modern card games such as bridge and poker.

Today there are several different types of card games and decks of cards. A standard deck of cards consists of 52 cards divided into 4 suits of 13 cards each, plus 2 jokers. Among the popular games played with a standard deck are bridge, gin rummy, hearts, poker, and I Doubt It. Over the years, a variety of games have been developed that use special decks of cards, including Authors, Uno, Rook, Old Maid, Go Fish, Flinch, and Mille Bornes.

Cards are very versatile and can be used in games involving two or more people, and even individuals. For individuals, there are countless variations of solitaire, or patience, games. With few exceptions, these involve placing a "tableau," or layout of cards, on a table and trying to build up piles of cards that match in color, rank, suit, and so on.

Word Games

Word games require players to make up words, to guess words or phrases, or to answer questions. Some of these games utilize special equipment including tiles, dice, game boards, timers, and so on. Others require nothing more than an imagination and perhaps a pen or pencil and a piece of paper. Some of the games that require little or no special equipment are sometimes referred to as "parlor games" because they were played in the parlor, or living room, before the invention of television.

Scrabble and Related Games. One of the most popular and well-known word games is Scrabble. The game of Scrabble has its origins in the 1930's with the games Lexico and Criss-Cross Words. These two games involved the random selection of lettered tiles; scores were based on the words formed from those letters. In the late 1940's certain changes were made to Criss-Cross Words and the new game was copyrighted and sold as Scrabble. Within a few years Scrabble had become tremendously successful.

Scrabble has been sold around the world in many languages, including Hebrew, Arabic, Japanese, and Russian. There has even been a version of the game in Braille (writing for the blind). International Scrabble tournaments are held, and there are Scrabble handbooks and dictionaries, and a Scrabble newspaper. There have also been various versions and spin-offs of the game, including Scrabble for Juniors and RPM—a speed game with a rotating game

Box for a Little Orphan Annie game, printed in the 1930's.

Go to the Head of the Class game board for the fifth edition, printed in 1949.

Box for the Howdy Doody Carnival game, printed in the 1950's.

board. Since Scrabble was invented, a number of related games have been developed, including Pictionary and Pictionary Junior, in which players draw pictures as clues to help their teammates guess words or phrases.

Pencil and Paper Games. A number of word games can be played with nothing more than a pen or pencil and a piece of paper. While most pencil and paper games involve the formation of words or phrases, a few involve drawing pictures or symbols.

Crossword puzzles are among the most common pencil and paper word games. Anagrams is a related game in which the letters of a word or phrase are combined or rearranged to form another word or phrase.

Other popular pencil and paper games include word building, dictionary, acrostics, and categories. In word building, players choose a keyword of several letters. Players then try to make as many words from it as possible, using each letter in the keyword in any order. A letter may only be used as many times as it appears in the keyword.

In dictionary, also known as lexicon or fictionary, the object of the game is to guess the correct definition of a word chosen from the dictionary. Players take turns finding a word that no one knows. The best words are often those that have humorous, strange, or unbelievable definitions. The person choosing the word reads the word aloud, and then everyone writes a definition for the word on a piece of paper. The person who chose the word then reads all the definitions, including the real definition. Each player chooses the definition he or she thinks is correct. Points are awarded to players who guess the correct definition or to players whose definitions are chosen by others. Points are totaled at the end of the game.

The object of acrostics is to think of words that begin and end with letters written vertically on the left and right sides of a sheet of paper. On the left side, a keyword is written vertically from top to bottom; on the right side, the same word is written vertically from bottom to top. Players must write words that have the same number of letters as the keyword.

Categories, or Guggenheim, is one of the best-known pencil and paper games. In this game, players first choose several different categories, such as animals, colors, rivers, states, and so on. Each player then writes these categories in a vertical column on a sheet of paper. One player then chooses a letter of the alphabet and all players write this letter at the top of a column to the right of the categories. The object of the game is to think of a word for each category that begins with the letter at the top of the column. The game is usually timed and the person who finishes first is the winner.

Questioning Games. A group of games related to word games are those that require players to answer questions. Twenty questions is a simple questioning game. In this game one player thinks of a person, place, or thing, and the other players must guess what it is. Each player is allowed to ask up to twenty questions to act as clues in helping guess the word. By asking questions such as Is it an animal? Is it a vegetable? Is it a mineral?, a player can narrow the choices of what the word might be.

A questioning game that has enjoyed great popularity since its recent invention is Trivial Pursuit. This game has many features of a race board game. Players move their pieces around a game board to reach a finishing point. A die is used to determine moves, and a player can continue moving as long as he or she correctly answers questions read from sets of cards accompanying the game. Squares on the game board represent different categories of questions, and each card contains one question for each category.

Marbles, rope jumping, and rolling hoops are games with very old origins that are played all over the world today. The version of marbles (*left*) played in Colombia, South America, would be recognized in the United States. The Double Dutch rope-jumping competitors from Brooklyn, N.Y. (*below*), could enter a contest anywhere. This youngster (*right*) keeps his hoop in motion in the Caroline Islands, West Pacific Ocean.

Activity Games

An activity game often requires some skill or dexterity. Jacks, pick-up-sticks, darts, and many marble games fall into this category. So do games such as hopscotch, rope-jumping games, tag, and Simon Says. The amount of skill or dexterity needed in an activity game varies from one game to another.

The game of jacks developed from early games using the knucklebones of sheep. Today, these knucklebones have been replaced by star-shaped metal objects called jacks. The game has remained relatively unchanged through the centuries, although there are several variations of it. The game involves throwing a jack or a ball up into the air and picking up other jacks before the thrown object reaches the ground.

In pick-up-sticks, also known as jackstraws, a bunch of sticks are thrown on the ground, floor, or some other flat surface. Then the players try to pick the sticks up one by one without moving any of the others. A player continues to pick up sticks until he or she accidentally moves another stick. The sticks are color-coded for different values, and the player with the most points wins.

The game of darts is thought to have originated in Europe during the Middle Ages. At that time archers carried short, heavy throwing arrows, which they threw at trees for practice. In the winter a section of a tree trunk could be hung on a wall indoors to continue practicing. Later, this activity became a pastime of royalty. The modern dart game dates from the end of the 1800's. In this game, darts are thrown at a round target with numbered sectors. Points are scored according to where the darts hit the target.

Games using marbles have been played since the time of the ancient Egyptians. Versions of marble games were also played in ancient Rome, and games using marbles were a popular pastime of schoolboys during the Middle Ages. There are dozens of different marble games today. The basic idea is for a player to flick a marble so that it hits an opponent's marble, or some other target, according to the rules of the particular game being played. A player generally keeps any marbles he or she manages to hit.

Hopscotch has been played since Roman times. Variations of the game have been

played for centuries by children in countries throughout the world. The game involves drawing a diagram of different spaces on the ground, throwing a marker of some sort onto various spaces, and hopping from space to space according to a specific sequence.

Rope jumping also has ancient origins. Although the exact origins are unknown, the first jumping games were perhaps contests in jumping across a stream or over a rock. In time, vines possibly were used to practice jumping skills. What is known for certain is that rope-jumping games are played by children in almost every country in the world. While there are many different variations in rope-jumping games, a common element in most is the chanting of some rhyme as children jump.

Tag games are played in some form by children everywhere. Some involve rituals that may go back to ancient superstitions—for example, being safe when touching wood or iron. The basic idea of tag games is that one person is "it" and tries to tag someone else to be "it." In some tag games, players are safe if they touch something, such as wood, or cement. In others, players are safe when they do something, such as whistle, stand on one foot, kneel, and so on.

The game Simon Says requires concentration and coordination. In this game players must do everything a leader does—but only if the leader first says "Simon says." It is important for players to pay attention, listen carefully, and realize that the actions a leader does are a mirror image of what they are to do.

Electronic Games

Among the most recently invented games are electronic games—computer or video games that use modern technology. In many of these games, one player can play alone, trying to better a previous score or competing against the computer or video terminal itself. Some of the games can be played by more than one person at a time as well, often by two players competing against each other.

Among the first electronic games were chasing games in which players tried to move around obstacle courses while keeping ahead of pursuers. One of the earliest chasing games was Pac Man. Another type of early electronic game was a simple tennis game in which a light on the screen was knocked back and forth between two bars. These games, as well as many that followed, challenged a player's ability to react quickly and with dexterity to the action on the screen.

Since these early electronic games first appeared, technological advances and sophisticated computer programs have greatly changed the world of electronic video games. While the first games could usually only be played in video arcades, now they can be played at home on personal computer systems or video game systems such as Nintendo.

Electronic video games are based on many sources, including traditional board games, television game shows or cartoon series, and original games designed for video. Since television and computers have become such an important part of our daily lives, electronic video games have become popular as well.

In electronic games such as this Atari Hard Driving game, the player is put in a "real" situation and competes against the computer in the video terminal.

Games have a long history in America. From games played by Native Americans to games brought by the early colonists to games of today, games of all types have played an important role in the lives of American people.

Games of the Native Americans

Long before Europeans came to America, Native Americans played various types of games. These games played an important role in Native American culture.

The games most commonly played among Native Americans include dice games, guessing games, and games of dexterity. Native American dice usually had two sides marked with colors and symbols. They were made of a variety of materials, including bones, shells, peach pits, stones, pottery, and beaver or woodchuck teeth. Dice were either thrown by hand or from a bowl or basket. In Native American guessing games, objects such as sticks or balls were hidden in the hands, in hollow tubes, or in the ground. Players then had to guess where the object was or guess its position.

Native American dexterity games were often tests of strength and hunting skills. They provided an opportunity for players to practice and improve their skills, and for young people to learn those skills. In the game of Hoop and Arrow, players shot or threw arrows at a rolling hoop or ring. Players scored according to the way the arrows fell. In Snow Snake, players threw darts along ice or snow or through the air to see which went farthest.

Games of the 1700's and 1800's

Settlers in the 13 colonies and the early United States certainly played many types of games, most of which were copied or brought from other countries. It was not until the 1790's that cards were manufactured in the United States, and there was little other game manufacturing there before 1843.

The mid-1800's was a time in which religion and morality were stressed, and games associated with gambling were frowned upon. In fact, dice were considered to be "tools of the devil." To avoid this association with dice, many early game makers used teetotums instead. Board games of this period were often designed to reinforce ideas of morality. The game Mansion of Happiness (1843) is an ex-

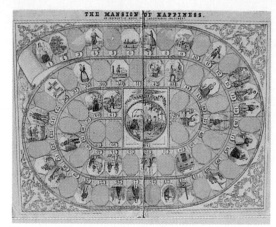

Mansion of Happiness game board, printed in 1843.

ample. The game was a race-type board game in which players moved along a spiraling path toward the Mansion of Happiness. When players landed on a space denoting a virtue, they moved ahead; when they landed on a space denoting a vice, they moved back. For example, landing on Idleness sent the player to Poverty, and players on the Road to Folly had to return to Prudence. The tone of the game can be summed up by two of the rules:

Teetotum

Whoever possesses Piety, Honesty, Temperance, Gratitude, Prudence, Truth, Chastity, Sincerity, Humility, Industry, Charity, Humanity, or Generosity is entitled to advance . . . toward the Mansion of Happiness. Whoever possesses Audacity, Cruelty, Immodesty, or Ingratitude, must return to his former situation . . . and not even *think* of Happiness, much less partake of it.

The Mansion of Happiness indicates something about leisure time in this period. While many games were played purely for enjoyment, games were often expected to be educational as well. In addition to moral teachings, many games of the 1800's were about history, geography, and authors. Many board games used maps, and card games often contained questions and facts.

Early Game Publishers

The game industry in the United States began in the mid-1800's with companies such as W. & S. B. Ives and McLoughlin Brothers.

W. & S. B. Ives, considered the first major game publisher, issued at least two dozen games in the mid-1800's, including Mansion of Happiness and Dr. Busby (a card game). McLoughlin Brothers published games noted for their beautiful covers, game boards, and cards. While other companies published games in the United States during the last half of the 1800's, none had the impact of McLoughlin and the "big three" of the game industry—Milton Bradley, Selchow and Righter, and Parker Brothers.

The Milton Bradley company was established in 1860 in Springfield, Massachusetts. Among its early successes was The Checkered Game of Life, and a pocket-sized version of this game was designed for soldiers in the Civil War. The company kept pace with rapid changes in education in the 1880's and 1890's and produced school supplies in addition to educational games for children and their families. Some Milton Bradley games include Concentration, The Game of Life, Battleship, Password, Stratego, and Yahtzee.

Selchow and Righter, originally established in 1867, patented Parcheesi, The Game of India. Except for this game, the company only sold games produced by other companies until 1927. In the 1950's, the company introduced Scrabble. More recently, it introduced Trivial Pursuit, one of the best-selling games of the 20th century.

The last of the "big three" game publishers, Parker Brothers, was founded in 1883 by George S. Parker. The company's 1894 catalog stated that its factory was "the only large building in America devoted exclusively to parlor games." Parker Brothers has produced such popular games as Boggle, Flinch, Masterpiece, Risk, and Sorry.

A Changing Society

By 1860, innovations in printing allowed games to be mass produced. When chromolithography was introduced in the 1870's, the hand-colored art on game boards and packaging all but disappeared. In the 1880's and 1890's, American society began to change rapidly as industrialization and immigration caused both a movement to cities and a growth of different cultures. In response, game companies expanded their efforts and produced a variety of well-made games. Although many games were still educational, fewer involved moral teachings, and games became accepted as a form of recreation for the family. Among the popular games introduced after 1900 were the card games Pit (1904) and Rook (1906), both created by Parker Brothers. Rook became the largest-selling card game in the world.

The Roaring Twenties was a boon to the game industry. The end of World War I allowed industry to turn from the war effort to the home front, and Americans had earned the right to enjoy their leisure. Uncle Wiggly, a game that had been created in 1916, became as popular as the books on which it was based. Mah-jongg, Chinese checkers, and jigsaw puzzles also became very popular. Many events, including the discovery of King Tut's

Mah-jongg, a popular tile game played in China for centuries, being enjoyed on the balcony of a building in San Francisco (*left*). A strategy game with ancient origins, Chinese checkers is often played on colorful game boards like the one shown above.

This Wheel of Fortune game (*far left*) is played with the popular TV show. The Centipede board game (*left*) is based on an early 1980's video game. A Dick Tracy game board from the 1930's (*below*) displays characters from the famous comic strip.

tomb, the first transcontinental airmail route, Charles Lindberg's transatlantic flight, and American's love for the automobile, became the subject of games. Games continued to reflect what was happening in society.

During the Great Depression in the 1930's, games provided inexpensive entertainment during troubled times. Backgammon and jigsaw puzzles were quite popular at this time. Games that stressed learning, such as Go to the Head of the Class, were also popular, and Monopoly became one of the most popular games of all.

During World War II, war games and games promoting patriotism and the United States became popular. Among these was the Game of States, published by Milton Bradley. Chutes and Ladders, Candyland, Clue, and Scrabble were also introduced during this period. Scrabble was to become the most popular word game in history.

The Impact of Popular Culture

Games have often reflected popular culture and have been based on radio, film, literature, famous people, and other sources. Games were based on such radio programs as "Fibber McGee and Molly" and "The Charlie McCarthy Show." The Wonderful Game of Oz was based on the book *The Wonderful Wizard of Oz*. Other games based on popular literature include Treasure Island, the Hardy Boys Treasure Game, and the Nancy Drew Mystery Game. More recent games have been based on movies such as *Star Wars* and the Indiana Jones series. Famous people, such as Donald Trump and the rock group Duran Duran, have also been the subjects of games. Cartoon and comic book characters, such as Dick Tracy, Donald Duck, Mickey Mouse, and Yogi Bear, have all found their way into games.

Perhaps the most significant impact on games in recent years has been the popularity of television, which changed the course of American games. Television has had many different effects: It offered a leisure activity that took time away from pastimes such as playing games. On the other hand it allowed game manufacturers to reach a mass market with advertisements, and it affected the content of the games that were produced. Games began to be based on popular television shows, especially game shows. This trend continues today with games based on television shows such as *The Simpsons* and *Miami Vice*, and *Jeopardy* and *Wheel of Fortune*.

▶THE FUTURE OF GAMES

Today people have more leisure time and more ways to fill that time. Our daily lives are very different from the lives of people in earlier times. Families are smaller, people are busier, and less time is spent reading or participating in family activities, including playing parlor games.

As electronic computer and video games become more popular, the publishers of traditional board and card games have begun to look for gimmicks, such as three-dimensional games, to recapture people's interest. With society continuing to change, it is difficult to predict what will happen to games in the future. While board and card games may always be around, games of the future may be dominated by electronic and computer technology and by technologies yet to be invented.

BRUCE WHITEHILL
Author, *Games: An Illustrated Resource Guide*

See also BACKGAMMON; CARD GAMES; CHARADES; CHECKERS; CHESS; CROSSWORD PUZZLES; DARTS; DOMINOES; JACKS; MARBLES; PARTIES (Games); VIDEO GAMES; WORD GAMES.

GANDHI, INDIRA (1917–1984)

Indira Gandhi was prime minister of India and one of the outstanding woman political leaders of her time. She dominated Indian politics from 1966 until her death by assassins' bullets in 1984.

Gandhi was born on November 19, 1917, at Allahabad, in Uttar Pradesh state. Her father, Jawaharlal Nehru, was the first prime minister of independent India. She was educated at schools in England and Switzerland as well as in India. In 1942 she married Feroze Gandhi (no relation to Mohandas K. Gandhi), a lawyer. They had two sons, Rajiv and Sanjay.

Gandhi was briefly involved in the movement that led to Indian independence in 1947. After Nehru died in 1964, she served as minister of information and broadcasting under his successor, Lal Bahadur Shastri. She became prime minister following Shastri's death in 1966.

Unmatched as a politician, Gandhi exercised a powerful hold over millions of Indians, particularly in the countryside. India's quick victory over Pakistan in 1971, during the civil war between West and East Pakistan, increased her popularity. In 1975, however, a high court ruled that she had violated election laws in 1971 elections. Refusing to resign, Gandhi declared a state of emergency. She suspended constitutional government and ruled virtually as a dictator from 1975 to 1977.

As prime minister of India, Indira Gandhi dominated her country's political life from 1966 until her assassination in 1984.

She fell from power in 1977 elections, but returned to office in 1980.

During the next four years, Gandhi was faced with growing political unrest, especially in the states of Jammu and Kashmir, Assam, and Punjab. In Punjab extremists from the Sikh religious group sought to break away from the Indian union. As violence increased, Gandhi, in June 1984, ordered military action against armed Sikh agitators barricaded in the Golden Temple, the Sikh shrine at Amritsar. This action worsened a situation that had already become explosive. Four months later, on October 31, 1984, Gandhi was shot to death by two of her Sikh security guards. She thus became the second of India's great political leaders to die by assassination. She was succeeded as prime minister by her son Rajiv.

BALKRISHNA G. GOKHALE
Author, *The Making of the Indian Nation*

See also GANDHI, RAJIV; INDIA, History (Recent History); NEHRU, JAWAHARLAL.

GANDHI, MOHANDAS KARAMCHAND (1869–1948)

Gandhi was modern India's greatest spiritual and political leader. It was mainly through his efforts that India won independence from Britain. A shy, gentle, frail man, Gandhi tried to teach his people to avoid violence and to struggle for independence by peaceful means. Many Indians considered Gandhi a saint. They called him *Mahatma*, meaning Great Soul.

Gandhi was born in Porbandar, India, on October 2, 1869. His large family belonged to the Hindu merchant caste (class). In India early marriages were customary, and Gandhi was married at the age of 13. When he was 18, he left for London to study law.

In 1893, Gandhi started a law practice in South Africa. To protest the harsh treatment of Indians in South Africa, he led a campaign of civil disobedience. He was sent to jail but won some reforms from the government.

Gandhi returned to India in 1915. During World War I, he helped the British. But after the war ended in 1918, he began a movement of nonviolent resistance to British rule to win self-rule for India. He became a leading figure in the Indian National Congress, a political party working for Indian independence.

Gandhi's methods included fasting (refusing to eat), peaceful disobedience, and boycotting (refusing to buy) British goods. Once, to protest a salt tax, he led his followers to the sea, where they made salt from seawater. He was jailed many times for his anti-British ac-

Mohandas K. Gandhi was a leader in India's struggle for independence from Britain. He helped achieve this goal in 1947 through a policy of nonviolent protest.

tivities. In jail he would often fast as a sign of protest. The British, fearing he would starve to death, usually released him quickly.

Gandhi also worked to improve social and economic conditions in India. He fasted for better treatment of the untouchables (Hindus without caste) and to keep peace between warring Hindus and Muslims.

Independence came to India in 1947. Because the Hindus and Muslims could not agree, the country was divided into separate nations—India and Pakistan. On January 30, 1948, as he walked to his evening prayers, Gandhi was shot and killed by a Hindu fanatic opposed to partition.

ROBERT I. CRANE
Syracuse University
See also INDIA, History (Mahatma Gandhi).

GANDHI, RAJIV (1944–1991)

Rajiv Gandhi was prime minister of India from 1984 to 1989. He succeeded his mother, Indira Gandhi, in office after her assassination in 1984. He, too, was killed by assassins, while seeking re-election in 1991.

Gandhi was born in Bombay on August 20, 1944. He was the elder son of Indira and Feroze Gandhi, and a grandson of Jawaharlal Nehru. Gandhi was educated in India, and in England. In 1968 he married the Italian-born Sonia Maino. They had a son, Rahul, and a daughter, Priyanka. In 1972, Gandhi began his career as an Indian airline pilot. He showed no political ambition, until the death of his younger brother, Sanjay, in an air crash in 1980.

Gandhi gave up his pilot's job, and in 1981 ran for and won the seat that his brother had held in the Indian Parliament. He served as general secretary of his mother's Congress Party and became its president in 1983. Chosen prime minister after his mother's death in 1984, he won an overwhelming victory for his party later that year, and became prime minister in his own right.

Gandhi began well, promising to fight corruption, streamline the government, and im-

Rajiv Gandhi succeeded his mother, Indira Gandhi, as prime minister of India, serving from 1984 to 1989.

prove the economy. However, he was soon caught up in a scandal involving arms purchases for the Indian army. His use of Indian forces in the violent separatist movement by Tamils in Sri Lanka was also controversial. In 1989 elections, his party suffered defeat and Gandhi resigned, becoming leader of the opposition.

When new elections were called for in 1991, Gandhi began a vigorous campaign to bring his party back to power. But on May 20, 1991, he was killed by a terrorist bomb at Periambur, near the city of Madras.

BALKRISHNA G. GOKHALE
Author, *The Making of the Indian Nation*
See also GANDHI, INDIRA; NEHRU, JAWAHARLAL.

GANGES RIVER

The Ganges River is the famed sacred river of India. It starts high in the Himalayas of northern India, at a point about 10,000 feet (3,000 meters) above sea level. The main headwaters of the Ganges are the Alaknanda and Bhagirathi rivers. These are fed by the melting snows and glaciers of the Himalayas. After passing through mountains for about 100 miles (160 kilometers), the Ganges leaves its narrow gorge to enter its plain at Hardwar. From there it flows southeast across northern India into Bangladesh, finally emptying into the Bay of Bengal.

Throughout its course of about 1,600 miles (2,600 kilometers), the Ganges receives water from many tributaries, draining a region about one-fourth the size of all India. Some of the large tributaries are the Jumna and Son rivers on the west, and the Ramganga, Gogra, Gumti, Gandak, and Kosi rivers on the east. The Ganges is joined by the Brahmaputra River in Bangladesh. Together these rivers have built the Ganges-Brahmaputra Delta, covering most of Bangladesh and part of India.

During the summer months, rains from the southwest monsoon fall over India. At this time the Ganges carries a great amount of water and is several miles wide in many places. Flooding is common in a number of sections of the plain and is often a serious problem in the delta. The width of the river is reduced in the dry season.

Several hundred million people live in the valley of the Ganges. Most of them are farmers, who live in thousands of villages. The cultivation of food grains and other crops is their main occupation. Other people live in the towns and cities, where they work in industries, business, schools, colleges, hospitals, and government. Some of the important cities of the Ganges Valley are New Delhi, Allahabad, Kanpur, Banaras, and Calcutta.

This enormous population can live in the Ganges Valley because the land is flat and there are fertile soils in many areas. However, the Ganges River is of vital importance in providing sufficient water to irrigate crops. A large system of canals carries water from the Ganges and its tributaries to the wheat-growing areas of the north and to the rice lands in the southeast Ganges Valley.

Hindus travel long distances to bathe in the waters of the Ganges River.

Reverence for the Ganges River is an important part of Hinduism. Ancient Hindu literature says the Ganges sprang from the feet of the god Vishnu. To Hindus the river is *Ganga Mai* ("Mother Ganges"), the mother of all rivers. Bathing in the Ganges is of great religious importance to Hindus. They believe the river has the power to purify the soul by washing away all sins, and that drinking its water cures illness.

At many places along the Ganges there are *ghats* (flights of steps leading into the water). Here devout Hindus bathe before praying. The *ghats* are also used for meditation, for the cremation of Hindus after death, and for the scattering of their ashes in the river. Holy cities are located at a number of special places on the banks of the Ganges. Each has its temples and *ghat*. Among the holy cities that attract large numbers of pilgrims are Hardwar, Allahabad, and Banaras. One of the most celebrated religious bathing centers in India is at Allahabad, where the Jumna River flows into the Ganges. Many Hindus believe this is the holiest place in the world. Every twelve years, millions of pilgrims gather here to cleanse their souls or to die near the most sacred of rivers.

DAVID FIRMAN
Towson State University

GARBO, GRETA. See MOTION PICTURES (Profiles: Movie Stars).

GARDENS AND GARDENING

Making a garden is one of the pleasantest of pastimes.

Even your first garden can be a success if you plan it carefully and work at it faithfully. In the beginning it is best to select flowers or vegetables that are easy to grow in your area. Then there will not be any bare patches in your garden to discourage you. It is best, too, to start with a small garden so that you will be able to care for it properly.

Gardening is a year-round activity. You can start in the winter by planning your garden, work on it through the spring and summer, and gather your harvest in the fall.

Planning is one of the most important steps. It depends on the plot of ground you have to make into a garden and on the kind of garden you like best.

▶ WHAT KIND OF GARDEN DO YOU WANT?

If you would like to have a flower garden, you can plant either a bed or a border of flowers. A bed can be any shape you like, but for a beginner a rectangular garden is easiest to work with. In it you might plant rows of tall flowers for cutting, like asters, snapdragons, marigolds, and zinnias.

Or you might have an informal garden made up of masses of flowers of many heights, colors, and fragrances. Gardens of this kind are called English, or old-fashioned, gardens. Hollyhocks, foxgloves, marigolds, stock, candytufts, and pansies are some of the flowers usually grown in them. If you have a big flower garden, it is nice to have a grass path or two leading through it. Then the garden is tied in with the rest of the yard.

A border of low-growing flowers can be planted to edge a walk, lawn, or driveway or to set off a garden of taller-growing flowers.

If you decide to raise vegetables, you will probably want to start with a small garden where you can raise just enough for your family's use. This is called a kitchen garden.

It is also possible to raise flowers and vegetables together. Flowers can be used as a border around a vegetable garden, and certain vegetables and herbs are nice in a flower garden or around the edges of it. Carrots look good in a flower garden, because they have lovely, graceful foliage. Peppers are decorative, and kale has beautiful curly green leaves. Herbs like parsley, savory, basil, sweet marjoram, sweet lavender, and thyme can be grown with your flowers or separately in an herb garden. If you have a trellis or fence, you can train climbing flowers like morning glories and sweet peas or vegetables like cucumbers and red cherry tomatoes to grow on it.

▶ SELECTING THE PLOT

Once you have decided on the kind of garden you would like, the next step is selecting the best place for it. It is easier to take care of a garden if it is near the house and near a source of water. The spot you select should have sunlight at least 5 or 6 hours a day. A sheltered spot with a southern exposure is best of all.

The ground should be almost level, with just a little slope for drainage. Try to stay away from trees, shrubs, and stones. It is hard to work around them, and tree roots may rob your garden of moisture. The best soil is well drained, loose, and high in humus content. Humus is soil in which leaves and other vegetable or animal matter have decayed.

▶ PLANNING YOUR GARDEN

The success of a garden depends a great deal on the planning that is done beforehand.

First map out your garden in detail by drawing it to scale. You can use a scale of ½ or ¼ inch to a foot. Your plan should show the plants you intend to grow, where you are going to place them, the number of rows you will have, and the amount of space between each row. Be sure to keep in mind the size of each plant when it is fully grown so that you will not have an overcrowded garden.

If you are raising flowers, you might start with a garden 3 feet by 12 or 15 feet. Do not make it any wider than 4 feet, or you will not be able to lean across it to work on the flowers

---

This article will help you plan, plant, and care for a garden. The descriptions and photographs will help you learn about and recognize many popular garden plants. Related articles on gardening include FERTILIZERS; LAWNS; PLANT PESTS; and WEEDS. Vegetable and fruit gardening are covered here and in the articles VEGETABLES and FRUITGROWING. By using the index you can find specific articles on many different fruits and vegetables.

For information and ideas on indoor gardening, see the articles HOUSEPLANTS and TERRARIUMS. Special gardens grown for research and public display are described in BOTANICAL GARDENS. If you want information on plant biology or specific plant features, refer to the article PLANTS.

Floribunda roses.

Larkspur.

A formal garden bordered by sweet alyssum.

Border of rudbeckia, sweet alyssum, petunias, and phlox.

Vegetable garden.

Azalea garden.

PLAN FOR A FLOWER GARDEN

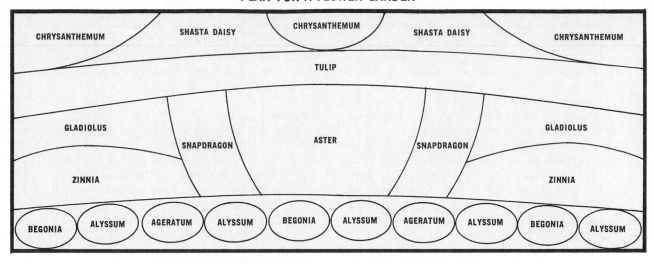

in the center of the bed. For a vegetable garden a good size is 12 feet by 16 feet. You will have to stand between the rows to weed, so leave at least a foot between them. If you are raising larger vegetables, you may have to leave as much as 3 feet.

If the ground slopes, plan the rows so that they run across the slope like the rows of benches in a football stadium, rather than up and down. Then rainwater will be caught and held, and the soil will not wash away.

Annuals, Biennials, Perennials

Before you decide where to place each kind of flower and vegetable, there are several things to consider. The first is the number of years a particular plant will live. Some plants grow from seed, bloom, and die all in 1 year. These are called annuals. Some plants complete their growth in 2 years. They are called biennials. Other plants live for a number of years. These are called perennials.

In a flower garden biennials and perennials

ANNUALS

Ageratum	Nicotiana
Balsam	Pansy
Candytuft	Petunia
China aster	Portulaca
Cornflower	Snapdragon
Cosmos	Stock
Impatiens	Sweet alyssum
Larkspur	Sweet pea
Marigold	Verbena
Nasturtium	Zinnia

PERENNIALS AND BIENNIALS

Bleeding heart	Oriental poppy
Canterbury bell	Peony
Chrysanthemum	Phlox
Columbine	Primrose
Delphinium	Rose
Dwarf iris	(bedding, climbing)
English daisy	Shasta daisy
Foxglove	Sweet william
Hollyhock	Viola
Lily of the valley	Violet

BULBS, CORMS, RHIZOMES, AND TUBERS

Canna	Hyacinth
Crocus (spring and autumn)	Iris
Dahlia	Jonquil
Daffodil	Lily
Gladiolus	Narcissus
Grape hyacinth	Tulip

SHRUBS

Azalea	Mock orange
Beauty bush	Mountain laurel
Boxwood	Privet
(American and English)	Rhododendron
Chinese redbud	Rose of Sharon
Dogwood	Saint-John's-wort
Flowering quince	Scotch broom
Forsythia	Spirea
Hibiscus	(bridal wreath)
Hydrangea	Sweet shrub
Lilac	Viburnum
Magnolia	Virgin's bower
Malva, or mallow	Witch hazel

should be planted where they can stay for more than 1 year. But some annuals should be planted among them. This is because many perennials bloom early in the spring. The annuals, like zinnias and marigolds, bloom much later, but they continue to bloom all summer long. By planting some annuals among the perennials, you will have flowers throughout the growing season.

In a vegetable garden, plan to keep the perennials like asparagus, rhubarb, and strawberries separate from the annuals. (The strawberry is a fruit, but it may be grown in the vegetable garden.) Place them together on one side of the garden where they will not interfere with the rest of your gardening. On the other side, plant together all the vegetables that will be ready for harvesting at about the same time.

Consider the Height of the Plants

Another thing to consider in deciding where to place the different kinds of flowers and vegetables is the height to which each plant will grow. Flowers show off well if they are arranged according to height: the tallest flowers at the back of the garden, the shorter flowers in front of them, and the low-growing border flowers at the very front. While you are arranging your flowers according to height try to place them so that the colors look attractive together too.

In a vegetable garden, tall plants, like sweet corn, beans raised on poles, and tomatoes tied to wooden stakes, should be placed so that they do not shade the shorter plants. If the rows in your garden run from east to west, place the taller-growing plants to the north. If your rows run north and south, place the taller plants in the center of the garden or on the north end.

Choose the Right Planting Time

On the plan of your garden you will also want to include a planting date for each kind of flower and vegetable. The instructions on seed packets will guide you. Always read and follow these instructions carefully. Some seeds can be put in the ground before the last killing frost in the spring. Others must not be planted until the ground is warm. Seeds that are planted later in the season must have enough time to mature before the first frost in the fall.

You will need to know the dates of the last killing frost in the spring and the first killing frost in the fall in your area. You can get this information from your local agricultural agent, your state school of agriculture, or the United States Department of Agriculture.

Equipment

You will need seeds and bulbs from a reliable seed firm or nursery. You will also need a spade or a shovel for turning over the soil, a hoe for weeding and breaking up the soil around the plants, a garden rake, and a trowel for transplanting (digging up plants and moving them to another spot).

In addition, you may need fertilizer or manure for poor soil, lime for acid soil, twine and stakes to tie up tall plants, and a small duster or sprayer to keep plants free from bugs.

▶ MAKING THE GARDEN

Now you are ready to begin the actual work of gardening. This includes the preparation of the soil, planting, and transplanting.

Preparing the Soil

If you are planning to make a garden in the spring, and grass is growing on the spot you have chosen, turn over the ground in the previous fall. If there are leaves you can collect around the yard, turn them under the ground, where they will rot during the winter and nourish the soil.

You do not need a fertilizer for rich soil. But if the soil is poor, you can enrich it in the spring with compost, manure, or a commercial fertilizer. Compost is made by piling fallen leaves or lawn clippings in a sheltered spot and letting them rot. This mixture can then be spread on the ground. If you use manure, you will need 100 pounds for every 100 square feet of garden. If you use a commercial fertilizer, follow the directions for its use.

When you spade your garden, dig about 10 or 12 inches deep. Dig when the ground is dry and crumbly. If you work when the earth is wet, it will cake. Do not spade the entire garden at once. Just prepare a section at a time for planting.

After you have spaded the soil, hoe and rake it until it is smooth. Small seeds, like carrot, radish, and lettuce seeds, should be

Rose gardens.

Formal layout of rose garden.

Gardens at Birr Castle, Ireland.

Grass and flower design at an Italian villa.

Luxembourg Gardens, Paris, France.

Gardens of the Villa d'Este, Lake Como, Italy.

Gardens at Versailles near Paris.

Japanese garden surrounding a pond.

Spanish moss in Charleston, South Carolina.

Garden in the grounds of Christ Church College, Oxford, England.

Rock garden bordering steps.

Rock garden and woods.

Hilltop rock garden.

Lilac with dogwood tree in background.

Azaleas.

Forsythia.

Flowering quince and field of narcissus.

Rhododendron with mountain laurel in background.

Hydrangea and lilies.

Geraniums, petunias, zinnias, and marigolds used in window and ground planting.

Geraniums and petunias in a window box.

Hanging baskets in Rotterdam, the Netherlands.

Raking the soil.

Making a furrow for seeds.
Sowing a row of seeds.

planted in finely raked soil. For larger seeds or small plants, called seedlings, the soil may be coarser.

Planting Seeds

When you are ready to mark off the rows in your garden, place a string on the ground as a guide. You can use the handle of your hoe to make a furrow—a long, shallow groove in which to plant small seeds. A corner of the blade of the hoe can be used to make a furrow for larger seeds.

Many people make the mistake of planting seeds too deep in the ground. Just think of the way wild flowers grow. Their seeds fall right on top of the ground. Most garden flowers should be planted ¼ inch deep. A good general rule is to plant a seed at a depth of three or four times its width.

Cover the seeds with light soil so that the little plants can push their way up easily. Plant more seeds in each row than the number of plants you expect to have in that row. Not all the seeds will germinate, or sprout. If you find you have too many plants in a row, they can be thinned out and transplanted later on.

Some seeds do not grow well if they are planted in an open garden. They need special

conditions of warmth, moisture, and darkness in order to germinate. They must be started in wooden flats, or boxes, in the nursery, in pots in the house, or in a sheltered part of the garden. When they develop into seedlings, they can be transplanted to the part of the garden where they will stay. This group of seeds includes flowers such as snapdragons, giant and double petunias, and ageratum; and vegetables such as tomatoes, peppers, and eggplants. (Most home gardeners buy small vegetable plants to set out. They do not try to raise them from seed.)

Transplanting

Seedlings are ready for transplanting when they have one or two pairs of leaves. When you take up seedlings to transplant them, be sure that there is a good ball of soil around the roots. Be careful not to damage the roots or the tops of the plants. For each plant dig a hole twice as wide and twice as deep as the ball of soil. Set the plant a little deeper in the ground than it was originally so that the roots are not exposed. But be careful not to place the plant so deep in the ground that the growing point, or stem, is covered.

Planting Bulbs, Corms, Rhizomes, and Tubers

Some of the most colorful flowers in the garden and a number of vegetables are raised from underground stems, rather than from seeds. There are several types of underground stems. They are known as bulbs, corms, rhizomes, and tubers.

A **bulb** is short and rounded. It is made up of layers of overlapping leaves. In the center of the leaves is a bud, which will grow into a plant. The leaves contain food to nourish the bud as it grows. Onions, lilies, and many spring flowers, including tulips, narcissus, and hyacinths, all grow from bulbs.

Spring-flowering bulbs are planted in the fall. Some are planted earlier than others, so it is important to follow the growing instructions for the particular kind you buy. A general rule for planting bulbs is to place them in soil 2½ times as deep as the bulbs themselves. Plant them stem-end up and root-end down. When the plants have bloomed and their leaves have died, bulbs go through a period of dormancy (rest) before their roots start to grow again in the fall. Some bulbs can be left in the ground to bloom year after year.

Corms look like bulbs, but instead of being made up of layers of leaves, they are a solid mass of food for the growing plant. The crocus and the gladiolus are both corms. Spring-blooming crocuses are planted in the fall, and fall-blooming varieties are planted in August. The corms should be planted 3 or 4 inches deep. Crocuses look best when they are planted 2 or 3 inches apart in clumps, rather than in rows.

The gladiolus blooms in the summer. The corms (usually called bulbs) can be set out in

Transplanting broccoli seedlings.

Crab apple seedling.

a number of plantings from early spring through early summer so that there are blooms all summer long. The corms should be planted from 3 to 6 inches deep, depending on their size. Gladiolus corms will not survive the winter if they are left in the ground, so they must be lifted when their blooming season is over and stored in a cool, dry place.

Another kind of underground stem is the **rhizome**. It looks like a long, thick root. Irises and cannas, the brilliant summer flowers often seen in formal public gardens, grow from rhizomes.

Irises bloom in the spring and early summer. They should be planted in the late summer and early fall. The rhizomes are planted so that they lie along the ground close to the surface. They are never planted upright as a bulb is. The ground should be pressed down firmly after planting. Rhizomes grow longer each year and develop new buds. After several years irises should be lifted and divided.

Cannas are planted in the spring when the danger of frost is past. In cool climates they must be taken out of the ground in the fall.

The potato and the vegetable known as the Jerusalem artichoke are examples of another underground stem—the **tuber**. Tubers, like corms, are solid masses of plant food. They develop buds called eyes. New plants grow from these eyes. You can grow potatoes by cutting up a potato and planting the pieces that have eyes. Tubers are planted deeper in the ground than rhizomes.

Some plants, like the dahlia and the sweet potato, grow from a swollen underground root rather than from a stem. This root is often called a tuber, but it is more correct to call it a tuberous root.

Bulbs.

Tubers.

▶ CARE OF THE GARDEN

Beautiful flowers and delicious vegetables are the gardener's reward for the care he gives his garden all summer long.

Watering

The garden should be watered as soon as seeds and bulbs are planted. Most flowers and vegetables need about an inch of water a week. If less than that amount of rain falls, give your garden a good watering once a week. Be sure to soak it thoroughly so that the water goes all the way down to the roots of the plants. It is a good idea to water in the early morning or late afternoon. If you water in the middle of the day, when the sun is hottest, the moisture will disappear too quickly.

Mulching

After your plants are above the ground, hoe or rake the soil around them very slightly when it is dry. This will make what is called a dust mulch. A half inch of dust mulch keeps the ground moist near the roots of the plants. You can also shade the soil from the sun by placing leaves, straw, or grass clippings on the ground around your plants. Or you can use peat moss, peanut hulls, buckwheat hulls, corncobs, or sawdust. These are all called mulch materials.

Weeding and Cultivating

If you use enough mulch, you will not have to cultivate your garden (break up the soil around the plants), and there will be few weeds to pull. If you have a garden of low-growing plants that cover the ground, you need not cultivate, either. The few weeds that appear can be pulled out by hand.

In a garden without mulch, which must be cultivated, be careful not to hoe the ground when it is wet. It will cake, and the plants will have difficulty pushing their way through it.

It is a good idea to spray your plants from time to time with a good fungicide-insecticide combination. Start when the plants are a few inches high. Do not wait until plant diseases or garden pests appear.

Harvesting

Vegetables should be harvested when the crop is at its peak. Pick the vegetables when the plants are dry, and store them in a moist, cool place.

▶ GARDEN FLOWERS

If you are going to have a flower garden, start with the flowers you like best. But there are other things to consider, too, in making your selections.

It is wise for a beginning gardener to plant seeds that are easy to grow. Marigolds, zinnias, sweet alyssum, and nasturtiums are among the easiest flowers to grow.

Some flowers grow better in certain parts of the country than they do in others. Sweet peas, larkspur, and California poppies, for example, grow better where the summers are fairly cool. Petunias, portulaca, asters, marigolds, nicotiana (flowering tobacco), sunflowers, cosmos, and zinnias all do well where the summers are hot.

Another thing to consider is the season when flowers will bloom. If you are careful to choose some spring, some summer, and some fall flowers, your garden will be in continuous bloom for many months.

Spring Flowers

Most of the earliest spring flowers grow from bulbs and corms. Often before the last snows have melted, low clumps of lavender, purple, yellow, and white crocuses appear. Crocuses can be planted in the lawn as well as in the garden. They will come up year after year if their leaves are allowed to wither before the grass is cut. After the crocuses the members of the narcissus family begin to bloom. There are the narcissus itself, a fragrant flower with white petals around a short center crown, or cup; the daffodil, which has bright yellow petals around a deep center cup; and the yellow jonquil, which grows in clusters on a single stem.

Then the hyacinths appear. These are short, fragrant spikes of blue, white, or rose-colored flowers. They are especially pretty when they are planted in informal clusters. Tulips are an important part of any spring garden. They have been cultivated for centuries. Today they bloom in almost every color from pale ivory to deep purple. There are some two-toned tulips, and the fringed petals of the parrot tulip are often flecked with green. Yellow, white, and purple irises add color to the garden in the late spring. It is believed that the fleur-de-lis, which was the symbol of royal France, was an iris.

Many favorite spring flowers are perennials. Columbines, primroses, English daisies, violets, and lilies of the valley are in this group. Wild blue and white violets can be transplanted and grown in the garden. The lily of the valley, with its sweet-smelling white flowers shaped like tiny bells, grows well in a shady spot. Each year the plants increase. One of the largest and most striking of the spring perennials is the peony. Its flowers are made up of velvety white, pink, or deep-red petals. The plant, which is 2 or 3 feet tall, is like a shrub or bush.

A number of other spring flowers must be planted every year or 2 years for the best results. Richly colored pansies and delicate-blue forget-me-nots are in this group. Both are low-growing and combine well with spring bulbs. Sweet William, a relative of the carnation, is one of the most brilliant of spring flow-

Massed tulips and daffodils.

Tulips and other spring plants in Keukenhof Gardens, the Netherlands.

White hyacinth and grape hyacinth.

Crocuses in the snow.

Lilies of the valley.

Pansies.

Wisteria framing doorway and window.

Redbud tree.

Peony borders.

Poppies with background of foxgloves.

added advantage: the more they are cut, the more flowers they produce. Among all the bright colors, the fuzzy ageratum adds a misty note of blue.

The taller annuals include the cutting flowers like zinnias, marigolds, and spiky snapdragons, which come in white and shades of yellow, pink, and red. In this group, too, are four-o'clocks, which open every afternoon at 4; blue cornflowers, or bachelor's buttons; and nicotiana, the heavily perfumed white tobacco flower. One of the tallest annuals is the cosmos, a flower of Mexican origin that resembles a daisy. Although it looks delicate, it blooms until the first frost.

A number of other summer favorites are either biennials or perennials. Many of the old-fashioned garden flowers are in this group. There are white, pink, and blue Canterbury bells; blue delphinium; and purple, yellow, and white foxgloves. All three produce graceful spears of blossoms. The clove-scented phlox has clusters of bright flowers with contrasting eyes like the sweet William. Lemon-yellow, orange, or red day lilies bloom for only a day, but as one lily fades another blooms on the same stem. Red, yellow, and white hollyhocks, which may reach a height of 9 feet, make a colorful background for the summer garden.

The rose is the best loved and most fragrant of all the summer flowers. It has a woody stem and is actually a shrub. Roses have been cultivated for many hundreds of years. Bouquets of dried roses have been found in Egyptian tombs. Today there are more than 1,000 varieties of cultivated roses. They have all been developed from the five-petaled wild rose. Most of the roses grown in gardens today are double flowers. This means that they have many petals. The home gardener raises roses from plants rather than seeds.

Cultivated roses are found in every shade from silvery white to deepest purple, although there is no true blue. Roses are divided into three large groups: bedding roses (those that are planted in beds), climbers, and shrubs. Bedding roses include tea roses, hybrid teas (those bred from two different varieties), floribundas, and such old-fashioned types as the French, moss, and damask roses. Climbing roses grow along fences and walls. They include the ramblers, which can be trained

ers. Each stalk of the plant has a rounded cluster of white, pink, or red blossoms. The blossoms have eyes, or centers, of a contrasting color.

Summer Flowers

Just as bulbs are the stars of a spring garden, annual plants are the stars of a midsummer garden. Gardeners prize annuals, because they produce a great many flowers. The flowers are brightly colored and make a beautiful display. Many of them are excellent for cutting as well.

The low-growing annuals are used for both beds and borders. A popular edging plant is the lacy sweet alyssum, with its white or lavender blossoms. Spicy petunias bloom all summer long. The portulaca carpets the ground with vivid red, pink, yellow, white, and purple flowers. Yellow, orange, and red nasturtiums are always favorites. They are so gay and easy to grow. Dwarf French marigolds and dwarf zinnias are colorful and have an

Snapdragons.

Sweet peas.

Portulaca in blossom.

Zinnias.

Petunias and geraniums bordering a porch.

PLANTING CHART FOR POPULAR FLOWERS AND VEGETABLES

FLOWERS (SEEDS)	WHEN TO PLANT	WHERE TO PLANT	SPACE BETWEEN PLANTS	BLOOMING SEASON
Ageratum	Early spring[1]	Sun	10–12 in.	Summer to fall
Bachelor's button	Early spring	Sun	8–12 in.	Early to middle summer
Candytuft	Spring,[1] early fall[2]	Sun	8–12 in.	Midsummer
China aster	Early spring[1]	Partial shade or sun	10–12 in.	Summer to fall
Cosmos	Spring,[1] fall[2]	Sun	10–12 in.	Summer to fall
Hollyhock	Early spring, fall[2]	Sun	24 in.	Spring to early summer
Larkspur	Spring,[1] fall[2]	Sun	6–8 in.	Summer to fall
Marigold	Spring[1]	Sun	10–14 in.	Summer to fall
Nasturtium	Spring[1]	Sun	8–12 in.	Summer to fall
Pansy	Late Summer[1,2]	Partial shade or sun	6–8 in.	Spring to summer
Petunia	Spring[1]	Sun	12–14 in.	Summer to fall
Phlox	Spring[1]	Sun	6–8 in.	Summer to fall
Poppy	Fall[1,2]	Sun	6–10 in.	Spring to summer
Snapdragon	Spring,[1] fall[2]	Sun	6–10 in.	Summer to fall
Stock	Early spring[1]	Sun	12 in.	Summer
Sweet alyssum	Spring	Sun	12 in.	Midsummer to frost
Sweet pea	Spring,[1] fall[2]	Sun	6–8 in.	Midsummer
Zinnia	Spring[1]	Sun	8–12 in.	Summer to fall

[1]Plant in cold frames or flats for early blooming.　　[2]For next year's bloom.

VEGETABLES	NEEDED FOR 25-FT. ROW	DISTANCE APART Rows	DISTANCE APART Plants	EARLIEST PLANTING TIME	READY FOR HARVEST AFTER SOWING
Bean, lima (bush)	2 oz.	18 in.	6 in.	10–15 days after last frost	70–90 days
Bean, snap (bush)	2 oz.	18 in.	4 in.	After last frost	45–65 days
Beet	½ oz.	12 in.	1 in.	Before last frost	45–80 days
Carrot	¼ oz.	12 in.	1 in.	Before last frost	65–80 days
Corn	1 oz.	24 in.	24 in.	After last frost	60–100 days
Lettuce	¹⁄₁₆ oz.	12 in.	1 in.	Before last frost	60–90 days
Onion	¼ oz.	12 in.	1 in.	Before last frost	130–150 days
Parsley	¹⁄₁₆ oz.	12 in.	6 in.	Before last frost	65–90 days
Pea	4 oz.	18 in.	2–3 in.	Before last frost	40–80 days
Radish	¼ oz.	12 in.	½ in.	Before last frost	20–50 days
Spinach	¼ oz.	12 in.	3 in.	Before last frost	30–60 days
Squash	¹⁄₁₆ oz.	36 in.	36 in.	After last frost	75–120 days
Tomato	8 plants	36 in.	36 in.	5–15 days after last frost	100–140 days

The information on planting time for flowers and vegetables is general. Read instructions on seed packet.

over arches and trellises. Shrub roses are large types that grow in a spreading, bushy form. Some reach a height of 15 feet.

Two summer flowers are grown from underground stems, the gladiolus and the lily. The gladiolus is one of the best cutting flowers. Its long spikes of blossoms are both colorful and long-lasting. Of the many varieties of lilies, the tall golden-banded lily is a good choice for a summer garden. It has fragrant white blossoms banded in gold.

Late Summer and Fall Flowers

Among the flowers you will find in late summer and fall gardens are dahlias, asters, marigolds, and chrysanthemums. If you plant dahlias where they will have lots of sunshine, you will be rewarded with quantities of blossoms. There are both single and double dahlias in a wide range of colors and sizes. Some dahlias are tiny pompons of petals. Other blooms are the size of saucers. Asters look like daisies, but they have several rows of petals. Year after year, perennial asters will fill the fall garden with white, pink, and lavender flowers. Chrysanthemums, like dahlias, come in a variety of colors and sizes, and may be either single or double. Shasta daisies and marguerites are both chrysanthemums. The chrysanthemums are among the last flowers to fade from the garden in the fall.

▶ GARDEN VEGETABLES

Of all the vegetables grown, the average family uses only about 25. From that number it is not difficult to select the ones you would like to have in your garden. There are leafy vegetables, or the foliage crops, such as celery, cabbage, lettuce, and spinach; the root crops, which include beets, radishes, carrots, and turnips; the edible seed crops, such as beans, corn, and peas; and the vegetable fruits, such

Marigolds with background of ageratum.

Shasta daisies, phlox, nemesia.

Varieties of chrysanthemums.

as tomatoes, cucumbers, cantaloupes, peppers, and squash.

If you raise vegetables, do not plant the same kind of crop in the same part of the garden each year. The soil will lose much of the elements that that particular crop takes from it. If you plant a foliage crop in one part of the garden the first year, then plant a root crop there the next year, and a seed crop in that section the third year.

The vegetables that you and your family prefer and the size of your garden have a great deal to do with the plants you decide to grow. Carrots, beets, beans, radishes, and lettuce can all be grown close together, so they are all good choices for a small kitchen garden.

Tomatoes, sweet corn, squash, and cucumbers need more space and are good choices for a larger vegetable garden. But if you are especially fond of any one of these, you might be willing to give it the space it needs, even in a small garden.

Do not try to raise potatoes if you are a beginner. Excellent potatoes can be bought at the store. Spend your time instead on vegetables like sweet corn, peas, or tomatoes, which are especially delicious when they are homegrown. It is wise, too, to avoid planting vegetables that are difficult to grow. Cauliflower and celery are in this category.

Find out whether your particular climate and soil are well suited to the vegetables you would like to raise. Cabbage, for example, does best in a cool, moist climate and rich soil. Lettuce and spinach cannot stand heat, so they are raised early in the spring or late in the summer. Beets do not do well in an extremely warm climate, unless planted early. But tomatoes, cucumbers, eggplant, and peppers all thrive in heat. The seeds of some plants germinate quickly, and those of others more slowly. In a small garden in which you are trying to use every inch of ground to advantage, you can plant in the same row seeds like radishes that sprout quickly and seeds like beets that germinate more slowly. This is called intercropping. The first crop is eaten by the time the second is ready.

If you would like to have a continuous supply of a certain vegetable, you can plant it more than once in a season. An early crop, a summer crop, and a late crop of peas, beets, snap beans, carrots, and lettuce are often grown. In the late summer there may be enough left over to can. But if this is your first garden, you might prefer to try just one planting.

▶ GARDEN FRUITS

Many popular fruits, such as apples, peaches, pears, plums, and cherries, are grown on trees in orchards. But a number of small fruits, like berries and melons, are grown in the garden. Fruits have one disadvantage for the gardener who is starting on a small scale. They require a large amount of space in which to grow.

But if you would like to have at least one fruit in your garden, you might try strawberries. Even one row of strawberry plants will yield a large number of juicy red berries. Buy the plants and set them out in the early spring. The plants should be placed a foot apart. Strawberry plants develop runners, which spread over the ground, so leave about 3 feet between rows. It is important to keep the strawberry patch well weeded. The first year the plants will not bear fruit, but the second year they will bear generously.

Red and black raspberries, blackberries, red and black currants, and blueberries all grow on bushes. Currants need a moist, cool climate, and blueberries need acid soil. All of these berry bushes must be set 3 or 4 feet apart in rows 6 to 8 feet apart.

Grapes grow on vines that are trained over wire or wooden arbors. A vine does not produce grapes until it is 2 years old, but then it will bear for 50 years or more.

Melons must be planted from seed each year. Cantaloupes, honeydew melons, and watermelons need a long, warm growing season and plenty of room for their sprawling vines. In cool parts of the country, the seeds may have to be started in a protected place, then transplanted to the garden where they will grow.

Before you do any planting, it is best to learn the particular climate, soil conditioners, and kind of care your plants require. Then if you plan the garden carefully and tend the plants faithfully, you should have a picture-book garden on your very first try.

DAVID BURPEE
President, W. Atlee Burpee Co.

See also FLOWERS; PLANT PESTS; PLANTS.

JAMES A. GARFIELD (1831-1881)
20th President of the United States

FACTS ABOUT GARFIELD

Birthplace: Orange, Ohio *(right)*
Religion: Disciples of Christ
College Attended: Western Reserve
  Eclectic Institute (now Hiram College),
  Hiram, Ohio; Williams College,
  Williamstown, Massachusetts
Occupation: Teacher
Married: Lucretia Rudolph
Children: Eliza (died 1863), Harry A.,
  James R., Mary ("Molly"), Irvin,
  Abram, Edward (died 1876)
Political Party: Republican
Office Held Before Becoming President:
  U.S. Congressman
President Who Preceded Him:
  Rutherford B. Hayes
Age on Becoming President: 49
Term of Office: March 4 to September 19,
  1881 (died in office after being shot by
  · Charles J. Guiteau)
Vice President: Chester A. Arthur
President Who Succeeded Him: Chester
  A. Arthur (succeeded to the presidency
  September 20, 1881, after the death of
  Garfield)
Age at Death: 49
Burial Place: Cleveland, Ohio

J A Garfield.

During the 1880 presidential election campaign, Garfield was portrayed by a Republican cartoonist as a farmer, cutting a swath to the White House with a scythe labeled "honesty, ability, and patriotism."

GARFIELD, JAMES ABRAM. James A. Garfield served as president of the United States for only a little more than six months. On July 2, 1881, less than four months after taking office, Garfield was shot as he waited for a train at a Washington, D.C., railroad station. He died on September 19, 1881, becoming the fourth U.S. president to die while in office. It was a tragic end to the career of a man who had risen from a boyhood of poverty to become a college president, state senator, Civil War general, U.S. congressman, and finally president of the United States.

▶EARLY YEARS AND CAREER

Garfield was born in a log cabin in what was then the pioneer town of Orange, Ohio, on November 19, 1831. He was the youngest of five children of Abram and Eliza Ballou Garfield. When James was 2 years old, his father died, and James's mother was left with the difficult task of raising the young children in the rough frontier country. Life was hard for them, and all the children had to work.

They were able to go to school for only three months each year, but James showed an early interest in learning and read a great deal.

When James was 16, he left home and went to Cleveland, where he hoped to get work as a sailor on the ships that sailed the Great Lakes. He could not get a job on the big sailing ships, but he was hired to work on a canalboat carrying cargo between Cleveland and Pittsburgh. One of his jobs was leading the horses that pulled the boat along the canal. Garfield later recalled that he fell into the canal 14 times before he learned how to handle the team of horses. His career as a sailor ended when he became ill with malaria and had to return home.

When he recovered, young Garfield decided that he wanted to be a teacher. He attended Geauga Seminary, in Chester, Ohio, and then studied at Western Reserve Eclectic Institute (now Hiram College), in Hiram, Ohio. To support himself, he taught school and did odd jobs. When he was 23, he left Ohio to complete his education at Williams College, in

Williamstown, Massachusetts. He graduated from Williams with honors in 1856.

College President and Ohio Senator. After graduation, Garfield returned to teach at the Eclectic Institute. A year later, when he was only 26, he became president of the school. While he was teaching, Garfield studied law. He became interested in politics and spoke out about the problems facing the country at the time. The 1850's were years of bitter dispute between the North and South over the question of slavery and states' rights. Garfield joined the Republican Party, which had been founded in 1854 in opposition to the expansion of slavery into the western territories of the United States. In 1859 he was elected to the Ohio Senate. There he denounced slavery and called for the preservation of the Union.

Lucretia Rudolph Garfield. These were busy years for Garfield. Besides his other duties, he was a preacher in the Disciples of Christ Church. In 1858 he married Lucretia Rudolph. "Crete," as he called her, had been his childhood friend, a fellow student, and pupil. The Garfields had seven children in all, of whom two died as infants.

Civil War Service. When the Civil War broke out in 1861, Garfield volunteered for the Union Army. He received a commission as lieutenant colonel and helped raise a regiment of Ohio volunteers. Many of the men were his old students. Garfield had no military experience, but he was willing to learn. He studied military textbooks, and he drilled his men with a textbook in one hand.

In December 1861, Garfield was given command of a brigade in Kentucky. He was ordered to attack the Confederate forces under General Humphrey Marshall, an experienced soldier. At the battle of Middle Creek he defeated Marshall and forced him to retreat from Kentucky. It was not a great victory, but it was welcome news in the North, for up to this time the Union Army had won few victories. Garfield was promoted to brigadier general and fought at the bloody battle of Shiloh in Tennessee.

While his military reputation was growing Garfield became ill and had to leave the field. But he was soon active again as chief of staff to General William S. Rosecrans. He fought at Chickamauga in Georgia and for his courage and leadership was promoted to major general.

Above: When the Civil War broke out in 1861, James A. Garfield volunteered for the Union Army. Commissioned a lieutenant colonel, he took part in several battles and rose to the rank of major general.

Above right: Lucretia Rudolph, a childhood friend and fellow student of Garfield's, had married him in 1858. Garfield called her "Crete."

Right: This photograph of Garfield and his youngest daughter, Mary ("Molly"), was taken in about 1870, when he was serving in the U.S. House of Representatives.

▶**CONGRESSMAN**

In 1862, while still in the Army, Garfield was elected to the U.S. House of Representatives. He remained in the Army until December 1863, when he resigned his commission and took his seat in Congress.

Garfield served in the House of Representatives for 17 years, including a period as House minority leader. He was particularly interested in matters affecting the freed blacks in the South and in education.

The Crédit Mobilier Scandal. In 1872, during the administration of President Ulysses S. Grant, Garfield became involved in the scandal of the Crédit Mobilier, a railroad construc-

IT MAKES HIM SICK.

tion company. Garfield and other politicians, including former Vice President Schuyler Colfax, were accused of having taken bribes from the company in exchange for political favors. Garfield denied the charge, which was never proved. But some Republicans demanded that he resign from Congress. Garfield, however, made a tour through the villages of his Ohio district, defending his conduct to the satisfaction of voters.

Compromise Candidate. In 1880, Garfield was elected to the U.S. Senate. Before he could take his seat, however, he unexpectedly won the Republican presidential nomination.

In 1880 the Republicans met in Chicago to pick a candidate for president to succeed Rutherford B. Hayes. The two great rivals for the nomination were former President Grant and Senator James G. Blaine of Maine. Grant was backed by a group of Republicans known as the Stalwarts, led by Senator Roscoe Conkling of New York. Blaine was supported by a group called the Half-Breeds.

At the Chicago convention the Grant and Blaine forces were deadlocked. Finally Blaine decided to give his support to Garfield, who had impressed the delegates with his speeches. On the 36th ballot, Garfield was nominated as the candidate for president. Chester A. Arthur, a Conkling supporter, received the nomination for vice president.

During the election campaign, the old Crédit Mobilier scandal came back to haunt Garfield. The number 329 (he was charged with having received $329 from the company) was carried on posters, painted on walls and windows, and printed in newspaper headlines by his opponents. The election was very close. Garfield beat his Democratic opponent, General Winfield Scott Hancock, by fewer than 10,000 popular votes. But he received 369 electoral votes to Hancock's 155.

▶PRESIDENT

A Divided Party. Garfield began his administration as the head of a divided party. He had offended the powerful Senator Conkling by appointing Blaine, a Half-Breed, to the post

Above: A political cartoon of Garfield, referring to the Crédit Mobilier scandal, appeared during the 1880 presidential campaign. *Below:* The Republican ticket of 1880 included Garfield for president and Chester A. Arthur for vice president. *Right:* Garfield was inaugurated as president on March 4, 1881, but died a little more than six months later from an assassin's bullets.

On July 2, 1881, President Garfield was shot while waiting for a train at the Washington, D.C., railroad station. Secretary of State James G. Blaine, accompanying the president, pointed out the assassin, Charles J. Guiteau, a disappointed office seeker. Garfield died on September 19, 1881, succeeded in the presidency by Vice President Chester A. Arthur. Guiteau was tried, convicted, and hanged, even though many people thought him insane.

of secretary of state. Other Half-Breeds were given important government jobs, while the Stalwarts generally received only minor posts. Their dispute became worse when Garfield appointed William H. Robertson, Conkling's worst political enemy, collector of customs for New York.

At the time, a more serious situation faced the president. Certain post office officials were accused of cheating the government on western mail routes. These were the so-called Star Route frauds. The men were brought to trial. But before the case could continue, the nation was shocked by the news that President Garfield had been shot.

The Assassination. On the morning of July 2, 1881, Garfield, accompanied by Secretary of State Blaine, was preparing to leave Washington to visit Williams College. As they waited at the Washington railroad station, a man approached Garfield from behind and shot him twice. The man, Charles J. Guiteau, was a Stalwart who had been refused a government post.

Garfield was nursed at the White House and then at a summer resort cottage at Elberon, New Jersey, where his family was staying. He died at Elberon and was buried in Cleveland, Ohio. Vice President Chester A. Arthur succeeded to the presidency. Guiteau was arrested and tried for murder. He was convicted and hanged in 1882, even though many people thought he was insane.

▶AN AROUSED NATION

Garfield's friends collected a large sum of money to help the president's widow and her five children. One of their sons, James R. Garfield, later became secretary of the interior under President Theodore Roosevelt. A second son, Harry A. Garfield, became president of Williams College.

Garfield became president at a time when there was a great need for reform in politics. Although his tragic death cut short a promising political career, it aroused the nation to the necessity for such reform. The murdered president became a symbol of this need to the people of the United States and to the presidents who followed him.

Reviewed by RICHARD B. MORRIS
Columbia University
Editor, *Encyclopedia of American History*

IMPORTANT DATES IN THE LIFE OF JAMES A. GARFIELD

1831   Born in Orange, Ohio, November 19.

1856   Graduated from Williams College.

1857–1861   President of Western Reserve Eclectic Institute.

1858   Married Lucretia Rudolph.

1859   Elected to the Ohio State Senate.

1861–1863   Served in the Union Army.

1863–1880   Served in the U.S. House of Representatives.

1881   Inaugurated as the 20th president of the United States, March 4; shot by Charles J. Guiteau, July 2; died in Elberon, New Jersey, September 19.

GARIBALDI, GIUSEPPE (1807–1882)

Giuseppe Garibaldi, Italy's great patriot and revolutionary hero, was born on July 4, 1807. Italy was then divided into many small states under different rulers. The king of Sardinia ruled Nice, where Garibaldi was born (it is now part of France). Like another great Italian patriot, Giuseppe Mazzini, Garibaldi dreamed of a free and united republic of Italy.

In 1834, while serving in the Sardinian navy, Garibaldi joined Mazzini in an uprising against the king. The uprising was crushed. Garibaldi was condemned to death, but he escaped to South America. There, during a 14-year exile, he fought in wars of liberation in Brazil and Uruguay.

In 1848, Garibaldi returned home to join the fight for freedom in Italy. Revolutions broke out in all the Italian states, but they were put down by Austria and France. Garibaldi was again forced into exile. He went to the United States, where for a time he lived in Staten Island, New York. In 1854 he returned to Italy and resumed his lifelong struggle to liberate and unite his country.

By now, Garibaldi had given up his ideal of a republic. In 1859 he supported King Victor Emmanuel II of Sardinia in a war against Austria in northern Italy. The next year, Garibaldi led a volunteer force of 1,000 guerrillas—the famous Redshirts—to victory against the Bourbon king in Sicily and Naples, and in 1861, Victor Emmanuel II became the first king of a united Italy.

Garibaldi was a national hero, loved for his honesty and fiery spirit. In 1874 he was elected to the new Italian Parliament. But he was a soldier, not a politician, and after a short time he resigned. He could have been wealthy. Instead, he lived a simple life as a farmer on the island of Caprera, near Sardinia, saved from poverty by help from his admirers. He died there on June 2, 1882.

EMILIANA P. NOETHER
University of Connecticut
See also MAZZINI, GIUSEPPE; VICTOR EMMANUEL.

GARLAND, JUDY. See MINNESOTA (Famous People); MOTION PICTURES (Profiles: Movie Stars).

GARNER, JOHN NANCE. See VICE PRESIDENCY OF THE UNITED STATES.

GARRISON, WILLIAM LLOYD. See MASSACHUSETTS (Famous People).

GARY. See INDIANA (Cities).

GASES

All matter exists in three basic forms: solids, liquids, and gases. The ground under our feet is a solid, the ocean is a liquid, and the air we breathe is made up of gases. In fact, air is a mixture of primarily two gases—78 percent nitrogen and 21 percent oxygen—but it also contains small amounts of argon, carbon dioxide, neon, helium, and other gases.

Like all matter, gases are made up of tiny particles called molecules. Gases, like liquids, have no definite shape. They fill any container regardless of its size or shape. The molecules of a liquid or a solid are so close together that they touch. That is why they cannot be compressed, or squeezed into a smaller space. (The amount of space a substance or an object occupies is known as its volume.) Gases, on the other hand, can be compressed to about $\frac{1}{1000}$ of their normal volume because their molecules are far apart.

Gas molecules are in constant motion. The higher the temperature, the faster they move. If they are inside a container, they are constantly bumping into and bouncing off its walls. This is similar to what happens when you throw a tennis ball against the side of a building. The tennis ball exerts a small force on the building each time it hits and bounces from it. A molecule also creates a small push each time it hits and bounces from the wall of its container. Each collision produces only a tiny push, but there are about 25 thousand quadrillion molecules in each cubic centimeter of a gas. The tiny pushes from all these collisions make up the **pressure** of the gas.

At sea level, the pressure of our atmosphere is enough to support a column of mercury 30 inches (76 centimeters) high or a column of water 34 feet (10 meters) high. This fact is the basis for the working of a **barometer**, a device that uses a column of mercury to measure air pressure. The barometer was invented by Italian physicist Evangelista Torricelli in 1643.

To demonstrate that air pressure can support a column of water, fill a test tube or a long tube that is sealed at one end with colored water, as shown in Figure 1. Put your thumb over the open end of the completely filled tube and then turn it upside down in a pan of water. Be sure that the end of the tube covered by your thumb is under the water before you remove your thumb. As you will observe, the colored water, which is supported by air pressure, remains in the tube.

▶ THE THREE GAS LAWS

There are three fundamental laws in science for all gases. In 1662, English scientist Robert Boyle discovered the first of these laws. Known as **Boyle's law**, it states that at a constant temperature, the volume of a gas varies inversely with the pressure on it. That is, if you double the pressure on a gas, you reduce its volume by half; if you triple the pressure on a gas, you reduce its volume to one-third of what it was; but if you reduce the pressure on a gas by half, you double its volume, and so on. This can be demonstrated with a cylinder that contains a gas and is sealed by a movable piston, as shown in Figure 2a. If weights are added to the piston, the volume occupied by the gas will grow smaller. If enough weights are added to the piston so that the pressure on the enclosed gas is doubled, as in Figure 2b, then the volume of the gas will be reduced by half.

You can see how the first gas law, or Boyle's law, works by first drawing some air into a large plastic syringe that does not have

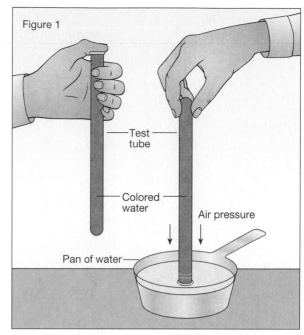

Air pressure can support a column of water. You can demonstrate this by placing a test tube filled with colored water upside down in a pan of plain water.

a needle. First pull the piston outward and seal the open end of the syringe with your finger, as shown in Figure 3. Then push the piston farther into the cylinder. You can feel the increase in pressure as you squeeze the gas. If you release the piston, it will spring back to its previous position. Boyle called this the "spring of air."

The second gas law, known as **Charles' law**, was discovered by French scientist Jacques Charles in 1787. Charles found that at a constant pressure, a gas at 0°C expands by $\frac{1}{273}$ of its volume for each degree the tem-

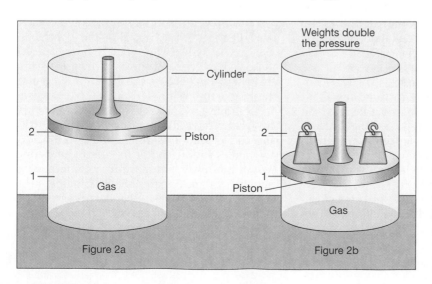

When you increase the pressure on a gas, it reduces in volume. On the left, gas is sealed inside a cylinder by a movable piston. On the right, weights have been added to the piston so that the amount of pressure on the gas is doubled. This reduces the volume of the gas by half.

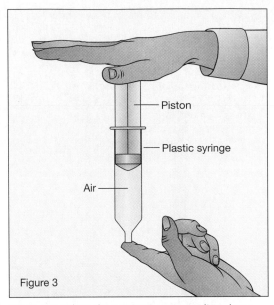

Figure 3

When you reduce the pressure on a gas, its volume increases. To demonstrate this, push the piston into the syringe and then release it. As the pressure is reduced, the compressed gas pushes the piston back to its original position.

perature of the gas increases as measured on the Celsius scale. For each degree the gas decreases in temperature, the volume of the gas contracts by the same fraction.

You can demonstrate Charles' law quite easily. Place an empty soda bottle and a balloon that has not been inflated into a refrigerator for a few minutes. Then pull the neck of the balloon over the mouth of the bottle as you remove it from the refrigerator. Leave the bottle in a warm room for a few minutes. As its temperature rises, the gas in the bottle expands and partially inflates the balloon. Put the bottle back into the refrigerator, and as its temperature cools, the gas in the bottle contracts and the balloon deflates.

By combining the laws of Boyle and Charles, scientists predicted the **third gas law**. The third gas law states that at a constant volume, the pressure of a gas at 0°C increases by $\frac{1}{273}$ for each degree it increases in temperature as measured on the Celsius scale. For each degree it decreases in temperature, the pressure decreases by the same fraction. This law was confirmed by French chemist Joseph Gay-Lussac.

By the mid-1800's, Scottish mathematician and physicist Lord Kelvin (William Thom-

son) had devised a temperature scale, now known as **Kelvin's absolute temperature scale**, that eliminates negative temperatures. On Kelvin's scale, 0 is the lowest possible temperature—one that is equal to –273°C. Since kelvins and degrees Celsius are the same size, 273 on Kelvin's scale is equal to 0°C. Using Kelvin's absolute temperature scale, Charles' law states that the volume of a gas at a constant pressure is directly proportional to the absolute temperature. That is, if the absolute temperature doubles, so does the volume of the gas. Thus the third gas law states that the pressure of a gas at constant volume is directly proportional to the absolute temperature. If the absolute temperature doubles, so does the pressure of the gas.

▶ **THE GAS LAWS AND MOLECULES**

In terms of the actions of molecules, the gas laws make sense. The pressure of a fixed volume of gas increases with rising temperature, as stated in the third gas law, because the faster-moving molecules hit the walls of the container with more force and therefore raise the pressure. Just the opposite happens as temperature decreases. The molecules move more and more slowly, and the pressure decreases.

When the pressure on a confined gas increases at a constant temperature, the volume decreases, as stated in the first gas law (Boyle's law), and the pressure of the enclosed gas increases. If the molecules are in a smaller volume, they strike the walls of the container more frequently because they have less distance to travel between collisions. The increased number of collisions per second creates a greater pressure.

If the pressure on a gas is kept constant—for example, by using a cylinder and a movable piston of fixed weight—the volume of the gas increases with the temperature, as stated in the second gas law (Charles' law). This happens because the faster-moving molecules hit the piston with more force, causing it to move upward. As the gas expands, the molecules have to travel farther before striking the piston. This reduces the number of molecules hitting the piston at any one time. When the fewer but more forceful molecules achieve balance with the unchanging pressure exerted by the piston, expansion stops but the volume has increased.

Another property of a gas is that lighter molecules move faster than heavier molecules. This faster motion compensates for their smaller mass. Lighter molecules would strike the walls of a container with less force than heavier molecules if it were not for their greater speed. Their added speed causes lighter molecules, such as hydrogen, to exert the same average pressure as heavier molecules, such as carbon dioxide, at the same temperature.

Because of differences in molecular speed, the heavy molecules that make up dense gases **diffuse**, or spread through space, more slowly than gases that are less dense. Diffusion has caused some objects in outer space, such as the moon, to lose any atmosphere they may once have had. The gases simply spread out into space. The reason that this has not happened on Earth is that its gravity is strong enough to hold some gases within its atmosphere.

To demonstrate that gases really do diffuse, have someone open a bottle of perfume at least 1 yard (1 meter) away from you. After a short time, you will smell the perfume. This is because its molecules have diffused from the bottle through the air to your nose.

Gravity is not the only force pulling on molecules. Gas molecules exert small attractive forces on one another. If the temperature is lowered, the gas molecules move less rapidly. If the temperature is lowered enough, the attraction between the slower moving molecules pulls them together, forming a liquid. Very low temperatures are required to change air, for example, into a liquid. At about –328°F (–200°C), air liquefies. Some gases, such as hydrogen and helium, must be cooled to even lower temperatures before they will liquefy.

▶ GASES IN INDUSTRY

A number of gases are used in industry to make a wide range of products, from steel girders to foods to electronic devices to medicines. Do you ever use a computer or a cellular phone? Oxygen, nitrogen, and noble gases are used in making the computer chips inside these devices. Do you like soft drinks that fizz? The fizz in these drinks is produced by carbon dioxide. Air itself is widely used as an industrial gas. Compressed air is used to run drills and other machinery. Air is mixed with fuel to make it burn in internal combustion engines, the type used in most automobiles.

Most gases used in industry occur in the atmosphere naturally. The gases are separated from one another through a process known as **fractional distillation**. The air is first purified and then cooled to about –330°F, or –200°C, which converts it to a liquid. The liquid air is then heated to boiling. Each gas—nitrogen, oxygen, argon, xenon, neon, and krypton—has a different boiling point. (For example, the nitrogen and oxygen in liquid air can be separated because nitrogen will boil, or change back to a gas, at a lower temperature, –321°F, or –196°C, than oxygen, –297°F, or –183°C.) Once the gases are purified, they are used in manufacturing. Those companies that use large quantities of nitrogen or oxygen build their own air-separation plants. Other companies usually buy the gases they need from industrial gas-supply companies.

Nitrogen

Nitrogen is especially important to industry because it is **inert**, meaning that it will not react chemically with most metals and many other materials. Manufacturers of electronic devices, petrochemicals, plastics, and pharmaceutical products are some of the industries that use nitrogen. Nitrogen is tasteless and harmless. For that reason, it is used inside the containers of some foods in order to keep their flavors from being changed by the oxygen of the air. Liquid nitrogen is used by food packagers to freeze food quickly. Liquid nitrogen is also used in hospitals for certain types of surgery and for preserving biological materials.

Oxygen and Oxy-Fuel Mixtures

Oxygen and oxy-fuel mixtures are used to help reduce air pollution. Industries that require high-temperature combustion, such as glassmaking and steelmaking, now burn oxy-fuel mixtures in their furnaces. An oxy-fuel mixture contains very little nitrogen and is rich in oxygen. The oxy-fuel mix burns cleanly and does not create nitrogen oxide emissions.

When oxygen is used to replace air during a wide range of chemical-processing applications, such as the bleaching of pulp and paper, it eliminates the formation of many pollutant gases. Oxygen is used in medicine, in pharmaceutical products, and for space exploration, where it keeps astronauts alive in the spacecraft's cabin and fuels the rocket during lift-off and beyond. Oxygen is also used for waste incineration, for welding and cutting metals, and in fish farming.

Hydrogen

Hydrogen, the lightest gas, was once used to fill blimps. But hydrogen is very flammable in the air, so helium or hot air is now used. Hydrogen has been increasingly used as an energy source because it is clean-burning and thus nonpolluting. By the year 2000, it may be used to power fleets of buses, taxis, and delivery vehicles. However, concerns about their high cost and safety may prevent the widespread use of hydrogen-fueled engines.

Hydrogen is important as a food additive. It is added to liquid oils, such as soybean, fish, cottonseed, and corn, to convert these oils into semisolid products such as shortening, margarine, and peanut butter. It is used in chemical processing, primarily to manufacture ammonia and methanol, and also to change nonedible oils from liquids to semisolids for use in soaps, insulation, plastics, and ointments. Hydrogen is used to produce sorbitol, a compound used in cosmetics, adhesives, and vitamins A and C. In the aerospace industry, hydrogen is used to fuel spacecraft and to power life-support systems and computers. In the process of doing this, it produces drinkable water for astronauts as a by-product.

Fluorocarbons

Fluorocarbons, a group of very useful gases created by scientists, are compounds that

---

Did you know that...

every time you turn on your television set you have "tuned into" a series of products that were produced with gases? Oxygen and oxy-fuel combustion technologies are used to melt the glass for the picture tube. The copper wires inside the television set are produced in furnaces that use oxygen. The plastic cabinet of the set may have been molded into shape and then quickly cooled with nitrogen. Neon-helium and krypton-neon-helium mixtures are used in the remote control you use to locate the program you want to watch. These gases generate the infrared rays that are sent to the television receiver, telling it to change channels or to adjust the volume of the program you are watching.

contain the elements fluorine and carbon. Freon is the best known of these gases. In a liquid form, fluorocarbons are used as refrigerants. Many scientists have expressed their concern about possible dangers from the widespread use of fluorocarbons. There is some evidence that these gases destroy the ozone gas in the stratosphere, which may cause global warming. The ozone in our atmosphere prevents dangerously high amounts of the sun's ultraviolet light from reaching the Earth. Fluorocarbons are no longer used in the United States as propellants to spray materials out of aerosol cans.

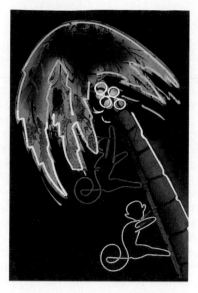

Many of the noble gases are used in what are called neon signs because they give out bright, vibrant colors when an electric current is sent through them.

Noble Gases

The noble gases, which are sometimes called inert gases, are found in nature in very small amounts. These gases—argon, helium, krypton, neon, radon, and xenon—have certain qualities in common. They are nonexplosive and can be made to conduct electricity when subjected to high-frequency electric fields. Because they emit colored light when they are electrically charged, they are used in lighting, in lasers, and in medical imaging. They are also used in laboratory research. Except for radon, each noble gas gives out a color when excited by electricity: argon gives out a reddish blue; helium gives out white, yellow, or violet; krypton gives out yellow, green, or violet; neon, a red-orange; and xenon, blue or a blue-green.

Argon is a nontoxic, nonreactive, and nonflammable gas used primarily in the production of aluminum, steel, and metal alloys; in producing lasers; and for welding and cutting metals. It is also used to fill incandescent and fluorescent light bulbs. Argon is not a good conductor of heat, so it is used by window manufacturers in double-paned, insulated windows to improve the energy efficiency of the windows.

Helium, in its liquid form, is the coldest liquid on Earth. Because it will not liquify until it reaches –452°F (–269°C), helium is used for scientific experiments that require extremely cold temperatures. In its gaseous form, helium is used as a tracer in detecting gas-line leaks because its tiny molecules easily pass through the smallest holes. Helium is also used for welding, for cooling magnetic resonance imaging machines that help doctors make medical diagnoses, for balloon inflation, and for deep-sea diving.

Krypton, a dense gas that is a poor conductor of heat, is used in the powerful lamps on airport landing strips and in lamps for other places where very bright light is needed. There are thin metal wires, called filaments, inside these krypton lamps. When electric current flows through the filaments, they become very hot. Since krypton is a poor conductor of heat, the filaments glow brightly.

Neon glows red-orange when electricity is sent through it at a high enough voltage. It is the most commonly used gas in advertising signs.

Radon, which occurs naturally in the ground, becomes hazardous when it seeps into buildings. Because it is radioactive, it can be absorbed into the lungs and, with prolonged exposure, can lead to lung cancer. As a result, special tests have been devised to determine if there are harmful levels of radon in buildings.

Xenon, which is the rarest of the noble gases, is often used in electron tubes. If its pressure is reduced and a high enough electric voltage is used, xenon is a good conductor of electricity. Like krypton, xenon can be used in powerful lamps.

ROBERT GARDNER
Author, *Science Projects about Chemistry*

DONNA PIERPONT
Marketing Communications Manager, Praxair, Inc.

See also ATMOSPHERE; BOYLE, ROBERT; FUELS; HYDROGEN; LIQUID OXYGEN AND OTHER LIQUID GASES; LIQUIDS; MATTER; NEON AND OTHER NOBLE GASES; NITROGEN; OXYGEN AND OXIDATION; SOLIDS.

GASOLINE

Since the early 1900's, when automobiles were first mass-produced, gasoline has become one of the world's most important fuels. In addition to its use as a fuel for most cars, trucks, buses, and boats, it is also used in some airplanes and in machines such as lawnmowers.

How Gasoline Is Obtained. Gasoline, like the crude oil it comes from, is a mixture of many different **hydrocarbons**—substances composed only of hydrogen and carbon atoms. To separate gasoline from other hydrocarbons, crude oil is distilled in an oil refinery. In the **distilling process**, crude oil is first boiled. As the vapors cool within the tall columns of the refinery, molecules of various sizes change into different liquids. These liquids become various petroleum products such as gasoline, diesel fuel, or jet fuel.

When crude oil is first distilled, gasoline makes up 15 to 25 percent of the refined product. A process called **cracking**, in which large molecules are cracked into smaller ones at very high temperatures under controlled conditions, allows refiners to produce additional gasoline from the less valuable refined products. As a result, gasoline makes up more than half of the total output of oil refineries in the United States.

Characteristics of Gasoline. Gasoline is often dyed. It actually looks like water before the dyes are added. Gasoline also has a distinctive odor, and it burns very easily, making it dangerous if handled carelessly. In an automobile engine, gasoline is mixed with air in the carburetor or fuel injector and then sprayed into the cylinder, where heat turns it into a vapor. The car's spark plugs ignite this vapor, producing gases that expand with great force. The force of these expanding gases pushes the piston down to turn the crankshaft and move the car.

If the gasoline-air mixture burns unevenly, the engine makes a sharp rattling sound called pinging or knocking. Knocking reduces the engine's power and increases engine wear. Gasoline is rated according to how much it is likely to produce knocking. These ratings are called octane numbers. The term "octane" refers to iso-octane, a type of hydrocarbon. Regular-grade gasoline generally has an octane number of 87, which is equivalent to 87 percent iso-octane. Premium gasoline may have an octane number ranging from 91 to 94. When used in the same conditions, gasoline with a high octane number produces less knocking than one with a low number. Special substances called **additives** are often mixed with gasoline to prevent knocking. Other additives help clean the engine, prevent rust, and stop ice from forming in the gas tank in cold weather.

Gasoline and Pollution. The burning of gasoline releases substances, including carbon monoxide, that contribute to air pollution. In order to reduce pollution, most cars now use unleaded gasoline. Oil companies must supply different gasolines depending on the season and quality of the air in a particular area. In winter in certain areas, gasoline containing more oxygen helps control carbon monoxide. In summer, gasoline that evaporates more slowly helps control smog. In areas with high levels of ozone pollution, the use of a "reformulated gasoline" has been required since 1995. The amount of potential pollutants in this gasoline has been reduced by the refiners. Eventually, reformulated gasoline will be produced that contains even lower levels of pollutants.

From Refinery to Consumer. After gasoline is produced at a refinery, it is transported by pipeline or barge to terminals, which consist of large storage tanks and equipment for reloading the gasoline. Those terminals located near the ocean may also receive shipments of foreign-produced gasoline in large ships called tankers. From the terminals, the gasoline is pumped into tank trucks for delivery to service stations, which sell directly to individual users.

For motorists, gasoline is still more economical than alternative fuels or electric-powered vehicles. New technologies have increased the availability of crude oil, easing fears that supplies were running out, and the improved quality of gasoline has reduced pollution. As a result, gasoline will probably remain the most important transportation fuel for many years to come.

CHERYL J. TRENCH
Petroleum Industry Research Foundation

See also FUELS; KEROSENE; PETROLEUM AND PETROLEUM REFINING.

GASOLINE ENGINES. See INTERNAL-COMBUSTION ENGINES.

GAUGUIN, PAUL (1848–1903)

The restless spirit of the French painter Eugène Henri Paul Gauguin drove him to faraway places. A successful stockbroker, he gave up his career to devote his life to painting and to seek the simple beauty he saw in the lives of primitive peoples.

Paul Gauguin was born in Paris on June 7, 1848, and moved to Peru with his family when he was 3 years old. The excitement of his four years in Lima, the capital of Peru, had a great impact on the little boy. At 17 he joined the merchant marine and went to sea for six years. Then he returned to France, filled with memories of strange and beautiful lands.

The White Horse, painted by Paul Gauguin in 1898, is now in the Louvre, Paris.

He settled in Paris and became a stockbroker. On pleasant Sundays he could be seen strolling in the park with his Danish wife, Mette, and their five children, all healthy, proud, and well dressed.

Gauguin enjoyed the art of Camille Pissarro and other French artists known as the impressionists. He collected their works, took up painting, and in 1880 exhibited with them. Three years later he left his job and told Mette that he planned to devote all of his time to art. Gauguin was accustomed to success and was certain that he would succeed in painting; Mette was not. She never forgave her husband for what she thought was the sacrifice of his family for a selfish whim. In the end, the couple separated.

As an artist, Gauguin was unable to sell his work and now faced a life of poverty and desperation. By 1886 the expense of city life had become so demanding that he left Paris and went to an artists' colony in Brittany, a region in northwestern France. After a year he traveled to Panama, where he worked as a laborer. Then he went to the tropics of Martinique, where he could live and paint in freedom. After a year in Martinique, Gauguin returned to Brittany, ill and penniless.

Gauguin's style was influenced by the picturesque surroundings of Brittany as well as his memories of voyages to exotic places. He was also helped by Japanese ideas, as interpreted by his friend the artist Vincent van Gogh. Gauguin's work was characterized by flat, simple forms in intense colors that were often outlined in black. His paintings portrayed his feelings toward the natural and the mysterious.

In 1891, Gauguin had raised enough money to go to the primitive South Sea island of Tahiti. The lush forests, the beautiful people, and the calls of strange birds haunted him. He decided to stay and share the simple life of the Tahitians.

Although his paintings capture the beauty of Tahitian culture, Gauguin could not completely understand or be happy in this primitive society. He suffered years of poverty and sickness. On May 8, 1903, he died on Hiva Oa, one of the Marquesas Islands, alone and unaware of the mark his painting would make on modern art.

Reviewed by FRANK GETLEIN
Author, *The French Impressionists*

GAUSS, CARL FRIEDRICH (1777–1855)

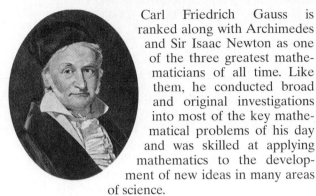

Carl Friedrich Gauss is ranked along with Archimedes and Sir Isaac Newton as one of the three greatest mathematicians of all time. Like them, he conducted broad and original investigations into most of the key mathematical problems of his day and was skilled at applying mathematics to the development of new ideas in many areas of science.

Born on April 30, 1777, in the Duchy of Brunswick (now part of Germany), Gauss came from a poor family of gardeners, masons, and weavers. He was a child prodigy who could read and compute by the age of 3. His abilities were recognized by his teachers, who brought him at 14 to the attention of the Duke of Brunswick. The duke paid for Gauss's higher education and supported him financially after Gauss earned his doctorate in 1799. When the duke died, Gauss needed to earn his own livelihood. In 1807 he became director of the Astronomical Observatory at Göttingen University in Germany, where he remained for the rest of his life.

Gauss had a facility with languages and considered devoting his life to philology, the study of language. At the age of 19, Gauss made a discovery that gave him a reputation in mathematics and convinced him to pursue it as a career.

Since the time of the ancient Greeks, mathematicians had explored ways to construct regular polygons using a compass and straightedge. (Polygons are figures made up of straight line segments with all sides and angles equal.) But no one had ever found a way to construct a regular polygon with a total number of sides that was not a multiple of 3, 4, or 5. Using the rigorous logic that characterized all his work, Gauss discovered a way to construct a regular polygon with 17 sides. Later he developed the general theory that established which regular polygons can or cannot be constructed.

It was an astronomical investigation, however, that made Gauss known outside the world of mathematics. On January 1, 1801, the asteroid Ceres was first observed, but astronomers soon lost track of it because they did not know how to calculate its orbit. Gauss found a way to determine Ceres' orbit based on only a few sightings and a series of complex calculations he did himself. It was an extraordinary feat in the days before computers. Using Gauss's data, astronomers found Ceres exactly where he predicted it would be. Gauss's method is still used today to calculate the orbits of objects in space.

Gauss's contributions to mathematics were in almost every branch of the subject. His doctoral thesis of 1799 provided the first proof that all equations formed by adding and multiplying integral powers have a solution. This is now called "The Fundamental Theorem of Algebra." In 1801 he published *Disquisitiones Arithmeticae (Arithmetical Researches)* in which he completely restructured the theory of numbers. An interest in surveying led to his theory of how to describe all curved surfaces mathematically. His ideas also helped further the development of statistics, probability theory, and topology.

Gauss made many other mathematical discoveries that he described in his notebooks or wrote about to friends but chose not to publish. Many of his findings were later rediscovered by other mathematicians, who were often annoyed to learn that Gauss had discovered them first.

During the last twenty years of his life, Gauss devoted much of his time to scientific research. He and a colleague built a working telegraph more than a decade before Samuel Morse built his first model telegraph. Among Gauss's other inventions were the heliotrope, a surveying instrument used to send signals by reflected light, and a device for measuring the intensity of a magnetic field.

Over his lifetime, Gauss received numerous honors and prizes and was so esteemed that he was often called the Prince of Mathematicians. A modest man, Gauss lived simply and quietly, never seeking the fame or awards that were bestowed upon him. He was married twice and raised six children. On February 23, 1855, he died of heart failure at the age of 77.

BRYAN H. BUNCH
Coauthor, *The Timetables of Science*

See also MATHEMATICS, HISTORY OF; NUMBER PATTERNS.

GAZA STRIP. See PALESTINE.

Among the largest gears made are double helical gears (*above*) used to drive hot mill rollers that squeeze steel, making it progressively thinner. Among the tiniest gears are spur gears (*inset*) used to drive each tuft of an electric toothbrush.

GEARS

What do automobiles, electric tooth brushes, airplanes, electric can openers, helicopters, photocopiers, missiles, robots, and roller coasters have in common? The answer is gears. Without gears, none of these devices would work.

Gears are wheels with teeth that are used to transmit motion and power from one part of a machine to another. Although an integral part of many machines, often they are not visible, and many people may not even realize that gears are working. Yet all of us use devices that depend on gears to operate.

The principle behind gears is similar to the principle behind levers. In both, two different forces interact to create power and motion. (To read about levers, see WORK, POWER, AND MACHINES in Volume W-X-Y-Z.)

▶ HOW GEARS WORK

Most gears are mounted on axles, or shafts. If two or more gears are working together, this is called a train of gears. When the teeth of gears working together interlock, they are said to be engaged, or meshed. When gears are meshed, the turning of one gear will cause another gear to rotate, which is how motion and power are transmitted from one gear to another.

When two gears of different sizes mesh together and turn, they transmit power and speed at a given relationship known as the **gear ratio**. This ratio is based on the relationship between the diameter of the larger gear and that of the smaller gear. The smaller gear is called the **pinion**. A pair of gears in which the diameter of the larger gear is six times larger than that of the smaller gear is said to have a gear ratio of 6:1 (six to one). This means that the smaller gear will turn six times as fast as the larger gear, but the larger gear will deliver a turning force, or **torque**, six times as great as the smaller gear. Gear ratio is also determined by the number of teeth on each of two gears. For example, if a large gear has 180 teeth and a small gear has 30, the gear ratio will be 6:1 (180:30 = 6:1).

A good example of how gear ratio works and can be used to great advantage can be found in ten-speed bicycles. The power to make the bicycle move comes from the person who is pedaling, so only a small amount of power is available. The rider uses the bicycle's gears to vary the relationship between the turning speed of the wheels and the amount of force needed to make them turn. When riding on a smooth, level surface, only a small amount of force is needed to make the wheels turn, so the rider selects a high gear. This allows the wheels to turn faster with fewer turns of the pedals. In this case, a smaller gear on the wheel turns faster than a larger gear on the pedal, but the pedal delivers greater torque. When going up a hill, a much larger force is needed to turn the

HELICAL GEARS

SPUR GEARS

HERRINGBONE GEARS

WORM GEARS

BEVEL GEARS

wheels, so the rider chooses a low gear. This allows the wheels to turn slowly with more turns of the pedals. In this case, a smaller gear on the pedal turns faster than a larger gear on the wheel, but the wheel delivers more torque. This same principle is used in automobile transmissions, which contain a series of gears that produce different gear ratios depending on driving conditions.

Some gears use a small force traveling at high speed to create a large force that travels at a much lower speed. Such gears are called **speed reducers** or **torque multipliers**. In some cases, gears are used to do just the opposite. A large force traveling at low speed is used to create a small force that travels at a much higher speed. These gears are called **speed increasers**.

▶ TYPES OF GEARS

The type of gear used in a machine depends on the purpose of the machine and the type of power supply available. **Spur gears**, the most common type, transmit power between parallel shafts. They have straight teeth parallel to the shaft. Spur gears are used in simple machines that operate at low speeds, such as electric can openers or office machines. Some automobiles also use spur gears to transmit power from the engine to the wheels.

There are three kinds of gears used primarily for machines that operate at high speeds, such as helicopters or jet airplanes, or for large machines that transmit huge amounts of power, such as the machines in steel mills. **Helical gears** are similar to spur gears except that their teeth are twisted instead of straight. **Spiral bevel gears** have straight teeth set at an angle to the shaft. These two gears can be

used to transmit power between parallel shafts or between shafts at different angles to one another. **Herringbone gears** have teeth that form a V-shaped pattern. Herringbone gears are used to transmit power between parallel shafts.

Worm gears have a threaded cylinder, called the worm, that resembles a screw. These gears allow small motors to exert large turning forces. They are used in model trains and slot racing cars and in hand-operated machines, such as winches and fishing reels.

▶ HISTORY OF GEARS

Gears have been in use for thousands of years. In the first century B.C., Ctesibius, a Greek mathematician living in Egypt, built a water clock with gear wheels. The first known mill that used gears was built about 27 B.C. The Chinese used crude wooden gears in a type of compass known as a south-pointing chariot, which dates back at least to the 200's A.D. Over time, people developed ways to use gears in clocks, waterwheels, windmills, and machines of war. Many of these early applications were relatively simple. Then in the late 1400's and early 1500's, Leonardo da Vinci suggested uses for gears that were far more advanced than most people of his time could imagine. For example, one of his ideas was for a helicopter-like machine. But many of Leonardo's ideas were not put to use until hundreds of years after his death.

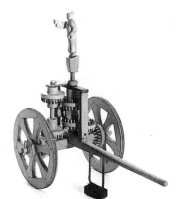

South-pointing chariot

For centuries gears were made of wood or wood inset with stone teeth. Occasionally a metal like iron, tin, or bronze was used. It was not until precision gear-cutting machines were invented in 1855 that metal gears came into wide use. Since then, gears have been used in many remarkable and useful devices.

RAYMOND J. DRAGO
Drive Systems Technology, Inc.

See also AUTOMOBILES; LOCOMOTIVES; TRANSMISSIONS; WORK, POWER, AND MACHINES.

GEESE. See DUCKS, GEESE, AND SWANS.

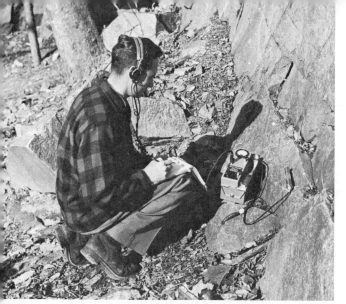

Prospecting with a Geiger counter.

GEIGER COUNTER

Today, Geiger counters are a familiar sight. We see pictures of scientists using them in laboratories. Engineers work with Geiger counters in nuclear power plants. Prospectors looking for uranium take them into the hills. As the prospectors search about, their Geiger counters make a clicking sound every once in a while. But if the prospectors come upon some uranium, the clicking increases until it becomes very fast.

The reason is that uranium gives off tiny amounts of energy and matter called radiations. Uranium is one of a small group of chemical elements that give off such radiations. These elements are called radioactive elements. When the radiations from these elements enter a Geiger counter, they cause it to click.

Radiations cannot be seen. In small amounts they cannot be felt on the skin. A Geiger counter, or some similar instrument, is needed to tell when they are present.

Some radiations have so much energy that they can pass into or through solid materials. In large amounts they can damage the human body. Hence the Geiger counter is often used as a safety device. It can indicate whether a dangerous amount of radiation is present.

▶ INVENTION OF THE GEIGER COUNTER

The Geiger counter was developed in 1908 by Hans Geiger (1882–1945), a German scientist working with the British scientist Ernest Rutherford. Radioactivity had been discovered only twelve years earlier. The new invention proved useful to scientists studying radioactive substances. Using a Geiger counter, they could detect radiations given off by radium and other materials they worked with. By placing counters around a radioactive substance, they could find out in what directions it gave off radiations. The Geiger counter used today is sometimes called the Geiger-Müller counter, or G-M counter. It is similar to a model that was perfected by Geiger and Walther Müller in 1928.

▶ HOW DOES A GEIGER COUNTER WORK?

A Geiger or Geiger-Müller counter consists of a glass cylinder with a wire running through it. The wire is part of an electronic circuit. The cylinder is airtight and is usually filled with a gas other than air, often argon. When radiations enter the cylinder, they cause the gas to break up into electrically charged particles. Some of the particles hit the wire and produce a pulse of electricity. The electric pulse is usually amplified and produces a clicking sound in a loudspeaker. Each click is a signal that some radiation has entered the Geiger counter.

HOW A GEIGER COUNTER WORKS

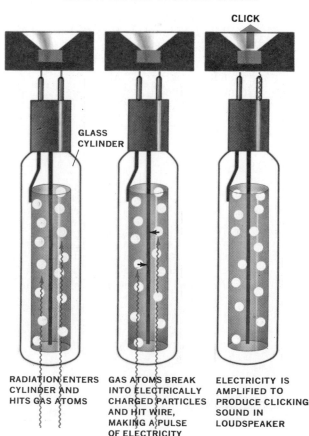

CLICK

GLASS CYLINDER

RADIATION ENTERS CYLINDER AND HITS GAS ATOMS

GAS ATOMS BREAK INTO ELECTRICALLY CHARGED PARTICLES AND HIT WIRE, MAKING A PULSE OF ELECTRICITY

ELECTRICITY IS AMPLIFIED TO PRODUCE CLICKING SOUND IN LOUDSPEAKER

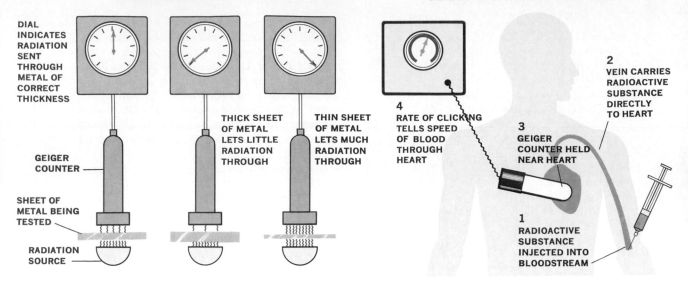

DIAL INDICATES RADIATION SENT THROUGH METAL OF CORRECT THICKNESS

THICK SHEET OF METAL LETS LITTLE RADIATION THROUGH

THIN SHEET OF METAL LETS MUCH RADIATION THROUGH

GEIGER COUNTER

SHEET OF METAL BEING TESTED

RADIATION SOURCE

4 RATE OF CLICKING TELLS SPEED OF BLOOD THROUGH HEART

2 VEIN CARRIES RADIOACTIVE SUBSTANCE DIRECTLY TO HEART

3 GEIGER COUNTER HELD NEAR HEART

1 RADIOACTIVE SUBSTANCE INJECTED INTO BLOODSTREAM

▶ USES OF THE GEIGER COUNTER

Many people in industry, medicine, and scientific research depend on Geiger counters in their work.

For example, Geiger counters are used to measure the thickness of sheet metal. As a sheet moves between a radiation source and a counter, radiations are sent through the sheet. The number of radiations is always the same. If the sheet is too thin, a lot of radiation passes through the sheet. The counter shows that too much radiation is passing through. If the sheet is too thick, not much radiation passes through it. The counter shows that few radiations are passing through the sheet. In either case, the machines producing the metal sheets are then adjusted.

In medicine one use of the Geiger counter is to check the flow of blood through the heart. A small amount of a radioactive substance is injected into the bloodstream. A Geiger counter is then held near the heart. The radiations from the injected substance cause the counter to click. The rate of the clicking tells the speed of the blood through the heart.

Geiger counters help geologists to search for radioactive minerals. And they warn people who work with X-ray apparatus if they are exposed to dangerous amounts of radiation. The counters are also useful in tracing radioactive materials that have been lost, spilled, or stolen. In fact, Geiger counters are valuable whenever radioactive materials must be located or measured.

Reviewed by SERGE A. KORFF
New York University

See also ATOMS; RADIATION.

GEMSTONES

All through history people have valued stones of great beauty. When early people found brightly colored stones, they thought the stones had special powers. They used such stones to decorate themselves. Through the centuries more and different gemstones have been discovered over the face of the earth. Owning gems has brought wealth and importance. Great rulers have had gemstones set into their weapons and their crowns. Many other people have worn them with pride.

In order to qualify as gems, stones must have beauty, they must be hard and tough enough to take considerable wear, and they must be rare enough for people to prize. Diamonds, rubies, and emeralds have all these qualifications to a marked degree and are the most prized gems.

Gemstones, with only four exceptions, are minerals. Minerals are inorganic combinations of chemical elements that are found naturally in the earth. ("Inorganic" means that they were not formed from living things.) They usually have a crystal structure. Four gemstones are made of organic materials formed by plants or animals. These four exceptions are pearl, amber, coral, and jet.

When a mineral has a definite form and regularly arranged outer surfaces, and when its atoms are lined up in a regular arrangement, the mineral is a crystal. Crystals also have a definite inside pattern that is always the same. As every mineral has its own definite crystal form, we can usually know the mineral by the shape of its crystal or its inside pattern.

▶ PHYSICAL PROPERTIES OF GEMSTONES

The beauty of a gemstone depends on one or more of four things: its color, its brilliancy, its "fire," or its special optical features, like the play of color in a fine opal. "Brilliancy" and "fire" sound like the same thing, but they are not. Brilliancy means the stone's shininess, or ability to reflect light. Fire is the rainbow effect caused by the breaking up of white light into different wavelengths. The glittering colors seen in a diamond when it is turned are an example of fire. A mineral may be called a gemstone if it is outstanding in even one of these characteristics. The main attraction of jet, for instance, is its deep black color.

Color

Gemstones can be found in almost any color. Rubies are intensely red, and emeralds are intensely green. Topaz is often a warm golden-yellow. Turquoise is valued for its light-blue color alone, for it is opaque and thus does not transmit any light. Some stones, such as tourmaline, change in color when viewed from different angles.

Brilliancy

Brilliancy is the amount of light that is reflected from a gemstone. The term brilliancy refers only to the quantity of light flashing, not to its color. The brilliancy of a stone depends on its refractive index, the clearness of the stone, its polish, and the way it is cut. The refractive index measures a gem's ability to bend, or refract, the light that passes through it. Diamonds, although they do not have the highest refractive index, are brilliant because they are highly transparent. They can also take a very high polish.

Fire

The intense colors that flash from a diamond in sunlight are called its fire. These colors come from the separation of light by the stone into the individual colors of the spectrum. Only transparent stones that have brilliancy can flash fire. Gemstones that show a high degree of fire include the diamond, zircon, and demantoid garnet.

Hardness and Toughness

Each gemstone has a characteristic hardness and toughness. Hardness is the gem's resistance to scratching or wearing away. Toughness is its resistance to breakage. Unless a gemstone is fairly hard and tough, it is not practical for use as a stone in a ring, where it would receive hard wear.

Hardness is measured according to the Mohs' scale, named for the German mineralogist Friedrich Mohs (1773–1839). On this scale the hardest mineral is rated 10, and the softest is 1. Each mineral on the list can be scratched by the minerals with a higher number. Since diamond cannot be scratched, it is 10. Talc can scratch nothing and is 1.

MOHS' SCALE	
10	Diamond
9	Corundum (Ruby and Sapphire)
8	Topaz
7	Quartz
6	Feldspar (Orthoclase)
5	Apatite
4	Fluorite
3	Calcite
2	Gypsum
1	Talc

Toughness depends on a gemstone's resistance to fracture and cleavage. The cleavage of a gemstone refers to the way in which it breaks in certain definite directions, leaving a fairly smooth surface. Diamonds are sometimes cut on their lines of cleavage.

Unusual Effects in Appearance

Among the unusual effects in appearance for which many stones are valued are chatoyancy, the cat's-eye effect; asterism, the star effect; opalescence, milky or pearly reflections from the inside of a stone; and play of color.

Chatoyancy is a single bright band of light

across the top of a stone polished to a curved surface. The word *chatoyant* is French and means "shining like a cat's eye." The best example of this effect can be seen in a cat's-eye chrysoberyl. When this gemstone is turned, it resembles an eye opening and closing. Quartz, tourmaline, and beryl also may show this effect.

Asterism is a special type of chatoyancy that results when several sets of the cat's-eye effect appear in one stone. Six rays are produced when three cat's-eye lines cross at the center of a stone. This star—*aster* is the Greek word for star—appears in the popular star sapphires and rubies. Other star materials are quartz, garnet, and beryl.

Opalescence is the pearly reflection from the inside of a gemstone. Opalescence is usually found in an opal, as might be guessed from the name. It can be best seen when the stone is cut with rounded surfaces. The effect is caused by the reflection of light from many tiny gas-filled cavities in the stone. A milky blue floating light that appears in moonstones is called adularescence.

The unique **play of color** in some opals makes them very desirable gemstones. The many different colors in these stones form a beautiful patchwork. As the stone is turned or seen from another direction, the color of each patch changes. This change is similar to the color change in soap bubbles.

▶ FORMATION OF GEMSTONES

Gemstones are formed by the same natural processes that form all minerals. But they are formed under unusually good conditions that yield transparent stones without faults. (Not all gemstones are transparent, however.) Most minerals in nature contain impurities that have kept them from forming perfect crystals. The three methods by which gemstones are formed are: cooling and crystallization from molten (hot, melted) rock; developing out of a solution; and the action of heat, pressure, and moisture upon rocks.

▶ WHERE ARE GEMSTONES FOUND?

Diamonds are usually found in long and narrow vertical rock masses called pipes. These pipes contain **blueground**, a bluish-gray hard rock. Blueground is often called **kimberlite** for the Kimberley diamond mines in South Africa, where it is found in great amounts.

Many diamonds are found at or near the surface in **dikes**. A dike is a long, thin, wall-like mass of rock. It is formed from molten material that enters cracks in older rocks and then cools and becomes solid.

Pegmatite dikes in Brazil, Madagascar, and California produce many fine gemstones. The material in these dikes is coarse and has many crystals in it. Important gemstones found in pegmatite dikes include aquamarine and other varieties of beryl (but not emeralds), tourmaline, topaz, and quartz.

When molten rock at great depth meets some impure limestone, it usually changes the limestone into marble. The impurities that were present may then form gemstones. Gemstones formed this way are corundum (rubies and sapphires), spinel, and a type of garnet. The finest rubies and sapphires found anywhere in the world today are mined in Burma.

Burma produces a bewildering number of gemstones—not only the usual rubies and blue sapphires, but sapphires of many other colors, star sapphires and star rubies, spinel, topaz, peridot (olivine), garnet, quartz, and many other rare gems. Ceylon, another famous gem source, has long been called the Island of Gems. Almost all the major gemstones except diamonds and emeralds are found there. The finest emeralds ever found come from Colombia, in South America.

▶ SYNTHETIC GEMSTONES

Today substitutes for gemstones can be produced. There are two kinds of substitutes: synthetics and imitations. A synthetic gem has the same chemical makeup and the same crystal structure as the gem being copied. Imitations look like the natural gem but do not have the same basic structure. Even though synthetic gemstones are so much like the gemstones copied, there are tests by which a natural gem can be discovered.

Some synthetic gems are grown in a high-temperature mixture of melted chemicals. Others are grown from solutions under high pressure. But in the chief method used today, a mixture of powdered chemicals is fed slowly into an intensely hot flame. The powder melts and falls onto the tip of a heat-resistant rod. A crystal forms at the tip of the rod and grows in a shape something like a carrot's. The crystal is then cut and polished into final shape.

TESTING GEMS

Gem testing is one of the duties performed by a gemologist, who is an expert in the science of gemstones. The gemologist grades gemstones and judges their value. With a very powerful microscope he can identify synthetic gems by the type and shape of materials enclosed in the crystal as it grew. To test gemstones he may observe the degree to which a stone bends light (refractive index), its weight, and the light effects it has.

CUTTING GEMSTONES

The beauty of a gemstone often depends on the way it is cut. Poor cutting decreases the value of a stone. To be truly brilliant a gem must have balanced measurements and a high polish. Poor cutting usually leaves a transparent stone with a "window," or a spot in the center through which objects can be seen. With proper cutting, brilliant reflections should appear across the entire stone. These reflections also help to develop the strength of color, or fire, in a stone, as well as its brilliancy. This method of cutting is called **facet** cutting and is used only with transparent stones.

The **cabochon** cut is the method of smoothing and rounding out a stone. Long ago, before men learned facet cutting, all gemstones were given cabochon cutting. The only stones now cut in this way are opaque stones and stones with special cat's-eye effects, asterism, or opalescence.

GEM MINERALS

Diamond. The diamond is called the king of gems. The beauty of this gemstone comes from its fire and brilliancy, as most diamonds are colorless. The few diamonds that do have color, like the blue Hope diamond and the apple-green Dresden diamond, are especially valuable.

Many of the famous diamonds have come from India, once the chief place to get diamonds. In the 1720's, after the supply in India had been mined out, diamonds were discovered in Brazil. The South African deposits came to light in 1867, and since then Africa has been the chief source of diamonds.

Corundum (Ruby and Sapphire). The red ruby and the blue sapphire are transparent varieties of the mineral corundum. These gemstones have little fire and depend on color for their beauty. All transparent corundum that is not red is called sapphire. The sapphire is usually blue, but there are also white sapphires, pink sapphires, and yellow, or golden, sapphires. According to folklore, the sapphire has many magical properties and is used by witches in their enchantments. The ruby was thought to give courage, prevent impure thoughts, preserve chastity, and kill poisonous reptiles that it touched.

Beryl. The mineral beryl includes the gemstones **emerald**, **aquamarine**, **golden beryl**, and **morganite**. All these stones are transparent.

The bright grass-green emerald, traditionally a symbol of eternal life, is one of the most valuable gemstones. A very good emerald is of greater value than a diamond of the same size. Old stones came from the ancient mines of Cleopatra in Upper Egypt. When Spaniards conquered Peru, they found great quantities of emeralds there. In the 1550's they found the mines in Colombia that are now the main source of emeralds.

It is very unusual to find a flawless emerald. Even synthetic emeralds have flaws.

The word "aquamarine" means "seawater" and describes perfectly the color of most of these stones. Some aquamarine is pale blue. This stone typically is free from visible flaws and makes very attractive jewelry.

Morganite is the name for rosy or pink beryl. Yellow or golden beryl has a golden-yellow color.

Topaz. The topaz has long been considered a symbol of fidelity. This gemstone is known for its warm golden glow. But not all yellow stones are topaz. A yellow quartz, called citrine, is sometimes mistakenly called topaz. Nor is all topaz yellow. Some is perfectly colorless, faintly tinted, pink, or blue.

The stones are found principally in pegmatite dikes and cavities in granite. Many come from Brazil.

Garnet. Garnet is a common mineral, but garnets of gem quality are rare. There are garnets in many colors. **Pyrope**, used as a gem, is a beautiful deep pure red. **Almandite** is perhaps the best known of the garnets. It is usually a dark brownish- or violet-red. **Rhodo-**

January—garnet.

February—amethyst.

March—aquamarine.

April—diamond.

May—emerald.

June—pearl.

July—star ruby.

August—peridot.

September—sapphire.

October—opal.

November—topaz.

December—turquoise.

Opal.

Garnet.

The pictures on this page show rough gemstones and polished gems cut from each.

Amethyst.

Aquamarine.

CURIOUS BELIEFS ABOUT GEMSTONES

Opals bring disaster, rubies remove evil thoughts, turquoise brings good fortune—these are some of the superstitions that people have about gemstones. Superstitions about gems have existed since earliest times. Sometimes beliefs about the same stone have differed. For instance, Europeans in the Middle Ages believed that diamonds were a symbol of the sun and of innocence. In Persia during the same period of time diamonds were believed to be a source of sin and sorrow and to have been created by the devil.

There are many different beliefs about the influence of gems on love and marriage. Turquoise used to be popular because it was thought to prevent disagreement between a husband and wife. Aquamarine promotes the love of married couples. The women of ancient Rome wore amethysts to assure their husbands' love. Topaz is a symbol of loyalty. Those who wear it are said to be devoted to their husbands or wives for life. A diamond must be given in love or it will lose its value. An emerald is a symbol of success in love and so can be used in an engagement ring.

Some stones are believed to have the power to cure or prevent illness. Amethyst is considered especially effective against headache and toothache. Diamonds are believed to cure leprosy, insanity, and nightmares. When placed in a wound, a bloodstone or a ruby is said to stop the flow of blood. Agate reduces fever. A carnelian tightens loose teeth. Some people believe that a carnelian can cure tumors and strengthen the voice. Opals or sapphires strengthen failing eyesight.

Various stones were (and are) worn as amulets—ornaments used as protection against evil. Sapphire was originally believed to give protection from spirits of darkness and to encourage pure thoughts. The Chinese put jade bracelets or anklets on their children to protect them from harm. The Hindus use pearls for an especially strong charm to protect themselves against all evils. The garnet, because it is the color of blood, is believed to make its wearer incapable of being wounded or injured.

Some amulets are worn to protect against human enemies. The aquamarine protects against enemies in battle and in lawsuits. The sapphire preserves its wearer from the envy and fury of his enemies.

There are many other special amulets. An opal necklace is supposed to guard the life and color of blond hair. A turquoise is said to be a prime charm against falling from a horse.

Some gems are supposed to give warning of poison. In the presence of poison an emerald will burn, an opal will turn pale, and a ruby will become cloudy. Diamonds repel poison, as well as witchcraft and madness. Sapphire also protects one from poison. A poisonous reptile placed in the same glass with a sapphire is supposed to die from the rays of the gem.

A gemstone may also be worn as a talisman, an object that magically produces positive qualities in its wearer. Both aquamarine and amethyst are used to quicken the intellect. Carnelian restrains anger and gives a man dignity and courage in battle. Muslims traditionally believe that the carnelian preserves tranquility in the midst of turmoil and keeps its wearer happy and blessed. The olive-green peridot is worn as a talisman to give its wearer full reason and a merciful disposition. However, the peridot does not exert its fullest power unless it is set in gold. Sapphire is a stone of very good omen, bringing health, wealth, and strength. Either plain or starred, it has been called one of the luckiest of talismans.

A very special quality credited to the amethyst by the Greeks is that of keeping a wine drinker sober. The theory stemmed from the legend of Bacchus and Diana (Artemis). According to the legend, Bacchus, the god of wine, became inflamed with love for a beautiful nymph. She, wanting to escape the drunken god, fled to Diana, the patron goddess and protectress of maidens. Diana protected her by changing her into a white stone statue. Later Bacchus was sorry he had chased her. As a sign of affection for her, he poured an offering of purple wine over the statue. As the statue turned from white to purple, Bacchus vowed that anyone who wore an amethyst would be immune from drunkenness.

lite, a combination of pyrope and almandite, looks like a pale almandite.

Spessartite. Spessartite yields some of the most colorful stones: pale orange-yellow, orange, orange-red, and even deep red. **Grossularite** has two major gem varieties. One is a transparent orange-brown, like topaz. The other is a translucent, jadelike green. **Andradite** gems are the most spectacular. One of these, called **demantoid**, is a lovely bright green. It is the most valued gemstone of the garnet family.

Zircon. Zircon is available in a wide range of colors, most of them rarely seen in jewelry. The brilliancy and fire of the colorless zircon are second only to a diamond's. Another beautiful zircon is a transparent and brilliant greenish-blue stone unlike any other natural stone. Golden-brown zircons have a special warmth of color. There are also brown, brownish-red, and gray zircons.

Opal. A famous English art critic once wrote that "Opal shows the most glorious colors to be seen in the world, save only those of the clouds." The opal sometimes holds all these colors in one stone. But there are many varieties of opal. The finest come from Australia. These have a black background with vivid colors. Next in value and beauty are white opals that also come from Australia. Fire opals from Mexico are usually yellows, reds, and browns. A valuable black opal is sometimes found in Nevada.

Whole logs of opalized wood have been found in North America. But gem opals are found in quantity in only two countries—Australia and Mexico. Beautiful opal in Mexico was being cut and polished by the Aztecs long before America was discovered by Europeans.

Quartz. Quartz is the commonest of all minerals. It has been found in nearly every kind of rock and includes more gemstones than any other mineral.

Rock crystal is transparent, colorless quartz. It has been cut into vases and crystal balls. When cut for necklaces and other jewelry it is called rhinestone. Much of what is sold now as rhinestone jewelry is really made of cut glass.

One of the most beautiful forms of quartz is the lovely purple or violet **amethyst**. The name comes from the Greek word meaning "not

drunk." The Greeks believed that anyone who drank wine from an amethyst cup would not get drunk.

Citrine is a yellow or yellowish-brown quartz. It is often sold as topaz-quartz or, incorrectly, as topaz. Rose quartz is usually a translucent pink stone. Many rose-quartz stones show asterism, the star effect. Smoky quartz is a well-crystallized smoky yellow or dark-brown quartz. **Tiger's-eye** is a quartz with a cat's-eye effect that comes in deep brown in nature. It is dyed to blue or red colors.

There are certain kinds of quartz that are known as **chalcedony**. All these stones are translucent, occur in solid or mixed colors, and have unusual markings. Some of these are agate, onyx, bloodstone, sardonyx, carnelian, and petrified wood.

Jade. Jade is the most important precious stone in China. The Chinese believe that it represents the virtues of charity, modesty, courage, justice, and wisdom. They use it for intricately carved objects of great beauty.

Jade includes two different minerals that look alike: **nephrite** and **jadeite**. Nephrite, the more common, is most often a dull green or dark green, and sometimes is found in white, bluish, yellowish, black, or reddish shades. The finer of the two jades is jadeite, which comes from Burma. Jadeite is usually white or emerald green and sometimes brown, orange, red, or black.

Chrysoberyl. The mineral chrysoberyl forms two unusual gemstones: **alexandrite** and **cat's-eye**.

Alexandrite is a transparent stone that is green or blue-green by daylight and becomes red in artificial light. It was named for Czar Alexander II of Russia when it was discovered in the Ural Mountains of Russia in 1833. The cat's-eye is a gem with chatoyancy. There are quartz cat's-eyes and beryl and tourmaline cat's-eyes, but the best cat's-eye is the chrysoberyl.

Tourmaline. One of the most striking minerals is the tourmaline. This gemstone has a wide range of colors—sometimes as many as five different colors appear in one crystal. It has become a very popular gem. Pink tourmaline is important to the Chinese. They often carve from it small art objects of religious importance. The gem also has an electrical attraction when it is hot. This was first noticed by some Dutch children who saw a tourmaline attracting ashes and straw when the sun shone hotly upon it.

Peridot (Olivine). The Roman naturalist Pliny in A.D. 70 mentioned a deposit of olivine on St. John's Island in the Red Sea. It is likely that even before this, big green crystals of olivine were being mined in Burma.

The word "olivine" comes from the olive-green color of many of the stones. Jewelers call this stone peridot. The yellow-green variety is called **chrysolite**.

Spinel. Spinel has often been confused with the ruby. Although the deep-red and transparent stone is the most popular of spinel gems, there are also blue, violet, green, and black spinels.

Turquoise. The bright color of turquoise is very popular in American jewelry of Navajo design. The Navajo kept pieces of turquoise with them at all times, believing that it brought them closer to the gods and kept them from harm. The Aztecs wore turquoise jewelry to reveal their rank.

The color of turquoise varies considerably, but sky-blue is the most prized color. The stone is usually opaque and somewhat waxy. In a fine-quality turquoise the color is permanent, but waxed turquoise often becomes discolored.

Feldspar. Feldspar is a very common mineral found in many rocks. Feldspar is usually opaque and not very attractive, but some lovely gemstones are found in it. One is **moonstone**. **Amazonite**, **sunstone**, and **labradorite** also come from feldspar. Moonstone is an unusual stone with a pearly luster and a floating blue light. Amazonite is a bright, jadelike green. Sunstone has a moonstone effect, with a reddish color and yellow and red reflections. Labradorite shows multicolored reflections as the stone is turned. It may be a glistening bright blue or glistening greens, golds, bronzes, or coppers.

Lazurite (Lapis Lazuli). The deep-blue lapis lazuli is not one mineral but a combination of many different minerals.

Since ancient times, lapis lazuli has been valued for its use as an ornamental gem and as a source of the pigment ultramarine. It is the "sapphire" mentioned in the Bible. In ancient Egypt the beautiful stone was used for inlaid work on vases and ornaments.

▶ ORGANIC GEMS

Pearl. The pearl is known as the queen of gems. This gem has a lovely soft glow in its natural state. A perfect pearl only needs to be drilled for stringing to be shown off beautifully. A pearl results from an irritation to an oyster or some other shellfish. When the oyster has an irritating object within its body, it gradually builds over it a lustrous coating called **nacre**, or mother-of-pearl. Mother-of-pearl is a shell-lining material that the shellfish normally develops. As the mother-of-pearl continues to cover the irritating object layer by layer, over the years it builds up a pearl. A cultured pearl is created when an irritating object, such as a large round bead, is put into the shell of a live oyster. A coating of mother-of-pearl grows over this.

Coral. Coral is used for necklaces, bracelets, and other beaded types of decoration. Coral is the hard, stony skeleton built by a small sea animal called a coral polyp. Coral may be red, pink, white, or black. The red, pink, and black kinds are the ones used as gems. Most gem coral is taken from water along the shores of the Mediterranean Sea and in the Sea of Japan.

Amber. Amber is a hardened resin that once oozed out of prehistoric trees. It is now found under layers of sand and gravel. For many years amber has been a well-known material. Much amber is purely transparent, but amber may contain perfect specimens of prehistoric insects that were trapped in the sticky resin ages ago.

Amber that is not suited for use as gems may be carved and is sometimes manufactured into combs, jewel cases, and other items. Most amber comes from deposits along the southern coast of the Baltic Sea.

Jet. A very hard and very black special variety of lignite, or brown coal, is known as jet. This gem is velvety black, light in weight, and warm to touch. In Victorian times, when black was commonly worn for funerals and for periods of mourning, jet was a popular gemstone for these occasions. Today the use of black jewelry is no longer limited chiefly to mourning, and many people may be seen wearing jet or imitation jet.

Reviewed by RICHARD T. LIDDICOAT, JR.
President, Gemological Institute of America

See also CRYSTALS; DIAMONDS; JADE; JEWELRY; MINERALS; ORES; PEARLS; QUARTZ; ROCKS.

GENEALOGY

It is a fact of life—you have two parents, four grandparents, eight great-grandparents, sixteen great-great-grandparents, and so on, back to the very beginnings of human existence. You probably know who your parents and grandparents are and where they came from. But who were your great-great-grandparents? Who were your ancestors in the 17th, 18th, and 19th centuries? Where did they live? How did you get here if they lived there?

People have been asking questions like these for thousands of years. The Bible has the stories of many families. The ancient Greeks and Romans kept track of their relatives—sometimes to show that they were related to the gods. The study of families and their relationships throughout history is called **genealogy**. The record of a particular family is also called a genealogy, or a **family tree**.

Right: A grandmother helps her grandchildren trace their family tree, using books and family records. Below: Alex Haley told the story of his search for his family's origins in the book *Roots*.

▶ GENEALOGY TODAY

Today more and more people are studying genealogy. Some of them are professionals. They earn their living tracing family trees for other people. In the United States, many genealogists belong to the American Society of Genealogists, founded in 1940. Some are elected to the National Genealogical Society, founded in 1903.

Many people who are not professional genealogists want to find out their ancestry because they want to join a society such as the Sons of the American Revolution, the Daughters of the American Revolution, or the Colonial Dames of America. Others want to know whether they are related to nobles or kings or queens.

But most people who become interested in genealogy want simply to find out for themselves who they are and where they came from. Many people in the United States started on this search because of a popular book written by Alex Haley (1921–92). This book, *Roots,* told about Haley's search for his family's origins in the United States and Africa.

TRACING YOUR FAMILY TREE

It is not always easy to trace your ancestors. But think of yourself as a detective. As any police detective will tell you, there is a great deal of work—discouraging at times—involved both in the hunt for clues and in following up on them.

Begin at Home

If you decide to trace your own family tree, start at home. Talk to your relatives, especially the older ones. Ask for facts—birth dates, names of parents, names of places where they lived, and so on. It is a good idea to prepare a fact sheet for each relative. It might look somewhat like this:

MY ANCESTORS

Name of Person _____

Relation to Me _____

Birth Date _____ Place _____

Father's Name _____

Mother's Name _____

Brothers' and Sisters' Names _____

_____

_____

Schools Attended _____

_____

_____

Occupations _____

_____

_____

Where He/She Lived _____

_____

Spouse's Name _____

Marriage Date _____ Place _____

Children: Number _____

    Name   Birth Date

_____   _____

_____   _____

_____   _____

You probably will not be able to fill in all the blanks on the fact sheet right away because you will not have all the information. But start a sheet even if all you know is the person's name. That makes him or her "real" to you. And as you go back several generations, the number of your ancestors will quickly increase. This will be confusing if you do not have a good system for recording information. If you could trace your family back to the year 1600, you would find about 65,000 ancestors!

Write down the stories that your relatives tell you as well—stories of what school was like, what games they played, what pets they had, how they were affected by wars or any other big events. You will discover that your relatives have done many interesting things. Perhaps some were famous.

Some relatives may live far away. Write to them. Describe your project and ask for their help. Send along copies of your fact sheet and ask them to fill out one for each relative that they know about.

Ask your parents and relatives for permission to see scrapbooks, family Bibles, diaries, letters, passports, birth and death certificates, marriage licenses. It make take some gentle nudging on your part to get people to remember where they have stored these things. But such papers can be very useful.

Use Public Records

After you have gathered as much information as possible from your family, you are ready to check public records. This is where tracing ancestors begins to become difficult.

In Europe, written records were not kept for most people until the 1500's. Before that time, some genealogies were made into poems or songs and recited on special occasions. But only the genealogies of nobles and kings were considered important enough to be remembered in this way. The family histories of most people were forgotten. Regular record keeping was not common in many countries until very recently.

Even when records exist, they may be incorrect or incomplete. Records may be wrong because the people who kept them were careless or made unintentional mistakes. For example, a person who could not read or write could not tell a record keeper how to spell his or her name. The record keeper would have to guess at the correct spelling. In such cases, many people with slightly different last names may actually be related to one another.

Sometimes records are lost or burned. A big fire in Chicago destroyed almost all the city and county records up to 1872. People may

Old, weathered tombstones sometimes provide valuable clues to a person's heritage.

Above: Immigrants in the early 1900's gave facts about themselves to immigration officers. Below: The Genealogical Department of the Mormon Church.

have changed their names—or immigration officials may have changed the names for them.

Black people in America have special problems when they try to trace their ancestors. Before the Civil War, most blacks in the United States were slaves. No one kept track of their last names. Records sometimes gave only the age and sex of the slave. In any case, slaves were not allowed to keep their African names, which might have given clues about their families and the places that they came from. After the war, many took their former owners' names.

But if you are fortunate, you will find that public records are available for many of your ancestors. They may include such things as land deeds, census records, wills, and military records. If you know, for instance, where and when some of your ancestors settled, you can check county and town records and perhaps learn where they bought land, how much they paid for it, and how long they kept it.

Churches and graveyards are also excellent sources of information. Churches have records of births, marriages, and deaths. Tombstones may give birth and death dates. They may also indicate family relationships and provide other information.

Other Help in the Search

Public libraries have many books that tell you how to trace your family tree. Government collections, such as the National Archives and the Library of Congress in Washington, D.C., are valuable sources. There are also many historical societies, genealogical societies, and other groups that have collections and libraries that are devoted to the subject. In the United States, one of the best of these is the Genealogical Department of the Church of Jesus Christ of Latter-Day Saints in Salt Lake City, Utah. It has about 60,000,000 names on record, including those of Mormons and non-Mormons. Other sources include the New England Historic Genealogical Society and the New York Genealogical and Biographical Society.

JENNY TESAR
Program Design, Inc.

Reviewed by KENN STRYKER-RODDA
Fellow, The American Society of Genealogists

GENERATORS, ELECTRIC. See ELECTRIC GENERATORS.

On the earth today there are more than 1,500,000 different kinds of living plants and animals and microbes. We are but one of these kinds of organisms, or living beings. Every kind of organism has a way of life that is its own. Even very similar kinds of living beings follow somewhat different ways of life. What makes each kind of living being and its way of life different from all others? Part of the answer can be found in the study of genetics.

Each kind of organism is called a species. When we observe just one species, we see that each of its many millions or billions of individual beings follows a similar path: it begins life, lives for a certain period of time, and then dies. Its length of life ranges from a few minutes in some microbes to thousands of years in some ancient trees.

Sometime during this span of life an organism performs its most important act: it reproduces and gives rise to new beings like itself. Some organisms are able to do this alone. Some can do it only with the help of another organism of the opposite sex. In either case, parents give rise to offspring, and so the species is continued on earth for another generation.

Life on earth is an unbroken chain. Each new generation is linked to the last one by a strand of living substance. Parent organisms give a part of themselves to start their new offspring along the path of life. The way a new individual develops depends on the "instructions" it receives from its parents. These instructions are found in large molecules called **genes**.

There are countless kinds and numbers of genes. Each species of organism contains many different genes. Parents pass along a set of genes each time they reproduce. But each set may be a little different from other sets of genes passed on by the same parents. Thus when parents produce a number of offspring, they will find each individual offspring more or less like themselves, yet each one may be distinct.

In the language of the genes is written the story of life. The study of genes—what they consist of, how they work, how they are passed from parent to offspring, and how they change—is called **genetics**.

GENETICS

Some small organisms seem to have very little shape. The flowing mass of living substance called an amoeba can be seen through a microscope. When it reproduces, the "parent" amoeba separates into two similar halves. By this process one parent amoeba divides into two "young," smaller amoebas. Each "young" amoeba is independent. It begins to take in food, and it grows. When it is large enough and "old" enough, it again divides into two new amoebas. Each new amoeba resembles its parent in appearance and way of life.

Like the amoeba, many other small organisms arise from a single parent. Among most of the larger plants and animals that you see every day, however, life begins in a different way. They have two parents—one male, one female. At certain times in life each parent produces special reproductive cells. Males produce sperm, and females produce eggs. Like most cells, each reproductive cell has a central part, the nucleus. The nucleus contains long, thin bodies called chromosomes. The chromosomes contain most of a cell's genes—its chemical instructions. The nucleus of a

The amoeba reproduces by dividing in half.

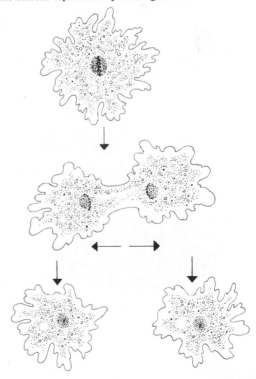

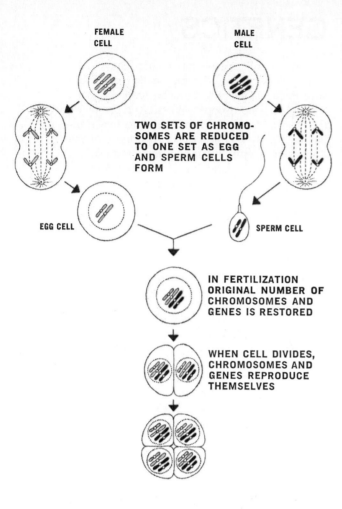

FEMALE
CELL

MALE
CELL

TWO SETS OF CHROMO-
SOMES ARE REDUCED
TO ONE SET AS EGG
AND SPERM CELLS
FORM

EGG CELL

SPERM CELL

IN FERTILIZATION
ORIGINAL NUMBER OF
CHROMOSOMES AND
GENES IS RESTORED

WHEN CELL DIVIDES,
CHROMOSOMES AND
GENES REPRODUCE
THEMSELVES

Sperm cells, below, surround a human egg cell. When a
sperm cell enters the egg, a new individual starts.

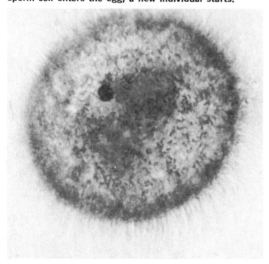

sperm cell carries a set of genes from the male parent. The nucleus of an egg cell carries a set of genes from the female parent.

Sperm cells are very tiny and can be seen only through a microscope. Egg cells may be somewhat larger, but many also are invisible to the unaided eye. Eggs that contain much stored material may be quite large, however. You can see the eggs of fish, amphibians, reptiles, and birds quite readily. The egg cells of many plants, on the other hand, may be hidden deep within the flowers.

A new individual begins when a sperm cell enters an egg cell. Once within the egg, the genes brought by the sperm join the genes of the egg. Two sets of genes are now contained within a single nucleus. The egg cell is then said to be fertilized. It has two sets of chemical instructions.

In time the fertilized egg divides into two cells. In preparation for this cell division, each gene in the nucleus reproduces itself. Each new cell thus gets the two sets of genes that were present in the fertilized egg. The cells continue to divide, forming more and more new cells. Each new cell in the developing organism contains a nucleus with one set of genes from the male parent and another set of genes from the female parent. These two sets of genes, working together, determine the hereditary (inherited) traits of the offspring. Each cell has in its nucleus its own genetic "control center."

This general pattern of sexual reproduction is the same in many forms of life, including humans. A new individual results from the joining together of male and female reproductive cells. Together these cells, through the genes they contribute, control the development of the new individual.

A new individual starts as a fertilized egg. But how does its development continue? What causes this small new cell to develop into a particular kind of animal or plant?

The answer can be found within the genes. Genes "tell" the cell exactly how to manufacture the molecules it needs. When these instructions are followed, the fertilized egg develops into a mature organism that resembles the parents. This process has been repeated again and again over the thousands and millions of years that life has existed on earth.

Each puppy in a litter resembles the parents but shows individual features.

▶ THE STUDY OF GENES

Each new organism resembles its parents, and yet it differs from them. Look at the puppies in a new litter, for example. Do they resemble the mother or the father? Or are the puppies like the mother in some ways and like the father in others?

The same question can be asked about human beings. Children may look like one parent or the other, but usually they have some features of each parent. Perhaps Johnny has his mother's nose, his father's ears, and his grandfather's eyes. Each person seems to be a mixture of traits. Some of them we recognize in other members of the family; others seem to be new. Johnny's sister may be quite different from Johnny, from her parents, and from her grandparents. Yet her traits, like Johnny's, are controlled by genes inherited from her ancestors.

The study of genes is called genetics. Genetics, a branch of biology, includes the study of heredity—how offspring resemble their parents outwardly, as well as in their blood types and other physical characteristics. It also tries to find how offspring may differ so much from their parents—the study of variation.

The first clues to the mysteries of heredity and variation were discovered in the 1860's by Gregor Mendel, an Augustinian monk and teacher in what is now the Czech Republic. When not busy with other duties, he carried out plant-breeding experiments in the tiny garden of the monastery. He crossed, or bred together, various kinds of pea plants and studied the number and kinds of offspring produced. For more than seven years he carefully crossed garden peas of many pure varieties. Most important of all, he kept careful records of the appearance of each parent and each offspring. From these records he was able to work out the first rules of heredity.

Gregor Mendel studying heredity in peas.

THE WORK OF MENDEL

In his early experiments Mendel crossed two plants that differed in only one trait. For instance, he crossed plants that produced only green seeds with those that produced only yellow seeds. In the first generation of offspring he found that all the plants produced yellow seeds. Then the first-generation plants were crossed with others of the same generation. Plants in the second generation of offspring produced some yellow seeds and some green seeds. Mendel repeated this cross many times and carefully recorded all the offspring. From the plants of the second generation he got 6,022 yellow seeds and 2,001 green seeds.

From the results of this experiment Mendel was able to draw two conclusions. First, when a plant producing yellow seeds was crossed with a plant producing green seeds, all the plants of the first generation produced only yellow seeds. Because the yellow-seed trait seemed to overshadow the green-seed trait, Mendel called the yellow-seed trait **dominant** to the green-seed trait. But since the green-seed trait reappeared in the next generation, he called it a **recessive** trait—it had disappeared from view only temporarily.

Mendel's second conclusion was based upon the number of dominant seeds and the number of recessive seeds that he obtained from second-generation plants. There were almost exactly three yellow for every green seed. This was a ratio of ¾ to ¼.

Mendel worked out an explanation for these results. He represented traits by letters of the alphabet. For instance, Y could stand for the dominant yellow-seed trait and y for the recessive green-seed trait. Today such letters are used to stand for the genes that control the traits of yellowness and greenness. Other letters may stand for genes that control other traits.

Two genes in each cell of the pea plants control the color of the seeds. In plants that always produce yellow seeds the genes are represented as YY. In plants that always produce green seeds the genes are yy. When these two kinds of plants are crossed, each reproductive cell carries one gene. In this way, for instance, a sperm cell from a yellow-seeded plant may carry one Y gene and an egg cell from a green-seeded plant may carry one y gene. When the sperm nucleus enters the egg, a Y gene and a y gene are contained in the fertilized egg. Since the Y gene is

ONE OF MENDEL'S EXPERIMENTS

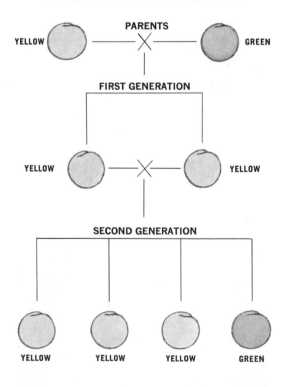

EXPLANATION OF THE EXPERIMENT

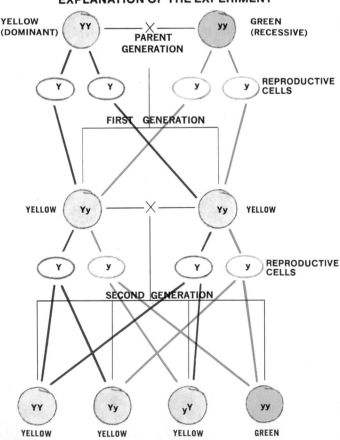

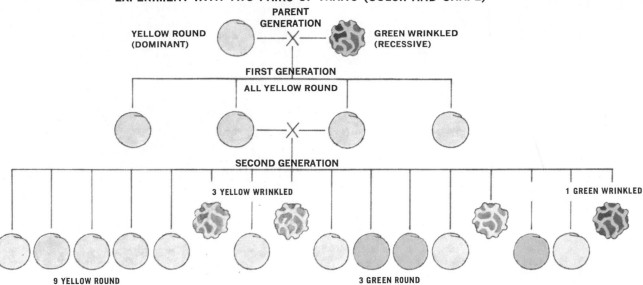

dominant to the *y* gene, only yellow seeds are produced by first-generation plants.

Each first-generation plant produces two kinds of reproductive cells in equal numbers; half have *Y* genes and half have *y* genes. Either kind (*Y* or *y*) of sperm nucleus may unite with either kind (*Y* or *y*) of egg nucleus. That is, *Y* can join with *Y*, *Y* with *y*, *y* with *Y*, or *y* with *y*. In ¾ of the resulting peas, the dominant gene *Y* is present, and the seeds are yellow. But in ¼ of the peas, only the two recessive genes (*yy*) are present. Then the seeds are green. This explains the ¾ to ¼ ratio that Mendel found in the second generation.

In further experiments Mendel crossed plants that differed in other traits. For example, he crossed tall plants with short plants. All the offspring were tall. He concluded that the heredity factor (now called a gene) for long stems was dominant to the factor for short stems. Then the first-generation plants were crossed. In the second generation, ¾ of the plants were tall and ¼ of the plants were short. The same rules of inheritance seemed to operate for color of seed.

▶ THE UNIT OF HEREDITY

Mendel based his rules on an important idea. This was the idea that a hereditary trait depended upon a single "factor." Each factor behaved independently, and it controlled a single trait. Each factor also remained "pure," or unchanged, from generation to generation. Even when the trait was not visible, the factor for that trait was unchanged and the trait

could reappear in a later generation. To find out if these factors (genes) behaved as independent units, Mendel studied two pairs of traits in the same plants. He knew from crossing various kinds of plants that the factor for round seeds was dominant to the factor for wrinkled seeds. He also knew that the factor for yellow seeds was dominant to the factor for green seeds.

Mendel crossed plants producing yellow, round seeds with those plants producing green, wrinkled seeds. In the first generation all plants produced seeds that were yellow and round. When the first-generation plants were crossed, Mendel found four kinds of offspring in the second generation. Some seeds were yellow and round; some were green and round; some were yellow and wrinkled; and some were green and wrinkled.

If genes are units, then those controlling seed shape should behave independently from those controlling seed color. The experiments showed that this is what happens. When the genes pass separately into reproductive cells, four kinds of reproductive cells are possible in either male or female parts of the plants. Since each of the four kinds of sperm cells can fertilize any of the four kinds of egg cells, 16 gene combinations are possible. But only four types of offspring appear. This is because one gene of each pair may be dominant to the others. Mendel obtained a ratio of $\frac{9}{16}$ yellow, round seeds to $\frac{3}{16}$ green, round seeds to $\frac{3}{16}$ yellow, wrinkled seeds to $\frac{1}{16}$ green, wrinkled seeds.

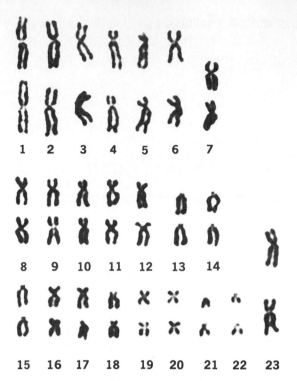

1 2 3 4 5 6 7

8 9 10 11 12 13 14

15 16 17 18 19 20 21 22 23

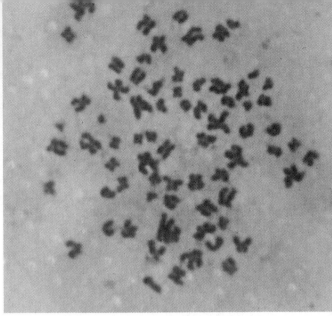

Left: The 23 pairs of human chromosomes arranged by pairs. The last pair (23) shows that these chromosomes are from a female. A male would have an X and Y chromosome instead of a pair of X chromosomes. Above: The 23 pairs in a cell.

Mendel reported his conclusions in 1865. His work was an entirely new approach to the problems of heredity. It provided a sound basis for future experiments in genetics. But scientists who knew about it did not understand or appreciate Mendel's work. Its importance was not recognized until 1900, 35 years after the work was completed.

Today scientists, from their study of genes, understand many more rules of inheritance. They know that Mendel's conclusions do not always apply. They also know a great deal about the chemistry of the genes. Their knowledge of heredity has been applied to the solutions of many practical problems.

Much has been learned about the way in which new varieties of living things arise. Some of the new varieties are of benefit to us. Most of today's foods, for example, come from plant and animal varieties that were unknown early in this century.

Scientists have also learned that certain chemical disorders in people are caused by defects in specific genes. Some of these disorders can be treated with special diets. The person is not permitted to have foods containing chemicals that his or her body cannot use.

The study of genetics leads from the tiny nucleus of the cell to the study of individuals and families to the study of huge populations of millions and billions of bacterial and mold cells and virus particles. Let us now look within cells to learn more about the genes themselves.

▶ LOCATING THE GENES

The genes had to be somewhere in cells, but where? Scientists who had studied cells looked for some part of the cell that behaved the way genes seemed to act. What was it in the cell that behaved independently and was found in both sperms and eggs?

The answer was found in the nucleus, which both sperm cells and egg cells possess. Within the nucleus of each cell are long, thin strands, or threads. (These become short and thick when cells divide.) When the strands are colored with special dyes, they can easily be seen through a microscope. These strands are called **chromosomes**, which means "colored bodies."

After a series of careful observations and experiments, scientists showed that the chromosomes carried the genes. And the behavior of the chromosomes explains results like those that Mendel found in his breeding experiments.

A sperm cell and an egg cell have one set of chromosomes each. A fertilized egg therefore has two sets of chromosomes. Each chromosome in the sperm set has a partner chromosome in the egg set. Thus chromosomes in body cells occur in pairs. The members of a pair are similar in size and shape.

Each kind of organism has a specific number of chromosome pairs in its body cells. One species of worm has only 1 pair. The fruit fly has only 4 pairs. Corn has 10 pairs, and humans have 23 pairs of chromosomes.

The chromosomes contain the genes. Since chromosomes occur in pairs, their genes are also paired. The chromosomes of a cell may contain hundreds of thousands of pairs of genes. Each gene pair controls one or more features of the organism. The genes are the cell's "master molecules." From their control centers in cell nuclei, genes exert their power over the life of cells and the organism composed of those cells. Some genes are now known to be outside the nucleus. Their nature and activities are still under study.

▶ HOW GENES CHANGE

Life has existed on earth for many millions of years. The kinds of life on earth today are different from those of long ago. The genes that control their growth and development are also different. The many changes scientists can observe must depend on changes in the genes themselves.

Genes usually produce exact copies of themselves for hundreds of cell generations. But genes do change, sometimes without apparent cause. A sudden and permanent gene change is called a **mutation**. When a

mutated gene reproduces itself, it makes copies of its new form. Under normal conditions of life, mutations of a particular gene are rare.

Because of mutations there is much genetic variety in the living world. When a gene mutates, its new action may cause a trait to develop in a different way. In human beings, for instance, eye color is gene-controlled. Because of past mutations, eyes may be blue, gray, hazel, green, brown, or black. The color and kind of hair is also under genetic control. Hair may be blond, red, brown, or black. It may also be straight, wavy, curly, or absent.

More mutations occur when organisms are exposed to certain agents. X rays and other kinds of radiation, for instance, may greatly increase the number of mutations in organisms. Certain chemical substances and high temperature may also increase the number of mutations that occur.

There are mutations that may be beneficial to an organism. They make it possible for the organism to live more successfully and to leave more offspring. But other mutations—most of them, in fact—are harmful to the organism. Fewer offspring are produced by the organism in which the mutations appear. Some mutations are so harmful that organisms containing them are not able to live and reproduce at all. Since most mutations are harmful, special precautions must be taken when people work with radiation and with substances

Fruit fly (Drosophila) has four pairs of chromosomes. Drosophila reproduces rapidly and is widely used to study effects of changes in the chromosome arrangement.

Corn has 10 pairs of chromosomes. At one stage in the process of cell division, chromosomes are arranged in long ribbons.

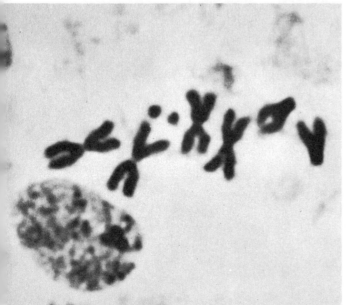

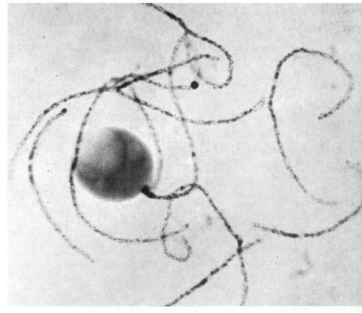

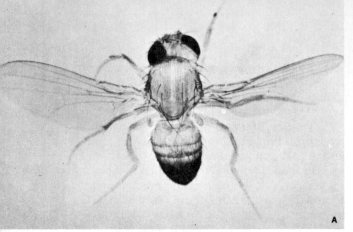

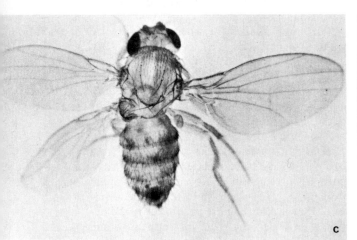

Radiation affects genes and can change patterns of heredity. All the flies above were exposed to radiation except A, which is a normal fruit fly. B is a four-winged fly with double body segment; C and D are three-winged flies with partly doubled segments.

that might cause mutations. The reproductive cells in particular should be protected. Mutations in these cells may be passed on to the next generation.

▶ HOW GENES WORK

The mystery of how genes carry out their remarkable work is now being solved. It has been known since 1944 that most genes are a special kind of nucleic acid, or chemical building block—deoxyribonucleic acid, or **DNA**. DNA is a large molecule, made up of four similar kinds of smaller molecules. These smaller molecules are hooked together into long, spiral chains. The arrangement of the four kinds of smaller molecules forms a chemical message, somewhat as the arrangement of letters forms a word. Many different words can be made from a few letters, and many different DNA messages can be made from a few chemical "letters."

The genes of a cell thus carry a set of messages. They are a library of information. They give the cells chemical instructions about how to manufacture certain kinds of molecules. These instructions are passed from DNA to ribonucleic acid, or **RNA**. RNA is similar to DNA in chemical structure.

RNA transfers the instructions out of the nucleus to certain structures in the cell called **ribosomes**. The ribosomes determine the way protein molecules are formed.

A protein molecule is made of a long chain of amino acids, which, like nucleic acids, are basic building blocks. There are about 20 kinds of amino acids. These may be arranged in many different ways in a protein molecule.

Proteins are of great importance to all cells. No cell can live without them, and each protein has a specific job to do in the cell. Some proteins make up the cell's basic structure and its membranes. Many others are enzymes. The complicated chemical reactions that take place in a cell are made possible by enzymes. Each enzyme controls a specific kind of chemical reaction at the ordinary temperatures of living organisms. Most of the chemical reactions in a cell depend on one or more enzymes.

It seems that most of the DNA instructions in a cell are for the arrangements of amino acids—and so for the manufacture of specific kinds of proteins. A small change in a DNA message can cause one amino acid to replace another. A change of even one of the hundreds of amino acids in a large protein molecule can result in a different kind of protein.

By controlling the kind of protein molecules that are manufactured, genes control most of the chemical reactions in a cell. A mutation in a DNA molecule can thus affect the entire life of the cell.

▶ HUMAN HEREDITY

Progress in understanding human heredity has been somewhat slower than with other organisms. This is partly because scientists cannot plan "experiments" in human heredity and because humans have few offspring. Scientists do obtain some information by tracing particular traits in members of a family. But memory about past generations is often unreliable. (Did your great-grandmother have blue eyes or were they brown?)

Nevertheless, scientists can often work out an idea of how a trait, such as straight or curly hair, is inherited. When both parents have straight hair, they usually have straight-haired children. When a straight-haired person marries a curly-haired one, they may have curly-haired children. The gene for curly hair thus seems to be dominant. But if the curly-haired parent carries the recessive gene for straight hair, some of the children may have straight hair. Curly-haired couples usually have some curly-haired children. But if each parent carries a recesssive gene for straight hair, some of the children may have straight hair. Observation of children of many such couples indicates

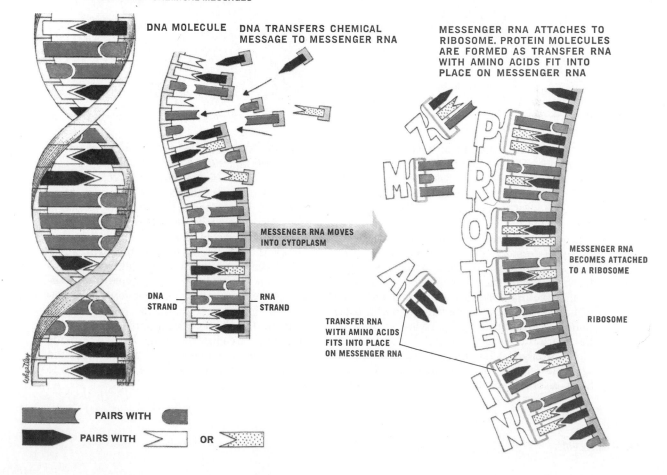

GENES ARE MADE OF DNA MOLECULES, WHICH CARRY CHEMICAL MESSAGES

DNA MOLECULE

DNA TRANSFERS CHEMICAL MESSAGE TO MESSENGER RNA

MESSENGER RNA ATTACHES TO RIBOSOME. PROTEIN MOLECULES ARE FORMED AS TRANSFER RNA WITH AMINO ACIDS FIT INTO PLACE ON MESSENGER RNA

MESSENGER RNA MOVES INTO CYTOPLASM

DNA STRAND

RNA STRAND

MESSENGER RNA BECOMES ATTACHED TO A RIBOSOME

RIBOSOME

TRANSFER RNA WITH AMINO ACIDS FITS INTO PLACE ON MESSENGER RNA

PAIRS WITH

PAIRS WITH   OR

TWINS

Twins are a pair of babies born to the same mother at the same time. They occur once in about 90 human births. They may be **identical twins**, alike in all ways, including their sex. Or they may be **fraternal twins**, alike in some ways, but no more so than non-twin brothers and sisters. Fraternal twins may be of the same sex or of opposite sexes. The two kinds of twins come about differently.

Every human being begins life as a fertilized egg cell, which divides to form two cells. During the division, each gene in the cell reproduces itself, so each of the new cells receives a set of similar genes. The two cells divide to form four cells, and these, too, have genes that are exactly alike. The cells remain attached as they continue to divide. In time a tiny mass of cells,

all exactly alike, is formed. The mass, called an embryo, goes on growing, developing into a baby.

Sometimes, however, the mass of cells splits in two at an early stage. Each half continues to develop, so two embryos are formed. The embryos are alike because the genes in their cells are alike. Each embryo continues to grow, developing into a baby. These babies are identical twins.

Fraternal twins result from the fertilization of two different egg cells. Within the mother's body, usually one egg cell at a time matures, ready for fertilization by a sperm cell. Sometimes two egg cells mature at the same time, and each of them is fertilized by a different sperm cell. The babies may have a few genes of the same kind, but most of their genes are different.

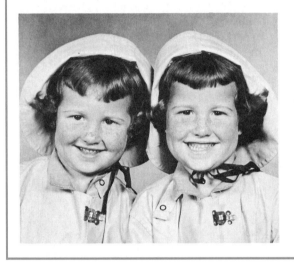 

that there are about three curly-haired children for every straight-haired one. This is the same ratio Mendel found in the second generation of his crosses of garden peas. The basic rules of heredity apply alike to people and to peas.

The way human traits are inherited is only partly understood. Many traits, such as body size and intelligence, seem to be controlled by more than one pair of genes. Environmental factors complicate our understanding of human heredity. For example, is Bill taller than John because of his genes or because he had a better diet in childhood?

Knowledge of human genetics has proved valuable in dealing with inherited diseases. Such disorders occur because a person has

one or more faulty genes. For example, sickle-cell anemia, a serious blood disease, and Tay-Sachs disease, which affects the nervous system, are inherited as recessive traits.

Married couples or people who intend to marry may be concerned about the possibility of their children inheriting a family disorder. Or the couple may have one child with a disorder and fear that another child might also be affected. They may go for **genetic counseling**. A genetic counselor is an expert on inherited disorders. Usually the counselor can estimate the chance that a particular disorder will occur or can suggest tests that can be made even before a child is born. The counselor can often assure a family that there is no need to worry.

GENES IN POPULATIONS

Scientists can study a hereditary trait in large or small groups of organisms. From such studies they can learn the relationships of various populations on earth to each other. For example, they know that genes determine specific types of blood. Human beings may have one of four blood types: A, B, AB, or O.

By taking a small sample of blood from many people in different countries all over the world, scientists learn which kinds of blood are most common in certain areas. They have found, for instance, that about 30 percent of the people in parts of Asia have type B blood. Yet in some American Indian tribes and among the aborigines of Australia there are no people with type B blood.

Apparently, these American and Australian groups have been separated for thousands of years from populations with genes for type B blood. Their people have not intermarried. If the populations had mixed, the gene for type B blood would be present in both populations. Genes that determine other blood types may be studied in the same way.

From such studies scientists learn how genes are distributed in various populations on earth. This can be done in all kinds of populations—such as beetles, flies, rodents, and plants—as well as in humans. Scientists also learn about changes that have occurred in the past.

GENETICS AND EVOLUTION

The term "evolution" refers to the changes that have occurred in life. Scientists who study evolution know much about genetics.

Individual organisms live for a relatively short time. But populations of organisms, which usually live in a particular environment, continue from generation to generation. At least, they continue as long as they produce offspring that can survive under changing conditions—for the earth is constantly changing, and the conditions of life also change.

Sometimes entirely new conditions make different traits valuable to a population. For example, scientists have observed some interesting changes in the peppered-moth population outside Manchester, England. In the middle of the 1800's this area was covered with fields and woods. Most of the moth population was lightly speckled. But the population also contained a few moths with dark-colored wings. The dark wings had appeared as the result of genetic mutations.

Then factories were built. They produced smoke and dirt. Soot settled on trees. As a result, moths with dark-colored wings had a better chance of surviving than moths with light-colored wings. It was harder for birds to see them against the sooty bark.

Thus the dark-colored moths were "selected" for survival. Fewer were eaten, and their numbers multiplied. Light-colored moths were easily seen against the black bark, and more of them were eaten. By the middle 1900's the peppered-moth population near Manchester was almost entirely dark-winged. Only moths with genes for dark wings had flourished under the changed conditions.

Evolution occurs chiefly through such natural selection. Natural selection in turn depends on the genes available in a population. For example, suppose there had been no genes for dark wings in the peppered-moth population. Then the population could not have adapted by that color change to the change in environment. It would probably have been eliminated entirely.

Left: Can you see the light-colored moth on tree bark? Right: Birds easily find light-colored moths on soot-darkened bark. Dark moths have a better chance to survive.

When natural selection operates over long periods of time, species of organisms gradually change. Sometimes all the members of one species belong to a single population. For example, almost all the whooping cranes left on earth are members of a single population that spends its winters in Texas and its summers in northern Canada.

Most species of organisms are made up of many populations. The human species, *Homo sapiens,* is one of these. Some of its populations have long been isolated on islands or in other hard-to-reach areas. These populations gradually developed a distinctive genetic nature and appearance. Today, travel and communication among human populations are easier. There are more marriages between individuals of populations that were once isolated. In the offspring of such marriages, the genes of populations that were once distinctive may be mixed together.

FRANK C. ERK
State University of New York at Stony Brook
See also BODY CHEMISTRY; CELLS; EVOLUTION.

GENETIC ENGINEERING

Long before the principles of genetics were known, early people began to domesticate wild animals and plants. They selected kinds of organisms that could be used for food or for doing work. They also domesticated organisms that gave them pleasure. This selective breeding was an early kind of genetic engineering—a deliberate effort to develop kinds, or strains, of organisms that would benefit human beings.

In time, many new strains of plants and animals were developed. Among these were new strains of cattle, horses, dogs, cats, wheat, rice, and corn. Each new strain was genetically different from its ancient ancestors and from closely related strains. For example, people developed breeds of horses to meet specific needs. Some of these were fast, sleek racehorses. Others were large, strong workhorses.

After 1900, when Mendel's principles of genetics were rediscovered, genetic engineering became a much more accurate science. Scientists worked hard to understand how genes work and how to use genes for specific purposes. They learned to breed pure strains of plants. Purebred strains are genetically constant. That is, all their offspring are exactly like the parents. The purebred strains did not always show desirable qualities. But when different purebreds were bred with one another, some of the offspring showed unusual vigor or higher yields. These strains were **hybrids**. They had genes from two or more different strains.

Hybrid corn strains developed by cross-breeding methods have almost completely replaced the kinds of corn that were grown earlier. The hybrid strains yield much more corn for a given piece of land. Their kernels are more nutritious. The plants also are uniform in size. This makes it possible to harvest the corn by machine.

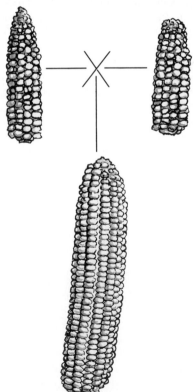

Hybrid strains of corn are produced by crossing pure strains. In only one or two generations, it is possible to obtain strains with desirable characteristics, such as large size or more nutritious kernels.

Through selective breeding, scientists eliminated genes that lead to disease and weakness. They favored genes that result in higher yields, resistance to disease, and the ability to withstand changing conditions of climate.

▶ MUTATIONS MADE TO ORDER

At first, scientists depended on natural mutations (changes) to produce the kinds of genes that could be used in developing new strains. Later, they learned to cause mutations by exposing parent individuals to radiation such as X rays. Even seeds could be x-rayed to produce new mutations. The offspring were examined for new genetic traits, especially for new traits that might be useful. Those offspring that had useful mutations could be used to develop new and valuable strains.

Millions of lives have been saved by one product of genetic engineering that was developed in this way. In 1928, the Scottish scientist Alexander Fleming discovered that *Penicillium* molds make a substance—called penicillin—that slows or stops the growth of some kinds of bacteria. Later, penicillin was found to be effective in killing certain bacteria that cause infections in people.

During World War II, penicillin was of great value in treating infections resulting from wounds. But the molds did not produce nearly enough penicillin to meet the need. In the laboratory some strains of *Penicillium* were x-rayed to cause mutations. The new strains of molds were tested to find any that might yield larger amounts of penicillin. In time, high-yielding strains of *Penicillium* were developed. Large amounts of penicillin were produced, purified, and used during the war. After the war, penicillin was released for general use.

▶ GENE SPLICING

In the 1940's, scientists proved that genes are made of a chemical called deoxyribonucleic acid (DNA). DNA molecules are very big compared to most other molecules. A DNA molecule is made up of many smaller molecules in a definite order, or sequence, like building blocks. When a cell divides, the DNA reproduces itself. Thus the DNA in the two new cells is exactly like that in the parent cell. The new cells contain the same genetic information as did the parent cell.

As scientists learned more about genetics, they began to pay more attention to bacteria and other micro-organisms. These are organisms so small that they can be seen only through a microscope. The tiny organisms are of genetic interest for several reasons. First, the genes of micro-organisms can be removed, purified, and studied more easily than the genes of higher organisms.

Second, it was discovered that DNA is found in several places in bacterial cells. For example, in *Escherichia coli* (*E. coli*), a harmless bacterium that lives in the human intestine, most of the DNA is organized into a single circular chromosome. More DNA is found in small rings called **plasmids**. Plasmids are very useful in manipulating genes.

Third, it also was discovered that *E. coli* and some other kinds of bacteria make special chemicals, or **enzymes,** that are able to cut through strands of DNA at specific places. With these enzymes, bacteria can cut the DNA of viruses that invade their bodies. Viruses are tiny organisms that grow and reproduce only when they are inside living cells. The bacterial enzymes cut the virus DNA into harmless fragments. Since they help to restrict, or limit, the growth of viruses, the enzymes are called **restriction enzymes**.

Scientists now know of dozens of kinds of restriction enzymes. They use these enzymes to learn more about DNA molecules. The enzymes also have made possible a dramatic new kind of genetic engineering called gene splicing. Using gene-splicing methods, scientists can take a gene from one organism and splice it into (make it part of) another organism's genetic material. Because gene splicing recombines DNA in new ways, it is also called **recombinant-DNA**.

▶ HOW GENES ARE SPLICED

A restriction enzyme "recognizes" a certain short grouping, or sequence, of building blocks in DNA. Different enzymes recognize different sequences. Scientists remove plasmids from bacteria and mix the plasmids with a specific restriction enzyme. The enzyme cuts the plasmids at a specific place. Each ring of plasmid is opened, and two sticky ends are formed.

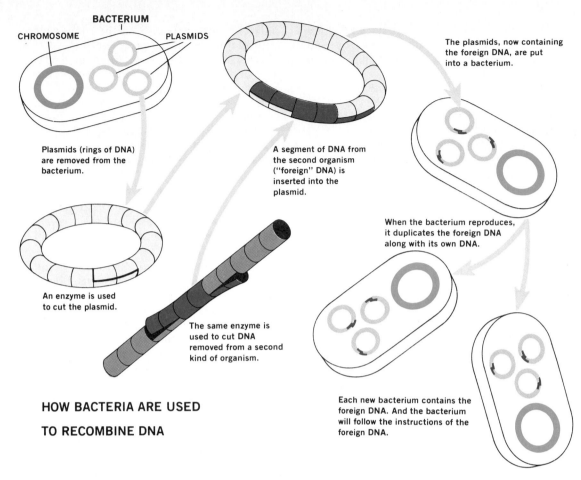

BACTERIUM

CHROMOSOME   PLASMIDS

Plasmids (rings of DNA) are removed from the bacterium.

An enzyme is used to cut the plasmid.

The same enzyme is used to cut DNA removed from a second kind of organism.

A segment of DNA from the second organism ("foreign" DNA) is inserted into the plasmid.

The plasmids, now containing the foreign DNA, are put into a bacterium.

When the bacterium reproduces, it duplicates the foreign DNA along with its own DNA.

Each new bacterium contains the foreign DNA. And the bacterium will follow the instructions of the foreign DNA.

HOW BACTERIA ARE USED TO RECOMBINE DNA

When the same restriction enzyme is used on another kind of DNA—say the DNA of a human being—it cuts that DNA at the same sequence of building blocks. The cut ends have the same shape as the plasmid ends. When this "foreign" DNA is put into the container holding the opened plasmids, some of it joins with the plasmid DNA. In this way, a "foreign" DNA fragment may become part of a plasmid. Its sticky ends attach to the plasmid's sticky ends, and the plasmid ring is once again formed.

The modified plasmids (recombinant DNA) can be taken up by bacteria. When the bacteria divide, the foreign DNA is reproduced along with the rest of the plasmid's DNA.

The building blocks of DNA are the same for most organisms. Therefore, pieces of DNA from quite different species can be spliced together. Almost any kind of plant or animal DNA can be inserted into plasmids.

Even synthetic DNA can be spliced into a cell's genetic material. This is DNA made entirely in the laboratory. It does not come from a living being.

▶ USES FOR GENE SPLICING

Genes are like directions in a do-it-yourself project. They tell a cell what to do. A gene, or fragment of DNA, may tell the cell to put together a certain protein. The protein will have the exact structure specified by the gene. Thus bacteria and other organisms are somewhat like factories. They manufacture the proteins specified by the DNA they contain.

Bacteria will manufacture not only their own proteins but also any protein specified by genetic instructions that have been spliced into their DNA. For example, scientists have spliced a certain gene from the cells of humans into the DNA of *E. coli.* It is the gene that specifies the making of insulin. Insulin is a protein normally made by the pancreas.

It helps to control the amount of sugar in the blood. In some people, the pancreas does not make enough insulin. As a result, these people suffer from diabetes. They must be given insulin from another source. Most of the insulin they use is obtained from cattle and pigs. But animal insulin is not exactly the same as human insulin. It can cause undesirable side effects in people who use it.

When the human insulin gene was spliced into the DNA of *E. coli,* the bacteria began to make insulin. The insulin made by the bacteria is exactly like the insulin made by your body. The bacteria-made insulin is now being tested. If it is proved to be safe, it will become available for use by people with diabetes.

From this one example, you can see that the potential value of gene splicing is great. Micro-organisms can be changed so that they manufacture chemicals needed by people. They can make these chemicals in large quantities and at reasonable cost.

Medical Products. Gene splicing may greatly improve health care. Besides human insulin, scientists have obtained other chemicals through gene splicing. One is human growth hormone, which controls body growth. Some people do not produce enough of this chemical. As a result, they do not grow to normal heights. Children who have this problem can be given growth hormone taken from the bodies of people who have died. But obtaining the hormone in this way is difficult and expensive. Using bacteria to make human growth hormone will mean that much more of the hormone will be available, at a much lower cost.

Another chemical made by gene splicing is interferon. Interferon is a protein made by the human body when viruses invade it. The interferon fights, or interferes with, the viruses. Some scientists believe that interferon may be useful in the fight against some kinds of cancer. Testing this belief has been difficult because interferon has been hard to obtain. Huge amounts of blood are needed to obtain a tiny amount of interferon. But now bacteria and yeast have been genetically engineered to produce human interferon. For the first time, enough interferon will be available to test fully its effects on cancer and other diseases.

Agriculture. Scientists have used gene splicing to develop a vaccine against foot-and-mouth disease. This serious disease is caused by a virus. It affects large numbers of cattle and other farm animals. Tests show that the vaccine is safe and effective against one common type of the virus.

Gene splicing is being used to improve plants. One of the scientists' goals is to improve the nutritional value of plants. Another goal is to improve the plants' resistance to disease. Still another important goal is to develop plants that can make their own fertilizer. Plants need nitrogen compounds to grow. Farmers have to add expensive fertilizers containing these compounds to fields in which they grow corn, wheat, oats, and most other crops. But certain bacteria, called nitrogen-fixing bacteria, can take nitrogen from the air and change it into the compounds that plants need. Biologists would like to take the nitrogen-fixing genes from the bacteria and splice them into the genetic matter of corn and other plants.

Industry. Scientists are using gene-splicing techniques to develop micro-organisms that manufacture certain chemicals that are important in industry. This promises to be cheaper than making the chemicals by traditional methods. Less energy would be needed. And the genetic method, unlike the traditional methods, would not pollute the environment.

▶ **IS GENE SPLICING SAFE?**

Some people believe that gene splicing could be harmful. They worry that new kinds of dangerous organisms could be created, either accidentally or on purpose. Government and private research organizations follow guidelines for gene splicing. Some kinds of experiments can be carried out only in laboratories that have special safety features. So far, there have been no known illnesses or other problems caused by gene splicing. But the valuable contributions that this technology can make are becoming more and more obvious. Over the next few decades, we can expect that products obtained by gene splicing and other kinds of genetic engineering will become a common part of our lives.

FRANK C. ERK
State University of New York at Stony Brook

GENETS, CIVETS, MONGOOSES, AND THEIR RELATIVES

In an African forest a catlike creature climbs nimbly up a tree and stalks a sleeping bird. With a sleek, spotted coat and long, ringed tail, the climber looks somewhat like a small leopard. But it is a genet.

Beneath the tree a larger, spotted animal with a ridge of hair rising along its back runs through the underbrush. Suddenly it pounces on a scurrying forest rat. This hunter is a civet, or civet cat.

In an Indian jungle a small, weasel-like mammal advances toward a cobra. Its hood spread wide, the snake rears and prepares to strike. It faces one of its most dangerous enemies—a mongoose.

In Borneo a beast that looks somewhat like a black bear cub with a bushy tail climbs through the branches of a tree. It opens its mouth and utters a series of loud howls. This creature is the binturong, or bear cat.

In southern Africa a slender animal falls asleep on top of a "tower" of other animals in its colony. This is the odd way in which a suricate, or meerkat, ends its day.

The genet resembles a cat in many ways.

A VARIED AND LITTLE-KNOWN FAMILY

Each of these five mammals is different from the others. Yet each is a member of the family Viverridae, one of the branches of meat-eating mammals. Genets, civets, and mongooses are the main members of this little-known family. But the group also includes many strange relatives of theirs. You have probably never heard of most of them.

In all, the family totals 100 or more species. All of them live in the Eastern Hemisphere. Many of them are African. Others live in tropical Asia and the islands of Indonesia. A number are found only on Madagascar. Two of them live in southern Europe.

Members of the Viverridae generally have long bodies and tails. Their legs are short, and their muzzles are pointed. Many of them have scent glands and can give off a musky odor. Some have sharp, sheathed claws, like cats, and are expert climbers. Most of them are no bigger than squirrels or domestic cats. The largest seldom weigh more than 12 or 14 kilograms (26 to 30 pounds). Usually active at night, they sleep during the day in burrows or in holes in trees. Meat eaters, many of them also eat insects, fruit, and vegetable matter.

As noted, some members of the family resemble small cats. Others remind us of weasels. Sometimes called weasel cats, they take the place of the true weasels in tropical areas of the Eastern Hemisphere. They are a confusing group. Many of them are known only by strange-sounding local names or by their scientific names.

This article will discuss each of the main branches of the family in turn.

GENETS AND LINSANGS

The various species of genets are about the size of small domestic cats. And they are like cats in many ways. Their faces and ears are catlike. They have long, ringed tails. Their claws, used for climbing and for seizing prey, are curved, and they can be drawn back into sheaths.

However, the genets are longer, leaner, and more lithe than the typical cats, and their legs are shorter. Their coats are handsomely spotted, with a black line down the ridge of the back. Expert climbers, they hunt by night for rodents, birds, and other small prey.

Most genets live in Africa, generally be-

tween eastern Africa and the Cape of Good Hope. But the European genet roams Mediterranean countries, from southern Spain to the borders of western Asia. The ancient Greeks are said to have tamed this species. They kept it as a house pet and expert mouser.

The linsangs of Asia are close relatives of the genets. They are even smaller and more slender. Also handsomely spotted or banded, they roam tropical areas of southeast Asia and the islands of Indonesia. One small species of African genet is often called the African linsang.

▶ CIVETS, THE MUSK CARRIERS

The civets, or civet cats, are found in both Africa and Asia. They are generally larger than genets and not so slender. Their bodies are long and somewhat flattened from side to side. They usually have a ridge of upright hair running down their backs. Ground dwellers, they have feet more adapted for running than for climbing. Many of them are as strikingly spotted or banded as the genets.

The Indian civet, one of the largest, may weigh 11 or 12 kilograms (about 25 pounds) and measure about 1 meter from the tip of its sharp nose to the end of its bushy, ringed tail. Civets produce a fatty, yellow substance called civet, or civet musk. They mark their territory with it. Its odor on rocks or trees warns other civets away.

Civet musk is valuable because it is an important ingredient of perfume. For this reason, the Indian civet and the African civet are often kept in captivity. The civet musk is in a double pouch that lies under the skin of the animal's abdomen. It is scooped out through an opening near the civet's tail. Today many perfume companies manufacture civet artificially.

One of the smallest civets is the rasse, which lives in eastern Asia. It has been introduced into Madagascar and other islands. The water civet, an unusual member of the family, lives along jungle streams of the Congo. It has a chestnut-brown body with white lips and throat. Its partially webbed feet are an adaptation for swimming and catching fish.

Right, top to bottom: The civet produces musk, used to make perfume. The African palm civet lives in tall palm trees. The binturong has a tail nearly as long as its body.

PALM CIVETS, OR "TODDY CATS"

The palm civets are close relatives of the true civets. Most of them are Asian, but one common form lives in western Africa. Their feet are adapted for climbing, and they spend most of their time in the treetops. They often make their homes in the tops of big palm trees.

The palm civets of India and Sri Lanka are often called toddy cats because they drink the palm sap, or "toddy," that the people collect. Their close relatives in southeast Asia and the neighboring islands are often called musangs. Another form, the masked palm civet of southern Asia, does not have the usual civet spots. But it does have a black and white pattern on its face. This gives it the appearance of wearing a mask.

The African palm civet has a thicker coat and bushier tail than most of its Asian relatives. It may have up to four young at a time, which the mother sometimes carries on her back. This civet is a very primitive animal. Its body-build closely resembles that of the prehistoric Miacidae. This family of early meat eaters lived some 50,000,000 years ago. They were the ancestors of all the many different kinds of meat-eating mammals living today.

THE BINTURONG, OR BEAR CAT

The binturong, or bear cat, is the largest of the Viverridae. Clothed in black shaggy fur, it has a body about 75 centimeters (2½ feet) long and a bushy tail almost the same length. It lives in jungles from southeastern Asia to Java, Sumatra, Borneo, and the Philippines. A night prowler, it lives mainly in the trees, where it often holds on with the tip of its tail. Slow and awkward on the ground, it moves in a flat-footed fashion, like a bear.

MONGOOSES

A great variety of mongooses live in Africa and Asia; one species also lives in southern Europe. Most of them have small heads with pointed muzzles, long bodies with short legs, and long tails. Unlike most of their relatives, they may be most active during the day, when

Left, top to bottom: A mongoose and a cobra—natural enemies—eye each other. The battle begins. The mongoose kills the cobra and begins to eat it.

Above: The fossa is a skilled tree climber. It lives only on the island of Madagascar. Right: An African mongoose. Most mongooses have slender bodies and long tails.

they hunt the snakes, rodents, and other small animals that are their main food. They usually live in burrows.

The best-known mongooses—about a dozen species—all belong to the group called *Herpestes*. One of these, the common mongoose, lives in southern Spain. The others are African or Asian.

Mongooses are famous for killing and eating poisonous snakes. Advancing cautiously toward the snake, the mongoose threatens it with bared teeth. The cobra rears and spreads its hood, opening its jaws. It strikes at the mongoose, but the little animal dodges. Before the cobra can strike again, the mongoose lunges forward and bites it at the back of the head. The mongoose usually wins because it is quicker than the cobra. When the snake has been killed, the mongoose eats it, poison sacs and all. But the mongoose usually dies if the cobra bites it.

Mongooses in the West Indies

Nearly a century ago mongooses were brought into Jamaica and other islands of the West Indies. The hope was that they would kill the rats that were killing the poultry. The adaptable rats soon took refuge in trees, where mongooses seldom ventured. The mongooses, in their turn, took to eating eggs, birds, and other small native animals. They did not control the rats but did much damage to many species that people needed. The same thing has happened in other areas where mongooses have been brought in. As a result, the United States has long forbidden anyone to bring mongooses into the country.

There are many other kinds of mongooses besides the common ones. One of these is the

African striped, or banded, mongoose, which dwells in burrows under termite towers. Another is the dwarf mongoose, which sometimes hunts in packs. Others are the marsh mongoose, the white-tailed mongoose, and the bushy-tailed mongoose. Near relatives of the mongooses are two little African mammals with strange names—the suricate, or meerkat, and the cusimanse. Both are burrowing animals that eat insects.

▶ **THE FOSSA AND OTHER RELATIVES**

The fossa is the largest meat eater of Madagascar. It looks like a thin, long cat and measures about 1.5 meters (5 feet) from its nose to the end of its tail. It is reddish brown and has short, smooth fur. Its face is like a cat's, and it has needle-sharp, curved claws. A skilled climber, it hunts by night for birds, lemurs, and other small game. Many scientists think that it forms a link between the civet family and the true cats.

Another member of the Viverridae is the otter civet, which lives in Malaysia, Java, and Sumatra. With a flat head, long body, thick fur, and partly webbed feet, it looks and acts like a small otter.

Among the other Viverridae is the anteater civet, or falanouc, of Madagascar. It has a slender, pointed muzzle and weak teeth. It eats mostly insects and fruit. Another is the striped civet of Madagascar, which has a number of black stripes down its back. Still another is the vontsira, also of Madagascar. This little beast has a reddish brown coat and a bushy tail. Graceful and active by day, it climbs through the trees like a squirrel.

ROBERT M. McCLUNG
Author, science books for children

GENGHIS KHAN (1167?–1227)

The world conqueror Genghis Khan was a military genius who is often compared to Alexander the Great and Napoleon. He created the greatest land empire in the history of the world. It was a huge rectangle stretching nearly 8,000 miles (13,000 kilometers) from the Sea of Japan on the east to Hungary in the west. From north to south, it extended more than 2,000 miles (3,000 kilometers), from the forests of Siberia to central Iran, the Himalayas, and China.

Genghis Khan was born in a felt tent in northeastern Siberia about the year 1167. He belonged to the nobility of a wandering Mongol tribe that had suffered painful defeats in wars with other Mongol tribes. He was named Temüjin. When he was only 13 years old, his father died. Temüjin and his family were deserted by their tribe, and they had to struggle to survive.

As a child, Temüjin had been engaged to Börte, the daughter of the chief of a faraway Mongol tribe. When they were married, she brought him a splendid black sable coat as part of her dowry. Temüjin gave the coat to an-other Mongol leader, Wang Khan, who took Temüjin into his army. Together, Wang Khan and Temüjin won many victories against the Tatars, a related tribe. Later, the two leaders quarreled. When Wang Khan died, Temüjin became the most powerful leader in eastern Mongolia. When he defeated the Naiman tribe in western Mongolia in 1204, he became the sole ruler of all the Mongols.

In 1206, Temüjin called a great council (meeting) of all the Mongol nobles. A leading *shaman* (priest) declared it to be God's will that Temüjin rule the world. The great council approved and named him Genghis Khan, meaning "Universal Ruler." Genghis Khan then drew up the Great Yasa, his code of laws based on traditional Mongol law. It stressed complete loyalty, strict discipline, and unity among the tribes. Those who disobeyed these laws were swiftly punished.

In 1207, Genghis Khan embarked on the first of a series of successful invasions. He divided his superb Mongol cavalry into tightly disciplined units led by his nobles; he himself led an elite group of ten thousand warriors. Members of the tireless Mongol cavalry were always prepared to plunge directly into battle, even after several days of hard riding.

Genghis Khan's military tactics were so effective that his campaigns met with little resistance. By 1215, he had captured Peking. He then turned his victorious armies to the west. By 1220–21, they had reached the shores of the Caspian Sea. The Mongol armies took thousands of captives back to Mongolia to serve the Mongol nobles.

Genghis Khan died in Kansu, Mongolia, in 1227. He left behind a vast, well-organized empire that included much of China, all of Central Asia, parts of what are now Iran and Iraq, and a kingdom in Russia. But this single empire did not last. It was divided among four of his many sons. They enlarged and developed it until Mongol power extended from Kiev, in Ukraine, to Korea. A grandson, Batu, conquered much of eastern Europe and the Volga region in Russia. Another grandson, Kublai Khan, founded the Yüan dynasty in China. Baber, one of Kublai Khan's descendants, became the first Mogul emperor of India.

ROBERT I. CRANE
Syracuse University

See also MONGOLIA.

GEOGRAPHY

How and why is one place on earth different from another? This is the most important question of geography, but there is certainly nothing new about it. People have always been interested in other places.

Ever since man began to walk the earth he has been eager to explore. Perhaps one of those early men lived in a cave in some isolated valley. He was curious about the other side of the mountains. Would there be valleys similar to his own? Would there be supplies of berries and fruit waiting to be gathered? Would there be animals that he might trap to add to his supply of food? And would there be other men with whom he might trade and exchange ideas?

Thousands of years ago this man set out to climb the mountains to see what was on the other side. In doing so he became the world's first geographer. Of course he did not think of himself as a geographer. He was only interested in the other side of the mountains. But this interest was geographic, for he was trying to find out about other places.

In time he discovered the best trails to neighboring valleys. He searched out the lowest passes through the mountains. And as his knowledge grew he tried to find ways of passing this knowledge on to his sons and his friends. But early man had no written language. The caveman could not write a book or a set of directions. Instead, as the group sat around their fire at night he told stories of the places and people he had seen. He described the land and its treasures. He told of the people and their ways of life. Sometimes he scratched crude maps on skins and on the walls of his cave. Or perhaps he made maps with shells or by tying sticks together in such ways as to point out the direction to other places.

Who was this first geographer of so many thousands of years ago? Of what places did he tell? No one will ever know. But such must have been the beginning of geographical knowledge.

▶ GAINING GEOGRAPHICAL KNOWLEDGE

It has taken thousands of years to gain all of our present knowledge about places on our earth. Today we have many ways of learning about places. We have books, magazines, and newspapers. We have television, radio, and records. We have movies and slides. All of these things help to bring other places right into our own homes. We also have automobiles, trains, ships, and airplanes that can move us rapidly from one place to another. We have many opportunities to learn how and why one place is different from another.

In the past gaining geographical knowledge was not so easy. Only a few men were brave enough to travel to distant places. How eagerly people must have listened to their tales of strange people and far-off lands. As their stories were told and retold they often became a curious mixture of fact and fantasy. But they were not useful to people who wanted the truth. Accurate information was necessary to change travelers' tales into geography.

To secure correct information about other places, travelers had to learn to observe carefully. This means that they had to train themselves to look carefully at the land and the way it was used by its people. Along with careful observation had to come accurate written reports. It was also important that the travelers' reports be written in an interesting manner. But it was even more important that their written reports be accurate. For only in this way could a reader of the reports gain true geographical knowledge.

Means of measuring distance and direction were also needed. It would do the traveler little good to observe carefully and write accurately if he did not know where he was, in what direction he had traveled, or how far he had come. So travelers began to add carefully drawn maps, with true reports of distance and direction, to their written descriptions of other places. This was the beginning of real geography.

The First Real Geographers

To travel is one thing. To observe, map, and report carefully is quite another. From the time of our first caveman, many people traveled. But it was the Greeks of more than 2,000 years ago who were the earliest real geographers.

The first of these real geographers was **Thales**. Thales was born in 640 B.C. and died in 546 B.C. He lived on the shore of the Aegean Sea and spent his lifetime as a traveler

Mont Blanc in the French Alps.

Spruce forests in California.

Atlantic coastline of South Africa near Capetown.

Kofa Mountains and desert in western Arizona.

and trader. Everywhere Thales traveled he asked questions. He observed carefully. He kept accurate notes of what he had seen and learned. He searched for good ways of measuring distance and direction so that he could draw accurate maps. By questioning other travelers Thales also collected information about places that he had not seen himself.

Greeks who lived after the time of Thales added to a growing fund of geographical knowledge. **Herodotus** wrote lengthy and accurate descriptions of the places he had seen. **Pytheas** learned to establish distance and direction accurately by observing the height of the sun at noon. Still another Greek geographer, **Eratosthenes**, worked out a means of calculating the earth's circumference (the distance around the earth). He also drew maps using lines of latitude and longitude so that places could be located more accurately.

Two other Greek geographers added much to geographical knowledge. One was **Strabo**, who wrote a great series of books, 17 volumes in all, entitled *Geography*. In his books Strabo brought together all the geographical knowledge that the Greeks had accumulated. Strabo's books were a kind of geographical encyclopedia.

The other Greek geographer was **Ptolemy**. Like Strabo, he called his book *Geography*. Ptolemy's *Geography* was mainly a book about map making. His book also contained lists of places and an atlas of maps. With the names of places went their latitudes and longitudes, so that they might be found easily on the maps.

Opening Up the World

Ptolemy was the last of the great Greek geographers. Although the Romans continued the Greek tradition of mapping, they added little in the way of geographical writing. Following the decline of the Roman Empire came a period of history known as the Middle Ages. In Europe little new geographical knowledge was added. In fact, much of the knowledge of the Greeks was forgotten. Some people of the Middle Ages even came to believe in a flat earth.

During the Middle Ages the Arabs of North Africa and Arabia became the best geographers and map makers. They continued to believe in the Greek idea of a round earth.

Finally in the 15th century there was a great new period in the growth of geographical knowledge. This century marked the beginning of the Age of Discovery. Expeditions sailed out across uncharted ocean waters to explore the coast of Africa. Ocean routes to the Far East were explored and mapped. Then European seafarers began to look toward the west and the Atlantic Ocean. Christopher Columbus, who had studied the writings of Ptolemy, began preparations for one of the greatest voyages of all time—a voyage that led to the discovery of the Americas.

Soon ships from all of the European countries bordering the Atlantic Ocean were sending expeditions to chart new lands. Within less than a century all of the continents except Antarctica and Australia had been sighted. For the first time men had real knowledge of the size of the earth, the location of continents and oceans, and the variety of the earth's land and its people.

The Coming of Modern Geography

Three names mark the beginning of modern geography. All three men worked during the 19th century. Karl Ritter and Alexander von Humboldt were Germans. John Wesley Powell was an American. Ritter became a specialist in the theory and writing of geography. But it was Humboldt and Powell who followed the Greek tradition of geography established 2,000 years earlier. They became the fathers of modern field observation.

At the beginning of the 19th century Humboldt explored the tropical portions of South and Central America. He crossed and recrossed the Andes mountains. He used the latest scientific techniques to make his careful observations and his maps.

Humboldt noted the distribution of plants in the Andes. He observed that certain communities of plants seemed to be found at specific elevations. He took temperature readings at these elevations. His findings led to the discovery that different kinds of plants are found in different temperature zones.

On the slopes of a snow-capped mountain on the equator, Humboldt saw every kind of plant that one would find in traveling from the equator to the polar lands. Humboldt also became the first geographer to prepare maps

SOME GEOGRAPHY TERMS

Alluvium—Earth material deposited by flowing water.

Altitude—Vertical distance above sea level.

Aquifer—Layer of rock that holds water and allows water to seep through the pores of the rock.

Arable land—Land that can be plowed for agriculture.

Archipelago—Group of islands.

Arctic Circle—Line of latitude around the north polar region at 66° 30′ N. **The Antarctic Circle** is a line of latitude around the south polar region at 66° 30′ S.

Arroyo—A stream bed that is usually dry.

Atmosphere—The air that surrounds the earth.

Atoll—Ring- or horseshoe-shaped island, usually made of coral, that surrounds a lagoon.

Axis of the earth—Imaginary line that extends through the center of the earth from pole to pole. The earth turns, or rotates, on this axis from west to east.

Bay—Arm of an ocean or a lake that extends into the land. A bay is usually smaller than a gulf.

Bedrock—Solid rock that lies beneath soil and subsoil.

Butte—Small, flat-topped hill formed where a hard-rock lid protects softer rock underneath from erosion.

Canyon—Steep-sided valley, usually cut by a river through soft rock.

Cape—Point of land reaching out into the sea.

Census—Official counting of the number of people living in an area.

Chinook—Dry, warm wind that slides over a mountain chain into a valley, melting winter snows and raising temperatures. **Foehn** is the name used in Europe for the same kind of wind.

Climate—The kind of weather that an area has over a long period of time.

Climatology—Study of climates.

Cold front—Front edge of a large mass of cold air.

Continental climate—Climate with hot summers and cold winters.

Continental shelf—Relatively shallow ocean floor bordering a continent.

Contour line—Line on a map joining all places of the same height above sea level.

Cordillera—Large group of mountain systems. Each system has several ranges composed of many peaks.

Crater—The hollow at the top of a volcano.

Crevasse—Deep, steep-sided crack in a glacier.

Culture area—Area containing people who share a similar way of life.

Delta—Fan-shaped plain at the mouth of a river.

Density of population—Average number of people living on each square mile of an area.

Dew—Moisture from the air, deposited on objects as the air cools.

Divide—A highland that separates two or more river systems. **A continental divide** is a mountainous ridge that separates rivers and streams that flow to opposite sides of a continent.

Doldrums, or calms—Regions of the ocean near the equator where the wind is very light.

Drainage basin—Land drained by a river system.

Drift—(1) slow movement of surface water caused by the wind or (2) material deposited by a glacier.

Dry farming—Way of farming without irrigation in areas where there is limited rainfall.

Dune—Hill or ridge of sand formed by the wind.

Ecology—Study of the relationship between living things and their surroundings.

Elevation—Height of an object above its surroundings.

Equator—Imaginary great circle, halfway between the poles, on the earth's surface. It divides the earth into the Northern and the Southern Hemispheres.

Equinoxes—Times of the year when days and nights are equal in length. The sun is then directly overhead at the equator. **The spring equinox** is about March 21, and **the fall equinox** is about September 21.

Era—Major division of time in the history of the earth.

Erg—Area of sand dunes in the Sahara.

Erosion—Wearing away of land by natural forces, such as wind and water.

Escarpment—Inland cliff or steep slope.

Estuary—Portion of a drowned river valley into which tides enter.

Fall line—Line connecting the waterfalls farthest downstream on a number of parallel rivers.

Fault—Huge crack, or fracture, in rock. The segment on one side of the crack has been pushed up or down.

Fiord—Long, narrow inlet of the sea, between high banks or cliffs.

Floodplain—Land bordering a river, formed by deposits of earth materials carried by the river.

Frost—Moisture in the form of ice crystals. The crystals form when moisture in the air is deposited at temperatures below freezing.

Geomorphology—Study of the physical features of the earth's surface.

Glacier—Mass or tongue of ice that moves slowly down a slope or a valley.

Great circle—Any circle on the earth's surface that divides the earth into hemispheres. The equator and lines of longitude are great circles.

Great-circle route—Transportation route that follows a great circle. The shortest distance between two points on the earth's surface is on a great circle.

Gross national product—Total value of the goods and services produced within a nation during a year.

Groundwater—Water found beneath the surface of the earth.

Growing season—Time of the year when plants can grow without being affected by frost.

Gulf—Large body of water extending into the land.

Habitat—Natural region in which a plant or animal lives.

Hail—Precipitation in the form of hard pellets of ice.

Headwaters—Origin, or source, of a river or a river system.

Hinterland—Land lying behind a coast or a city.

Horizon—More or less circular line where earth and sky seem to meet.

Horse latitudes—Belts of high pressure and calm, fine weather. They are found about 35° north and 35° south of the equator.

Humus—Soil material of animal and vegetable origin.

Iceberg—Large floating mass of ice that has broken away from a glacier or ice cap at the edge of the sea.

Ice floe—Sheet of floating sea ice.

Isobar—Line on a map joining places having the same atmospheric pressure.

Isotherm—Line on a map joining places having the same temperature.

Isthmus—Narrow strip of land joining two large land areas.

Jungle—Thick tangle of vegetation in tropical lands.

Lagoon—Shallow stretch of water partly or completely separated from the sea by a narrow strip of land.

Land breeze—Wind blowing from land to sea, usually during the night or the early morning.

Landform—A natural feature of the earth's surface. Plains, plateaus, and mountain ranges are major landforms. Hills, canyons, buttes, and cliffs are examples of minor landforms.

Latitude—Distance in degrees north or south of the equator. **A line of latitude** is a line on the earth's surface connecting points having the same latitude.

High latitudes are latitudes between 60° and the pole in the Northern and the Southern Hemispheres.

Low latitudes are latitudes extending north and south of the equator to 30° latitude.

Middle latitudes are the latitudes between the high and the low latitudes.

Lava—(1) molten material from the earth's interior that has reached the surface or (2) the rock formed from this material.

Leaching—Washing away of minerals from soil.

Leeward—Side away from the wind. **Windward**—Side against which the wind blows.

Legend—Key to the symbols used on a map.

Loam—A soil containing a mixture of sand and clay, along with silt and humus.

Loess—Fine earth material, usually deposited by the wind.

Longitude—Distance in degrees east or west of the prime meridian. **A line of longitude** is a line on the earth's surface connecting points having the same longitude.

Map—Plan, picture, or diagram showing part or all of the surface of the earth or the sky.

Map projection—Method by which the curved surface of the earth is represented on a flat surface.

Map scale—Ratio between distance on a map and distance on the earth.

Marine climate—Mild, humid climate found in lands near the ocean in the higher middle latitudes.

Mediterranean climate—Climate with mild, wet winters and hot, dry summers.

Meridian—Half circle on the earth's surface from the North Pole to the South Pole.

Mesa—Small, flat-topped hill with steep sides.

Meteorology—Science of the atmosphere used especially in forecasting weather.

Metropolitan area—Area of urban development that includes and surrounds a large city.

Monsoon—Wind system of the Indian Ocean and southern Asia that changes its direction from season to season.

Moraine—Rock material deposited at the ends or the sides of a glacier.

Mountain—Mass of land usually more than 1,000 feet in elevation.

Natural resources—Materials found on the earth that are useful to man.

Oasis—Fertile area in a desert.

Oceanography—Study of the oceans.

Pampas—Treeless plains in Argentina.

Parallel—Line of latitude.

Peneplain—Region made almost level by erosion.

Peninsula—Stretch of land almost surrounded by water.

Permafrost—Permanently frozen subsoil.

Piedmont—Region of foothills.

Plain—Nearly level or gently rolling region.

Plateau—Extensive area of land that stands above the level of the surrounding land.

Prairie—Treeless plain of tall grasses.

Precipitation—Moisture such as rain, snow, hail, or drizzle that is deposited on the earth.

A prevailing wind—Wind that blows most often in a given locality.

Prime meridian, or zero line of longitude—Meridian passing through Greenwich, England, from which longitude is measured.

Rain forests—Dense forests with little undergrowth that grow where rainfall is very heavy, as in the tropics.

Range—(1) grazing land for sheep and cattle or (2) line of mountain ridges.

Reef—Narrow ridge of rocks, coral, or sand at or near the surface of the water. **A barrier reef** is a long, narrow line of rocks or coral not far from land that separates a shallow lagoon from the sea.

Relative humidity—The amount of moisture in the air compared with the full amount that the air can hold at that temperature.

Relief—Difference in height between the highest and the lowest points at any place on the surface of the earth.

Rural—Having to do with the country.

Savanna—Tropical grassland containing scattered trees.

Sea breeze—Wind blowing from sea to land, usually during the day.

Sea level—Level that the ocean would reach if it were as still as the water in a pond. The height, or altitude, of land is always measured from sea level.

Silt—Fine earth and sand carried by water and deposited as sediment in river valleys, lakes, and deltas.

Sleet—Precipitation in the form of frozen raindrops or of melted and refrozen snowflakes.

Smog—Fog containing much smoke.

Snow—Precipitation in the form of ice crystals.

Soil—Loose material forming the upper layer of the earth's surface.

Solstices—Times of the year when there is the greatest difference between the length of days and nights. At that time the sun is farthest from the equator.

   Summer solstice—Around June 21.

   Winter solstice—Around December 21.

Steppes—Semiarid grasslands in the middle latitudes.

Strait—Narrow stretch of water connecting two larger bodies of water.

Swamp, marsh, or bog—Wet, spongy land. **A bayou** is a swampy watercourse in the southern United States.

Tableland—Plateau bounded by steep sides.

Taiga—The name given to forests in the high latitudes of the Northern Hemisphere.

Till—Rock material dragged along under a glacier and left behind when the glacier melts.

Topography—All the physical features of a region, such as roads, bridges, streams, lakes, hills, and valleys.

Trade winds—Winds blowing toward the equator from the horse latitudes, usually from the northeast in the Northern Hemisphere and from the southeast in the Southern Hemisphere.

Tropic of Cancer—Line of latitude lying 23° 30' north of the equator. **The Tropic of Capricorn** is the line of latitude lying 23° 30' south of the equator.

Tundra—Treeless Arctic plain.

Urban—Having to do with towns and cities.

Valley—Long, narrow depression in the surface of the earth.

Value added by manufacture—Difference between the price of a product and the cost of materials used to produce it.

Veld—Dutch word for field, referring to a grassland area in South Africa.

Wadi—Arabic word for a stream bed in a desert.

Warm front—Front edge of a large mass of warm air.

Waterpower—Energy obtained from falling water.

   Hydroelectric power—Energy produced by turning waterpower into electricity.

Watershed—Highland that separates two or more river systems.

Waterspout—Tornado over a water area.

Water table—Surface of groundwater.

Weather—Condition of the atmosphere from day to day.

Weathering—The breaking down of parts of the earth's crust by the action of such forces as wind and water.

Wind—Air in motion.

Winter wheat—Wheat planted in the fall and harvested in the early summer. **Spring wheat** is wheat planted in the spring and harvested in the late summer.

Grand Coulee Dam in Washington harnesses the Columbia River for power and irrigation.

Drilling for oil in the waters off Venezuela in the Gulf of Paria.

THE WATERS OF THE EARTH SERVE PEOPLE IN MANY WAYS

The Corinth Canal in Greece connects the Ionian Sea with the port of Athens (*above*).

Waters of the Great Salt Flats in Colombia, South America, are evaporated to obtain salt (*left*).

The Black Sea provides fish for a market in Istanbul, Turkey (*below*).

showing the distribution of population in the areas he explored. On his return to Germany, Humboldt wrote 29 volumes and drew hundreds of maps and charts, all based on his field observations.

Powell is best known for his exploration of the Grand Canyon. His reports on the western United States are masterful examples of field geography. His keen observations, detailed reporting, and careful maps set a high standard for generations of American geographers.

▶ WHAT IS GEOGRAPHY TODAY?

Geography is still concerned with the question of how and why one place on the earth differs from another. To find answers to this question geographers study the characteristics of specific places. Some of the problems that geographers study are these: Where is this place located? How is it located with reference to other places? What landforms, soils, plants, and animals are found here? What type of climate does this place have? What kind of home does it provide for man? How has man used the land? In using the land, how has man altered it? What patterns of land use can be noted? How did these land-use patterns come into being? Why is one area used for industry and another for agriculture? Why is the main business district of the town in one place and the residential district in another? How is this place like other places? How is it different? What do these likenesses and differences mean to man?

The modern geographer has help that was undreamed of in Humboldt's and Powell's time. Aerial photographs make it possible to map areas that cannot be surveyed on foot. Our increasing knowledge of the atmosphere gives us detailed climatic information. The careful work of government census workers provides information about the distribution of people, agriculture, and manufacturing. Data-processing machines enable the modern geographer to solve problems in hours that once would have taken years. With all these new aids the growth of geographical knowledge is tremendous.

▶ FINDING USES FOR GEOGRAPHY

To the earth's first people the home valley was the entire world. Man knew nothing of valleys beyond his own. A world outside his home did not exist for him. Even to the Greeks the world consisted only of the lands immediately surrounding the Mediterranean Sea. At the beginning of the Age of Discovery in the 15th century, the known world was Europe. Even now we are just beginning to get accurate maps of the antarctic continent. Detailed maps for vast areas of our earth's surface have still not been drawn.

Rapid transportation and communication have changed modern man's view of the world. Airplanes can take us to almost any part of the earth in little more than a day. As a result, in our time as never before in the past everyone must use and know geography.

Geography for Understanding

Each day news broadcasts and newspapers bring us reports from every part of the world. Geography provides the knowledge of a place that is necessary to understand the news.

Geography provides the means of understanding the variety of physical, biotic, and cultural patterns found on the earth's surface. **Physical patterns** include the distribution of climates, soils, water features, and landforms. **Biotic patterns** include the distribution of plants and animals. **Cultural patterns** include the distribution of the things that man has added to the earth's surface. These include cities, roads, farms, factories, mines, and the multitude of man-made features.

Geography helps us read with greater understanding. With increased ability to observe we get greater understanding from pictures and photographs. And of course geography will enable us to read and to use properly the geographer's chief tool, the map.

Geography provides ways of understanding the world. It helps us see how and why one place differs from another. It shows us how these differences influence our lives.

Geography for Citizenship

Geography involves every level of citizenship. It involves citizens in the local community. Voting on the location of new schools or new roads requires knowledge of the physical, biotic, and cultural patterns found in each community.

Geographical understanding is necessary in state and national affairs. There are geographical problems in selecting the location of a new

FORESTS AND DESERTS OF THE WORLD SERVE HUMAN NEEDS

Copper is mined in the Atacama Desert in Chile, South America.

Forests provide pulpwood for the manufacturing of paper.

Controlled cutting in Mt. Hood National Forest, Oregon, supplies lumber and preserves the forest for the future (*left*). Countries prospect for oil in the Libyan Desert (*above*). An irrigation canal in California's Imperial Valley turns the desert into fertile farmland (*below*).

dam. What is the best site for the dam? What is the best place for the storage of water in man-made lakes? What will be the effects on population distribution as the result of new navigation channels, more electricity, and flood control?

Geography plays a vital role at the international level too. The raw materials needed to keep factories running and people working come from all parts of the world. Manufacturing processes are so complex that no industrial nation can be self-sufficient. No nation can supply all of the raw material it needs from its own mines, forests, and farms. International trade is necessary. Understanding the resources and industrial potential of the world's nations requires geographical knowledge.

Geography and Other Fields of Learning

Geography contributes to an understanding of other fields of learning. In turn, these fields contribute to geography.

Geography is related to history. History deals with events that had special meaning in the past. Geography helps us to understand why they occurred in a particular place.

Geography is related to the natural sciences. Geography studies the distribution of plants and animals on the earth. This ties geography to botany and zoology. Geography deals with the distribution of landforms. This ties geography to geology. Geography is concerned with the variety of climates found on our earth. This ties geography to meteorology.

▶ GEOGRAPHY AS A CAREER

A person who earns his living at geography is called a professional geographer. Professional geographers have special skill and training in geography. Today there are a little over 2,000 professional geographers in the United States. There are good positions waiting for many more.

Geography is taught from the elementary grades through college and the university. There are many opportunities for teachers interested in geography.

Nearly 500 professional geographers work in government service. The majority work for the federal government. A large number have positions in the Department of Defense, especially in the Army Map Service. Others work in various intelligence agencies and in the Department of State. A number are also employed in the Departments of Agriculture, Commerce, and the Interior.

Some government geographers work with city and state planning agencies. Others find positions in state conservation departments, in surveying, and in a variety of map-making and map information agencies for the federal and state governments.

There are many opportunities in business for geographers. Geographers help to locate raw materials for manufacturing and find markets for the finished goods.

Geographers work for companies that publish atlases, maps, and textbooks. News magazines also need the special skills of the geographer, especially if he has talent in designing and compiling maps.

▶ THE DIVISIONS OF GEOGRAPHY

During the days of Thales and Herodotus one could be an expert on all geography. As recently as 200 years ago men wrote books that summarized all of the known knowledge about places on our earth. So much knowledge has accumulated today that it is impossible for any one person to know all of geography. Geographers usually specialize in one kind of geography and one particular part of the earth. A specialization in one kind of geography is called a systematic specialty. A specialization in one part of the earth is called a regional specialty.

Systematic Geography

There are many specialized systematic branches of geography. Here are brief descriptions of some of the more important ones:

Agricultural Geography. The agricultural geographer specializes in rural land use. Often he specializes in one crop or one type of farming or one farming region. For example, some agricultural geographers are interested in corn-growing, some in pioneer farming, and some in tropical agriculture.

Biogeography. Biogeography is the study of the geography of plants and animals. Biogeographers usually specialize in either plant geography or animal geography rather than both. Plant geographers investigate the geographical distribution of plants. They prepare maps that show patterns of plant distribution. The plant geographer then shows how climate, soil, and other environmental factors explain these patterns. The animal geographer's work is much like that of the plant geographer. He is interested in understanding the differences in animal populations from place to place on the earth's surface.

Cartography. Cartography is the science of map making. All geographers use maps. But all geographers are not specialists in cartography. Some cartographers specialize in the design of maps. Some specialize in the compiling of map information to be placed on maps. Map librarians specialize in the collection, classification, and storage of maps.

Climatology. Climatologists specialize in the study of world climates. They map, compare, and analyze climatic patterns.

Geomorphology. Geomorphology deals with the classification, description, and measurement of landforms. The geomorphologist studies mountain systems, broad plains, the shapes of hills and slopes and valleys, and the nature of coastlines.

Historical Geography. Historical geographers describe and analyze places as they were in the past. They examine the changes that occur through time in the geography of places.

Industrial Geography. Industrial geographers are particularly concerned with problems of industrial location. They seek answers to such questions as: Where should a manufacturing plant be located? What are the best sources of raw materials? Where are the best sources of labor?

Marketing Geography. Marketing specialists must be able to work out ways of getting goods to customers at the lowest possible cost. The marketing geographer works on such problems as store location. Before a store is built, the geographer studies population distribution and analyzes traffic flow. With the information that his research gives him he can suggest which corner of which side of the street would be the best store location.

Political Geography. Political geographers study nations or states. They anyalze political boundaries. They study the physical, biotic, and cultural patterns of nations to determine their strength and weakness.

Population Geography. Population geographers are interested in the arrangement and distribution of people. They try to analyze the make-up of the population of given places.

This involves studying the distribution of age groups, sexes, languages, religions, and races.

Resource Geography. Some geographers have been particularly interested in resources and their distribution. Many resource geographers give special attention to conservation.

Settlement Geography. Settlement geography has to do with the things men build as they occupy the land. These include such things as houses, roads, and towns. Their distribution takes on patterns, which can be studied and mapped.

Transportation Geography. This specialty, like marketing and industrial geography, is important in business. Transportation geographers study the movement of goods between one place and another. They prepare maps that show both the route that goods take and the volume of goods that travel over the route. Their work helps determine the efficiency of routes and means of transportation.

Urban Geography. Urban geographers study cities. This is an increasingly important field of study, for the world is becoming more urbanized. Some urban geographers try to map, describe, and define the various parts of a city. Some study the relationship of the city to the countryside and smaller communities surrounding it. Some work on problems involving the improvement of transportation facilities, housing, and industrial location within the city.

Regional Geography

In addition to a systematic specialty, most geographers have a regional specialty. They give their attention to a particular country or part of the earth. There are specialists in the regional geography of such areas as Brazil, Southeast Asia, and the Pacific Ocean island group called Polynesia.

The regional specialist must know the people of his region as well as the land. He must learn the languages of the region so that he can read its literature and talk with its people. As often as possible, the regional specialist visits his region to travel, to study, and to do research. Part of the job of the regional geographer is to help the people of the United States understand the land and the people of his regional specialty.

PHILLIP BACON
Teachers College, Columbia University

See also MAPS AND GLOBES.

GEOLOGY

Earth is the rocky planet beneath our feet. When you look around our planet you see mountains, valleys, rivers, cliffs, and many other interesting features. Perhaps you have wondered how these different features were formed. Geology is the science that studies the Earth's rocks, minerals, and fossils and the different physical features on and below the planet's surface. Geology is also the study of how the Earth has changed since it was first formed about 4.5 billion years ago. There are many different branches of geology. Each is concerned with studying a particular aspect of the Earth. These different branches of geology have developed only quite recently, but the history of geology itself goes back thousands of years.

▶THE HISTORY OF GEOLOGY

Over the last few thousand years, people have been trying to explain the geologic features of the Earth and their origins. According to some ancient myths, the Earth and its geologic features were created by magic or by gods. As time passed, however, people began looking for other answers to their questions about the Earth.

Early Origins of Geology

About 2,500 years ago, Greek scholars and philosophers made some of the earliest observations of the Earth. This was the beginning of the development of science. In the 500's B.C., Pythagoras reasoned that the Earth was a sphere because its shadow on the moon was round during a lunar eclipse. In about 200 B.C., Eratosthenes made the first measurement of the diameter of the Earth. Other ancient Greeks concluded that fossils of fish found in rocks high up in mountains meant that these rocks must have been on the bottom of the sea at one time. The philosopher Theophrastus wrote a very practical book on rocks and minerals and their use in building and art. Because the field of science progressed very slowly in ancient times, the book remained useful for nearly 2,000 years.

Although some Greek philosophers based their explanations of the Earth and its geologic features on observations of nature, many early ideas about geology were based on philosophical beliefs. For example, Empedocles proposed that all things are composed of earth, fire, air, and water. This idea also was included in the writings of Aristotle, one of the most important ancient Greek philosophers. Aristotle was so famous that no one challenged his ideas for nearly 2,000 years.

The Romans did not share the Greek interest in science as a way to explain natural phenomena. Roman writings on geology were more practical. They were concerned mostly with the location of different rocks and minerals that could be used for magic charms and rites, art objects, or building materials. The Roman writer Titus Lucretius Carus, however,

WONDER QUESTION

What is geomythology?

Until the invention of science, natural phenomena often were explained through made-up stories, or myths. Geomythology refers to the special myths that explain geologic events or landforms.

One common type of geomyth assumes that geologic features were made by a race of ancient giants. An old German geomyth, for example, explains that river valleys were formed by the feet of clumsy giants, and these valleys were filled by the giants' tears.

Some geomyths relate to ancient gods or devils. For example, in Ethiopia there is a volcanic crater lake known as Ara Shatan, "the Devil's Home." A local myth explains how, long ago, a devil and a sorcerer had a great fight on the spot. As the devil was about to lose, he stuck his spear into the ground and shouted, "Let this be the devil's home," and the ground collapsed to form the crater lake. According to legend, if a stone is tossed into the lake, it will be thrown out by the devil.

People and Events in the Early Development of Geology

Ancient Times Greek philosophers are among the first to discuss their observations about the Earth and natural phenomena.

45 B.C. In his teaching poem *De Rerum Natura*, which fills six books, Roman philosopher and poet Titus Lucretius Carus recognizes that rocks age and crumble:

Do we not see lumps of rock roll down torn from the lofty mountains, too weak to bear and endure the mighty forces of time finite?

A.D. 79 A letter describing Pliny the Elder's death during the eruption of Mount Vesuvius (*right*) provides the first accurate description of a volcano erupting.

A.D. 132 The first seismograph (model at *right*) is used to detect and record tremors caused by an earthquake.

A.D. 1130 The Chinese scholar Shen Kua recognizes how fossils (*far right*) are created and how they can lead to an understanding of past geologic events.

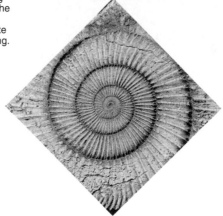

wrote a long poem that included theoretical explanations about geology.

The greatest source of information on ancient beliefs about geology is found in the 37-volume work called *Historia naturalis* ("Natural History"), written by the Roman scholar and naturalist Pliny the Elder. Pliny summarized many ideas from earlier philosophers and writers and reported on many things from his own travels around the Mediterranean. Pliny died in A.D. 79 while observing the eruption of Mount Vesuvius; his curiosity led him too close to the volcano, and he suffocated.

The Greeks and Romans were not the only ancient people to observe and wonder about geology and apply what they learned. In the 700's B.C., engineers in the Middle East mastered the practical side of geology and designed underground tunnels called **qanats** to carry water under the desert. Ancient Chinese writers also described and classified rocks and minerals. About A.D. 132, the Chinese scientist Chang Heng invented an early form of the seismograph, a scientific instrument used to detect earthquakes. About 1,000 years later, Shen Kua, a Chinese scholar, recognized the true nature of fossil plants and seashells. He believed that these fossils were proof that the climate had changed and that oceans must have covered the dry land at one time.

The Middle Ages

During the Middle Ages in Europe, there was little interest in geology or any other science. It was religion that had a strong influence on people's lives. The Christian church was very powerful during this time, and many Christians believed that the end of the world was near. Because of this belief, many Christians thought that science did not matter and that it was important for them to know only what was in the Bible.

1500's Georgius Agricola (*left*), a German physician working in the mining districts of Saxony, writes the first mineralogy textbook, *De Re Metallica*.

1795 James Hutton (*right*), a Scottish geologist, creates the foundation for modern geology with his theories of how the Earth constantly changes.

1815 The first geological map (*left*), created by English surveyor William Smith, identifies the strata and different rock types of England and Wales.

1830 Popular theory is challenged when English geologist Charles Lyell (*right*) authors and illustrates the three-volume *Principles of Geology* (illustration *above*).

1839 Charles Darwin documents his study of Galápagos Islands finches (*right*) in the *Journal of Researches*; his writings examine life-forms over time.

1. Geospiza magnirostris. 2. Geospiza fortis.
3. Geospiza parvula. 4. Certhidea olivacea.

Although science was not important to Christians at this time, it was important to the Muslims of the Middle East and North Africa. Muslim philosophers wrote books based on the knowledge of the ancient Greeks, especially Aristotle. They also added to scientific understanding by including their own observations and theories. The Arabian philosopher and doctor Avicenna proposed that mountains could be formed when land was lifted up by earthquakes and that wind, rain, and other forces could erode them, or wear them down. He realized that at one time, water must have covered parts of the Earth that are now dry land, and he also believed that meteorites were not formed on the Earth.

Toward the end of the Middle Ages, there was a reawakening of interest in geology. This occurred because of the practical experience of miners, who learned to recognize and use different kinds of rocks and minerals. In the 1500's, Georgius Agricola, a German doctor, wrote the first modern textbook on rocks, minerals, fossils, and metals. Another contributor to geology was Nicolaus Steno. He was a Danish doctor who, while working in Italy, discovered that rock **strata**, or layers, are like a timetable of the Earth's history. He proved that rock strata were originally horizontal, with the oldest layers of rock at the bottom.

In 1654, Irish bishop James Ussher had calculated the age of the Earth by adding together the ages of all the people mentioned in the Bible. He had concluded that the Earth was formed at nine o'clock in the morning on October 26 in the year 4004 B.C.

The 1700's and 1800's

By the 1700's, geology began to be taught in universities. One of the most famous geologists of the time was the German scholar Abraham Werner. Werner believed that all rocks had been formed from sediments of sand, mud, and other materials deposited in layers at the bottom of a vast, ancient ocean covering the entire Earth. From time to time, the water in this ocean withdrew, and the sediments that remained hardened into layers of **sedimentary** rock. According to Werner, these rock layers were stacked according to occurrence, from very ancient rocks at the bottom to more recent layers of loose gravel and sand that had not yet solidified. Werner argued that the flood described in the Bible had carved the Earth's mountains and canyons and that similar catastrophes explained the Earth's geologic history.

Scientists in Italy, where volcanoes erupt regularly, knew that Werner's idea was not correct. They knew that certain types of rock were formed when volcanoes erupted. But it was a Scottish geologist, James Hutton, who provided the correct theory for the origin of rocks. Hutton observed that rocks eroded to form pebbles. He also noted that some rocks contained pebbles, which must be fragments of older rocks. He concluded that there must be a balance between the formation and the destruction of rocks. Unlike Werner, who believed that all rocks formed early in the Earth's history, Hutton proposed that the Earth was constantly changing as a result of erosion and mountain-building forces. Hutton believed that these geologic forces occurred very slowly and that the Earth was much older than the 6,000 years determined from evidence in the Bible.

Another important advance in geology occurred in the 1800's as a result of the digging of canals and mines. At that time, the English engineer William Smith noticed that the same types of fossils occurred in certain rock strata throughout southern England. In 1815, he published a geologic map showing the relationships among strata of different ages. Soon geologists were making maps of much of Europe and eastern North America. Through their work, it became clear that there were many similarities in layers of rock types and fossils found in different places around the world. Geologists gradually developed a geologic time chart that summarized the changes in rock strata and fossils over time. The largest periods of time were called **eras**, and these were subdivided into **periods** and **epochs**.

French scientist Georges Cuvier discovered that there were many types of fossils in rock strata. He also discovered that only the youngest strata contained fossils of plants and animals that still existed; older rock strata contained fossils of many strange forms of life

A bold new theory was proposed by Alfred Wegener (*left*) in the early 1900's. He suggested that the continents were formed as one supercontinent, Pangaea, broke up into smaller continents that slowly drifted apart. He created a map in 1915 to illustrate his theory.

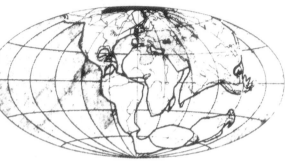

that had become extinct. Cuvier thought that these earlier forms of life must have died out suddenly as a result of some natural catastrophe. However, an English geologist named Charles Lyell thought that such catastrophes were not needed to explain geologic history. He believed, like James Hutton, that such geologic processes as volcanoes, earthquakes, and erosion could account for all of the Earth's geologic changes, both in the present and the past. Lyell wrote the first modern textbook of geology, converting many geologists to his and Hutton's views.

One young geologist who studied Lyell's book was Charles Darwin. While on a five-year expedition around the world, Darwin made careful observations of plants, animals, rocks, and fossils. One thing he noticed was that there were many species of finches living on different islands in the Galápagos Islands off the coast of South America. While these species of finches appeared similar, they were all slightly different. Darwin concluded that the birds originally had been one species but had evolved into different species over long periods of time because their source of food was slightly different on each island. He expanded this idea into a general theory of evolution, which offered an explanation for how all living things have appeared and disappeared over geologic time.

The Modern Age

In the late 1800's, scientists discovered that some elements are radioactive—that is, they decay, or break down, at identifiable rates. With this discovery, it became possible for scientists to measure the age of rocks by calculating the amount of radioactive decay that had taken place in the rocks' elements.

The first dating of rock using radioactive decay was done in 1907 by an American chemist named Bertram Boltwood. He discovered that some rocks were about 2.2 billion years old. Later measurements indicated that the Earth was formed about 4.5 billion years ago. Using this type of dating, which is also known as radiometric dating, scientists have been able to determine the ages of the many different rock strata and their fossils.

After Hutton, Lyell, and others had established the fundamentals of geology, it seemed to many that there was little left to be discovered. However, two questions continued to pique the interest of scientists in the 1900's: How did the continents form? And what led to mass extinctions?

Continental Drift. In 1912, Alfred Wegener, a German meteorologist, proposed a revolutionary idea. According to Wegener, originally there was only one large continent named Pangaea. Pangaea then fragmented into smaller continents that drifted apart very slowly. He suggested that the Atlantic Ocean had formed as the Americas moved westward and that India had moved northward to join Asia. Wegener's theory of continental drift was a brilliant scientific proposal, but it was widely ridiculed by many scientists.

No progress on Wegener's idea was made until 1956. It was then that British scientists mapping the direction of magnetism in rocks discovered that North America and Europe had drifted apart over the last few hundred million years. But overwhelming evidence to support Wegener came from the ocean floors themselves. In the 1950's, American geologists discovered long chains of mid-ocean mountain ranges and zones of fractured rock at right angles to them. In 1962, one of these geologists, Harry Hess, proposed a startling idea. Hess suggested that huge blocks of the Earth's crust containing continents and ocean floor move slowly over a deeper layer of rock. The mid-ocean mountains, he argued, were spreading areas where new crust was created. This process slowly pushed apart the huge blocks of the Earth's crust.

In 1963, the British scientists Frederick Vine and Drummond Matthews measured patterns of magnetism along mid-ocean ridges and proved that seafloor spreading actually occurs. Since the 1980's, it has been possible, using satellites, to determine the yearly movement of the Earth's crust by measuring the distance between Europe and North America.

Mass Extinctions. In 1981, the American physicist Luis Alvarez made a proposal that was as outrageous as Wegener's had

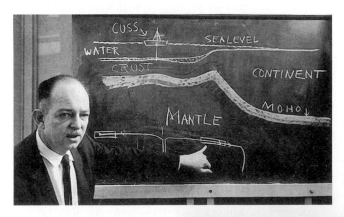

The work of Harry Hess (*above*) did much to explain the movements of the huge slabs of solid rock, called plates, that make up the Earth's surface.

Not all geologic changes occur slowly. One catastrophic event —an asteroid hitting the Earth—is thought to have wiped out the dinosaurs and many other species.

been nearly 70 years earlier. Based on geological evidence gathered by his geologist son Walter, Alvarez and a team of scientists proposed that the end of the Cretaceous period, which occurred about 65 million years ago, had been caused by a comet or an asteroid hitting Earth. As a result of the impact, the dinosaurs and many other species of animals and plants died. Scientists discovered more

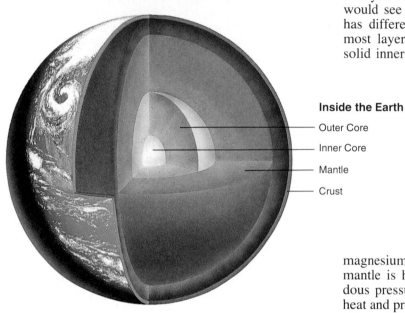

Inside the Earth

—— Outer Core

—— Inner Core

—— Mantle

—— Crust

geologic evidence to support this theory during the next ten years, such as the remnants of an ancient impact crater, about 200 miles (322 kilometers) in diameter, discovered in the Yucatan Peninsula of Mexico. With this and similar discoveries, scientists now understand that periodic impacts from asteroids are also a part of the Earth's normal geologic process.

▶THE EVER-CHANGING EARTH

Geologic forces have continuously changed the face of the planet. Scientists now know that these forces are generated by energy from the sun and from within the Earth itself. To help understand these forces, it is useful to look at the Earth's composition.

The Composition of the Earth

If you could cut a slice out of the Earth, you would see several distinct layers. Each layer has different physical properties. The innermost layer is the **core**, which consists of a solid inner core surrounded by a large liquid outer core. The entire core, which is very hot and consists mainly of iron and nickel, extends 2,100 miles (3,379 kilometers) from the center of the planet.

Surrounding the core and extending almost to the Earth's surface is the **mantle**, a layer of dense, heavy rock 1,800 miles (2,896 kilometers) thick. The mantle is made up of rocks that are composed mainly of silicon, oxygen, aluminum, iron, and magnesium. Although the temperature in the mantle is hot enough to melt rocks, tremendous pressure keeps the rocks solid. But the heat and pressure makes the mantle rocks flexible and allows them to flow slowly, carrying the layers of rock above like a raft on an ocean.

Above the mantle is the Earth's **crust**, a layer of solid rock. There are two main types of crust: the crust under the oceans and the crust of the continents. The crust under the oceans is a thin layer of dense volcanic rock called basalt and is about 3 to 4 miles (5 to 7

The Drifting Continents

Cambrian Period
600–500 million years ago

Devonian Period
400–345 million years ago

Permian Period
280–225 million years ago

kilometers) thick. The continental crust is much thicker. It averages about 22 miles (35 kilometers) thick, although the roots of mountains can extend as far as 60 miles (97 kilometers) into the mantle. There are many types of rock in the continental crust, but the most important is granite, a lightweight rock found most often in mountainous areas.

The Effect of Heat Within the Earth

The Earth's surface is formed and changed by geologic forces that are set in motion by the heat from inside the Earth. The Earth's core has a temperature of about 12,600°F (7000°C). The escape of this interior heat and the heat from radioactive decay provide the energy that forms mountains and volcanoes and causes earthquakes.

To understand how heat provides the energy for geologic forces, imagine the movement of boiling water in a pan. As water at the bottom of the pan becomes hot, it becomes lighter and rises to the surface. When the heated water reaches the surface, it moves to the side of the pan, cools, and becomes heavier, causing it to sink to the bottom. This movement caused by heating and cooling is called a **convection current**. A similar process is believed to exist inside the Earth. Convection currents bring hot material called magma up through the Earth's mantle toward the crust. As the magma cools, it circulates back into the Earth's interior. In places the magma breaks through the crust, creating volcanic eruptions. Geologists studying the ocean floor have discovered volcanic mountain chains where convection currents reach the Earth's crust. These underwater mountain chains are found in the middle of the Atlantic, Pacific, and Indian oceans.

Plate Tectonics. As magma erupts along the mountains on the ocean floor, it creates new crust and pushes existing rock sideways. This force, along with the horizontal movement of convection currents, is so great that it slowly moves huge blocks, or **plates**, of the Earth's surface. The geologic activity caused by the movements of these plates is called **plate tectonics**.

Although these plates move only a few inches a year, during the last few hundred million years they have moved thousands of miles around the Earth. A map of the Earth 150 million years ago would look very different from a map of today. Africa and Europe were joined to North and South America, and the Atlantic Ocean did not yet exist. Australia and Antarctica formed one large continent, and India was a large island. Earlier still, there was only one supercontinent named Pangaea (as had been proposed by Alfred Wegener in 1912), and the rest of the Earth was covered with water.

Today the Earth consists of seven large plates and several smaller ones. Most plates include parts of both continents and oceans. Geologists have also discovered that parts of Alaska, western North America, and other places are made up of dozens of small pieces of plates that have collided with and stuck to larger plates. Almost all earthquakes, volcanic activity, and mountain building take place where the edges of plates meet.

Tectonic Activity. When two plates collide, rocks are crumpled and crushed together, forming mountain ranges like the Andes and the Alps. If one plate consists of ocean-floor rocks, which are heavy, and the other consists of continental rocks, which are lighter, the ocean plate will dive under the continental

The continents of the Earth are constantly moving and changing the Earth's geography. The movements of the Earth's landmasses from the Cambrian period to the present are shown below (the names of ancient landmasses appear in red).

Triassic Period
225–190 million years ago

Cretaceous Period
135–65 million years ago

Quaternary Period
2 million years ago–present-day

one. As the ocean plate sinks, its rocks are heated and gradually melt. This molten magma then rises up through the overlying continent and forms a chain of volcanoes. Much of the magma, however, cools and becomes solid before it can erupt through the surface. When this happens, it forms massive bodies of volcanic rock within the Earth's crust called **intrusions**. As water and other liquids move through these heated intrusions, gold, silver, copper, and other minerals are concentrated into distinct layers.

Sometimes two plates slide past each other, creating what is known as a **fault zone**. The San Andreas Fault in California, the best-known fault on the Earth, is the boundary be-

Geologic Forces at Work

Changes on the Earth's surface occur as tectonic plates move slowly about on the hot mantle rock circulating beneath the crust.

New crust, created by molten rock from the underlying mantle, fills the space produced as neighboring plates move apart (*left*).

Volcanoes mark the site where one plate is driven deep into the mantle beneath another (*below*). The sunken rock melts, forming magma that rises and erupts through the crust.

The movement of hot mantle rock as it circulates through the mantle to the crust, cools, and then sinks back into the Earth's interior is called a convection current (*below*).

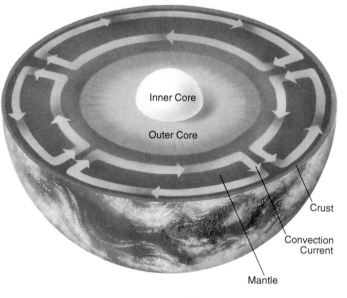

Inner Core

Outer Core

Crust

Convection Current

Mantle

A chain of volcanoes, such as those that became the Hawaiian Islands (*below*), is created as plumes of molten rock rise and erupt through the crust of a moving plate (*below right*).

tween the North American and Pacific plates. Plates do not move past each other continuously. Instead, they often stick together until the force of the plate motion ruptures them, causing an earthquake.

The Effect of the Sun

While heat from the Earth's interior is largely responsible for the geologic forces that build mountains and other landforms, the heat from the sun is responsible for the geologic forces that erode the Earth.

Erosion from Wind and Water. As the sun's heat warms the Earth's atmosphere, it causes the winds that move over the planet's surface. These winds pick up tiny pieces of rock and minerals from one place and deposit them as sediments at other places. Vast areas of the world are blanketed by such sediments. Over millions of years, these loose sediments harden into rock.

The sun's heat also evaporates water from oceans, lakes, and rivers, causing the formation of clouds. The rain that falls from these clouds acts like millions of tiny hammer blows, weakening and finally eroding rocks and soils and carrying the sediments downhill. As the sediment-laden water runs downhill, it cuts channels for streams and rivers to flow through. The Grand Canyon in northern Ari-

Mountains form when two plates carrying continents collide (*below*). Layers of rock crumble and fold during the slow collision, thrusting up great mountain ranges, such as the Himalayas (*right*).

Powerful earthquakes can occur at the boundaries, called faults, where plates slide past each other (*above*). The San Andreas Fault (*right*) forms the boundary between two large sliding plates.

Layers of rock, representing billions of years of Earth's history, are revealed as wind and water erode a bed of sandstone.

zona is a spectacular example of what erosion can accomplish.

Action of Glaciers. At various times during the Earth's history, the Earth has cooled. Snow and ice have collected in high mountains and around the North and South poles. In time, the accumulation of ice and snow forms **glaciers**, which are simply vast sheets or rivers of ice. During the last ice age (which ended about 10,000 years ago), thick sheets of ice spread across North America as far south as southern Illinois. These giant ice sheets crushed and polished the rocks they passed over. They also scraped away much of the soil underneath them and deposited it into mounds and ridges, called **moraines**, at the foot of the glaciers. The heavy weight of the glaciers also gouged out great valleys to form the Great Lakes. Along the seacoasts of Alaska, Scandinavia, and other areas, glaciers eroded steep-walled valleys. As the glaciers retreated, the valleys filled with sea water, forming deep inlets known by their Norwegian name of **fjords**.

The glaciers of the last ice age were so thick and heavy that they pushed down parts of the Earth's crust, which was flexible because of the hot mantle underneath. Now that most of the ice is gone, the once-covered land has been slowly rising. There are places where the Ice Age never ended. Greenland and Antarctica are still covered by thick ice sheets that push their rock surfaces below sea level.

During the last ice age, so much of the Earth's water was frozen into glaciers that the sea level was about 300 to 450 feet (91 to 137 meters) lower than it is today. The edges of the continents extended hundreds of miles farther out into the oceans, and rivers like the Mississippi and the Nile deeply eroded land that is now covered by the sea.

The gradual, powerful movement of glaciers are responsible for the moraines created along the edges of an Alaskan glacier (*below*) and a steep-cliffed fjord (*right*) dug out of the western coast of Norway.

All living things have the ability to change the face of the Earth through their actions. However, human beings—as they clear vegetation from the land, consume resources, and create pollution—have the most profound effect on the Earth's landscapes.

For nearly two hundred years, scientists wondered what caused the ice ages. Today, geologists and astronomers know that the advance and retreat of glaciers during the last ice age was due, in large part, to changes in the Earth's orbit around the sun. Over thousands of years, the gravitational pull of other planets changes the Earth's orbit so that the planet is sometimes closer or farther from the sun. In addition, the Earth wobbles on its axis as it spins, causing parts of the planet to be closer or farther away from the sun at different times. Together, these two factors significantly changed the amount of sunlight that the Earth received, which caused the ice ages.

The Effect of Plants and Animals

Plant and animal life can be considered unique geologic agents that have also changed the face of the Earth. Plants take carbon dioxide out of the atmosphere and release oxygen, which plays a role in the processes of erosion and the decay of plants and animals. Coral reefs and mangrove swamps protect shorelines from the action of waves, slowing the rate of coastal erosion. Trees, grasses, and other plant cover allow rainwater to seep into the ground rather than run off, thus slowing erosion on land. Microscopic plants and animals in the ocean die and fall to the seafloor, where they eventually form sedimentary rock. Human beings change the Earth by logging forests, damming rivers, reshaping landscape, and re-leasing carbon dioxide and other gases into the atmosphere (perhaps contributing to major climatic changes). No matter what happens as a result of plant and animal action on the Earth, the planet itself will survive. But the fate of humans and most other species of plants and animals is uncertain.

▶TYPES OF ROCKS

The processes that shape the Earth's surface can create different types of rocks. Geologists recognize three major rock types: igneous, sedimentary, and metamorphic.

Igneous rocks form as a result of the cooling of magma either within the Earth's crust or on its surface. When igneous rocks are formed within the Earth's crust, the rocks are called **intrusive**; when igneous rocks are formed on the surface, they are called **extrusive**. The most common igneous rocks are granite (intrusive) and basalt (extrusive).

Sedimentary rocks consist of small pieces of eroded rock and plant and animal remains. Most sedimentary rocks are formed on the ocean floor from fragments of eroded rock and sand deposited by rivers and the sunken remains of tiny sea animals and plants. Over time these loose sediments are compacted and cemented together to form layers of hard rock. Sedimentary rocks are the only type of rocks that contain fossils. Among the most common sedimentary rocks are sandstone, limestone, and shale.

Rock is created by geologic processes on and beneath the surface of the Earth. Magma cooling on the surface forms basalt columns (*far left*), a type of igneous rock; heat or pressure produce marble (*left*), a type of metamorphic rock; buried and compacted layers of sediment, which can include the remains of animals or plants, create sedimentary rock (*below*).

Metamorphic rocks are the rocks that have been changed from one form to another. They are formed from igneous or sedimentary rocks that have been subjected to intense heat or pressure or both, causing the characteristics of the rock to change. This heat and pressure usually occur as a result of some type of tectonic activity. Two common types of metamorphic rock are slate, which is formed from a sedimentary rock such as shale, and gneiss, which is formed from an igneous rock such as granite.

▶ GEOLOGY IN THE SOLAR SYSTEM

During the last thirty years, the field of geology has expanded to include the study of the solar system. In studying the Earth's moon and the other planets and their satellites, geologists have learned a great deal. The four giant gaseous planets—Jupiter, Saturn, Uranus, and Neptune—do not have solid surfaces and therefore do not have geologic activity. But their natural satellites and the planets Mercury, Venus, and Mars have provided geologists with opportunities to investigate geologic processes that are similar to those on Earth. They found that two types of geologic activity occur on nearly all solid worlds: volcanic action and impact cratering (the formation of craters by the impact of comets or asteroids on an object's surface).

Apparently most of the solid planets and satellites were hot when they were first formed.

They have also been heated by radioactive decay. On the smaller planets and satellites, the heat escaped into space rather quickly. But the larger ones retained heat long enough to melt parts of their interiors, leading to volcanic activity. There is evidence, for example, that the moon had extensive volcanic eruptions for its first billion years, while the satellites of Mars were too small for such activity. Mars was volcanically active for 3 to 4 billion years before its interior cooled enough for volcanic activity to end. The Earth is large enough so that volcanic activity has continued throughout its entire lifetime. Venus is about the same size as the Earth, and recent spacecraft images have revealed that lava flows and volcanic mountains dominate its surface.

When a comet or asteroid strikes the surface of a planet or satellite, the force of its impact excavates a crater. During the Apollo expeditions to the moon, scientists discovered impact craters of all sizes on its surface—from tiny ones that can be seen only with a microscope to huge ones 600 miles (965 kilometers) across. Geologic mapping on the Earth has revealed nearly two hundred large impact craters on our planet. Many more may lie hidden beneath the surface, or they may have been destroyed by erosion or tectonic activity. Photographs obtained during space probes to other parts of the solar system have revealed impact craters on nearly every solid satellite or planet that has been studied.

Other geologic processes have acted to varying degrees on other planets as well. Mars and Venus, for example, have dunes and other features formed by the action of the wind. Long channels on Mars suggest that it once may have had rivers that eroded the landscape. Scientists have also determined that Mars currently has polar ice caps. Large faults are seen on all solid planets and most satellites, indicating that earthquakes have occurred. Plate tectonics as found on the Earth, however, have not been found on any other planet.

▶ **THE GEOLOGIST AT WORK**

Geology is a broad field of study with many different specialties. Some geologists, however, also work as generalists who utilize a broad range of geologic knowledge. Many generalists work for the United States Geological Survey or state geological surveys, where they use their knowledge of various aspects of geology to make maps showing the distribution of different rock types, faults and other structural features, and mineral deposits.

The largest numbers of geologists work for oil companies, where they help locate deposits of oil and gas that can be used to make gasoline and to generate electricity. Many geologists also work at universities, where they teach and become experts in a specialized area of geology. For example, a few hundred geologists have the exciting and sometimes dangerous career in the special area of volcanology, the study of active volcanoes. Others specialize in historical geology and spend many months carefully digging up bones of dinosaurs and other extinct animals to better understand how they lived and how they died. Although geologists work outdoors a great deal, they also spend much of their time in laboratories, using microscopes, computers, and scientific instruments to learn more about the Earth's geologic processes.

Collecting rocks, gems, and fossils is a good way to learn about geology. But to prepare for a career as a geologist, students should take math and science courses in high school and major in geology or Earth sciences in college. Many jobs in geology require a

Studying fossils is one way geologists find out what occurred in past ages. Here a team carefully removes the remains of a mammoth from the Earth's crust.

master's degree or a doctor of philosophy degree. Geologists also need good writing and speaking skills so that they can explain their discoveries to others. In the past, most geologists were men, but many women are now active in every branch of geology.

▶ **GEOLOGY IN THE FUTURE**

All life on Earth is based upon the use of the planet's resources. In the future, geologists will continue to be needed to find such natural resources as oil, minerals, and even fresh water. They will also be needed to help develop ways of controlling and reducing pollution on land and water. As an increasing world population brings more people near volcanoes, earthquake faults, and flood plains, geologists will need to evaluate these hazards and devise plans to evacuate people quickly in times of danger. Future geologists also will increase their use of space satellites to monitor geologic activity on the Earth as well as on the other planets. In the next century, human beings no doubt will return to the moon and perhaps visit Mars. Geologists will be among the first settlers of these worlds.

CHARLES A. WOOD
University of North Dakota

See also CLIMATE; EARTH; EARTH, HISTORY OF; EARTHQUAKES; FLOODS; FOSSILS; ICE AGES; MINERALS; ORES; RADIOACTIVE DATING; ROCKS; VOLCANOES.

GEOMETRY

The word "geometry" comes from the early Greeks and means "to measure the Earth." Geometry can be used to measure the size of an atom, the size of the universe, or the size of everyday things around us. Anyone who builds a bridge, paints a house, or plants a garden uses geometrical measurement.

Geometry also includes the study of shape and space. Geometric shapes, from circles and spheres to squares and cones, appear throughout our environment, in natural objects and in objects made by people. Whenever we describe an object, give a direction, or view a work of art, we use our geometric sense of space.

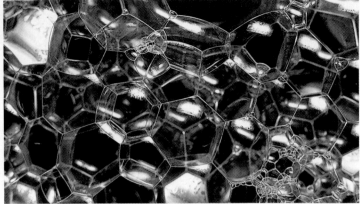

Geometric shapes of all kinds appear in natural objects. Several can be seen in these bubbles.

▶ EARLY GEOMETRY

Some of the earliest examples of the use of geometry come from the Babylonians from about 2000 B.C., who knew how to measure the areas and volumes of some geometric shapes. Clay tablets from their time reveal that the Babylonians also knew about what is now called the Pythagorean theorem, which explains the relationship between the sides of right triangles. We know that this relationship was recognized by the ancient Egyptians, who used it to measure their lands and to build the pyramids. From ancient Chinese manuscripts we know that the Chinese were also familiar with the Pythagorean relationship and that they studied and measured various geometric shapes.

The ancient Egyptians used their knowledge of the relationship between the sides of a right triangle to measure many things. A person called a rope stretcher would tie equally spaced knots in a rope, then tie the ends together, resulting in 12 knots and 12 equal segments between the knots. The rope stretcher then laid the rope out into a triangle with sides of 3, 4, and 5 segments. This produced what is called a right triangle, a triangle with one angle that can be used to make a square corner. From this starting point they could go on to make other measurements.

▶ EUCLIDEAN GEOMETRY

Geometry is often thought of as getting its start in Western culture in about 300 B.C., with the work of Euclid, a Greek mathematician. Euclid gathered together all of the mathematics that was known at the time and organized it into a collection called *Elements*. Euclid began by setting down the simplest mathematical assumptions or statements, which he called **axioms**. Then he reasoned that certain other statements, based on the axioms, must also be true. These statements he called **theorems**.

The system of using axioms as statements to be accepted without proof, then using the axioms to prove other statements, or theorems, was then used throughout all of mathematics and is still the way new mathematics is created.

In his *Elements*, Euclid also defined various geometric figures and described their basic properties, or characteristics. These figures included circles and other shapes made of straight or curved lines. Euclid also explained certain geometrical relationships and demonstrated how geometric figures can be constructed and measured. All of these ideas are still basic to an understanding of geometry, and they are the first things the student of geometry usually studies. This article will discuss the principal geometric figures.

▶ PLANE FIGURES

Euclid began his study of geometric figures with the **plane**. A plane is a flat surface like the top surface of a table, the outer side of a box, or a football field. We think of simple shapes, or figures, on the plane as enclosing part of the plane.

Any enclosed figure made from line segments is called a **polygon**. If the sides and the angles of the figure are all equal, it is called a **regular polygon**.

Angles

Angles are used in defining and describing many plane figures, so we will examine them before polygons. An **angle** is a wedge-shaped piece formed as an opening between two lines. Angles are measured with a protractor or an angle ruler, which are marked off in measures called **degrees**. The symbol ° is used for the word "degree."

Angles that make square corners and measure 90° are called **right angles**. If an angle measures less than a right angle, it is called an **acute angle**. If it measures more than a right angle, it is an **obtuse angle**.

Lines that meet at right angles are called **perpendicular**. If a pair of lines in a plane never meet, they are called **parallel**.

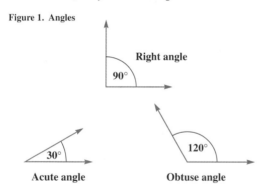

Figure 1. Angles

Right angle
90°

30°
Acute angle

120°
Obtuse angle

Triangles

The simplest polygon is the **triangle**, which is made of three line segments joined together. If all the line segments, or sides, are the same length, the figure is an **equilateral triangle**. All the angles in an equilateral triangle are also equal. If only two sides are the same length, the figure is an **isosceles triangle**. The two angles opposite the two equal sides of an isosceles triangle are also equal. Mathematicians working on computers often ask for a **random triangle**, one in which the lengths of the sides are unpredictable.

If one of the angles in a triangle is a right angle, the triangle is called a **right triangle**. The side opposite the right angle is called the hypotenuse. The other two sides are called legs. Examples are shown in Figure 2.

Triangles are widely used in science, navigation, and construction.

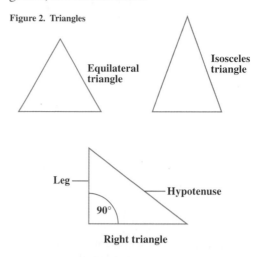

Figure 2. Triangles

Equilateral triangle

Isosceles triangle

Leg

Hypotenuse

90°

Right triangle

The Pythagorean Theorem

The Greek mathematician Pythagoras, who lived in the 500's B.C., worked out an important theorem about the relationships between the lengths of the legs and the length of the hypotenuse of a right triangle. Pythagoras first measured and then squared the lengths of the two legs of a right triangle. For example, if one leg measured 3 inches, he squared the 3 by multiplying it by itself, getting 3 x 3, or 9. If the other leg measured 4 inches, squaring the 4 produced 16. Pythagoras then added: 9 + 16 = 25. The sum, he discovered, was equal to the length of the hypotenuse squared. The length of the hypotenuse in this case would be 5 inches since 5 squared is 25.

Pythagoras' theorem can be stated this way: For any right triangle, the square of the length of the hypotenuse is equal to the sum of the square of the length of the sides.

Quadrilaterals

A figure with four line segments enclosing a plane is called a **quadrilateral** (see Figure 3). The word "quadrilateral" comes from a Latin word meaning "four-sided." One type of quadrilateral, the **parallelogram**, has opposite sides that are parallel and equal in length. When one of the angles in a parallelogram is a right angle, the figure is a **rectangle**. If all the sides of the parallelogram are the same length, the figure is a **rhombus**, and if one of the angles in a rhombus is a right angle, the figure is a **square**.

Figure 3. Quadrilaterals

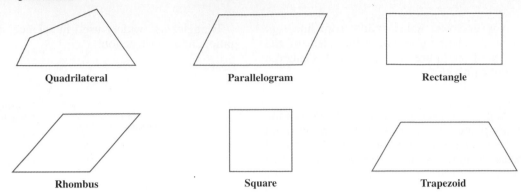

Quadrilateral   Parallelogram   Rectangle

Rhombus   Square   Trapezoid

A less common quadrilateral is the **trapezoid**. It has only two parallel sides and they are unequal in length.

If a quadrilateral can be placed in a circle so that all four corners lie on the circle, it is called a **cyclic quadrilateral**. Squares and rectangles are cyclic quadrilaterals.

Other Polygons

There are many other polygons that are classified according to their number of sides. One example is the regular five-sided polygon called a **pentagon**, which was studied by the Greeks for the relationships that can be found in its sides and angles. Regular six-sided polygons called **hexagons** have been used in ancient and modern times to tile floors because they fit together so well. Today, the common stop sign takes the shape of the regular eight-sided polygon, which is the **octagon**.

Circles

A portion of a plane can be enclosed by figures other than polygons. For example, all of the points that are an equal distance from a fixed point describes the figure called the **circle**. Circles can be found everywhere. Wheels, many coins, and the moon in its full phase all have circular shapes.

Figure 4 shows a circle with some of its parts. A line through the center touching both sides of the circle is the **diameter**. Half of the diameter is the **radius**. The distance around a circle is the **circumference**.

In Figure 4 we have placed six line segments, each the same length as the radius, around the inside of the circle. This demonstrates that the circumference of a circle is greater than six radii (the plural of radius), or three diameters.

To calculate the circumference of the circle, we multiply the diameter of the circle by a special number called **pi**. The symbol for pi is π and its value is approximately 3.14. If the diameter of the circle is 5 inches, for example, we multiply 5 x 3.14 to get a circumference of 15.7 inches, which is a little greater than three diameters.

Figure 4. Circle

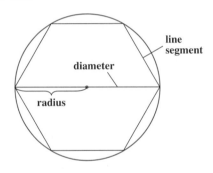

line segment

diameter

radius

Conic Sections

Menaechmus, a Greek mathematician who lived in the 300's B.C., is credited with the discovery of a group of curved plane figures that are formed by making slices through different sections of a cone. As Figure 5 shows, if

Figure 5. Conic Sections

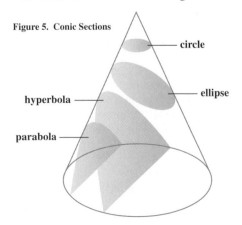

circle

ellipse

hyperbola

parabola

Figure 6. Platonic Solids

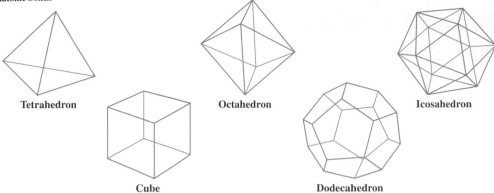

Tetrahedron

Octahedron

Icosahedron

Cube

Dodecahedron

you slice the cone straight across, the resulting section is a circle. If, instead, you slice the cone on an angle, you get an **ellipse**. Ellipses occur in the paths the planets take as they revolve around the sun, and in bridges, arches, and other constructions. If you increase the angle of the slice, you get a **parabola**, and increasing the angle even more yields a **hyperbola**. A baseball thrown into the air will travel in the path of a parabola.

▶ THREE-DIMENSIONAL GEOMETRY

While most basic geometry that is studied is two-dimensional—concerned with figures having only length and width—we live in a three-dimensional world. From soccer balls and tin cans to Egyptian pyramids and barnyard silos, almost everything around us has three dimensions—length, width, and height.

Regular Polyhedra

Euclid ended his geometric studies with an exploration of the three-dimensional figures called **solids** that can be constructed from two-dimensional polygons. For example, if you join four equilateral triangles together at their corners, you will produce a solid called a **tetrahedron** (see Figure 6). The four triangles make up the **faces** of the tetrahedron. The faces are joined at their six **edges**, and the edges end at four corners called **vertices**.

The tetrahedron is one of a group of solids called **polyhedra**. The singular of polyhedra is **polyhedron**. A polyhedron is a figure with flat faces and straight edges.

Two other polyhedra can be constructed from equilateral triangles: the **octahedron**, which has eight faces, and the **icosahedron**, with twenty faces.

One polyhedron, the **cube**, or **hexahedron**, has six faces and is built from squares. The

dodecahedron is constructed from regular pentagons and has twelve faces.

These five figures make up a special group called the **regular polyhedra**, or the **Platonic solids**. All the faces in a regular polyhedron are the same size and shape. The Greeks thought that the five regular polyhedra reflected the universe and its four elements—air, water, fire, and earth.

Other Solid Forms

Polyhedra that are not regular include the **prism** and the **pyramid** (see Figure 7). A prism has two parallel bases, or ends, and its other faces are parallelograms. A nonregular pyramid has one base that is not an equilateral triangle, and its other faces are triangles.

Not all solids are polyhedra with plane faces. Some solids include curved surfaces. The **sphere** is a solid with a curved surface. We see spheres in many types of balls used in sports and recreation. In a sphere, the dis-

Figure 7. Other Solids

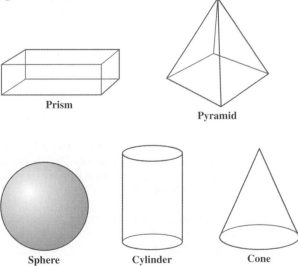

Prism

Pyramid

Sphere

Cylinder

Cone

HOW TO CONSTRUCT A POLYHEDRON

Polyhedra are easy to construct using hollow straws and lengths of string. To make a tetrahedron, you will need six straws.

1. Pass one length of string through three of the straws.
2. Form an isosceles triangle with the straws and tie them at the top with a knot.
3. Tie a length of string to each vertex, or corner, of the triangle.
4. Pass the length of string at each vertex through another straw.
5. Tie the three loose ends together.

How many vertices are there in your tetrahedron? How many edges? How many faces? (4, 6, and 4) You may want to try constructing other regular polyhedra using the same method.

tance from the center of the sphere to every point on its surface is the same.

The common can is a good model for another solid called a **cylinder**. The **cone** is probably most familiar to us in the form of the cone that holds scoops of ice cream.

▶ **MEASURING AREA AND VOLUME**

Measurement is an important part of geometry. From ancient times, geometers—

mathematicians who specialize in geometry—have concerned themselves with measuring the areas and volumes of geometric figures.

Area

Area is the amount of surface covered by a figure. It can be measured by first covering a shape with **standard unit squares**, such as square inches or square centimeters, and then counting the number of standard squares in the shape. The rectangle in Figure 8 has been covered with square centimeter units. How many square centimeters do you get by counting all the unit squares? There are 20 unit squares, so the area of this rectangle is 20 square centimeters.

If the shape is an orderly shaped figure such as a square, or the rectangle in Figure 8, there is a quicker way of counting the unit

Figure 8. Finding Areas

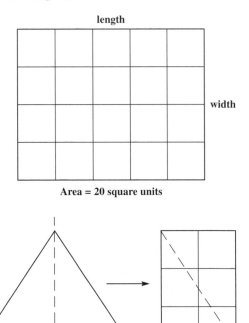

squares. Just multiply the number of squares in each row (5) by the number of rows (4) to get 5 x 4 = 20 square centimeters. This shortcut method for finding the area of a rectangle can also be stated in a mathematical equation called a formula. Since there are 5 square centimeter units along the length of the

Figure 9. Symmetry, Similarity, and Congruence

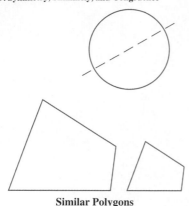

Similar Polygons

Figures with Symmetry

Congruent Triangles

shape and 4 square centimeter units along the width, the formula would then be written, Area = length x width, or $A = l \times w$.

If you want to find the area of a triangle or some other shape in which the unit squares do not fit well, you could estimate the number of unit squares. Or, for an isosceles triangle, for instance, you could cut the triangle down the middle into two pieces and refit the pieces into a rectangle, as in Figure 8. Then find the number of unit squares in the rectangle. Similar methods work for other shapes.

Students sometimes find it useful to use a small plastic sheet with a grid of standard squares marked on it to measure irregular shapes.

Volume

The amount of space a solid figure occupies or fills is its **volume**. The volume of a figure is measured using methods similar to those used for finding areas. The unit of measure for volume is the **standard unit cube** such as a cubic inch or a cubic centimeter. We can pack a figure, a rectangular box, for example, with unit cubes and then count the number of cubes in the box. Or we can use the quicker method of counting the number of unit cubes in the bottom of the box, then count the number of layers of cubes necessary to fill the box, and then multiply the two numbers. If the bottom of the box had 6 rows of inch or centimeter cubes and it had 4 cubes in each row, there would be 6 x 4, or 24 inch or 24 centimeter cubes. If it then took 3 layers to fill the box to its height, we would multiply 24 x 3 to get a volume of 72 cubic inches or centimeters. Or, instead, we could use the formula Volume = length x width x height, or it may be written $V = l \times w \times h$.

To find the volume of odd-shaped or irregular objects, we could estimate the number of unit cubes in the object. Another method would be to pour water into the object and then pour the water into a special container marked in cubic units.

▶ SIMILARITY, CONGRUENCE, AND SYMMETRY

Geometric figures that have the same shape but not necessarily the same size are called **similar**. In similar shapes, all corresponding angles are equal to each other. Whenever we build a scale model of an airplane or draw a map to scale, we are dealing with similar figures.

Two or more figures that have exactly the same size and exactly the same shape are called **congruent**. The tops of the student tables or desks in a classroom or the pages of a book are likely to be congruent to each other.

A figure is said to have **symmetry** if the parts of the figure on opposite sides of a point, line, or plane correspond exactly. Figure 9 shows examples of similarity, congruence, and symmetry.

▶ TRANSFORMATION GEOMETRY

Transformation geometry is concerned with those properties, or characteristics, of a figure that are not changed by certain rigid motions. Such motions are called **isometries**. The word "isometry" means "the same measure." An isometry, thus, is a movement of a figure to a new position, leaving all its measurements, including size and shape, the same.

One type of motion in transformation geometry is the **flip**, or **line reflection**. In a line reflection, every point in the figure is symmetrical to a corresponding point in the

Figure 10. Transformations

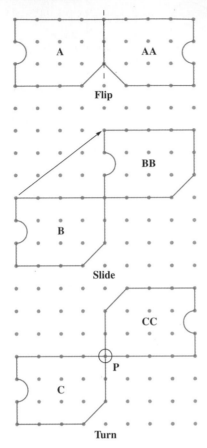

Flip

Slide

Turn

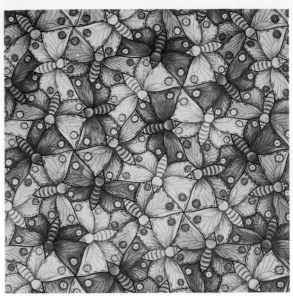

The artist M. C. Escher has created this tessellation using a single butterfly shape in three different colors. An important element of the design incorporates groupings of six butterflies in two alternating colors rotating around a point where their wings meet. The dots on the wings of the group are in the third color. For example, if the group contains blue and green butterflies, the wing dots are red.

image on the other side of a line called the line of symmetry. Look at Polygons A and AA in Figure 10. You can think of Polygon AA as being the flip side or mirror image of Polygon A. Polygon A has actually been flipped across the line of symmetry to form a congruent image.

In the motion called a **slide**, or **translation**, a figure is moved up, down, to the left or right, or diagonally. Figure 10 shows how sliding Polygon B on the diagonal results in the congruent slide image, Polygon BB. An arrow called a slide arrow indicates the direction of the slide motion.

If a figure is rotated, or turned, around a fixed point, the motion is called a **turn**, or **rotation**. In Figure 10, Polygon C has been rotated 180° around Point P to form the congruent image, Polygon CC.

Transformations can be used to create designs such as those made famous by the Dutch artist, M. C. Escher. These designs, consisting of interlocking shapes, are called

tessellations, or **tilings**. Escher made extensive use of flips, slides, and turns to create his designs, rendered as drawings, woodcuts, or paintings.

▶ **BEYOND THE THIRD DIMENSION**
The idea of dimension has long fascinated mathematicians. We can think about as many dimensions as we wish. Let us look at the simplest dimensional idea, which is the single point. We will say that the point represents zero dimensions.

Zero dimensions •

Imagine the point shifting through space a short distance to generate a line segment with 2 endpoints. Counting only endpoints and segments, we have 2 points and 1 segment, representing 1 dimension.

One dimension •———•

Now imagine the segment shifting in a new dimension to generate a square, a two-dimensional object. We now have 4 endpoints, 4 segments, and 1 square.

Two dimensions

Next, the square shifts perpendicular to itself to generate a cube with three dimensions. Now we have 8 points, 12 segments, 6 squares, and 1 cube.

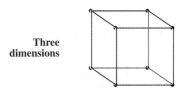

Three dimensions

We can put this data into a table to help us find some patterns. In one pattern, the number of points is doubled each time we shift the figure. That pattern is easy. Now look at what happened when the segment shifted, resulting in 4 points, 4 segments, and 1 square. The 4 points represent the 2 old points and 2 new points. The 4 segments represent the old segment, the new segment, and 2 new segments produced by the points that shifted.

Looking at the 6 squares that were generated in the shift from two to three dimensions, we can see that they were the old square, the new square, and 4 squares generated by the 4 shifting segments. In the table we can calculate the 6 by doubling the 1 directly above the 6 and adding the 4 to the left of the 1.

We can continue to extend the table by using the pattern of selecting a cell, or box, doubling the number above the cell, and adding the number to the upper left of the cell. To compute the numbers that would go in the row for the fourth dimension, we first

double the 8 points, giving us 16 points. The number of segments would be 2 x 12, or 24, plus 8, or 32. The number of squares would be 2 x 6, or 12, plus 12, or 24. The number of cubes would be 2 x 1, or 2, plus 6, or 8. This produces a four-dimensional figure called a **hypercube**, or **tesseract**. With a computer we can produce an image of a hypercube, formed as the result of shifting a cube.

Figure 11. Hypercube

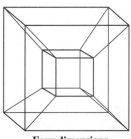

Four dimensions

In the hypercube you can easily find and count the 16 points. It is a little harder to count the 32 segments. Some of the squares look strange because of your point of view, but it is possible to find 24 squares. Of the 8 cubes, you can easily see the large outer cube and the small inner cube. The other 6 cubes are nested on the 6 sides of the small cube and are bounded by the large cube.

You could extend the table to describe a five-dimensional or a six-dimensional cube. These are more than fanciful ideas. Ideas and figures of more than three dimensions are used in some multidimensional statistical tests and in other fields of mathematics.

▶ NON-EUCLIDEAN GEOMETRY

Ideas about non-Euclidean geometry, a geometry that is different from that of Euclid, originated with the great German mathematician Carl Friedrich Gauss in the 1800's.

Table 1. Dimensions

Dimensions	Points	Segments	Squares	Cubes	Hypercubes
0	1				
1	2	1			
2	4	4	1		
3	8	12	6	1	
4	16	32	24	8	1

What is pi?

Early mathematicians knew they needed a special number that would enable them to calculate the area of a circle. This number, eventually called pi, defines the relationship between the diameter and the circumference of a circle. No one, however, had a good idea of the value of pi or of what quantity it represented.

In about 1650 B.C., the Egyptian scribe Ahmes described a problem having to do with the area of a circular field. He calculated that pi had a value of about $3\frac{1}{6}$.

The Greek mathematician Archimedes, who lived in the 200's B.C., inscribed, or drew, polygons whose areas could easily be

computed, inside and outside a circle. Using the areas of the polygons, he was able to calculate the area of the circle, and then calculate pi. Archimedes eventually used a 96-sided polygon and derived a value for pi of between $\frac{22}{7}$ and $\frac{223}{71}$, or about 3.14.

For years mathematicians all over the world used Archimedes' method, eventually inscribing polygons with thousands of sides. Then in 1579, the Frenchman François Viète calculated pi to 9 decimal places using a formula he invented and a polygon with almost 400,000 sides.

It was not until the 1700's that the Greek symbol for pi, π, came into common use, largely due to the writings of the Swiss mathematician Leonhard Euler. In 1766, Johann Lambert, a Swiss-German, proved that pi was an irrational number, a number whose decimal places never end.

Knowing they cannot get an exact value for pi has not stopped mathematicians from computing to more and more decimal places. The latest calculations, done by computer, carry the value to more than 2 billion decimal places. For most ordinary mathematics today, we use 3.14 or 3.1416 as a workable value for pi.

These ideas were subsequently worked out in detail by three other mathematicians—Nikolai Lobachevsky from Russia, János Bolyai from Hungary, and Bernhard Riemann, also from Germany.

One of Euclid's basic assumptions, the parallel postulate, had troubled mathematicians for years. It seemed to be more complicated than the other assumptions, and some mathematicians thought it should be classified as a theorem. The parallel postulate states that through any point not on a line, exactly one line can be drawn through the point parallel to the other line. Lobachevsky and Bolyai decided to find out what would happen if they made an alternative assumption to the parallel postulate. Their assumption stated that through any point not on a line, more than one line can be drawn through the point parallel to the other line. Riemann worked on another assumption, which stated that there were no parallel lines.

These ideas were developed into a new non-Euclidean geometry that forced mathematicians to change many former conceptions. The assumption had been that Euclidean geometry described our world very well. Non-Euclidean geometry, however, caused mathematicians and others to perceive the world in completely new and different ways and to develop new mathematical models with which to test their ideas. (More information about non-Euclidean geometry is in MATHEMATICS, HISTORY OF in Volume M.)

Geometers continue to explore alternative geometries, looking for new ideas, patterns, and models. This contributes to our mathematical knowledge and to the development of major applications in science and technology.

WILLIAM M. FITZGERALD
Professor of Mathematics, Michigan State University

See also MATHEMATICS; MATHEMATICS, HISTORY OF; TOPOLOGY; TRIGONOMETRY; WEIGHTS AND MEASURES.

GEOPHYSICS. See GEOLOGY.

GEORGE

George was the name of six kings of England and two kings of Greece. The first four English kings are often referred to as "the four Georges." The graceful style of architecture and decorative art known as the Georgian style emerged during their reigns (r. 1714–1830).

▶**KINGS OF ENGLAND, SCOTLAND, AND IRELAND**

George I (1660–1727) (r. 1714–27), the great-grandson of James I, was the first English king from the German House of Hanover. He was born George Louis on May 28, 1660, in Osnabrück, Hanover (in Germany). He succeeded his father as ruler of Hanover in 1698 and became king of England in 1714 upon the death of Queen Anne.

It might seem strange that a German should succeed to the British throne, but England's Act of Settlement of 1701 barred Catholics from becoming king or queen, and George was the nearest Protestant heir. In 1715, George I put down a Jacobite rebellion, an uprising led by those who wished to restore the Catholic Stuarts to the throne.

Because he spoke no English, George I allowed his ministers to conduct national affairs for him. This practice led to the establishment of the office of prime minister. (Sir Robert Walpole, the king's first prime minister, communicated with George in French.) George I died in Osnabrück on June 11, 1727.

George II (1683–1760) (r. 1727–60) was the son of George I. Born George Augustus on November 10, 1683, at Herrenhausen Palace in Hanover, he was the last ruling British monarch born outside the British Isles.

George II was a capable politician in his own right, but he was enormously influenced by his intelligent wife, Caroline of Ansbach, who persuaded him to retain his father's adviser, Sir Robert Walpole, as prime minister. George II played a larger role in England's foreign and military affairs than his father had. In 1743, during the War of the Austrian Succession, he became the last British monarch to command troops in the field.

In 1746, at Culloden Moor, the king's forces defeated a Jacobite rebellion led by Prince Charles Edward Stuart (also known as Bonnie Prince Charlie, or the Young Pretender). This was the Stuarts' last attempt to regain power in Britain.

George I, a German prince, ascended the British throne in 1714. Because he spoke no English, his ministers, most notably Sir Robert Walpole, conducted national affairs.

George II was the last British king to command troops in the field (1743). Toward the end of his reign, Britain entered into the Seven Years' War against France.

George II died of a stroke on October 25, 1760. Within three years of his death, England had defeated France in the Seven Years' War (1756–63). Under the leadership of George II's secretary of state, William Pitt the Elder, England took control of Canada and became the dominant foreign power in India.

George III (1738–1820) (r. 1760–1820) George II's grandson, was the son of Frederick, Prince of Wales, who had died before he could succeed his father. George III was born George William Frederick on June 4, 1738. He became Britain's longest-reigning king and was the last king of the American colonies.

George III eventually gained enough power to break the control of the Whigs, who had dominated Parliament since the reign of King George I. He appointed his own prime ministers, the Earl of Bute (1762–63), Lord North (1770–82), and William Pitt the Younger (1783–1801).

George III's controversial and oppressive policies contributed to the outbreak of the American Revolutionary War in 1775. When Britain lost that war, George became so bitter

George III lost the American colonies during the Revolutionary War, but he strengthened British imperial power in Africa and India.

The unpopular George IV served as Prince Regent during the final years of his father's reign. He was an extravagant and ineffective monarch.

he considered abdicating (giving up the throne). However, in spite of losing the American colonies, George III greatly expanded Britain's control in India, the West Indies, and Africa.

It is widely believed that George III suffered from porphyria, a rare illness whose symptoms resemble insanity. However, that diagnosis has been challenged. Nevertheless, he had numerous mental breakdowns and was permanently disabled after 1811. For example, it is said that once while driving near Windsor Castle, George III got out of his carriage and shook hands with the branch of an oak tree, which he mistook for the king of Prussia. After 1811 he lived in seclusion and died on January 29, 1820.

George IV (1762–1830) (r. 1820–30) was the eldest son of George III. He was born George Augustus Frederick on August 12, 1762, at St. James' Palace in London. Due to his father's illness, George took control of the throne in 1811, serving as Prince Regent (ruling prince) until George III's death in 1820. This period is known as the Regency.

George IV was very unpopular among his subjects, and his extravagant life-style brought the British monarchy into disrepute. His marriage to the widow Mrs. Maria Fitzherbert was considered illegal. He later married Princess Caroline of Brunswick but caused another scandal when he tried to divorce her.

George IV's most positive legacy was his patronage of the arts. He was responsible for the Regency style in art and architecture. He died in London on June 26, 1830, and was succeeded by his brother, William IV.

George V (1865–1936) (r. 1910–36) was the second son of Edward VII. He succeeded his father because his older brother, Prince Albert, had died in 1892.

He was born George Frederick Ernest Albert on June 3, 1865, at Marlborough House, in London. As a young man, George attended the Royal Naval Academy. In 1894 he married Princess (Victoria) Mary of Teck, who had been engaged to his older brother. George was devoted to his wife and children.

At the beginning of his reign, George V was called on to settle two controversial crises. The first concerned the reform of the House of Lords (1910–11), intended to control the power of its Conservative majority. The second concerned Irish home rule (1912–14) and the threat of civil war in Ireland.

During World War I (1914–18), while England was at war with Germany, George V changed the name of the British royal house from the German Saxe-Coburg-Gotha to the more patriotic, British-sounding name of Windsor. He was an extremely popular king at a time when many of the European monarchies were being swept away by wars and revolutions. He and Queen Mary maintained a solid sense of duty, which gave the British stability during turbulent times.

George V died on June 20, 1936. Fifty years passed before it was revealed that the king's personal physician had hastened his death with lethal injections. Although the injections undoubtedly were given to ease the king's pain and suffering, the news of this mercy killing caused enormous controversy.

George VI (1895–1952) (r. 1936–52) was the second son of George V. He unexpectedly became king after his older brother, Edward VIII, scandalized the world by abdicating the throne to marry an American divorcée, Wallis Simpson.

George VI was born Albert Frederick Arthur George on December 14, 1895, at Sandringham (the royal family's home in Norfolk). His family called him "Bertie."

Like his father before him, Bertie never expected to become king. He attended naval college and rose to the rank of lieutenant. During World War I (1914–18) he was on duty during the Battle of Jutland (1916), the largest naval battle of the war.

In 1920 he was made the Duke of York, and three years later he married Lady Elizabeth Bowes-Lyon, the daughter of a Scottish earl. As Duke and Duchess of York, they had two daughters, Elizabeth Alexandra Mary and Margaret Rose.

When Edward VIII abdicated on December 11, 1936, he seriously damaged the reputation of the monarchy. Therefore, after his coronation on May 12, 1936, George VI and his wife, Queen Elizabeth, set about repairing the good name of the monarchy. They were soon praised and admired for their warmth and sense of duty. During World War II (1939–45), George VI visited war zones, and he boosted civilian morale at home by remaining in London during the German bombing raids over the city.

George VI was the last emperor of India, as India gained its independence shortly after World War II ended. He died at Sandringham on February 6, 1952, and was succeeded by his daughter, the present Queen Elizabeth II.

KINGS OF GREECE

George I (1845–1913) (r. 1863–1913) was the second son of King Christian IX of Denmark. He was born Christian George in Copenhagen on December 24, 1845. In 1863, at the age of 17, he was elected King George (Georgios) I of Greece by the Greek National Assembly after the unpopular King Otto had been deposed (removed from the throne).

George I introduced a democratic constitution in 1864 and expanded Greek territory by conquering much of Thessaly and Epirus from the Turks in 1881. His family ties to members of the royal families of Denmark, Russia, England, Norway, and Sweden, gave Greece an influence in European affairs it might not have had otherwise.

George I was assassinated by a revolutionist in Salonika, Greece, on March 18, 1913. He was succeeded by his son, Constantine.

George V reigned during World War I. His visits to the British troops at the battlefront earned him enormous respect and popular affection.

George VI reigned during World War II. His courageous stand during the German air raids over London comforted his threatened subjects.

George I's grandson, Prince Philip, duke of Edinburgh, is married to Elizabeth II, the present Queen of the United Kingdom and Northern Ireland.

George II (1890–1947) (r. 1922–23; 1935–47) was the son of Constantine I. He was born in Tatoi, near Athens, on July 20, 1890. He married Princess Elizabeth of Romania in 1921.

Because of his pro-German sympathies during World War I, George was initially passed over for the throne. But when Constantine finally abdicated in 1922, George became King Georgios II. He was exiled the following year, and Greece was declared a republic in 1924.

George II was restored to the throne in 1935, but the country was governed under the dictatorship of Prime Minister Ioánnis Metaxás. Forced into exile after the Germans conquered Greece in 1941, George II returned in 1946. He died in Athens on April 1, 1947, and was succeeded by his brother Paul.

JEREMY BLACK
Author, *Eighteenth-Century Europe, 1700–89*

GEORGE, JEAN CRAIGHEAD. See CHILDREN'S LITERATURE (Profiles).

GEORGIA

Georgia was named in honor of King George II of England, who granted a royal charter establishing the colony in 1732. The largest state east of the Mississippi River and one of the South's industrial leaders, Georgia is often called the Empire State of the South. Two other nicknames—the Goober State and the Peach State—were inspired by two of the state's most famous crops: peanuts (often called goobers in the South) and luscious Georgia peaches.

State flag

Georgia is a part of the Deep South. It is bordered by Florida on the south, Alabama and Florida on the west, Tennessee and North Carolina on the north, and South Carolina and the Atlantic Ocean on the east.

The southern half of the state is a relatively flat coastal plain. Much of this section is sparsely populated, and the bulk of the land is used for forests, farming, and grazing livestock. Most of the northern half of the state is the Piedmont region, where the red clay hills of Georgia are located. While also containing forests and farms, this region is densely populated with a diversified (mixed) economy. Atlanta, by far the state's largest metropolitan area, spreads over a large part of the Piedmont. The Appalachian Mountains thrust into the extreme northern part of the state.

Georgia was one of the 13 original colonies, and it is a state steeped in history. In the decades before the United States Civil War, Georgia was a land of slavery and great cotton plantations. During the Civil War (1861–65), Georgia suffered widespread devastation.

In more recent decades, Georgia has experienced rapid economic growth, but many Georgians still treasure the slower-paced and more easygoing practices of the past. Good manners and southern charm are still highly valued social graces.

Georgia's long, hot summers, numerous lakes and rivers, and scenic beauty incline people to outside activities. Fishing, hunting, amateur sports, and outdoor arts and music festivals are common recreations.

A large majority of Georgia's people today live in urban areas. Atlanta's famed Peachtree Street, once a quiet and dignified residential area where wealthy Atlantans made their homes, is now a bustling thoroughfare. Most

Georgians work in office buildings, factories, restaurants, and shops, and about half of the population lives in suburbs.

The University of Georgia, chartered in 1785, was the first state-chartered university in the United States. The nation's first gold rush took place in Georgia in 1828. The first Indian newspaper, *The Cherokee Phoenix*, was published in Georgia, also in 1828. The Girl Scouts of America was founded in Georgia in 1912. In 1943 Georgia became the first state to lower the legal voting age to 18. These are only a few of the firsts that Georgia has been able to claim during its long history.

▶ LAND

The average elevation in Georgia is about 600 feet (183 meters) above sea level. The land slopes downward from the Appalachian Mountains in the north to the wetlands and coastal areas in the south. Most of the state's land is fertile and suitable for a variety of crops. Forests cover approximately 70 percent of the land area.

Land Regions

Georgia may be divided into three general land areas, two of which contain important subdivisions.

Opposite page, clockwise from left: Famous for its crops of mouth-watering peaches, Georgia is nicknamed the Peach State. The High Museum of Art is one of many cultural attractions in Atlanta, the state capital. Autumn foliage enhances the beauty of the Blue Ridge Mountains, which extend into northeastern Georgia.

State flower:
Cherokee rose

State tree:
Live oak

FACTS AND FIGURES

Location: Southeastern United States; bordered on the north by Tennessee and North Carolina, on the east by South Carolina and the Atlantic Ocean, on the south by Florida, on the west by Florida and Alabama.

Area: 58,910 sq mi (152,576 km²); rank, 21st.

Population: 7,058,000 (1994 estimate); rank, 11th.

Elevation: *Highest*—Brasstown Bald Mountain, 4,784 ft (1,458 m) in Union County; *lowest*—sea level.

Capital: Atlanta.

Statehood: January 2, 1788; 4th state.

State Motto: *Wisdom, justice, and moderation.*

State Song: "Georgia on My Mind."

Nicknames: Empire State of the South; Peach State.

Abbreviations: GA; Ga.

State bird:
Brown thrasher

Left: Rushing waters and mountainous terrain are among the natural features of northern Georgia. *Above:* A canoe trip is a delightful way to explore the wilderness of the Okefenokee Swamp. *Opposite page:* Live oaks draped with Spanish moss shade a path on Cumberland Island, one of Georgia's coastal islands.

The Coastal Plain covers more than half of the state and is composed of two large subregions. The smaller of the two, the lower coastal plain, includes the eight major barrier islands along the Atlantic Coast, Georgia's share of the Okefenokee Swamp (the remainder is in Florida), and other wetlands. The soil in this area is sandy, not very fertile, and poorly drained—it is not well suited to agriculture. In the 1800's, Georgians often referred to this part of the state as the "pine barrens" or "wiregrass," because much of it was largely barren (empty) of vegetation except for pine trees and tough grasses.

The larger portion of the coastal plain is the upper coastal plain. It is a gently sloping area with well-drained and mainly fertile soil. This area was once the land of cotton plantations. It is the state's most important farming area and now produces a variety of crops.

The Piedmont Plateau covers more than a third of the state. The line where the coastal plain and the Piedmont meet is called the fall line. It marks the point where rivers flowing from the hilly terrain of the Piedmont to the relatively level land of the coastal plain make waterfalls and rapids. The cities of Augusta, Columbus, and Macon are on the fall line.

Until well into the 1900's, the Piedmont was an agricultural region that contained many cotton plantations. Today the region is the most thickly populated part of Georgia. Most of the state's manufacturing is done there.

The Appalachian Plateau, the Blue Ridge, and the Ridge and Valley Region make up the northern portion of Georgia. The mountains and valleys of this area are extremely scenic, and most of the land is forested. Brasstown Bald Mountain in the Blue Ridge, at 4,784 feet (1,458 meters), is the state's highest point.

Rivers, Lakes, and Coastal Waters

Rivers form a large part of Georgia's boundaries. The Chattooga, Tugaloo, and Savannah rivers form all of the boundary with South Carolina. The Chattahoochee forms half of the boundary with Alabama. The St. Marys provides part of the boundary between Georgia and Florida.

Georgia's river systems drain in three directions. The Savannah, Ogeechee, Altamaha, Satilla, and St. Marys rivers all flow into the Atlantic Ocean. The Suwannee and Chattahoochee rivers drain toward the Gulf of Mexico. The small streams in the Blue Ridge drain into the Tennessee River, which flows toward the Mississippi.

All of the state's larger lakes were created by the construction of dams on the rivers.

Georgia has about 100 miles (161 kilometers) of coastline on the Atlantic Ocean. Along the coast are many islands. They are part of the chain of low islands known as the Sea Islands of South Carolina, Georgia, and Florida. Shallow lagoons separate the islands from the mainland. Some of the islands are noted for their beaches and vacation resorts.

Climate

Georgia's climate is described as a humid subtropical climate. Winters are usually cool and wet, and summers are hot and humid. In general, the highland areas of the north are cooler than other parts of the state.

The average January temperature is 40°F (4°C) in the northern Blue Ridge and 54°F (12°C) in the southern part of the state. In July the average Blue Ridge temperature is 75°F (24°C), and the south coastal area averages 81°F (27°C).

Rainfall in Georgia, which averages about 50 inches (1,270 millimeters) per year, ranges from 45 inches (1,143 millimeters) in the central and eastern part of the state to 65 inches (1,651 millimeters) in the Blue Ridge.

The growing season in Georgia is quite long. It ranges from about 190 days in the mountain areas to approximately 260 days in the southern part of the state. Over most of the state, the first frost occurs in mid-November and the last frost in late March.

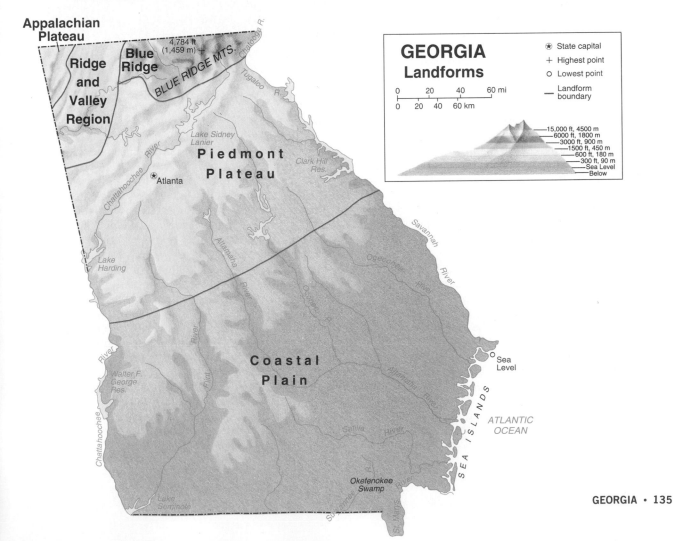

Left: Students relax in a pleasant spot on the campus of Georgia State University in Atlanta. The coeducational, state-supported institution was founded in 1913. *Below:* Young visitors to Kennesaw Mountain National Battlefield take a close look at a cannon. The scene of an important Civil War battle, Kennesaw Mountain is one of many historic sites in Georgia.

Plant and Animal Life

More than two thirds of Georgia is forested. The fast-growing pines are the most common trees. They are found in all parts of the state. Hickory, white oak and red oak, and maple are among the hardwoods that cover the mountains. Live oak, cypress, and palmetto are found along the coast and in swampy areas.

The Okefenokee Swamp is the home of alligators, deer, black bears, and many other animals. Rare birds in the area include the sandhill crane, ibis, barred owl, and water turkey. In the northern mountains there are many deer, foxes, squirrels, rabbits, opossums, and raccoons. Game birds such as wild turkeys, quail, ducks, and doves are also plentiful. The mountain lakes and streams are well stocked with trout, bass, pike, and other game fish. In the coastal waters there are shrimps, crabs, and oysters.

Natural Resources

In addition to water, forests, and wildlife, Georgia's natural resources include soils and minerals.

Since the 1930's, Georgia has practiced flood control, soil conservation, and reforestation. More recently, air quality, solid-waste management, and water management laws have been passed. The rapid population growth during the recent decades has, however, created many environmental problems.

Clays and stone are Georgia's most important minerals. Stone includes marble, granite, limestone, talc, and slate. The chief clays and claylike minerals are kaolin, fuller's earth, and bauxite. The metals include iron ore, barite, and gold. The fuels are coal and peat.

▶PEOPLE

Approximately two thirds of Georgia's 7 million people live in metropolitan areas, while one third live in rural areas.

Georgia's people are overwhelmingly Protestant in their religion. For many years the Georgia economy was dominated by plantation agriculture, which made it difficult for a new immigrant to acquire land. For this reason, and because for so long Georgia was a poor state that offered limited opportunity, the wide variety of ethnic and religious groups that helped to populate many other states rarely moved to Georgia. To be sure, Catholics, Jews, and members of other religious groups have always lived in Georgia and have contributed to the state's progress, but they remain a small minority.

About 70 percent of Georgians are white, and most originally came from northern or western Europe and especially from the British Islands. Almost all nonwhite Georgians are African Americans. Georgia's rapid growth since World War II has greatly increased immigration into the state, and the population is becoming more diverse.

Education

Georgia was slow to create an adequate system of public education. Not until the 1950's was the public school system fully established. Since the 1950's public schools have made enormous progress.

Beginning with the chartering of the University of Georgia in the late 1700's the state has established a broad-based system of higher education. The Georgia system includes five universities—the University of Georgia in Athens, Georgia Institute of Technology in Atlanta, Georgia State University in Atlanta, Georgia Southern University in Statesboro, and the Medical College of Georgia in Augusta—as well as numerous junior and senior colleges. All the state-supported institutions are governed by a single board of regents.

Georgia also contains many private colleges and universities. The best known are Emory University in Atlanta and the Atlanta University Center, which includes such important individual colleges as Morehouse and Spelman.

Libraries, Museums, and the Arts

Georgia has more than 50 regional and county library systems. Bookmobiles serve many rural areas. The largest library in the state is the Atlanta Fulton Public Library in Atlanta. Special libraries include the Georgia Historical Society Library in Savannah and the Jimmy Carter Presidential Library, housed in the Carter Presidential Center in Atlanta.

The Robert W. Woodruff Arts Center in Atlanta houses the Atlanta Arts Alliance, the Alliance Theater, the High Museum of Art, the Atlanta School of Art, and the Atlanta Symphony Orchestra. Other important art museums include the Callanwolde Fine Arts Cen-

Sports are a vital part of Georgia life. Several professional teams are centered in Atlanta; amateur sports such as college basketball are also popular.

ter in Atlanta, the Georgia Museum of Art at the University of Georgia, the Gertrude Herbert Memorial Institute of Art in Augusta, the Columbus Museum of Arts and Sciences in Columbus, and the Telfair Academy of Arts and Sciences in Savannah.

Sports

During the 1960's Atlanta became a professional sports center. The city is the home of the Falcons football team, the Braves baseball team, and the Hawks basketball team. Georgia is also a center for stock-car racing, a sport that originated in the southern states.

Most impressive, however, is the wide range of amateur sports. Virtually every com-

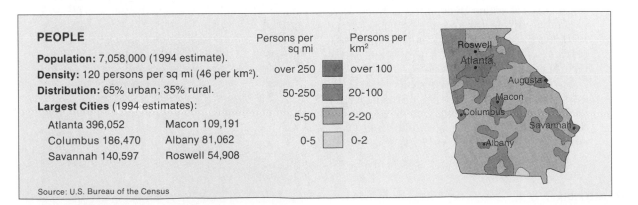

PEOPLE

Population: 7,058,000 (1994 estimate).
Density: 120 persons per sq mi (46 per km²).
Distribution: 65% urban; 35% rural.
Largest Cities (1994 estimates):

Atlanta 396,052	Macon 109,191
Columbus 186,470	Albany 81,062
Savannah 140,597	Roswell 54,908

Persons per sq mi	Persons per km²
over 250	over 100
50-250	20-100
5-50	2-20
0-5	0-2

Roswell
Atlanta
Augusta
Macon
Columbus
Savannah
Albany

Source: U.S. Bureau of the Census

Manufacturing: Textiles and clothing, transportation equipment, food products, paper and related products.

Agriculture: Poultry and eggs; livestock and dairy products; peanuts, tobacco, and soybeans; forestry products.

Minerals: Clays, gravel, sand, stone.

Services: Wholesale and retail trade; finance, insurance, and real estate; business, social, and personal services; transportation, communication, and utilities; government.

*Gross state product is the total value of goods and services produced in a year.

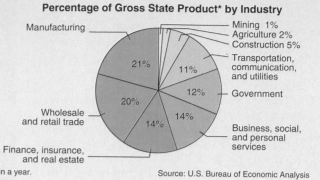

Percentage of Gross State Product* by Industry

Manufacturing 21%, 11%, Mining 1%, Agriculture 2%, Construction 5%, Transportation, communication, and utilities 12%, Government 14%, Business, social, and personal services 14%, Finance, insurance, and real estate 14%, Wholesale and retail trade 20%

Source: U.S. Bureau of Economic Analysis

munity has its organized softball league, hunting clubs, and similar groups. By far the most widely followed sport is football. Several college football teams have won national championships. High school football in the state not only attracts a wide following but is one of the nation's best programs.

▶ ECONOMY

Agriculture remained the base of Georgia's economy long after many other states developed economies based on manufacturing. During the 1900's, Georgia's economy has become far more diversified, with an increased dependence on service enterprises.

Services

Even in the heyday of "King Cotton," service enterprises were important to the Georgia economy because the financing, insuring, transporting, and marketing of the Georgia cotton crop were all essential services.

After World War II, as Georgians gained more wealth, wholesale and retail trade grew dramatically. As society became more complex, business, social, and personal services expanded. As government grew, so too did the number of government employees in Georgia. Today more than half of all employed Georgians work in these industries.

Because of Georgia's rapid growth in recent decades, real estate and public utilities have expanded, while transportation, finance, and insurance services remain important. These services employ more than 10 percent of the Georgia work force.

Several major service companies are headquartered in Georgia, mostly in Atlanta. They include Bell South, a telephone company; the Southern Company, a major utility; and Delta Air Lines.

Manufacturing

Textile manufacturing is Georgia's oldest and largest industry. The textile mills produce various kinds of cloth, thread, and yarn, which are then used to make clothing and other products. Originally, the textile mills relied on cotton grown in Georgia and nearby states, but today a wide variety of synthetic fibers are produced. The fall-line cities of Columbus, Augusta, and Macon are centers of textile manufacture, but textile and clothing factories exist throughout the state.

Other important industries are the processing and packaging of food and related products—often grown on Georgia farms—and the manufacture of paper and allied products—frequently from pine trees grown in Georgia forests. Lumbering and furniture production also rely on state forest resources.

Industries that have grown rapidly in recent decades include those producing chemicals, machinery, and particularly transportation equipment. Two large automobile assembly plants and the Lockheed Aircraft Corporation, all located in the Atlanta area, have been among the state's largest employers during most of the post-World War II period.

Several major industrial firms are headquartered in Georgia, including the Coca-Cola Company, which celebrated its one hundredth birthday in 1986.

Agriculture

Little more than 2 percent of Georgia's work force is employed in agriculture and forestry, but the enterprises are more important to the Georgia economy than such a figure suggests. As noted above, many of Georgia's most important industries—food processing and the production of paper, wood, and furniture—involve the manufacturing and processing of products from Georgia farms and forests. So, to a lesser degree, do textiles, chemicals, and other enterprises.

Georgia agriculture is richly productive. The state ranks high in the production of poultry and eggs, sales of which account for more than a third of Georgia's farm income. Also important are row crops, such as peanuts and soybeans; peaches, pecans, and other fruits and nuts; and cattle and dairy products.

Mining and Construction

Georgia is a leading producer of marble and granite. Tate in northern Georgia is famous for its marble quarries. Elberton in the northeast is known for granite. Georgia also leads the nation in production of kaolin—a white clay used in making white paper, porcelain, and other products. Kaolin is found along the northern border of the Coastal Plain. Chatsworth in the northwest is the center of talc mining in the state. Bartow County in northwestern Georgia produces barite, a mineral with a variety of uses.

The construction industry benefited from Georgia's economic development and today employs about 6 percent of the work force.

Transportation

Georgia has two natural deep-water harbors, at Savannah and at Brunswick. Savannah is a major port for international commerce. More than 100 steamship lines serve the two ports. Major inland ports are Bainbridge, on the Flint River; Augusta, on the Savannah River; and Columbus, on the Chattahoochee River. The Intracoastal Waterway extends the length of Georgia's coast.

Atlanta is one of the nation's major transportation centers. It has long been the chief railroad center of the Southeast. Today numerous railroad lines provide freight service within the state. Atlanta is the hub of several spokes of the interstate highway system. This system and other highways provide bus and truck routes throughout the state. The Atlanta airport vies with Chicago's O'Hare as the busiest in the United States. In addition, Georgia has more than 120 smaller public airports and about 160 private airports.

Opposite page: The Coca-Cola Company is one of many businesses headquartered in the Atlanta area. *Below:* The textile industry is the state's oldest and largest industry. *Right:* Georgia's trees provide the raw materials for such products as paper and furniture.

Places of Interest

Andersonville National Historic Site, in Andersonville, was a confederate stockade for Union prisoners during the Civil War. It is a memorial to all American prisoners of war. **Andersonville National Cemetery** is on the site.

Callaway Gardens, Pine Mountain, includes mountains, spring-fed lakes, and flower trails. Facilities are provided for boating, fishing, hunting, and golfing.

Carter Presidential Center, in Atlanta, has a museum that offers special displays to explain the office of the president to children.

Cumberland Island National Seashore, off the southeastern coast, has long stretches of beaches and sand dunes, as well as marshes and lakes.

Dahlonega Gold Museum, in Dahlonega, preserves buildings, mining equipment, and gold specimens from Georgia's gold-rush days.

Fort Frederica National Monument stands on a high bluff on St. Simons Island. The fort was built (1736–48) by James Oglethorpe to protect the British colonies against the Spanish.

Little White House, Warm Springs, was the Georgia home of President Franklin D. Roosevelt, who died there on April 12, 1945. The house remains largely as it was then.

Martin Luther King, Jr., National Historic Site, in Atlanta, preserves the grave and the birthplace and other structures associated with the civil rights leader Martin Luther King, Jr.

New Echota, near Calhoun, is the site of the capital of the last Cherokee Nation in Georgia. Here the first Indian newspaper was published in 1828.

Okefenokee Swamp, in southeastern Georgia, is maintained in its natural state. It includes the Okefenokee National Wildlife Refuge, operated by the United States Fish and Wildlife Service, and the Okefenokee Swamp Park, a wildlife sanctuary under commercial management.

Stone Mountain Park, east of Atlanta, surrounds Stone Mountain. A Confederate memorial, which was dedicated in 1970, is carved on the face of the mountain. The park provides facilities for boating, fishing, swimming, and camping. There are also several museums.

State Recreation Areas. The state park system includes more than 60 parks and other areas, ranging from Jekyll Island State Park's beaches to part of the Appalachian Trail at Vogel State Park. To obtain information on other recreational areas and places of interest, write to the Georgia Department of Natural Resources, Division of Parks, Recreation and Historic Sites, 205 Butler Street, S.W., Atlanta, Georgia 30312.

Confederate Memorial, Stone Mountain Park

Carter Presidential Center, Atlanta

Callaway Gardens, Pine Mountain

Above: Founded in 1733, Savannah is the oldest city in Georgia. Many of its historic buildings have been carefully restored. *Right:* Atlanta is Georgia's largest city as well as its capital. It is an economic and transportation center of the Southeast.

Communication

Georgia has approximately 30 daily newspapers and many weekly papers. The *Constitution* and the *Journal*, both published in Atlanta, have the largest number of readers. Station WSB in Atlanta was the South's first radio station. It was licensed in 1922. Today the state has some 300 radio stations and about 25 television stations. Cable stations of Atlanta's Turner Broadcasting System, including the Cable News Network (CNN), are popular nationwide.

▶CITIES

The massive Atlanta metropolitan area is Georgia's main economic, political, and social center. Other important cities include Columbus, Savannah, Macon, Albany, and Augusta.

Atlanta, the capital and largest city of Georgia, was founded in 1837. In 1864, during the Civil War, most of the town was burned. Modern Atlanta was built on the ashes. It became the state capital in 1868. Today the Atlanta metropolitan area contains nearly half of Georgia's people, and is a financial and transportation hub of the Southeast. An article on Atlanta appears in Volume A.

Columbus, the second largest city in the state, is the seat of Muscogee County in western Georgia. Located on the Chattahoochee River, it was founded in 1827 as a trading post. In the early days a textile plant was built at Columbus to make use of a nearby source of waterpower. Today textiles and clothing are among the many products manufactured in Columbus.

Savannah, Georgia's oldest city, was founded in 1733. It is situated on the Savannah River, not far from the Atlantic Ocean. Because of Savannah's location, it is a major seaport of the East Coast of the United States.

The original section of Savannah has been designated a national historic landmark. The many restored buildings in this area have made it an important tourist attraction.

Macon is a fall-line city located on the Ocmulgee River. It is a manufacturing and processing center that was founded in 1823. Because the city lies near the geographical center of the state, it is known as the Heart of Georgia.

Albany is a commercial and industrial center in southwestern Georgia. Situated on the Flint River, it serves as a trade center for the surrounding agricultural region and is the home of Albany State College. Albany was founded in 1836 and incorporated five years later.

Augusta is located on the Savannah River. Textiles and clay products are the leading manufactures. Goods are carried by boat and barge between Augusta and the port city of Savannah.

Augusta is Georgia's second oldest city. It was founded as a fort and trading post in 1735. During the Revolutionary War it was the capital of Georgia. Places of interest include the Augusta National Golf Club, home of the Masters Golf Tournament.

Atlanta's domed capitol building is the center of state government. The capitol also houses a state museum of science and industry and a state hall of fame.

▶GOVERNMENT

The present constitution went into effect in 1983. It is Georgia's tenth constitution.

The governor is the chief executive officer. The governor is elected for a 4-year term and may be re-elected for a second consecutive term. As director of the budget, the governor has considerable control over state spending.

The legislature is called the General Assembly and is composed of a senate, with 56 members, and a house of representatives, with 180 members. All members of the legislature serve 2-year terms.

At the top of the judicial system is the state supreme court, composed of seven justices elected in statewide elections to 6-year terms.

GOVERNMENT

State Government
Governor: 4-year term
State senators: 56; 2-year terms
State representatives: 180; 2-year terms
Number of counties: 159

Federal Government
U.S. senators: 2
U.S. representatives: 11
Number of electoral votes: 13

For the name of the current governor, see STATE GOVERNMENTS in Volume S. For the names of current U.S. senators and representatives, see UNITED STATES, CONGRESS OF THE in Volume U-V.

INDEX TO GEORGIA

• County Seat   Counties in parentheses   ★ State Capital

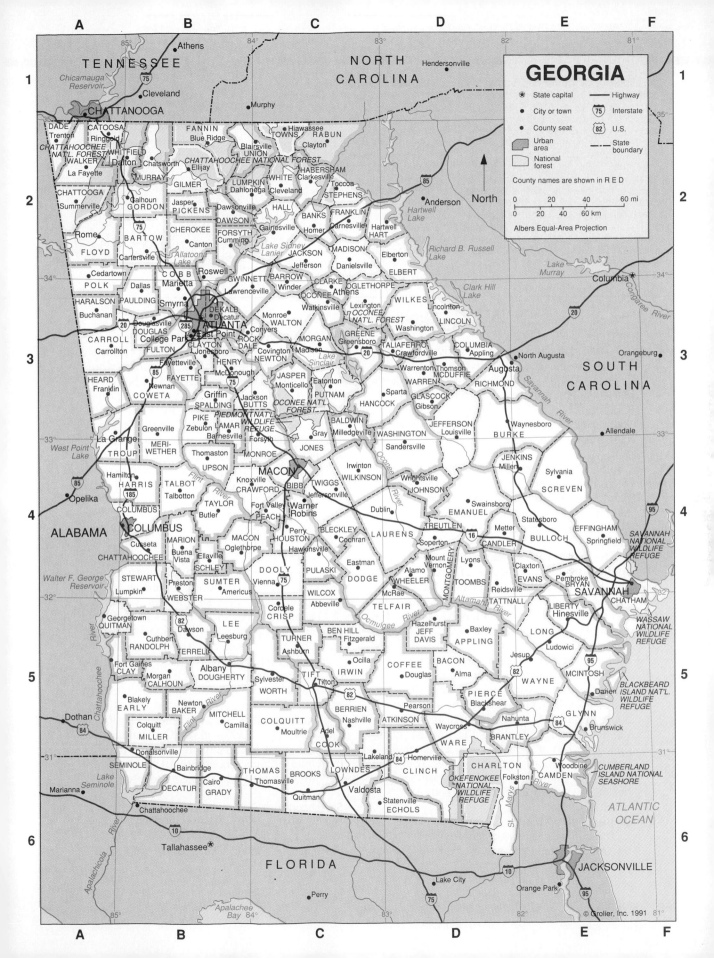

James Earl Carter, Jr. (1924–), 39th president of the United States, was born in Plains, Georgia. He served in the Georgia Senate and was governor of the state before his election as president in 1976. A biography of President Carter appears in Volume C.

Tyrus Raymond (Ty) Cobb (1886–1961), born in Banks County, was a professional baseball player. He was nicknamed the Georgia Peach. As a major league player, Cobb recorded a lifetime batting average of .367 and won twelve American League batting titles. He was one of five original members elected to the National Baseball Hall of Fame in 1936.

Rebecca Latimer Felton (1835–1930), born near Decatur, was the first woman to serve in the United States Senate. She was appointed in 1922 at age 87 to fill a temporary vacancy, serving for one day. During a long career of public service, Felton was an influential leader in the temperance and women's suffrage movements.

Henry W. Grady (1850–89), of Athens, was a journalist who won fame for his efforts to promote the development of the South after the Civil War. He also worked to improve relations between the North and the South.

Martin Luther King, Jr. (1929–68), born in Atlanta, was an important leader

Martin Luther King, Jr.

▶HISTORY

When the first Europeans arrived in Georgia, they found the land inhabited by two large groups of Mississippian Indians. The Cherokees lived in the northern highlands, and the Creeks occupied the remainder of the area. Both tribes practiced hunting and farming and constructed substantial towns.

Exploration and Settlement

In 1540 a Spanish expedition led by Hernando de Soto traveled through Georgia on an exploring excursion. The members of the expedition were the first Europeans to set foot on the Georgia mainland.

The first European settlers were the Spanish soldiers who established a fort on St. Catherine's Island in 1566. Thereafter the Spanish built forts and Catholic missions along the Georgia coast and on the Georgia islands. For a century the Spanish remained the dominant European influence in Georgia, although most of the land remained under Indian control.

In 1633, England asserted its claim on Georgia. Soon afterward the English established a settlement in the nearby area that became South Carolina. Spanish influence rapidly declined. In 1686 the Spanish abandoned the last of their Georgia settlements.

For almost half a century after 1686, the Europeans traded with the Indians of Georgia, but otherwise left them undisturbed.

English Colonization

The colony of Georgia was founded in 1733 by James Oglethorpe and named for George II, King of England. The king had good reason to grant Oglethorpe's request to start a settlement in America. A new colony would help stimulate trade and serve as a buffer between the English colony of South Carolina and Spanish-held Florida. In 1742, Oglethorpe defeated the Spanish at the Battle of Bloody Marsh on St. Simons Island. This battle ended Spanish influence in Georgia.

Oglethorpe had hoped to make the colony a haven for the "worthy poor" of England. This plan was rejected by Parliament, and few of England's poor ever went to Georgia. But some of the regulations set up by the Trustees for Establishing the Colony of Georgia reflect the noble ideals of Oglethorpe's original plan. The trustees banned slavery and hard alcohol from the colony and adopted policies to support communities of small farmers.

The noble experiment failed. In 1752 the trustees gave up the administration of Georgia, and it became a royal colony controlled by the king of England. By that time the ban on slavery and hard drink had been lifted.

As a royal colony, Georgia was the least populated and most remote of the 13 colonies. It played a relatively minor role in the Revolutionary War (1775–83). On January 2, 1788, Georgia became the fourth state to ratify the United States Constitution; it was one of only three states to do so unanimously.

Statehood and Development

The most important event in Georgia's early history as a state was the invention of the cotton gin. The gin was invented in 1793 by Eli

Flannery O'Connor

James Edward Oglethorpe

in the U.S. civil rights movement. A biography of King appears in Volume J-K.

Flannery O'Connor (1925–64), born in Savannah, is considered one of the most important modern southern writers. Her works include *Wise Blood* and *A Good Man is Hard to Find*.

James Edward Oglethorpe (1696–1785), the founder of Georgia, was born in London, England. In 1733, Oglethorpe and more than 100 settlers landed at what is now the city of Savannah. A biography of Oglethorpe appears in Volume O.

Sequoya (1770?–1843), also known as George Guess, was a Cherokee Indian scholar who created a system of writing for his people. A biography of Sequoya appears in Volume S.

Alice Walker (1944–), born in Eatonton, is a novelist, essayist, and poet whose works portray the hardships and triumphs of poor black people, especially black women. She received a Pulitzer prize in 1983 for her novel *The Color Purple*.

Andrew Jackson Young, Jr. (1932–), a civil-rights leader and politician, was mayor of Atlanta from 1982 to 1990. He also served as U.S. representative from Georgia (1973–77). Young was the first black to be appointed U.S. ambassador to the United Nations (1977–79).

Whitney, a northerner visiting Georgia. This machine, by separating the cotton fiber from the cotton seed, saved much labor and made cotton a profitable crop.

During the early 1800's, Georgia produced more cotton than anywhere else in the world. Most of it was grown on plantations and cultivated by African-American slave labor.

Cotton made many white Georgians rich, and it stimulated an increasing demand for land on which to grow it. The Indians were relentlessly pushed from the state to make room for more farms and plantations. General Andrew Jackson's victory over the Creeks during the War of 1812 opened large areas of Georgia to white settlement.

In 1828 gold was discovered in the Cherokee territory of northern Georgia, and many gold-seekers poured into the area. The settlement that grew up was named Dahlonega, from a Cherokee word meaning "yellow money." The discovery added to the desire for Cherokee lands. In 1838 federal soldiers

marched the last significant group of Georgia Cherokees to lands west of the Mississippi. This forced migration west was called the Trail of Tears because of the hardships and many deaths suffered on the way.

By 1860, Georgia contained more than 1 million people, 45 percent of whom were slaves. About one third of white families owned at least one slave, but only slightly more than 5 percent of white families were planters who owned 20 or more slaves. Nevertheless, the profitability of cotton agriculture made Georgia a relatively rich state.

Civil War and Reconstruction

In 1861, Georgia was the fifth state to secede (withdraw) from the Union and join the Confederate States of America. It became a major battleground in the war.

During 1864, General William T. Sherman's Union Army invaded Georgia, launching the attack from Chattanooga on the state's northwestern border and fighting a series of

In 1864, Union troops led by General William T. Sherman marched from Atlanta to Savannah, destroying everything in their path. The damage inflicted during the Civil War left the Georgia economy in ruins. Rebuilding the state was the main goal of the postwar years.

battles on the way to Atlanta. The city was captured in September 1864. In November, Sherman's troops burned Atlanta and began their famous march to the sea. Along the route from Atlanta to Savannah, the Union Army destroyed everything in its path in an attempt to drive a wedge through the center of the Confederacy. The Confederate states surrendered in April 1865.

Following the war, Republicans in Congress launched a bold program to "reconstruct" Georgia and the other Southern states. The Reconstruction period was a difficult one for the South. (See RECONSTRUCTION PERIOD in Volume Q-R.) Georgia was ruled by a series of military governors. Finally, in 1870, Georgia was re-admitted to the Union after it ratified the 14th and 15th amendments to the U.S. Constitution. These amendments granted citizenship to black Americans and guaranteed them the right to vote. But many white Georgians refused to accept the new social order, and some turned to violence to maintain white supremacy. The result was another failed experiment in Georgia: Blacks had gained their freedom but not equality.

From Reconstruction to World War II

The Civil War cost Georgia dearly. The loss of slaves, a valuable source of unpaid labor, combined with the extensive wartime destruction ruined the Georgia economy. Georgia moved from being one of the wealthiest states in the Union in 1860 to being one of the poorest states after the war.

Georgia's poverty greatly hindered the state's development during the late 1800's and early 1900's. Plantation agriculture and cotton production were restored, and Georgia grew more cotton than ever before. The cotton economy, however, never returned to prosperity. Georgia remained a predominantly rural and agricultural state. Many farmers, both black and white, became tenant farmers, or sharecroppers (people who farmed a landlord's land in exchange for a share of the crop). In 1920 more than two thirds of Georgia's farmers were tenants.

During the difficult period between the Civil War and World War II, many Georgians left the state in search of economic opportunity.

The Great Depression of the 1930's marked the final bankruptcy of cotton plantation agriculture in Georgia. There was a massive exodus off the Georgia farms, as hundreds of thousands of rural Georgians abandoned agriculture.

Modern Georgia

World War II (1939–45) was a turning point in Georgia history. Wartime spending greatly enlarged Georgia's industrial base. Older industries, such as the manufacture of cotton textiles and wood products, expanded. New industries, such as aircraft construction and chemical manufacture, developed.

Georgia cities, fed by the migration from farms and newcomers from outside the state, grew rapidly. By the mid-1970's, Georgia and other southern and southwestern states were known as the Sun Belt, a region of vigorous population and economic growth.

Such developments helped increase the state's wealth. Today the standard of living is approximately equal to the national average.

The most important social development in modern Georgia was racial desegregation. In Georgia and other states, blacks still had not gained equal status with whites more than a century after the Civil War. State laws discriminated against blacks and segregation practices kept them separate from whites. In 1954, the U.S. Supreme Court ruled that segregation in the public schools was unconstitutional. But this decision had little effect at first. In the mid-1950's, black southerners launched the civil rights movement to protest discrimination peacefully. Atlanta was the headquarters of the movement and the home of its leading figure, Martin Luther King, Jr. By the end of the 1960's, desegregation had become a reality in Georgia.

In 1976, Georgians saw one of their own elected to the White House when Jimmy Carter became the first Georgian elected president of the United States.

Georgia's urban areas continued to grow during the 1980's. Atlanta, in particular, strengthened its position as one of the nation's major cities. As it entered the last decade of the 1900's, Georgia, like the rest of the nation, searched for solutions to social problems, especially issues of poverty and unemployment, education and health care, the environment, and civil rights.

NUMAN V. BARTLEY
University of Georgia
Author, *The Creation of Modern Georgia*

GEORGIA, Republic of

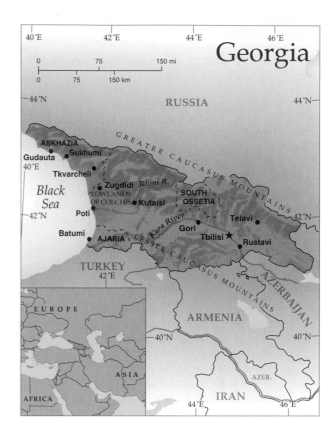

Georgia

Georgia is a country located in the western part of Transcaucasia, a region lying in the Caucasus mountain range that separates Europe and Asia. Its neighboring countries are Russia on the north, Turkey on the south, and Armenia and Azerbaijan, the two other Transcaucasian republics, on the southeast. On the west, Georgia is bounded by the Black Sea.

In ancient times, Colchis, or western Georgia, was famed as the site of the legendary Golden Fleece, the prize sought after by the Greek hero Jason and the Argonauts. The Romans gave the country the name "Georgia," although its people call their land Sakartvelo. Long fought over by competing empires, Georgia fell to Russia in the 1800's. It was briefly independent, between 1918 and 1921, before being absorbed into the Soviet Union. With the breakup of the Soviet Union in 1991, Georgia regained its independence.

The People. The Georgians, who call themselves Kartveli, are the original inhabitants of the region whose roots can be traced back some 3,000 years. The Georgian language belongs to the Caucasian language family. Georgia adopted Christianity in the A.D. 300's and has its own national church within the Eastern Orthodox Church. There is a small but important Muslim community, found mainly in the southwestern part of the country. Georgia also has a small number of Jews.

Georgians make up about 70 percent of the population. Other nationalities include Abkhazians and South Ossetians (who have their own autonomous regions), Armenians, Russians, Azeri Turks, and Greeks.

Georgia lies in the high mountains of the Caucasus range, which separates Europe and Asia. The shepherd at right tends his flock in one of the country's mountain pastures. Formerly a republic of the Soviet Union, Georgia regained its independence with the breakup of the Soviet Union in 1991.

In appearance, Georgians are often slender, with dark hair and eyes and strong facial features. They have been variously described as proud, hospitable, easygoing, fond of poetry and of the fine wine of the country.

More than half the people live in urban areas (cities and towns). Tbilisi, the capital and largest city, has a population of about 1.25 million.

The Land and Climate. Georgia is situated between the Greater Caucasus mountain range on the north and the Lesser Caucasus in the south. In the west the mountains widen, giving way to the lowlands of Colchis (Kolkhida). The major rivers are the Kura and Rioni. It is a varied land of great natural beauty—majestic forest-covered mountains, deep valleys, numerous mineral and hot springs, and warm, sunny beaches on the Black Sea coast.

The high wall of the Greater Caucasus shields Georgia from the cold winds of the north, while in the west the country is open to the warm air of the Black Sea. The result is a mild, often subtropical climate.

The Economy. Georgia has a diverse industry that includes the manufacture of railway locomotives, trucks and other heavy vehicles, chemical fertilizers, and synthetic fibers. Its chief mineral resources are manganese, of which it has some of the world's richest deposits, and coal.

Georgia has only limited farmland. But it produces grains, tea, citrus fruits, and grapes, chiefly in the Black Sea region, as well as wines (including champagne) and brandies.

Early History. The first Caucasian kingdoms arose here in the 500's B.C. It was the site of early Greek settlement and later became a part of the Roman Empire. Georgia was divided between the Persian and Byzantine empires in A.D. 562. After the Byzantine decline, Georgian monarchs created an independent state, which reached its height between the 1000's and early 1200's.

Between the 1500's and 1700's, Georgia was overrun by the Ottoman Turks and was again divided, this time between the Turks and Persians. A third power, Russia, joined in the struggle for Georgia and the rest of Transcaucasia. It annexed eastern Georgia in 1801, and then gradually took over the rest.

Soviet Rule. After revolutions in Russia in 1917, Georgia declared its independence, on May 26, 1918. In 1921, however, Red Army troops occupied the country, which was incorporated into the Soviet Union. A native Georgian, Iosip Dzhugashvili, who took the name Joseph Stalin, ruled the Soviet Union from 1924 until his death in 1953.

Independence and Government. Georgia's proclamation of independence from the Soviet Union in 1991 was followed by civil war between rival political factions. As a result, President Zviad Gamsakhurdia, who had been elected by popular vote, was ousted. He was replaced as head of state in 1992 by Eduard Shevardnadze, who had served as the last Soviet foreign minister. There was also continuing conflict with rebel South Ossetians, demanding unification with North Ossetia, a part of Russia, and with Abkhazians demanding independence.

Georgia's constitution, adopted in 1995, provides for a president, elected for five years, as head of state and chief executive. The government is led by a minister of state who is accountable to the president. The legislature is the Parliament, which is elected for four years. Shevardnadze was elected president under the new constitution in 1995.

ALEC RASIZADE
The W. Averell Harriman Institute
Columbia University

GERBILS. See GUINEA PIGS, HAMSTERS, AND GERBILS.

GERMAN MEASLES. See DISEASES (Descriptions of Some Diseases).

FACTS and figures

REPUBLIC OF GEORGIA is the official name of the country.

LOCATION: Western Transcaucasia.

AREA: 27,000 sq mi (70,000 km²).

POPULATION: 5,500,000 (estimate).

CAPITAL AND LARGEST CITY: Tbilisi.

MAJOR LANGUAGES: Georgian (official), Russian.

MAJOR RELIGIOUS GROUPS: Christian (Eastern Orthodox), Muslim.

GOVERNMENT: Republic. **Head of state**—president. **Head of government**—minister of state. **Legislature** —Parliament.

CHIEF PRODUCTS: Agricultural—grains, tea, citrus fruits, grapes, wines. **Manufactured**—railway locomotives, trucks, chemical fertilizers, synthetic fibers. **Mineral**—manganese, coal.

MONETARY UNIT: Lari (1 lari = 100 tetri).

GERMANY

For some forty-five years, between 1945 and late 1990, the German people lived in a divided land. During most of that period, Germany was made up of two separate states: the Federal Republic of Germany (known as West Germany) and the German Democratic Republic (or East Germany). The two Germanys were divided not only by a border, but by opposing political systems as well. West Germany had a democratic form of government. East Germany was a Communist state.

The division of Germany was a result of its defeat in World War II. In 1945, at the end of the war, Germany was divided into four zones of occupation by the victorious Allies—the United States, Britain, France, and the Soviet Union. In 1949, West Germany was formed from the U.S., British, and French zones; and East Germany from the Soviet zone.

In October 1990 the two Germanys were reunited. The new unified German government, which took office in 1991, maintains the democratic traditions established by earlier West German governments.

▶THE PEOPLE

Origins. The Germans are descended from the various Germanic peoples who arrived in northern and central Europe at least 2,000 years ago. The origin of the Germanic peoples is unclear. But they are known to have been organized into tribes that migrated to the region over a period of many centuries. They developed a common language, culture, and customs that distinguished them from other peoples of Europe. See the separate article on the German language in this volume.

Religion. The Protestant Reformation began in Germany. Religious battles once turned Roman Catholics and Protestants against each other, but they now live peacefully side by side.

Northern Germany is mostly Protestant, and southern Germany is mainly Roman Catholic. About 500,000 Jews lived in Germany before World War II. Most Jews who were not able

Looking like a fairy-tale castle, Neuschwanstein lies high in the Bavarian mountains. The castle was built for King Ludwig (or Louis) II of Bavaria but remained unfinished at his death in 1886.

to escape from the country were murdered in concentration camps by the Nazis during the war; few survived. Only about 30,000 Jews live in Germany today. The practice of religion was discouraged in East Germany during the years of Communist rule.

Education. Education has always been respected in Germany. Famous universities founded at Heidelberg (1386), Leipzig (1409), and Rostock (1419) helped to set standards that were followed by universities all over the world.

Elementary schools in the former West Germany are controlled and supported by the various *Länder* (states). Children are required by law to attend school full-time from the age of 6 to 15 or 16, depending on their course of study.

After four years of primary school (*Grundschule*), students go on to one of four kinds of secondary schools. About 60 percent attend a *Hauptschule* for another five or six years. This type of school provides a general education. Most *Hauptschule* graduates then attend a vocational school part-time for three years while they learn a trade. Other students, after passing an examination, may attend an intermediate school (*Realschule*) for six years or a senior high school (*Gymnasium*) or comprehensive high school for nine years. *Realschule* graduates usually train for a career in business. The *Gymnasium* prepares students for entrance to a university.

Education in the former East Germany was controlled by a ministry of education. Children were required to attend school for at least ten years. Since the reunification of the two Germanys, the East German educational system has been gradually adapted to the former West German system.

Germany has numerous schools of higher education, including dozens of universities.

▶WAY OF LIFE

The great majority of Germans live in urban areas (cities and large towns). Aside from Berlin, the capital and most populous city, the largest cities are in western Germany. It is the most densely populated part of the country and one of the most densely populated areas in Europe.

Many urban areas had to be rebuilt after the destruction of World War II. There is still a housing shortage, especially in the west because of the millions of immigrants who fled there from the eastern region.

Reducing Regional Differences. Life in most of western Germany's cities, towns, and villages has become much the same, although the pace of life is faster in the cities. In the small villages, people still take pride in local customs and they may wear traditional dress on

Some faces of Germany. *Opposite page, from left:* A quizzical-looking young Bavarian; *Oktoberfest* celebrants downing the famed Munich beer; a mother and daughter, both grape-pickers, from the Saar. *Above and right:* A couple from the former East Germany; a young woman from the northern port city of Hamburg; and North Rhine-Westphalians, made up as clowns, at the pre-Lenten carnival of *Fasching.*

holidays and other special occasions. Regional dialects can still be heard. But, with a few exceptions, the great historical differences that once existed among the regions have all but disappeared.

There are several reasons for this development. In the postwar period, millions of refugees from the east settled throughout Germany, including Protestants in traditionally Catholic areas and Catholics in Protestant areas. In addition, the boundaries of the former West German states were drawn up in most cases by the Western allies—the United States, Britain, and France—who were not especially interested in keeping the country's historic regions intact.

Television has also played a major role in reducing regional differences. People throughout the country watched the same television programs or listened to national radio networks. There were fewer programs with a regional emphasis.

Standards of Living. Whether they live in urban or rural (country) areas, the people of the former West Germany generally have a high standard of living. Many families own their own homes and most have automobiles,

television sets, and other modern electronic appliances. In part, these Germans can live so well because families are small and women often work before and after they have children. Nearly all jobs are open to women and they have full legal equality with men.

The standard of living in the former East Germany was much lower. This led many East Germans to move to West Germany before 1961, when the border was closed, and after 1989, when it was reopened. Like West Germany, the former East Germany is highly urbanized and women make up a large part of the work force. Since the reunification of the country, the federal government has provided much-needed financial assistance to the hard-pressed eastern sector, as it probably will have to for years to come.

A Changing Society. Traditional family life, dominated by the father, once played an important role in German society. By the late 1960's, however, many young people in Germany, like those in the United States and other countries, had rebelled against parental authority and traditional ways of life. They favored greater equality between men and women in marriage. Most were more liberal politically than their parents. Many were active in peace movements and in organizations to protect the environment.

Food and Drink. Each region of Germany has its own specialties. Bavaria is famous for its *Knödel* (dumplings). The Hamburg area is known for its delicious seafood dishes. Westphalian pumpernickel, or black bread, and German rye bread are also popular in many other countries. Venison (deer meat), rabbit, and other kinds of game are served in many parts of Germany. Cold fruit soups are another German specialty. Favorite foods all over Germany include *Wiener schnitzel* (breaded veal cutlet), pork chops, herring, and *sauerbraten* (beef marinated in vinegar and spices before roasting). Sausages, in all their many varieties, are served everywhere, from little street stands to the finest restaurants. However, Germans have become more health-conscious in recent years. They eat less fatty foods and prefer a more balanced diet.

Beer and wine are the favorite alcoholic drinks. Germany is famed for its beers and its white wines. The best-known German wines come from the Rhine and Moselle river regions. Non-alcoholic beverages, including spa or mineral waters, are consumed even more widely.

FACTS and figures

FEDERAL REPUBLIC OF GERMANY (Bundesrepublik Deutschland) is the official name of the country.

LOCATION: North central Europe.

AREA: 137,803 sq mi (356,910 km²).

POPULATION: 79,500,000 (estimate).

CAPITAL AND LARGEST CITY: Berlin.

MAJOR LANGUAGE: German.

MAJOR RELIGIONS: Protestant, Roman Catholic.

GOVERNMENT: Republic. **Head of state**—president. **Head of government**—chancellor. **Legislature**—federal parliament, consisting of the Bundesrat (Federal Council) and the Bundestag (Federal Diet).

ECONOMY: Chief agricultural products—wheat, rye, oats, barley, sugar beets, potatoes, hops, wine grapes, livestock. **Chief manufactures**—iron and steel, motor vehicles, electrical equipment, precision instruments, optical equipment, plastics, pharmaceuticals (medical drugs), china, glass, textiles, processed foods. **Chief minerals**—coal, lignite (brown coal), potash, iron ore, petroleum, natural gas.

MONETARY UNIT: Deutsche Mark (1 mark = 100 pfennigs).

Sports and Festivals. Soccer is the favorite German sport. Gymnastics, swimming, horseback riding, tennis, and handball are also popular. Winter sports, such as skiing and ice-skating, draw thousands of families to the Bavarian Alps and other winter resorts. Many Germans enjoy hiking.

Germans love celebrations. During the months of September and October, the Rhineland celebrates the wine harvest. There are weeks devoted to the music of Ludwig van Beethoven in Bonn and to Johann Sebastian Bach at Ansbach. Richard Wagner's operas are performed at Bayreuth in July and August. Berlin is the site of numerous film, theater, and music festivals. During the *Oktoberfest* in Munich, large amounts of food and beer are consumed. The annual Children's Festival at Biberach always draws large crowds.

Many small medieval towns in the south present historical plays. The passion plays, which are usually given at Easter time, dramatize Christ's last days on earth. The most famous passion play is presented in the Bavarian village of Oberammergau. It has been staged in the summer every ten years since the 1630's to celebrate the town's deliverance from the Black Plague.

The pre-Lenten season is celebrated with carnivals in Munich, Cologne, and some other areas. But the most important German holiday is Christmas. During this season the kitchens have a delicious smell of homemade fruitcake, *Lebkuchen* (gingerbread), and all kinds of cookies. Christmas trees are decorated with silvery strands of "angel hair" and many white candles. On Christmas Eve, church bells ring, carols are sung, and gifts are exchanged.

Cultural Heritage. Germany has made impressive contributions to the arts and sciences over the centuries. Many German writers, composers, philosophers, painters, architects, and scientists have had an impact far beyond the country's borders. During the years of Nazi rule in Germany (1933–45), however, scores of artists and scientists fled the country or were forced into exile. Many lent their talents to their adopted countries, but they left a void in Germany that lasted well into the postwar period.

For more information on this topic, see the following articles in this volume: GERMANY, ART AND ARCHITECTURE OF; GERMANY, LANGUAGE OF; GERMANY, LITERATURE OF;

The Moselle River (*above*) crosses western Germany before flowing into the Rhine. The two river regions are famed for their scenic beauty and their fine white wines. The Zugspitze (*top left*), in the Bavarian Alps, is Germany's highest peak. Lowland areas in southwestern Germany (*left*) are suitable for growing grain and raising dairy cattle.

GERMANY, MUSIC OF. Also see the Index for separate subject entries and biographies.

▶THE LAND

Germany's location has played an important role in its history. Situated in the very heart of Europe, it has few natural frontiers to mark its borders. Its location and lack of natural barriers have led to numerous invasions of Germany and also to German invasions of its neighbors. In area, Germany ranks sixth among the nations of Europe, after the Russian Federation, Ukraine, France, Spain, and Sweden.

Landforms. Germany can be divided into three distinct geographical regions—the northern lowlands, the central uplands, and the southern mountains.

The northern German lowlands slope toward the Baltic and North seas, Germany's only areas of seacoast. In the plains of the northern lowlands, forests alternate with meadows and marshy lakes. The few hills of this region do not rise more than 1,000 feet (300 meters) above sea level.

In the central German uplands, deep river valleys alternate with forested hills. Many of the forests and hills, painted houses, and turreted castles of the region were used as settings for the Grimm brothers' fairy tales. The highest peak in the central uplands is Brocken, which rises to 3,747 feet (1,142 meters) in the Harz Mountains.

Southern Germany has more rugged mountains. It is the land of the Black Forest and the Bavarian Alps. The Black Forest, in the southwest, is a mountainous region running along the Rhine Valley to the Swiss border. It is not really black, but very dark green—the color of the dense fir trees that cover the slopes. The tallest peak, the Feldberg, reaches a height of 4,898 feet (1,493 meters).

The Bavarian Alps in southeastern Germany are one of Europe's favorite winter playgrounds. Alpine lakes and steep slopes attract thousands of tourists, who come for the skiing and other winter sports. The Zugspitze, the highest peak in all Germany, at 9,718 feet (2,962 meters), is in the Bavarian Alps.

Rivers and Lakes. The Rhine River, with a total length of about 820 miles (1,320 kilometers), is the chief river of Germany and the most important commercial waterway in Western Europe. It rises in the mountains of Switzerland and empties into the North Sea. Other important German rivers—such as the Main, the Moselle, and the Neckar—flow into the Rhine. In northern Germany, branches of the Rhine interlock with those of the Ems and Weser rivers to form a network of water highways. Throughout the Rhineland, medieval castles and fortresses dot the steep, wooded hillsides. It was along the banks of the Rhine that the Romans planted the first vineyards in Germany, which now provide the grapes for the famed Rhine wine.

The Weser River flows across northwestern Germany into the North Sea. It is linked with the Elbe River by canal. The Elbe, which rises in the Czech Republic, flows northwestward across northern Germany and empties into the North Sea. The Oder River, which forms part of Germany's border with Poland, also rises in the Czech Republic. It joins the Neisse River south of Frankfurt an der Oder (Frankfort on the Odor) and is linked to the Spree and Elbe rivers by canals.

The Danube, one of Europe's major rivers, rises in the Black Forest of southwestern Germany and flows through seven other countries before emptying into the Black Sea. This river is important for transportation and is a source of hydroelectric power.

The lakes of the northeastern lowlands are set amid sand or peat or are ringed by marshes. In the south, alpine lakes sparkle in deep valleys cut by glaciers. Germany's largest lake, Lake Constance, lies on its border with Austria and Switzerland.

Climate. Most of Germany has a fairly mild climate without extremes of temperature. Winter fogs and dark, cloudy days are common in the northern lowlands. Northern cities like Hamburg and Berlin have average winter temperatures of around 36°F (2°C). Summer temperatures average 64°F (18°C) or more. Inland regions farther south and east normally have hotter summers and colder winters.

Rainfall generally increases to the south. There is usually more rain during the summer. The northern plains average from 20 to 40 inches (500 to 1,000 millimeters) of rain a year. More than 75 inches (1,900 millimeters) of rain or snow fall in the Bavarian Alps each year. From the Harz Mountains south, peaks are usually snowcapped all winter.

Mineral Resources. Germany's most important mineral is coal, which is the basis of its steel industry and is also used to generate electric power. Hard coal is mined chiefly in the Ruhr and Saar districts, which have some of the largest deposits in Western Europe. Lignite, or lower-grade brown coal, comes mainly from eastern Germany.

Small quantities of other minerals, including iron ore, copper, lead, and zinc, are mined elsewhere. Germany also produces much of the world's potash, used in making chemical fertilizers. Some petroleum and natural gas are found in the northwest, but Germany must import much of its supply of petroleum.

▶THE ECONOMY

Germany's defeat in World War II destroyed its once-thriving economy. But within less than twenty years, partly as a result of Marshall Plan aid from the United States, West Germany achieved an economic miracle, raising its standard of living to one of the highest in the world. East Germany also recovered, but at a much slower rate, and by the time of reunification in 1990, its economy had badly declined.

Agriculture. Only a small percentage of the German labor force is engaged in agriculture. Nevertheless, the country is largely self-sufficient in food production. Most farms in the former West Germany are small. But the government has encouraged the redistribution of land to enable farmers to work single large tracts conveniently and economically. Farmers often join together in co-operatives to buy machinery, seed, and fertilizer and to get better prices for their crops. East Germany formerly had collective farms run by the government, which decided how much each farm must produce and set the prices to be paid.

Modern agricultural methods, machinery, and improved uses of fertilizer help farmers produce more on the same amount of land. The chief crops are wheat, rye, oats, barley, hops (used in making beer), potatoes, sugar beets, and wine grapes. The raising of live-stock, including cattle, pigs, sheep, horses, and poultry, is also important.

Manufacturing. Germany is one of the world's leading industrial nations. Nearly 45 percent of the work force is employed in this sector of the economy.

Germany's Ruhr district is the industrial heart of Western Europe. Its rich coal mines provide energy for factories in such industrial centers as Essen and Dortmund. Germany ranks among the chief steel producing countries, and it is Europe's leading automobile manufacturer. People the world over were familiar with the distinctive Volkswagen "beetle" and many owned (or hoped to own) such German-made luxury cars as the BMW, Mercedes-Benz, and Porsche.

Germany has long been famous for precision instruments, cameras, and lenses. It is also a major producer of electronic equipment, chemicals, pharmaceuticals (medical drugs), and medical and other scientific equipment. It is the second largest producer of plastics, after the United States. China, glass, textiles, office and kitchen equipment, and aircraft are other important manufactured goods. However, German products face increasing competition from Japan and other industrialized nations.

East Germany's slower economic recovery was due partly to the fact that West Germany retained the industrial Ruhr district when the country was divided. In addition, entire factories were moved from the eastern sector to the Soviet Union as war reparations. Still, East Germany became an important industrial region in its own right. Before 1990, the eastern region had a centrally planned economy. The state owned and operated most industries and decided what goods to produce and in what amounts. East Germany became the leading producer of heavy machinery in the former Communist bloc of Eastern European nations. The production of machinery was emphasized to serve the needs of these countries and the Soviet Union. The price paid by the East German people for this was a chronic shortage of consumer goods.

Germany is one of the world's leading manufacturing countries. Its heavy industry is centered in plants like this one in the Ruhr (*right*). Automobiles, such as the popular Volkswagen (*below*), are a chief export. Grapes for the famed Rhine and Moselle wines are grown in carefully tended vineyards (*below right*).

72

The eastern part of the city was the seat of government of East Germany. The western part was closely linked to West Germany. See the separate article on Berlin in Volume B.

Eastern Germany. Leipzig and Dresden are other important cities in eastern Germany.

Neon lights illuminate a busy intersection in Berlin (*left*), Germany's capital and largest city. The twin spires of its great cathedral rise over the city of Cologne (*below*). Situated on the Rhine, Cologne dates from Roman times. A statue of the composer J. S. Bach (*opposite page*) stands before the church of St. Thomas in Leipzig, where he wrote some of his greatest music.

With reunification, the transformation of the eastern sector's economy to a free enterprise system, like that in the west, was begun. In the transition period, this led to serious economic problems in the east, including high unemployment.

Transportation and Communications. Germany has an extensive highway, railroad, and canal system, linking various parts of the country. Trucks compete with railroads in the transportation of goods. The German airline, Lufthansa, serves all international routes.

Germany has over 1,200 daily newspapers. There are 11 national and regional radio and television stations run by the federal postal system, and several privately owned ones.

▶MAJOR CITIES

Berlin was the capital of Germany from 1871 to 1945, and again became the national capital in 1990. Between 1945 and 1990, Berlin, like Germany itself, was divided in two.

Leipzig is the site of one of the oldest German universities and industrial fairs. It was the home of the composer Johann Sebastian Bach for the last 27 years of his life, when he wrote much of his greatest music. Dresden has given its name to a highly prized, delicate china that is really made in the nearby town of Meissen. Three fourths of the city of Dresden was destroyed during World War II, but it is now an important industrial center.

Although smaller in population, Frankfurt an der Oder is an important railroad junction linking Germany with Poland and other Eastern European countries.

There are several other cities of great historic interest in eastern Germany. Weimar is honored as the city in which the poet and dramatist Johann Wolfgang von Goethe spent most of his life. Wittenberg is known as the birthplace of the Protestant Reformation. Jena is a famed university town, as well as a center for making glass and optical equipment.

Western and Northern Germany. The university town of Bonn was the capital of West Germany between 1949 and 1990. Bonn is also famed as the birthplace of the composer Ludwig van Beethoven.

Germany's two busiest ports, Hamburg and Bremen, are in the north. Both are also important shipbuilding and manufacturing cities. The great cities of the Ruhr—Essen, and Dortmund—have long been centers of heavy industry. Düsseldorf, a center of commerce, is noted for its fashion industry. Cologne, like many other cities on the Rhine, was founded by the Romans. Its cathedral is the most famous Gothic building in Germany. Heidelberg, a university town, has attracted visitors for hundreds of years.

Central and Southern Germany. Among the most interesting cities of central and southern Germany are Frankfurt am Main, Nuremberg, Stuttgart, and Munich. Frankfurt, the birthplace of the poet Goethe, is a center of banking, commerce, and transportation.

Nuremberg dates from the Middle Ages. The old walls, towers, and palace have been restored to look much as they did when the great artist Albrecht Dürer was born there in 1471. Stuttgart is a center of the automobile and publishing industries. Munich, in Bavaria, is one of the most visited cities in Germany. It has world-famous art collections and historic treasures, which can be seen in its many museums.

JOHANN SEBASTIAN BACH

GOVERNMENT

The two Germanys had separate constitutions from 1949 to 1990. The West German constitution provided for the accession, or joining, of other parts of Germany to West Germany. On October 3, 1990, East Germany merged with West Germany and disappeared from the political landscape. The united country retained the official name of West Germany—the Federal Republic of Germany— as well as its constitution and form of government, with only slight changes.

Germany today is a federation of 16 *Länder* (states). The legislature is a federal parliament, made up of two chambers—the Bundestag (Federal Diet) and the Bundesrat (Federal Council). The Bundestag is the major body, responsible for passing the country's laws. Its members are elected by the people for 4-year terms. The Bundesrat delegates are elected by the *Länder* cabinets.

The Bundestag elects a chancellor, who heads the government. The chancellor is usually the leader of the largest political party in the Bundestag. A president, who serves as head of state but has little political power, is elected for five years by a convention made up of members of the Bundestag and the state legislatures.

Each state has its own government, which administers national laws and provides for education, police, and internal security.

HISTORY

Early History. Germany was at the edge of European history until the year 58 B.C., when Julius Caesar led the Roman armies to the Rhine River. The Roman legions clashed with the German tribes, who fought back stubbornly. In A.D. 9 a Roman army was decisively defeated by the Germans at the Battle of the Teutoburger Wald, limiting Rome's expansion. Unable to conquer the German tribes north of the Rhine, the Romans built a line of forts and walls along the lower Rhine and other rivers. They founded many towns and brought Roman civilization to this region.

When the Western Roman Empire collapsed in the A.D. 400's, Germanic tribes moved across Europe in large numbers. As the tribes took Roman towns, they mixed with Romans and learned Roman ways. Many became Christians. The Alemanni, the Saxons,

GERMANY

and the Franks were among the largest groups. One Christian tribe, the Franks, began to conquer and unite other tribes. They built up a large empire in Germany and Gaul (part of present-day France).

Charlemagne. Charlemagne, who is called Karl der Grosse (Charles the Great) in German, was the most powerful of the Frankish kings. Charlemagne was able to bring most of western Europe under his control. As he conquered various tribes, he converted them to Christianity. Under his rule the Franks cleared forests, built roads and bridges, and set up schools and monasteries. On Christmas Day, in the year 800, Pope Leo III crowned Char-

lemagne emperor of the lands that would become known as the Holy Roman Empire. The territories ruled by Charlemagne were also known as the First Reich (First Empire). See the article on Charlemagne in Volume C.

Treaty of Verdun. After Charlemagne died, his son and grandsons fought over who was to be emperor. The Treaty of Verdun (843) settled the matter by giving his grandson, Louis the German, the eastern part of the empire—from the Rhine to the Elbe (later Germany). Another descendant took the west (later France), and another took the center (later the Low Countries, parts of France, and most of Italy).

The German States

Schleswig-Holstein
Mecklenburg-Western Pomerania
Bremen
Hamburg
Lower Saxony
Berlin
Brandenburg
North Rhine-Westphalia
Saxony-Anhalt
Saxony
Thuringia
Hesse
Rhineland-Palatinate
Saarland
Bavaria
Baden-Württemberg

LÄNDER (STATES) OF GERMANY

Baden-Württemberg
Bavaria
Berlin
Brandenburg
Bremen
Hamburg
Hesse
Lower Saxony

Mecklenburg-Western Pomerania
North Rhine-Westphalia
Rhineland-Palatinate
Saarland
Saxony
Saxony-Anhalt
Schleswig-Holstein
Thuringia

But many of the Holy Roman emperors who followed Otto wasted their strength in fighting with the popes over church reforms and in trying to rule Italy. This left Germany divided into small feudal states ruled by petty princes. The power of these local rulers grew because the emperor was often away from Germany.

Frederick I, known as Frederick Barbarossa ("Red Beard"), was crowned emperor in Rome in 1152. He succeeded in uniting the warring sections of Germany, and under him the empire reached a peak of power. He weakened the position of his cousin, Henry the Lion of Saxony, and won some control over the pope and northern Italy. Frederick has become a legendary figure. Some Germans say he never died but sleeps in a cave, with his beard still growing, and will return one day. After Frederick I, local princes grew stronger again. During the reign of Frederick II, who died in 1250, the Holy Roman Empire declined in size and importance.

In 1356 a law was passed that assured the German imperial princes the right to elect the emperor. As a result, the emperor had little real control. He simply presided over a loose league of many independent states. By the 1400's, the Holy Roman emperor was usually a member of the Habsburg royal family.

See the articles on the Holy Roman Empire and the Habsburgs in Volume H.

The Hanseatic League. During the Middle Ages, some north German cities grew strong and their merchants rich. These large cities became free cities. The most important were Hamburg, Bremen, and Lübeck. To protect themselves and to regulate trade, these cities

Within the empire each area had its own ruler. The Saxons were especially strong, even though Charlemagne had fought for years to convert and subdue them. Under Henry I (Henry the Fowler), who became their ruler in 919, the Saxons instead of the Franks became the kingmakers. They were the leaders of the empire for about one hundred years.

The Holy Roman Empire. In 955 the Saxon king Otto I (Otto the Great) defeated the Magyars, whose raids had plagued Germany for about fifty years. Because of this victory, he was hailed as the savior of western Christendom. In 962 Otto was crowned Holy Roman emperor by the pope.

The mass migration of Germanic peoples hastened the fall of the Western Roman Empire in the A.D. 400's.

Some important figures in early German history. *From far left:* Charlemagne (742–814) unified most of western Europe under his rule. Frederick I (1123?–90), called Barbarossa ("Red Beard"), brought the Holy Roman Empire of German states to its height of power. Martin Luther (1483–1546) was a leader of the Protestant Reformation. *Opposite page:* Frederick II (1712–86), known as the Great, a musician as well as a military commander, made Prussia a major power.

and others formed an organization called the Hanseatic League. For centuries the league controlled trade on the Baltic Sea and with the Scandinavian countries.

The Reformation. Until the 1500's the rival German states were united by the Roman Catholic religion. But in 1517 a priest named Martin Luther nailed a list of 95 theses—his disagreements with the church—on the door of a church in the town of Wittenberg. Luther's theses criticized what he believed to be wrongdoing in the church and demanded reforms. The pope dismissed him from the church. His followers, called Protestants or Lutherans, split away from the Roman Catholic Church. North Germans flocked to the Protestant banner. South Germans and Austrians continued to worship as Roman Catholics. In 1555 the Peace of Augsburg brought an uneasy truce between the two groups. The two faiths were considered equal and each prince was given the right to choose the religion for his land. But the peace did not last.

The Thirty Years' War. In 1618 the Protestant nobles of Bohemia rebelled when the emperor sought to re-establish Roman Catholicism. This touched off the Thirty Years' War (1618–48). Other countries were drawn in until most of Europe was involved. The war devastated Germany, where most of the fighting took place. One third of the population may have died as a result of the war, which ended with the Peace of Westphalia.

See the article on the Reformation in Volume Q-R. An article on Martin Luther appears in Volume L, and one on the Thirty Years' War in Volume T.

The Rise of Prussia. The Peace of Westphalia had lessened the importance of the Holy Roman Empire. Under the rule (1640–88) of the "Great Elector," Frederick William, the state of Brandenburg took over the leadership of the alliance of northern states. Frederick William's son Frederick I took the title of king of Prussia in 1701. Prussia developed a strong army and an efficient government. Its royal family, the Hohenzollerns, were to become the first rulers of a united German nation.

Under Frederick II (the Great), who reigned from 1740 to 1786, Prussia became a major European power. Frederick took Silesia from Austria. He fought Austria, Russia, France, and Sweden in the Seven Years' War (1756–63), and annexed part of Poland.

Frederick the Great was also a patron of the arts, as were many of the German rulers. The 1800's were a period of great German cultural achievements, particularly in music and literature.

See the article on Frederick the Great in Volume F.

Two Revolutions. The French Revolution, which broke out in 1789, and the rise of Napoleon drew Prussia into war again. Napoleon crushed Prussia in 1806–07. But an alliance of Prussia, Russia, Austria, and Britain eventually defeated Napoleon in 1814. The Congress of Vienna (1815), which met to restore peace in Europe, made Germany a loose confederation of states. Prussia gained the Rhineland with the Ruhr coal deposits.

In 1848 revolutions aimed at establishing more representative government swept across much of Europe. German liberals gathered in Frankfurt am Main and drew up a constitution, calling for a German federal state with a constitutional monarchy under the king of Prussia. But the reformers were divided among themselves, and the king himself rejected the Frankfurt Constitution.

Bismarck and Unification. Prince Otto von Bismarck, chancellor to King William I of Prussia, succeeded in unifying Germany by force of arms.

Under Bismarck, Prussia won quick victories over Denmark in 1864 and Austria in 1866. The defeat of Austria gave Prussia the leadership of the German states. In 1867, Bismarck organized the North German Confederation, uniting German states north of the Main River. The king of Prussia became president of the confederation.

In 1870, Bismarck turned Prussia's military against France, maneuvering the French emperor, Napoleon III, into war. In the Franco-Prussian War (1870–71), France was quickly defeated. Bismarck forced it to give up most of the territory of Alsace-Lorraine and pay an indemnity equivalent to $1 billion.

The south German states now joined Prussia's confederation, and all of Germany was united in the Second Reich (Second Empire) when King William I was crowned kaiser (emperor) in 1871. See the article FRANCO-PRUSSIAN WAR in Volume F.

The Empire. Germany prospered under Bismarck's leadership, becoming the strongest power on the continent. As long as Bismarck was chancellor he kept a balance of power in Europe. But William II, who became kaiser in 1888, was young and ambitious. In 1890 he forced Bismarck to resign and began running the empire in his own way.

See the article on Bismarck in Volume B.

William II speeded Germany's overseas colonial growth, seizing several African lands and Pacific islands. He also made Germany a leading commercial and naval power. Britain and France, which already had established powerful colonial empires, saw their interests threatened. Germany's construction of the Berlin-to-Baghdad railway increased its role in Middle East affairs. Its support of Austria-Hungary's policy in the Balkans region of southeastern Europe put Russia on guard. As a result of two crises in the North African state of Morocco (in 1905–06 and 1911), Britain, France, and Russia formed an alliance, the Triple Entente, to counter the Central Powers —Germany and Austria-Hungary.

World War I (1914–18). In 1914 a Serbian nationalist assassinated the Archduke Francis Ferdinand, the heir to the throne of Austria-Hungary. The assassination led to an explosive conflict between the rival European powers. Germany backed Austria-Hungary's declaration of war against Serbia (now part of Yugoslavia). In turn, the nations of the Triple Entente declared war on the Central Powers. Japan entered the war on the side of the Entente, or Allied, powers. Italy joined the Allies in 1915, and the United States did so in 1917. The Turkish Ottoman Empire and Bulgaria sided with the Central Powers.

German armies advanced quickly into Belgium and France in the first month of the war. But the conflict then settled into a military stalemate between the two sides, punctuated by fierce battles for a few miles or just a few yards of ground. Finally, in November 1918,

DROPPING THE PILOT.

A political cartoon of 1890 depicts the young German emperor, William II, dismissing the aging Otto von Bismarck, who as chancellor had guided Germany (like a ship's "pilot") to unification and power. The headstrong William led Germany to defeat in World War I (1914–18), ending the short-lived monarchy.

an exhausted Germany accepted the Allied armistice terms, ending the fighting. In Germany itself, a left-wing revolution led to the overthrow of the imperial government of Kaiser William, who fled to the Netherlands, where he lived in exile until his death in 1941.

The Treaty of Versailles. The peace treaty, the Treaty of Versailles, signed in 1919, imposed severe penalties on Germany. It stripped Germany of Alsace-Lorraine and all of its overseas colonies. Part of the Rhineland was to be occupied for a number of years by Allied forces. The treaty created the Polish Corridor —a narrow strip of land that cut off East Prussia from the rest of Germany, in order to give a restored Poland access to the sea. Many German-speaking people were left outside the newly drawn boundaries. Germany was lim-

ited to an army of 100,000 soldiers, and was forced to pay the Allies the equivalent of $33 billion in reparations.

For more information on the origins of World War I and Germany's role in the war, see the separate article in Volume W-X-Y-Z.

The Weimar Republic. In 1919 a popularly elected national constituent assembly met in the city of Weimar and drew up a constitution that made Germany a republic. Friedrich Ebert was named president. Because the constitution had been written in Weimar, the postwar government of Germany has come to be known as the Weimar Republic.

The new government faced serious challenges. It was threatened by political extremists on both the left and the right, who often battled each other. Many Germans bitterly resented the harsh terms of the peace treaty. Democracy and the Weimar Republic were connected in their minds with their defeat.

In the early 1920's, inflation made German money almost worthless. Many people were unemployed, hungry, and desperate. Some Germans began to think that democratic government could never bring them prosperity.

In the mid-1920's, however, Germany experienced several years of normalcy. Gustav Stresemann, who as foreign minister had worked hard for international understanding, was able to obtain a reduction in the reparations payments. In 1925, Germany was one of the signers of the Locarno Pact, which sought to maintain world peace and stability. The next year Germany became a member of the League of Nations.

But hopes for economic recovery were dashed by the worldwide Great Depression, which began in 1929 and hit Germany especially hard. By 1933 more than 6 million people were out of work. Germans began to listen to the promises of Adolf Hitler, the leader of the German National Socialist Workers' Party.

The Rise of Hitler and the Nazis. The Nazis, as the National Socialists were called, were fanatic patriots who promised to make Germany rich and great again. They demanded revision of the Treaty of Versailles and return of the lost territories. As conditions grew worse, they got more votes. In April 1932, the aging Paul von Hindenburg, a military hero of the war, was re-elected president. The National Socialists and their allies soon became the strongest party in the Reichstag, or parlia-

Germany's economy collapsed after its defeat in World War I. Inflation was so great that paper money became almost worthless. It was cheaper for a housewife in the 1920's to light her stove with millions of marks in German currency than to use the money to buy fuel.

ment. Von Hindenburg was persuaded to name Hitler chancellor in January 1933. The Weimar Republic had ended and the Third Reich had begun.

In March 1933, the Reichstag granted Hitler dictatorial powers. He soon began to take charge of all aspects of German life. The Nazi party became the sole legal political party. Democratic organizations, such as trade unions, were crushed. Storm troopers and the Gestapo (the secret police) hunted down political opponents of the regime and threw many of them into concentration camps. By 1934, with Von Hindenburg dead, Hitler was the unquestioned *Führer* (leader) of Germany—a Germany that had become a police state.

Nazi ideology included the concept of Germans as a "master race." Under the Nuremberg Laws of 1935, German Jews became second-class persons. They lost their citizenship, were barred from many professions, and were forbidden to marry non-Jews. Pre-war persecution of the Jews reached its height in November 1938 with the widespread destruction of synagogues (houses of worship) and Jewish properties. Many Jews, along with non-Jewish Germans, fled the country.

The Road to War. Hitler soon adopted an aggressive foreign policy aimed at territorial expansion. He began expanding the German army and adding to its armaments, something forbidden under the Versailles treaty. In 1936 he sent German troops into the Rhineland, which had been demilitarized under the terms of the treaty. That same year he formed an alliance with Italy and Japan. In 1938, German troops marched into Austria, which was annexed to Germany.

Hitler then turned to Czechoslovakia, which had a considerable German minority. At the Munich conference of 1938, Hitler met with British, French, and Italian leaders and demanded territorial concessions from Czechoslovakia. This was agreed to by the Western leaders. Nevertheless, in March 1939, German troops invaded what remained of Czechoslovakia, and Hitler made the historic provinces of Bohemia and Moravia a German protectorate.

World War II (1939–45). Britain and France, militarily weak, had tried to appease Hitler in order to maintain peace. However, when German armies invaded Poland in September 1939, the two countries declared war on Germany.

The first years of the conflict saw remarkable successes by Hitler, whose armies quickly conquered most of the European continent, from the English Channel to the borders of the Soviet Union. But these successes led Hitler to overreach himself. In June 1941 he invaded the Soviet Union, in spite of a Soviet-German nonaggression pact. This, together with the entry of the United States into the war in December 1941, marked the beginning of a slow but sure decline in Hitler's fortunes. Eventually, Germany came under attack from the west by U.S. and British forces and from the east by Soviet armies. With many of its cities destroyed by bombing, Germany was forced to surrender. The signing of the surrender documents took place on May 7, 1945. Hitler did not live to see the destruction of his Third Reich. He had committed suicide, along with several other Nazi leaders, a week earlier.

For a detailed account of the origins of World War II and the course of the war itself, see the article in Volume W-X-Y-Z. An article on Adolf Hitler appears in Volume H.

The Nuremberg Trials. War-crimes trials of the surviving Nazi leaders were held in the city of Nuremberg between 1945 and 1946.

The Nazis, led by Adolf Hitler (with arm outstretched in the Nazi salute), came to power in the early 1930's. Promising to restore Germany's greatness, Hitler built a huge army with which to conquer Europe. His invasion of Poland in 1939 set off World War II.

Allied Occupation. The war left Germany in ruins, a land of bombed cities filled with starving, homeless people. The victorious Allies divided Germany into four occupation zones. Northwest Germany, including the Ruhr, was the British zone. The United States zone was in southern Germany. France took over southwestern Germany. The Soviet Union occupied the east and much of central Germany. The Soviet Union also administered part of East Prussia, and Poland administered the section up to the Oder-Neisse line. Berlin, the seat of the Allied Control Council, lay deep inside the Soviet zone. Berlin was also divided into four occupation sectors.

The Allied aims for Germany were disarmament, democratization, and denazification. But a peace conference never took place. A split developed between the Soviet Union and the Western Allies. The Communist Party took control in the Eastern Zone. Britain and the United States combined their zones and in 1948 issued a new currency. This was the start of a unified West Germany. The Soviet Union issued new currency for its zone.

Early in 1948, the Soviet representative walked out of the Allied Control Council meeting in Berlin, making co-operation between East and West on political and economic matters nearly impossible. In the early summer of 1948, the Soviets blocked all roads into West Berlin. For about a year the United States and Britain supplied Berlin by airlift.

By the war's end in 1945, a defeated Germany had been devastated, with many of its cities in ruins. Here, children play amid the rubble of Berlin.

The charges included crimes against humanity and violations of the established laws of war. Among the atrocities with which the Nazi regime was charged was the extermination of 6 million Jews. Gypsies and other persecuted groups had suffered the same fate. Millions of people had perished under German occupation, while many others had been deported to Germany as forced labor.

In the main trial, 22 Nazi leaders were accused. Twelve were sentenced to death. (Hermann Goering, one of the top leaders and head of the air force, took poison before his sentence could be carried out.) Three were acquitted (that is, found not guilty) and the remainder received prison terms. Lesser Nazi officials were tried before subsequent war-crimes tribunals.

The Cold War between the Soviet Union and the Western countries had begun.

Creation of West Germany. In 1949 the Allied military government ended, and the Western zones of occupation were combined to form the Federal Republic of Germany (West Germany). But an Allied High Commission was still the final source of political authority.

West Germany made a rapid recovery from the war with the help of the Marshall Plan. It also managed to take care of about 10 million people from East Germany and the former German eastern territories. Under the leadership of Konrad Adenauer, who served as chancellor from 1949 until 1963, West Germany became one of the most prosperous industrial nations in the world. The Allied High Commission ended in 1955, and West Germany became fully independent. It then joined the North Atlantic Treaty Organization (NATO). In 1957, West Germany was one of six nations to sign the Treaty of Rome, which created the European Economic Community (Common Market). West Germany had allied itself firmly with Western Europe, both militarily and economically. Ludwig Erhard, the former minister of finance, succeeded Adenauer as chancellor. Erhard further strengthened West Germany's ties with Britain and the United States.

The first attempts to improve West Germany's relations with East Germany were made by Kurt Kiesinger, who served as chancellor from 1966 until 1969. This policy was continued and expanded by Chancellor Willy Brandt. He called the new approach to Eastern Europe *Ostpolitik* (Eastern policy). During Brandt's time in office (1969–74), West Germany signed a treaty with the Soviet Union that renounced the use of force to reunify the two Germanys. Trade between West Germany and the Soviet Union and its allies continued to increase after Helmut Schmidt became chancellor in 1974. In the early 1980's, people began to worry about rising unemployment and inflation, even though both were low by world standards. Schmidt's government split apart in 1982, and Helmut Kohl became German chancellor.

Development of East Germany. The German Democratic Republic (East Germany) was also established in 1949. The leading figure in the new government was Walter Ulbricht, who became head of the Socialist Unity (Commu-

nist) Party in 1950 and chairman of the Council of State, or head of state, in 1960.

East Germany's economic recovery in the years immediately after World War II was slow. Many fled the country, and there was a serious shortage of skilled labor. Ulbricht continued the Soviet policy of nationalizing industry and agriculture (placing them under government control). In 1950, East Germany

Germany from 1871 to the Present

The division of postwar Germany by the victorious Allies is reflected in this warning sign (*left*) in Berlin. Jubilant Germans (*above*) celebrated the reunification of their country in 1990.

became a member of the Council for Mutual Economic Assistance (COMECON), linking its economic activities with those of the Soviet Union and its allies in Eastern Europe.

Soviet tanks crushed a brief revolt in East Germany in 1953. The Soviet Union proclaimed East Germany a fully sovereign state in 1954. The following year, it became a charter member of the Warsaw Pact.

By 1961, as many as one thousand people a day were fleeing East Germany. To stop the westward tide, the East German government closed its entire border with West Germany in 1961. A wall was erected between the eastern and western sectors of Berlin, a move that was strongly condemned by the West.

Ulbricht resigned as party chairman in 1971. He was succeeded by Erich Honecker, who became chairman of the Council of State in 1976. During the 1970's, East and West Germany signed a series of agreements intended to begin the normalization of relations between them. In 1973 both East and West Germany were admitted to the United Nations. In 1987, Honecker became the first East German head of state to visit West Germany.

Reunification: One Germany. The political reforms begun in the Soviet Union in the late 1980's spread to Eastern European Communist nations in 1989. In East Germany there were increased demonstrations by the people, demanding greater freedom. Honecker was forced to resign, replaced by moderate Communist leaders. The new leaders opened the Berlin Wall, permitting East Germans to cross freely to the West for the first time since 1961. Demands for more political changes, however, led to the downfall of the Communist government and to the election of a non-Communist coalition government in March 1990. A monetary union of the two Germanys went into effect in July 1990. A treaty with the former Allied powers, officially ending their status in Germany, was signed in Moscow on September 12, 1990.

The merger of East Germany with West Germany on October 3, 1990, marked the birth of a new united Federal Republic of Germany. In December 1990, the first free all-German election since 1932 gave conservative and liberal parties a solid majority to govern again. In early 1991, Helmut Kohl began another term as chancellor. One of the greatest challenges facing the new government is to bring the economic level of people in the former East Germany up to that of Germans in the west.

Dorothea Spada
Die Stuttgarter Zeitung
Gerard Braunthal
University of Massachusetts, Amherst
Author, *West German Social Democrats, 1969–1982*

Pages from two German illuminated manuscripts: the Gospels of Otto III (*left*), created in the late 900's, and the Berthold Missal (*right*), which dates from the 1200's.

GERMANY, ART AND ARCHITECTURE OF

Germany's position in the center of Europe has made the country a crossroads for European ideas, trade, and art. Because they lived in the center of the continent, German artists were influenced by the art of other countries. But the German artists always gave the foreign forms a German look. For example, during the Renaissance, German painters followed the lead of the Italians, painting lifelike figures in realistic settings. But German artists never stopped using the strong lines and bright colors favored by their ancestors.

▶THE MIDDLE AGES

When the Roman Empire in the west came to an end in the A.D. 400's, Germanic peoples established kingdoms in parts of Europe formerly under Roman rule. The Germans were greatly influenced by the way of life in Roman Europe. They tried to copy Roman art and architecture. They accepted the Christian religion. They turned their artistic skills to making Christian art but used the geometric and detailed decoration that characterized the early art of the Germanic people.

One of the most powerful of the Germanic tribes, the Franks, ruled much of what is today France and Germany. During the rule of the Frankish kings, ivory carvings and illuminated manuscripts became important art forms. Illuminated manuscripts were religious books written and illustrated by hand—most often in monasteries. Some of the most beautiful manuscripts of all time were created in Germany during the 700's, 800's, and 900's. Geometric and detailed forms were used to decorate manuscript pages. Handsomely painted letters spelled out stories and prayers from the Bible.

In the middle of the 900's, art in Germany began to develop individual characteristics. The Germans remained more faithful to older art forms than did other people. The strong religious feeling of the Germans was expressed in their art. They depicted the human body in twisted shapes to show the suffering and devotion of the Christian saints.

The Romanesque period (about 1000–1250) was a time of great artistic activity. The Rhine Valley was an important trade route, and the people who lived there were in constant touch with Lombardy, a region of Italy, where the Romanesque style began. In the ca-

Left: The Abbey Church of Maria Laach has the round arches characteristic of Romanesque architecture. *Right:* This statue of St. Kunigunde is an example of German Gothic sculpture.

thedrals of Speyer, Worms, and Mainz there are many round arches and arched ceilings typical of Romanesque architecture.

The Gothic style began in France toward the end of the 1100's but did not influence German art for over 50 years. The cathedral of Cologne (begun in 1248 and finished in 1332) was a large and richly decorated building similar to the French cathedral at Amiens. This effect of overpowering size can also be seen in the later cathedrals at Ulm and Freiburg. A person standing in a Gothic cathedral feels tiny beneath the high, heaven-pointing arched ceilings.

German sculpture of the Gothic period also followed French work. But instead of being carved almost flat against the church walls, German Gothic sculpture stood out from the walls. The statues of religious figures were made to look quite real.

The Gothic style was well suited to the tastes of the German people. Germans liked the high, slender, orderly look of Gothic churches and the rugged, emotional style of Gothic sculpture.

▶ 1400'S AND 1500'S

The Renaissance, which began in Italy about 1400, was marked by a renewed interest in humans and their world. (During the Middle Ages the world of religion and the church had been of central importance.) Science, philosophy, and the arts were all influenced by this people-centered movement, called **humanism.**

But humanism was not an easy idea for Germans to accept. The Renaissance did not take hold in Germany for more than 100 years after it began in Italy. Even then German art kept much of its Gothic character.

In the paintings of the north German artists, realistic and often gruesome details were combined with subjects from medieval fairy tales. The rounded human forms in these paintings show the influence of the Renaissance.

It was in the southwest area of present-day Germany that the first influence of the new Renaissance style of realism was felt. The *Magdalene Altar* (1431) by Lukas Moser in a church at Tiefenbronn is the earliest known German painting to place the human figure in a realistic setting. Other painters began to use realistic forms and correct perspective. But the stiffness of the figures and the use of bright colors kept a Gothic feeling in their work.

The master artist Albrecht Dürer (1471–1528) understood the history of German art. A great scholar and international traveler, he combined the good qualities of Italian Renaissance art with the Gothic art of the north. More than any other artist, he created for north central Europe its own Renaissance style.

Dürer was a fine painter, but he was even more outstanding as a printmaker. His woodcut prints and engravings show how well he combined the several influences on German art. He was interested in Renaissance humanism, in showing the correctly proportioned human body in lifelike settings. But still he stressed the beauty of jagged lines and the ruggedness of Gothic art. His great works have had a lasting influence on the art of Germany.

During the life of Dürer southern Germany was Europe's most important center of sculpture. Wooden altars were carefully carved with very detailed designs. The late Gothic wood sculpture was covered with carved groups of flowers. And the sculpture was often brightly painted. This custom of painting sculpture lasted many years in Germany.

Hans Holbein the Younger was renowned for his highly detailed and lifelike portraits, such as this painting of Anne of Cleves, fourth wife of England's Henry VIII.

St. Anthony at Nuremberg, an engraving by Albrecht Dürer, shows the artist's skill as a printmaker. Dürer's art combined the ideas of the Renaissance with northern traditions.

The Isenheim altarpiece, painted about 1515, is the masterwork of Matthias Grünewald. The grim crucifixion scene on the center panel is in the spirit of medieval German religious art.

This portrayal of Cardinal Albrecht of Brandenburg as the scholarly hermit St. Jerome was painted in 1525 by Lucas Cranach the Elder, a popular court painter.

There were many fine German artists at that time, including Martin Schongauer (1453?–91), a brilliant woodcutter, engraver, and painter. Lucas Cranach the Elder (1472–1553) painted portraits, mythological subjects, and scenes of court life. The portraits by Hans Holbein the Younger (1497?–1543) were realistic. Holbein went to England and had a great influence on English portrait painting. The style of Matthias Grünewald (1485?–1530?) is the most unusual of all. His well-known Isenheim altarpiece is grim and richly colored.

▶THE BAROQUE AND ROCOCO PERIODS

During the baroque and rococo periods (1600's and 1700's) many fine buildings were constructed. A number of south German and Austrian architects who worked during the first half of the 1700's copied their basic style from the French and Italians. But the buildings of the Germans and Austrians were more richly decorated. The palaces by Johann Lukas von Hildebrandt (1668–1745) had the solidity and rich decoration of the baroque and the ornamental features of the French rococo.

Rococo was outstanding for its extremely fancy, shell-like designs. One could almost say that rococo wore one sequin too many. Decoration covered almost everything, even when simplicity would have better suited the building. For example, the huge monastery at Melk, designed by Jacob Prandtauer (1660–1726), was as richly decorated as a gingerbread palace. The church of St. John Nepomuk in Munich, by the Asam brothers (Cosmas Damian Asam, 1686–1739, and Egid Quirin Asam, 1692–1750), is an outstanding example of the late rococo style.

Many times the work of the painters and sculptors was so fanciful that it was hard to tell whether a wall or ceiling was real or just decoration. The interiors of Dominikus Zimmermann's (1685–1766) Pilgrimage Church at Wies and of Neumann's Vierzehnheiligen Church are like enormous wedding cakes. In Germany in the 1700's both nobility and peasants felt that the house of God should be built with the same splendor as the dwellings of earthly rulers.

▶ 1800'S AND 1900'S

In the late 1700's and early 1800's the Germans were active in a new European art movement. The movement was called **neoclassicism**, a return to the art of ancient Greece and Rome. Asmus Jacob Carstens (1754–98) liked to combine a classical style with Christian content. He admired the work of Raphael (1483–1520), the Italian Renaissance painter.

Neoclassicism quickly developed into the romantic movement of the 1800's. **Romanticism** was a way of viewing the world. The romantics loved nature and the distant past. The romantic artist Caspar David Friedrich (1774–1840) painted ruins of Gothic churches in forests, views of distant, misty mountain peaks, and lonely beaches. But others, like Philipp Otto Runge (1777–1810), and Arnold Böcklin (1827–1901), used classical subjects to produce romantic art.

German art of the 1900's has often been a protest against imitation. Modern German artists have felt art of the late 1800's was too concerned with the past. The works

Above: The interior of the Benedictine Cloister Church in Ottobeuren, Bavaria, with its elaborate design and rich decoration, is typical of the German rococo style. *Below: Easter Morning*, by romantic artist Caspar David Friedrich, creates a solemn and mysterious mood.

Ernst Ludwig Kirchner, a member of the expressionist group Die Brücke, used simplified forms and flat areas of bold color in his *Self-Portrait with Model* (1907).

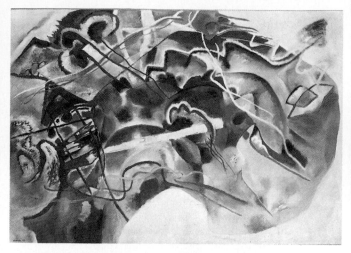

Two other German expressionist artists led a group called The Blue Rider. Wassily Kandinsky's colorful abstract canvases, like *Painting with White Border* (*top right*), consist of freely painted forms rather than realistic images. Franz Marc's *Little Blue Horse* (*bottom right*) is one of his series of brightly colored animal paintings.

of a very few, such as the artist Käthe Kollwitz (1867–1945) and the Viennese architect Adolf Loos (1870–1933), had some of the qualities of modern art. Then about 1905 the influential **Die Brücke** ("The Bridge") group was formed in Dresden by Ernst Ludwig Kirchner, Erich Heckel, and others. The young artists of Die Brücke were influenced by primitive art and by early German woodcuts. They tried to express the feeling of modern life in their art through the use of bright, intense colors and simple shapes. At first glance, these vivid colors and simple outlines seem childish and crude. But the art of Die Brücke, called **expressionism,** became one of the most important styles of the early 1900's.

Another group of expressionist artists, called **The Blue Rider,** was formed in Munich in 1911. It was led by Franz Marc (1880–1916), the Russian-born Wassily Kandinsky (1866–1944), and the Swiss artist Paul Klee (1879–1940). The artists of The Blue Rider were greatly influenced by the cubist painters in France. They believed in the importance of experimentation and originality in art. Gradually some of the artists of The Blue Rider moved from representing scenes and objects realistically to painting forms and colors that did not create a realistic image. This kind of painting is called abstract. Abstract expressionism was later to become a major movement in the history of modern art.

The Fagus shoe factory (1911), designed by architect Walter Gropius, was one of the first buildings to have glass and metal walls, later a common feature of architecture of the international style.

Gottfried Boehm, a leading German architect of the late 1900's, designed a complex of buildings in Cologne, Germany, combining a church, library, and youth center.

The **Bauhaus,** a German design school founded by the architect Walter Gropius (1883–1969), completed the trend of modern German art toward abstraction. The Bauhaus was established in 1919 in Weimar and was later moved to Dessau. Students were trained in painting, sculpture, and architecture. They also learned to design products for everyday use. Germany had made great advances in industry. But too often the objects produced were neither as attractive or as useful as they might have been. The designers of the Bauhaus redesigned anything that they thought could be made more beautiful. They gave new shapes to skyscrapers and steam irons, chairs and containers, textiles and toys. Even the printed page was made more attractive be-cause of Bauhaus experiments with printing methods. The ideas of the Bauhaus designers influenced product design throughout the world.

Like the Bauhaus designers, many architects from the school also influenced their field, especially after leaving Germany before World War II. In particular, Walter Gropius and Ludwig Mies van der Rohe (1886–1969) contributed much to the clean, strong lines of the international style, an architectural style that dominated commercial building during the second half of the 1900's.

ROBERT WELSH
University of Toronto

See also ARCHITECTURE; GOTHIC ART AND ARCHITECTURE; PAINTING; SCULPTURE.

GERMANY, LANGUAGE OF

The German language is spoken by some 120 million people. It is the official language of Germany, Austria, and Liechtenstein and is one of the official languages of Luxembourg and Switzerland. Many of the world's great works of philosophy, science, and literature were written in German, as well as masterpieces of opera and song.

German is a major language in the family of Germanic languages, which includes Dutch, Scandinavian languages, and English. All Germanic languages belong to a larger family of languages called Indo-European.

▶**EARLY GERMAN**

The first writing in German began in the A.D. 700's. At that time there was no standard form of German, and each writer used his region's own dialect, or way of speaking. These dialects differed greatly from each other. Dialects in the south were called High German, and in the north, Low German. Therefore the language of the period ending about 1100 is called Old High German or Old Low German.

One of the oldest monuments of the German language is the Codex Argenteus (about A.D. 500), a translation of the four Gospels into Gothic, an early form of German.

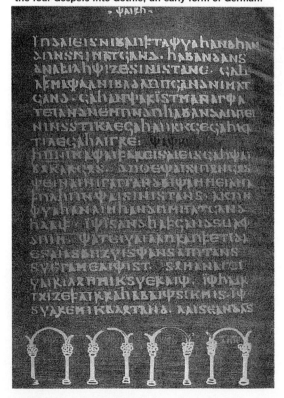

The greater share of the German writing of this early period consists of translations or adaptations of Latin originals. Since the knowledge of writing was largely confined to the monasteries, where Latin was the official language, original works in this early German are exceedingly rare. The emperor Charlemagne (742?–814) is said to have had the old Germanic poetry written down. If he did so, little of it has remained. Since most of the writing was done in the monasteries of southern Germany, it is mainly in the Old High German dialects. Only one Old Low German dialect, called Old Saxon, was widely written.

Latin influence on the development of the German language has a long history, dating back to the southward movement of German tribes and their contact with Roman culture, politics, and military power. This influence is seen in many early German words—*Fenster* (window) from the Latin *fenestra*, *Pfund* (pound) from *pondus*, and many more.

▶**MIDDLE PERIOD**

The language of the period from about 1100 to the end of the 1300's is called Middle High German in the south and Middle Low German in the north. The use of German in literature increased greatly during this period, especially in the south. Between 1170 and 1300 French influence was especially important. German princes and kings and their courts copied French manners. Writers, in turn, produced courtly epics patterned after French models. As a result, the influence of the French language was very great, as in *falsch* (false) from the French *faux*, *klar* (clear) from *clair*, *fein* (fine) from *fine*, and *tanzen* (dance) from *danser*. In this period, also, the endings of noun and verb forms were greatly simplified.

Most of the literature was composed in a special literary form of the Middle High German language. Since few people could read or write, and since there were no printed books, the use of this literary language was extremely limited. It could not be considered in any way a standard language that most people could speak or even understand. As before, only the various dialects were in spoken use.

In northern Germany, Middle Low German developed no important literature. Writing was used chiefly for town records and in commerce. Its most important single use was as the official commercial language of the Hanseatic League. The chief centers of this merchant's league were Lübeck and other northern German cities. From them Middle Low German spread throughout Scandinavia, the Baltic countries, and northern Russia as a business language in trading centers.

The years from about 1350 to 1600 were the most important in the development of the present German language. This span included the end of the Middle High German period and the beginning of the New High German period. There was a great increase in the use of German for all sorts of writing. The emperors of Germany began to use it more and more in state documents. Particularly important was the German written by several rulers: Charles IV, whose capital was Prague; the Hapsburg emperors in Vienna, especially Maximilian I; and the prince elector of Saxony, Friedrich the Wise. The German of their official forms varied slightly because of the differences in the dialects on which they were based. But all the rulers tried to make their language clear in their dealings throughout the empire.

Martin Luther's Influence. The Protestant Reformation in Germany had a great influence on the development of a standardized German language. Its leader, Martin Luther, translated the Bible into the German of east central Germany, already used officially in upper Saxony. Luther's Bible translation, as well as his many other writings, did much to establish a single common German language and formed the basis for modern German. There had already been many other translations of the Bible into some form of German. Since the official language of the Church was Latin, however, the translations had had little effect on the development or spread of a standard form of German. The language of east central Germany had another advantage over the many southern forms of High German. East central German was based on a language that was already somewhat mixed, since this part of Germany had been settled by speakers of different German dialects.

The invention of printing played a major part in the development of a standard form of German during this period. Printing enabled Luther's writings, and especially his Bible translation, to reach a much wider public. The printers naturally wanted to print their books in a language that could be read by as many people as possible.

SOME EVERYDAY GERMAN WORDS

one	eins	twenty	zwanzig
two	zwei	twenty-one	einundzwanzig
three	drei	hundred	hundert
four	vier	and	und
five	fünf	book	Buch
six	sechs	father	Vater
seven	sieben	house	Haus
eight	acht	kindergarten	Kindergarten
nine	neun	mother	Mutter
ten	zehn	school	Schule

In the 1600's the standard language of Luther and his imitators spread still more. Its use reached beyond the territory affected by the Protestant Reformation, into German Switzerland and into southern and western German areas that had remained Catholic. During the same century scholars attempted to make the grammar regular and to decide between different usages. Most of the grammars written were based on Luther's language or on the works of authors attempting to follow his usage.

▶ **MODERN GERMAN**

By the end of the 1600's the standard High German language resembled the German of today. Yet people in various parts of Germany still pronounced it differently, according to the sounds and structures of their local dialects. In fact, this situation continued well into the 1800's. The Protestant Reformation had its greatest success in northern Germany, where the native language was Low German. The northern German pronunciation of the standard language, then, became the most widely accepted. It is the one now generally taught in schools in Germany, the United States, and elsewhere.

Although the basic grammar of the German language did not change after 1700, changes in style and vocabulary took place. These were due to the work of the great authors of the 1700's and 1800's, who helped develop the expressive qualities of the German language.

French continued to influence German vocabulary, especially in the 1600's and 1700's. English has left its imprint on German, especially in the 1800's and 1900's. Since World War II, German has borrowed many words from American English, including boom, comeback, knockout, team, and teen-ager.

GEORGE S. LANE
University of North Carolina

Reviewed by FERDINAND A. RUPLIN
Author, *Basic German: A Programmed Text*

GERMANY, LITERATURE OF

German is spoken in an area larger than Germany itself. When the German states were united in 1871, Austria and Switzerland remained independent. However, since these countries still use the same language and share many common interests with Germany, their writers are included here.

▶ EARLY GERMAN LITERATURE

In early times the German tribes celebrated their gods and heroes in songs of praise. These were handed down by word of mouth, so we have no record of most of them. However, *Hildebrandslied* (*The Song of Hildebrand*) was written down by monks about A.D. 800. It tells of a famous hero whose son did not recognize him after a long absence and challenged him to a fight. The song is not in rhyme, but many words begin with similar consonants, giving a pleasing sound.

When the Germans became Christians, monks began to write regularly in German as well as in Latin. A monk named Otfried von Weissenburg wrote a version of the Gospels about 870. *Der Heliand* (*The Savior*; about 830) by an unknown author makes Christ into a German chieftain.

In the 900's the monks once again wrote almost entirely in Latin, but they dealt mainly with worldly affairs. *Waltharius Manufortis* (*Walther of the Strong Hand*; about 930) tells how a German hero escaped with his bride from the Huns and then fought 12 warriors. *Ruodlieb*, written after 1050, is the account of a German knight's adventures.

▶ A GOLDEN AGE

A reform of the monasteries ended this worldly literature. But not long after, knights themselves became writers. They wove Christian and knightly themes into remarkable literary works, resulting in a short but glorious golden age (1180–1220) of German literature.

The courtly romance developed from French and Celtic tales of King Arthur and from other romantic tales. These romances celebrated the ideals of courtly love and chivalry. *Erec* (1180) and *Iwein* (1202), by Hartmann von Aue, taught knightly restraint. *Poor*

Walther von der Vogelweide, seen here in an illustration from an early manuscript, wrote some of the greatest German lyric poetry of the Middle Ages. He is the best known of the German minnesingers, poets who were also musicians.

Henry (1195) was Aue's best romance. A knight is stricken with leprosy as punishment for his worldly pride. Only the blood of an innocent girl can save him. The daughter of one of his men offers herself. When Heinrich refuses to accept her sacrifice, God forgives and heals him.

In about 1210, Gottfried von Strassburg wrote an ageless love story about Tristan and Isolde. Tristan courts lovely Isolde of Ireland for his uncle, Mark, King of Cornwall. During their journey to Cornwall the young people share a magic drink and fall in love. But their love brings them only unhappiness. Wolfram von Eschenbach is known for his *Parzival*, also written about 1210. A simple lad grows up to become the mighty knight of the Holy Grail. He is unsuccessful in his quest for the cup Jesus used at the Last Supper until he learns to place his faith in God.

The courtly romances also inspired new treatments of myths from the time of the Germanic migrations. *Nibelungenlied* (*The Song of the Nibelungs*; about 1200) was the best known. It has become the national epic. Loyalty and revenge are its themes.

The greatest lyric poet of the time was Walther von der Vogelweide. He wrote courtly love poetry and political verse.

▶ LATE MIDDLE AGES AND RENAISSANCE

Toward the end of the 1200's knighthood began to crumble. Important writers no longer lived at the courts of kings and nobles. Instead, the cities became centers of culture.

Much writing was done by **meistersingers**, or mastersingers, tradesmen who formed guilds for the writing of songs and poetry. The best-known meistersinger was Hans Sachs, a shoemaker in Nuremberg. Meistersingers wrote simple adventure stories that lacked the beauty and originality of the courtly romances. With the coming of printing, these stories soon became very popular. Along with the old heroes, new figures appeared who reflected the changing times. Till Eulenspiegel was a rascal and a jack-of-all-trades who always managed to outwit the narrow-minded townsfolk. Dr. Faust was a wicked magician who gained his powers by selling his soul to the devil. This simple literature did not try for beauty but attempted to make its readers better people.

Unlike the worldly literature, religious writing improved during the late Middle Ages. Meister Eckhart and other Dominican monks wrote inspiring sermons. They taught that God was in man's heart. Passion plays showing the life of Christ were performed in town squares.

The cultural flowering known as the Renaissance reached northern Europe in the 1500's. Great changes took place in many fields. The leading figure of the Renaissance in Germany was Erasmus of Rotterdam. His polished essays, written in Latin, reflect Renaissance **humanism** (the study of human life and achievements). Martin Luther was the leader of the Reformation, a major reform movement in the Christian church. He translated the Bible into the German of his day, thus helping to establish the form of the modern German language. Biographies of Erasmus and Luther can be found in the appropriate volumes.

▶ **1600'S AND 1700'S**

The Thirty Years' War (1618–48) left Germany poor and weak. Two thirds of the people were killed. The princes became stronger than

The great German religious reformer Martin Luther also influenced the development of his country's language and literature. His German translation of the Latin Bible was widely read throughout Germany and helped to standardize the language.

ever, and court poets were favored. Martin Opitz tried to improve literary style by setting up strict rules, but the writing grew flowery and false. There were a few good writers, like Andreas Gryphius, who wrote tragedies as well as lively comedies such as *Herr Peter Squentz* (1658).

The wordy dramas of Daniel Casper von Lohenstein are filled with murder and torture. The novels of the time concentrated on the policies of rulers and on heroic deeds rather than on the development of character. An outstanding exception was *Simplicissimus* (1669) by Hans Jacob Christoph von Grimmelshausen. *The Cherubic Wanderer* (1674), a collection of short religious poems, was written by Angelus Silesius, a Catholic mystic.

In 1730 a strong-willed reformer named Johann Gottsched tried to improve German writing by laying down rules based on reason. He used French writing as a model. His influence produced good structure but dull writing.

After 1750, German writing made great progress. Four writers stand out, Gotthold Ephraim Lessing turned from France to England and particularly to Shakespeare for inspiration. His *Minna von Barnhelm* (1767) is a masterpiece of German comedy. *Nathan the Wise* (1779) is a stirring plea for religious tolerance.

Friedrich Klopstock gave new dignity to poetry. Inspired by Milton, he wrote an epic about Christ, called *The Messiah* (1748–73). His odes reveal great poetic skill. Johann Herder, a theologian, believed that folk poetry was the direct expression of the soul of a people. This attitude had a deep effect on later writers. Herder collected folk poetry of many countries in his *Voices of the Nations in Song* (1807). Christoph Wieland proved that the German language could have wit and grace. One of his best works is the romance *Oberon* (1780).

Two giants of German literature, Johann Wolfgang von Goethe (*left*) and Friedrich Schiller (*above*), wrote landmark works of prose and poetry that inspired later writers.

Goethe and Schiller. Germany's two greatest writers were Johann Wolfgang von Goethe and Friedrich Schiller. Their early writings, rebellious and idealistic, were part of a movement called *Sturm und Drang* ("Storm and Stress"), which influenced many other young writers.

Goethe's lyric poetry is wonderfully fresh and natural. His early plays had a loose structure and fiery heroes taken from history. Goethe's world-famous novel, *The Sorrows of Young Werther* (1774), reflects the excited emotions of its author. Goethe worked for most of his life on his masterpiece, *Faust* (Part I, 1808; Part II, 1831). In Goethe's drama, Faust is a scholar in search of the best in human knowledge and experience. He challenges the devil to make him give up this search. Faust thus represents humanity's endless striving.

Goethe's later works include many fine ballads, as well as lyrics expressed in forms and images of Asian countries. His novels—*Wilhelm Meister's Apprenticeship* (1795), *Wilhelm Meister's Wanderings* (1821), and *Elective Affinities* (1809)—and his autobiographical works, reflect his feelings of social responsibility. A biography of Goethe appears in this volume.

Friedrich Schiller received his early schooling in a military academy. His hatred of the academy's rigid discipline is shown in his early dramas. Like Robin Hood, the hero of *The Robbers* (1781) seeks to take justice into his own hands. The hero of *Fiesco* (1783) stirs up a revolution and wavers between love for his people and desire for power. In *Intrigue and Love* (1784), a love affair is crushed because it interferes with political schemes.

Schiller's next two plays show a deepened interest in history. The plot of *Don Carlos* (1787) concerns the Dutch struggle for religious freedom. *Wallenstein* (1798–99) portrays the tragic end of the Austrian general, Albrecht von Wallenstein.

The later dramas are about moral rather than political freedom. *Maria Stuart* (1800) tells how Mary Queen of Scots overcame her passionate nature to win a moral victory over Queen Elizabeth I. *The Maid of Orleans* (1801) deals with Joan of Arc's triumph over her love for a young Englishman. In the play that has become the national drama of Switzerland, *Wilhelm Tell* (1804), the Swiss people fight for their independence.

Schiller's polished and highly dramatic ballads are unique in German literature.

▶**ROMANTICISM**

Toward the end of the 1700's a new generation of writers placed their faith in imagination, turning away from everyday reality to seek an ideal world. They were the romanticists. The brothers August and Friedrich Schlegel founded the literary journal *Athenaeum,* which published the works of the romanticists. The lyric poet Novalis (Baron Friedrich von Hardenberg) wrote the beautifully sad *Hymns to the Night* (1797) and a dream novel, *Heinrich von Ofterdingen* (1802). Ludwig Tieck revived the spirit of the Middle Ages in *Franz Sternbalds Wanderungen* ("The Wanderings of Franz Sternbald"; 1798). Jean Paul Friedrich Richter wrote rambling tales, rich in imagination and humor. E. T. A. Hoffmann allowed his fancy to create modern fairy tales and weird horror stories like those of Edgar Allan Poe.

When Napoleon conquered Prussia in 1806, romantic poets like Ernst Moritz Arndt, Theodor Körner, and Friedrich Rückert urged Germans to unite against the common foe. Other authors inspired national pride by awakening interest in Germany's past. Achim von Arnim and Clemens Brentano made collections of folk songs. The Grimm brothers, Jacob and Wilhelm, wrote books about the old German heroes and collected three volumes of fairy tales (1812; 1815; 1822). A biography of the Grimms appears in this volume.

Several writers used polished, classical form but were romantic in spirit. Friedrich Hölderlin wrote poetry that showed his love for ancient Greece. Heinrich von Kleist expressed his feelings in patriotic dramas, including *The Prince of Homburg* (1810) and *Die Hermannsschlacht* ("Herman's Battle"; 1809). He also wrote a fine comedy, *The Broken Jug* (1806), and excellent short stories. Franz Grillparzer, Austria's most famous dramatist, was most romantic in his *Ancestress* (1817).

The later romantic writers included many good poets like Joseph von Eichendorff, Heinrich Heine, and Eduard Mörike. Their poems were usually simple in form, easy to understand, and of a delicate mood. A biography of Heine appears in Volume H.

▶ REALISM

About 1830, German writing grew more realistic. Writers increasingly dealt with social and economic issues. A group of writers known as the Young Germans attacked the conservative political systems of the day. Heine belonged to this group, as did Heinrich Laube and Karl Gutzkow. Fiery political poetry by Ferdinand Freiligrath and Georg Herwegh heralded the revolution of 1848.

Friedrich Hebbel was a fine tragedian. He was interested in periods when new ideas arose. This is the basic theme found in all his plays. *Herodes und Mariamne* (1849) and *Gyges and His Ring* (1854) mirror the conflict between ancient and modern views. *Agnes Bernauer* (1851) and *Maria Magdalene* (1844) tell the stories of women who suffer because of the old-fashioned thinking of their times.

Two plays by Georg Büchner, *Danton's Death* (1835) and *Woyzeck* (1836), have been hailed as forerunners of modern drama. *Woyzeck* is one of the first dramatic studies of a murderer to explain his deed in social and psychological terms.

After 1850, many novelists wrote realistic stories about the regions of their birth. Theodor Storm described Schleswig-Holstein. Adalbert Stifter and Peter Rosegger wrote about Austria, and Berthold Auerbach wrote about the Black Forest. Fritz Reuter and Wilhelm Raabe pictured the North German scene. Raabe also

Traditional German fairy tales collected by the brothers Jacob and Wilhelm Grimm have become famous throughout the world. This engraved title page is from the first edition, published in 1812.

treated the problems of the German emigrants to the United States.

The Swiss clergyman Jeremias Gotthelf described people of his day in great novels. He was succeeded by the sly humorist Gottfried Keller. Keller's *Green Henry* (1854) is one of the best novels of the 1800's. It tells of a boy who failed as an artist but overcame his romantic notions. Another Swiss, Conrad Ferdinand Meyer, wrote dramatic stories set in the past.

The philosopher Friedrich Nietzsche wrote about his ideal of the superior human being. Convinced that everyone was becoming less vital and creative, Nietzsche felt that great people should ignore rules and vigorously pursue their own goals. His book *Thus Spoke Zarathustra* (1883–85) was widely read.

Theodor Fontane was a journalist who also wrote beautiful novels about social relations. In his *Effie Briest* (1890), an aristocratic young wife is divorced by her husband, separated from her young daughter, and scorned by society when a brief love affair she had long ago is discovered.

After the German states were unified in 1871, the growth of industry caused people to move to the cities. Soon there was a large working class with many problems. Gerhart Hauptmann dealt with these problems in his early plays, including *Before Dawn* (1889) and *The Weavers* (1893), using a realistic style. But he found realism was not always the best way to show the sadness and tragedy of life, so he used other styles as well. Hauptmann wrote one excellent comedy, *The Beaver Coat* (1893), about a thieving but lovable washerwoman who outwits a narrow-minded judge.

The Austrian playwright Arthur Schnitzler won fame for his moody, impressionistic dramas. Some deal with love and courtship—*Anatol* (1893) and *Liebelei* ("Dalliance"; 1895) —and some with the responsibilities of marriage—*The Lonely Way* (1904) and *Intermezzo* (1905). Others deal with the problem of truth and illusion—*The Green Cockatoo* (1895) and *The Veil of Beatrice* (1900). Another Austrian, Hugo von Hofmannsthal, was a master stylist. He is best known for his ver-

The Threepenny Opera (1928) is a bitingly witty attack on social conditions in Germany before World War II. It was a popular success among the very people it satirized, the German middle class. The play, by Bertolt Brecht with music by Kurt Weill, is based on *The Beggar's Opera* (1728), a satirical play by the English writer John Gay.

sion of the medieval play *Everyman* (1911). It has been performed many times at the Salzburg Festival. Hofmannsthal also wrote the librettos for a number of operas by Richard Strauss, such as *Der Rosenkavalier* ("The Cavalier of the Rose"; 1911).

Carl Zuckmayer also wrote realistic plays dealing with social problems. *The Captain of Cöpenick* (1931) pokes fun at the Germans' respect for uniforms. *The Devil's General* (1946) is a tense drama dealing with war guilt in Nazi Germany. *Das Kalte Licht* ("The Cold Light"; 1955) is a drama about the atomic bomb.

▶ EXPRESSIONISM

About 1910 a new generation rejected realism entirely. They were known as expressionists because they wanted to express their innermost feelings through their writing. (Expressionism began as an art movement. To read more about this movement, see the article EXPRESSIONISM in Volume E.) The most famous German expressionists were the playwrights Georg Kaiser, Ernst Toller, and Fritz von Unruh. Kaiser's most successful play, *From Morn to Midnight* (1916), is the story of a modern Faust who looks in vain for happiness and goodness. Toller's *Hinkemann* (1922) is a drama about a crippled war veteran. Von Unruh's powerful drama *A Family* (1916) shows how war destroys moral and cultural values.

Franz Werfel was a more religious expressionist. His plays, such as *Mirror Man* (1920) and *Jaurez and Maximillian* (1924), teach love of all humankind. His novel *The Song of Bernadette* (1941) tells about the simple maid of Lourdes to whom the Virgin appeared in a lonely grotto.

Bertolt Brecht began as an expressionist. When he became a Marxist, he switched to a new kind of realism, which he called "epic theater." His plays try to teach rather than to please. But they are so original that they are performed everywhere. His greatest hit was *The Threepenny Opera* (1928). This was a witty attack on middle-class society. While a refugee from Nazi Germany, Brecht wrote the great plays *Mother Courage* (1941), *The Good Woman of Setzuan* (1942), and *The Life of Galileo* (1943).

Brecht's influence is seen in the plays of the Swiss dramatists Max Frisch and Friedrich

Thomas Mann, one of the great German novelists of the 1900's, won the Nobel prize for literature in 1929. Among his masterworks is *The Magic Mountain* (1924).

Dürrenmatt. Frisch's first great success was *The Firebugs* (1958) a grotesque comedy telling how a silly man helps two criminals set fire to his own house. Dürrenmatt's bitter comedy *The Visit* (1956) coats with humor its message that people are brutal and selfish.

▶ MODERN FICTION

The novelists Thomas Mann and Hermann Hesse both won the Nobel prize for literature. Both were genuinely concerned with the problem of the artist in relation to society and with the tragic destiny of Germany. Mann's greatest novels include *Buddenbrooks* (1901), *The Magic Mountain* (1924) and *Dr. Faustus* (1947). Mann lived in the United States during World War II and became an American citizen. Hesse was a sensitive, sad writer with a deep religious awareness. His novels, including *Siddharta* (1922) and *Steppenwolf* (1927), tell the story of Hesse's spiritual development and his desperate struggle to reconcile idealism with the real world.

An even more tortured artist, Franz Kafka, wrote novels and stories that were quiet and clear in manner but filled with nightmarish situations. In "Metamorphosis" a salesman

The novels and stories of Franz Kafka, an Austrian who wrote in German, portray people caught in nightmarish situations. His haunting works, including *The Trial* and *The Castle*, capture the isolation and anxiety of modern life.

awakens one morning to discover that he has been changed into an enormous bug. In *The Trial*, written in 1914, a man is convicted but never finds out his crime. Kafka's world is a strange and horrible place in which people seek vainly for a meaning to existence.

The Austrian Robert Musil devoted many years to writing *The Man Without Qualities* (1930–43). This long and ironic novel sought to reveal the attitudes among people in Austria and Germany that led to World War I. Erich Maria Remarque wrote popular novels about war and its aftermath. The best known of these, *All Quiet on the Western Front* (1929), is a story about young German soldiers that pleads the insanity of war.

Perhaps the most unusual modern novel was written by Hermann Broch. In *The Death of Virgil* (1945), Broch tries to re-create all the

The German writer Christa Wolf has dealt with problems confronting modern Germany, such as the aftermath of World War II and the role of women in society. Her novels include *Childhood Patterns* (1977) and *No Place on Earth* (1982).

thoughts of the dying poet during his last 24 hours.

The poets Rainer Maria Rilke and Stefan George were pessimists. Rilke's *Duino Elegies* and *Sonnets to Orpheus,* both written in 1923, are poetic masterpieces.

The Postwar Period. At the end of World War II (1939–45), two separate German states were created: the Federal Republic of Germany (West Germany) and the German Democratic Republic (East Germany).

Most of the West German writers who gained fame after the war belonged to the Gruppe 47, a writers' club organized in 1947. The novels of Heinrich Böll usually describe conditions in Germany during and after the war. He received the Nobel prize for literature for *Group Portrait with Lady* (1971). Günter Grass in his *Tin Drum* (1959) tells the story of a dwarf who refused to grow up. In *Speculations about Jakob* (1959), Uwe Johnson directs his attention to the problems of the two Germanys. Siegfried Lenz won wide recognition for his novel *Deutschstunde* ("German Lesson"; 1968) which describes a young German trying to overcome his past.

In East Germany, censorship imposed by the state limited freedom of literary expression. Through the years some outstanding writers—including Karl Krolow, Sarah Kirsch, and Reiner Kunze—emigrated to the West. Others, like the folk singer and poet Wolf Biermann, were expelled from East Germany. East German writers who were widely read in both parts of Germany include Hermann Kant, Ulrich Plenzdorf, and Christa Wolf. Kant's *The Auditorium* (1966) describes the lives of a group of working-class students. Plenzdorf wrote a modern version of Geothe's *Werther* novel, *The New Sufferings of Young W* (1973), in which the young hero loves blue jeans and the music of Louis Armstrong. Wolf's novels—including *Childhood Patterns* (1977) and *Kassandra* (1983)—treat such themes as German guilt over World War II, problems in postwar East Germany, and women's place in modern society.

The reunification of East and West Germany in 1990 marked the beginning of a new era in German literature.

HERBERT W. REICHERT
Formerly, University of North Carolina
Reviewed by RUSSELL E. BROWN
SUNY Stony Brook

GERMANY, MUSIC OF

The music of Germany and Austria is an important part of today's concert repertory. As a result of the common language and historical background of these two countries, their musical cultures have been closely related. "German music" usually refers to the music of Austrian as well as German composers.

The symphonies, concertos, and chamber works of the great composers of Germany and Austria are highly regarded for their depth of feeling and the splendor of their form. German composers have also produced masterpieces of opera and song.

A German minnesinger entertains an appreciative audience in this illustration from an early manuscript. The minnesingers, who were poets as well as musicians, performed their songs of love and chivalry in the castles of the nobility. They produced much of the nonreligious music of medieval Germany.

▶ MIDDLE AGES

Religious Music. In Germany as in the rest of Europe, the Roman Catholic Church played an important role in the development of music during the Middle Ages (500–1500). The earliest-known church music, called **chant**, or **plainsong**, consisted of a single line of melody sung to Latin texts without any harmony or instrumental accompaniment. This is called **monophonic** music.

One of the most important German composers of chant was Hildegard von Bingen, who was the abbess of a large convent near the town of Bingen in Germany. Hildegard wrote beautiful lyric poetry, which she set to music. Much of her music still survives.

After the year 1200, composers added voices and music to the chant. This style of music, in which two or more melodies are sung or played at the same time, is called **polyphonic** music. Composers' skill in this art steadily increased throughout the Middle Ages and into the Renaissance.

Secular Music. German composers also were involved in the composition of monophonic secular (nonreligious) music. During the 1100's and 1200's, an important group of poet-musicians appeared called the **minnesingers**, or love-singers. The minnesingers, many of whom were no-

blemen, traveled from castle to castle singing their songs. They sang mostly about love and chivalry but also about nature, the changing of seasons, religion, and even politics. *Palestine Song*, written about 1200 by Walter von der Vogelweide (Walter of the Bird Pasture) is one of the few original minnesinger melodies that has survived until today.

▶ RENAISSANCE

The cultural flowering known as the Renaissance began in Germany in the 1500's. During that time, monophonic compositions were written by **meistersingers**, or mastersingers, artisans or tradesmen who formed guilds dedicated to the writing of poetry and music. The meistersingers believed that anyone who followed certain rules of composition could pro-

Hans Sachs, the most famous of the Renaissance meistersingers, is portrayed here in a woodcut from 1545. The meistersingers were German tradesmen who tried to carry on the tradition of the medieval poet-musicians. They formed guilds to encourage the writing of songs and poetry.

duce wonderful poems and songs. Following the rules, however, did not always enable the meistersingers to produce great works of art. One of the more talented meistersingers was the shoemaker Hans Sachs. Some 300 years later, the composer Richard Wagner made Sachs the hero of his opera *Die Meistersinger von Nürnberg* (1868).

German Renaissance composers were influenced by important new developments in polyphonic music from Italy, France, and the Netherlands. In the 1500's and 1600's, many polyphonic works were heard both inside and outside the church. One important composer of the late 1500's was Hans Leo Hassler. Hassler studied music in Italy but spent most of his life in Germany. Michael Praetorious was an important composer who also wrote about music. His *Terpsichore* (1612) is a set of dances for instruments alone.

Reformation. A major reform movement, known as the Protestant Reformation, occurred in the church during the 1500's. It was begun in Germany by Martin Luther. One of Luther's beliefs was that worshipers should take part in the performance of sacred music and should understand every word they sang. He therefore replaced Latin chants with German hymns, called **chorales**. Luther himself wrote some chorales, such as the great *Ein' feste Burg* ("A Mighty Fortress"; 1529). The chorales are still sung today. Through Luther's influence, music became a central part of daily life in Germany.

▶ **BAROQUE**

The baroque period, beginning in the late 1500s and lasting into the first half of the 1700's, was an important phase in the development of German music. German baroque music is known for its forcefulness, excitement, and elaborate structure.

Early and Middle Baroque. During the 1600's and early 1700's, many German composers were influenced by music from other countries. One such composer was Heinrich Schutz, the most famous German composer of the 1600's. Schutz studied in Venice, learning techniques of Italian music and transforming them to suit the German language and musical style. Schutz composed the first German opera, *Dafne*, in 1627.

During the 1600's organ music became increasingly important, particularly in northern Germany. German craftsmen built magnificent church organs, and composers wrote pieces for these new and improved instruments. Dietrich Buxtehude was one of the best-known organ composers of the 1600's.

The High Baroque. Baroque music reached the peak of its development in the works of Johann Sebastian Bach, George Frederick Handel, and George Philip Telemann. Bach composed in every form of music known in his time except opera. He came from a long line of Protestant church organists and was

Johann Sebastian Bach, one of the greatest German composers of the baroque period, is also among the most important composers of all time. More famous in his lifetime as an organist than as a composer, his genius was not widely recognized until after his death.

probably the greatest performer and composer of organ music who ever lived. Many of his works have been lost, but well over 1,000 have survived. They include about 200 church cantatas—compositions for voices and instruments that were written for Sundays and important holidays. Bach was an excellent teacher of the harpsichord and the clavichord (early keyboard instruments). The pieces he wrote for his pupils, such as *Inventions* (1723) and the *Well-Tempered Clavier* (Book I, 1722; Book II, 1738–42), are masterpieces of keyboard music.

Unlike Bach, who spent his entire life in Germany, Handel was well traveled. He was born in Germany and received his early training from German composers. However, he studied in Italy and spent most of his adult life in England. Like many other baroque composers, Handel devoted much of his attention to the writing of opera and, later, to **oratorio**. An oratorio is a dramatic work performed by chorus, soloists, and orchestra without any stage action. Handel achieved immense success with his oratorios; his *Messiah* (1747) has become a pillar of our musical life. Handel also wrote much fine orchestral music. His music has a warm, singing quality that shows the influence of his studies in Italy.

During his lifetime, Telemann was probably the most famous German baroque composer—his fame surpassed even that of Bach. Telemann wrote an extraordinary number of musical compositions for both instruments and voices. He was the director of the Leipzig Collegium Musicum, a famous music society, which performed popular weekly concerts. Telemann wrote many works for this group and helped to popularize public concerts in Germany.

▶ CLASSICAL ERA

While Bach, Handel, and Telemann were writing their greatest works, a younger generation of composers was working out new musical ideas. Many of these composers rejected the complex style of their parents' generation, preferring music that was light, graceful, and immediately pleasing to their audience. This style was called *style galant*, or "gallant style." At this same time, many composers were writing short compositions for orchestra called symphonies. The German court at Mannheim boasted one of the best symphony orchestras of its time. Composers there developed new and exciting orchestral techniques that would show off the skills of this orchestra.

Among the important composers of the early classical period were the sons of the great Johann Sebastian Bach. The oldest, Carl Philip Emmanuel Bach, was known for his highly emotional and romantic style of music. He worked for many years at the Berlin court of the Prussian King Frederick the Great. Another of Bach's sons, Johann Christian Bach, moved to London, where he became well known for his operas and keyboard concertos.

During the latter part of the 1700's a great center of musical activity grew up in Vienna, Austria. Here were written many masterpieces of music that are now regarded as classical because of their flawless design and great beauty of form. Among the composers working in Vienna were Christoph Willibald Gluck, Franz Joseph Haydn, Wolfgang Amadeus Mozart, and Ludwig van Beethoven.

Gluck. Despite important developments in the composition of instrumental music, opera continued to be important in the classical era. Christoph Willibald Gluck was an important classical composer of opera. His ambition was to simplify opera and increase its dignity and dramatic effect. Gluck believed that much opera of his day was unnatural and unrealistic. Instead of filling his arias (solo songs) with flowery ornaments, Gluck used simple, elegant melodies that he felt would express emo-

Two great German classical composers were (*left*) Wolfgang Amadeus Mozart, who as a child prodigy performed with his father and sister, and (*right*) Ludwig van Beethoven.

tion more realistically. An example of one of Gluck's "reform" operas is his *Orfeo and Eurydice* (1762), which is still performed today.

Haydn. Like Gluck, Franz Joseph Haydn was a reformer, but his main achievements were in fields other than opera. Haydn was largely self-taught. As a young man he played the violin with a group performing at a nobleman's castle. For these musicians he wrote his first string quartets—works for two violins, viola, and cello. Haydn wrote string quartets all his life, often experimenting with new and bold compositional techniques.

Haydn also excelled as a composer of symphonies. During his lifetime the symphony was to become the most important form of orchestral music and would remain so for the next 100 years. Haydn's first symphonies, composed when he was in his 20's, followed the fashion of the time. They were brief works in several movements, or sections. His Symphony No. 104, written in 1795 when he was 63, is a masterpiece in four highly developed movements. Because of his important contributions in this area, Haydn is often called the father of the symphony.

Although Haydn also wrote a number of operas and other vocal works, he was particularly well known for his oratorios. One, *The Creation* (1798), depicts the creation of the world, the animals, and Adam and Eve. Another, *The Seasons* (1801), describes the seasons of the year in four contrasting parts.

Mozart. As a very young child, Wolfgang Amadeus Mozart showed amazing musical talent. He began to compose at an age when he was still unable to write notes without splashing the page with ink. The young Mozart was also an accomplished violinist and pianist. At the age of 6, he traveled throughout Europe with his father and talented sister, performing for kings and queens. Mozart was well acquainted with Haydn, and the two exchanged many ideas about musical composition.

In addition to writing many wonderful piano concertos, symphonies, and chamber music, Mozart was also one of the greatest opera composers that ever lived. Mozart's gift for bringing characters to life through his music can be seen in his comic opera *The Marriage of Figaro* (1786). In *The Magic Flute* (1791), Mozart created a delightful fairy-tale world; the opera also expresses important messages about humankind, truth, and justice.

Beethoven. Ludwig van Beethoven is probably the most esteemed of all German composers. He wrote many different kinds of music, including chamber music, opera, and piano sonatas. He is especially well known for his nine symphonies. Beethoven's early works were in very much the same style as those of Haydn and Mozart. His later works, however, were much longer and more complicated, full of excitement and tension.

While still a young man, Beethoven began to lose his hearing. In his later years he was almost totally deaf. While Beethoven experienced great personal sadness and despair over the loss of his hearing, the tragedy did not hinder his composing career. Many of his best and most adventurous works were written after he had lost his hearing.

Beethoven introduced many new ideas into his music. One of his boldest ideas was to use a chorus and solo singers in the last movement of his Ninth Symphony (1823). The first three movements are played in the usual way, by the orchestra alone. In the fourth movement, chorus and soloists suddenly enter with Beethoven's setting of the *Ode to Joy*. The text, from a poem by the German poet Schiller, tells all people to be happy and to love one another. The effect of this choral movement has been imitated by later composers but never equaled.

▶**THE ROMANTIC AGE**

Beethoven's Ninth Symphony pointed the way for the composers of the romantic period. Romantic composers aimed at producing unfamiliar, unexpected, and startling effects. They favored vocal music, and even when they wrote for instruments alone they liked their works to express an idea or tell a story. Romantic music dominated the 1800's and even part of the 1900's.

Song and Piano Music. One of the earliest romantic composers was Franz Schubert. While he made many important contributions to the music of the early romantic era, Schubert is probably best remembered for his many songs. The German **lied** (plural: **lieder**) is a solo song for voice and piano, set to German poetry. Franz Schubert wrote more than 300 lieder. His gift for inventing melodies never seemed to fail him, and he could express the mood of a poem with only a few notes. Schubert helped turn the lied into an important art form, and many later composers were influ-

Robert and Clara Schumann were outstanding composers of piano music and songs (lieder), forms that flourished in German music during the romantic period.

enced by his work. Schubert and his colleague Robert Schumann also wrote a number of **song cycles**. A song cycle is a group of songs, performed together, that tells a story or expresses a single idea. Schubert's *Winterreise* ("Winter Journey"; 1827) and Schumann's *Dichterliebe* ("A Poet's Love"; 1840) are two of the best-loved romantic song cycles.

Schumann was also well known for his piano music. His own career as a pianist was cut short after he accidentally injured his hand while attempting to devise a method to improve the strength of his fingers. Nevertheless, he continued to write piano music throughout his career. Schumann liked to write sets of miniature piano pieces called **character pieces**. Character pieces are brief piano works that use music to create a mood, express an idea, or describe a character. Schumann's *Carnaval* (1835) is a set of 21 character pieces for piano solo. Each one represents a different character at a Mardi Gras costume ball.

Schumann's wife Clara was a well-known pianist and composer of songs and piano pieces. After her husband's death, Clara continued her concert career and played Robert's music throughout Europe.

Program Music. While many composers continued to write symphonies in the tradition of Haydn, Mozart, and Beethoven, others were looking for a new means of expression.

Some romantic composers wrote orchestral music that expressed ideas from nature, literature, history, or fine arts. Sometimes the story behind the music was explained to the audience in a printed concert program, and the music came to be called **program music**. Some of the earliest pieces of program music were orchestral introductions to plays and operas. One of these, an overture to *A Midsummer Night's Dream* (1826), by Felix Mendelssohn, is a particularly magical work. The characters and events of Shakespeare's comedy are skillfully portrayed. Even the braying of the donkey can be heard.

Franz Liszt, a later composer, wrote many works for orchestra depicting poems, paintings, or drawings. He called these works **symphonic poems**. The *Faust Symphony* (1854), one of Liszt's largest works, deals with the old legend of Faust, who promised his soul to the devil in exchange for eternal youth.

The idea of the symphonic poem was further developed by Richard Strauss. Strauss called his works in this form **tone poems**. In his *Til Eulenspiegel* (1895), the music expresses the merry pranks and sad end of a mischievous young man. In *Don Quixote* (1897), a solo cello plays the part of the Don, while a viola represents his servant, Sancho Panza.

Brahms. Johannes Brahms, one of the greatest composers of the second half of the 1800's, had a different outlook. He was not interested in opera, and his compositions did not tell stories or paint musical pictures. Brahms wanted instead to build on the classical traditions of Haydn, Mozart, and Beethoven. His piano works, chamber music, concertos, and four symphonies are all works of extraordinary beauty. His *German Requiem* (1868) for chorus, solo voices, and orchestra, which mourns the death of his mother, is one of the finest works of its kind.

The New Book of Knowledge contains biographies of many of the composers discussed in this article. Consult the appropriate volumes to find the following entries:

BACH, Johann Sebastian	MAHLER, Gustav
BEETHOVEN, Ludwig van	MENDELSSOHN, Felix
BRAHMS, Johannes	MOZART, Wolfgang Amadeus
GLUCK, Christoph Willibald	SCHOENBERG, Arnold
HANDEL, George Frederick	SCHUBERT, Franz
HAYDN, Franz Joseph	SCHUMANN, Robert
LISZT, Franz	WAGNER, Richard

A scene from *Das Rheingold*, one in a cycle of four music dramas by the romantic composer Richard Wagner. The theme was taken from German myth and legend.

the words. Meanwhile, the orchestra interprets what the singers say and do on the stage. Short musical themes called **leitmotivs** represent characters, objects, and situations in the drama. In *Die Walküre* ("The Valkyrie"; 1856), for example, when the hero Siegmund finds a sword, a trumpet plays a short tune, or leitmotiv. This same leitmotiv is then heard whenever the sword is used or mentioned throughout the opera. This way of writing operas proved to be very successful and influenced many other composers.

The operas of Richard Strauss, including *Salomé* (1905) and *Der Rosenkavalier* (1911), were also innovative, with unusual plots and expressive music.

Later Romantic Composers. Like Beethoven, Wagner had an enormous influence on later musicians. The Austrian Anton Bruckner was a famous organist and an admirer of Wagner. Rather than writing music dramas, Bruckner wrote nine long symphonies. With the exception of his last symphony, which he did not live to finish, all of Bruckner's symphonies follow the traditional four-movement plan used by Mozart, Haydn, and Beethoven. Bruckner followed Wagner's example by using a very large orchestra and writing works that were quite long. He was also very influenced by Wagner's use of harmony and sense of drama.

A second important symphonic composer of the late 1800's was Gustav Mahler, another fervent admirer of Wagner. Mahler's symphonies, unlike those of Bruckner, were often programmatic, vividly depicting nonmusical elements such as the call of a cuckoo bird or a procession of animals. Mahler often followed the example of Beethoven, adding voices to his symphonies. The last movement of Mahler's Fourth Symphony (1899) is a beautiful orchestral song that describes a child's view of paradise.

The songwriter Hugo Wolf was one of the most unusual composers of the late romantic era. He belonged to the same circle of musicians that included Wagner, Mahler, and Bruckner, but his main interest was in writing songs. Wolf's songs are built on the same tradition of German songwriting that Schubert had raised to such perfection. However, he added to this the dramatic and harmonic intensity of Wagner. Each of his songs is like a music drama in miniature.

Opera and Music Drama. German romantic music found its most characteristic expression in operatic works. *Der Freischutz* (1821; "The Marksman"), an opera by Carl Maria von Weber, was one of the most successful of early romantic operas. It was based on a German legend and used melodies with a folksong character. More important were the achievements of Richard Wagner, who wrote both the librettos (texts) and the music for his operas. He called his operas **music dramas**, to show that he thought the story as important as the music. The stories are based on old legends dealing with dwarfs and giants, maidens in distress and gallant knights, and sorcerers and magicians.

Wagner's operas are very different from those of other composers. The singers usually sing almost as though they are speaking, to make it easier for the audience to understand

Innovative German composer Arnold Schoenberg (*left*), shown conducting in this sketch, was a pioneer of atonal and twelve-tone music. The techniques he developed gave modern composers new means of musical expression.

The title page of Paul Hindemith's 1922 *Suite for Piano* (*right*) was illustrated by the composer. Hindemith used the language of modern music to compose works inspired by musical forms of the past.

▶THE MODERN ERA

Three of the most important composers of the early 1900's—Arnold Schoenberg, Alban Berg, and Anton Webern—worked in Vienna. Like the earlier Vienna-based composers Haydn, Mozart, and Beethoven, they profoundly influenced the music of later generations. Thus they are often referred to as the composers of the Second Viennese School.

Led by Schoenberg, the composers of the Second Viennese School sought new means of musical expression through the use of **atonality**. Atonality literally means an absence of tonality. In atonal music, there is no one central tone. All notes are considered equal and can be arranged in new and exciting ways. Atonal music can sound quite harsh and dissonant on first hearing. It seemed appropriate to express the turbulence that many felt in the early decades of the new century.

One of the most important works of the Second Viennese School was Schoenberg's *Pierrot lunaire* (1912) for instruments and singer. In this work, the singer uses a combination of singing and speech called *sprechstimme* ("speech voice"). The same technique was used by Berg in his atonal opera *Wozzeck* (1914–21). This opera deals in a shockingly realistic manner with the unhappy life of a soldier. Webern was also an accomplished composer in the new style. His works are unusual for their complexity and shortness.

Later 1900's. During the turbulent years before World War II, many German composers immigrated to the United States and made important contributions to American musical life. Arnold Schoenberg taught musical composition at the University of California. Paul Hindemith, another great German composer, taught at Yale University, and the Austrian Ernest Krenek taught at Vassar College. Kurt Weill, who composed the music for Bertolt Brecht's famous play *The Threepenny Opera* (1928), wrote Broadway musicals.

In the second half of the 1900's, many composers turned to revolutionary new methods of composing. Two modern German composers who achieved international renown were Karlheinz Stockhausen and Hans Werner Henze. Stockhausen believed that the orchestras of the 1800's were no longer adequate to express musical ideas. He used electronic sounds in such works as *Hymnen* ("Anthems"; 1966–67) and was one of the first composers to experiment with **chance music**, in which some element of the music is chosen at random. Unlike Stockhausen, Henze used a modern musical language to compose traditional types of works such as ballet, symphony, and opera.

KARL GEIRINGER
Author, *The Bach Family*
Reviewed by WENDY HELLER
New England Conservatory of Music

GERMS. See MICROBIOLOGY.

GERONIMO (1829–1909)

One of the most daring fighters of the American Indian wars was the Apache leader whom the Mexicans called Geronimo. His real name was Goyathlay, meaning "one who yawns." Geronimo grew up in Arizona and New Mexico. Brave and wise, he became a medicine man of the Chiricahua Apache.

The Chiricahua often crossed the border to trade with the Mexicans. On one such expedition Geronimo's mother, wife, and children were killed. The young brave swore vengeance. For several years he led brutal raids against his Mexican enemies.

Meanwhile, American settlers were inflicting great cruelties on the Indians. In revenge Geronimo led fierce raids on American settlements. Soon just the sound of his name was enough to terrorize the settlers.

General George Crook of the United States Army finally succeeded in capturing Geronimo. But Geronimo escaped, and General Crook was replaced by General Nelson Miles. By 1886, after years of bitter fighting, Geronimo knew his cause was hopeless and surrendered to General Miles. The defeated Indian chieftain and his followers were sent to join other Apache in Florida.

In 1894 the Apache were moved to a reservation at Fort Sill, Oklahoma. Here Geronimo devoted himself to farming and seeking better education for Indian children. Late in life he adopted Christianity.

Geronimo died at Fort Sill on February 17, 1909. His name lives on as a battle cry used by paratroopers as they jump from their planes.

Reviewed by DANIEL JACOBSON
Michigan State University

GERRY, ELBRIDGE. See VICE PRESIDENCY OF THE UNITED STATES.

GERSHWIN, GEORGE (1898–1937)

George Gershwin, one of America's most original composers, was born in Brooklyn, New York, on September 26, 1898. At 15 he had learned to play the piano so well that he left high school to become the youngest "song plugger" ever hired on Broadway. His job was demonstrating songs for the customers of a music publisher.

George also composed his own songs. In 1919, at the age of 20, he wrote his first big hit, "Swanee." In the same year he received excellent reviews for his first New York musical comedy, *La, La, Lucille.* Several Broadway and London musicals and revues followed.

The American composer George Gershwin first gained fame for writing popular Broadway musicals. His *Rhapsody in Blue* (1924), a concert work that incorporates elements of jazz, is a landmark in the history of American music.

In 1924 George wrote *Lady, Be Good!*, his first big musical comedy success. The lyrics were written by his older brother, Ira, who became his chief collaborator. Their other Broadway successes included *Tip-Toes* (1925), *Oh, Kay* (1926), *Funny Face* (1927), *Strike Up the Band* (1929), and *Girl Crazy* (1930). They also wrote the first Pulitzer prizewinning musical, *Of Thee I Sing* (1931).

Early in 1924 George was asked to write a concert piece for Paul Whiteman's jazz orchestra. In less than three weeks he composed *Rhapsody in Blue*, which created a sensation in American musical history. The following year he wrote his Concerto in F for piano and orchestra and in 1928 a tone poem called *An American in Paris.*

In 1935, after twenty months of hard work, George finished *Porgy and Bess*, a folk opera about blacks in the American South. The next year he and Ira went to Hollywood and wrote three film musicals. George died of a brain tumor there on July 11, 1937.

The music of George Gershwin lives on. Annual all-Gershwin concerts are held in nearly every large city in America. In Europe, too, no American composer's works are more frequently played.

IRA GERSHWIN

GETTYSBURG ADDRESS

On November 19, 1863, the National Soldiers' Cemetery at Gettysburg, Pennsylvania, was dedicated. The new national cemetery occupied part of the battlefield where, three months earlier, an estimated 50,000 men had been killed or wounded during one of the bloodiest battles of the U.S. Civil War.

Thousands of people gathered on Cemetery Hill for the official parade and speeches. Then, President Abraham Lincoln rose to deliver his eloquent two-minute address that is remembered as a powerful expression of the American ideal of liberty. Lincoln passionately believed that American democracy was "the last, best hope of the earth." He believed that the secession of states from the Union could not be tolerated. At Gettysburg, while honoring the dead, Lincoln urged the living to prove to the world that American democracy would not fail and that it would not "perish from the earth."

ARI HOOGENBOOM
City University of New York,
Brooklyn College

LINCOLN'S GETTYSBURG ADDRESS

Fourscore and seven years ago our fathers brought forth on this continent a new nation, conceived in liberty, and dedicated to the proposition that all men are created equal. Now we are engaged in a great civil war, testing whether that nation, or any nation so conceived and so dedicated, can long endure. We are met on a great battlefield of that war. We have come to dedicate a portion of that field, as a final resting place for those who here gave their lives that that nation might live. It is altogether fitting and proper that we should do this. But, in a larger sense, we cannot dedicate — we cannot consecrate — we cannot hallow — this ground. The brave men, living and dead, who struggled here, have consecrated it, far above our poor power to add or detract. The world will little note, nor long remember, what we say here, but it can never forget what they did here. It is for us the living, rather, to be dedicated here to the unfinished work which they who fought here have thus far so nobly advanced. It is rather for us to be here dedicated to the great task remaining before us — that from these honored dead we take increased devotion to that cause for which they gave the last full measure of devotion — that we here highly resolve that these dead shall not have died in vain — that this nation, under God, shall have a new birth of freedom — and that government of the people, by the people, for the people, shall not perish from the earth.

GETTYSBURG, BATTLE OF. See Civil War, United States.

GEYSERS AND HOT SPRINGS

Some parts of the world have natural hot water. If the water shoots up out of the earth, it is called a geyser. If it bubbles up quietly, it is called a hot spring.

▶HOT SPRINGS

Water in a hot spring can be pleasantly warm. At Warm Springs, Georgia, the temperature of the water is about 87 degrees Fahrenheit. The water in hot springs can also be much hotter. At Hot Springs, Arkansas, the water temperature is 143 degrees. And in Yellowstone National Park, Wyoming, the water in many of the hot springs is almost boiling.

Some springs are hot because their water circulates far down in the earth, where there is great heat. The hot springs in Georgia and Arkansas are of this type. Most hot springs, though, are found where there are active volcanoes. New Zealand and Japan, which have many hot springs, are two such places. There, molten rock coming up from deep inside the earth brings heat to the surface. Rainwater seeping down through the ground gets hot. If this water comes to the surface, it is a hot spring.

The water of a hot spring carries many minerals dissolved in it. This usually gives the water an unusual smell and taste. Some doctors believe the mineral water in hot springs is helpful in treating certain diseases, such as arthritis. Many people go to these hot springs for their health. A place where hot springs are used for health purposes is called a spa. The spas at Banff in the Canadian Rockies, Hot Springs in Arkansas, and Baden-Baden in Germany are some of the most famous in the world. Japan and Mexico also have some popular spas.

Iceland has thousands of hot springs. Water from many of them is piped into homes for heat and hot water. Most of the homes in the capital city of Reykjavik get their heat and hot water in this way. In Iceland, water from hot springs is also used to heat greenhouses, where flowers, vegetables, and fruit are grown.

In New Zealand the steam from underground hot springs is harnessed to make electricity.

▶GEYSERS

A geyser is a special kind of hot spring. Our word "geyser" comes from the name of one hot spring in Iceland. The name of the spring probably came from the Icelandic word meaning "to gush."

A geyser spurts hot water and steam into the air from an opening in the ground. It plays like a fountain for a while, then dies down.

Every geyser is different. The water in some geysers rises only 1 or 2 inches. In others it rises hundreds of feet. Some geysers erupt every few minutes, giving off small streams of water. Some erupt only once every few years. There are geysers that play for hours, while others play for only a few minutes.

Some geysers erupt so regularly that a schedule of their display times can be listed. One of these is the geyser in Yellowstone National Park that is called "Old Faithful." It plays about every 66 minutes. Its water and steam gradually rise until they reach a height of about 150 feet. Then the geyser dies down and is quiet again.

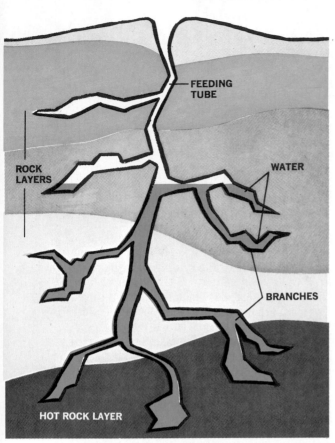

How a geyser looks underground. The feeding tube must be narrow for a geyser to play.

FEEDING TUBE

ROCK LAYERS

WATER

BRANCHES

HOT ROCK LAYER

Riverside Geyser in Yellowstone Park, Wyoming, erupts 80 to 100 feet into the air every 6 to 9½ hours.

Geysers are rare. Nearly all the world's geysers are in Iceland, New Zealand, and Yellowstone National Park.

Why a Geyser Plays

A geyser has a special "plumbing system." This consists of a long, vertical passage, called a feeding tube. The tube leads from hot rocks deep in the earth to an opening at the surface. Usually, several underground branches lead out from the main tube. The tube must be quite narrow for a geyser to work.

When the geyser is quiet, the feeding tube is filled with water. The water in the lower part of the tube is heated by the hot rocks. Since the feeding tube is narrow, most of the hot water stays at the bottom. It cannot circulate as water ordinarily does when it is heated from below.

The water at the bottom of the tube becomes hotter and hotter. But it cannot boil because of the pressure of the column of water above it. (Pressure changes the boiling point of a liquid—an increase in pressure raises the boiling point.) Finally, when the water does boil, it begins to drive the column of water upward. This releases some of the pressure on the water near the bottom, and more of it turns to steam. Steam and hot water erupt upward, pushing all the water out of the tube.

When the steam reaches the cooler air, it condenses back to water. Most of this water, plus water thrown out during the eruption, drains back into the feeding tube. The tube fills again. The water heats, turns to steam, and erupts again.

Water from geysers also carries minerals dissolved in it. The most common mineral is silica, in a form called geyserite. It deposits around the mouth of the tube and piles up, making a crater. The craters take many forms and add to the strangeness and beauty of a geyser area.

REBECCA B. MARCUS
Author, *First Book of Volcanoes and Earthquakes*

Reviewed by CLIVE R. B. LISTER
Geophysical Consultant
Ocean Science and Engineering, Inc.

GHANA

Ghana is a nation in West Africa. It is situated on the southern coast of the great western bulge of Africa, bordering the Gulf of Guinea, an inlet of the Atlantic Ocean. Ghana gained its independence in 1957. It was formed from the British colonies of the Gold Coast and British Togoland and named Ghana after an ancient African empire.

▶THE PEOPLE

There are more than a dozen ethnic groups in Ghana, and over 50 dialects are spoken. The main groups in the center and south are the Ashanti, Brong-Ahafo, Fanti, Ewe, and Ga. The Dagomba and Mamprusi live in the north. Most of these people are farmers, and many still live in walled villages, originally designed to ward off enemy attack.

Language and Religion. English is the official language, although many African languages also are spoken. Nearly half the people are Christians, and many others follow traditional African religions. About 12 percent of the population are Muslims.

Way of Life and Education. Village families usually live in houses of baked earth with roofs of straw or corrugated iron. A staple food is a porridge called *fu-fu,* which is made from cassava, a starchy root plant. Both men and women wear gaily patterned cotton robes. The most prized robes are made of *kente,* cloth woven of cotton and silk yarn.

About 35 percent of the people now live in urban areas. Many Ghanaians in the cities wear Western-style clothes, but some still prefer their colorful traditional dress.

Education has been compulsory since 1961. Children attend three levels of school—primary, middle, and secondary. There are numerous teacher-training colleges and technical institutions. The leading universities are the University of Ghana at Legon, near

The campus and grounds of the University of Ghana at Legon, a suburb of Accra.

Accra; Kumasi University of Science and Technology; and the University of Cape Coast. Ghana's literacy rate (the number of people who can read and write) is rising. Many adults, however, still cannot read or write, and the government holds classes in many villages to combat adult illiteracy.

The Arts. The people of Ghana once had a flourishing artistic tradition in wood carving and in objects made of gold and brass. But little remains of this heritage. Ghanaians are noted for their talent in music and dance. Painting, drama, and fiction are more recent developments. Almost all publications in Ghana are in English.

▶THE LAND

Ghana is bounded by the Ivory Coast on the west, Burkina on the north, Togo on the east, and by the Gulf of Guinea on the south. Along its coast are sandy beaches, mangrove swamps, and clumps of waving coconut palms. Inland on the coastal plain, farmers grow limes, bananas, coffee, rice, sugar, corn (maize), yams, cassava, peanuts, and other crops. A dense tropical forest covers southern Ghana. The trees are big, and their leaves form a green, roof-like cover. The shaded land between these trees is ideal for growing cacao. The gold that gave the area its former name, the Gold Coast, lies in the forest region. Early prospectors scraped it out of the ground with simple tools. Today it is mined from deposits deep beneath the earth's surface. Rough diamonds used for drilling are found in sandy soils near rivers. There are bauxite and manganese deposits in the south.

In the center and north, the forest changes to open savanna (grassland). Here the trees are smaller and farther apart, and grass grows between them. Farmers raise cattle and plant corn, yams, and peanuts. They dread the harmattan, a dry, hot wind that blows dust in from the Sahara and shrivels up their crops. Farther north no rain falls from October to May, and the soil turns into sand.

Elephants, rhinoceroses, lions, and many other beasts used to live in the forest and savanna. But big game hunters and ivory traders have almost wiped them out.

The Volta River, the largest in Ghana, rises in low hills and runs a curling course to the sea. In the mid-1960's, a great dam was built

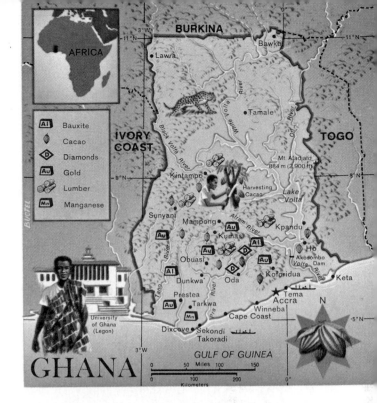

across the Volta, providing hydroelectric power for agriculture and industry.

▶THE ECONOMY

Most Ghanaians are farmers. They grow yams, cassava, rice, sorghum, millet, and nuts for their own use. Ghana's chief cash crop is

Cocoa is often called the "brown gold" of Ghana.

cacao. Farmers cut off the ripe cacao pods in November and December, and children collect them. The beans—from which cocoa is produced—are shelled and left on banana leaves to ferment. Then they are dried, packed, and carried to depots for shipment. Ghana was once the world's leading supplier of cacao. But many of the cacao trees are old and no longer produce abundantly. The price the government pays farmers for cacao is so low that many of them have shifted to growing maize (corn) or other crops. Some have left their farms altogether and moved to the cities in search of better-paying work. In addition, many years of neglect have left Ghana's transportation system in such poor condition that it is hard to get the cacao to market. For all these reasons, cacao production has declined, although cacao is still a major export.

Ghana also exports gold, diamonds, and manganese. Bauxite is smelted into aluminum before it is sold abroad. Among Ghana's traditional industries are forestry, fishing, and the making of handicrafts. Various kinds of consumer goods are manufactured. But industrial output is low because factory owners find it hard to get the spare parts and imported raw materials they need to keep their machinery running.

Above: Processing cacao requires a large amount of hand labor. The cacao seeds are removed from the pods, fermented, and then dried in the sun before they are shipped to market. **Below:** Fishermen bring in their catch from the waters of the Gulf of Guinea.

The capital and largest city in Ghana is Accra. Kumasi, Ghana's second largest city, is the major commercial and transportation center of the interior. Tema, Ghana's chief port, has grown from a tiny fishing village to one of the largest ports in western Africa. Sekondi-Takoradi (formerly two separate towns) is another port. There are no natural harbors along Ghana's coast. For centuries, ferries were used to carry cargoes and passengers from ships to the shore.

▶HISTORY AND GOVERNMENT

Early History. The ancestors of today's Ghanaians probably began moving into the area from the grasslands to the north by about A.D. 1200. It seems likely that they provided gold to traders from the great Mali and Songhai kingdoms to the north. The gold was so abundant that what is now Ghana came to be known as the Gold Coast after the Portuguese arrived there in 1471. After that time, the various European nations competing for trade and territory in Africa built a number of forts along the coast.

A hydroelectric power plant at Akosombo, on the Volta River, began operation in 1966. It supplies power for aluminum smelting and other industrial activities.

FACTS and figures

REPUBLIC OF GHANA is the official name of the country.

LOCATION: Western Africa.

AREA: 92,099 sq mi (238,537 km²).

POPULATION: 18,000,000 (estimate).

CAPITAL AND LARGEST CITY: Accra.

MAJOR LANGUAGES: English (official), various African languages are also spoken.

MAJOR RELIGIOUS GROUPS: Christian, traditional African, Muslim.

GOVERNMENT: Republic. **Head of state and government**—president. **Legislature**—National Assembly.

CHIEF PRODUCTS: Agricultural—cacao, corn, yams, cassava, peanuts, limes, bananas, coffee, rice, sugar, oil palms, coconuts. **Manufactured**—processed cacao and other foods (including fish), textiles, vehicles, cement, paper, chemicals, refined petroleum. **Mineral**—gold, diamonds, bauxite (aluminum ore), manganese.

MONETARY UNIT: New cedi (1 cedi = 100 pesewas).

The Slave Trade. In the 1500's, Spain turned to Africa as a source of labor because the Indian peoples in the Spanish colonies of the Americas refused to work for their conquerors. Dutch and Portuguese traders signed contracts with the king of Spain to supply African slaves. The English later shipped African slaves to their plantations in the West Indies and in what is now the southern United States. The Gold Coast became a source of slaves as well as gold.

The Ashanti. At the time, the Ashanti were the most powerful people in the region. Their armies defeated rivals, captured their people, and marched them to the coast to be sold to the highest European bidder in exchange for guns, rum, cloth, and beads.

The victors in African wars often sold their captives as slaves, and slaves in Africa were generally treated well. One in every eight of the millions of Africans shipped across the ocean died during the voyage. Unlike slaves in Africa, those who survived had little hope of regaining their freedom.

Finally British reformers exposed the evils of the slave trade. In 1807 the British government made slavery illegal in British possessions. The Civil War ended slavery in the United States, and the slave traders went

Ghanaians shop for fish at a local market. Fishing is a traditional occupation.

out of business. British merchants continued to buy timber, palm oil, and gold, and in 1844 the Fanti and other tribes signed a treaty placing their part of the Gold Coast under British protection.

The Ashanti, who had built up a powerful kingdom in the interior, resented this bond between the British and the Fanti. Fighting broke out between the British and the Ashanti in 1873. The British captured and destroyed the Ashanti capital, Kumasi, and exiled their ruler. But they did not capture the Ashanti's most sacred possession—a golden stool that was said to have come from the sky and to contain the soul of the Ashanti nation.

Gold Coast Colony.   In 1901, after a second war with the Ashanti nation, the British united the Ashanti region with the neighboring territories that were under British protection and formed the Gold Coast Colony. After World War I the British sent a governor, Sir Gordon Guggisberg, who understood the needs of the people. He formed a council in Accra and enlisted educated Africans to advise on local problems. He helped build schools, hospitals, roads, and railways. In 1924 the exiled Ashanti chief was allowed to return.

During World War II the people of the Gold Coast proved their loyalty to the British by providing ports and air bases. A large number of volunteers fought with the British Army. The people of the Gold Coast learned much about the rest of the world during the war. And when the war ended, they began to claim the right to govern themselves.

In answer to their demand, the British government granted the country a new constitution in 1946. It provided for larger African representation in the government of the colony. But this did not satisfy the people because it fell short of self-rule.

Kwame Nkrumah.   At this time a young man named Kwame Nkrumah returned to the Gold Coast from his studies in the United States and Great Britain. Nkrumah formed the Convention Peoples Party (CCP), with the slogan "Self-government Now."

The British proposed a second constitution, but it, too, blocked self-government. In protest Nkrumah called a general strike that brought the colony to a standstill. He and eight of his supporters were arrested and sent to prison.

In 1951 the Gold Coast held its first general election. Nkrumah was in jail, but his Convention Peoples Party won a sweeping victory. Realizing that Nkrumah had wide popular support, the British released him, and in 1952 he was elected first prime minister of the Gold Coast.

Independence and After.   The Gold Coast won its independence on March 6, 1957. The previous year the people of neighboring British Togoland had voted to join the new nation, which was renamed Ghana.

In 1960, Ghana became a republic, with Nkrumah as president. The country had economic problems, and there was growing criticism of Nkrumah's rule. In 1966 he was overthrown in a military coup. Although civilian rule was restored in 1969, army officers again seized power in 1972. There were two more military coups in 1979. The leader of the second coup, Flight Lieutenant Jerry J. Rawlings, returned power to a civilian government. But he staged another coup in 1981, charging the civilian leaders with corruption. A new constitution was approved in 1992 and elections held, the first in many years in which opposition parties were allowed to take part. Rawlings was elected president in 1992 and re-elected in 1996.

KATHERINE SAVAGE
Author, *The Story of Africa*

GHOSTS

A ghost is the spirit of a dead person that somehow makes itself known to the living. Scientists have found no evidence that ghosts exist, and most people today dismiss the idea. But belief in ghosts is ancient, and stories of ghosts are still common.

▶ **GHOSTS IN ANCIENT TIMES**

People have always regarded the dead with a mixture of awe and fear. To ancient people, the body of a dead person was like an empty house. The air was filled with evil spirits and demons looking for a home. If the body was not properly protected by the correct magical and religious ceremonies, these spirits might take it over, with terrible results.

Today we know that this cannot happen. But in prehistoric times, graves were often covered with heavy stones. This was not merely a way to mark the grave site. It was a way of keeping someone or something from getting into—or out of—the grave. Sometimes bodies were wrapped or tied to make sure that they would not leave the grave.

Ancient people also wondered what happened to the spirit of a person who had died. Obviously, the spark that had once made the person a living being had gone—but where? And what powers did the spirit have?

Among the ancient Greeks and Romans, it was believed that if a body was not given a proper burial its spirit would walk the earth to trouble the living. One of the oldest written accounts of a ghost was set down nearly 2,000 years ago by the Roman writer Pliny the Younger. He told the story (which he believed to be true) of a haunted house in Athens. The house was troubled by the ghastly figure of an old man, who dragged chains and moaned. Finally one brave man followed the ghost and watched as it pointed to a particular spot on the ground. When the place was dug up, a skeleton was discovered, with rusted chains still clinging to the bones. The remains were carefully collected and buried with the proper ceremonies, and the house was never again troubled by the ghost.

Not all people have regarded ghosts with fear. In some societies, the spirits of dead ancestors have long been believed to protect the family. Shrines might be set up in homes to honor these ancestors.

Spirits haunt miserly Ebenezer Scrooge in *A Christmas Carol*, by Charles Dickens. Here, Scrooge sees the ghost of his former business partner, Jacob Marley.

Various forms of ancestor worship have traditionally been important in a number of African and Asian societies. In some cases, a particularly powerful person might actually come to be regarded as a god after his or her death and have power far beyond the immediate family. In the voodoo religion of Haiti, for example, many of the numerous gods that are worshipped were originally the spirits of powerful priests and priestesses of the religion.

▶ **GHOSTS IN THE MIDDLE AGES**

The spread of Christianity through Europe did not greatly change people's ideas about ghosts. Officially, the Christian Church did not recognize ghosts, and it tried to discourage belief in them. But the ancient beliefs continued anyway. And throughout the Middle Ages and into later times, belief in ghosts became thoroughly mixed up with belief in magic and witchcraft.

In Europe, most ghosts were thought to be the spirits of people who had died suddenly, often by violence. Frequently they were believed to have returned to earth to complete some unfinished task. There were many, many tales of ghosts of individuals who had been murdered returning to haunt and accuse their murderers. More than one murderer confessed to the crime out of fear of being haunted by the ghost of the victim.

Other stories told of ghosts who returned to help their heirs discover a hidden will or buried treasure. And whenever an evil person died, stories that the person had returned as an evil and dangerous ghost might quickly spread.

▶ SCIENCE AND GHOSTS

About 200 years ago, many educated people in the West began to seriously doubt the existence of ghosts. The development of scientific methods of research, which require facts and evidence as the basis for beliefs, helped create these doubts. It was no longer possible to accept an idea just because a lot of people had accepted it for a long time.

Some people thus set out to gather evidence to scientifically prove the existence of ghosts. However, this turned out to be very difficult to do. Most of the accounts of ghosts were old and impossible to check or came from distant places or unreliable sources. Ghosts never seemed to show up when a group of competent observers was on hand.

A movement called **spiritualism** (or spiritism) seemed to offer the scientifically minded some basis for a belief in ghosts. Spiritualism began in the United States in the 1840's and soon spread throughout much of the world. The basic idea behind spiritualism was that certain individuals, called **mediums**, could regularly and reliably communicate with the spirits of the dead. This was usually done during a gathering called a **séance**.

At a séance, spirits might make their presence known in a variety of ways. The medium might go into a trance, and a spirit would take control of his or her body. The spirit might speak through the medium, knock on a table, or move things around the room. Or the spirit might even appear physically, as a glowing and ghostly form.

In 1882 a group of scientifically minded men and women in Britain formed the Society for Psychical Research to investigate séances and other possible evidence that the dead might somehow communicate with the living. (The word "psychical" comes from the Greek word *psyche*, or soul.) A similar society was formed in the United States a few years later.

The researchers soon discovered that most mediums were fakes, and that most of the ghostly happenings of the séance were the result of trickery. However, a number of psychical researchers were convinced that at least some of the mediums were genuine. Some researchers also felt that they had collected other evidence of ghosts—for example, accounts from believable witnesses who were convinced that they had seen or otherwise experienced encounters with ghosts.

The researchers did not win many supporters in the scientific community, however. Today the vast majority of scientists say that the case for ghosts is at best unproved. Spiritualism now has only a small following, and séances are rarely seriously investigated anymore. But researchers still investigate reports of ghosts.

The most common reports of ghosts today involve a type of spirit called a **poltergeist**. (The word "poltergeist" comes from German words meaning "knocking spirit.") In a typical poltergeist case, a house is afflicted with strange noises, and small objects are mysteriously moved and thrown about. Often poltergeist activity seems to center around a young person. In many cases trickery has been proved, but in some cases the cause of the disturbances remains unclear.

▶ GHOST STORIES

Even if scientists and many other people do not believe in ghosts anymore, ghost stories are just as popular as they ever were. Chilling (and sometimes humorous) tales of ghosts have formed the basis for a number of popular novels and films in recent years. And ghosts have played important parts in some of history's most famous works of literature, including the *Iliad* by the ancient Greek poet Homer and William Shakespeare's plays *Hamlet* and *Macbeth*.

Probably the most famous ghost story in all English literature is also the most famous Christmas story: *A Christmas Carol*, written in 1843 by Charles Dickens. Dickens even subtitled his tale *A Christmas Ghost Story*. Today we associate the telling of ghost stories with Halloween. But a century or more ago, the traditional time for telling ghost stories was Christmas Eve.

DANIEL COHEN
Author, *The Encyclopedia of Ghosts*

GIANTS

Can you imagine a person twice or more as big as anyone else? Many people have imagined that an entire race of such persons once walked the earth. These were the giants—creatures like humans but vastly larger and stronger.

▶GIANTS IN MYTHS AND LEGENDS

Giants play roles in many ancient myths and legends. Often, old tales tell how giants battled gods or human heroes. And ancient ruins and even features of the landscape have been taken for the work of legendary giants.

Giants and Gods. The Titans of ancient Greece were giants who existed before people —and even before the gods. They were the children of Uranus (Heaven) and Gaea (Earth). Some of the Greek giants represented aspects of nature, such as water, air, and earth.

Zeus, the king of the gods, was the son of one of the Titans, Cronus. Before he could lead the gods, Zeus had to overcome Cronus. This he did in a long battle, in which he and the other gods defeated the Titans and imprisoned them in a mountain.

In Scandinavian mythology, too, the giants were a race that preceded the gods. Most of the stories in Scandinavian mythology are about battles between gods and giants. The god Odin outwits the giants, and the god Thor defeats them with his hammer. In one of the best-known stories, Thor defeats a giant named Hrungnir, whose heart is made of stone. But Thor's greatest enemy is the Midgard Serpent, a huge snake of the giant race. The Midgard Serpent lies deep in the sea surrounding the earth. A story that was popular among the Vikings tells how Thor once caught the serpent on the end of a fishing line.

At the end of the world, Scandinavian stories say, the gods and the giants will fight to a standstill. The world will be destroyed by fire but will rise again. In this new world there will be only gods and humans, no giants.

Giants and People. Especially in Europe, it was commonly believed that giants lived before people. The medieval historian Geoffrey of Monmouth wrote that Britain was settled by Brutus, prince of Troy, at a time when giants still lived there. Brutus killed all the giants but two, whose names were Gog and Magog.

Many legends tell how ancient heroes fought evil giants. In this illustration by N. C. Wyeth, the French knight Sir Roland prepares to battle the giant Ferragus.

These he brought to London, where he made them stand guard outside the royal palace. At least since the early 1400's, enormous wooden statues representing Gog and Magog have stood in London. They must be very popular, for they have twice been destroyed by fire and each time rebuilt.

The idea that giants might have been an older, larger race of humans has lived on in many stories in folklore. A story commonly told in Europe tells of a giant girl who sees a human farmer plowing a field. Thinking that the farmer and his plow and oxen are toys, she picks them up and shows them to her father. He sternly orders her to put them back where she found them. They are not toys, he says, but the creatures who will inhabit the earth after the giants.

Some legends say that the giants have not disappeared. Instead, they have moved somewhere far away. Sometimes they moved because they could not stand the sight of a church or the sound of church bells. One legend tells of a man who travels far away and visits an old giant who used to live where the man lives now. The giant wants to shake the man's hand, but the man hands him an iron staff. The giant squeezes the staff so hard that it melts!

Giants Formed the Landscape. Many people have believed that giants who lived long ago helped form the landscape. Large boulders were said to have been tossed by giants who were angry at one another, and marks in rocks were said to have been made by giants' fingers. Potholes in rocks, which were formed by the movement of glaciers and can be several feet wide and deep, are sometimes called giants' kettles.

The idea that giants shaped the earth is reflected in many place names. Part of the Sudeten mountain range, between the Czech Republic and Poland, is called the Giant Mountains. A mountainous section of northern Norway is called Giant Land. In Northern Ireland a large formation of rock columns is called the Giant's Causeway. Legends tell that it was a stairway for the giants.

American legends tell that the giant lumberjack Paul Bunyan made some of the largest mountains and rivers, including the Rocky Mountains and the Mississippi River. Besides these impressive feats, he was famous mostly for his exaggerated size and abilities. For example, he lived in a cave ten times as large as Mammoth Cave, the huge and famous cavern in Kentucky. He climbed the tallest mountains in six strides. Paul Bunyan's companion was a giant blue ox, Babe. Babe could drink rivers dry and wore shoes so heavy that men carrying them sank into solid rock.

As the lumberjacks had their tales of Paul Bunyan, so cowboys sang songs of Pecos Bill. Although Pecos Bill was not as large as Paul Bunyan, he was just as strong, for he dug out the Grand Canyon and the Rio Grande.

Giants as Master Builders. Besides features of the natural landscape, giants were thought to have built many large or tall buildings. Ancient ruins, when they were large, might be taken for the work of giants. And hundreds of years after churches and cathedrals were built, the details of the actual construction were sometimes forgotten. Then people imagined that giants were the builders. For example, stories were told about the building of the cathedrals in Trondheim, Norway, and Lund, Sweden, and about many smaller churches in Scandinavia and Germany. In most of these stories, a giant agrees to build the church, but he is to be paid with the life of a person. Only by guessing the giant's name can the human hero of the story avoid paying the giant with his life. But while he is out walking, the hero overhears the giant's wife talking to her children, and she mentions the giant's name. And so the church is built, but the giant does not get a human life in exchange for all of his hard work.

Giants and Heroes. Because of the great strength that people imagined them to have, giants were fearsome opponents. Many stories tell how they were defeated by brave heroes. One of the most famous of these tales is the story of David and Goliath in the Old Testament of the Bible. Goliath was the champion of the Philistines and was said to have been about 9 feet 6 inches (300 centimeters) tall. He wore heavy armor and carried a mighty bronze spear with a thick wooden shaft.

Goliath challenged the Israelites to send someone to fight alone with him. If Goliath won, the Israelites would serve the Philistines; but if Goliath lost, his people would serve the Israelites. The young shepherd David fought the duel. But instead of a sword or a spear, he carried only a slingshot and a few smooth stones. David shot a stone and struck the giant in the forehead. When Goliath fell, the Philistine army fled.

Giants were the opponents of the heroes of many fairy tales. One of the most beloved of these tales is the story "Jack and the Beanstalk." Jack and his mother have almost no food left, so she sends him to town to sell their cow. Instead, he exchanges the cow for some beans. When he plants them, a huge beanstalk grows to the sky. Jack climbs it and comes to a magical land where a giant lives in a vast castle. Helped by the giant's foolish wife, Jack steals such valuable objects as a hen that lays golden eggs, bags of money, and a talking harp. When the giant chases him, Jack climbs down the beanstalk and quickly chops it down. The giant is still high up in the beanstalk, and he falls to his death.

According to this and other tales, giants were strong but easy to outwit. For example, several tales tell of a hero who challenges a giant to squeeze water out of a stone. After the giant has squeezed a few drops from a large stone, the hero squeezes a cheese (or, in some stories, an egg) and gets much more liquid. Another tale tells of a hero who challenges a giant to a stone-throwing contest. The hero throws a bird when it is his turn, and the bird flies much farther than the giant's stone.

In yet another story, a hero gets into an eating contest with a giant. Instead of eating his food, the hero stuffs it into a bag under his shirt. In that way he "eats" much more than the giant. When the giant wonders how someone so small can eat so much, the hero says that he always opens his stomach to let the food out after a big meal. He then cuts open the bag. The foolish giant tries the same and cuts open his stomach. The folklore of the world is filled with many similar stories of stupid giants and clever heroes.

▶GIANTS IN LITERATURE

In literature, a number of authors have created characters that were giants. Often, the author uses a giant as a way of arguing a point.

In the 1500's, the French writer François Rabelais wrote a novel about two giants, Gargantua and his son, Pantagruel. (The English word "gargantuan," meaning "huge," comes from this work.) Through the adventures of these giants, Rabelais mocked the society of his time and presented his own philosophy.

The English writer Jonathan Swift used giants in a similar way in his book *Gulliver's Travels*. The book tells of four worlds that are visited by a traveler named Lemuel Gulliver. In one of these worlds, called Brobdingnag, the people are as tall as the tallest buildings in our world. They can hold Gulliver in one hand. To them, the affairs of our world seem trivial. In another world, Lilliput, Gulliver finds that the inhabitants are only 6 inches (15 centimeters) tall. Here Gulliver is the giant! (An excerpt from this story accompanies the biography of Swift in Volume S.)

▶A GIANT HOAX

Although a rare medical condition called gigantism can make people grow to unusual size, giants belong properly in myths, legends, and other stories. In the 1700's, some scientists uncovered large fossil bones they thought belonged to giants. In fact, the bones were those of dinosaurs. In the same way, all other evidence of giants has proved false.

The hero of *Gulliver's Travels*, by Jonathan Swift, is no bigger than the average person. But he is a giant to the tiny inhabitants of Lilliput.

Such evidence figured in one of the most famous hoaxes in the United States. In 1869, workers digging a well in Cardiff, New York, unearthed the stone figure of a man 12 feet (365 centimeters) tall. Many people believed that the figure was an ancient giant that had turned to stone. Others thought that it might be an idol or some other kind of statue from long ago. The owner of the property where the Cardiff giant was found quickly put the figure on display and charged admission.

In time, however, it was revealed that the giant had been carved out of a block of gypsum by a stonecutter. The stonecutter had received the gypsum from a relative of the man on whose property the giant was found. In short, the Cardiff giant was a fake.

You can still see the Cardiff giant at the Farmer's Museum in Cooperstown, New York. But you can see real giants only in the pages of books or in your imagination.

JOHN LINDOW
University of California, Berkeley

See also FOLKLORE; MYTHOLOGY.

GIBRALTAR

The Rock of Gibraltar has stood throughout the centuries as a symbol of strength and endurance. We often call a strong, courageous person a Rock of Gibraltar.

Gibraltar is a British Crown Colony on a peninsula in southwestern Europe at the entrance to the Mediterranean Sea. It is a narrow strip of hilly land, 1.2 kilometers (¾ mile) wide and nearly 5 kilometers (3 miles) long. At its highest point, it rises to almost 430 meters (about 1,400 feet) above sea level. One end of the peninsula is attached to Spain. The other extends into the Strait of Gibraltar.

Because it looms over the western entrance to the Mediterranean Sea, Gibraltar has had great military importance. A map shows why the Rock has played such an important role in European history. As a fortress, it controlled the sea-lanes from Europe to western and southern Africa.

Today Gibraltar is a modern and fully equipped fortress. The best military minds have worked to make Gibraltar almost unconquerable. Many underground passages and ammunition and storage vaults have been built into the Rock. The gun batteries of the fort are skillfully camouflaged. There are water reservoirs, tunnels, and a hospital.

The town of Gibraltar is located on the west side of the peninsula. Its deep harbor is well protected from storms and is a perfect gathering place for a large fleet. About 30,000 people and a company of British soldiers live in the town. The ancestors of the people were Spanish, Italians, and Portuguese.

Gibraltar imports most of its food. It has no large industry and depends for income on tourism, shipping fees, and British defense spending and aid. There is an airport in the northern part of the peninsula.

Gibraltar was known to the ancient Greeks as one of the Pillars of Hercules. From about A.D. 710 until the latter part of the 15th century, Gibraltar was in the hands of the Moors, who were Arab Muslim invaders. It was taken by the Spanish in 1462. In 1704, Gibraltar was occupied by the English, and it has been a British possession ever since.

In the 1960's the United Nations instructed the British to "decolonize" Gibraltar. Instead, the British held a referendum. The majority of the people voted to remain part of Britain. The Spanish Government called the referendum illegal and placed restrictions on the colony. In 1969 the border between Spain and Gibraltar was closed. When it was partly opened in 1982, local people could leave to shop in Spain.

In 1985 the border was fully reopened, the result of an agreement between Spain and Britain. The agreement gave Spaniards the right to work and own property in Gibraltar and called for negotiations to determine which nation would govern the colony in the future.

ANTHONY SAS
University of South Carolina

Gibraltar is a British colony and a major military base. Guns hidden within the Rock of Gibraltar control the passage of ships into and out of the Mediterranean Sea.

GIBSON, ALTHEA (1927-   )

From a childhood in one of New York City's poorest neighborhoods, Althea Gibson rose to become one of the top international tennis players of the 1950's. Her success helped win acceptance for black players in the major tennis tournaments, and her aggressive style of playing helped make women's tennis the competitive sport it is today.

Along the way, Gibson built up an impressive record of major wins and "firsts." She was the first black woman player to compete in United States national tennis championships and the first black to win a major tennis title. In 1957 and again in 1958, she won the United States women's singles title at Forest Hills, New York, and the women's singles championship at Wimbledon, near London, England. She was also a member of the winning women's doubles teams at Wimbledon for three years in a row, in 1956, 1957, and 1958.

Althea Gibson was born in Silver, South Carolina, on August 25, 1927. She grew up in the Harlem section of New York City, where she learned to play paddle tennis in the Police Athletic League "play street" program. In 1941 she began to play tennis, and in 1944 and 1945 she won the junior girls' championship of the American Tennis Association (ATA), a group for black players. Two years later she captured the ATA women's championship—a title she held for ten years.

Gibson studied at Florida Agricultural and Mechanical University from 1949 to 1953. In 1950, her performance in tournaments sponsored by the United States Lawn Tennis Association earned her entry into the national championships at Forest Hills. She lost in the second round, but her entry marked an important step for black players.

After college, Gibson worked as an athletic instructor for two years. Then, in 1955, she was chosen as a member of a team of United States tennis players who were sent abroad on a goodwill tour. While playing overseas, she perfected her game and began her rise to the top of international amateur tennis.

Besides winning her first Wimbledon women's doubles title in 1956, Gibson scored victories at major tournaments in France, Italy, and several Asian countries. In 1957, she was the world's number one woman player. After her singles and doubles wins at Wimbledon,

As one of the top international tennis players of the 1950's, Althea Gibson helped win greater acceptance for black players in major tennis tournaments.

she returned to the United States and captured the women's national clay court championship. Then she went on to win the women's singles title at Forest Hills. She successfully defended her Wimbledon and Forest Hills titles the next year. She was also a member of the victorious United States Wightman Cup team in 1957 and 1958.

Gibson became a professional tennis player in 1959. While she continued her tennis career, she also played on the women's professional golf tour during the 1960's. And beginning in the 1960's, she held various positions in state and local recreation programs in New York and New Jersey.

Sportswriters of the 1950's described Gibson's tennis playing as a "combination of deftness and power" and gave her credit for the "best serve in women's tennis." After her 1957 Wimbledon victories, she was honored with a ticker-tape parade in New York City. She received many other honors during her career. The Associated Press twice named her woman athlete of the year. She was named to the National Lawn Tennis Hall of Fame in 1971 and to the Black Athletes Hall of Fame in 1974. She is the author of *I Always Wanted to Be Somebody* (1958).

Reviewed by FRANK V. PHELPS
Contributor, *Biographical Dictionary of American Sports*

GIFT WRAPPING

Gifts and gift wrapping are meant for each other. One is not complete without the other. Yet the custom of wrapping gifts in colorful paper and tying them with gay ribbons and bows is comparatively new.

It is hard to say when this delightful custom originated, but before 1800 most people throughout the world presented their gifts unwrapped. Centuries ago the Chinese used silk as gift wrapping, but the first widely used materials were brown paper and twine.

It was during the Victorian era (1837–1901), when elaborate decoration was popular, that a new art was born—the art of wrapping attractive gift packages. White tissue paper (which had been used primarily to wrap silverware) became popular as gift wrapping, and colored twine was used to brighten the packages. When colored crepe paper and colored tissue were imported from England in

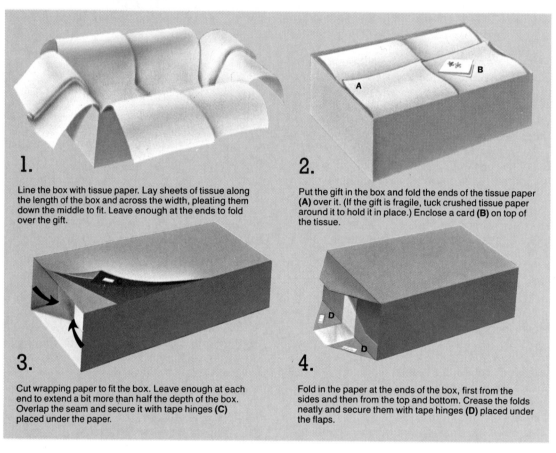

1.
Line the box with tissue paper. Lay sheets of tissue along the length of the box and across the width, pleating them down the middle to fit. Leave enough at the ends to fold over the gift.

2.
Put the gift in the box and fold the ends of the tissue paper **(A)** over it. (If the gift is fragile, tuck crushed tissue paper around it to hold it in place.) Enclose a card **(B)** on top of the tissue.

3.
Cut wrapping paper to fit the box. Leave enough at each end to extend a bit more than half the depth of the box. Overlap the seam and secure it with tape hinges **(C)** placed under the paper.

4.
Fold in the paper at the ends of the box, first from the sides and then from the top and bottom. Crease the folds neatly and secure them with tape hinges **(D)** placed under the flaps.

A ribbon tie is easy to make.

1. Hold the ribbon a few inches from the end. Bring it around the length of the box and then around the width.

2. Cut the ribbon off, leaving several inches, and knot it securely. Make the bow separately, and use the ribbon ends to tie it in place.

1.

2.

1.
To make the bow, pinch the ribbon between your thumb and forefinger as you form the loops.

2.
Secure the bow by wrapping a piece of wire around the center of the loops. Twist the ends of the wire together to hold it in place.

There are many ways to make your gift especially attractive. Here are two ideas:

Use ribbon of a color that contrasts with the color of the wrapping paper — pale blue ribbon with pink paper, for example.

For a humorous touch, cut advertising slogans from old magazines and paste them onto the paper.

1. To wrap a round box, cut the paper as you would for a rectangular box. Place the box on its side and roll the paper around it, securing the paper with tape hinges under the seam.

2. Pleat the ends of the paper down, so that they lie flat. Secure them with decorative seals to give the package a finished look.

1890, many people started to use this new material for wrapping their packages. Soon ribbon was used in place of twine.

In 1901 the first holiday tag was introduced in North America. It was like the plain shipping tag we know today, except that a holly design was printed on it. It proved to be so popular that by 1903 two more holiday tags were introduced—one with a bell design and the other with Santa Claus's smiling face. The following year gummed seals using these three designs appeared on the market.

During this same period the first printed gift-wrapping paper was manufactured. It was a Christmas design of holly. Today there are gift wraps, tags, and ribbons for many occasions. Basic instructions for wrapping gifts appear with this article. A little imagination and practice will soon make your gifts ''too pretty to open.''

NATALIE LEYDEN
Dennison Manufacturing Company

GILBERT AND SULLIVAN OPERETTAS

In the spring of 1875 a London stage manager named Richard D'Oyly Carte was faced with a problem. His company was performing *La Périchole*, an operetta by the popular French composer Offenbach. But *La Périchole* was not quite long enough to fill an evening. D'Oyly Carte desperately needed another piece to add to the program. He asked William S. Gilbert, a successful playwright, and Arthur Sullivan, a well-known composer, to write a short operetta for him. Working furiously, they put together *Trial by Jury* in three weeks' time.

London had never before seen a courtroom drama like *Trial by Jury*. The bewigged judge and lawyers sang and danced merrily about the stage; the defendant led the jurors in song. It was a sensational success, overshadowing the Offenbach operetta, which was supposed to be the more important part of the program.

Trial by Jury was the first success of the remarkable musical partnership of two very different men. Gilbert, the older, was born in London in 1836. He was a lawyer by profession, but enjoyed writing plays and light verse. He finally abandoned the law entirely for a career as a writer. Sullivan was born in 1842, also in London. He had an excellent academic training in music, and was headed toward a career as a composer of serious concert and religious music. Strikingly different in personality, Gilbert and Sullivan sometimes quarreled bitterly. Nevertheless, they continued to write comic operas together for more than twenty years.

After the success of *Trial by Jury*, D'Oyly Carte rented a theater and gathered a company of singers to perform new operettas written by the partners. The first of these, *The Sorcerer* (1877), had a fair reception. It was followed by *H.M.S. Pinafore* (1878), in which Ralph Rackstraw, a simple British sailor, wins his captain's beautiful daughter, in spite of the efforts of the captain, the evil Dick Deadeye, and the first lord of the Admiralty and a vast number of "his sisters and his cousins and his aunts."

Though the first-night audience loved *Pinafore*, the next performances were poorly attended. It looked as if the piece would have to close. But Sullivan saved it by including some of the catchiest tunes from *Pinafore* in a concert he conducted at Covent Garden. The audience liked the music, and many came to D'Oyly Carte's theater to hear the whole operetta. After this shaky start, *Pinafore* went on to become a complete success. It ran for more than seven hundred nights in London, and was performed all over the United States.

When at last the audiences for *Pinafore* began to fall off, it was replaced by *The Pirates of Penzance* (1879), with its "modern Major-General" and his lovely daughters, and its choruses of gentle, poetry-loving pirates and timid policemen. *The Pirates* ran for

about a year, and was followed by *Patience* (1881), which made fun of some silly fashions of the day in literature and art.

By this time the operettas had made so much money that D'Oyly Carte built a new, larger, and more modern theater for his Gilbert and Sullivan productions, named the Savoy; hence the operettas are often called the Savoy operas, and enthusiastic admirers of Gilbert and Sullivan are known as Savoyards.

The first new operetta to be staged at the Savoy was *Iolanthe* (1882). It was a brilliant sight. The theater was ablaze with electric lights—the first ever to be used in a London theater. The women in the chorus were dressed as fairies, with wands and crowns tipped with lights. The men wore the flashing coronets and bright-colored robes of the House of Lords. *Iolanthe* contains some of Gilbert's best lyrics and Sullivan's loveliest melodies. It was another great success.

After *Iolanthe* came *Princess Ida* (1884), which pokes fun both at a poem by the poet laureate, Lord Tennyson, and at the notion of college education for women. *Princess Ida* was not quite as successful as its predecessors, and some people wondered whether Gilbert and Sullivan's spring of wit and melody might be beginning to run dry.

Their answer was *The Mikado*, perhaps the best of the Savoy operas, which opened in 1885 and ran for nearly two years. In 1887 came *Ruddigore*, followed in 1888 by *The Yeomen of the Guard. The Yeomen* is the most

serious of the operas and the only one with a partly unhappy ending. Next came *The Gondoliers* (1889), which takes place in Venice. The story pokes good-natured fun at kings, noblemen, and common folk alike.

During the successful run of *The Gondoliers*, Gilbert and Sullivan had a serious quarrel. For some years they had not been working together smoothly. Sullivan kept pressing Gilbert to write more serious librettos for him. He wanted to be known as a composer of grand and serious operas and at times looked down on the Savoy operas as trifles unworthy of his genius. Gilbert resented the criticism of his stories. It did not help matters that Sullivan had been knighted by Queen Victoria in 1883, while Gilbert had not.

For four years Gilbert and Sullivan wrote no new operettas. Then D'Oyly Carte brought them together again, and they wrote *Utopia Limited* (1893) and *The Grand Duke* (1896), neither of which was very successful.

So ended this remarkable partnership between two men whose talents, unlike their personalities, were perfectly matched. Nobody has equaled Gilbert's skill at unexpected and amusing rhymes and rhythms. His stories, abounding in both sentiment and humor, still retain their charm.

Sullivan contributed a rare gift for melody and orchestration, but the wit in his music should not be overlooked. He loved to parody familiar musical styles, such as church music, Italian opera, or English madrigals. And in almost every opera, Sullivan inserted a number in which two melodies are cleverly combined. In *Patience*, for example, the ladies sing a sweet, slow song. Then some dashing cavalry officers sing a fast, spirited number. And before we know what has happened, both songs are going at the same time and fit together perfectly.

Sullivan died in London in 1900; Gilbert, who was finally knighted in 1907, died in 1911. The original D'Oyly Carte Opera Company gave its last performance in 1982 after more than a hundred years of operation as a troupe. But new productions of Gilbert and Sullivan operas are still being staged all around the world for enthusiastic audiences.

THOMAS W. PERRY
Boston College

GINSBURG, RUTH BADER. See SUPREME COURT OF THE UNITED STATES (Profiles).

In the paintings of Giotto, such as *Madonna Enthroned* (*above*) and the fresco *The Lamentation* (*right*), holy figures are portrayed realistically and show strong human emotions.

GIOTTO DI BONDONE (1267–1337)

The Italian painter Giotto di Bondone was the most important artist of the late Middle Ages. Unlike other artists of his day, he painted realistic figures whose faces and gestures show strong human emotions. Giotto's work looked forward to the painting styles of the Renaissance.

Very little is known about Giotto's early life. He was born about 1267 in a remote mountain village in Tuscany, Italy. He is believed to have studied art in Florence, probably with Cimabue, a leading Florentine artist. Giotto began to work on his own about 1300.

One of Giotto's earliest works was a large altarpiece painted for the Church of Ognissanti (All Saints) in Florence. It depicts the Virgin Mary seated on a throne and surrounded by saints and angels. The holy figures are painted in a way that was revolutionary for that time. In most paintings of the Middle Ages, figures appear flat and one-dimensional. Giotto's figures seem three-dimensional and almost real, with the solidity and weight of sculpture. Many people were amazed at Giotto's skill.

About 1305, Giotto was called to the town of Padua, near Venice. He was commissioned by one of Padua's wealthiest citizens to paint the inside of the Arena Chapel with a series of frescoes—wall paintings done on wet plaster —depicting the life of Christ and his parents.

Giotto's frescoes in the Arena Chapel are among the most important paintings in the history of Western art. Artists before Giotto had painted Christ as a superhuman figure, but Giotto showed the human side of Christ. In the frescoes, Christ experiences the same strong emotions of friendship, joy, fear, and sorrow felt by all of us. Giotto's skill at painting men and women who seem to be alive helped him tell his stories in an effective way. The Arena Chapel frescoes were imitated by many other artists and thus had a very strong influence on the development of Italian art.

About 1330, Giotto painted two chapels in the church of Santa Croce in Florence. In one of the chapels Giotto painted scenes from the life of St. Francis of Assisi. In the other he painted stories from the lives of St. John the Baptist and St. John the Evangelist.

In 1334, Giotto was placed in charge of the building of the Cathedral of Florence. He designed the bell tower (*campanile*) that stands beside the cathedral. He died in 1337, before the tower was completed.

BRUCE COLE
Author, *Giotto and Florentine Painting 1250–1375*

GIRAFFES

The giraffe is by far the tallest land animal in the world. Its legs are so long that a grown person can walk under a giraffe's body without ever bending over. The giraffe's neck is nearly 6 feet (2 meters) long. Surprisingly, it contains only seven bones—the same number as in the necks of human beings and most other mammals.

Fully grown male giraffes may reach a height of about 18 feet (5.5 meters). Females are a bit shorter at 15 feet (4.6 meters) tall. These tall animals are also quite heavy. The males weigh more than 2,600 pounds (1,180 kilograms), while the females weigh about 1,750 pounds (800 kilograms).

Giraffes are found only in Africa south of the Sahara. They live on the open plains, or savannah, where there are scattered trees and bushes on which they can feed. As a rule, giraffes are not found in extreme desert areas, in dense woods or jungles, or on mountains.

▶PHYSICAL DESCRIPTION

Nine kinds of giraffes live in different parts of central and southern Africa. Each has distinctive spotting. For example, the Masai type has spots with many jagged edges. The reticulate giraffe has evenly shaped blotches separated by narrow pale lines. All types of spotting act as camouflage. For example, when a giraffe is standing among the leaves and branches of trees, a lion may not notice it is there—especially if the lion is upwind and cannot smell the giraffe.

The spots of the giraffe cover all of its body except for its lower legs and upper head. Its hair is short, except for the hair in its long black tail, its brown mane, its eyelashes, and around its short horns.

Both male and female giraffes have horns. The horns are unlike those of cattle or deer because of their covering of skin. Under the skin, the horn is made of bone. The hairs around the horns are worn down in older males who hit each other with their horns during fights, called sparring matches. The females do not fight, so the hairs around their horns remain fairly long. For this reason, it is possible to tell the sex of an adult giraffe by looking at its horns.

Because of their long legs, giraffes are unable to trot, a movement that would cause their front and back legs to interfere with each other. Giraffes usually get around by walking, although they also can gallop. A galloping giraffe can reach speeds of up to 35 miles (56 kilometers) per hour.

▶ACTIVITIES

Giraffes feed on many kinds of trees and shrubs. They stretch up to high tree branches above them or reach down to low bushes. Many of the plants they feed on have thorns, but these do not bother giraffes. They gently pluck leaves, flowers, and fruits from among the thorns with their thick, mobile lips and long tongue. Like cattle, giraffes chew their cud while they rest after a meal.

Giraffes spend most of the day feeding, especially in the dry season when they must visit a large number of trees and bushes to obtain enough food. They also spend hours each day resting, either while standing or lying down.

To lie down, giraffes first go down onto their front legs—like a cow does—and then fold their hind legs down beside their body.

Tall enough to look into a second-floor window, the giraffe towers over all other land animals. It can feed on branches and treetops higher than other animals can reach.

When a giraffe finds water, its long legs and long neck make bending over to drink a bit of a challenge (*left*). Young giraffes stay close to their mother (*above*) who provides milk, helps protect them from such predators as lions and leopards and teaches them to find food.

To stand up, giraffes straighten their hind legs first and then their front legs. These are difficult movements for animals with very long legs. For this reason, young giraffes lie down more often than do older ones.

Giraffes are curious animals. If they see a person sitting under a tree, they may snort at it to see how it reacts. Females may also call to their calves with a gentle lowing sound (like that of a cow), but in general giraffes make few vocal noises.

In order to drink, giraffes stretch their front legs sideways or bend them so that they can reach the water with their mouth. They have an efficient circulatory system that enables the heart to push blood far up to the brain when the animal is standing upright. It also prevents a rapid increase in blood pressure at the brain when the giraffe lowers its head to drink or eat.

▶LIFE CYCLE

Giraffes mature when they are about 4 years old. A female, or cow, is able to mate every two weeks. A single calf is born after growing in its mother's body for 15 months. The newborn is as tall as a full-grown person and weighs about 110 pounds (50 kilograms). It can stand within an hour of birth and walk and suckle soon after. It has horns of soft cartilage that slowly turn to bone.

A young giraffe accompanies its mother for many months. The calf may join other young, but its mother is never very far away. Giraffe herds may consist of just a few animals or of a dozen or more, with individuals occasionally joining or leaving the group.

Large males, or bulls, wander about by themselves, meeting up with different groups of giraffes for a few days or weeks at a time. A male giraffe may roam an area of about 40 square miles (100 square kilometers). The range of females is somewhat smaller. The less food available, the greater the area giraffes must cover to survive.

The lion is the only nonhuman predator of adult giraffes, but even a lion may hesitate to attack a large male. Giraffes have been known to kill lions by kicking and trampling them to death.

Young giraffes are preyed on by lions, leopards, cheetahs, and crocodiles. A crocodile can grab the nose of a young giraffe as it leans down to drink and pull it into the water where it drowns. Many young die in their first year of life. Giraffes thrive in zoos, where they may live to be almost 30 years old. Few in the wild survive that long.

▶GIRAFFES AND PEOPLE

Although giraffes were once widely spread across the African plains, many have been killed off. In the past, hunters in Africa killed giraffes for food. Native people made shields, drums, whips, bracelets, and buckets out of their skin. They made sewing thread and guitar strings from the tendons of the giraffe's leg muscles and fly switches from the long tail. Today, some giraffes live on private game farms, but most live in national parks where they are protected from hunters.

ANNE INNIS DAGG
Co-author, *The Giraffe: Its Biology, Behavior and Ecology*

Girls Clubs provide opportunities for girls of all backgrounds and abilities to explore their interests. Members are encouraged to achieve their full potential in such areas as science, math, creative writing, photography, and career development.

GIRLS CLUBS

During the mid-1800's, many young American women moved from the country to the cities to find work in textile mills and factories. Away from their families for the first time, many were lonely and sometimes frightened. Girls clubs were formed to provide safe gathering places for these young women.

Since that time, the girls-clubs movement has grown and expanded its goals. More than 200 chapters of Girls Clubs of America serve over 250,000 members who are 6 to 18 years old. These girls, of all backgrounds and abilities, are helped and encouraged to achieve their full potential.

Girls Club Programs

The core program is called "Going Places." It focuses on six areas of activity: Careers and Life Planning; Health and Sexuality; Leadership and Community Action; Sports and Adventure; Self-Reliance and Life Skills; and Culture and Heritage. Programs within these areas include AIDS Education and Operation SMART (Science, Math, And Relevant Technology).

The programs are designed to help girls become responsible, confident adults and achieve economic independence and personal fulfillment. Peer counseling and leadership training are part of the programs. Members help in programs for younger members.

Annual awards are offered to local Girls Clubs for developing new programs. Individual members receive awards and scholarships for excellence in such areas as creative writing, photography, and career development.

The Organization of Girls Clubs

Girls Clubs are located in cities, suburbs, and rural areas. Some clubs are in specially designed centers that have swimming pools or gymnasiums. Others are in remodeled churches or houses. The clubs are open every day after school, in the evenings, on weekends, and all day in the summer. Many clubs offer day camp programs in the summer.

Each club has a professionally trained director and a trained staff. There are also adult volunteers who are concerned about the community and the girls who live there.

Girls Clubs of America is based in New York City. Four regional Service Centers support individual Girls Clubs. The National Resource Center in Indianapolis, Indiana, is a training and research facility and has the nation's largest source of information on girls' activities and interests.

History

The clubs that originally formed to help young working women expanded their activities. They began to offer programs for younger girls who had no place to play except the city streets. Some clubs had classes in cooking and sewing, provided homes for orphans, and established kindergartens and public playgrounds.

In 1945, representatives of 19 clubs united to form a national organization, the Girls Clubs of America. It takes a leading role in supporting the rights of girls of all backgrounds and abilities and in helping all girls become informed, creative, and active members of society.

GIRLS CLUBS OF AMERICA

Right: An adult leader stands with U.S. Girl Scouts from five age levels (*clockwise from upper left*)—Senior, Junior, Cadette, Brownie, and Daisy. *Above:* Three pins display Girl Scout insignia. The top pin shows the emblem of the World Association. The lower pins show contemporary and traditional emblems of the Girl Scouts of the United States.

GIRL SCOUTS

Girl Scouts of the United States of America (GSUSA) is the largest voluntary organization for girls in the world. Its 3,000,000 members participate in programs that encourage self-discovery through activities in the outdoors, science, the arts, and with other people. Girl Scouts have fun, make new friends, and acquire new skills. They develop self-confidence and understanding of themselves and others.

Girl Scouts of the U.S.A. is part of the World Organization of Girl Guides and Girl Scouts, which is composed of national organizations in 112 countries. Through the World Association, more than 8,000,000 girls around the world are linked together.

Wherever they are, Girl Scouts and Guides are united by a spiritual and moral code, called the Girl Scout Promise and Law. This code has been adapted to every country where a Girl Scout or Girl Guide movement exists. In the United States, it reads as follows:

THE GIRL SCOUT PROMISE

On my honor, I will try:
To serve God and my country,
To help people at all times,
And to live by the Girl Scout Law.

THE GIRL SCOUT LAW

I will do my best:
—to be honest
—to be fair
—to help where I am needed
—to be cheerful
—to be friendly and considerate
—to be a sister to every Girl Scout
—to respect authority
—to use resources wisely
—to protect and improve the world around me
—to show respect for myself and others
        through my words and actions

▶MEMBERSHIP AND ORGANIZATION

Each Girl Scout belongs to a small group that is sometimes called a troop. Girls can also take part in programs and activities individually under the guidance of an adult adviser. Interested adult volunteers and leaders encourage the Scouts to try a wide variety of projects and activities. As the girls work together, they learn to be both members and leaders in group activities.

Girl Scout activities are financed through membership dues and through various projects and sales. The national organization is supported by donations, membership dues, and by sales of equipment.

Girl Scouts are ages 5 through 17 or are in kindergarten through grade 12. They are grouped in five levels according to age or grade. Each group has its own mix-and-match uniform—a set of co-ordinated articles of clothing. This allows a girl to choose how she would like to look and still be in uniform. All U.S. Girl Scouts wear a badge showing three girls' faces silhouetted on a trefoil (a three-leaved design resembling a cloverleaf).

The Five Levels of Girl Scouting

Daisy Girl Scouts. This group is for girls who are 5 and 6 years old or who are in kindergarten or first grade. They participate in small service projects such as planting flowers and caring for pets. They keep a scrapbook of their yearly activities and are awarded a certificate at the end of the year. Daisy Girl Scouts

Scouting means getting involved in many activities. Here, Daisy Scouts (*above*) make bird feeders. Brownies (*left*) water a garden. And Junior Girl Scouts (*right*) lend a hand in a community recycling drive. Activities like these are intended to help Girl Scouts develop skills and values as they have fun.

wear a blue tunic over their regular clothing. The group was named for Juliette Gordon Low, founder of Girl Scouts of the U.S.A., whose childhood nickname was Daisy.

Brownie Girl Scouts. These girls are age 6 through 8 or are in first, second, or third grade. Their activities help them see themselves as part of their community, to learn about themselves and about people and things in the world around them. The *Brownie Girl Scout Handbook* introduces activities in each of the five worlds of interest. By completing certain groups of activities, the Scout earns a patch to wear on her brown uniform.

Junior Girl Scouts. These girls are age 8 through 11 or are in third through sixth grade. *The Junior Girl Scout Handbook* has many activities through which the Scout can earn badges and signs, which she wears on her uniform sash. These activities include horseback riding, working with computers, and cooking. Other badges may be earned in subjects such as leadership, communication, service to society, healthy living, and technology. Junior Girl Scouts wear green uniforms.

Cadette and Senior Girl Scouts. Cadette Girl Scouts are 11 through 14 years old or in grades six through nine. Senior Girl Scouts are 14 through 17 years old or are in grades nine through twelve. These Scouts are introduced to exciting new challenges to develop and test their leadership skills, to explore careers, to travel, and to find themselves and their place in the world around them. *The Cadette and Senior Girl Scout Handbook* includes sections on how to keep fit and healthy, managing time and money, family relationships, dating, and dealing with peer pressure. It also has Leader-

Outdoor activities have always been an important part of Scouting. *Above:* Scouts gather in a friendship circle at a Girl Scout camp. *Right:* On overnight camping trips, the Scouts help plan the trip and bring their own gear.

In-Training and Counselor-In-Training projects and ways to plan for the future and careers. This handbook is used to help girls complete activities in its companion book, the *Cadette and Senior Girl Scout Interest Projects.* Working on interest projects is one of the ways Scouts have fun, expand friendships, increase their skills and knowledge, and give service to the community. Cadette and Senior Girl Scouts wear blue uniforms.

Girl Scout Programs

Girl Scout activities are in five categories, or Worlds—the World of Well-Being, the World of People, the World of Today and Tomorrow, the World of the Arts, and the World of the Out-of-Doors. A Scout may choose the program that interests her.

The World of Well-Being has activities related to physical and emotional health, nutrition, living with others, the home, safety, consumer awareness, and similar topics.

In the World of People, a girl learns concern for community needs. She is encouraged to develop awareness of the various cultures in her society and around the world. She develops pride in her own heritage.

The World of Today and Tomorrow introduces girls to the metric system, carpentry, scientific experiments, and to ideas about their future as working women.

The World of the Arts includes activities in the visual, performing, and literary arts. These activities help a girl develop appreciation of the many art forms and things of beauty in the world around her and also develop her own personal tastes. She learns to express herself through these arts.

The World of the Out-of-Doors expands traditional Girl Scout activities involving camping, nature, and conservation. There is an emphasis on ecology and understanding the environment.

The Girl Scout organization publishes a series of booklets on contemporary issues. The series complements other Girl Scout program materials. The booklets help adults present activities that enhance the girls' self-esteem as they learn skills that include communication, problem solving, stress management, personal safety, and family living.

Camping

For most girls, camping trips, cookouts, and the chance to be out-of-doors with girls their own age are among the most exciting things about being a Girl Scout. When Girl Scouting was started, it was rare for females to go camping—but Girl Scouts did. In 1921 they pioneered in organized camping.

Today there are more than 400 Girl Scout resident camps and other outdoor facilities around the country. In addition, almost 400,000 day campers—nonmembers as well as Girl Scouts—participate in Girl Scout day camps and other facilities.

Girl Scouts do three kinds of camping—day, resident, and troop or small-group camping. All three provide fun, adventure, appreciation of the outdoors, and a chance to learn to get along with others in a new setting.

At day camp, girls of different backgrounds and ages come together at a site in their community and return home in the evening. Day camps are usually located within easy reach of their homes. Teenage Girl Scouts often conduct day camp sessions during the summer for younger girls and boys in the community.

A resident camp is a live-in camp, where girls share tents or cabins with other girls for stays of a week or more. At resident camps, girls can enjoy a wide variety of activities, such as swimming, backpacking, hiking, canoe trips, camp crafts, competitive sports, and bicycle trips. Some camps feature petting zoos and horses. Others have sailing, snorkeling, or other waterfront activities.

When girls go troop or small-group camping, they plan together with their leader and are responsible for bringing their own gear—bedrolls, food, cooking utensils, and other equipment they may need.

A Girl Scout group may plan everything from overnight or weekend camping to trips that take them abroad, particularly into Canada or to Our Cabaña, the world center at Cuernavaca, Mexico. Traveling groups often visit the Girl Scout national centers—Juliette Gordon Low Girl Scout National Center in Savannah, Georgia, and Girl Scout National Center West in Wyoming—or national parks. They may also visit the Edith Macy Conference Center in Briarcliff Manor, New York, where they camp in the John J. Creedon Camp of Tomorrow. This camp serves as a training and testing site for many new concepts and

Cadette and Senior Girl Scouts wear blue uniforms. At this age level, Scouting activities help girls explore careers and plan for the future.

equipment that will be used in outdoor education throughout the country. Adult Girl Scouts also go to the Camp of Tomorrow, where they learn outdoor skills to teach the members of their home councils and troops.

Wider Opportunities

Each year, many teenage girls travel beyond their own communities to attend events called Wider Opportunities. These events are sponsored by the national Girl Scout organization or by local Girl Scout councils and are held at camps, college campuses, and other sites throughout the United States. They include workshops in such subjects as music, art, aeronautics, human relations, ecology, competitive sports, dance, theater, communications, and oceanography. Girls also work with disabled children and in community action projects.

In 1968, Girl Scouts of the U.S.A. acquired 15,000 acres (6,000 hectares) of primitive land in Wyoming's Big Horn basin. This land became Girl Scout National Center West. Since then, thousands of girls each summer have participated in the "Wyoming Trek"—from one to two weeks of primitive camping.

BROWNIE AND JUNIOR PROFICIENCY BADGES

Brownie Try-Its

Science Magic

Sports and Games

Dabbler Badges

People

Arts

Well-Being

Today and Tomorrow

Outdoors

Proficiency Badges

Wider Opportunities

Group Sports

Food, Fibers, and Farming

Science in Action

Healthy Eating

Architecture

Troop Camper

Community Health & Safety

Theater

Traveler

Girl Scouting Everywhere

Swimming

Communication Arts

My Community

Pet Care

Water Wonders

Horseback Riding

Program consultants from all over the United States are on hand at Center West to help girls enjoy such activities as archaeological digging, backpacking, horseback riding, fishing, hiking, and studies in ecology, geology, and Indian lore.

Teenage Girl Scouts also may be selected to take advantage of international travel opportunities. The girls visit the world centers, attend jamborees, or visit families abroad. They share experiences with Girl Scouts and Guides of other countries.

Wider Opportunities give girls the chance to meet and know people who may think and act differently from themselves. Through this program, they become aware of some of the problems facing the world today. The hope is that perhaps one day they can help to solve some of these problems.

▶ GIRL GUIDES OF CANADA

Girl Guides in Canada share many of the goals and activities of Girl Scouts and Girl Guides worldwide. Canadian Girl Guides are divided into groups by age—Sparks, age 5; Brownies, ages 6 to 9; Guides, ages 9 to 12; Pathfinders, ages 12 to 15; and the Senior Branches. This last group consists of Junior Leaders, ages 15 to 17; Cadets, ages 15 and older; and Rangers, ages 15 to 17. Junior Leaders volunteer their time to work with the younger groups. Cadets participate in a two-year leadership training program. Rangers plan and carry out projects that emphasize their development at home, in the community, and on camping trips. Cadets and Rangers take part in international Girl Guides events.

The Girl Guides of Canada offers a program for girls who cannot attend regular meetings because they live in remote areas or have physical disabilities. These girls are known as Lones. They participate through the mail in the regular program for their age level.

▶ HISTORY

When Robert Baden-Powell founded the Scouting movement in England in 1908, it was intended for boys. But from the beginning, girls were determined to be included. In 1909, at the time of a large Boy Scout rally in the Crystal Palace in London, a number of eager girls showed up at the rally, calling themselves ''Girl Scouts'' and clamoring to join.

Baden-Powell recognized the need for an organization for girls. But he thought that they should have a program designed especially for their needs. He asked his sister, Agnes Baden-Powell, to help organize the Girl Guides. Thus, from the earliest days, the Boy Scouts and the Girl Scouts and Girl Guides have been two separate and independent organizations.

British girls did not keep Guiding to themselves for long. The idea spread rapidly, traveling to such distant places as Australia, Canada, and South Africa. Girl Guide groups were also established in several European countries.

CADETTE AND SENIOR INTEREST PATCHES

Dabbler Patches

People   Arts   Well-Being   Today and Tomorrow   Outdoors

Interest Patches

Travel   Audiovisual Production (basic)   Leadership   Tune in to Well-Being   Creative Writing   Entrepreneurship   Global Understanding   Pets

Emergency Preparedness   Camping   The Law   Audiovisual Production (advanced)   Invitation to the Dance   Fashion Design and Clothing   Child Care   Women's History   Music   Computers

In 1912, Juliette Gordon Low started the first group in Savannah, Georgia, with 18 girls. In the next ten years many new troops were organized, and membership grew to 50,000. The name was changed to Girl Scouts of the United States of America.

Girl Scouting differs from country to country, just as people and customs differ. But it developed in each country as a nonpolitical movement emphasizing belief in a supreme being, devotion to country, service to others, and love of the outdoors.

▶ THE WORLD ASSOCIATION

In 1919, Girl Scouting became truly international with the formation of the International Council. A year later, the first international conference was held. The World Association of Girl Guides and Girl Scouts (WAGGGS) came into being in 1928, with organizations from 28 countries as founding members.

The World Association is administered through the World Bureau in London, England. The World Association holds world conferences every three years. It also sponsors world camps and study groups for girls and leaders of member countries.

The association maintains four world centers, where members of all nationalities may stay—to work and play together and learn about one another's homes, customs, and lives. Each center has its own character, which influences the activities held there. Activities include special sightseeing expeditions and classes where members can learn about the culture of the area.

Our Chalet, near Adelboden, Switzerland, was the first world center, opened in 1932. There Scouts can ski, hike, or take part in mountain-climbing expeditions.

Our Cabaña, in Cuernavaca, Mexico, has a well-equipped crafts room and a swimming pool. The center holds study sessions on the crafts and history of Mexico. Sangam, newest of the four world centers, is situated at Poona in Maharashtra state, India. In Sanskrit, *sangam* means "going together." This center offers Girl Scouts and Girl Guides an opportunity to study arts and crafts of India.

Pax House is a program and training center in London, England. While taking part in programs and training there, girls can enjoy the nearby art galleries, museums, theaters, and other cultural attractions.

The World Association emblem—a gold trefoil (cloverleaf design) on a bright blue field—symbolizes the three parts of the promise. It is used on the World Association flag and the world badge.

THE GIRL SCOUTS OF AMERICA

GISH, LILLIAN. See MOTION PICTURES (Profiles: Movie Stars).

GLACIER NATIONAL PARK

Glacier National Park, located on the border between Montana and Canada, is a wild and beautiful area in the heart of the Rocky Mountains. The park covers more than 1 million acres (404,680 hectares) of glacial valleys, clear blue lakes, and lofty mountains. Its highest peak, Mount Cleveland, rises 10,466 feet (3,190 meters) above sea level.

Every year, nearly 2 million people visit Glacier National Park. Many arrive by train, while others drive the spectacular Going-to-the-Sun Road through the park into Canada. To really see the natural features, however, most visitors hike along the park's 730 miles

Glacier National Park is one of the most popular vacation spots in the United States. St. Mary's Lake, pictured above, is just one of its many attractions.

(1,175 kilometers) of trails. Boating, fishing, and cycling are permitted, and visitors may stay at eight different campgrounds.

Natural Features. Glacier National Park takes its name from the glacial movement that formed many of the region's natural features. During the Ice Age, glaciers carved U-shaped valleys out of streambeds and canyons, eroded mountainsides to create cliffs, and formed lakes in the valleys. The park still contains numerous glaciers that are fed by heavy snowfall. The rivers and streams in the park are clear and cold.

Much of Glacier National Park is rich in plant and animal life. Because of the changes in elevation from mountains to valleys, vegetation varies considerably. Trees range from fir and lodgepole pine on the western side to red cedar and hemlock in the southeastern part of the park. Large animals include bears, deer, elk, goats, moose, and wolves. Indeed, Glacier is one of the few remaining areas in the continental United States with significant grizzly bear activity. Among the smaller animals are marmots and beavers. Birds include eagles, hawks, and woodpeckers.

History. For many centuries, Native Americans, notably the Blackfoot tribe, hunted wild animals such as buffalo in the region. In the 1700's, European trappers came to hunt beaver and other fur-bearing animals. Then in the late 1800's, surveyors for the Great Northern Railroad found a route through the mountains at Marias Pass. Settlement expanded after the railroads were built. As a result, conservationists such as Kootenai Brown in Canada and George Bird Grinnell in the United States encouraged their governments to set aside some of this area to preserve the wildlife and the natural conditions. In 1895 the Canadians established Waterton Lakes National Park. The U.S. Congress established Glacier National Park on May 11, 1910.

The northern boundary of Glacier National Park is also the southern boundary for Canada's Waterton Lakes National Park. In 1932 the two nations came together to establish Waterton-Glacier International Peace Park, the world's first international park dedicated to peace between nations. Although each park is separately administered by its own nation, Glacier/Waterton has special status as the first International Biosphere Reserve in the world. The two parks coordinate efforts to protect ecological diversity, to guard against stress on the environment caused by increasing numbers of visitors, and to serve as a model of the positive relationship that exists between the American and Canadian people.

WILLIAM R. LOWRY
Washington University

GLACIERS

In 1840 the scientist Louis Agassiz put forward a startling idea. After studying the glaciers in his native Switzerland, he concluded that vast sheets of ice—like the Swiss glaciers but far larger—once covered much of northern Europe and helped carve the landscape there.

Agassiz was not the first scientist to suppose that the glaciers had once been larger. But he was the first to prove that glaciers actually moved across the land, carrying rock and shaping the earth. Moreover, he found that the ridges, boulders, and other features left behind by known glaciers were just like features found in areas far from the ice—evidence that these areas, too, had once been ice-covered.

Since the time of Agassiz, scientists have learned a great deal about glaciers and their effects. And the idea of ice ages—times in the distant past when great blankets of ice stretched not only across northern Europe but across much of North America and other areas—is widely accepted today.

▶ HOW GLACIERS FORM

A glacier is a huge mass of ice, so thick that it moves under the pressure of its own weight and the force of gravity. Glaciers can develop wherever the amount of snow falling in winter is greater than the amount that melts in summer. As snow builds up over many years, the lowest layers are compressed by the layers above. They slowly change, first to a dense material called **firn** and eventually to ice.

This change to ice takes place very slowly in regions where it is cold all year and the snow rarely melts. At the South Pole, for example, snow does not turn to ice until it has been buried for several hundred years and is at a depth of about 300 feet (90 meters). Ice forms somewhat more quickly in areas where there is some melting during the warm months. This is because **meltwater** (water from melted snow) trickles down to the lower layers, where it freezes into ice.

Eventually the ice becomes so thick and heavy that it begins to move downhill under the force of gravity. It can do this because, under pressure, ice is not a rigid solid like steel. It can flow, or **creep**—but very slowly. (This type of movement is sometimes called **plastic flow**.) When the mass of ice is thick enough to flow, it is called a glacier.

Most glaciers move very slowly. New ice is constantly formed at the glacier's origin, or accumulation basin. But the leading edge (or

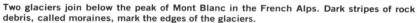

Two glaciers join below the peak of Mont Blanc in the French Alps. Dark stripes of rock debris, called moraines, mark the edges of the glaciers.

snout) of the glacier slowly moves into warmer regions where it may begin to melt. Or it may reach the sea and **calve** (break off), forming icebergs.

If the amount of ice lost through melting and calving is equal to the amount of new ice that forms, the glacier will remain the same size for many years. The position of the snout will change only gradually, advancing if the climate grows colder or retreating if the climate grows warmer. But there are a few glaciers that periodically surge. Every ten or twenty years, the glacier moves forward very quickly for a year or two, perhaps advancing several miles. Then the snout melts back to its previous location.

As a glacier slowly moves across land, it picks up rocks and dirt and carries these materials along. A glacier can actually break rock and reshape the land through the tremendous pressure of its ice, the effects of freezing and thawing, and the grinding action of the debris it carries. Where a glacier flows over rough or very steep terrain, huge cracks called **crevasses** may open in the ice. Some of these cracks may be 100 feet (30 meters) deep or more.

▶TYPES OF GLACIERS

Glaciers can be classified in various ways. Usually, however, they are grouped according to their size and shape into three basic types: valley glaciers, ice caps, and ice sheets.

Valley Glaciers

There are valley glaciers in many parts of the world—even near the equator, in the high mountains of South America, East Africa, and New Guinea. Valley glaciers begin when snow builds up in hollows high in the mountains. As the name suggests, they flow down valleys to warmer regions, where the melting is much greater. Over many years, these rivers of ice may carve the mountain hollows into round bowls called **cirques** (or **corries**) and reshape the valleys through which they flow.

Because they quickly reach warm areas as they travel down the mountains, most equatorial glaciers are short—usually only a mile or two (under 3 kilometers) long. Valley glaciers in the western United States are also quite small. Most of these are in the Rocky, Cascade, and Olympic mountain ranges. Farther north, in the Canadian Rockies and in Alaska, the valley glaciers are much larger. Many extend down to the sea, so that they are often called **tidewater glaciers**.

A VALLEY GLACIER

Valley glaciers form in high mountain hollows, where ice carves the rock into round bowls called cirques. As the glacier flows downhill, rock debris is carried along, forming moraines. Deep crevasses develop over steep terrain. Piles of debris and pools and streams of meltwater mark the glacier's snout, or end.

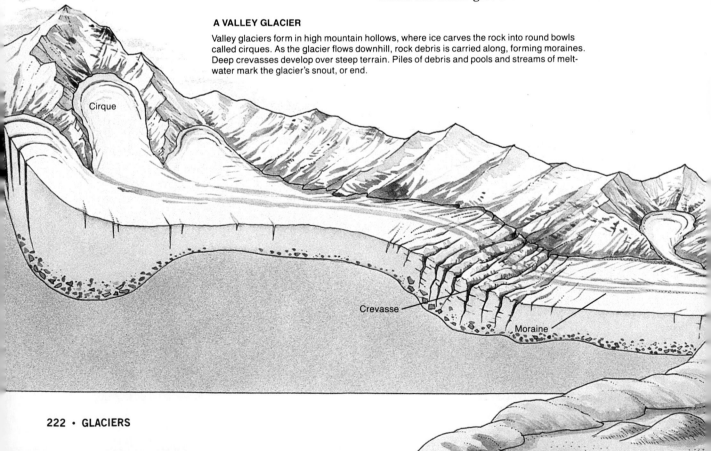

The biggest valley glaciers in North America include the Malaspina and Columbia glaciers, both in southern Alaska. (Large glaciers form less readily in northern Alaska, where the temperatures are lower but the annual snowfall is less.) The Columbia Glacier has a total area of about 400 square miles (more than 1,000 square kilometers). The lowest 15 miles (24 kilometers) form a **tongue** that extends into Columbia Bay. This tongue formerly ended on an offshore bank of sand and gravel that had been carried down to the sea and deposited by the glacier itself. But in recent years, the amount of melting has increased, and the tongue has receded so that it is no longer pinned on the gravel bank but floats in the water of the bay. It breaks off easily into icebergs and is expected to keep receding until the snout of the glacier is on land.

The Malaspina Glacier is confined to a relatively narrow valley in the coastal mountains for much of its length. The glacier then flows out onto a level coastal plain where the ice spreads into a flat lobe about 20 miles (32 kilometers) wide. This part of the ice is called a **piedmont glacier**. (The term "piedmont" comes from French words meaning "foot of the mountain.")

Even larger valley glaciers are found in the Himalayas. Many are more than 50 miles (80 kilometers) long. There are also large valley glaciers in the Alps, in Scandinavia, in the Caucasus and Ural mountains (between Europe and Asia), and in New Zealand.

Ice Caps and Ice Sheets

When a glacier covers a high mountain plateau and pushes out in all directions, it is called an ice cap. And when an ice cap grows to cover vast areas of land, it is called an ice

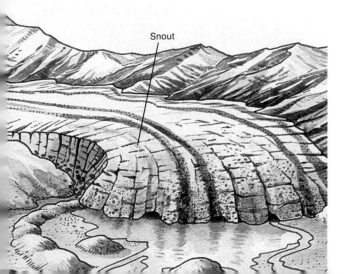

The tips of tall mountains poke through the vast Antarctic Ice Sheet. Altogether, the ice covers an area half again as large as the United States.

sheet. There are two continental ice sheets. One covers more than 80 percent of Greenland, and the other covers about 97 percent of Antarctica.

The Greenland Ice Sheet is about 700,000 square miles (1.8 million square kilometers) in area—almost three times the size of Texas. About half of the edge of the ice sheet ends on land, and in these places there is quite a lot of melting each summer. Around the rest of the ice sheet, the ice flows all the way to the sea, forming **outlet glaciers** where it pushes through the coastal mountains. One of these, the Jacobshavn Glacier, is the fastest known glacier—it moves up to 4 miles (more than 6 kilometers) a year and forms great numbers of icebergs as it calves into the sea.

In places the Greenland Ice Sheet is almost 2 miles (about 3 kilometers) thick. The top surface rises to an elevation of about 9,000 feet (almost 3,000 meters) above sea level. But the bottom surface rests on ground that is close to sea level—and well below sea level in some places. The areas where the land is lowest and the ice is thickest are in the middle of Greenland. Before the ice sheet formed, the middle of Greenland was a plateau about 2,000 feet (600 meters) above sea level. But the tremendous weight of the ice has depressed the crust of the earth. This process is called **isostatic adjustment**. If the ice were removed, the land would rise (quickly at first, and then more slowly) until it reached its previous position.

The Antarctic Ice Sheet is even larger than the Greenland Ice Sheet. Altogether, the ice that covers nearly all of the continent, flows through the mountains at its edges, and extends into the surrounding seas has an area of nearly 5.4 million square miles (14 million square kilometers)—half again as large as the United States. In it is locked up nearly 70 percent of all the fresh water on earth. In places the ice is about 2 miles (3 kilometers) thick. Because extremely low temperatures prevent melting, ice has built up even in areas where the annual snowfall is very small.

The Antarctic Ice Sheet is more complicated than the Greenland Ice Sheet. It is actually two ice sheets—an eastern sheet and a western sheet—separated by the Transantarctic Mountains, which extend across the continent. The eastern ice sheet, which is the larger, faces the Indian and Atlantic oceans. Under it are mountains and deep troughs.

In the western ice sheet (which faces the Pacific Ocean) the bottom of the ice is well below sea level in many places. Even if the ice were removed and the land were to rise, much of it would still be below sea level. Scientists think that this part of the ice sheet formed over an area of shallow seas and islands; thus it is sometimes called a **marine ice sheet**.

The Antarctic Ice Sheet's outlet glaciers include the steep and heavily crevassed Beardmore Glacier, one of the world's longest outlet glaciers. Where the ice sheet extends into the sea, it forms huge **ice shelves**. The largest of these, the Ross Ice Shelf, is as big as France. Enormous icebergs break off the ice shelves. One that was spotted in 1987 was bigger than the state of Rhode Island.

▶ GLACIERS AND THE ICE AGES

Since the idea of ice ages was first put forward in the 1800's, scientists have learned much about the past climate of the world. In the Greenland and Antarctic ice sheets, they have drilled deep holes and drawn out cores of ice formed long ago. From these samples and from cores of sediment taken in similar ways from the ocean floor, as well as from evidence on land, they have learned that huge ice sheets covered large areas of land at several times in

Near the snout of a glacier, meltwater carves eerie channels and caves in the ice. Meltwater from glaciers feeds cold mountain streams and lakes.

the earth's history. Each of these ice ages included **glacial periods**, in which the ice sheets advanced, and **interglacial periods**, in which the ice melted and drew back.

In the past three million years, there have been four glacial periods, each followed by an interglacial period. The most recent glacial period began about 75,000 years ago. Ice sheets covered much of northern Europe and northeastern Siberia. Southern Alaska, western Canada, and the northwestern parts of the continental United States were covered by the Cordilleran Ice Sheet. Another glacier, the Laurentide Ice Sheet, covered much of Canada east of the Rockies and extended south to the Ohio River in the United States.

The Laurentide Ice Sheet reached its largest size about 17,000 years ago, and its thickest part was over what is now Hudson Bay. There the ice sheet depressed the earth's crust, as the Greenland Ice Sheet does today. The ice began to retreat 10,000 to 11,000 years ago, and 8,000 years ago all the ice was gone from the Hudson Bay area. But the land in this area is still rising very slowly—a few inches in a century.

The enormous ice sheets of the past had many other effects. As they moved back and forth, they eroded the land and left deposits of rock and dirt—material known as **glacial till**. In places the glacial till was piled into ridges called **moraines** and mounds called **drumlins**. Glaciers also carved out valleys and carried huge boulders hundreds of miles from their places of origin. At times, so much of the earth's moisture was frozen in ice sheets that sea levels were much lower than they are today. Between Siberia and Alaska, the seafloor was exposed, so that a bridge of land connected North America to Asia.

We live in an interglacial period. Scientists do not know if—or when—this period will end and ice sheets will again advance. But in recent years, there has been more concern about another trend: For the past hundred years or so, the worldwide average temperature has grown steadily warmer.

Many scientists have traced this warming to a buildup of carbon dioxide, methane, and other gases in the earth's atmosphere. (Many of these gases are produced by human activities, such as burning gasoline and other fossil fuels.) When these gases build up high in the atmosphere, they produce what is called the **greenhouse effect**—that is, they trap the sun's heat much as the glass of a greenhouse does.

If the warming trend continues, the temperatures may rise enough to melt the great ice sheets of the world. This could cause sea levels to rise by perhaps 200 feet (60 meters), changing the world's coastlines and drowning many large cities. If only the western part of the Antarctic Ice Sheet melted, sea levels could rise some 20 feet (6 meters), enough to flood many coastal cities.

COLIN BULL
Formerly, The Ohio State University

See also ICE; ICE AGES.

GLADSTONE, WILLIAM EWART (1809–1898)

William E. Gladstone, one of Great Britain's most famous prime ministers, was born on December 29, 1809, in Liverpool, England. After graduating from Oxford University in 1831, young Gladstone thought of becoming a clergyman. But at his father's suggestion he entered politics. In 1832 he was elected to Parliament. He served almost continuously in the House of Commons for the next 63 years. Gladstone married Catherine Glynne in 1839. They had eight children.

Gladstone began his political career as a Tory, or Conservative, in the cabinet of Prime Minister Sir Robert Peel (1788–1850). After Peel died, Gladstone became a leader of the Peelites, as Peel's followers were called. In 1852 the Whigs (opponents of the Tories) formed a joint government with the Peelites, who had broken with the regular Tories. Gladstone became chancellor of the exchequer, an office he held twice. He stood out as a brilliant orator as well as an expert on finance. Gradually the Whigs were transformed into the Liberal Party. In 1867, Gladstone became leader of the party. When the Liberals won the election in 1868, he became prime minister.

In all, Gladstone served four times as prime minister. He was a man of strong moral convictions, and it was said that he acted like a clergyman as well as a politician. His name is associated with many reforms that helped make the British government more democratic and efficient. He extended the right to vote to workers left out of an earlier Tory reform bill and helped bring about church and land reforms in Ireland. He also did much to improve the civil service and the Army. He established an elementary school system open to all children. His great political opponent was Benjamin Disraeli, the Tory leader and prime minister.

Gladstone's greatest struggle in Parliament was for a law that would give home rule to Ireland. Twice he introduced an Irish Home Rule bill, and twice it was defeated. He did succeed in making it more difficult for British landlords to evict their Irish tenants, and he reduced the power of the Anglican Church in Ireland. The second defeat of the Irish Home Rule bill was in 1893. Gladstone resigned as prime minister the next year and retired in 1895. He died on May 19, 1898, and was buried in Westminster Abbey.

Reviewed by DAVID C. LARGE
University of Reading (England)

See also DISRAELI, BENJAMIN.

GLANDS

What do crying, eating dinner, and climbing a rope have in common? They all involve the work of glands—specialized tissues or organs that produce, or secrete, various chemicals. Some of these chemicals help in body functions such as digesting food, keeping the eyes and skin from drying out, and flushing dust and soot from the breathing passages. Other chemicals, called **hormones**, work with the nerves to control and co-ordinate body functions. Hormones help keep the blood flowing and determine whether foods are used for energy or stored as starch or fat. They help us grow and develop and have children.

Other animals have glands, too. These include some glands that people do not have. Glands in shrimp and lobsters produce chemicals that control molting (the shedding of the animal's shell and the production of a new shell). Insects have molting chemicals, too, as well as glands that control metamorphosis (the change from an immature form, such as a caterpillar, to a mature form, such as a butterfly). In some snakes, venom glands secrete a poison that the snake can inject with its bite. Even plants have glands. Glands in flowers, for example, produce sugary nectar.

Humans have two main kinds of glands: exocrine glands and endocrine glands.

▶ **EXOCRINE GLANDS**

Exocrine glands secrete their chemicals through tiny tubes (or **ducts**) that lead directly to the place where they will be used.

Goblet Cells. When you have a cold, your nose may be filled with a thick liquid called **mucus**. You feel uncomfortable. But by producing mucus, glands in the lining of your nose are actually helping to get rid of germs and other harmful materials. Each of these glands consists of just a single cell, called a goblet cell because it is shaped like a wineglass.

Goblet cells are found in the linings of the breathing passages, the digestive system, and the urinary and reproductive passages. They help keep these delicate linings smooth and moist. In the breathing tubes, the flow of mucus carries out dust, smoke, bacteria, and other particles that we breathe in. (Some mucus is always being secreted, but the amount increases when you have a cold.) The mucus in the stomach forms a protective barrier against stomach acid.

Tear Glands. Exocrine glands may be simple, one-celled structures such as the goblet cells, or they may be more complex. Tears, for example, are secreted by almond-shaped structures, the tear glands (or **lacrimal** glands), just above the outer corners of the eyes. Tears are not just water. They contain salts, proteins, and even a special bacteria-killing chemical.

Tears may spill out of your eyes when you are very happy or sad. They are produced in small amounts all the time, however. Each time you blink, you squeeze some tears out of the tear glands into tiny tear ducts on the underside of your eyelids. The eyelids spread these watery secretions over the surface of the eye. Tears protect the eyes from drying out and wash away dust and other tiny particles. Then the tears drain down into the nose.

Glands of the Skin. Two kinds of exocrine glands are found in the skin. **Sebaceous glands** (or oil glands) empty into the tubes from which hairs grow. Their oily secretions help keep the skin moist and smooth. **Sweat glands** secrete a watery fluid containing salts and various body wastes. Sweat flows through ducts to openings (or **pores**) in the skin surface, where it evaporates. Water carries away heat when it evaporates, so sweating helps cool the body in addition to getting rid of wastes.

There are two kinds of sweat glands. **Eccrine** sweat glands produce quite watery secretions. They work harder when it is hot and when you exercise or are frightened or upset. The increase in sweating is caused by messages from nerves and by hormones produced in endocrine glands. Eccrine sweat moistens the palms of your hands and the soles of your feet and helps them grip better. (This is how exocrine glands help you climb a rope.) **Apocrine** sweat glands secrete a thicker, sticky fluid containing various chemicals. These chemicals send out scent messages about emotions and body cycles. Apocrine sweat is the main source of body odor.

Digestive Glands. A number of exocrine glands help in digestion. When you smell food (or even think about eating), your mouth begins to water. Three pairs of **salivary glands** are pouring their secretion, saliva, into your mouth. The **parotid** glands are the largest and are located just in front of the ears. Their ducts empty into the mouth in the upper jaw. The **submaxillary** glands in the lower jaw have ducts that open just behind the lower front teeth. The ducts of the **sublingual** glands open under the tongue. Saliva contains enzymes that help digest starch.

In the stomach, glands produce hydrochloric acid, enzymes, and other digestive juices that help digest protein and fat. Many enzymes work in the small intestine to digest starches, proteins, and fat. Some of these are produced in the intestine, but others are formed in an organ called the **pancreas** and flow through ducts to the intestine. Glands in the liver produce **bile**, which flows to the small intestine and helps break up fats.

Mammary Glands. In women, the mammary glands in the breasts produce milk, a special secretion to nourish a baby. The milk flows through ducts to the nipples. Milk production is controlled by hormones, and it takes place only following the birth of a baby.

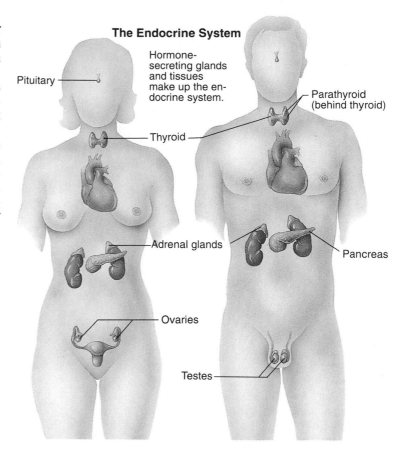

The Endocrine System

Hormone-secreting glands and tissues make up the endocrine system.

Pituitary

Thyroid

Parathyroid (behind thyroid)

Adrenal glands

Pancreas

Ovaries

Testes

▶ENDOCRINE GLANDS

Endocrine glands are ductless glands. They secrete their chemicals, the hormones, into the bloodstream. The bloodstream carries the secretions to where they will do their work.

The endocrine glands are found in various parts of the body. They are not connected, but they work together closely. The hormones of one endocrine gland may act on other endocrine glands and on exocrine glands, causing them to start or stop producing their own secretions. The endocrine glands also work with the nervous system to control many body functions. Together, these glands form what is sometimes called the **endocrine system**.

The Pituitary Gland. The pituitary gland is a pea-sized gland at the base of the brain. Its secretions help control the other endocrine glands and their effects on major body functions. Pituitary **growth hormone** controls the growth of the body. Other pituitary hormones stimulate the secretion of hormones by the thyroid gland, the adrenal cortex, and the sex glands. Pituitary hormones also stimulate the

production of milk and help prepare the body for pregnancy.

The Hypothalamus. The hypothalamus is the part of the brain that contains many important control centers for the nervous system. The hypothalamus produces hormones that start or stop the production of hormones by other endocrine glands. For each of the pituitary hormones, it produces a **releasing hormone** that turns on the secretion and an **inhibitory hormone** that stops the secretion.

The hypothalamus also produces two hormones that are stored in the pituitary gland and released as they are needed. **Vasopressin** raises the blood pressure and increases the amount of water retained by the body. **Oxytocin** makes the uterus contract when a baby is born and then stimulates milk production.

The Thyroid Gland. The thyroid gland is located in the neck. Its hormones act on all parts of the body. They regulate the rate at which body cells burn food for energy. One thyroid hormone helps control the amount of calcium in the blood. It works together with the tiny **parathyroid glands**, which are found inside the thyroid gland.

The Adrenal Glands. An adrenal gland sits like a cap on top of each kidney. Each adrenal gland has two parts. The outer layer, the **adrenal cortex**, secretes hormones that help regulate the levels of sugars, proteins, minerals, and body fluids. It also produces certain sex hormones. The secretions of the adrenal cortex are regulated by the pituitary gland.

The inner layer, the **adrenal medulla**, secretes hormones of a different kind. These are the "fight or flight" hormones, which help the body react to emergencies. The hormone **epinephrine** (or adrenaline), for example, makes the heart beat faster, raises the blood pressure, widens the breathing passages, and increases the amount of sugar in the blood to supply more energy for the muscles and the brain.

Other Endocrine Glands. The pancreas is really two organs in one. Some of its cells act as exocrine glands, producing digestive juices. Other cells act as endocrine glands, producing two hormones involved in the body's use of sugar. **Insulin** helps body cells use sugar. It also causes the liver to take the sugar glucose out of the blood and store it in the form of starch. **Glucagon** causes the liver to break down starch and send more sugar into the blood.

The male and female sex organs produce the male and female cells (sperm and ova, or egg cells) that can combine to start a new life. These organs are also endocrine glands. The **testes** of a male produce male sex hormones such as **testosterone**. The **ovaries** of a female produce female sex hormones such as **estrogens** and **progesterone**. The sex hormones help the body to develop and mature, and they are involved in all stages of reproduction.

The role of the **pineal gland**, a small gland in the brain, is not entirely clear. It produces **melatonin**, a hormone that is thought to be related to skin pigment and perhaps mood.

Certain other organs also act as endocrine glands. The stomach and small intestine produce hormones that stimulate the flow of digestive juices. Hormones produced by the kidneys help regulate blood pressure and the production of red blood cells. The **thymus gland** helps special kinds of white blood cells develop. These cells form part of the body's defense against disease.

▶**DISORDERS OF GLANDS**

The "swollen glands" that develop with a cold are not really glands. They are swollen lymph nodes, in which white blood cells are fighting infection. (These nodes are part of the lymphatic system, which is described in the article CIRCULATORY SYSTEM in Volume C.)

Glands do swell in **mumps**, an infection caused by a virus. Mumps usually affects the salivary glands, although in adults it sometimes causes other glands to swell. A person generally becomes immune to mumps after one infection—that is, he or she cannot get mumps again. A vaccine can be used to produce immunity without the illness.

Acne results when bacteria grow in the oils produced by the sebaceous glands. Pores become plugged when oil and other matter build up. Acne is most common during the teen years, when the skin tends to be oily.

If the mucus-producing cells in the lining of the stomach or intestine are not active enough (or if the stomach produces too much acid), the delicate lining tissues may be irritated. The result may be a sore called an **ulcer**.

In certain disorders, an endocrine gland produces too much or too little of its hormones. Many parts of the body may be affected when this happens. For example, when the pituitary gland does not produce enough growth hormone, a child will be very short. If the gland produces too much growth hormone, a person may grow abnormally tall.

When a baby's thyroid gland produces too little of a hormone called thyroxine, a form of mental retardation may result. In adults, too little of this hormone can make a person gain weight and feel listless, while too much can make a person lose weight and feel nervous.

Diabetes is a serious disease caused by a lack of the hormone insulin. Without this hormone, the level of sugar in the blood rises. The effects can be severe if the disorder is not treated.

Many endocrine disorders are successfully treated by administering hormones or substances that help control the production of hormones. For example, insulin is given to people with diabetes. Special diets may also help this condition.

ALVIN and VIRGINIA SILVERSTEIN
Co-authors, *The Endocrine System*

See also BODY, HUMAN; BODY CHEMISTRY; DIGESTIVE SYSTEM.

GLASS

The story of glass is old and mysterious. Primitive people used a natural black volcanic glass called obsidian for arrowheads, knives, and tools, and for decoration. The luxury-loving Emperor Nero (A.D. 37–68) was so enchanted by the beauty of glass that he paid 6,000 sesterces (about $2,500) for two small cups.

The sparkling brightness of glass, as well as its many uses, comes from its rather peculiar properties. Its base is pure silica sand. Silica sand is composed of the mineral quartz, a compound of the elements silicon and oxygen. Soda ash and lime or potash and lime are added to the sand. These act as fluxing agents—that is, they cause the materials to fuse (melt) at temperatures of about 2600 degrees Fahrenheit.

Each of the fluxing agents has a special function. The soda and potash lower the melting point. Lime stabilizes and hardens the glass. By adding other substances, glass can be adapted for special uses. Lead gives glassware its clear, sparkling beauty. Borax keeps glass from expanding and cracking, so that it can be placed over a direct flame without breaking.

Glass naturally has a greenish cast because of the iron present in all sand. Clear glass has been **decolorized** by adding selenium (a non-metallic element somewhat like sulfur). The selenium gives glass a red tint that balances out the green. Other colors can be obtained by adding different chemical oxides to the ingredients. Cobalt is put in for blue, gold for ruby, manganese for purple, chromium or iron for green, and uranium for yellow.

▶ HISTORY OF GLASS

The time and place of the discovery of the combination of materials and heat that makes glass are uncertain. The Roman natural historian Pliny (A.D. 23–79) wrote that this important event occurred along the coast of Syria around 1200 B.C. According to his account, some Phoenician seamen moored their small wooden boat on the sandy coast and cooked their evening meal onshore. Since they could not find large enough rocks to hold their cooking pots, they used blocks of niter, a form of soda, from their cargo. After their fires died down, they were amazed to find that the niter had fused the sand underneath into a glassy substance.

Actually, glass had been discovered long before 1200 B.C. The oldest man-made glass that has been found is a deep-blue charm used to keep away evil spirits. Archeologists date this charm at about 7000 B.C. All very early glass articles seem to have been beads and inlays for metal jewelry. Indeed, glass appears to have been used first as a gem valued equally with the natural stones that ancient man considered precious. Excavations in a cemetery in the ancient Babylonian city of Ur along the Euphrates River unearthed a large quantity of glass beads. Diggers at Tel el Amarna in upper Egypt found the **glass factory**, or **glass house**, of Amenhotep IV, who reigned in 1400 B.C. Here they found tubes and strips of opaque (cloudy) as well as partly clear glass.

The first glass drinking mugs and flasks were made on a sand-clay core. The core was molded into the desired shape and held together with a cloth fastened around a rod. The glassmaker dipped the core into a pot of molten glass until the core was covered with it. After the glass had cooled, the rod was removed and the sandy core scraped out.

Coinlike medallions were made by pouring molten glass into a mold. The glass was gathered on the enlarged head of an iron rod called a **punty**, much as one would gather molasses on a knife blade by turning it in a jar of the syrup. The workman held the **gather** of glass over the mold and let the proper amount of glass run into the mold. Some objects were also cut from solid pieces of glass.

Many treasured objects were made in these crude ways, but they were so expensive that they were only for the very rich. Not until the discovery of the **blowpipe** was glass changed from a luxury into a product that people of simpler means could enjoy.

Some adventuresome man must have substituted a hollow pipe for his usual punty. He found that if he puffed through the pipe, the gather of molten glass would blow out like a bubble. By the 1st century A.D., glassblowing was a common practice. A better-quality glass could be made into new and larger shapes more economically by this method. The first pieces of blown glass were made without

Persian bowl, 4th century B.C. Corning Museum.

Roman vase, 2nd or 3rd century A.D.
Corning Museum of Glass, New York.

Venetian chalice (1465?)
decorated with *Adoration of the Magi*. Civic
Museum, Bologna.

Latticinio (lace-glass) vase;
Venice, around 1600.

molds and with only simple hand tools to aid the imagination and skill of the craftsman.

Later, wooden molds were developed that allowed the craftsman to turn out glass objects of consistent size and shape.

With the same tools that are used in making handmade glass today, glassmakers of the Roman Empire achieved a degree of skill that has never been surpassed. They developed a clear crystal as well as a wide variety of richly colored glass.

The Romans decorated their glass in many ways. On the still soft, warm glass of one color they sometimes wound strands of different-colored glass in vertical, horizontal, or spiral "cording." Often the horizontal strands were pulled down by a simple hook tool into loops or half-moons. Small gobs of glass molded into seal-like decorations were pressed on the glass or geometric or flowered patterns were cut in with sandstone wheels. Colorful enamels were also fired, or baked, on the glass.

One of the most interesting effects was created by covering crystal glass with a layer of colored glass (such as ruby glass). This process is known as **casing**. When a pattern was cut through the overlay of ruby, the sparkling design of crystal made a beautiful contrast with the colored glass. Many of these techniques of cutting and casing are still in use today.

Crude glass bottles continued to be made after the fall of the Roman Empire, but the skill and techniques perfected by the Romans were lost. Gradually, craftsmen in Venice began experimenting with glass, and in the 15th century they developed a clear crystal that once again turned glassmaking into an art. Fabulous prices were paid for Venetian goblets and bowls.

The Venetians used many of the Roman techniques and created new ones of their own. A design known as **latticinio** demanded particular skill. Rods of colored glass were laid around a mold. Then the mold was covered with glass of a different color, and blown. A second bubble with rods going in a different direction was often then blown inside the first. The finished glass had a rectangular mesh of different-colored bands lying inside it. Latticinio was very difficult to make, because the two soft bubbles of glass might at any moment lose their shape. Another Venetian technique

was to roll a bubble of glass over broken bits of glass of a different color. Glass made this way was known as **ice glass**.

In order to keep the skills of their craft a secret, Venetian glassblowers were forbidden to leave Venice. But kings and nobles of other lands enticed the craftsmen to their courts by promising them wealth. Soon beautiful glass was being made throughout Europe.

In France the Venetian glassmakers combined their art of mirror-making with the French glassworkers' techniques for making huge pieces of flat glass. The Venetians had discovered they could turn a piece of glass into a mirror by coating one side with tin and mercury. Until that time mirrors had been made mainly of polished metal. The Venetian mirrors commanded a large price because they were a novelty and also because they appealed to man's natural vanity. For almost the first time, a person could see what he really looked like. Mirror-making required great skill, because the glass had to be clear and flat.

Glassmakers in France had worked out several techniques for making flat glass. One method had actually been developed by the Romans hundreds of years earlier. The Romans had made flat window glass by pouring molten glass over a flat surface covered with sand and then rolling the glass smooth. By the end of the 17th century, French glassworkers also knew how to make flat glass in this difficult and dangerous way. The glass had to be poured from pots onto large tables, where iron bars kept the hot glass from running off the table. The bars could be moved to make different-sized pieces of glass. Once the glass was on the table, it was spread to the right thickness. After the glass had cooled, it was ground and polished.

Flat glass was also blown by an ingenious process known as **crown**. The craftsman gathered a gob of glass and blew it into a cylindrical bubble. Then he attached a punty rod to the bubble. By spinning the punty, he flared the bubble into a flat piece of glass. Unfortunately, the punty left a thick bull's-eye in the middle of the glass. When the bull's-eye was cut out, only a fairly small piece of glass was left. Larger pieces of glass were made by blowing the glass and then letting it swing out into a long cylinder. The cylinder

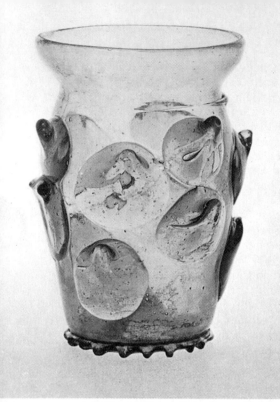

Left: German glass called a *Nuppenbecher*, 15th or 16th century. Corning Museum.
Right: Dutch tumbler known as a *roemer* (around 1700).

English enameled goblets (1760–70).

German tumbler, early 19th century, etched with a view of the city of Meissen.

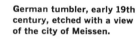

was cut lengthwise. When it was reheated, the glass was pressed into a flat shape. Blown plate glass was made in France by Venetian craftsmen for Louis XIV's famous Hall of Mirrors at Versailles.

Southern European craftsmen created the glowing stained-glass windows that gave Gothic churches so much of their beauty. These craftsmen painstakingly worked different-colored pieces of glass into beautiful patterns. Then they set the bits of glass in soft lead strips to hold them together. This craft was begun in the 12th century and reached its height in the 14th century.

Although both the Romans and the Venetians had developed a clear glass, it did not have quite the sparkling quality of glass made today. In 1673 an Englishman, George Ravenscroft, added lead to glass, and this was the beginning of modern glassmaking. Lead makes glass sparkle. **Lead crystal** is also softer and easier to cut than earlier types of glass. Glassmakers were soon putting their skill to cutting glass designs that showed off the play of light on lead crystal.

English craftsmen added more and more lead to the crystal. This made the glass heavier and allowed deep geometric patterns to be cut into the glass. The famous Irish Waterford crystal goblets are examples of this kind of work.

The American glassmaker Henry William Stiegel (1729–85) also cut glass in elaborate patterns. His glass was lighter than either English or Irish glass, and not all of it was in the same style. He was particularly famous for producing glass in beautiful colors. Stiegel glass is said to be the first lead glass of high quality produced in America.

Glassmaking was the first industry in America. In 1608 the colonists at Jamestown built a glass house there because of the availability of fuel and materials. The colonists had come to America to find gold. Instead they found nothing but huge forests and the sand along the seashore. In desperation the starving colonists decided to use the natural resources—wood, sand, and lime—to make glass to export to England. They did produce some glass, but disease and attacks from Indians destroyed the struggling colony's interest in glassmaking. By 1624 tobacco had replaced glass in the trade with England.

▶ **MANUFACTURE OF GLASS TODAY**

Handmade glassware is made today much as it was in the beginning. Materials are purer, and melting furnaces have been improved. But the skilled glassworker still follows the same steps that the ancients did.

Watching its production is a fascinating experience. The furnace room is lit mainly by the light from the glowing molten glass in the furnace openings and by the roaring fires in the smaller **glory holes**. Glory holes are smaller furnaces where the glass is reheated and polished while it is being worked toward its final form.

There are men everywhere, moving about with no apparent pattern. Actually, the men are highly organized. If glass is followed through all the steps of its creation, it is obvious that these scattered workmen are members of a team, or **shop**. Each man contributes a part in the making of a single glass.

First, a **gatherer** shoves the end of his blowpipe into a pot of hot, glowing glass and gathers up just the right amount of glass. As he carries the **gather**, or gob of hot glass, away from the furnace, he must turn the pipe constantly to keep the hot glass from running off it. On a metal plate called a **marver** he rolls the glass back and forth, shaping it into a conelike mass called a **parison**. Then, raising the pipe like a trumpet, he puffs a breath of air into it to start the bubble, and hands the pipe to the blower.

The **blower** is the head of the shop, and his job demands the most skill. The blower holds the pipe with the cone end down, alternately blowing and shaping the bubble. He lets the glass stretch out until the bubble seems to him to be the right shape. As he blows, the pipe must be continually turned to let the glass run out evenly. One little misjudgment, one second of delay, and the glass is ruined. Seemingly at the last possible moment, he dips the bubble in the mold and blows it out into a perfect copy of the mold's shape.

Stems can be made in several ways. One of the methods is to so shape the cone that it has some extra glass on its end. The blower, after partly forming the glass, sits down in a special chair. He spins the blowpipe on the two long arms of the chair. Then he takes a simple U-shaped iron tool called a **pucellas**. With the tapered legs of the pucellas he cuts a groove around the tip of the cone, to make a knob. Holding the tool on the knob while constantly turning the pipe, he draws, or pulls, a stem from the extra glass on the cone. He shapes the stem into a straight column or forces it to bulge slightly into a pleasing shape called a lady-leg stem. With the hot stem dangling from the partly shaped goblet, the blower carefully puts the goblet back into the mold and again blows out the bowl.

The foot is made from a small gather of glass dropped upon the knob on the bottom of the stem. A particularly skilled craftsman called the **foot-setter** flattens the glowing bit of glass. Then he grasps it in a hinged tool made of two pieces of wood or carbon and squeezes out a perfect, delicate circular foot. It is hard to imagine that such beautiful creations can be made with just an iron blowpipe, a punty to gather the foot glass, and a few simple tools to pull the stem and shape the foot.

Although the skill and speed of the workers make the process seem easy, it is not. Long training is necessary. The blower began as a **carrier**. It is the carrier's job to take the finished piece from the last craftsman and carry it to the cooling oven, or lehr. The carrier gradually worked through the more complicated jobs until he finally became head of the shop. The head of the shop sometimes lets the other men practice at blowing until they, too, are qualified to move on.

Inside the lehr, the glass is allowed to cool very slowly and evenly. This process is called **annealing**. If the glass were allowed to cool quickly, it would crack. In modern plants a traveling lehr is used for annealing. The glass travels through the oven on a slowly moving conveyor belt.

Often blown glass is decorated by **cutting**. Guide points are first inked on the glass to give the cutter starting and stopping points. In this way the cutter can make his cuts of equal lengths for flowered or geometric patterns. He holds the glass against the wheel, and the cut is made in an instant. But even with the guide points, the cutter has only his trained eye and sense of judgment to reproduce the design. The process has not really changed since the days of the Romans, except that synthetic cutting wheels have now replaced the early sandstone wheels.

Etching is another kind of decoration. Etched glass is made by wrapping a paper pattern around the glass and coating the part that is not covered by the pattern with an acid-resistant substance. When the glass is dipped in acid, the acid cuts out the pattern from the glass that has been left unprotected.

The cutter guides the glass as the pattern is cut by the spinning wheel.

Victorian vases, late 19th century, England.

Pint flask with portrait of Benjamin Franklin, 19th century. Kensington Glass Works, U.S.A.

Tiffany vases (1896), United States.

Pressed glass pitcher (1829–32). Fort Pitts Glass Works, United States.

Pressed Glass

The technique of pressing glass in molds was known long ago. But this way of making glass lagged behind the development of blowing. Small objects, such as feet for blown bowls, were sometimes pressed, but the process of pressing was not perfected until an American, Deming Jarves (1790–1869), developed a handpress for making glass around 1825. Jarves was the founder of the Boston and Sandwich Glass Company.

Today a **gatherer** gathers a gob of hot glass on a punty, an iron rod with an enlarged head. After winding up the gob on his rod, he balances the liquid mass by turning it back and forth as he carries it to the press.

The **presser** has an empty mold waiting for the hot glass. When the gatherer has let the right amount of glass run off his punty, the presser cuts the stream with a pair of shears. Quickly he pushes the mold into the press and pulls the lever, which lowers the plunger into the mold cavity. The plunger forces the liquid glass into shape.

From the mold the piece goes into the "glory hole" for its trial by fire. Mold imperfections are literally burned off, and the glass takes on a glittering polish. The glass comes out of its bath of flame soft and ductile (easily shaped). The last craftsman, the **finisher**, coaxes and forms the hot glass into its final shape with a simple wooden paddle. The glass is still so soft that a skillful craftsman can shape it in any way desired. For instance, the edges of a flat plate can be turned up until the plate has become a bowl.

▶ MECHANIZATION OF GLASSMAKING

Handmade glass requires a large amount of highly skilled labor, which of course raises its cost. The demand for lower-priced window glass, bottles, and many other industrial items caused manufacturers to look for cheaper methods of making glass. About 1900, glass manufacturing began to be mechanized, bringing costs down. Today the manufacture of machine-made glass is one of the larger mass-production industries.

Many kinds of glass items are now made automatically. The raw materials are fed into one end of a huge rectangular furnace. The ingredients move through the furnace until completely melted, and the molten glass flows out in a steady stream, much as toothpaste flows from its tube. The temperature of the melting ingredients must be kept exactly right to keep the glass continuously flowing. As much as 250 tons of glass can come out of one of these furnaces every 24 hours.

Automatic shears cut gobs of exact size from the stream. The gobs drop into a waiting mold on a multi-station press. This machine carries the gobs through a series of operations that form and shape the glass. When the article is finished, it is mechanically put in an annealing lehr to be slowly cooled.

This process is highly automated, and each step of the operation must be carefully timed. Some machines press, some blow, and some press and blow. Each operation is really reproducing the motions and procedures of a handworker.

Sheet (window) glass is drawn from the surface of a similar furnace. The wide sheet travels up into a tall tower, passing through an annealing lehr. A cutting machine at the top of the tower trims the sheet and cuts it into lengths. The temperature of the glass and the speed at which it is drawn determine the thickness of the sheet.

Plate glass flows through large iron rollers set to produce the proper thickness. The rollers mar the glass a little. So as the glass is moved away from the furnace on a long conveyor, it is ground and polished on both sides to restore its luster. Another way to make plate glass is to float it on a bath of molten metal alloy. The bath presents a perfectly flat surface to support the glass, and it does not cause the defects that occur in rolling. Plate glass made by this process does not need to be polished.

Tubing and rod also are drawn by machine. The glass flows from the furnace over a ceramic cone called a mandrel and is pulled out along a series of roller supports. If air is blown through the mandrel, the tubing comes out hollow. Again the temperature of the glass and rate of pull determine the size of the tubing. Tubing can pass over the pipe at the rate of 40 miles per hour.

Uses of Glass

Glass is essential to lighting. Without the light bulb our homes would be dreary places at night. Our streets would not be safe. No automobile, train, or airplane could operate after sunset.

The commercial uses of glass are almost endless. Glass is an excellent container for many kinds of foods and beverages, because it does not corrode.

Glass is vital to science. Laboratories use many glass items, from simple test tubes to complicated beakers, flasks, valves, and their connecting tubing. Microscopes must have glass lenses. Tubes to hold electric wiring are essential to the growing field of electronics. A glass ceramic called Pyroceram withstands such extreme temperatures that it has many uses in space programs.

Panes of glass can be made so tough that they are bulletproof. Another type of glass bends as readily as spring steel. Glass can be made so porous it will float. It can be made into insulating wool.

Glass has become an exciting structural material. Sheets or tiles of different-colored glass make good wall panels for showers or bathrooms. Glass blocks can be put in masonry walls where light is needed. Window glass is made so large that it often serves as outside walls on modern buildings.

Glass fiber, known as **fiberglass**, is a long-lasting as well as fireproof material. Fiberglass can be spun into clothlike material for curtains and many other uses. And fiberglass, when impregnated with plastic, is one of the strongest materials known. Bodies of some sports cars and the hulls of many pleasure boats are made out of it. It is also used for the shafts of golf clubs and fishing rods.

Windows of specially made glass, and other parts also made of glass, were built into the Apollo vehicles that carried men to the moon.

ROBERT F. HANNUM
President, Fostoria Glass Company

See also BOTTLES AND BOTTLING; OPTICAL INSTRUMENTS; STAINED-GLASS WINDOWS.

GLAUCOMA.   See EYE (Disorders of the Eye).

GLENN, JOHN H., JR. (1921–)

On February 20, 1962, astronaut John Glenn became the first American to orbit the Earth. In 4 hours and 56 minutes, in a space capsule called the *Friendship 7*, Glenn circled the Earth three times before splashing down into the Atlantic Ocean.

John Herschel Glenn, Jr., was born on July 18, 1921, in Cambridge, Ohio, and grew up in New Concord. An honor student and athlete, Glenn studied chemistry at Muskingum College before entering the Naval Aviation Cadet Program in 1942. As an officer in the U.S. Marine Corps, Glenn flew almost 150 combat missions during World War II and the Korean War, earning 6 Distinguished Flying Crosses and 18 Air Medals. After the wars, Glenn became a military test pilot. On July 16, 1957, at an average speed of 726 miles (1,169 kilometers) an hour, he made the first transcontinental supersonic (faster than the speed of sound) flight.

In 1959, Glenn became one of the nation's first seven astronauts when the National Aeronautics and Space Administration (NASA) asked him to join the Mercury space program. He made his historic orbit of the Earth in 1962, on the program's third mission. Glenn left the space program in 1963

and retired from the Marine Corps a year later. He became a successful businessman and remained a consultant for NASA.

In 1974, after two failed attempts to enter politics, Glenn, a Democrat, won election to the U.S. Senate. Opposed to the spread of nuclear weapons, he wrote the Nonproliferation Act of 1978. He won re-election in 1980 and 1986. And from 1987 to 1995 he served as chairman of the Senate Governmental Affairs Committee.

In 1990 the Senate Ethics Committee investigated Glenn and four others, known as the Keating Five, for alleged abuse of power. But the committee concluded that Glenn had not acted improperly, and in 1992 he was re-elected to the Senate by an overwhelming majority.

AMOS J. LOVEDAY, JR.
Ohio Historical Society

With its streamlined shape and long, slender wings, a glider can fly great distances without an engine (*above*). Inside the glider (*right*), the pilot steers with a control stick and floor pedals. Dials indicate the glider's altitude and airspeed.

GLIDERS

Gliders are winged, motorless aircraft that soar on the wind as silently and gracefully as eagles. Also known as **sailplanes**, gliders use currents of rising air to remain aloft.

Like an airplane, a glider has wings, a fuselage (body), a tail assembly, and landing gear. The glider's long, tapered wings usually extend across the top of the fuselage. A clear canopy covers the cockpit.

Skilled craftspeople construct most modern sailplanes of fiberglass. Fiberglass allows for long, thin wings, light weight, and a streamlined design. (For a more detailed description of the structure of an airplane and how it flies, see the articles AIRPLANES and AERODYNAMICS in Volume A.)

A glider must be launched into flight. This is usually accomplished by towing the glider to an altitude of between 1,000 and 2,000 feet (300 to 600 meters) behind an airplane. A 200-foot (60-meter) towrope links the glider to the airplane ahead. Once the desired altitude is reached, and currents of rising air have been found, the glider is released from the tow plane.

A glider is controlled much like an airplane. The pilot moves a stick and pedals inside the cockpit to operate movable wing and tail surfaces. Moving these surfaces while in flight will make the glider climb, dive, or turn.

Every glider is also equipped with an airspeed indicator, an altimeter (which shows altitude), and a compass. Another important instrument called a variometer shows the rate at which the glider is climbing or descending.

SOARING

The goal of every glider flight is to soar as long as possible on rising air, or **updrafts**. Since a glider has no engine, it must use energy available in the environment.

Gravity pulls the glider toward the ground. But as the glider falls, air moving past the wings creates a force that offsets the effect of gravity. This force is called **lift**. Because lift does not completely offset gravity, the glider follows a downward, or descending, flight path. But even in still air without updrafts, a glider can fly a long distance without losing much altitude. For example, if a high-performance glider started soaring at an altitude of one mile (1.6 kilometers), it would glide as much as 40 miles (64 kilometers) before it reached the ground.

Usually the pilot can locate and use updrafts to gain altitude. There are three types of updrafts used by glider pilots: ridge lift, wave lift, and thermal lift.

A strong wind blowing steadily against a mountain ridge is swept upward, producing a narrow band of rising air called **ridge lift**. Gliders can fly long distances in the ridge lift along a range of mountains.

Wave lift, like ridge lift, is produced by a wind flowing against a mountain. However, in the case of wave lift, air flows up and over the mountain, like water over a rock.

The third and most common form of lift is **thermal lift**. Updrafts result from uneven heating of the earth by the sun. Dark, flat, or open areas such as parking lots, rooftops, and plowed fields absorb more heat from the sun than tree- or water-covered areas, for example. The air above these warm areas is heated and becomes lighter than the surrounding air. This light air, which rises in the form of a column or bubble, is called a **thermal**.

Thermals are often indicated by puffy, white cumulus clouds. Glider pilots steer toward such clouds, then circle in the strong updrafts under them to gain altitude. Once in a thermal, the pilot checks his variometer to determine the strength of the lift. If the lift is not strong enough, the pilot will leave the thermal and fly to the next cumulus cloud.

The strongest part of a thermal is generally located in the center of the column, with weaker lift around it. In order to use the strongest lift in a thermal, the pilot must bank (tilt) his glider steeply and turn tight circles in the turbulent, rising air. Soaring birds, such as hawks, often indicate where the best part of a thermal is located.

Cumulus clouds can quickly form into dangerous thunderheads with lift so strong that it can suck a glider up inside the storm. Because of these powerful updrafts, and the turbulence and lightning associated with them, glider pilots avoid thunderstorms.

Every soaring flight ends with a landing. The glider lands on a single wheel which is retracted (pulled up into the fuselage) during flight and extended for landing. Because they are able to fly at very low speeds, gliders can land in short spaces. On flights that end far from the point of takeoff, gliders often must land in fields or pastures. Then the pilot radios his or her crew, which brings the glider trailer

Most hang gliders consist of a triangular fabric sail attached to an aluminum frame about 30 feet (9 meters) wide. The pilot steers with a control bar.

to wherever the glider has landed. In most cases, a glider can be disassembled and loaded in the trailer in 15 minutes. The trailer is towed back to the airport and the glider is reassembled for the next flight.

HANG GLIDERS

Hang gliders were the ancestors of modern sailplanes. The earliest flights in heavier-than-air craft were made in the 1800's in hang gliders constructed of wood and fabric. As more efficient designs were developed, hang gliders were virtually abandoned. Then in the 1970's, hang gliding became a popular sport in the United States.

Like sailplanes, hang gliders are capable of soaring flight. The typical hang glider is made of an aluminum frame over which synthetic fabric is stretched. The pilot straps him- or herself into a harness and typically launches the hang glider by running down a hill until reaching a speed fast enough to fly. The pilot controls the flight of the hang glider by pushing and pulling on a control bar, and by shifting body weight to the left and right.

▶HISTORY OF GLIDING

People have always been fascinated by the idea of flying. According to ancient Greek mythology, Daedalus and his son Icarus escaped imprisonment by flying with wings made of waxed feathers. In the late 1400's, Leonardo da Vinci designed a flying machine after he studied the flight of birds.

One of the most famous of the early glider pilots was Otto Lilienthal (1848–96), a German engineer. He steered his glider by shifting his body forward and backward, and from side to side. Lilienthal died in a glider crash after making more than 2,000 flights during the 1890's. Octave Chanute (1832–1910), an American engineer, developed the use of movable control surfaces to steer a glider.

Orville and Wilbur Wright (1871–1948; 1867–1912), American inventors, were inspired by the work of Lilienthal and Chanute. Before their first successful powered flight in 1903, the Wrights learned much about flying by building and testing gliders.

Gliders were first used for military purposes by Germany in World War II. Since World War II, however, military use of gliders has been limited to flight training.

TERRY FRAZIER
University of North Carolina
Contributing Editor, *Soaring* magazine

See also AVIATION.

Gloves come in an amazing variety of sizes and shapes. *Clockwise from right:* ski glove, baseball glove, golf glove, hockey gloves, boxing gloves.

GLOVES

Gloves have been used since very ancient times. There are many different kinds of gloves, each with its own special use or purpose. Some are decorative covers for the hands. Others are worn to provide warmth. Many kinds are made to protect the hands. Steelworkers, meat cutters, fire fighters, and astronauts are among the many workers who need special hand coverings. People who handle materials such as stone and rough wood wear heavy cotton or leather gloves to guard against scrapes, blisters, and splinters. Homemakers and industrial workers wear rubber and plastic gloves to guard their hands from water and strong chemicals. In golf, tennis, skiing, and snowmobiling, as well as in many other sports, special gloves are used. Among these are boxing gloves, catchers' mitts, and the padded gloves of hockey players.

Gloves are made of various materials, such as leather, wool, synthetic fibers, vinyl, and rubber. The finest gloves are still made by hand although this skill is rapidly disappearing. Many former European glove-making centers, such as those in France, have been replaced by centers in Asia, which today manufacture a large portion of the world's glove supply. The major glove-manufacturing countries are the United States, the Philippines, Italy, Taiwan, and Korea.

Most American dress gloves are made in Fulton County in New York State, especially in the cities of Gloversville and Johnstown. The industry was begun in this area in 1760 by Scottish glove makers who were persuaded by the British Government to immigrate there. Industrial gloves are made mainly in the Midwestern states.

JAMES H. CASEY, JR.
National Association of Glove Manufacturers

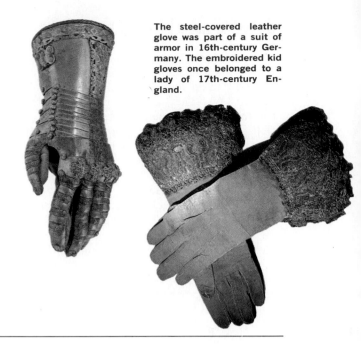

The steel-covered leather glove was part of a suit of armor in 16th-century Germany. The embroidered kid gloves once belonged to a lady of 17th-century England.

GLUCK, CHRISTOPH WILLIBALD (1714–1787)

The great opera composer Christoph Willibald Gluck was born in Erasbach, Bavaria, on July 2, 1714. His early education prepared him to be a church musician; he studied Latin, voice, and the organ. He showed such talent he was sent to Prague to study further. Prince Lobkowitz, who employed his father as a forester, hired Gluck to lead his private orchestra. In 1736 the prince brought the young musician to Vienna.

There his talent won him an invitation to go to Italy to learn to write operas. His first opera was given in Milan in 1741. Its success brought him offers to write more operas and to visit London. On his way home to Vienna, Gluck visited Paris, where he heard French operas by Rameau. These works gave him ideas on how opera could emphasize drama instead of being merely concerts in costume like the old-fashioned Italian operas.

Gluck returned to Vienna in 1748 to develop his ideas about reforming opera. After several tries he wrote *Orpheus and Eurydice* (1762). It was so simple and moving that it made a deep impression on his audience. Gluck had equal success with *Alceste* (1767). For this opera he wrote a preface explaining his reforms.

Even though there were many who disliked Gluck's new ideas, he continued to win the friendship of important people. The Austrian empress made him director of her court theater. Her daughter, Marie Antoinette, was Gluck's pupil before she became queen of France. Marie later asked him to come to Paris. Gluck arrived there in 1773 and rewrote *Orpheus and Eurydice* and *Alceste* in the French language.

Gluck and an Italian composer named Piccinni became the center of a famous dispute. Those who liked the old Italian style invited Piccinni to Paris as Gluck's rival. To settle the dispute both Gluck and Piccinni wrote operas called *Iphigenia in Tauris* (1779). Gluck's opera was a masterpiece that Piccinni could not equal, and his victory helped convince many people of the value of his reforms.

In that same year, Gluck returned to Vienna in poor health. He lived there as an invalid but continued to compose until his death on November 15, 1787. Today Gluck's early works are largely forgotten, but his reform operas remain important. They influenced such great composers as Mozart, Berlioz, and Wagner.

Reviewed by WILLIAM ASHBROOK
Philadelphia College of the Performing Arts

GLUE AND OTHER ADHESIVES

A stamp on an envelope, a piece of plywood, tiles on a floor, sandpaper, a book, and a Band-Aid on your elbow all have something in common. They are all held together by substances that we call adhesives.

If you spill honey or jam on your fingers, the fingers get sticky. That is, they are adhesive. Adhesives are sticky substances. They are used to stick (bond) two things together. They are used in place of nails, screws, or bolts. Sometimes they are used together with nails, screws, or other fasteners. The two things joined may be the same, such as two pieces of paper, or they may be different, such as wood and metal.

The two things to be stuck together must be clean and properly prepared. The adhesive must be the proper one for these materials, and it must be correctly applied. A good, strong bond should then be formed. The bond may be stronger than the bond obtained from mechanical fasteners because the stress is spread over the whole surface rather than just at the point held by a nail or screw. Another advantage of an adhesive is that it does not weaken the bonded materials by poking holes in them.

Adhesives are made from many different materials. Some are made from animal by-products such as hides, bones, and blood. Others are made from vegetable starches or sugars. Still others are made from such materials as natural rubber, synthetic rubber, and a wide selection of chemicals found in petroleum, natural gas, and even sand.

Glue is an impure form of the protein gelatin. It is one of the oldest adhesives known. It was by far the most important adhesive until the latter part of the 1800's. Even today people incorrectly call all adhesives "glue." Glue is obtained by cooking animal hide or bone. It can also be made from the skin or bones of fish that are not oily. Glue makes a very strong joint, but it is not waterproof. It readily dissolves in hot water.

Mucilage is a mixture of water and the natural gums of certain plants. It is a liquid adhesive, and it is not very strong. It is used mainly for cementing paper.

Paste is a mixture of flour or starch and water. It makes a good adhesive for paper and is cheap and easy to prepare. Paste also is safe for small children to use.

Cement usually means the material used in concrete, but the term also is used for a number of adhesives that are made from chemicals, rather than from animal or vegetable materials. The cements usually are in solution in chemical solvents such as alcohol, rather than in water. In a broad sense, the term "cement" can mean any adhesive.

▶ **WHAT MAKES ADHESIVES STICK?**

Adhesives act in three different ways to join materials. They may penetrate the tiny surface pores of the materials and hold them together physically, as a burr sticks to clothing (**mechanical** bonding). The adhesive may act by means of powerful but little-understood forces of attraction between its molecules and the surface molecules of the pieces being joined (**intermolecular** bonding). With certain materials, the adhesive actually unites chemically with the surface molecules of the pieces being joined (**chemical** bonding).

Whether adhesives are used in industry or in household projects, the surfaces to be joined must be clean and must fit each other closely. The strength of the bond depends to a great degree on the surface areas that are actually in contact with the adhesive. If the surfaces do not fit closely, the adhesive may shrink away in drying and leave only small patches actually bonded. Grease and dust also cause poor bonding by keeping the adhesive from coming into contact with the surface. Very rough or splintery surfaces give a poor bond. But the adhesive often grips better if the surfaces are slightly roughened. A thick layer of adhesive is no guarantee of a strong joint. In fact, it may actually weaken the bond by keeping the surfaces apart or by preventing the adhesive from wetting the surfaces completely.

Most adhesives require pressure to hold the parts being joined in place until the adhesive has set. By bringing the surfaces into close contact, pressure also helps to give a stronger bond. Some adhesives also require heat, and few will work well at temperatures below 20°C (68°F). A new field of adhesives consists of melted solids that bond as they cool. These are called **hot melt** adhesives.

TYPES OF ADHESIVES

Adhesives may be classified in many ways. One of the most usual ways is according to origin (animal, vegetable, or synthetic). Adhesives may also be classified according to the materials they are used to join (wood, paper, or metal, for example), speed of drying, resistance to water, and in many other ways.

HISTORY OF ADHESIVES

The sticky qualities of certain substances have long been known. Primitive peoples used resins and plant gums to stick things together. Glue has also been known for thousands of years. Egyptian carvings dating from 1500 B.C. show people using glue to join pieces of wood.

The introduction of plywood (around 1875) created a need for adhesives that could stand water better than the old, familiar animal glue. Albumin and casein, both known for centuries but little used, met the need. Albumin (a protein found in blood and egg whites) was known to the Romans. Casein (the milk protein that turns into cheese) was used by the ancient Chinese.

Albumin glue reached new importance in World War I, when it was used to hold together the wood-and-canvas airplanes of the period. It remained the leading aircraft glue until aircraft manufacturers began making metal airplanes.

The boom in the use of plywood also brought vegetable adhesives into general use. Most vegetable adhesives are based on cornstarch. Tapioca, potato, and other starches also are used. Soybean glue differs from other vegetable adhesives in being a protein, not a starch.

The great change in adhesives came with the development of synthetic resins. (Natural resins come mostly from trees.) These new resins were first introduced in the 1920's. But they did not come into widespread use until the 1930's, when ways were found to manufacture them cheaply. They proved to be stronger, cheaper, and more durable than natural adhesives. And they stood up against water, mold, and fungi as well. The newest synthetic resins are so strong that they are used in bonding the metal skins of some airplanes and missiles.

Pressure-sensitive tapes are another fairly

Many adhesives are specially prepared and packaged for use in artwork and other projects.

recent development. These rely mainly on rubber-based adhesives. They are widely used in homes, schools, and stores for such jobs as mending torn pages and sealing packages. But their main use is in the automobile and appliance industries. Here they are used in painting to mask (cover) parts that should not be painted. They also are used to apply thin pieces of trim to dashboards and other parts of the interiors of new automobiles.

WHAT IS THE BEST ADHESIVE?

Advances in chemical technology have made it possible to create adhesives with almost any combination of characteristics. Yet there is no one adhesive that is best for all tasks. Different uses call for different qualities in the adhesive. The adhesive used to seal a paper envelope does not need to be so strong and durable as the adhesive that holds together the parts of a rapidly whirling helicopter rotor blade. In some cases durability and strength can actually be a drawback. Masking tape and adhesive bandages would not be of much use if they could not be removed when they were no longer needed. On the other hand, a missile would not get very far if it were held together by masking tape. Engineers and scientists have learned from experience that the best results are gained by experimenting with adhesives and using the adhesive that is found to be best suited for the particular job.

Reviewed by THOMAS F. MITCHELL
Darling & Company

See also CHEMICAL INDUSTRY; PLASTICS; RESINS; WOOD AND WOOD PRODUCTS.

GNEISS. See ROCKS (Metamorphic Rock).

GOATS

Goats may have been the first hoofed animals that were ever tamed. In the Biblical town of Jericho, people kept tame goats as long ago as 6,000 or 7,000 years before Christ. People still raise goats in many places throughout the world. Different kinds of goats also live in the wild.

Like cows, goats are kept for their milk. They are also bred for meat, hair, and hide. Many tame goats have been trained to pull carts.

The earliest goats were animals of steep hills and mountainsides in Asia. Later they spread to North Africa and southern Europe. The lands they lived in were either hot and dry or cold and barren, with few plants.

From these wild ancestors domestic goats have inherited two unusual traits. They are very surefooted. And they will eat almost any plant material. Goats like grass, leaves, twigs, and berries. They will eat bitter desert plants and also lichens. They may nibble dry wood, rope, cotton cloth, and cigarettes.

When climbing, a wild goat can cling to the tiniest ledges of a cliff that is almost straight up and down. Tame goats will often climb high walls or play on a barn roof. Goats have a very good sense of balance. The two large hooves on each of their feet are shaped like cups. These leathery hooves can grip a surface.

Ibex (wild goats) have hooves that are perfect for climbing the rocky Swiss Alps.

Goats are so closely related to sheep that some are hard to tell apart from sheep. But there are differences. The male, or billy, goat has a beard and a strong odor. The sheep has neither. Usually only male sheep, or rams, have horns. Both male and female goats have horns, except for some dairy goats that have none. Most male goats have big horns that curve back toward their shoulders. The female, or nanny, goat's horns are smaller.

Goats are far more lively and curious than sheep and make interesting pets. The young of goats are called kids.

Some wild goats are called **ibex**. Ibex live in small herds in Spain, the Alps, North Africa, and Asia.

Reviewed by ROBERT M. MCCLUNG
Author, science books for children

See also HOOFED MAMMALS.

GOBI DESERT. See DESERTS.

GODDARD, ROBERT HUTCHINGS (1882–1945)

Robert Goddard, the father of American rocketry, was born on October 5, 1882, in Worcester, Massachusetts. When Robert was still a baby, his family moved to a suburb of Boston. There his father ran a small factory. He passed on to his son a keen interest in scientific matters.

Robert began very early to invent and experiment. He was always making new kinds of kites and trying them out. He performed chemical experiments in an attic workshop. He tried but failed to send up a hydrogen-filled aluminum balloon.

In 1898 the family returned to Worcester. There Goddard's interest in rocketry began.

He started reading science-fiction stories about space travel.

In those days, of course, there were no space rockets. Rockets had been used only as fireworks or as weapons of war. But Goddard came to believe that a piloted rocket might one day reach the moon or another planet. He spent almost all of his life trying to make this dream come true.

After high school he studied and taught at Worcester Polytechnic Institute and at Princeton University. At Princeton he became ill with tuberculosis. After recovering in 1914, he taught physics at Clark University in Worcester.

THE FIRST EXPERIMENTS

Throughout Goddard's college years, ideas of space travel and rocketry had never left his mind. The fireworks rockets then in use were gunpowder rockets. The gunpowder burned inside its casing, or tube. The gases produced by the burning gunpowder shot out of the rocket tube. This caused the rocket to shoot ahead.

Goddard had experimented with gunpowder rockets in college. He continued these experiments as a professor at Clark. He hoped to design rockets that could carry measuring instruments to very high altitudes. The instruments would tell how hot or cold it was high in the atmosphere. And they could find out how air pressures change at different altitudes. If rockets proved useful for this purpose, people would be more likely to support rocket research.

Goddard could pay for only a few experiments out of his salary. In 1916 he decided to write a report of the work he had done. If he could interest a scientific organization in his work, they might provide the money he needed. He sent the report to the Smithsonian Institution in Washington, D.C. The Smithsonian decided to give him $5,000 to carry on his research.

In 1919 the Smithsonian published Goddard's rocket report. It was called *A Method of Reaching Extreme Altitudes*. It was full of mathematics and was not very interesting reading to the general public. In its pages, however, Goddard suggested a way of reaching the moon. Build a multistage rocket, he said. Each stage would contain a rocket engine. The most powerful stage (called the first stage) would be placed on the launching pad. The next most powerful stage would be placed on top of the first stage, and so on.

Goddard figured out that such a rocket could go all the way to the moon. If it carried a load of flash powder, this could be exploded on the moon and seen through telescopes from the earth.

The newspapers seized on this small part of Goddard's report, ignoring the solid scientific thinking in the rest of it. Stories were written about "the moon rocket man," as one reporter called him. Goddard had always tended to keep to himself. Now he became even more

Robert H. Goddard lecturing on space flight at Clark University.

determined to keep his ideas to himself. For this reason, Goddard's achievements in rocketry did not become well known during his lifetime.

THE LIQUID-FUEL ROCKET

In the early 1920's Goddard began to experiment with a new kind of rocket. Its engine burned liquid fuel and liquid oxygen instead of gunpowder. Goddard figured out that a liquid fuel, such as gasoline, would produce much more power than gunpowder. He hoped to see this new type of rocket rise to the "extreme altitudes" he had predicted.

During this period Goddard married Esther Kisk, who had been a secretary at Clark University. She became his most valuable assistant. Not only did she act as his secretary, but she kept a motion-picture record of his rocket work for the next 20 years.

Mrs. Goddard was with her husband on March 16, 1926, to film the takeoff of the world's first liquid-fuel rocket. The rocket was 3 meters (10 feet) long. A small motor with a nozzle was attached to the top of the rocket. As fuel was ignited in the motor's combustion chamber, exhaust gases shot out through the nozzle. The rocket rose 12.5 meters (41 feet), dipped toward earth, and crashed 56 meters (184 feet) away. It was a short flight but the first made by a liquid-fuel rocket.

Goddard used a farm near Auburn, Massachusetts, as a launching site. In 1929 he built another, bigger, rocket. It, too, was launched from the Auburn farm and roared along close to the earth with a lot of noise and flame. People complained about the risks to their families, so Goddard conducted his next tests at Fort Devens, Massachusetts. News of this move appeared in the newspapers.

One person who read about it was Charles A. Lindbergh, the famous aviator. Lindbergh thought that rockets might supply power for airplanes. He persuaded Daniel Guggenheim, a wealthy man interested in flying, to give money to Goddard for rocket research.

Goddard set up an experimental research station near Roswell, New Mexico. In New Mexico rocket tests could be made all year round. There Goddard developed larger and better rocket engines and steering devices. In 1935 one of his rockets flew at the speed of sound for the first time. During World War II, Goddard was called to the U.S. Naval Academy at Annapolis, Maryland. He developed a liquid-fuel jet device to assist flying boats (a kind of airplane) in taking off from bodies of water. He asked the government to develop rockets for use as long-range weapons. Although Goddard was one of the world's leading rocket experts, the United States did not act on his suggestion.

Robert Goddard died on August 10, 1945. Shortly after his death, the United States started a large rocket program for military defense. It was only then that people began to realize the importance of Goddard's work. In 1959 he was honored with a Congressional medal. In 1962 the Goddard Space Flight Center, in Greenbelt, Maryland, was dedicated.

In 1969 the first person stepped onto the moon. And then, in 1976, small spacecraft were landed on the planet Mars. The rockets that made these events possible used many of Goddard's ideas. At last Goddard's dream had come true.

Reviewed by MILTON LEHMAN
Author, *This High Man: The Life of Robert H. Goddard*

GODS AND GODDESSES. See GREEK MYTHOLOGY; MYTHOLOGY; NORSE MYTHOLOGY.

GOETHE, JOHANN WOLFGANG VON (1749–1832)

Goethe is to Germany what Shakespeare is to England, Dante to Italy, and Cervantes to Spain—the country's greatest literary genius. Goethe was born in Frankfurt on August 28, 1749. His father was a prosperous lawyer who was more interested in the arts and sciences than the practice of law. Goethe's mother was a gifted storyteller. Her tales and a puppet theater given to him by his grandmother opened a world of fantasy for the boy.

Under his father's guidance, young Goethe was educated at home. During the Seven Years War (1756–63), when the French controlled the city, Goethe had his first exposure to French theater and culture. He began his university studies at Leipzig when he was 16. From 1770 to 1771 he studied law at Strasbourg and read Homer and Shakespeare. Between 1771 and 1775, he wrote his first major poems and the highly successful novel *The Sorrows of Young Werther* (1774), a romantic tale told in letter form.

In 1775, Goethe went to Weimar as companion to young Karl August, Duke of Sachsen-Weimar-Eisenach. He became a member (and later president) of the Duke's cabinet, administering state projects ranging from road building to theatrical productions. In addition he furthered his own interests in botany, mineralogy, anatomy, and optics.

Between 1786 and 1788, Goethe traveled in Italy. This country, particularly Rome, had a stimulating effect on him. He completed two major plays there, *Iphigenia in Tauris* and *Egmont*. When he returned to Weimar, he began to dedicate more time to writing.

After 1794, inspired by his friend the dramatist Friedrich Schiller, Goethe began a highly productive period of creativity. He published *Faust, Part I* (1808) and the novels *Wilhelm Meister's Apprenticeship* (1795–96) and *The Elective Affinities* (1809).

Goethe wrote some of his finest poems in his old age and completed his masterpiece, *Faust,* in 1831. Toward the end of his life, Goethe's house became a mecca for writers from all over the world. He died in Weimar on March 22, 1832, and was buried in the family tomb of the Dukes of Weimar.

ROBERT SPAETHLING
University of Massachusetts

See also FAUST LEGENDS.

GOLD

Since ancient times, gold has been one of the most wanted things on earth. People have left their homes and traveled into unknown wildernesses in search of gold. Wars have been fought and kingdoms have risen or fallen because of gold. Columbus was looking for gold when he discovered America.

People have always valued this shiny, yellow metal not only because it is beautiful but because it is scarce. If iron were as scarce as gold, it would be just as treasured.

▶ WHAT IS GOLD?

Gold is a soft, yellow metal. Its chemical symbol is Au, from the Latin word for gold, *Aurum*. Gold is one of the heaviest chemical elements. It is more than 19 times as heavy as water.

Gold is one of the most easily worked metals. It is so easy to shape and hammer that 1 gram (less than $1/25$ ounce) of pure gold could be formed into a wire about 1.6 kilometers (1 mile) long. Gold can be hammered into sheets as thin as 0.000076 millimeter ($3/1,000,000$ inch).

Unlike most metals, gold does not tarnish in the air. It remains bright and shiny indefinitely. People probably first valued gold for this special quality.

Gold is one of the least chemically active metals. It reacts with only a few acids. Gold does dissolve in aqua regia, a mixture of hydrochloric and nitric acids, although neither acid alone attacks it. Gold also dissolves in a solution of potassium cyanide or sodium cyanide. The elements chlorine, fluorine, bromine, and iodine combine with gold in the presence of moisture, forming chemical compounds. With mercury, gold forms a liquid alloy that is called an amalgam.

▶ USING GOLD AS MONEY

The most common use of gold has always been as money. Ships loaded with gold from the New World were in constant danger of attacks by pirates who carried their booty to island hideouts. Whenever the pirates managed to return to Europe, their stolen gold made them rich. Although coins also were made of metals other than gold, the value of gold coins was never questioned. But gold did not become a standard for a country's money until 1821, when Britain adopted gold as its official currency.

By 1914, gold was the measuring stick for almost all the currencies in the world. By having one standard of value, countries were able to trade more easily with one another. Dollars from the United States, francs from France, and marks from Germany all had a set value in gold. The currencies could be changed into gold at any time. This system was known as the **gold standard**. Because of economic difficulties after World War I, most countries had gone off the gold standard by 1933. Countries such as the United States, Germany, and France store part of their government gold holdings. This gold is called a **reserve**. It is held in refined bars of uncoined gold known as **bullion**. Today the gold reserve is not used to back up international trade because of differences of opinion among governments on how this gold should be valued.

▶ OTHER USES OF GOLD

After its use as money, the next most important use of gold is in jewelry and the arts. Gold is made into rings, watchcases, pins, and earrings. It also is used as a plating, or coating, for costume jewelry. Pure gold is called 24-karat gold. The karat mark on jewelry tells the number of parts out of 24 that are gold. The standard jewelry alloys (combinations of gold with other metals) in the United States are 10, 14, and 18 karat. This means that the weights of

---

BASIC FACTS ABOUT GOLD

CHEMICAL SYMBOL: Au.

ATOMIC WEIGHT: 196.967.

SPECIFIC GRAVITY: 19.32 (nearly 20 times as heavy as water).

COLOR: Golden yellow when pure; impurities cause various shades of yellow.

PROPERTIES: Very soft and easily shaped; extremely resistant to corrosion; nonmagnetic; excellent conductor of heat and electricity; reacts with very few chemicals.

OCCURRENCE: Very thinly distributed in earth's crust and seawater; concentrated in veins in quartz rock and in alluvial deposits.

CHIEF ORES: Usually found in metallic form; often found as impurity in ores of copper, iron, lead, and other metals; also found combined with tellurium as the mineral calaverite.

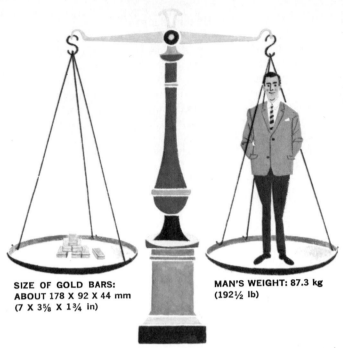

SIZE OF GOLD BARS:
ABOUT 178 X 92 X 44 mm
(7 X 3⅝ X 1¾ in)

MAN'S WEIGHT: 87.3 kg
(192½ lb)

Gold is one of the heaviest of all materials. Seven bars of gold weigh as much as this man.

in chemical-industry equipment that must resist very corrosive liquids or gases.

Gold Alloys

Gold is too soft to be used by itself, except in thinly applied coatings for decorative use. It is almost always alloyed with another metal. The metals most commonly alloyed with gold are copper, nickel, and silver. Other metals sometimes used are palladium, platinum, and zinc. For jewelry and dental work, gold is usually alloyed with silver and copper.

In jewelry the color of gold is important. Changing the amounts of copper and silver in the gold alloy changes the color of the gold. For instance, an 18-karat alloy (75 percent gold and 25 percent silver and copper) can be changed from green to a greenish yellow and then to yellow and finally to a reddish shade by replacing the silver with more and more copper. Zinc makes reddish alloys more yellow. White gold, which has been used as a substitute for the more costly platinum in jewelry, is really a gold-nickel alloy. A typical 18-karat white gold (75 percent gold) contains 17.3 percent nickel, 5.5 percent zinc, and 2.2 percent copper.

▶**WHERE GOLD IS FOUND**

Gold is present in very small quantities all through the earth's crust and in seawater. But it is too thinly concentrated to be worth extracting from these sources.

In some areas gold became concentrated in veins in quartz rock. Sometimes the gold occurs in the form of big chunks and veins of solid metal. More often it is scattered through the rock in tiny particles.

This gold-bearing rock was often exposed to the atmosphere and gradually weathered away to gravel and sand. The weathered rock and the gold it contained were carried away by running water and dumped in the beds and along the banks of streams. These beds of water-borne sand and gravel are called **alluvial deposits**. Gold found in alluvial deposits is usually in the form of gold dust or small chunks of solid gold called nuggets. Some nuggets are quite large—one containing 85 kilograms (187½ pounds) of gold was found in Australia—but most nuggets are the size of pebbles. Alluvial deposits that contain valuable minerals are called placers.

gold in these alloys are 41.66, 58.33, and 75 percent. Articles marked "gold-filled" or "rolled gold plate" are made of a base metal (usually brass) covered on one or more surfaces with a gold alloy.

Very thin sheets of gold are known as gold leaf. They are used for decorative purposes— to gild wood, plaster, ceramics, glass, and other substances.

About 15 percent of the gold not used for money is used in dentistry. This use dates back at least 3,000 years. Gold does not corrode, or rust, in the mouth. It is easily worked into the intricate shapes that are needed to replace or reinforce teeth. Today a variety of gold alloys is used for dental work. Some of these alloys are soft and are used for fillings. Others are hard and strong and are used to replace parts of teeth.

Gold has many industrial uses. Because it is a good conductor of electricity and resists corrosion, it is used for electrical contacts in switches. Electroplated gold has many uses in electronic devices, such as on wave guides for radar, on electron-tube grids, and on electrical contacts.

Because gold does not corrode, it is sometimes used in laboratory equipment and

In the course of time, some of the alluvial deposits were covered over with soil. Others remained at the surface of the earth, where people could easily find them. These surface alluvial deposits of gold were probably people's first source of gold.

Gold is also found in a few minerals and in the ores of some other metals, particularly those of silver, copper, lead, and uranium. The gold is recovered as a by-product of refining these metals.

▶MINING TODAY

As the surface deposits were worked out, organized mining companies equipped with the latest machinery took over from individual prospectors. This was particularly true of the hard-rock mines, where the gold was still trapped in the quartz. Tunnels and shafts have been blasted to reach the gold-bearing rock layers. The rock is then crushed so that the ore can be treated. Some gold mines reach extreme depths. Mines in the Rand area of South Africa go down as deep as 3,700 meters (12,000 feet).

Gold is also recovered from deep riverbeds and the ocean floor by dredges. One type of dredge is used to mine deeply buried placers on dry land. The dredge is brought overland in pieces and assembled at the digging site. The dredge slowly chews its way ahead, digging up tons of dirt and gravel a day.

▶EXTRACTION AND REFINING

Gold dust and nuggets from stream beds can be recovered by the simple process of washing. But gold that is mined from hard-rock deposits or that occurs in mineral compounds must be extracted by chemical action. One of the oldest extracting processes, called **amalgamation**, was invented by the Romans. It is still used to a limited extent. Amalgamation is based on the fact that mercury can dissolve gold and a few other metals. The crushed ore is treated with mercury, which dissolves some of the gold in the ore. The liquid amalgam, as it is called, is separated from the crushed rock by squeezing it through leather bags. Then the amalgam is heated. The mercury boils off, leaving the gold.

The process most often used today is the **cyanide method**. Gold-bearing ores are crushed and treated with a solution of sodium cyanide. This chemical dissolves out the

WONDER QUESTION

What is "Fool's Gold"?

"Fool's gold" is a nickname for a mineral called **iron pyrites**, or simply **pyrite**. This mineral, a compound of iron and sulfur, is sometimes found as shiny, yellow, metallic-looking crystals in rocks. Often these crystals have been mistaken for gold, hence the name "fool's gold." Iron pyrites can be distinguished from gold by a number of simple tests. Iron pyrites is quite brittle and will shatter from a hammer blow; gold will simply flatten out. Iron pyrites decomposes when heated; gold melts. On a piece of unglazed white porcelain, iron pyrites leaves a greenish-black streak; gold leaves a yellow streak. The name "fool's gold" is also applied to the shiny, yellow mineral **chalcopyrite**, an ore of copper that also contains iron and sulfur.

precious metal, leaving the crushed rock as a sludge. The solution is then filtered and treated to separate the gold.

Gold is very seldom pure. It usually contains some silver, copper, or iron. The process of purifying the gold is called **refining**.

Modern gold refining is done by two methods. In one method the impure gold is treated with **sulfuric acid**. The gold is not affected by this acid, but silver, copper, and other metals are dissolved away.

The other method is **electrolytic refining**. The gold is dissolved in water solutions that contain nitrates or chlorides, and an electric current is passed through the solution. By properly controlling the strength of the current, the gold can be deposited on one of the electrical terminals while the other metals remain dissolved.

World Production. Slightly more than half of all the gold mined today comes from South Africa. The world's richest gold deposits were discovered there in 1886. The Ural Mountains of Russia are another rich source. Gold is also mined in Canada, the United States, central Africa, Australia, the Philippines, South America, Japan, Mexico, and India.

Reviewed by J. SCOTT WEAVER
Columbia University

See also GOLD, DISCOVERIES OF; METALS AND METALLURGY; MINES AND MINING; MONEY.

GOLD, DISCOVERIES OF

The news that gold has been discovered sometimes starts a gold rush. When that happens, thousands of people rush to the scene of the discovery to look for gold. It is like a big treasure hunt. Everybody dreams of getting rich overnight. Towns and cities spring up; some disappear, but others remain and flourish. Mines are developed, providing work for the townspeople. Gold rushes have created communities and mining industries in Australia, South Africa, New Zealand, Canada, the United States, and many other places.

Man's Long Search for Gold

Gold is a magic word. "Gold! Gold! Gold! Gold!" wrote the poet Thomas Hood. "Bright and yellow, hard and cold." It is the mythical treasure of King Midas and of Jason and his Argonauts. Many countries use gold as a standard of value for money.

Before the discovery of America most of Europe's gold had come first from the Mediterranean region, then from Africa. During the 16th century the search for treasure brought Spanish explorers to Central and South America. They hoped to find a golden land, *El Dorado*. Instead they found the treasure of the Aztecs and Incas in Mexico and Peru and shipped it back to Spain. From the New World flowed more gold than the world had ever seen up to that time. Until about 1800 South America supplied most of the world's gold.

▶ UNITED STATES

Gold was discovered in North Carolina about the year 1799, and the first gold rush took place in Georgia in 1829. But the age of the big gold rushes really began with the discovery at Sutter's mill, Coloma, California, in 1848.

California

On January 24, 1848, James Marshall was working at Captain John Sutter's mill. It was located about 40 miles up the American River from Sutter's Fort (near Sacramento). Noticing something yellow shining in the water, Marshall picked it up and excitedly reported his find to Sutter. They tested it. It was gold!

At first the news did not stir up much interest. But in May a businessman, Sam Brannan, showed his gold to the people of San Francisco. This was like a spark setting off a bonfire. Doctors, lawyers, merchants, tailors—anyone who could—rushed off to hunt for gold in the streams near Sutter's Fort.

Rumors of the discovery reached eastern newspapers. When President James K. Polk (1795–1849) announced it in his December, 1848, message to Congress, easterners, too, caught the gold fever. They began going west by thousands, singing to the tune of "Oh, Susanna"

> I shall soon be in San Francisco
> And then I'll look around,
> And when I see the gold lumps there
> I'll pick them off the ground.

During 1849 gold hunters, 80,000 strong, poured into California, which in 1850 became a state. In 3 years San Francisco grew from a village to a city of over 25,000 people, with fine homes, hotels, and an opera house.

The **forty-niners**—as the gold hunters were called—came to California by three different routes. Some of them sailed around Cape Horn, the southern tip of South America. This meant a dangerous 6-month voyage. Ships often were overcrowded and did not carry enough fresh food. Many travelers drowned or died from disease. When the ships arrived, crews left them and ran off to the diggings where gold had been found. Over 500 ships were left at anchor in this way in San Francisco Bay. Not all were American ships, for the forty-niners came from all over the world.

Gold hunters who wanted a quicker route sailed to Central America. They crossed to the Pacific through the jungles of the Isthmus of Panama or Nicaragua. Then they waited for a ship to take them to the West Coast. Altogether about 39,000 men and women took these two sea routes.

Over 40,000 took the land trails across the continent, headed for Sacramento, as the song said, "with my washbowl on my knee." In May, 1849, a steady stream of wagon and mule trains pulled out of St. Joseph and Independence, Missouri. Most of these gold hunters were farmers or town dwellers and knew very little about pioneering. Much of the equipment they brought along was useless and had to be thrown away on the journey. Almost one out of eight adventurers died on the way to "Californi-o."

Most of California's gold was found in the gold-bearing sands and gravels of stream beds. These deposits were easily worked by **placer mining**. All that was necessary was to separate the **gold dust** or larger **nuggets** from the sand by washing it in a pan or with a hose or by using a **dredge**. You do not have to dig mines or use complicated machinery for this type of mining.

A forty-niner prospected along a stream by **panning gold**. He scooped up sand or gravel and water into a bowl or pan and shook it around. Then he tilted the pan to let the water carry off the sand, leaving the heavier gold in the pan. If the prospector had a **lucky strike** (or struck **pay dirt**) and his pan **showed color**, he **staked a claim** at the spot where he found the gold.

Prospectors later found that they could clear more gold-bearing earth if they rocked a **cradle** or washed gold with a **long tom**. Groups sometimes tried to wash gold out of the hills by turning a powerful hose onto a hillside. This washed the earth down into a ditch, where they could separate the gold from the dirt.

Life in the mining camps was hard. Men lived in tents and huts made of pine branches. They stood in icy water to pan gold. But each man hoped to **strike it rich**. One man's claim produced $40,000 worth of gold in a single month. A rich find was the Calaveras Nugget, which weighed 162 pounds and was worth $43,534. In the peak year 1852 California's goldfields produced gold worth $80,000,000.

Life also was full of disappointments. As more prospectors arrived to stake claims, there was less gold for everyone. Prices for food and lodging were high. There were shootings too. The gold hunters had to form their own courts to punish criminals and men who took other prospectors' claims.

By the middle 1850's the best placer gold deposits had been used up. Much of the remaining gold was deep underground in layers, or veins, of rock (usually quartz) called **lodes**. This gold could not be mined without machinery.

Nevada and Colorado

Unlike other American frontiers, the gold rush frontier moved eastward instead of westward. In 1859 two men began working their claim near Virginia City, Nevada. They found considerable gold in the gravel mixed with "blue stuff." This "blue stuff" turned out to be almost pure silver. News of the discovery brought a rush of **fifty-niners** to the Comstock Lode, as it was called. Although chiefly silver, this was the richest find in mining history.

Colorado also had a gold rush in 1859. Wagons with signs reading "Pike's Peak or Bust" rolled in from Missouri. Very little gold was found at first, and soon the wagons were rolling eastward again. This time the signs read "Busted, by Gosh!" But even as the fifty-niners headed home, a rich strike was made at Clear Creek. By 1860 a real gold rush was in full swing. Strikes at Leadville and other places followed. The discovery at Cripple Creek in the 1890's led to one of the last American gold rushes. Like the Comstock, the Colorado mines produced great fortunes.

Other Gold Discoveries in the Rockies

Strikes in Idaho, near Lewiston and Boise, brought gold hunters from Nevada, Colorado,

---

SOME GOLD RUSH TERMS

Cradle—Device used for washing gold. Sand was put on a piece of metal with holes in it that covered the cradle. When the sand was washed off, the gold caught on slats in the cradle underneath the metal.

Diggings—Name for the place where gold is found.

Dredge—Machine with a series of buckets that scoop up gravel from a riverbed.

Forty-niners—Men and women who went to California in the gold rush of 1849. **Fifty-niners**—Those who went to Colorado in the gold rush of 1859.

Gold dust—Name given to grains of gold in powder or dust form.

Gold rush—Mass movement of people to a place where gold is discovered.

Lode—Layer or vein of rock, usually quartz.

Long tom—Wooden trough 12 to 25 feet long used by miners for washing gold from sand or gravel. The sand was washed through holes in a piece of iron attached to one end. The gold caught on the slats in the box underneath the metal.

Lucky strike—Finding a large amount of gold on your claim.

Nugget—Lump of gold.

Pan gold—Wash sand or gravel with water in a pan until it is washed away, leaving the heavier gold in the pan.

Pay dirt—Earth, sand, or gravel where gold is found.

Placer mining—Surface mining for gold.

Prospect—Hunt for gold or other minerals.

Show color—Gold dust left in the pan after it has been washed shows up as a streak of yellow.

Stake a claim—Indicate (by driving stakes into the ground) the boundaries of the area claimed by a prospector hunting for gold.

Strike it rich—Find a rich deposit of gold.

and California. Bannack, Montana, was the scene of a gold rush in 1862.

During the 1870's a strike in the Black Hills of South Dakota not only brought in gold hunters but helped to start a war as well. For years there had been rumors of gold in the Black Hills, but the government had given the land to the Sioux Indians. Although soldiers tried to keep miners out, they managed to slip in anyway. By 1875 a gold rush was under way. One of the towns that sprang up was Deadwood, famous for Wild Bill Hickok and Calamity Jane. The Indians tried in vain to drive the white men from the area. The Sioux lost the battle of Wounded Knee in 1890 and with it the last great Indian war of the West.

▶ CANADA AND ALASKA

A gold strike on British Columbia's Fraser River in 1858 brought a rush of 25,000 prospectors. Others followed at the news of discoveries in the Cariboo Mountains 4 years later.

The Klondike River, a branch of the Yukon River, was the area of North America's last gold rush. It started in 1897. By the early 1900's Nome and Fairbanks in Alaska were the centers of gold strikes. Placer mining was used mostly, but frost created a special problem for Alaskan miners. They had to stack blocks of frozen gravel and wait for the ice to melt.

▶ AUSTRALIA AND NEW ZEALAND

One of the most important events in the early history of Australia was the discovery of gold. In 8 years the country's population doubled. The first major discovery was made by E. H. Hargraves near Bathurst, New South Wales, early in 1851. Later the same year finds at Ballarat and Bendigo in Victoria set off the gold rush of 1852. In 1869 a nugget weighing about 157 pounds was found in Victoria. The "Welcome Stranger," which was the name given to it, lay only a few inches deep in a rut made by a cart.

Many discouraged California prospectors headed for Australia. There they prospected with pans and other simple tools, as they had in California. But there was a difference. Although American discoveries had been made on government land, the government did not interfere with the gold hunters. In Australia, on the other hand, they had to get a license from the government to hunt for gold on public land.

Gold was found in every state in Australia, but the richest deposits were those in Victoria and Western Australia. The big rushes in Western Australia began with the discovery of gold at Coolgardie in 1864. Even bigger deposits were found at Kalgoorlie, where the famous Golden Mile was discovered in 1893. Kalgoorlie is still one of the world's great goldfields.

The earliest important discovery of gold in New Zealand came in 1852, at Coromandel on North Island. Not until 1861 was a permanent goldfield found, at Tuapeka, in Otago on Smith Island. Most of these deposits were worked by dredging.

Here as elsewhere, gold mining brought in many settlers. By the end of the 19th century the gold rush period was disappearing in Australia and New Zealand as well as in North America.

▶ SOUTH AFRICA

Gold was found on the Witwatersrand (or the Rand) in the Transvaal in 1886. This was one of the last great gold discoveries outside North America. The Rand is one of the world's largest and richest goldfields. Some of the deposits are more than 8,000 feet deep. Mining the gold took money and machinery. Businessmen were needed to run the mines. Gold mining and diamond mining became the basis of South Africa's wealth.

Not all gold discoveries started big gold rushes, and gold rushes have not always made lots of gold hunters rich. Some rushes were only important for adventure and excitement and for the stories they provided such writers as Mark Twain and Bret Harte. But all important gold discoveries have influenced the economy of the country in which they were made, and sometimes the world economy as well. One lasting effect of the discoveries of gold in the American West and elsewhere was to speed up settlement. People came to hunt for treasure and stayed to build a country.

ELISABETH MARGO
Author, *Taming of the Forty-Niner*

GOLDFISH. See FISH AS PETS.

GOLDWATER, BARRY. See ARIZONA (Famous People).

GOLF

Although the exact origin of the game of golf is unknown, we know that people have played games with balls and sticks since ancient times. Some historians think that the first true golfers were ancient shepherds who passed the time by using their wooden staffs to knock small stones into holes. In the 1200's the Dutch played a game similar to hockey called *Colf*, and the strong trading ties between the Dutch and the Scots during the 1400's may account for the migration of a similar game from Holland to Scotland, where it then grew into the game played today. There is no question that the modern game of golf was born in Scotland.

An aerial view of a golf course, which can be 9 holes or a standard 18 holes numbered to indicate the sequence in which the course should be played.

▶ HOW GOLF IS PLAYED

The game of golf is played by hitting a small ball with a club from a specifically marked area, the **teeing ground**, across a grassy field, the **fairway**, and into a small hole in a manicured area of grass, the **green**. This whole area is also referred to as a hole. The object of the game is to get the ball from the teeing ground into the hole in as few hits, or **strokes**, as possible. A standard golf course is made up of 18 holes, numbered 1 through 18. A golfer plays each hole in order, recording the number of strokes taken for each hole. A round of golf consists of playing 18 holes or 9 holes, depending on the size of the golf course. The number of strokes—the scores—for each hole are added up to get a final score for the number of holes played in the round.

Equipment

A golf ball is about half the size of a baseball, no less than 1 2/3 inches (4.27 centimeters) in diameter, and is designed to fly long distances. Made by molding a high-impact plastic cover around an energized rubber core, a golf ball can travel more than 300 yards (274 meters) in the air when struck by the strongest players. Hundreds of small dimples in the cover enhance the ball's aerodynamic qualities. For maximum visibility, most golf balls are white.

The rules state that a golfer may carry no more than 14 golf clubs at a time. A **set of clubs** has four categories: woods, irons, wedges, and a putter. Each category is different, but the basic construction is the same: Each club has a rubber **grip** for the hands; a **shaft**, which is usually made of steel or graphite; and a **clubhead**, usually made of steel, which makes contact with the ball.

With the exception of the putter, every golf club has an angled **clubface** that lifts the ball into the air at impact. This angle is called **loft**. Generally, the less loft a club has, the longer the shaft and the longer the ball will fly. A number, usually from 1 to 11, which refers to the loft, is stamped on the bottom of most clubs. The lower the number, the less loft the club carries. The longest-hitting club in a set is usually a 1-wood, with the least loft, typically 8 to 10 degrees, and the longest shaft, usually 43 to 45 inches (109 to 114 centimeters). A 2-wood club carries 4 degrees more loft in the clubface and has a shaft that is one-half inch shorter. This produces a slightly shorter shot that rises faster in the air. The numbering continues through to the shortest, most lofted clubs, the wedges, numbered 10 and 11, which produce the shortest, fastest-rising shots of all.

Woods are so named because for years they were made with wooden heads. In the early 1980's, manufacturers began making the heads out of stainless steel. Today, heads made of wood are rare. Woods have the

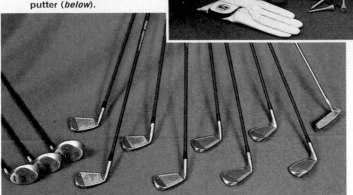

Some of the equipment used for the game of golf: shoes with metal cleats, a golf glove, a golf bag and clubs, club covers, golf balls, and tees (*right*). A golfer may carry no more than 14 clubs at a time. Shown here is a typical set of clubs: the 1-, 3-, and 5-woods, the 3- through 9-irons, a wedge, and a putter (*below*).

useful around the green. Here, **chips**—short, controlled shots that fly a very short distance and roll most of the way to the hole—and **pitches**—shots that fly slightly farther than chips—are required. There are three types of wedges. The pitching wedge is the least lofted and is used for short approach shots, chips, and pitches. The sand wedge is designed specifically for play from sand bunkers. The lob wedge, the shortest and most lofted club in the entire set, is used for high-flying, soft-landing short shots around the green.

A putter has little or no loft and is used to roll the ball across the green and into the hole. For control, putters usually have the shortest shafts, at 32 to 34 inches (81 to 86 centimeters), allowing the golfer to crouch directly over the ball while lining up a shot.

longest shafts in the set, and they can send the ball farther than irons. They also have their own subcategories: the driver (also known as the 1-wood) is used to hit the ball off a tee; fairway woods (3-, 4-, and 5-woods) are slightly shorter and more lofted than the driver and are used for long shots from the fairway; and utility woods (6-, 7-, 8-, and 9-woods) are shorter and more lofted than the average fairway wood and are used for shorter shots from the fairway. Utility woods are also used for long shots from the **rough**, an area of longer grass that makes it more difficult to make clean contact with the golf ball. The standard set of clubs has a driver and two or three fairway woods. Utility woods, while valuable, are usually optional.

Irons were once made of iron, giving them their name, but for years they have been made of steel. They are shorter than woods and are used for shorter shots from the fairway and rough that are intended to reach the green. Irons have their own subcategories: long irons (1-, 2-, 3-, and 4-irons), mid-irons (5-, 6-, and 7-irons), and short irons (8- and 9-irons). Most sets come with irons 3 through 9. The 1- and 2-irons are optional.

Wedges, which look like irons, are the shortest, most lofted clubs in the set and are

The Golf Course

Each hole on a golf course is assigned two numbers—the hole number, 1 through 18, which indicates the sequence in which the course should be played, and the par number, usually a 3, 4, or 5. **Par** refers to how many strokes it should take a professional golfer to hit the ball from the teeing area into the hole. For the most part, a hole's par is based on how long it is. If the green is close enough that a player should be able to reach it in one shot from the tee, the assigned par is 3, allowing for two putts once the green is reached. If two shots are required to reach the green from the teeing area, the assigned par is 4, and if three shots are required, the par is 5. On most courses, the pars of all 18 holes add up to a number from 70 to 72.

A teeing ground is a distinct area marked by shorter grass and objects, usually big colored balls, called **tee markers**. To begin any hole, the ball is placed on a **tee**, or 2-inch (5-centimeter) peg, between the tee markers. On par-3's, the object is for the tee shot to finish on the green, as close as possible to the flagstick, which marks the hole. On par-4's and

The longer the golf club, the longer the backswing and the farther the golf ball will fly. Notice the difference at the top of the swing between a driver used off the tee (*right*) and a mid-iron used in the fairway (*below*).

-5's, the object is for the tee shot to finish in the fairway, an alley that can be as narrow as 25 yards (23 meters) or as wide as 100 yards (91 meters) that runs most of the way from the tee to the green. The fairway is short grass, from which it is easy to hit the ball. It is usually bordered by rough.

The green has the shortest grass of any spot on the course. It is like a carpet, making it easy for the ball to roll toward the hole. The hole is 4 1/4 inches (10.8 centimeters) across and at least 4 inches (10 centimeters) deep. Surrounding the green is a slightly longer apron of grass, called the **fringe**, and outside the fringe is usually rough.

Virtually all golf courses have **hazards**, areas that challenge, or even penalize, the golfer whose ball lands in them. The most common hazards are **sand bunkers**, large pits in the ground filled with sand. Sand is less stable than grass and makes a solid swing and contact with the golf ball more difficult. Sand bunkers, or sand traps, as they are less formally called, are often strategically placed near the green or in the fairway. Also

common to many courses are water hazards, usually marked with red stakes. These can be creeks, streams, ponds, lakes, or any other bodies of water. Sections of land marked with white stakes are designated as out of bounds. These may be residential or heavily wooded areas in which golfers are not allowed to hit shots. Hitting the ball into a water hazard or out of bounds costs the golfer penalty strokes.

The Rules of the Game

The first official "Rules of Golf" were drawn up in 1754 at the Royal and Ancient Golf Club of St. Andrews in Scotland. Today, the R & A is the governing body of European golf, while the United States Golf Association (USGA), founded in 1894, serves the same purpose in the United States. Each organization has its own set of rules, both somewhat different from the first rules drawn up in 1754 but virtually identical to each other.

Although the object of the game is fairly simple, the fact that so many things can happen during a round can make the rules complicated to follow. Both the USGA and the R & A publish a rule book that covers the entire game. Because there are no referees in golf, all players must read the rule book and know the rules. Here are some of the basic rules in golf.

Each hole begins between the two markers on the teeing ground, and the golfer has the option of placing the ball on a tee. Every time a swing is made with the intention of hitting the ball, it counts as a stroke. There are no "do overs" or "don't counts."

Except for tee shots, whenever the ball is in play—not out of bounds or in a water hazard—it must be played from where it sits. There are two exceptions to this rule. One refers to areas marked as ground under repair or to **free-drop** areas like cart paths or around

Short shots count just as much as long ones. Here, a golfer hits a pitch shot with a wedge, the shortest, most lofted club in a set.

sprinkler heads. In these cases, the player is allowed to move the ball without penalty to the nearest playable area that is no closer to the hole. Another exception refers to what are called **unplayable lies**, when the ball is in play but is almost impossible to hit. For example, when it is stuck in the branches of a bush, the ball may be moved to the nearest playable area no closer to the hole, but one stroke is added to the score as a penalty.

When golfers play in a group, the order of play is determined by who is farthest from the hole after the tee shot. That person plays first. On each teeing ground, the golfer with the lowest score on the previous hole hits first. This is called **having the honor**.

The most common penalties are given when the ball is hit into a hazard. Each type of hazard has a different set of rules. Water hazards add two strokes to a score—the stroke that hit the ball in the water and a penalty stroke. The ball is then played from a spot closest to where it first entered the hazard. Out of bounds also costs the golfer the original stroke plus a penalty, but the ball must be played from the same spot as the original stroke. This is called a **stroke-and-distance** penalty. Sand bunkers carry no penalty, but it costs the golfer one stroke if, in making the escape shot, the club touches the sand at any time other than on impact with the ball. For example, if the golfer rests the club on the ground during the set up, a penalty is given.

All golf courses have hazards—areas that challenge and sometimes penalize the golfer whose ball lands in them. This player is hitting the ball from a sand trap.

On the green, the flagstick should be taken out of the hole before putting; if the ball hits the flagstick, a one-stroke penalty is given. If a putted ball hits another golfer's ball, the penalty is also a stroke. When other members of the group are putting, each golfer marks his or her ball by placing a small, flat object, such as a coin, behind the ball, and then picks up the ball. There is no penalty for hitting another golfer's mark.

Handicaps and Competition

Golf is a sport in which players of all abilities can play with each other and compete on an equal level. This is made possible by the **handicap system**, administered by the USGA, which gives players of lesser ability a cushion of strokes so they can compete with better players. A complicated mathematical formula is used to compute the handicap. The basic idea is that a player who takes an average of 80 strokes per round "spots," or gives an additional, 10 strokes to the player who averages 90 per round, allowing for a fair match.

A golfer prepares to putt the ball as his playing partner tends to the flagstick, which should be taken out of the hole before putting.

Competition in golf has two basic forms: **match play** and **medal play**, also known as **stroke play**. Match play pits a golfer or team head-to-head against another golfer or team, and it is played hole by hole. Each hole is a competition in itself; the player or team who wins the most holes wins the match, regardless of what the total score is. Medal, or stroke, play pits the golfer against the golf course; each golfer plays her or his best, counting every stroke, and the player or team with the lowest total score wins. Most tournaments, both professional and amateur, are stroke-play competitions. A few, including the U.S. and British Amateur championships, are match-play competitions.

▶ THE HISTORY OF GOLF

The Honourable Company of Edinburgh Golfers, which convened for the first time in Edinburgh, Scotland, in 1744, was the first organized golf club on record. However, the modern game originated at the Society of St. Andrews Golfers, formed in 1754 and later renamed the Royal and Ancient Golf Club of St. Andrews. It was here that the first set of official rules was drafted and it was determined that a golf course should be 18 holes.

Golf came to the Americas in the late 1800's. The first North American golf club on record was in Canada—The Royal Montreal Golf Club, which was formed in 1873. The first club in the United States was the St. Andrews Club in New York, formed in 1888. In 1894, representatives from five of the first American golf clubs drew up a charter and formed the United States Golf Association.

From the beginning, golf in the United States has been associated with wealth. The charter clubs of the USGA were all formed in historic and wealthy communities: St. Andrews, at Hastings-on-the-Hudson, New York; Newport Country Club, in Newport, Rhode Island; the Country Club, in Brookline, Massachusetts; Shinnecock Hills Golf Club, in Southampton, New York; and Chicago Golf Club, in the suburb of Wheaton, Illinois.

Tournament Play

A turning point for golf in America occurred in 1913. After 72 holes of regulation play in the U. S. Open, an unknown 20-year-old, American amateur Francis Ouimet, was tied with two legendary British professionals, Harry Vardon and Ted Ray. Ouimet was not given much chance in the 18-hole playoff, but he shocked the world by not just winning, but by whipping the pros. The final scores were Ouimet 72, Vardon 77, Ray 78. A former caddie from a modest background, Ouimet became the first amateur to win the U.S. Open and legitimized golf as a game that everybody could play.

Robert Tyre "Bobby" Jones, Jr., was the next person who became a major influence in golf. In the 1920's he was considered the best player in the game. However, he never turned professional, choosing instead to remain an amateur and to play competitive golf strictly for pleasure. In 1930, Jones won what was then golf's Grand Slam: the U.S. Open, the U.S. Amateur, the British Open, and the British Amateur. He retired from competition that same year, having set a standard for playing the game with integrity.

The PGA Tour

After Jones, professional golfers became the heroes of the game. The Professional Golfers' Association of America (PGA) was created in 1916, and in the 1940's and 1950's, players such as Ben Hogan, Sam Snead, and Byron Nelson captured the imagination of sports fans worldwide. Hogan worked tirelessly on his game, returning from a near-fatal auto accident to win the U.S. Open in 1950, despite barely being able to walk. Snead, who learned to play by swinging a sapling, is still considered the most natural player in the world.

However, the person perhaps the most responsible for increasing the popularity of golf was Arnold Palmer. Palmer turned professional in 1955 and won fans with his emotional, aggressive play and likable personality. During his career professional golf became a weekly event on television, and Palmer's charisma spread nationwide. After Palmer, the dominant player was Jack Nicklaus, considered by many to be the best United States golfer ever to play the game. Nicklaus won his first U.S. Open in 1962 at the age of 22. By 1986, he had won 18 major championships and 70 PGA Tour events. Since Nicklaus, no single player dominated the game the way he and Palmer did. Johnny Miller in the early 1970's and Tom Watson from the late 1970's to the early 1980's were considered the best players of those times. But since Watson, no golfer has been considered a dominant player for more than a year. Some of the most successful golfers in the 1990's included Greg Norman, Nick Price, Curtis Strange, and Nick Faldo. All have won multiple championships and contended in many others.

Women in Golf

Just as they did in many areas of society, women struggled for equal rights on the golf course. In 1894, a group of women opened the first all-female golf club in Morris County, New Jersey. A year later, they were bought out by the club's male financial backers and were allowed to play only at specified times that would not inconvenience male members of the club. In 1899, the Country Club, one of the charter members of the USGA, instituted the following restrictions against women: They could not play on holidays, Saturdays, or before 2:00 P.M. on week-

Great Players in the History of Golf

The World Golf Hall of Fame was dedicated in 1974 at Pinehurst, North Carolina. Male and female golfers are chosen on the basis of playing ability or service to the game. In 1986, the Professional Golfers' Association (PGA) took over operation of the Hall of Fame. The Ladies Professional Golf Association (LPGA) operates a separate Hall of Fame based in Daytona Beach, Florida. In order to qualify, a player must be a member of the LPGA for at least 10 years and win at least 30 LPGA events, including 2 majors. In 1998, both the World and LPGA Halls of Fame will move to the PGA Tour's World Golf Village, located outside Jacksonville, Florida. All of the golfers profiled are in one or both of these Halls. A biography of Bobby Jones is in Volume J-K.

PATTY BERG (1918–) won more than 80 tournaments during her competitive career, including a record 15 major championships. During the early years of the LPGA Tour, Berg served as its president and most dominant player, winning the Vare Trophy for low-scoring average in 1953, 1955, and 1956, and leading the money list in 1954, 1956, and 1957. She was elected to the LPGA (1951) and World Golf (1974) Halls of Fame in their inaugural years.

PATTY BERG

MILDRED "BABE" DIDRIKSON ZAHARIAS (1914–56), one of the greatest athletes of all time, won 1 silver and 2 gold medals in track and field at the 1932 Olympics before taking up golf. As an amateur, she won 17 consecutive tournaments, and as a pro, she helped found the LPGA. She won 31 of 128 scheduled events between 1949 and 1955 on the LPGA Tour, including 3 U.S. Women's Opens. She was elected to the LPGA (1951) and World Golf (1974) Halls of Fame.

MILDRED "BABE" DIDRIKSON ZAHARIAS

WALTER HAGEN (1892–1969) was America's first dominant professional golfer. A gifted, confident shotmaker, "the Haig" won 11 major titles between 1914 and 1929, including 5 PGA Championships, 4 of them consecutively. In 1922, he became the first American to win the British Open, and from 1927 to 1939, he served as captain of the American team in the Ryder Cup (a semi-annual competition between a team of U.S. and a team of European professionals). He was elected to the World Golf Hall of Fame in 1974.

WALTER HAGEN

BEN HOGAN

NANCY LOPEZ

BYRON NELSON

JACK NICKLAUS

ARNOLD PALMER

BEN HOGAN (1912–97), one of the most expert hitters of all time, won the U.S. Open in 1948, 1950, 1951, and 1953, the British Open in 1953, and the Masters and PGA titles each twice. His successful return to golf after a near-fatal car accident inspired the movie *Follow the Sun*. In 1953, Hogan was elected to the PGA Hall of Fame.

NANCY LOPEZ (1957–) was the first player ever to be named LPGA Rookie of the Year and Player of the Year in the same year—1978. She won 9 tournaments that year and 8 the next, and in 1983, she became the youngest golfer, male or female, to pass the $1 million mark in career earnings. After winning 35 titles, including 2 LPGA Championships, Lopez was elected to the LPGA (1987) and World Golf (1989) Halls of Fame.

BYRON NELSON (1912–), one of golf's greatest players, dominated the PGA tour during the years of World War II (1939–45). In 1945, he won 18 tournaments, including 11 in a row. Nelson's scoring average that year was an incredibly low 68.33 for 120 rounds. Nelson also won 4 major championship titles between 1937 and 1942 when the tour was at full strength. He was elected to the World Golf Hall of Fame in 1974.

JACK NICKLAUS (1940–), known as the Golden Bear, is regarded as the greatest U.S. golfer ever to play the game. After a distinguished amateur career, he won 70 titles on the PGA Tour and 18 major championships, including 6 Masters, 5 PGA Championships, 4 U.S. Opens, and 3 British Opens. Also a designer of golf courses, Nicklaus was elected to the World Golf Hall of Fame in 1974.

ARNOLD PALMER (1929–) and his aggressive style of play led golf's charge onto television in the early 1960's. In the final round of the 1960 U.S. Open, Palmer shot a 65 to close the 7-stroke gap between the leader and himself and win. During his career, he won 61 tour events and 6 other majors, including 4 Masters. His other great contribution—as an ambassador for the game—cannot be measured. He was elected to the World Golf Hall of Fame in 1974.

GARY PLAYER (1935–), the first foreign player to make a big impact on the PGA Tour, went from South Africa, his native country, to England before coming to the United States in 1958. An incredibly hard worker dedicated to health and physical fitness, Player won more than 120 events worldwide, including 21 PGA Tour events. He is one of only four men to win all 4 major championships at least once, including 3 Masters and 3 British Opens. He was elected to the World Golf Hall of Fame in 1974.

GENE SARAZEN (1902–), among golf's best during the 1920's and 1930's, won a total of 7 championships. He is one of only four men to win all 4 major championships. His most famous victory came in 1935, when he made a double-eagle (3-under par) on the 15th hole of the final round of the Masters to tie Craig Wood, whom he beat the next day in a playoff. Sarazen is also credited with the invention of the sand wedge. He was elected to the World Golf Hall of Fame in 1974.

SAM SNEAD (1912–), considered the greatest natural player of all time, possessed a flowing swing that hit the ball for distance with finesse. This natural ability propelled him to a PGA Tour record of 81 total victories, which he won between 1937 and 1965. He won 3 Masters titles, 3 PGA Championships, and 1 British Open. At age 67, he became the first player to shoot his age in a PGA Tour event, shooting 67 in the second round of the 1979 Quad Cities Open. Snead was elected to the World Golf Hall of Fame in 1974.

LEE TREVINO (1939–) was a driving range pro before bringing his skills and his sense of humor to the PGA Tour in 1967. In 1968 he beat Jack Nicklaus in an 18-hole playoff to win the U.S. Open, and a legend was born. Between 1968 and 1984, he won 5 major titles, and in 1971, he won the U.S., Canadian, and British Opens in the span of 4 weeks. He was elected to the World Golf Hall of Fame in 1981.

HARRY VARDON (1870–1937), one of the most accurate golfers of all time, revolutionized the golf swing with the Vardon grip, in which the pinkie of the right hand overlaps the forefinger of

GARY PLAYER

GENE SARAZEN

SAM SNEAD

LEE TREVINO

HARRY VARDON

GLENNA COLLETT VARE

TOM WATSON

KATHY WHITWORTH

MICKEY WRIGHT

the left. Between 1896 and 1914, Vardon won a record 6 British Open titles. In his memory the U.S. and European PGA Tours present the Vardon Trophy each year to the player with the lowest scoring average. He was elected to the World Golf Hall of Fame in 1974.

GLENNA COLLETT VARE (1903–89), America's first great woman golfer, won the U.S. Women's Amateur a record 6 times between 1922 and 1935. A lifelong amateur, Vare also won 6 Eastern Amateurs and 6 North and South Amateur titles. In 1953, the LPGA Tour named its annual prize for lowest scoring average the Vare Trophy. She was elected to the World Golf Hall of Fame in 1975.

TOM WATSON (1949–), known as the person who toppled Jack Nicklaus from pro golf's mountaintop, won 20 tournaments between 1977 and 1980 and was PGA Player of the Year all 4 years. Of his 32 victories, 8 are major titles, including 5 British Opens, 2 Masters, and 1 U.S. Open—in 1982, when he beat Jack Nicklaus by holing an improbable shot from off the green on the 71st hole. He was elected to the World Golf Hall of Fame in 1988.

KATHY WHITWORTH (1939–), with 88 official LPGA victories to her credit, has won more titles than any professional golfer, male or female. Between 1965 and 1973, she led the money list 8 times, winning 10 tournaments in 1968 and 8 tournaments in 1963, 1965, 1966, and 1967. Whitworth won the LPGA Championship 3 times and in 1981 was the first LPGA player to pass $1 million in career earnings. Whitworth was elected to both the LPGA (1975) and World Golf (1982) Halls of Fame.

MICKEY WRIGHT (1935–), who raised public awareness of the LPGA Tour and helped it grow, dominated the tour in the early 1960's by winning 49 tournaments from 1960 to 1964. Included in her 82 career victories are 13 major titles. Wright was the first to win back-to-back U.S. Women's Opens (1958, 1959), and she won 4 LPGA Championships (1958–64). She was elected to both the LPGA (1964) and World Golf (1976) Halls of Fame.

MAJOR GOLF COMPETITIONS

AMATEUR

The **U.S. Amateur Championship** (men's and women's) is a match-play competition of America's best amateurs. The **British Amateur Championship** (men's and women's) is a match-play competition of Europe's best amateurs. The **U.S. Mid-Amateur** (men's and women's) is a match-play championship for amateurs aged 25 or over. The **U.S. Amateur Public Links Championship** (men's and women's) is a match-play championship for players with no private-course privileges. The **Walker Cup** is a biannual match-play competition between a team of the top male amateurs from the United States and a team of Europe's best. The **Curtis Cup** is a team match-play competition for women between the best U.S. amateurs and the best European amateurs.

PROFESSIONAL

The **PGA Tour**, the leading professional tour for men, the **LPGA Tour**, the leading professional tour for women, and the **PGA Senior Tour**, the professional tour for men aged 50 or over, all hold tournaments from January to December. They also hold annual qualifying schools to select new members. The **Masters**, the first of golf's four major

Tiger Woods, 1997 Masters winner

championships for men, features an international field and is held every April in Augusta, Georgia. The **Nabisco Dinah Shore Championship**, the first major championship of the year for the LPGA, is held every March in Rancho Mirage, California. The **U.S. Open** (men's and women's), the national championship, is open to both professionals and amateurs. It is held in June for men and is the second of four majors; for women, it is held in July and is the third of four majors. The **LPGA Championship**, the championship of women professionals, is held every May and is the second major of the year. The **British Open**, Europe's national championship for male professionals and amateurs, is held every July and is the third major of the year. The **PGA Championship**, the fourth major competition for male professionals, is held each August. The **Du Maurier Classic**, the fourth major competition for women professionals, is held every August in Canada at rotating courses. The **Ryder Cup**, a match-play competition between a team of top U.S. professionals and a team of Europe's best, is held biannually. The **Solheim Cup**, a professional team competition between American and European women, is held every other year at rotating sites.

---

days. This discrimination was all too typical of private country clubs in the early years, and in some clubs it still exists.

Despite the discrimination, women's golf has survived and produced many exceptional players over its long history. Glenna Collett Vare won the U.S. Women's Amateur six times between 1922 and 1935. Vare's opponent in the final match of the 1935 U.S. Amateur was Patty Berg, a 17-year-old who went on to become one of the first female professional golfers and to win 15 major championships. Berg was one of seven women who formed the Ladies Professional Golf Association (LPGA) in 1949. Also included in that

group was Mildred "Babe" Didrikson Zaharias, perhaps golf's greatest athlete. Winner of two gold medals and one silver medal in track and field at the 1932 Olympics, Zaharias took up golf soon after and quickly mastered the game. Her popularity and many accomplishments made women's golf popular, but her career and contributions were cut short when she died of cancer in 1956.

The LPGA Tour went on to become the world's showcase for women's golf. Mickey Wright's dominance of the tour from 1960 to 1964 (in 1963 she won 13 of the 32 tournaments) attracted media interest and brought recognition to the tour. Wright was succeeded by Kathy Whitworth, who won her first tournament in 1963 and would go on to win 87 more titles. In 1978, Nancy Lopez, a rookie, won nine tournaments, including five in a row. She went on to win 35 tournaments. In the 1990's the LPGA Tour had no single, dominant player. As on the men's PGA Tour, there have been a handful of outstanding players, among them Beth Daniel, JoAnn Carner, Pat Bradley, and Patty Sheehan.

▶ **GOLF—A GAME FOR A LIFETIME**

Because you can never be too young or too old to play golf, it is a game for an entire lifetime. It is not a game that can be mastered in a few days. Every course, every round, every shot is different, and there are always new things to learn, no matter how good you become. The first rule is to realize that it will take time to learn how to play golf.

The best way to learn the basics of the game is to take a few lessons from a PGA professional. Almost every course, whether private or public, has a resident PGA pro who teaches golf and offers lessons. Reading magazines or books can also be helpful, but the best instruction comes from a trained professional in a one-on-one situation. After learning the fundamentals, it is up to you to put them to use. Golf is a game of experience. Practicing is important and can be fun, but the best way to continue to improve your game is to play it a lot.

Many courses have programs that give juniors a place to meet other golfers their age as they learn the fundamentals. A typical junior program offers equipment, tournament play, and instruction. A big part of the process is etiquette, playing in a manner that respects other players and the golf course. As you learn the game, make golf etiquette a priority; it will make the game more enjoyable for you to play and make you more enjoyable to play with.

JONATHAN ABRAHAMS
Author, *First Tee, A Beginner's Guide to Golf*

GOMPERS, SAMUEL (1850–1924)

Samuel Gompers is considered the father of the labor movement in the United States. Through his efforts, American workers achieved higher wages and better working conditions than they had known before.

Born on January 27, 1850, in London, England, Samuel left school at the age of 10. When he was 13, the family immigrated to New York City, where Samuel found work in his father's trade, as a cigar maker. In 1864, when Samuel was 14, he became one of the first members of the Cigar-Makers' International Union. In 1875 he was elected president of his local branch.

An economic depression in the 1870's weakened the cigar union's negotiating power, and a strike in 1877 for higher wages and better working conditions failed. When the economy revived, Gompers helped reorganize his union, making it stronger and more efficient. It became a model for other labor organizations.

In 1886, 25 trade unions throughout the United States combined to form the powerful American Federation of Labor (AFL). Samuel Gompers was elected its first president and served for nearly forty years (1886–94; 1896–1924).

Gompers felt that labor's goals should be obtained by negotiating with employers and by putting pressure on the politicians. Labor, he said, should "reward its friends and punish its enemies" with votes. A forceful leader and dramatic speaker, Gompers was proud of his strength, boasting that he was "built of oak."

By 1920 the AFL had more than 4 million members. Although he worked to better the working conditions for women and children, he did not believe union membership should be extended to them, nor to African Americans or unskilled laborers.

In 1867, Gompers married Sophia Julian. They had five children who lived to adulthood. After his wife died in 1920, he married Grace Neuscheler. On December 13, 1924, Samuel Gompers died in San Antonio, Texas.

Reviewed by GERALD KURLAND
Author, *Samuel Gompers: Founder of the American Labor Movement*

See also LABOR MOVEMENT.

GONORRHEA. See DISEASES (Descriptions of Some Diseases).

GOODALL, JANE (1934–)

Jane Goodall, born on April 3, 1934, is a British zoologist who is best known for her studies of chimpanzees in the wild. Through her work, Goodall was able to transform the way scientists viewed the relationship of animals and human beings.

Goodall's studies began in 1960 in what is now called Gombe National Park, in Tanzania, Africa. Within her first five months at Gombe, Goodall made some surprising discoveries. Chimpanzees were not strictly vegetarians as previously thought. They hunted animals and ate their flesh. They also made tools. Goodall watched as chimpanzees selected long blades of grass or stripped twigs of bark. Once prepared, the implements were used to capture insects, such as termites.

Goodall began her observations without formal scientific training. Her strong interest in animals and keen intuitive sense were enough for anthropologist Louis Leakey to sponsor Goodall and send her into the wilds to study the chimpanzees. But for her findings to be taken seriously by other scientists, Goodall had to secure the proper academic credentials. In 1965, she earned her doctorate from Cambridge University in England.

During the next ten years, Goodall and her staff won the trust of many chimpanzees and made close observations of their behavior. The emphasis on the actions and responses of individual animals became a hallmark of Goodall's research.

By the 1970's, Goodall had gained worldwide recognition for her work. She continues doing research on the chimpanzees at Gombe. As an author, she has written both popular and scientific books about her research, including *My Friends, the Wild Chimpanzees* (1967) and *In the Shadow of Man* (1971). Since the mid-1980's, Goodall has also been involved in lobbying efforts to improve the conditions for chimpanzees captured or bred for medical research. She is also working to get chimpanzees listed as an endangered species.

ELIZABETH KAPLAN
Science Writer

GOOD FRIDAY. See EASTER.

GOODMAN, BENNY. See ILLINOIS (Famous People).

GOODYEAR, CHARLES (1800–1860)

Charles Goodyear invented the process of vulcanization, which transformed rubber from a useless material into a very valuable one.

Goodyear was born on December 29, 1800, in New Haven, Connecticut. As a young man he joined his father's hardware company and in 1826 started his own, but both companies failed. In 1834 he began experimenting with rubber. The trouble with rubber then was that it got sticky and soft when it was warm and hard as a board when cold. Goodyear set out to solve these problems.

He was already in debt from his other business ventures, but Goodyear borrowed money for his rubber experiments. He had married Clarissa Beecher in 1824 and had a growing family. The Goodyears and their seven children often had to depend on friends and neighbors for food. Several times Goodyear was put into debtors' prison because he could not pay the money he owed. By 1837, Goodyear had found a way to process rubber so that it was not so sticky. To advertise his product, he made and wore clothes and shoes made of rubber. He also made rubber piano covers and tablecloths.

Goodyear continued his experiments, trying to find a way to strengthen rubber. Finally, in 1839, he accidentally found a better way of making rubber so that it would not be affected by temperature. This process became known as vulcanization. Goodyear obtained a patent on the process, but he made little profit from it, because many others used it without paying him.

In 1851, Goodyear went to Europe to publicize his rubber, but his trip was a failure. He died, deeply in debt, in New York City on July 1, 1860.

Reviewed by TERRY S. REYNOLDS
Michigan Technological University

See also RUBBER.

GORBACHEV, MIKHAIL (1931–   )

Mikhail Sergeyevich Gorbachev was the last political leader of the Soviet Union. After coming to power in 1985, he introduced radical reforms that led his country toward democracy and a free market economic system. But he was unable to solve the Soviet Union's deep-seated economic problems or to control the nationalistic forces that his policies had unleashed. When he stepped down as its president in 1991, the Soviet Union had already ceased to exist.

Early Years and Career.   Gorbachev was born on March 2, 1931, in the village of Privolnoye in the Stavropol region of southern Russia. He studied law at Moscow State University, where he joined the Communist Party and met his future wife, Raisa, whom he married in 1956. After graduating in 1955, he returned to Stavropol, rising steadily in the ranks of the party. In 1978 he was called to Moscow as an expert in agriculture. In 1980 he was made a full member of the Politburo, the highest decision-making body in the Soviet Union. He had become close to the powerful Yuri Andropov, who was Communist Party leader from 1982 to his death in 1984. When Andropov's successor, Konstantin Chernenko, died in 1985, Gorbachev was chosen to head the party.

Soviet Leader.   Gorbachev quickly embarked on a sweeping program of economic and political reforms (*perestroika*) and a new policy of openness in the media (*glasnost*). He encouraged intellectuals to speak out freely and called for honesty in the writing of Soviet history.

Among his chief aims were improved relations with the United States and other nations. He met three times with President Ronald Reagan, and in 1987 concluded a nuclear arms limitation treaty with the United States. In 1988–89, Gorbachev withdrew Soviet troops from Afghanistan, where they had been fighting since 1979 to support an unpopular Communist government. He restored relations with China in 1989, after more than thirty years of hostility between the two countries. He also refused to intervene in the affairs of former Soviet allies in Eastern Europe, when, beginning in 1989, they replaced their Communist regimes with more democratic governments. For his achievements, Gorbachev was awarded the Nobel Peace Prize in 1990.

Domestic Crises.   At home, by contrast, Gorbachev was faced by growing crises. In his drive for economic efficiency, he had called for less control by government planners and more reliance on supply and demand and other market forces. He also had convinced the Communist Party to give up its monopoly on power and compete with other political groups for the support of the people. But his policies failed to revive the economy, now close to collapse, and by reducing the power of the party, he had weakened Soviet unity.

Gorbachev's power was enhanced by his election as president of the Soviet Union by the Congress of People's Deputies in 1990. But his inability to carry out effective economic reforms eroded his support. By early 1991 the revolution that he had begun was out of control, as one by one the Soviet republics declared their independence.

End of the Soviet Union.   In August 1991, Communist hard-liners opposed to Gorbachev's reforms attempted a government coup, holding Gorbachev a prisoner for three days. The plot failed, largely due to the resistance of Boris Yeltsin, leader of the Russian republic and Gorbachev's chief rival. After his release, Gorbachev resigned from the party. Early in December, Yeltsin announced the formation of the Commonwealth of Independent States, which included most of the former republics, and the end of the Soviet Union. On December 25, 1991, Gorbachev formally resigned from office. He returned briefly to public life in 1996, when he ran, unsuccessfully, for president of the Russian Federation.

RONALD GRIGOR SUNY
University of Michigan

GORDY, BERRY, JR. See MICHIGAN (Famous People).

GORILLAS.   See APES.

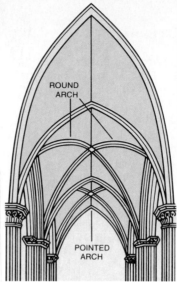

ROUND ARCH

POINTED ARCH

Ribbed vaulting and the pointed arch allowed Gothic architects to build magnificent churches that seemed to reach toward the sky. The awe-inspiring effect can be seen in Cologne Cathedral, Germany (*far left*), which was begun in 1248.

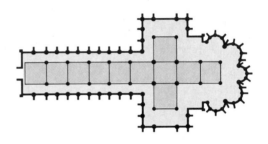

To make a ribbed vault, the plan of the church was divided into square sections called bays. Round arches spanned the bays diagonally from corner to corner. The use of pointed arches at the sides of the bays provided more space and enabled all the arches to reach the same height.

GOTHIC ART AND ARCHITECTURE

The style of art known as Gothic developed in Europe during the Middle Ages. It was mainly a method of building: Gothic characteristics appeared first in architecture. Many of the world's great cathedrals and churches were built in the Gothic style between the 12th and 16th centuries.

Gothic cathedrals are tall, their arches soar heavenward, and rays of sunlight pour through high, stained-glass windows and bathe the wood, masonry, and marble. Walls, columns, entrances, and doors are carved with figures and scenes from the Bible. Not only great cathedrals and abbeys but hundreds of smaller churches were built in the style. The Gothic style became popular throughout Europe. It spread to houses and castles and then to painting, sculpture, and the decorative arts.

Although it had a spirit of its own, Gothic architecture was in many ways based on the earlier style known as Romanesque. Romanesque architecture had preserved much of the style of Roman times. Little by little the plans of Roman public buildings were changed to suit the needs of the Christian religion. The result of these changes was Romanesque architecture.

The people who made Gothic art did not call it by that name. To them the work they did was simply the new fashion—the only possible style that could be used for buildings and objects, paintings and carvings, lettering and goldsmith's work. The term ''Gothic'' was first used during the Renaissance period,

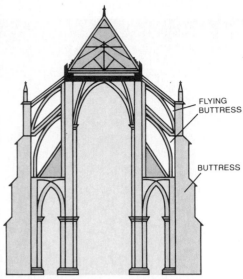

The weight of the vaults on the walls of Gothic buildings tended to force the walls outward, a concept called thrust. Buttresses built against the outside walls received the thrust from the vaulting. As buildings became higher, arch-shaped structures called flying buttresses were used to brace the walls.

The Cathedral of Notre Dame in Paris was built between 1163 and 1250. The aerial photograph at left clearly shows the flying buttresses that arch up from the buttresses to support the high walls.

which followed the Middle Ages. For some time the Gothic style was described as modern, in contrast to the classical Roman, which was called antique. But to provide it with a name of its own, people of the Renaissance took the word "Gothic" from the Goths, the people who had overrun the Roman Empire. Renaissance people thought, quite wrongly, that the Goths had brought this style with them.

▶ BACKGROUNDS OF THE GOTHIC

Three architectural features are typical of the Gothic. These are the pointed arch, the ribbed vault, and the flying buttress.

It is the pointed arch that most clearly makes Gothic building look different from Roman and Romanesque work. In the older style the semicircular, round arch was used

everywhere. But Gothic architects did not invent the pointed arch. It had been used much earlier in the Near East. It was used by Muslim artists in Asia, Africa, and even in parts of southern Europe. The use of the pointed arch in Europe started very soon after the First Crusade (1099), when Jerusalem was captured from the Muslims. Thousands of crusaders from Western Europe saw buildings and works of art entirely different from those that they were used to. Though they did not believe in the Muslim religion, there was no reason why they should not imitate the art that pleased them. This explains the arrival of the pointed arch in Europe.

The Europeans used the pointed arch in a new way. Medieval buildings were constructed with **vaults**—ceilings made by con-

Orvieto Cathedral (*left*), begun in 1290, is an outstanding example of Italian Gothic architecture. Notre Dame at Laon, France (*right*), an early Gothic building, was begun about 1160. It has some of the characteristics of the preceding Romanesque period.

tinuous arches of heavy columns. Architects of the late Romanesque period had experimented with the **ribbed vault,** which allowed them to build much higher churches. The plan of the church was divided into square sections called bays. At each corner a pier (large pillar) was built. Diagonally from corner pier to corner pier, round arches were built. Because the diagonal of a square is longer than its side, round arches on the sides of a bay would not be as high as the round arches that spanned the bay diagonally. It was found that pointed arches at the sides and round arches at the diagonals would all reach the same height. This system of building is called ribbed vaulting.

The weight of the vaults on the walls tended to force the walls outward. This is called **thrust.** To support the walls, structures called

buttresses were built against the outside of the walls. As ribbed vaulting enabled the construction of higher buildings, it became more difficult to resist the thrust from the arches. To support the additional weight of a higher building, buttresses had to be taller and to project more and more from the wall. Architects discovered that a fairly low buttress could be used to support the taller walls by means of a sloping arch, reaching up from the buttress and pressing against the outside of a higher wall. This kind of buttress is called a **flying buttress.**

When the flying buttress had been added to the ribbed vault and the pointed arch, all the main parts of Gothic architecture were there. As far as we know, all three were first used together at Durham Cathedral, in the north of England, about the year 1093. In spite of this,

Durham Cathedral was not yet Gothic in style, for round arches were still used in the cathedral.

▶THE FIRST GOTHIC

Within a very few years, probably between 1132 and 1144, a new church was built at the abbey of St. Denis, near Paris. This church is the first existing example of the Gothic style. It was a royal abbey, where the kings of France were buried in tombs that can still be seen. At that time the abbey was ruled by a great abbot named Suger, who was greatly interested in art of every kind. Suger wanted to make his church the finest and the most beautifully decorated in the Christian world.

Although Abbot Suger was a monk dedicated to a life of holiness, he did not believe that God's house should look bare and poor. Suger was fond of people—from the king to the beggar—and wanted them all to come to the services at his church. He insisted on rebuilding the much older St. Denis Church, which was small and old-fashioned.

Suger would not let any difficulty stand in his way. He arranged for the stone to be quarried—dug from the ground. He needed long wooden beams for the roof but was told such great timbers were not to be had; so he went out himself and searched in the forests until he found trees big enough to supply the beams he wanted. In the end he succeeded in getting the church built. It was dedicated in the presence of King Louis VII, on July 11, 1144.

▶THE SPREAD OF GOTHIC

King Louis liked what he saw, and his approval must have been one of the chief reasons for the rapid spread of the new fashion in building. Within five years after the dedication of St. Denis, an addition was made to the old west front of the cathedral of Chartres, about 50 miles (80 kilometers) from Paris. The work must have been done by the same artists who had worked for Abbot Suger. One of them even signed his name, Rogerus, behind one of the carved statues at Chartres. He was probably the chief of the masons, or stonecutters. Today we would call him the architect of the cathedral. He is the earliest Gothic architect whose name we know.

Within a few years great churches in the new style were being built all over north-eastern France. In Paris the Cathedral of Notre Dame was begun in 1163. It was completed around 1250. During the second half of the 12th century, the abbey at Pontoise and the abbeys of St. Martin-des-Champs, in Paris, and St. Remi, in Reims (Rheims), and the cathedrals of Sens, Noyon, Laon, Senlis, and Soissons were built. These early Gothic buildings still looked Romanesque in many ways.

It was not until near the year 1200 that Gothic architecture became completely different from Romanesque. The pure Gothic can be seen in France at Bourges Cathedral, begun about 1192, and in England at Lincoln Cathedral, built from 1192 to 1350. Slender **piers** (pillars) and buttresses were used, and great windows were decorated with stained glass to color the light as it poured into the churches.

▶THE INTERNATIONAL GOTHIC

By the 13th century the Gothic was the only style of building throughout northwestern Europe. The designs of vaulting, buttresses, and windows first produced by Gothic architects were imitated by other artists. The pointed arch is found again and again as a frame for paintings and ivory carvings. It is stamped on book covers and worked in metal for caskets and shrines. As time went on, the details of Gothic style developed and changed, first in the greater buildings and later in the smaller works of art.

The earliest Gothic windows had been narrow, but with a pointed instead of a round top. Then they became so large that it was necessary to put stone supports inside them to hold the glass firmly. These supports formed smaller pointed arches, circles, cloverleafs, and more complicated shapes. The stone patternwork inside each window is known as **tracery.**

Tracery, a typically Gothic form, was used at Reims (Rheims) Cathedral in 1211 or 1212 by the mason Jean d'Orbais. Reims Cathedral was the church where the coronations of French kings took place. It was this important royal connection that gave the new window tracery of Reims its great prestige.

While Reims Cathedral was being built it was visited by many architects. Impressed by the beauty of the new Gothic tracery, they made sketches of it. Among these architects

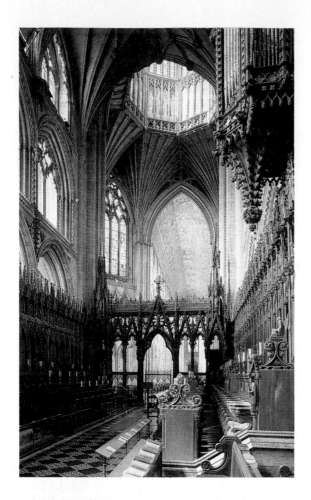

Supports in Gothic windows were carved in decorative patterns called tracery, seen here in the choir of Ely Cathedral, England. A form of tracery was also used along the walls and inside the octagon in the ceiling.

was Villard de Honnecourt, whose sketchbook can still be seen in the National Library in Paris. Honnecourt thought that the Reims windows were the most beautiful he had seen anywhere—and he had traveled across Europe through Switzerland and Germany and as far as Hungary. Other architects at the time were making sketches too, and the idea of tracery spread to many distant places.

Tracery may have been introduced to England by an architect called Master Henry, who had worked at Reims and who became the chief architect to King Henry III. He used tracery for the windows of Westminster Abbey, which he designed in 1245. Here the kings of England were to be crowned and buried. The new fashion was approved by the English king and was quickly adopted across the country. In France traceried windows like those at Reims were called the *style rayonnant* ("radiant style"). This term was used to describe a style of decorative art that was based on tracery. It referred, however, to decorative objects as well as to windows. Many people think that it represents the highest development of Gothic style.

Gargoyles, Cathedral of Notre Dame, Paris

WONDER QUESTION

What are gargoyles?

Fanciful stone figures called gargoyles are often seen on the roofs or eaves of Gothic buildings. Sometimes frightening, sometimes humorous, they include real and imaginary animals, imps and demons, and caricatures of people such as knights, monks, and religious pilgrims. Originally, a gargoyle was a plain waterspout that extended out from a rain gutter and directed water away from the building. (The term comes from the French word *gargouille*, which means "throat.") In time, the spouts were carved in the shapes of grotesque animals or humans, with the water flowing through the mouth of the figure. According to superstition, the gargoyle frightened away evil spirits as well as serving its practical purpose. After lead drainpipes were invented in the 1500's, gargoyles continued to be used as decoration. They are examples of the imagination and inventiveness of Gothic sculptors.

To this flowering of the Gothic belong the famous French cathedrals of Reims, Amiens, and Beauvais, in the north, while the same style was carried down to the south, through Limoges and Rodez to Narbonne.

During the Middle Ages many artists moved from place to place and from country to country, all over Europe, taking with them the latest ideas and the newest fashions in art. In Spain the *style rayonnant* influenced the design of the cathedral of Leon. There most of the glorious colored glass designed and made for the traceried windows still survives. In Germany, Cologne Cathedral was begun in 1245, but it was not finished for more than 600 years. French masons, under the architect Étienne de Bonneuil, were called far away to Uppsala, in Sweden, to design the cathedral that was built between 1270 and 1315.

Gothic Sculpture

Buildings in Gothic times supplied the framework into which all other arts fitted. Leaves, flowers, conventional patterns, and large statues were carved into the stonework of buildings. These statues were usually of saints or persons from the Bible: the prophets of the Old Testament and the kings of Judah, Christ and the Twelve Apostles, the story of the Crucifixion, Christ seated in judgment. Many of the architects who designed the buildings were also sculptors and carved the most important statues themselves. Others— and this became more common as time went on—only drew the general design of the statues and had sculptors carve them. The statues were not made just to stand on pedestals and be admired as fine art. They were always an important part of the design of the building.

Sculpture was used everywhere on Gothic churches. Figures of saints stood around the piers; scenes from the old and new testaments were carved above doorways. People were depicted more realistically during the Gothic period than during the Romanesque. The folds and wrinkles of garments were shown falling in a natural way. The faces of the statues had expressions, and their almond-shaped eyes seemed to look in one direction or another. This was unlike Romanesque sculpture, which was stiff and not naturalistic.

Gothic carvers often combined beautiful, natural-looking, and saintly figures with

Radiant stained-glass windows filled much of the wall space in Gothic cathedrals. Light poured through the glass, bathing the interior of the church in color. Circular "rose" windows, such as this one from Chartres Cathedral (13th century), are especially beautiful.

A closer look at a stained-glass window reveals the detail with which scenes, usually from the Bible, were depicted. Such scenes were important tools in teaching Christian beliefs to medieval people—many of whom could not read. This 13th century example from Canterbury Cathedral, England, shows the three wise men following the star to Bethlehem.

imaginary demons, imps, or other invented creatures. Sometimes these creatures were grotesque and sometimes they were funny. The Middle Ages was a time when the church had absolute authority, but that did not stop people from remembering the old legends and superstitions that had been passed down from their ancestors.

Gothic Painting

The earliest Gothic paintings were decorations on the walls of buildings. Later, stained-glass windows often took up much of the wall space, leaving no room for painting on a large scale. Smaller paintings on panels of wood were made to be placed above altars in churches. Other examples of Gothic painting are found in hand-decorated books called **illuminated manuscripts.** At first the paintings were mainly of religious subjects. Later the artists painted studies of real life. Plants and

animals and people served as models. It was during the Gothic period that artists stopped copying older forms and started basing their designs on shapes in nature.

▶GOTHIC ARCHITECTS

Abbeys, castles, and cathedrals called for many men to work together. The machinery—cranes and other hoisting devices, scaffolding, ladders, tools for centering arches and vaults—had to be taken care of and operated by specialists. The organization of such work was like that of modern construction groups, even as far back as the 12th century. All were under the direction of the architect.

The medieval architect was much like a modern architect. Then as now he had to make designs and prepare plans and other drawings of a building before it was begun. The plans of the vaults, buttresses, and window tracery all had to be worked out by

Many art forms flourished in Gothic churches. The statues at left, carved in the 13th century, are from the west entrance of Reims Cathedral. They depict a scene from the life of the Virgin Mary. The 15th-century Spanish painting at right was part of an altarpiece.

geometry before the stones could be cut to their proper shape. It was the architect who prepared full-size drawings of moldings that the masons used as patterns. When—as was often the case in the Middle Ages—special builders were employed, it was the architect's duty to check and control all construction.

Who were these architects? Most of them were stonemasons by training, able to shape stones for buildings. Often they were also able to carve both decorations and statues. Most of their training took place while working on a job. Under a master they learned how to choose stone from the quarry, how to cut it, how to draw, and how to design a building according to the traditions of the period and place. They were mostly well-educated men, who could read and write Latin as well as the language of their own country.

The best examples of an architect's skill, apart from the buildings themselves, are his drawings. Beautifully drawn on great sheets of parchment or paper, they were carefully preserved until the building was complete. Some of these drawings still exist at Cologne, at Vienna, and especially at Strasbourg.

▶THE LATER GOTHIC

The later Gothic was less fresh and less individual than it had been in the 12th and 13th centuries. There was less chance for invention. The rules for the design and proportions of every part of the building became too difficult for one man to master.

In the 15th century the clear rules for the proportions of architecture laid down by the Roman architect Vitruvius Pollio in the 1st century B.C. were again studied. It was natural that these simple rules should have been preferred by many people to the Gothic system, which required years of practice and study and which few but the architects themselves could understand at all. Gothic architecture and Gothic art had spread all over the western and northern parts of Europe. Gothic art even influenced the quite different forms of art of the Byzantine world to the east and the world of Islam to the south. But the Gothic style had never really taken root in Italy, the home of Roman architecture. There the round arch and the ancient orders of architecture were never altogether abandoned. The people of the Renaissance, reading the ancient manuscripts of

Beautifully decorated books called illuminated manuscripts were written and illustrated by hand. This page is from a 13th-century French picture Bible.

Latin literature and looking at the ruins of Roman buildings, started a new fashion for imitating the classical style.

The Gothic style was changed little by little. Architects had to learn the rules of Roman architecture and put aside the principles of the Gothic. So it was that Gothic art slowly passed away. But in the years between 1100 and 1600, it produced the greatest number of large buildings that the Western world had ever seen. Almost all the cathedrals of Western Europe were built in the Gothic period. Before revolution, war, and fires did their damage, Gothic cathedrals had contained the greatest quantity of art of one kind ever made.

JOHN HARVEY
Winchester College (England)

See also ARCHITECTURE; FRANCE, ART AND ARCHITECTURE OF; ILLUMINATED MANUSCRIPTS; SCULPTURE; STAINED-GLASS WINDOWS.

GOULD, JAY. See RAILROADS (Profiles).

The United States Congress is the lawmaking body of the U.S. government. It is composed of the House of Representatives and the Senate, shown here in a joint session.

GOVERNMENT, FORMS OF

Most of the world's people belong to political groups called nations or countries. Within the borders of each nation, the people are organized to keep order among themselves, provide certain common services (such as education, communications, and transportation), and protect themselves from attack by hostile countries.

Every one of the world's independent countries has its own form of government. Although many nations have similar kinds of government, each has the freedom to run its affairs in its own way. The people of one country do not have to answer to any other country for the type of government they choose for themselves.

Since the earliest years of human history, groups of people living together have needed rules to regulate their daily lives. Small, pre-industrial societies chose chiefs or other leaders to make and enforce the rules by which they lived. The people themselves took no part in the rulemaking; they left everything to their leaders. However, as cultures developed, people became interested in helping to make the rules or laws that governed them, because they

had so much at stake. Little by little they developed the idea of choosing leaders who would draw up laws that they wanted and thought suitable. The people also began to put into operation their own systems for enforcing these laws. They had learned how to create a government.

▶THE POWER OF GOVERNMENT

The governments that people establish for themselves can influence—and even change—their lives in many ways.

Governments decide such matters as what kinds of property should be publicly owned (that is, owned by the state in the name of the people) rather than privately owned and how much a person must pay in taxes. Governments can set educational requirements, place limits on immigration, and conscript (draft) citizens into military service. The availability of public libraries, museums, and other cultural institutions, hospitals, and parks is at least partly dependent on government.

▶THE POWER OF THE PEOPLE

Because those who run the governments of the world have such great power, nothing is more important to citizens than the choice of able leaders, for human happiness depends to a considerable degree on the kind of laws that governments enact.

In earlier societies political power was often accompanied by superior force. Governments today are sometimes ruled by leaders who have taken power by force, but such leaders are considered to govern illegally. Legal governments are those to which the consent of the governed has been freely given, usually through elections. Elected leaders are expected to take into account the economic and social needs of the people as well as their customs and traditions.

When a government reflects these needs and traditions, the people tend to have faith in it and a willingness to abide by its laws. If not, they may vote their leaders out of office and elect new ones. In most modern nations there are also agreements or understandings between the government and the governed. One basic form of agreement is a constitution, which defines (and limits) what a government can do and how it can do it. Constitutions may be written or unwritten, with unwritten constitutions usually based on a large body of established laws and custom.

▶ **TYPES OF GOVERNMENT**

Aristotle's Definitions. The ancient Greek philosopher Aristotle (384–322 B.C.) said that "The true forms of government . . . are those in which the one, or the few, or the many govern, with a view to the common interest. . . ."

A government run by one person Aristotle called a **monarchy**. Government by the few he called an **aristocracy**. Government by the many was a **polity**—or what we now call a constitutional democracy.

Although Aristotle considered these the true forms of government, he believed that each could be bad as well as good.

For example, a monarchy ruled only for the purpose of increasing the monarch's wealth and power became a **tyranny** and the ruler a **tyrant**. When the ruling few in an aristocracy ruled only for their own benefit, Aristotle referred to such a government as an **oligarchy**. Oligarchic governments were more common in his time than today. But although such governments did not necessarily begin as corrupt or tyrannical, Aristotle saw them as inevitably becoming so.

To describe rule by the many, Aristotle drew on the Greek word *demos*, meaning "common people." He called government by the common people a **democracy**. Aristotle did not regard democracy favorably, however, for he believed that government by the masses could lead to disorder or lawlessness.

Autocracy. Like many other terms used in government, autocracy is derived from Greek roots, in this case those for "self" and "rule." An autocrat was a ruler with unlimited authority. **Absolute monarchy**, a related term, refers to a monarch who ruled without checks on his or her power. The two terms were combined in the former emperors of Russia, who used "autocrat" as part of their title. Absolute monarchies exist today only in some of the states of the Arabian Peninsula. Another related term for autocracy, more commonly used in the past, is **despotism**, or rule by a **despot**.

Modern Democracy. Present-day democratic government differs significantly from the democracy practiced in ancient Greece, particularly in the city-state of Athens, where democracy reached its height. All male Athenian citizens were expected to participate directly in their government, in the making of laws as well as in choosing officials.

The modern democratic state is usually a **republic**, in which the people do not take a direct role in legislating or governing but elect representatives to express their views and wants. A democratic government exists when these representatives are freely chosen by the people, whose demands are then recognized by the duly elected government.

In addition to free elections, true democratic governments have other standards by which they can be measured. One is freedom of speech, under which people may criticize their governments without fear of persecution. Another is the peaceful and orderly transfer of political power when new leaders are elected to office.

A **constitutional monarchy** is a democratic government in which the monarch is retained as the ceremonial head of state but has little or no political power. Constitutional monarchies evolved from absolute monarchies, whose powers were gradually reduced and whose functions are now limited by a constitution. Probably the best-known constitutional monarchy is that of the United Kingdom, which has an unwritten constitution.

Queen Elizabeth II presides at the opening session of the British Parliament. In a constitutional monarchy, as head of state, she serves mainly as the living symbol of the nation.

Totalitarian Government. As a form of government, **totalitarianism** is of fairly recent origin. The term came into use in the 1920's and 1930's to describe the regimes of Fascist Italy and Nazi Germany, until their destruction in World War II. Following the war's end in 1945, the name was increasingly used in describing the government of the Soviet Union and the newly created Communist states of Eastern Europe.

A totalitarian government, as its name implies, is characterized by its total control over all aspects of its citizens' political and economic activities. Although often used interchangeably with **dictatorship** to indicate a non-democratic form of government, totalitarianism is even more rigorous in its controls. It is also marked by a distinct ideology, or set of beliefs, as in Fascism, Nazism, or Communism. The term **authoritarian government** is sometimes used for a similar form of government, but one that does not exert such absolute control over its peoples' lives.

The disintegration of the Soviet Union in late 1991 brought about the collapse of the Eastern European Communist governments. The result was their replacement by more genuinely democratic ones.

▶CLASSIFYING GOVERNMENTS

Democratic or Not? It is not always easy to tell if a country's government is democratic or not by its outward appearance, since many non-democratic governments have the trappings of democracy. The former Communist nations of Eastern Europe, for example, called themselves people's republics or people's democracies, had written constitutions, had legislatures to pass laws, and held elections. But real political power was concentrated in the hands of a small group, the top leadership of the Communist Party, which decided policy that was then automatically approved by the "official" organs of the government.

Election Procedures. One way to determine if a government is representative of its people is by its election procedures. In a democratic state, elections are held at regularly scheduled intervals, voters choose from a number of candidates, and vote is by secret ballot. The secret ballot is essential so that voters will not be unduly influenced or pressured, or fear retribution for the choices they make.

By contrast, there is the directed election, used by political leaders who, although they may have come to power legally, do not wish to be unseated. Essentially, in such an election the government in power so controls the election campaign that it cannot be defeated. In another kind of directed election, only one candidate is offered for each political office, giving voters no choice.

Political Parties. The structure of a country's system of political parties is a strong indication of its status. Democratic nations have at least two major political parties, and some have numerous parties that represent a wide range of interests. In most non-democratic countries there is only one legal party—that of the government in power. Even if other political parties are permitted, they merely go along with the policies of the dominant party.

Parliamentary Government. Modern democratic governments can be classified into two broad categories. One is parliamentary government, also known as **cabinet government**, whose model was the British parliamentary system. In parliamentary government there is a concentration of responsibility. The government is headed by a prime minister (or premier), who is usually the leader of the political party winning a majority of seats in election to the parliament. Where multiple political par-

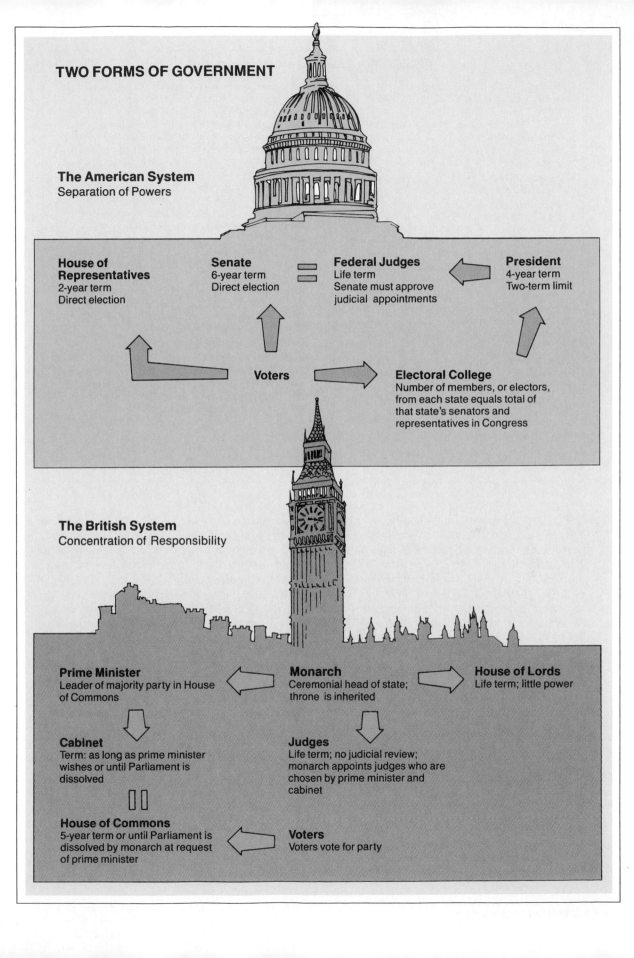

TWO FORMS OF GOVERNMENT

The American System
Separation of Powers

House of Representatives
2-year term
Direct election

Senate
6-year term
Direct election

Federal Judges
Life term
Senate must approve judicial appointments

President
4-year term
Two-term limit

Voters

Electoral College
Number of members, or electors, from each state equals total of that state's senators and representatives in Congress

The British System
Concentration of Responsibility

Prime Minister
Leader of majority party in House of Commons

Monarch
Ceremonial head of state; throne is inherited

House of Lords
Life term; little power

Cabinet
Term: as long as prime minister wishes or until Parliament is dissolved

Judges
Life term; no judicial review; monarch appoints judges who are chosen by prime minister and cabinet

House of Commons
5-year term or until Parliament is dissolved by monarch at request of prime minister

Voters
Voters vote for party

Some Other Terms Used in Government

Abdication—The formal relinquishing of power. A monarch abdicates by giving up all claims to the throne.

Alien—Someone who resides in a country but is not a citizen of that country.

Amendment—A change made in a bill, law, or constitution.

Amnesty—The act by which a government pardons, or forgives, a political or other offense against it.

Anarchism—A political theory that considers organized government to be evil and advocates its destruction. The term anarchy refers to disorder or lawlessness due to the breakdown or absence of governmental authority.

Apportionment—The allocation of seats in a legislature based on population.

Autonomy—A term meaning self-government.

Bicameral legislature—A legislature made up of two houses or chambers. The U.S. Congress is bicameral, consisting of the Senate and House of Representatives.

Bill—Proposed legislation. In the United States a bill becomes federal law after it is approved by the Congress and signed by the president.

Bureaucracy—The body of nonelected officials who perform the administrative functions of a government.

Cabinet—The officials heading the major departments of a government, appointed by and serving as advisers to a president or prime minister.

Due process of law—The individual's legal protection against arbitrary action by a government. It is provided for in the U.S. Constitution.

Federalism—A type of government under which political power is shared by central (or federal) and local authorities, with specific powers delegated to the central government. The United States has a federal form of government.

Filibuster—An attempt by lawmakers to block legislation by delay or other procedural tactics.

Impeachment—An official charge of wrongdoing brought by a legislature against an officer of government.

Plebiscite—A vote held by all eligible persons of a country or region, often to determine nationality or form of government.

Referendum—The principle of deciding an important issue by popular vote. Also the vote itself. A new or revised constitution is sometimes submitted to the people for approval in a referendum.

Suffrage—The right to vote.

Unicameral legislature—A legislature consisting of just one house or chamber.

Veto—A term usually referring to rejection of a bill by a chief executive. In the United States, the president may veto legislation, but the veto can be overridden by a two-thirds vote of both houses of Congress.

---

ties exist, a majority may not be achieved, and the largest party usually forms a **coalition** government with one or more smaller parties. The prime minister and cabinet form the government but are responsible to the parliament, of which they are members. If defeated on an important measure, the government must call new elections. In any event, elections must be held at scheduled periods.

Presidential Government. The presidential form of government, typified by that of the United States, is based on the **separation of powers**. Political power is distributed among three branches of government—executive (the president), legislative (the Congress), and judicial (the Supreme Court and other courts). This division of authority, or system of **checks and balances**, serves to limit the power of government, which is defined by a written constitution.

▶**THE FUTURE**

In past ages, the common people were afraid even to dream of a better way of life. If their ruler was an absolute monarch, they had no choice but to bow to that ruler's command. But in our own time, even the most autocratic governments have been forced to give some attention to the people's consent.

The Declaration of Human Rights, issued by the United Nations, stresses above everything—although it lacks legal force—the duty of governments to treat their people justly. It also charges the people to develop a voice in the running of their governments. The United Nations also holds that the sooner all nations and their people follow such action, the closer the countries of the world will come to realizing the goal of an international community dedicated to enduring peace, social growth, and economic plenty.

ROBERT RIENOW
State University of New York at Albany
Author, *Introduction to Government*

See also COMMUNISM; DEMOCRACY; ELECTIONS; FASCISM; PARLIAMENTS; PRIME MINISTER; SOCIALISM; UNITED STATES, GOVERNMENT OF THE.

GOVERNORS OF THE UNITED STATES. See STATE GOVERNMENTS.

Blind Man's Buff (1789?) by Goya. Prado, Madrid.

GOYA, FRANCISCO (1746–1828)

The brilliantly imaginative painter Francisco José de Goya y Lucientes was one of Spain's greatest artists. He was born on March 30, 1746, in Fuendetodos, a village near Saragossa, Spain. He studied near his home, traveled abroad for several years, and returned to Spain in 1771. Two years later he married Josefa Bayeu, the sister of a Madrid artist.

By 1775, Goya had moved to Madrid. His work was soon appreciated in the capital, and he was asked to design tapestries for the royal tapestry looms. Goya depicted the gaiety of Madrid festivals in reds and yellows and the peaceful gardens of the palace in blues and greens. Pleased with the tapestries, the court continued to order work from Goya. In 1786 he was appointed the king's painter. Goya enjoyed the luxury of court life and impressed the royal family with his charming manner.

Suddenly, in 1792, Goya suffered an illness that left him deaf forever. His art began to show his bitterness. In a series of etchings called the *Caprices*, he mocked court life. His portraits of the royal family, although richly painted, present an unflattering picture of Spain's rulers. After the invasion of Spain in 1808 by Napoleon's army, Goya's art became even more grim. His painting *The Third of May, 1808*, which shows a group of Spaniards about to be shot by a French firing squad, is an attack on the brutality of war. His *Disasters of War* etchings and other works are filled with nightmarish images representing the cruelties of society and the evils of war.

Goya painted his royal patrons only rarely now, and he feared their politics. In 1824 he retired to Bordeaux, France. He died there on April 16, 1828, at the age of 82.

Reviewed by FRED LICHT
Author, *Goya: The Origins of the Modern Temper in Art*

The writer Kenneth Grahame called on childhood memories of the English countryside to create the setting for his beloved children's book *The Wind in the Willows.*

GRAHAME, KENNETH (1859–1932)

Kenneth Grahame lived two lives. He was one of the most important bankers in Europe and also one of the greatest writers of children's literature. He was born in Edinburgh, Scotland, on March 8, 1859, the third of four children. When he was 5, his mother died and the children were sent to live with their grandmother.

Although "Granny Ingles" showed little affection for the children, her comfortable old house with its oak beams, its gardens, and the river Thames nearby all made a lifelong impression on young Kenneth. Years later he would bring the river and woods to life again by populating them with Rat, Mole, Toad, Badger, and the other remarkable characters in *The Wind in the Willows.*

Grahame was too poor to be able to attend the university, so in 1879 he went to work as a clerk in the Bank of England. He also began to write essays and sketches. In 1893 he published his first book, *Pagan Papers,* a collection of essays. Between 1894 and 1897 he also wrote for *The Yellow Book,* a well-known literary magazine.

Grahame won fame as a writer of children's books with *The Golden Age* (1895) and *Dream Days* (1898). Both books reflect the rich imaginative life he created to make up for the unhappiness of his childhood. They tell the story of five orphaned children living in a country house with unloved relatives. The children separate themselves from their adult caretakers by acting out stories from their books.

In 1898, Grahame became the secretary of the Bank of England. The next year he married Elspeth Thomson. Their only child, Alastair (nicknamed "Mouse"), was born in 1900. Grahame's most famous book, *The Wind in the Willows* (1908), began as stories told to Alastair, who was then 4 years old. It is a story of friendship, home, and exploration.

The character of Mole is like a child investigating the world for the first time. He has a friendly tutor in the person of Rat, who lives on the edge of the river in a wonderfully cozy home. Badger is a philosopher who lives deep in the Wild Woods. He hates society but becomes friends with Mole and Rat. Another friend is Toad, a reckless fellow who lives in Toad Hall when he is not in jail as the result of some prank. Mole and Rat come to understand that the song of the wind in the willows is one of Life and Death and the peace that nature offers.

Kenneth Grahame retired from banking in 1908. He wrote little in his later years and died on July 6, 1932, at his home in the village of Pangbourne, on the Thames River.

RICHARD KELLY
University of Tennessee

▶ **THE WIND IN THE WILLOWS**

In this episode from *The Wind in the Willows,* Toad has persuaded Rat and Mole to take to the Open Road with him in a gypsy caravan. But Toad unexpectedly discovers an even more exciting mode of travel.

They were strolling along the highroad easily, the Mole by the horse's head, talking to him, since the horse had complained that he was being frightfully left out of it, and nobody considered him in the least; the Toad and the Water Rat walking behind the cart talking together—at least Toad was talking, and Rat was saying at intervals, "Yes, precisely; and what did *you* say to *him*?"—and thinking all the time of something very different, when far behind them they heard a faint warning hum, like the drone of a distant bee. Glancing back, they saw a small cloud of dust, with a dark centre of energy, advancing on them at incredible speed, while from out of the dust a faint "Poop-poop!" wailed like an uneasy animal in pain. Hardly regarding it, they turned to resume their conversation, when in an instant (as it seemed) the peaceful scene was changed, and with a blast of wind and a whirl of sound that made them jump for the nearest ditch, It was on them! The "poop-poop" rang with a brazen shout in their ears, they had a moment's glimpse of an interior of glittering plate glass and rich morocco, and the magnificent motorcar, immense, breath-snatching, passionate, with its pilot tense and hugging his wheel, possessed all earth and air for the fraction of a second, flung an enveloping cloud of dust that blinded and enwrapped them utterly, and then dwindled to a speck in the far distance, changed back into a droning bee once more.

The old grey horse, dreaming, as he plodded along, of his quiet paddock, in a new raw situation such as this simply abandoned himself to his natural emotions. Rearing, plunging, backing steadily, in spite of all the Mole's efforts at his head, and all the Mole's lively language directed at his better feelings, he drove the cart backwards towards the deep ditch at the side of the road. It wavered an instant—then there was a heart-rending crash—and the canary-coloured cart, their pride and their joy, lay on its side in the ditch, an irredeemable wreck.

The Rat danced up and down in the road, simply transported with passion. "You villains!" he shouted, shaking both fists. "You scoundrels, you highwaymen, you—you—road hogs!—I'll

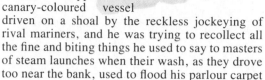

have the law on you! I'll report you! I'll take you through all the courts!" His homesickness had quite slipped away from him, and for the moment he was the skipper of the canary-coloured vessel driven on a shoal by the reckless jockeying of rival mariners, and he was trying to recollect all the fine and biting things he used to say to masters of steam launches when their wash, as they drove too near the bank, used to flood his parlour carpet at home.

Toad sat straight down in the middle of the dusty road, his legs stretched out before him, and stared fixedly in the direction of the disappearing motorcar. He breathed short, his face wore a placid, satisfied expression, and at intervals he faintly murmured "Poop-poop!"

The Mole was busy trying to quiet the horse, which he succeeded in doing after a time. Then he went to look at the cart, on its side in the ditch. It was indeed a sorry sight. Panels and windows smashed, axles hopelessly bent, one wheel off, sardine tins scattered over the wide world, and the bird in the birdcage sobbing pitifully and calling to be let out.

The Rat came to help him, but their united efforts were not sufficient to right the cart. "Hi, Toad!" they cried. "Come and bear a hand, can't you!"

The Toad never answered a word, or budged from his seat in the road; so they went to see what was the matter with him. They found him in a sort of trance, a happy smile on his face, his eyes still fixed on the dusty wake of their destroyer. At intervals he was still heard to murmur "Poop-poop!"

The Rat shook him by the shoulder. "Are you coming to help us, Toad?" he demanded sternly.

"Glorious, stirring sight!" murmured Toad, never offering to move. "The poetry of motion! Here to-day—in next week to-morrow! Villages skipped, towns and cities jumped—always somebody else's horizon! O bliss! O poop-poop! O my! O my!"

GRAIN AND GRAIN PRODUCTS

Grain is the world's most important crop. A field of waving grain means food for people and animals. Without grain the world could not support the large number of people that live in it. Half the people of the world depend on rice to fill their stomachs. The other half eat breads made from wheat or rye. Many people eat foods made from corn or oatmeal. Grains are so important that many ancient peoples believed they were given to people by gods. The ancient Roman goddess Ceres was believed to be the giver of grain. Our word "cereal" comes from her name.

The cereal grains, as these food grains are often called, are members of the enormous family of grasses that grow throughout the world. Many different foods are made from cereal grains. A special kind of wheat called durum is used for manufacturing spaghetti and macaroni. Porridge is made from oatmeal (ground or rolled oats). Corn is used to make a bread called corn pone, for cornmeal mush, and for hominy. Cakes, cookies, biscuits, and crackers, as well as bread, are made from wheat flour. Noodles, dumplings, and other similar products are also made from flour. And flour is used to thicken soups and sauces.

Grains are equally useful as feed for animals. The animals eat the grain, and we eat the animals or their products. Cattle fed partly on grain give us milk and beef. Pigs eat large amounts of grain and give us pork and bacon. Chickens, turkeys, and ducks also eat grain and provide us with eggs and meat.

Many non-food products are also made from grains. Some of the straw (dried stalks) provides pulp for paper products. The starches and glutens contained in the grain may be used for cloth, chewing gum, chemicals, and soft drinks. Furfural, a liquid that may be obtained from corn, rice, or oatmeal, is used in making nylon and plastics and in many other ways.

▶WHEAT

Wheat probably originated in southwestern Asia and spread from there to Europe, Russia, China, North America, and other parts of the world. It is the most widely grown of all cereals. Wheat grows well in hot countries, like India, and in cold countries, like Canada. It grows in the mountains and in low river valleys. Large crops are produced where rain is plentiful, but wheat also grows quite well with only a little rain.

The wheat of the world varies in quality depending on the temperature and the humid-

The world's three principal grains are wheat, corn, and rice. Far left: Vast fields of golden wheat stretch to the horizon in Kansas. Center: Grain-storage silos stand ready to receive the ripening corn. Above: Rice plants flourish in terraced paddies in Indonesia.

ity of the area where it is grown. Wheat grown in drier areas is very hard and high in protein content. This wheat is the most valuable for breadmaking. Wheat grown under heavier rainfall and lower temperature is soft, low in protein, and high in starch. This wheat makes the best flour for cakes and pastry. The best wheat for milling (grinding into flour) and baking must be fully ripe when it is cut. It must also be dry so that it will store well. When much rain falls during harvesting, the grain may become so wet that it sprouts. It is then useless for breadmaking.

To be turned into the food we eat, wheat must be milled into flour. In earlier times this was done with simple stone tools. In modern mills the wheat is gradually crushed into a fine powder, or flour, by grinding it between pairs of steel rollers. After each grinding the fine flour is sifted out and the coarser particles are reground. About three quarters of the wheat grain is turned into white flour. The remaining quarter, mainly bran (the outer coat of the wheat), is generally used for animal feed. Rye is milled in much the same way as wheat. Rye flour is usually grayish brown, but the very palest rye flours look like wheat flour.

Noodles made from wheat flour are a favorite food in Asia, eastern Europe, and North America. Dough is formed into thin sheets and then is cut into narrow strips. Noodles may be cooked at once in boiling water, or they may be used in soup. They may also be dried so that they can be stored for cooking at some later date. Dumplings are similar to noodles, except that the dough is shaped into balls rather than strips.

Spaghetti and macaroni are made from durum wheat, which is a different variety from bread wheat. A granular product called semolina is milled from the wheat and mixed into a very stiff dough. This dough is forced under pressure through small holes or slits in a metal plate. As the dough leaves the holes it may be cut into short or long pieces. Spaghetti is in the form of thin rods. Macaroni is thicker but has a hollow in the middle. Various designs can be made by using holes of different patterns. These products, which are all forms of "pasta," are then dried and packed. They store well and can be used to make many tasty dishes. Some spaghetti, macaroni, and other pasta products are cooked with sauces and canned.

RICE

Rice probably originated in southern India thousands of years ago, spreading eastward into China and later westward into Persia (Iran) and Egypt. Today, rice is more important than wheat in China, Japan, Korea, the Philippines, India, and other countries of east Asia and the Middle East. It is also an important food in Brazil, in humid areas of central Africa, and in the countries around the Caribbean Sea.

Rice can be grown only where the temperature is warm throughout the year and where there is plenty of water. It can be grown on dry land, but it is often grown on land covered by water. Flooding the rice fields helps to control many kinds of weeds. The water is usually drained away for the harvest. Traditional methods of growing rice require laborious handwork. Although the workers are paid very little, so many of them are needed that the cost of the rice is still high. Rice can be grown more cheaply by using farm machines, as in the United States.

Rice is threshed to separate the rice kernels from the chaff, or seed coat. Then the hulls are removed. In the United States this process is followed by polishing the kernels until the bran comes off and the rice is a creamy white. In Asia, rice is sometimes eaten without having been polished. When the bran is still on, the rice has a slightly brownish color and is called brown rice. It has greater food value than white rice, but it tends to spoil during storage.

In many of the countries of Asia, people eat meals mainly of rice. The rice is boiled, and the water is drained off. As the cooked kernels tend to stick to each other, it is not difficult to pick up a good mouthful with chopsticks. The rice is eaten from a separate rice bowl, and it is quite polite to hold this bowl close to the mouth. The rest of the course, which may be fish and vegetables, is served on a plate. Thus rice is eaten with the meal much as bread is in other countries.

It is generally thought that the Chinese eat mainly rice. This is true of the southern part of China. But north of the Yangtze River the main crop is wheat, and the northern Chinese eat relatively little rice. In Japan, where rice has been the main cereal, the habit of eating bread and rolls made from imported wheat is steadily increasing.

CORN

Corn was found in Central America and was carried back to Europe by the Spaniards. Wild corn has been traced in Mexico to approximately 5200 B.C. Present varieties of corn do not grow wild, because the seeds (grains) are completely covered by husks that must be removed if the seeds are to receive soil, sun, and water. Corn grows under a wide range of climates and temperatures. It is a very efficient cereal because it gives a high yield of grain for each hectare of land on which is it planted.

Corn is also called maize or Indian corn. This grain, which was found growing in North America by the first settlers, is still the biggest crop of the continent. The United States grows half the world's crop. Some 80 to 90 percent of the United States crop is used to feed livestock.

When corn is to be milled, the grain is washed and then split to separate the germ and bran from the white, starchy endosperm. The germs, which are relatively large, yield a valuable edible oil. The endosperm may be used in two ways. First, it may be ground into coarse fragments called hominy or hominy grits. These are used to make bread, hot cakes, and similar types of food. Second, it may be ground and suspended in water. The mixture is allowed to flow over long tables and the rolling motion separates the protein from the starchy particles. As starch is heaviest, it settles out on the tables and is recovered for use in industry.

BARLEY

Barley is one of the oldest grains used by people. It was used in ancient Egypt and China and in southern Europe until Christian times, when wheat and rye became popular. It will grow in high mountain areas, in cold weather, and in short seasons. It can stand heat and drought. About the only conditions under which barley will not grow well are hot, humid weather and poor soils.

The grain of barley plants grown in rich soils and dry air will have more protein than grain from plants grown elsewhere. The protein-rich barley is "hard." "Soft," starchy barley is preferred for making malt (grain that has been soaked and allowed to sprout and is used in brewing).

Most barley is used as a substitute for corn to feed livestock. About a quarter of the crop

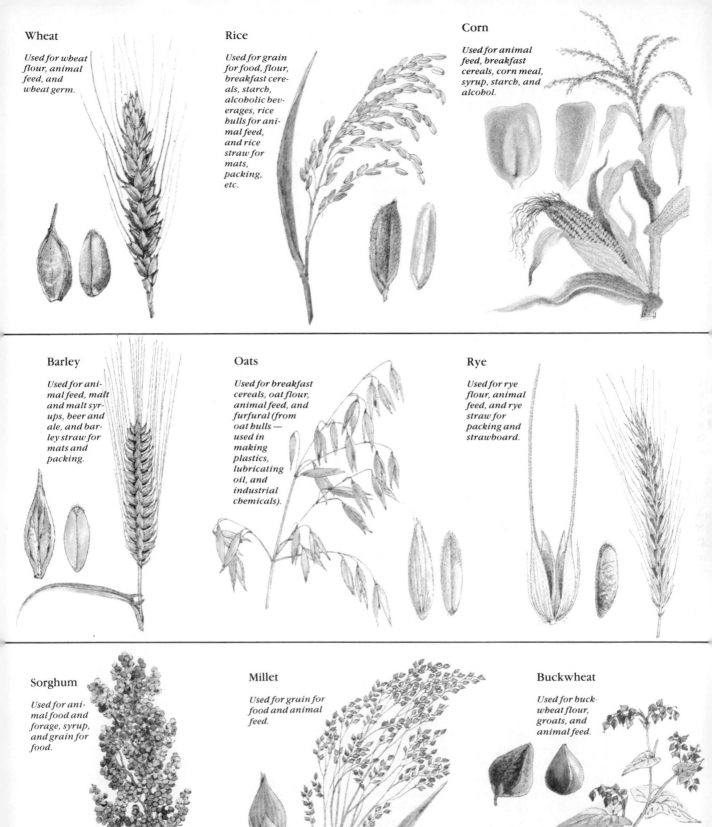

Wheat

Used for wheat flour, animal feed, and wheat germ.

Rice

Used for grain for food, flour, breakfast cereals, starch, alcoholic beverages, rice hulls for animal feed, and rice straw for mats, packing, etc.

Corn

Used for animal feed, breakfast cereals, corn meal, syrup, starch, and alcohol.

Barley

Used for animal feed, malt and malt syrups, beer and ale, and barley straw for mats and packing.

Oats

Used for breakfast cereals, oat flour, animal feed, and furfural (from oat hulls — used in making plastics, lubricating oil, and industrial chemicals).

Rye

Used for rye flour, animal feed, and rye straw for packing and strawboard.

Sorghum

Used for animal food and forage, syrup, and grain for food.

Millet

Used for grain for food and animal feed.

Buckwheat

Used for buckwheat flour, groats, and animal feed.

in the United States is used to make malt, which is used for brewing and for breakfast foods, malt syrups, and candies. Pot and pearl barleys are used for soups and stews. A little barley is turned into flour for baby food.

▶OATS

Oats are one of the most widely grown grains. We hear little about oats because most of the crop is used for animal feed. In North America and Europe, oats are widely grown because they are suited to many more types of soils and climates than most grains are.

The nutritional content of hulless oats is higher than that of wheat. Most people eat oats in the form of rolled oats (oatmeal) or oat granules. Oat flour seldom is used for making bread because it does not mix well with yeast or other materials that lighten dough or make it rise.

▶RYE, SORGHUM, MILLET, AND BUCKWHEAT

In parts of the world that are too cold, too hot, or too dry for growing wheat, corn, rice, oats, or barley, other cereals can be grown. These are rye, sorghum, and millet. They also are planted in many parts of the world for special uses.

Rye often is grown in cold areas. It resists cold weather better than any other grain known. It will grow in sandy soil that is not fertile enough for other crops. Rye flour alone is used to make the black bread of eastern Europe. In North America, rye bread is made from a mixture of rye and wheat flours.

Sorghum is grown as food for human beings mostly in Africa and Asia. In the United States and Canada it usually is used for live-stock feed. The plant grows well even on very dry land. It grows best in warm climates.

Millet forms a large part of the diet of some African and Asian peoples. It can be grown on poor soils with little rainfall and needs almost no care. In North America, millet is used in animal and poultry feed.

Buckwheat is also used as a grain although it is not one of the cereal grasses. It is actually a distant relative of rhubarb. In North America it is used for pancake flour and breakfast cereal. The Japanese use it for noodles. In eastern Europe and Russia buckwheat is commonly used. A popular Russian and eastern European cereal called "kasha" is often made from buckwheat.

▶DRY CEREALS

Almost all the cereal grains are used either separately or in mixtures for making breakfast cereals. Flakes are a common form. But all sorts of products, flavored in different ways and differing in texture and shape, are now available. All are made mechanically by automatic machinery. Packing is also automated.

Puffed rice and wheat are "shot" or "exploded." This is usually done by putting the grain into a cannon. The muzzle is then sealed with a tight cap. Steam pressure is built up inside the cannon, the cap is suddenly released, and the kernels shoot out with a loud bang into a wire net screen. The steam inside the kernels expands suddenly when the pressure is released, and the kernels are then blown up to several times their normal size. Sometimes the kernels are puffed in a pressure chamber instead of in a cannon. In North America, durum wheat is preferred for puffing because of its large kernels.

▶NUTRITIONAL VALUE OF CEREAL FOODS

Most of the foods made from cereals are similar in nutritional value. In considering the nutrition value of cereal products, the water content is disregarded. About 50 to 70 percent of most grain products is made up of starch and sugars. These are used by the body to produce energy for our physical and mental work. The proteins in grain products are also a useful part of the diet for body-building. But the cereal proteins do not have the best combination of amino acids for nutrition. The amino acids are the building blocks of which proteins are composed. People who eat meat, vegetables, fruit, milk, and eggs in addition to cereal grains are more likely to grow strong and healthy. People who live almost completely on grain can keep themselves alive, but they tend to be smaller and less healthy than people with a more varied diet.

▶BEVERAGES MADE FROM GRAINS

Beer and whiskey are usually made or flavored with malt that is made from barley. In addition, malt extract, a thick syrup, is used in baking, in various breakfast cereals, in candies, and in the cloth industry.

To make malt, barley is first soaked in water. The kernels are then allowed to sprout and grow under cool, moist conditions for a few days. After the kernels have sprouted they are called malt. The malt is dried in a kiln, or oven. Small shoots are rubbed off and sifted out. Malt looks just like barley, but the kernel is now brittle and easily broken; many chemical changes have occurred in it. A water extract of ground malt, called wort, is used to make beer.

The best Scotch whiskey is made entirely from barley malt. Bourbon whiskey is made partly from corn; and Canadian whiskey, partly from rye. Gin and vodka are made mainly from grain alcohol (alcohol distilled from grains).

▶INDUSTRIAL USES OF GRAINS

Industrial alcohol made from grains is used for making many things: lacquers, varnishes, enamels, shellac, plastics, explosives, polishes, adhesives, solvents, foods, drugs, dyes, perfumes, rubbing alcohol, liniments, cleaners, and preservatives. It is used in antifreeze and brake fluids. It is also used as a solvent in almost all chemical research laboratories. This is only a short list of some of its many uses.

Cereal grains, mainly corn, are the principal source of starch. This starch is used in making candies, chewing gum, and baking powder and in brewing beer. Starch is also used in laundries, to make cloth, to give weight and a good finish to paper and paper boxes, and to produce explosives, chemicals, and adhesives. By boiling it with acid, starch can be broken down into sugars. Starch sugars are used in baked products, drugs, soft drinks, jams, jellies, ice cream, and other foods. Sugary syrups are used in the same products and for tanning leather. They are also used in making adhesives, textiles, tobacco, and many other things.

Furfural is an important industrial liquid produced largely from oat hulls. One of its most important uses is in the production of nylon. Furfural is also used to refine oils, such as diesel, vegetable, and lubricating oils. It is used in the production of synthetic rubber and innumerable other industrial products. Some antiseptics for medical use are made from it. Many compounds of furfural are being tested for other medical products.

▶GRAIN STORAGE

For thousands of years, people have stored grain in order to make sure that they would always have food available. Today, grain is often stored until the grower wishes to sell it, usually to take advantage of higher prices. Grain is also stored to maintain feed supplies for animals throughout the year.

A **grain elevator** is a tower equipped to lift, store, and discharge grain. In North America, the two most commonly stored grains are wheat and corn. Elevators also store oats, barley, rice, sorghum, and other commodities.

Farm trucks carry grain to elevators and are unloaded. Conveyors then move the grain to storage bins within the elevator. Pneumatic, or blower, equipment is sometimes used to unload and transport the grain.

Huge grain elevators are a common sight in the farmlands of the American Midwest and the Canadian Prairie Provinces.

Because wet grain can decay and spoil other grain, fans or other driers are often used to keep the grain dry. Grain elevators may also have equipment for cleaning, grinding, and mixing grain.

Grain dust is highly combustible, so huge explosions are always a possible danger at grain elevators. It is necessary to reduce the amount of dust created and to avoid producing any flames or sparks. Some grain elevators have dust-collecting devices.

The major use of grain elevators began in the second half of the 19th century. Elevators now are common sights at railroad junctions in grain-producing areas, at grain markets, at major lake ports and seaports, and at grain-milling centers.

▶ BREEDING CEREAL GRAINS FOR THE FUTURE

Plant breeders all over the world are steadily improving cereal grains. Scientists have found out how to produce dwarf varieties of wheat and rice. These represent a major advance and are now widely grown in many countries.

Dwarf varieties of wheat and rice produce much more grain than older varieties. The stiff leaves catch the sunlight. The plants remain short and strong when a great deal of fertilizer is used and extra water is supplied by irrigation or rain. Under the same conditions older varieties are too tall and weak. The plants fall over under wind and rain. They do not ripen well, and they are difficult to harvest without serious loss.

Hybrid corn is another great achievement. When pollen from one variety of corn fertilizes a second variety, the seed thus produced is a hybrid. Some hybrids with carefully selected parents produce much more grain than either parent.

Hybrids of sorghum and pearl millet are also produced. Progress is being made in developing hybrids for wheat and barley.

Wheat and rye have been crossed to produce an entirely new crop called triticale. The name is a combination of the Latin words for wheat and rye. When two different species are crossed, the seed generally fails to develop or is sterile. It will not germinate, or sprout, and produce a crop. This problem was solved in the case of triticale by years of difficult research. Triticale grain is high in protein and has potential as human food. However, specific markets have not yet been developed. Current production is limited and is primarily in the western United States and Canada. The grain serves primarily as animal feed.

Some people are interested in expanding the use of seeds from plants like amaranth, quinoa, and other non-grassy (broad-leaved) species. Amaranth was once widely grown for grain by Indian civilizations in Central and South America. They used its seeds for food and in their religious ceremonies. Quinoa is still grown in the high Andes in South America. Its seeds are used for food and for fermenting to make beer. Both amaranth and quinoa may be helpful in the developing areas of the world, particularly in mountainous areas where other grains grow poorly. But neither will replace or rival the major cereal grains for their uses in human diets.

In breeding improved strains of cereal grains, plant scientists must make sure that new varieties are resistant to the many diseases that attack all crops. In addition, good quality must accompany high yields. Improvements in the nutritive value of grains are being made. All these developments will help to produce more cereal grain to feed the rapidly growing population of the world.

▶ HISTORY

Cereal grains were discovered many centuries before the birth of Christ. In open spaces early people probably found some tall grasses with seeds that were good to eat. It is likely they learned to grow these grasses themselves after they saw plants grow from seeds dropped around the camping site. The best plants with the largest heads and grains would have been selected for seed. Down through the ages this type of selection has been continued. Because of it grains have continuously improved. In the 20th century, science has helped to improve grains. Developing healthier and more productive grain plants is a science in many parts of the world.

Some facts are known about the very early history of grains. The Bible and other Hebrew books written before the birth of Christ speak of wheat and barley. Pictures on Egyptian monuments provide early records of flour milling. Seeds of barley and wheat have been found with mummies in tombs. Kernels of primitive wheats have been found in excavating a site in Iraq that was inhabited about

Left: Farmers stand on a pile of surplus grain, the overflow from elevators in the background. Right: People in famine-stricken Ethiopia receive grain from other countries.

5000 B.C. These kernels are dead and black with age, but they are easily recognized by their shape. Experts think that grain was widely grown for food long before these early records. Some stones for grinding grains have been found that are thought to be 75,000 years old.

When people learned to grow grain crops, they could settle down in one place. Closely related families probably gathered together for protection. A fort could be built for defense against other people. Permanent houses were built for better protection from the weather. As related groups banded together, larger and larger areas came under the control of one leader. Countries with royal rulers slowly developed.

Until the time when grain was grown, all people had to search for food. One person wandering in search of food could not find enough to feed other people. One family could not raise very many animals until they had grain crops to feed the animals. When grain was grown, food became more readily available. And some people were free to make pottery, become priests, or do other special work. Grains have been of great importance in the development of modern civilization.

Wheat, corn, rice, barley, and other grains are just as important today as they were in much earlier times. The number of people in the world is increasing very rapidly, and all must have food to eat. Farming with machines —such as tractors or combines that cut and thresh in one operation—increases the amount of grain that can be produced. Chemicals that kill weeds and chemicals that protect grains from insects during storage help to increase food supplies. But still greater increases must be made if all people are to be well fed.

Throughout human history, famines have developed when populations grew faster than food production. Famines have also occurred when droughts, floods, or insect and disease outbreaks caused grain crop failures. Irrigation and modern pest-control technology have reduced this risk. But famine still threatens in developing countries where rainfall is erratic. In the 1980's, drought in central and western Africa led to widespread crop failures, causing millions of people to starve to death. Government policymakers must join with scientists and engineers to develop plans and technology to overcome the age-old problem of famine.

J. ANSEL ANDERSON
Agriculture Canada

Reviewed by WILLIAM D. PARDEE
Cornell University

See also BEER AND BREWING; BREAD AND BAKING; CORN; FLOUR AND FLOUR MILLING; OATS; RICE; RYE; STARCH; WHEAT.

GRAMMAR

Grammar describes the way a language works. English grammar tells how English works in communicating ideas. Ideas are generally expressed in sentences. Sentences are made by grouping and arranging words. Therefore, grammar is the study of words in sentences.

In earlier years grammar was thought of as a set of laws governing a language. From this point of view the person who knew the laws of English and used them in speaking and writing would use English correctly. The person who did not follow the laws would be incorrect. Grammar was taught in order to make correct speakers and writers. This idea of grammar developed in England in the 18th century. Scholars of that period wrote many books setting forth the "rules" of correct English. Some of the rules came from Latin, a language they knew and admired. Other rules came from their personal feelings or prejudices. They did not form their rules from a scientific study of English. Because English changes from one period to another, some of these rules no longer apply. The rules do not govern the language. Today it seems wiser to base grammar upon seeing how English is used in speech and writing.

▶ THREE KINDS OF MEANING

Three kinds of meaning occur when words are used to express ideas: (1) the meaning of each word by itself; (2) the meaning of a word when it changes its form (like *man, men; go, goes*); (3) the meaning of words as they are arranged in a certain order. Grammar is based on observing these different kinds of meaning.

Word Meanings

Words are symbols for ideas. Every word has some meaning; most words are symbols for a group of ideas. A dictionary contains a collection of the meanings expressed by words. For example, one high school dictionary gives 30 meanings for the word "head." The basic meaning is "the top part of the human body where the eyes, ears, and mouth are." The other meanings are formed from this meaning and are symbols of closely related ideas. But "head" is a symbol only for English speakers.

For the same basic idea a German says *der Kopf,* a Frenchman says *la tête,* a Russian says *golová.* Each language has its own symbol for this idea.

In most languages a single word used alone has very little meaning. If you say to a friend, "Head," he will probably be puzzled. If you say, "My head," he will be less puzzled, and if you say, "My head aches," you have expressed a thought in a sentence that has a great deal of meaning. When you arrange words into a sentence, you have created a pattern that is a basic element of grammar.

Sometimes a single word can mean much if it becomes the symbol for a complete thought. For example, if someone says to you, "When do you go to camp?" you may answer, "Tomorrow." This single word then becomes the signal for a whole sentence, which is, "Tomorrow I shall go to camp." If you listen closely to conversation, you will observe that ideas are often expressed by a single word or a few words that represent a complete sentence.

The Forms of Words

The changing forms of certain words signal their meanings. Early English had many of these changing forms; only a few survive in modern English. Here are some examples still in use:

Noun:	boy, boy's, boys, boys'
	mouse, mouse's, mice, mice's
Adjective:	large, larger, largest
	good, better, best
Verb:	go, going, goes, went, gone
	look, looking, looks, looked
	am, is, are, was, were, be, being, been
Pronoun:	I, my, mine, me
	you, yours
	he, his, him; she, hers, her; it, its
	we, our, ours, us
	they, their, theirs, them
	who, whose, whom

Each of these forms signals a certain meaning that we understand when we hear the words spoken or read them. English-speaking children learn most of these forms before they go to school. People whose native tongue is not English find these forms difficult to use correctly. An important part of grammar is knowing the meanings signaled by the changing forms of words like these.

Patterns of Words

A third type of meaning comes from the order in which words are used. Compare these word groups:

(1) Dog frightened the cellar hid in the.
(2) The frightened dog hid in the cellar.

We know the words in pattern 1, but they make no sense. The same words arranged into pattern 2 give a clear meaning. Why? Because there is an expected pattern, or structure, of English sentences that gives meaning. In this structure there are two essential parts: a doer, or actor, and an action. In pattern 2 "dog" is the actor; "hid" is the action. The other words tell us something about the dog and something about the action. In grammar the doer-actor is called the subject; the action is called the verb. Patterns of words called sentences contain these essential parts. The order in which the words are arranged gives different meanings. Compare these two statements:

(1) The baby crawled over the kitchen floor.
(2) The kitchen floor crawled over the baby.

The words are the same, but the order in which we place them makes a great difference to the baby. Meaning is largely governed by the order in which we arrange words.

▶ ENGLISH SENTENCE PATTERNS

Although the different combinations of words that make sentences are almost beyond number, they are all based upon four patterns. Each pattern contains a subject and a verb. The first two patterns have verbs indicating an action.

Pattern I. *The boy runs.* The subject, "boy," does an act. He runs. So "runs" is the verb. In grammar this kind of verb is called **intransitive** because the action is confined to the subject.

Pattern II. *The girl baked a cake.* The subject, "girl," does an act, "baked," that is performed upon an object, "cake." In this kind of sentence the verb is called **transitive** because the action performed by the subject carries over to a person or thing acted upon, called the object. The largest number of English sentences follow this pattern.

The next two patterns use verbs that show a connection instead of an action.

Pattern III. *Mary is kind.* The verb "is" has the name "linking verb" because it connects the subject, "Mary," with a describing word, "kind," called an adjective.

Pattern IV. *John is our captain.* Here the linking verb "is" connects the subject, "John," with another name, or noun, "captain."

No matter how long and complicated it may be, every English sentence is based upon one of these patterns or a combination of two or more. Here are some longer sentences illustrating each pattern:

I. The weary hikers slept in a tumbledown cabin at the edge of the forest.
II. A famous traveler from South America delivered an interesting lecture to a rapt audience.
III. The passengers on the delayed train were hungry and thirsty.
IV. The distinguished-looking man at the head of the procession was the newly elected chancellor of the university.

▶ PARTS OF SPEECH

The words that form sentences are classified into parts of speech by what they do in the sentence. In traditional grammar there are eight parts of speech: noun, pronoun, adjective, verb, adverb, preposition, conjunction, and interjection. Modern grammarians speak of four main word classes: noun (including pronoun), verb, adjective, and adverb. The first two (noun and verb) create the frame of the sentence, and the second two (adjective and adverb) are the principal modifiers. Other words are important for making longer sentences. They are called "function words" or "structure groups." Among these are:

Determiners such as *the, a, an, this, these, those, that.*
Prepositions such as *of, by, for, with, over, under, beyond.*
Conjunctions such as *and, but, either . . . or, for, yet, still.*
Auxiliaries (used to help other verbs) such as *is, was, were, has, had, shall, will, would, could.*
Subordinators such as *when, while, as, since, because, whereas.*
Relatives such as *whose, whom, that, which.*
Intensifiers such as *so* (good), *very* (fine).
Sentence starters such as *well, now, oh, why.*

▶ WHAT IS GOOD ENGLISH?

Since rules do not govern English, grammar cannot set up rules for good, or "correct,"

English. Yet there are choices to be made in the words and phrases we use in speaking and writing. Some kinds of English are considered better than others. Here are examples of some choices in forms and phrases:

Where *was* you?	Where *were* you?
He *done* his work.	He *did* his work.
She *ain't* here.	She *isn't* here.
I *seen* him.	I *saw* him.
Between you and *I*.	Between you and *me*.
I *can't hardly* talk.	I *can hardly* talk.
There's three chairs here.	*There are* three chairs here.

Educated people do not use expressions like those in the first column. They use those in the second column, because other educated people expect them to do so. Good English is acceptable English; that is, it is acceptable to those who know the language customs of persons of education and culture. The choices made by educated people determine what is "standard English." Another way to say this is that "standard English" is the dialect of the educated speakers.

One modern grammarian has defined good English in this way: "Good English is that form of speech which is appropriate to the purpose of the speaker, true to the language as it is, and comfortable to speaker and listener. It is the product of custom, neither cramped by rule nor freed from all restraint; it is never fixed, but changes with the organic life of the language." To become a user of good English, a person must wish to speak accurately and acceptably and must observe the choices made by cultivated speakers and writers.

We can improve our English by reading good books, listening attentively to the speeches and conversation of educated persons, and patterning our own speech habits on these models.

ROBERT C. POOLEY
Author, *Teaching English Grammar*
See also PARTS OF SPEECH.

GRAMMAR IN A NUTSHELL
Anonymous

Three little words you often see
Are Articles—A, An, and The.

A Noun's the name of anything,
As School, or Garden, Hoop or Swing.

Adjectives tell the kind of Noun,
As Great, Small, Pretty, White or Brown.

Instead of Nouns the Pronouns stand—
Her head, His face, Your arm, My hand.

Verbs tell something being done—
To Read, Count, Laugh, Sing, Jump or Run.

How things are done the Adverbs tell,
As Slowly, Quickly, Ill, or Well.

Conjunctions join the words together,
As men And women, wind Or weather.

The preposition stands before
A Noun, as In or Through a door.

The Interjection shows surprise,
As Oh! how pretty! Ah! how wise!

The Whole are called Nine Parts of Speech,
Which reading, writing, speaking teach.

GRAND CANYON NATIONAL PARK

One of the scenic and geologic wonders of the world is the Grand Canyon in northern Arizona. The Grand Canyon is a huge gorge cut by the Colorado River over a period of millions of years. And the work of the Colorado River is far from complete. Each day the river and the forces of weathering combine in a process that continually widens and deepens the Grand Canyon.

Because of its scenic and scientific value, the area was designated a national park in 1919. In 1975 the Grand Canyon National Park was enlarged. It now includes areas formerly designated as the Grand Canyon and Marble Canyon national monuments.

The Grand Canyon is nearly 450 kilometers (280 miles) long and almost 2 kilometers (over 1 mile) deep. It varies in width from about 2 to 29 kilometers (over 1 mile to 18 miles). The land that rises from the canyon's floor is higher than any peak in the Appalachians.

García López de Cárdenas became the first European to see the Grand Canyon in 1540. John Wesley Powell (1834–1902) conducted the first boat trip down the rapids of the Colorado River and through the gorge in 1869.

Millions of visitors come each year to see the vastness
and magnificent colors of the Grand Canyon, a
spectacular gorge that was carved by the Colorado River.
The different shaded bands are layers of rock, including
sandstone, limestone, and lava that were deposited over
a period of a billion years. When most people think of
the Grand Canyon, they think of a hot and dry desert.
Once in a while, however, a dusting of snow will lend an
entirely new perspective to the Grand Canyon's beauty
and diversity.

There are many activities one can enjoy while visiting the Grand Canyon. *Top left:* Mules carry a packer and his belongings down one of the scenic trails. *Top right:* A cross-country skier enjoys solitude as he skis up to a point overlooking the canyon. *Left:* Boaters crash through rapids on the Colorado River. *Above:* Hikers walk down a trail to the bottom of the canyon.

Each year millions of people visit the Grand Canyon. Several trails lead to the bottom. Visitors can either hike down or ride on the backs of mules. The most scenic trails are Bright Angel Trail and the Kaibab Trail. A suspension bridge crosses the canyon. Visitors to the area often visit the nearby Hopi, Navajo, and Havasupai Indian reservations.

Each rock layer of the Grand Canyon holds a record of geologic history millions of years old. As the Colorado River cut deeply, forming the gorge, rock surfaces were exposed. Embedded in these surfaces are fossils. The fossils and the exposed rock layers give information on how the earth and life on it evolved.

The canyon also has several different climates, stacked one on top of the other. From top to bottom, the climate gets warmer. Near the top, where it is coolest, there are blue spruce and aspen trees. Lower down, there are yellow pines. On the floor of the canyon, where it is desertlike, the most common plants are cacti.

Reviewed by GEORGE W. CAREY
Rutgers, The State University of New Jersey

GRAND FORKS. See NORTH DAKOTA (Cities).
GRAND RAPIDS. See MICHIGAN (Cities).
GRANITE. See ROCKS (Igneous Rock).
GRANT, CARY. See MOTION PICTURES (Profiles: Movie Stars).

ULYSSES S. GRANT (1822-1885)

18th President of the United States

FACTS ABOUT GRANT

Birthplace: Point Pleasant, Ohio
Religion: Methodist
College Attended: U.S. Military
  Academy, West Point, New York
Occupation: Soldier
Married: Julia Dent
Children: Frederick Dent,
  Ulysses Simpson, Ellen
  Wrenshall, Jesse Root
Political Party:
  Republican
President Who
  Preceded Him:
  Andrew Johnson
Age on Becoming
  President: 46
Years in the Presidency: 1869-1877
Vice President: Schuyler Colfax (first
  term); Henry Wilson (second term,
  died 1875)
President Who Succeeded Him:
  Rutherford B. Hayes
Age at Death: 63
Burial Place: Grant's Tomb, New York
  City

DURING GRANT'S PRESIDENCY

Above: The first U.S. transcontinental
railroad system was completed, when
the tracks of the Union Pacific and
Central Pacific railroads were joined
at Promontory, Utah (1869). The air
brake for railroad cars was patented by
George Westinghouse (1869). The 15th
Amendment to the Constitution, prohib-
iting the denial of voting rights because of
race, color, or previous condition of slavery, was ratified (1870). *Above left:* The
Department of Justice was created (1870)
and placed under the office of the attor-
ney general. *Below:* The telephone was
developed (1876) by Alexander Graham
Bell. Colorado was admitted to the Union
as the 38th state (1876).

GRANT, ULYSSES SIMPSON. On February 16,
1862, during the Civil War, a Union soldier
carried a message from his general to the bat-
tle-weary Confederate forces defending Fort
Donelson in Tennessee. The Confederate
commander had asked for terms upon which
he could surrender the fort. The 39-year-old
Union general, Ulysses S. Grant, replied that
only ''an unconditional and immediate surrender'' would be accepted. This phrase, and the
man who said it, at once captured the attention
of the country. U. S. Grant became Unconditional Surrender Grant.

The surrender of Fort Donelson was an important victory for the North. For Grant it was
also a great personal victory after years of failure. Within two years he would become commander of all the Union armies, and a few
years later president of the United States.

▶ EARLY YEARS

Grant was born on April 27, 1822, at Point
Pleasant, Ohio, the eldest son of Jesse Root
Grant and Hannah Simpson Grant. He was
named Hiram Ulysses, but he was always
called Ulysses.

Ulysses loved horses. Almost as soon as he
could walk, he learned how to ride. By the
time he was 7 or 8 years old he could handle a
team of horses. Because he did not like working in his father's tannery, he did most of the
work on the family farm, especially taking
care of the animals. As a boy, he was thrifty,
thoughtful, and hard-working, but not always
too clever in business matters.

West Point. In 1839 Grant's father obtained
an appointment for him to the U.S. Military
Academy at West Point. The congressman
who made the arrangements mistakenly referred to him as Ulysses Simpson Grant, and
the name remained with him ever afterward.

At West Point his record as a student was
only average, although he was good in mathematics and drawing. But he impressed everyone with his expert horsemanship. In 1843,
Grant received his commission as a brevet second lieutenant. He did not like military life,
however, and he expected to leave the Army

Julia Dent (*above*) married Ulysses S. Grant in 1848, when he was a young army lieutenant. In 1864, Grant (*right*) was a lieutenant general and had been appointed by President Abraham Lincoln to command of all the Union armies in the Civil War.

after a few years of service to become a teacher of mathematics.

Early Military Career. Grant requested duty in the cavalry, but there were no openings. Instead, he was assigned to the 4th Infantry Regiment. He was in Texas when war with Mexico broke out in 1846.

Grant was not in sympathy with the aims of the Mexican War. He felt that the United States was not completely right in its actions and was bullying a smaller nation. However, as a soldier, he fought bravely in nearly all the major battles of the war and was promoted to first lieutenant.

Julia Dent Grant. As soon as the war ended in 1848, Grant asked for leave. In August 1848, he married Julia Dent (1826–1902), the sister of one of his classmates at West Point. Julia was to be a source of strength to Grant for the rest of his life. Grant had since given up the idea of teaching and had decided to stay in the Army for a time.

In 1852, Grant was ordered to the Pacific Coast. Because his pay as a lieutenant was so low, he could not afford to take his wife and young son with him. In 1853 he was promoted to captain. But even a captain's pay was too low to support his family in the West. Grant was lonely and homesick. According to army gossip, he began to drink, although there is no official record to support this. After quarreling

with his commanding officer, Grant resigned from the Army in 1854.

Years of Failure. Grant settled with his family in Missouri, intending to become a farmer. He started a farm on land owned by his wife and labored for three years, but bad economic conditions and illness made him quit. He then became a partner in a real estate agency. However, his lack of business experience forced him to give it up. He ran for the office of county engineer but was defeated.

In desperation, Grant took a job as a partner and clerk in a leather goods store operated by his two brothers in Galena, Illinois. But his civilian life soon was to be interrupted by war.

▶ **CIVIL WAR GENERAL**

The growing troubles between the North and the South came to a head with the election of Abraham Lincoln to the presidency in 1860. In December 1860, South Carolina seceded from the Union and was soon followed by other Southern states who formed the Confederate States of America. On April 13, 1861, Fort Sumter fell. Two days later President Lincoln called for 75,000 volunteers for the Army. The Civil War had begun.

Grant offered his services to the Union and was commissioned colonel of the 21st Illinois Volunteer Regiment. In August 1861, Grant read in a newspaper that President Lincoln had made him a brigadier general. Communications were so slow that he had received no notice of the promotion before.

Trial and Acclaim. Grant's first real battle in the Civil War took place at Belmont, Missouri. His troops drove the Confederate forces from their camp and destroyed it. But the Southerners counterattacked with additional forces, and Grant had to retreat. It was a bitter lesson, but he learned from it. His next campaign led to the capture of Fort Donelson. The surrender of this important fort made Grant a hero in the North, and President Lincoln promoted him to major general of volunteers.

During the years of war that followed, Grant was both criticized and praised. After the costly battle of Shiloh, in which Union and Confederate losses totaled over 20,000, Lincoln was asked to remove him from command. But the president refused, saying, "I can't spare this man—he fights." Actually, the Confederate forces were so beaten at Shiloh that they evacuated the vital fortified railroad center of Corinth, Mississippi, about a month later.

Union Army Commander. Grant repaid Lincoln's confidence by capturing the Confederate stronghold of Vicksburg, Mississippi, in 1863, giving the Union forces control of the Mississippi River. In 1864, Grant was promoted to the rank of lieutenant general and was given command of all the Union armies. He proceeded to hammer the Confederate forces in Virginia under General Robert E. Lee. It was a long, bloody campaign, for Lee was a great general. But the Southerners were greatly outnumbered, and on April 9, 1865, Lee surrendered to Grant at Appomattox Court House, Virginia.

A grateful U.S. Congress appointed Grant a full general. He was the first man to hold this rank since George Washington.

For a full account of the Civil War and Grant's role in it, see the article CIVIL WAR, UNITED STATES, in Volume C.

▶PRESIDENT

Because of Grant's great popularity, the Republicans nominated him for the presidency in 1868. Grant disliked politics and did not actively campaign, but he easily defeated the Democratic candidate, former New York governor Horatio Seymour. Grant won re-election in 1876, defeating Horace Greeley, a New York newspaper editor and publisher.

Political Scandals. Modest and unassuming, Grant tried to run the government the only way he knew—as a military operation. But his presidency was marked by scandal and corruption because he did not always choose the best men for political jobs. He was so honest himself that he found it hard to believe that anyone

Grant and his family sat for this photograph in 1868, at the time of his nomination by the Republicans for the presidency. At the rear, from left to right, are Mrs. Julia Dent Grant, daughter Ellen (Nellie), youngest son Jesse Root, and son Ulysses Simpson. The eldest son, Frederick Dent, is seated at right.

The remains of Ulysses and Julia Grant lie in a magnificent tomb in New York City. Dedicated in 1897, Grant's Tomb was built with money donated by thousands of ordinary people. Over the entrance to the building are carved the words spoken by Grant at the end of the Civil War: "Let us have peace."

he trusted could betray him. Yet in one case Grant's own brother-in-law involved him in a financial scandal. His personal secretary also was implicated in one of the most notorious scandals, that of the Whiskey Ring, which sought to evade U.S. taxes in the manufacture of whiskey.

Achievements. At home, Grant supported the rights of the freed blacks in the South. He opposed the recently-organized Ku Klux Klan (KKK), which sought through acts of terrorism to prevent blacks from voting. The most notable achievement of his administration, however, was the settlement of the *Alabama* claims dispute with Britain in 1872. The *Alabama* had been one of several Confederate warships built by Britain during the Civil War.

The United States demanded compensation for damages done to the Union merchant marine by these ships and was awarded $15.5 million.

▶**LATER YEARS**

Upon leaving the White House in 1877, Grant and his family went on a two-year tour around the world. After returning to the United States, Grant was supported by some Republicans to run for the presidency again, in 1880, but he lost the nomination to James A. Garfield.

Grant's last years were difficult ones. He lost the little money he had through bad investments. Penniless, he began to write his memoirs to provide for his family. Congress restored him to the retired list, with his old rank of general, to help relieve his financial burdens. But by this time Grant had little time left, for he was dying of cancer. Although in great pain, he continued to work on his memoirs. He finished them about one week before he died on July 23, 1885, at Mount McGregor, New York. His body and that of his wife, Julia, lie in a magnificent tomb, built especially for him, in New York City.

Grant's presidency in the years following the Civil War came at a time of political turmoil for the United States. Although he was not successful as president, he remains one of the great American military leaders. His personal qualities were more than admirable, and it is for these he should be remembered.

Reviewed by ULYSSES S. GRANT 3RD
Maj. General, U.S. Army (ret.)

GRAPEFRUIT. See ORANGE AND GRAPEFRUIT.

IMPORTANT DATES IN THE LIFE OF ULYSSES S. GRANT

1822	Born at Point Pleasant, Ohio, April 27.
1843	Graduated from West Point.
1846–1848	Fought in the Mexican War.
1848	Married Julia Dent.
1854	Resigned from the Army.
1861	Returned to military service at the outbreak of the Civil War.
1862	Capture of Fort Donelson.
1863	Capture of Vicksburg.
1864	Promoted to lieutenant general; appointed commander of the Union armies.
1865	Received General Robert E. Lee's surrender at Appomattox Court House, Virginia, April 9.
1866	General of the Armies.
1869–1877	18th president of the United States.
1885	Died at Mount McGregor, New York, July 23.

GRAPES AND BERRIES

It is no accident that berries and grapes are found almost everywhere they will grow. Their bright fruits especially attract birds, who carry the seeds far and wide. Men, too, have long been fond of grapes and berries. Berries, once gathered from wild plants, are now also cultivated on a large scale.

▶ **GRAPES**

Grapes have been grown by man since the dawn of recorded history. Grape vineyards are often mentioned in the Old Testament. The Egyptians left many pictures that showed their use of grapes for wine. Wine was a common drink of the Greeks and Romans, who even had a god of wine, named Bacchus. Throughout history grapes and wine have been a part of a cultivated society—in its religious celebrations and in the celebration of life itself.

The world grows more grapes than it does any other kind of fruit. Many grapes are eaten fresh, and many are dried to make raisins. But most grapes are crushed, and their juice is fermented for wine.

The European or Old World grape is grown in nearly all countries except in the tropics or where the winters are very cold. It is best suited to areas where the temperature is moderate and mild, like the area around the Mediterranean Sea. Large quantities of this kind of grape are raised in France, Italy, Germany, Hungary, Spain, and Portugal. In the United States the European grape is the chief grape of California where most of the grapes in the country are raised.

Many kinds of grapes are native to North America. The first colonists in New England tried to grow the European-type grape, but the vines died from the cold in winter and from plant diseases. By breeding the native kinds of grapes, many new varieties were developed. These improved American varieties grow well in the eastern part of the country and in the Pacific Northwest.

The roots of the American grape are resistant to an insect that causes great damage to European grapes. This insect, called phylloxera, wiped out many vineyards in Europe. Most European vineyards now graft European vines onto the hardy, phylloxera-resistant roots of American grapes. The words "American" and "European" refer to the original home of the grape variety. Both kinds are grown throughout the world, the choice of variety depending on local climates and soils.

Among the hundreds of grape varieties there are great differences in the size of the fruit, color, season of ripening, and quality. Grapes may be white (really pale yellow), red, or almost black (deep blue or purple). Among the American kinds the Concord grape is the most important. It is used for making juice and jellies and for eating. Other American grapes good for eating fresh are the Delaware, Niagara, and Fredonia.

The Thompson Seedless, called Sultanina in Europe, is the main grape used for making raisins. It is the most important European-type grape in the United States. It is also a popular grape for eating fresh. Other important European varieties for eating fresh are the Emperor, Flame Tokay, Ribier, and Malaga. These are grown in California, South Africa, Australia, Chile, and elsewhere.

Wherever grapes are produced, there are many varieties grown for wines. Red and white varieties are used for white or light-colored wines. Black varieties are used for red wines. Some of the white varieties used are Semillon, Colombar, Green Hungarian, and Franken Riesling. A few leading black varieties are Zinfandel, Refosco, and Barbera.

The Vine

Grapes grow on woody vines. Each vine develops a main **trunk**, side branches called **arms**, and leafy stems called **shoots**. The 1-year-old shoots are called **fruiting canes**. To develop the growth of large fruit clusters on the fruiting canes and also to develop new shoot growth, older canes are pruned yearly.

Plants must be supported, at least when young, by tying them to stakes or trellises. Some varieties of the European grape, if staked for several years, form a trunk that is large and sturdy enough to support the top.

Grape Culture

Grapes are a favorite fruit for growing in home gardens, as well as for commercial growing. They are ideal for home gardens with limited space, as they may be trained to grow against fences and arbors.

New plants are grown from plant cuttings of the canes. Cuttings usually develop good roots. Some varieties of grapes have roots that are attacked by tiny eel-like "worms." In such cases, cuttings of these varieties are grafted or budded onto the vines of strong, resistant roots from other varieties of grapes.

The plants are placed 8 to 10 feet apart in rows 10 to 12 feet apart. The plants grow best when the ground is cultivated. Pruning, or controlling growth of the plant by trimming, is done to make it possible for the plant to produce larger clusters of larger and sweeter fruit. Vines generally bear fruit the third season after they are planted. Vines that are well cared for may live for many years.

Spraying or dusting is necessary in most areas if insects and diseases are to be controlled. Fertilizers are needed to keep the vines healthy and productive.

Grapes to be eaten fresh are usually marketed at once. Some varieties of fresh grapes may be held in cold storage for 6 to 8 months. Grapes for making raisins are dried. For making wine, grapes are crushed immediately after harvest. A considerable quantity of juice is made from grapes. By-products may be jelly or brandy made from the skins, salad oil and tannin made from the seeds, and cream of tartar from the stems.

▶ STRAWBERRIES

Many people think that the strawberry is the finest of all berries. It is the most popular in home gardens and the most popular for commercial growing. An English doctor of the 16th century once said, "Doubtless God could have made a better berry, but doubtless God never did."

There are good reasons why strawberries are so popular. They are beautiful to look at and delicious to taste. They are easier to grow than most fruits. Few diseases or insects disturb them. It takes only a short growing time until the plants produce fruit. For the amount of land it takes to grow them, they produce a large number of berries.

Strawberries are native to many parts of the world. They are found growing wild over much of Europe, as well as in North and South America. The present large cultivated berries were developed from two kinds of wild berries—one from the Pacific coast of South America and the other from the eastern United States. Many different varieties are now grown. Early, midseason, and late varieties bear fruit in the spring and early summer. Everbearing varieties ripen until late fall. The time when the fruit develops depends on the temperature and rainfall the plants receive.

While most of the strawberries grown are the large cultivated varieties, some of the small, dark, fragrant, and very sweet wild varieties are also grown, especially in France. Many people prefer them to the large ones.

Plants set out in spring or summer will produce a crop in early summer of the following year. Strawberries are perennials—that is, they live for a number of years—but the first two or three crops are the best. The soil around the plants cannot be hoed easily, as the plants spread all over the ground. Weeds are better killed by chemical weed killers that do not damage the strawberry plants. In areas where winter temperatures fall below 15 degrees Fahrenheit, the plants are mulched—covered with straw—in the winter to keep them from being injured by the cold.

Strawberry plants send out runners that root. The rooted plants are called daughter plants, and the plants sending out the runners are called mother plants. Plants that grow in hill systems, where the daughter plants are trimmed out, produce the largest and finest berries. The matted-row system, where runners are allowed to set, grows the largest number of berries.

Strawberries are marketed fresh or are frozen after adding sugar. Frozen berries are sold in stores or made into such products as preserves and ice cream.

▶ RASPBERRIES AND BLACKBERRIES

Anyone who has ever picked blackberries or raspberries knows that they grow on prickly bramble plants. Because the berries are deliciously juicy, sweet, and tender, many people willingly suffer the pricks and scratches of picking them. Brambles are found growing wild throughout the temperate zones. Both blackberries and raspberries are native to Asia, Europe, and North America. Many varieties have been developed for commercial use.

The fruit is made up of a number of little fleshy parts. Raspberries may be black, yellow,

Strawberries

Grapes for eating fresh

Red raspberries

Blueberries

Grapes are grown for wine in these vineyards along Lake Geneva, Switzerland.

This cranberry bog is flooded for the harvest. When the berries are raked, they rise to the surface of the water and may be removed easily.

red, or purple. Blackberries are usually black, but some varieties may be amber or red. Dewberries, loganberries, youngberries, and boysenberries are some well-known varieties of the blackberries grown in the United States.

Blackberries are often confused with raspberries. It is easy to tell the small wild blackberry from a red raspberry, but a larger, cultivated blackberry may look very much like a black raspberry. The best method for telling the difference is to pull a berry off the stem. When a raspberry is ripe it pulls off from the plant in a thimble shape, leaving its center behind. (In some places the raspberry is called a thimbleberry because of this shape.) When a blackberry is picked, its center does not separate from the rest of the fruit. The fruit of cultivated blackberries may grow up to 1½ inches long. Raspberry fruit may grow up to 1 inch long.

The stems of raspberries and blackberries are called canes. Canes grow for 1 year, blossom and bear fruit the next year, and then dry up and die. New canes grow each year.

Raspberry plants can stand more cold than blackberries. Some kinds grow very well in the North but die out in warm climates. Blackberries are better suited to moderate weather and grow southward to the tropics. The finest blackberries grow in South America. Dewberries, loganberries, and boysenberries are especially suited to mild, dry weather.

Blackberries and raspberries are eaten fresh. Many are canned or frozen. They are favorites for making jams, jellies, and preserves. Some blackberries are used for making wine.

▶ CRANBERRIES

The Pilgrims who landed at Plymouth Rock found cranberries growing in the swamps and lowlands nearby. The Indians used them for food, and the Pilgrims found that they made an excellent sauce—especially for meat.

Cranberries (the word comes from the old name "crane berries"—perhaps because cranes like to eat them) have a small wild form, called the lingonberry, or mountain cranberry, that grows in Britain, northern Europe, and Siberia, as well as in North America. The larger cultivated form is native only to the boggy areas of North America.

Cultivated cranberries are now grown in large quantities in places where there is peaty soil or acid muck—in Cape Cod, Massachusetts; in New Jersey; and in Wisconsin, Oregon, and Washington.

The round or oval red berries, about ¾ inch in diameter, grow on vines that trail on the ground. The vines are usually flooded with water during the winter, to protect them from the cold. When the berries ripen in the fall, they are picked with a special handrake or by machines that look something like an old-fashioned lawnmower.

Cranberries are sold fresh, canned, or made into juice. They are used in relishes, sauces, molded salads and desserts, and pies.

▶ BLUEBERRIES AND HUCKLEBERRIES

Bears in Maine have been photographed as they stripped the berries from blueberry bushes with their teeth. Many people share the bears' fondness for the berries. Sweet, tender blueberries are appearing on the markets in ever-increasing quantities.

Certainly blueberries and huckleberries are among the best of the small fruits. These delicious round berries are native to North America. The wild berries are small, about ⅓ inch in diameter, and have a fine flavor. In New England, Michigan, and other areas, many of the wild berries are still picked in large quantities for sale.

In 1906 the United States Department of Agriculture began work to develop improved blueberries for commercial growing. The work was highly successful. Fruit of the improved berries is from ½ to 1 inch in diameter. It was learned that areas in which blueberries are to grow must have an acid soil. Now berries are grown commercially in New Jersey, North Carolina, and Michigan.

Real blueberries are various shades of blue and contain many very small seeds. Huckleberries are dark blue to black and have 10 nutlike seeds in their fruit. (In some areas blueberries are called huckleberries.) Both huckleberries and blueberries are sold fresh. They are also frozen or canned. These berries are especially delicious in pies or muffins.

J. R. MAGNESS
Former Head Horticulturist
United States Department of Agriculture

See also WINE.

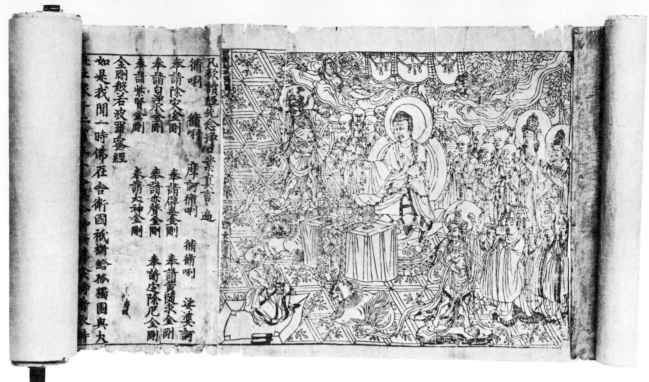

A woodcut from a page of the *Diamond Sutra*. Chinese, dated A.D. 868. British Museum, London.

GRAPHIC ARTS

The term "graphic arts" usually refers to drawing and printmaking. It comes from the Greek *graphikos,* which means "able to draw or paint." The graphic arts include the techniques used to make prints. An artist makes prints when he wants several copies of a single drawing. He carves his drawing into a slab of metal or wood. He can also burn it into metal or stone with acid. He then inks the slab and prints it onto paper with a press. Many copies can be made, and each is an original work of art.

Pictures that we see in books or buy in printshops are not original works of art; they are reproductions. The original painting or drawing has been photographed and reproduced by mechanical methods. An artist's print, however, is original art because it has been made directly from the woodblock, plate, or stone that the artist himself prepared.

▶ HOW PRINTS ARE MADE

There are three principal methods of making prints. The oldest is the **relief** method. In relief printing the print is made from a raised surface. Woodcuts are the most popular form of relief printing. The artist cuts from a block of wood with tools called **gouges**. He cuts away the background from his design. The raised design is then inked and printed.

A second printing method is called **intaglio** and is the reverse of relief printing. In intaglio printing, such as etching, the print is made from the lines or areas which have been cut or burned away. After the drawing has been carved or etched into a metal plate, the plate is covered with ink, then rubbed with a clean rag to remove the ink from the raised surfaces. Damp paper is placed on top of the plate, and when paper and plate are run through the press, the paper lifts the ink from the lines.

The third method is known as the **planographic** process. The print is made from a flat surface that has not been etched or carved. **Lithography** is the most common type of planographic printing. Slabs of limestone are most frequently used, although lithographs can be made from metal sheets. A drawing is made on the stone with a greasy crayon. The stone is then treated with various materials that make all but the crayon lines resist ink. The greasy drawing absorbs ink. When the paper is printed, the image the artist drew is lifted from the stone.

ORIENTAL WOODCUTS

Woodcut printing is the oldest well-known graphic art. By the 7th century A.D. the Chinese had begun to make religious woodcut prints. However, Chinese artists never became print designers. Paintings of the Oriental masters were copied by highly skilled cutters, but original work was never designed especially for woodcuts. The Japanese learned woodcutting from the Chinese and Koreans. But unlike Chinese prints, Japanese designs were made especially for the woodcut. One man designed the print, another cut the block, and a third printed.

When Westerners think of Japanese prints, they most often have in mind those of the ukiyoe school. The first of these prints was created in black and white around A.D. 1660. About 80 years later the Japanese began printing in three colors. A separate block was needed for each color. Around 1765 the full color print, using 8 to 11 blocks, was developed.

The names associated with Japanese prints are those of the designers; the cutters and printers are unknown. The artist drew his design on thin paper that was glued to the block of wood as a cutting guide. After the cutter carved the block, the printer brushed on the ink.

One of the big differences between the Oriental and Western woodcut is the way changes of shade are made. In Eastern work, watercolor is brushed on the surface of the block as in a painting. In the West, shading is created by cut, or engraved, lines.

EARLY EUROPEAN WOODCUTS

In Europe during the Middle Ages woodcuts were used to stamp fabric designs. The inked woodblocks were placed on top of the cloth and struck with hammers. Playing cards and religious pictures were the first products of European printers. After the invention of movable type, Bibles and history books were adorned with woodcut illustrations.

THE INVENTION OF ENGRAVING

The art of engraving, an intaglio process, was developed around the beginning of the 15th century. In engraving, a pointed tool called a **burin** cuts lines into a copper or zinc plate. Decorative engraving on metal, such as armor, was an old practice, but it is not known who first pulled a print from an engraved plate. The process seems to have been discovered independently in Italy and Germany.

Italian goldsmiths used an engraving technique called **niello**, in which hollowed lines were filled with enamel. There is a legend that intaglio printing was discovered when a laundress set her wet wash down on some drying niello ware. When she lifted her wash, the enamel design had been printed on her laundry. It is more likely that the process came from the goldsmiths' custom of rubbing paper over their work as a record of the design.

The painter Andrea Mantegna (1431–1506) was the first great Italian engraver. A man who lived at the same time, Marcantonio Raimondi (1475?–1534?), became famous for his prints of the paintings of Raphael and other masters, and his copies of Dürer's prints.

ETCHING, DRYPOINT, AND WOOD ENGRAVING

The leading graphic artist of northern Europe was Albrecht Dürer (1471–1528), a master of woodcut and engraving. In the second decade of the 16th century a new

The Knight, Death, and the Devil (1513). An engraving by Albrecht Dürer. Brooklyn Museum, New York.

Two Clowns. An etching from the series "Balli di Sfessania" (1622), by Jacques Callot. Metropolitan Museum of Art, New York.

Diogenes, a woodcut by the Italian artist Ugo da Carpi (1450?–1525?). Metropolitan Museum, New York.

The Blindness of Tobit (1651), an etching by Rembrandt. Pierpont Morgan Library, New York.

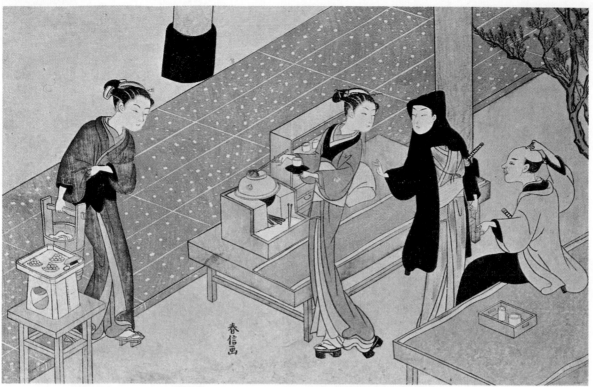

Osen of Kasamori. Woodcut by Suzuki Harunobu (1725?–1770). Tokyo National Museum.

process, etching, was invented, and Dürer quickly tried it. Etchings are printed by the intaglio method used for engraving. But instead of the lines being gouged out by hand, the plate is covered with a solution called **ground.** When the ground dries, it protects the plate with a water-resistant film. The drawing is scratched through the ground with a needle, and the plate is placed in a bath of water and acid. Where the ground has been scratched away, the acid etches the metal. The first etchings were on iron and had lines of equal width. Today copper and zinc plates are used.

Dürer was among the first to try another new technique, drypoint. In drypoint a sharp needle scratches the design directly into the plate; no ground is needed. Drypoint is often combined with etching or engraving on one plate. It differs from engraving in that the line is printed from a rougher edge.

Wood engraving was also invented in the 16th century. It is relief-printed, as the woodcut, but the cross grain—the end rather than the top—of a hardwood, such as box or cherry, is used. Also, engraving burins rather than gouges cut out the wood. A wood engraving usually is printed as white lines on black and a woodcut as black on a white background, but this is not a certain indication of the method used.

▶**PRINTS IN THE 17TH AND 18TH CENTURIES**

Peter Paul Rubens (1577–1640) kept a stable of engravers making plates of his work. He corrected the proofs but did none of the cutting. However, he may have made several etchings. His talented pupil, Sir Anthony van Dyck (1599–1641), etched the *Iconography,* a portrait series of the hundred most famous men of his day.

The Dutchman Hercules Seghers (1589?–1640?) is known for the imaginative and emotional quality of his work. He was a great technical experimenter, especially in color etchings. His work was admired and owned by Rembrandt van Rijn (1606–69), considered by many to be the greatest etcher who ever lived. Rembrandt produced many works on various subjects: portraits, nudes, landscapes, religious themes, and still lifes. Before Rembrandt, prints were usually first designed in another medium, such as pencil or ink. But Rembrandt began working directly on the

Divan Japonais (1892), a lithograph by Henri de Toulouse-Lautrec. Museum of Modern Art, New York.

Tarantelle (1943), engraving and soft-ground etching by Stanley William Hayter. Museum of Modern Art, New York.

Left: The General, aquatint and collage by Misch Kohn. Right: Triple Dip (1952), by Ben Shahn, silk and color screen. Museum of Modern Art, New York.

Por que fue sensible. Aquatint from "Los Caprichos" (1799), by Goya. Hispanic Society of America, New York.

The Scream (1895). Lithograph by the Norwegian artist Edvard Munch.

plate. This allowed him to express his ideas in one creative act. He was also a master of the drypoint.

Mezzotint

The mezzotint technique of printmaking was invented in the middle of the 17th century in Germany. With a many-toothed tool called a **rocker**, the artist covers an entire copper plate with tiny dots. The plate then prints a solid black. Next the grain is ground away; the more an area is rubbed, the lighter it becomes. Mezzotint portraits were popular in England in the 18th century, and the technique was called "the English manner."

Soft-Ground Etching

In the 17th century a technique developed using soft ground. Soft ground is made of a wax or some other nonhardening substance. With this ground the artist can make softer lines than with hard ground. He places a piece of paper or fabric on top of the ground-coated plate and draws on it. The drawing lifts the ground from the plate. When the plate is etched, fuzzy lines are made.

Aquatint

Aquatint was a major advance in intaglio printing. Developed around 1768, this process produces a range of grainy values from silver-gray to intense black. A coating of special powder is dusted onto the plate and heated. The plate is protected by the powder, but the metal in between the grains of powder can be etched. The plate is etched a number of times until the desired darkness is achieved. Because the method was adaptable to color printing, it almost completely replaced the mezzotint color process.

▶ GRAPHICS IN THE 19TH CENTURY

The leading graphic artist at the beginning of the 19th century was the Spanish painter Francisco Goya (1746–1828). He perfected the aquatint and combined it with other techniques to create many powerful prints. His *Disasters of War,* a series of prints, depicts the evils of the Napoleonic wars. These prints are unusually vivid comments on misery and cruelty. Goya was an experimenter: late in his life he was among the first to try lithography, a new technique.

Lithography

Lithography was invented about 1798 by Aloys (or Alois) Senefelder (1771–1834), a German. He made his discovery while seeking an inexpensive method of reproducing plays and musical scores. Lithography was first used for commercial purposes.

The lithograph first won popularity in France. It was less complicated and less costly to use than woodcuts or the intaglio process, and better suited to mass production. The new merchant class used it to print political propaganda, decorations for walls, and illustrations for books.

The hero of lithography is the French artist Honoré Daumier (1808–79). He drew more than 4,000 cartoon lithographs for the newspapers. Daumier understood human behavior very well. He attacked anyone who made him angry—lawyers and kings included. He went to jail in 1832 for his caricature of King Louis Philippe. The great French romantic painter Eugène Delacroix (1798–1863) also produced a number of fine etchings and lithographs. But otherwise lithography fell into disuse.

Toward the end of the 19th century, three other French artists—Pierre Bonnard (1867–1947), Jean Édouard Vuillard (1868–1940), and especially Henri de Toulouse-Lautrec (1864–1901)—put new life into color lithography. Toulouse-Lautrec's posters for the famous café the *Moulin Rouge* ("Red Mill") influenced later lithography, printing, and even painting.

▶MODERN GRAPHICS

The invention of photography and photo-engraving ended the use of prints to reproduce paintings. Techniques such as mezzotint are seldom used anymore. Other processes, such as line engraving, are now used to make original prints.

Since the end of World War I there has been a trend toward experimenting with the graphic techniques. By exploring all the possibilities of a process, artists make prints that are more than just reproduced drawings. The United States has been a center of this interest, but much of its force has come from Stanley William Hayter (1901–88), an Englishman. Located in Paris from 1927 to 1939, his Atelier 17 (Studio 17) encouraged experimentation, especially in intaglio. Hayter began to influence American graphics when he moved to the United States in 1940.

The main emphasis since World War II has been on color printmaking. Prints are made with combinations of techniques: one color may be printed from a woodblock, and another from an aquatint plate. Countless materials are used for printing: plaster, linoleum, rough-textured fabrics, and even dried glue. Glue prints are easily made at home on a piece of wood or heavy cardboard. A design is drawn with a tube of Duco cement or white wood glue. When the glue is thoroughly dry (which takes a day or two), it is inked with a roller. A piece of absorbent paper—such as newsprint or Japanese rice paper—is placed on top of the design and rubbed with the back of a wooden spoon. The design then appears on the paper. Many copies can be made in this way.

Serigraphy

The newest printing medium, serigraphy, or silk screening, developed from one of the oldest, the stencil. On a tightly stretched silk screen the areas not to be printed are blocked out with glue or lacquer. Ink is then forced through the parts of the screen that have not been blocked out. A separate stencil is needed for each color.

Most 20th century artists have made prints. Prints are seldom made today in great quantities, since they are no longer created for mass-produced publications. A print—designed, carved, or etched, and printed by the artist himself—is a precious work of art. But unlike a painting, of which there is only one "original," a print yields 25 or 50 originals. For this reason an artist's print usually costs less than one of his paintings. Many great art collections have been started with the purchase of a single print.

RICHARD W. IRELAND
The Maryland Institute College of Art

See also ENGRAVING; ETCHING; ILLUSTRATION AND ILLUSTRATORS; LINOLEUM-BLOCK PRINTING; SILK-SCREEN PRINTING; WOODCUT PRINTING.

GRAPHS

A graph is a visual display of information, or data. Because graphs can make large amounts of even complicated information clear and easy to understand, they are one of the most useful tools for communicating such information.

▸ **BAR GRAPHS**

One kind of graph is the **bar graph**, or **bar chart**. A bar graph is generally used to display and compare the number of people or things in a category, or group. If you owned an ice cream store, for example, it would be useful for you to know which ice cream flavors are the most popular among your customers and be able to compare which groups preferred which flavors.

To make the graph, first collect data about your customers' preferences. Then organize and summarize that information in a table, as in Figure 1.

Flavor	Frequency (Number of People)
Vanilla	40
Chocolate	30
Strawberry	15
Chocolate Chip	10
Coffee	5

Figure 1. Table of Ice Cream Preferences

Next draw a simple bar graph to display the results. One way to start is by drawing a frame for your graph. The horizontal and vertical sides of the frame are called the **axes** of the graph. On the bottom, or horizontal, axis (singular of axes), write the name of each category, in this case, the different flavors of ice cream. Be sure to leave equal spaces, or intervals, between the categories.

The left, or vertical, axis shows **frequency**, or how many people or things fit into each category. Here the frequency is the number of people who prefer a certain flavor. Next set up a scale—a set of numbers at equal intervals—along the vertical axis. Since 40 is the highest frequency in the table and 5 is the lowest, you might want to number the vertical axis from 0 to 50 in equal intervals of ten.

The last step is to draw a rectangular bar to show the number of people in each category. Although the bars will have different heights, they should all have the same width. The bar graph in Figure 2 shows what the results of this survey might look like. Another way to draw a bar graph would be to use horizontal instead of vertical bars.

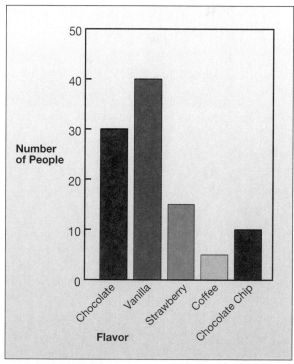

Figure 2. A Bar Graph

At a glance you can tell that many customers prefer vanilla or chocolate, but few like coffee the best. Although the table provides the same data, it is quicker and easier to get the information from the bar graph.

A double-bar graph can be used to make a side-by-side comparison between two groups. The graph in Figure 3 was drawn to show if adults and children prefer different flavors of ice cream. Note that it uses three-dimensional bars. To read the graph correctly, you must match the front edge of the top of the bar with a number on the vertical axis.

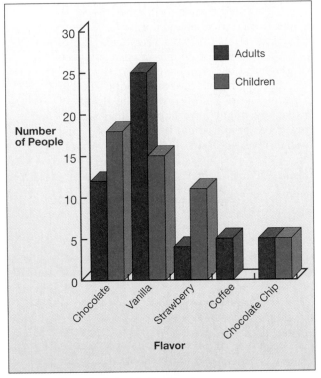

Figure 3. A Double-Bar Graph

This graph shows that adults seem to enjoy vanilla more than children do, that no children in the survey prefer coffee ice cream, and that children and adults seem to like chocolate chip equally well.

▶ PICTOGRAPHS

Pictographs, sometimes called pictograms or picture graphs, are similar to bar graphs. Pictographs, however, present data in an interesting way by using icons, or images, instead of solid bars to display the number of people or things in a category. In the pictograph in Figure 4, images of dogs, hamsters, cats, and fish are used to show the types of pets owned by youngsters in one school. The

key indicates that each image represents 10 animals, so you can see the children in this school own 50 dogs and only 20 fish.

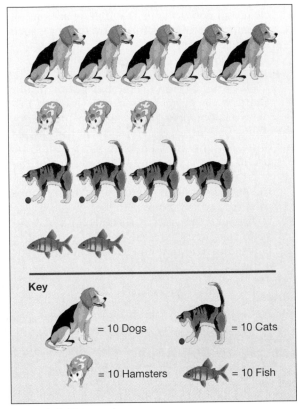

Figure 4. A Pictograph

▶ PIE CHARTS

Pie charts, also called circle graphs or area graphs, display information organized by category, too. The pie chart, however, emphasizes how each category is related to a topic or question. Each "slice," or section, of the pie represents a category, and the size of each section is determined by the percentage of people or things in that category.

In the pie chart in Figure 5, the topic is the ways people use to get to work. Each section of the chart represents an individual method. In a pie graph the sections must be the correct size in relation to each other and to the whole. For example, as Figure 5 shows, 40% of the commuters surveyed drive to work. Not only is this piece 40% of the whole circle, it is also twice as large as the piece that shows that 20% of the people take the bus.

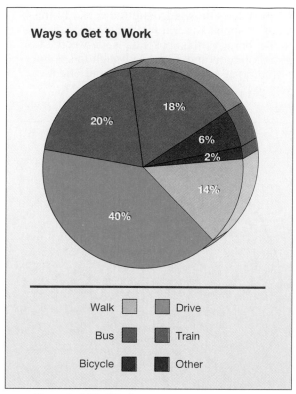

Ways to Get to Work

18%

6%

2%

20%

14%

40%

Walk ▢ Drive ▨

Bus ▨ Train ▨

Bicycle ▨ Other ■

Figure 5. A Pie Chart

drawn contains no height greater than 70 inches. These numbers progress from bottom to top in intervals of ten.

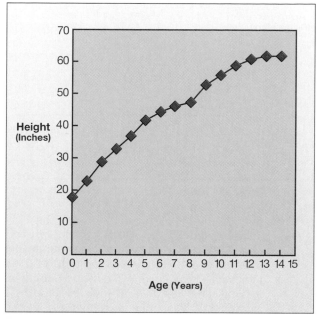

Figure 6. A Line Graph

When you read a pie chart, always add the percentages to make sure that they total 100%. If the values are not given in percentages, the numbers must still add up to the total number of people or things that were counted.

▶ **LINE GRAPHS**

Line graphs show the relationship between two kinds of information and often show a trend, or a pattern of change.

A line graph is constructed by plotting points, or dots, on a grid, then connecting the points to form a line. Numbers, instead of categories, are written on the horizontal axis. As in a bar graph, the scales in a line graph are drawn to include the smallest and largest numbers in the data.

The line graph in Figure 6 traces the height of a girl from birth to age 14. The numbers 0 to 15 have been placed on the horizontal axis, but we are only concerned with the girl's height from her birth, age 0, to age 14. On the vertical axis, a reasonable range of heights has been set, from 0 inches to 70 inches, because the data from which this graph was

You can see that the girl was 18 inches tall at birth and about 52 inches at age 9. The graph also shows the relationship between the girl's age and her height as a pattern of growth. Notice that the line goes in an upward direction from left to right, indicating that the girl's height increased steadily during this time period. You can also see that the line rises steeply between the ages of 8 and 11, showing that she had a "growth spurt" during these years. It also shows that her growth appeared to slow down, or level off, as she approached age 15.

▶ **SCATTER PLOTS**

A **scatter plot** is similar to a line graph in that it allows us to compare two sets of numbers. But a scatter plot shows patterns in groups, or clusters, of unconnected points rather than by a line. We might be interested in the question "Do taller people tend to have longer arm spans than shorter people?" A scatter plot can show the correlation, or relationship, between two sets of data—in this case, between arm spans and height.

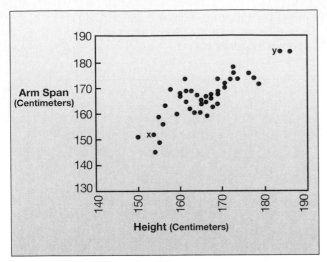

Figure 7. A Scatter Plot

on the circles drawn around the clock. In this study, it appears that a likely time for a baby to be born at this hospital is between the hours of noon and 5 P.M. Although this is not a traditional graph, it is a clear and effective way to present the data.

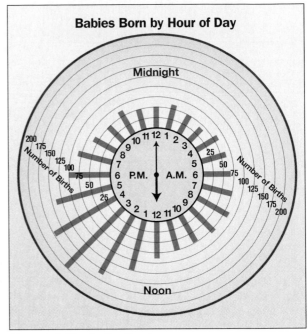

Figure 8. A Circular Bar Graph

Each point in the scatter plot in Figure 7 represents a person with a particular height and arm span. The point to the right of the *x* indicates a person who is about 154 centimeters tall and has an arm span of about 152 centimeters. The point next to the *y* represents a person 183 centimeters tall with an arm span of 185 centimeters. General trends in this data are shown by how the points are clustered—shorter people tend to have shorter arm spans and taller people tend to have longer arm spans.

Scatter plots are also useful in allowing us to make predictions. Based on Figure 7, you might predict that a person who is 185 centimeters tall will most likely have a longer arm span than one who is 165 centimeters tall.

▶ OTHER TYPES OF GRAPHS

There are other types of graphs besides the ones described above, including **stem and leaf graphs**, which are used mainly for tallying scores and other measurements, and **box and whisker graphs**, which give information about the range of a set of numbers, as well as where the numbers are clustered.

Sometimes unique graphs are created for special purposes. The graph in Figure 8 shows patterns in the times of day that babies were born at one suburban hospital over a period of one year. In this graph, bars are set around a circular clock face, one bar for each of the 24 hours in a day. The frequencies, or numbers of babies born at that hour, are shown

▶ MISLEADING GRAPHS

Graphs are extremely useful as ways of presenting data, but they can sometimes be misleading. Graphs can be inaccurate or improperly constructed. Even a careful person may read a number incorrectly or add numbers instead of subtracting them.

Sometimes a graph may be drawn that emphasizes certain features to make a particular point. The pictograph in Figure 9, for example, compares the number of boxes sold of two different brands of cereal at a particular supermarket. In the graph on the top, the numbers on the vertical axis indicate that twice as many boxes were sold of Tasty Flakes than of Poppin' Oats. The visual image, however, can lead to a different interpretation. In the graph on the bottom, you can see that four boxes of Poppin' Oats can fit into the box of Tasty Flakes, giving the visual message that four times as many boxes of Tasty Flakes

Figure 9. How a Graph Can Be Misleading

what that person or group may have to gain by presenting the data in a particular way. If it is available, it is also a good idea to compare a graph to the table of information it came from to be sure one is consistent with the other.

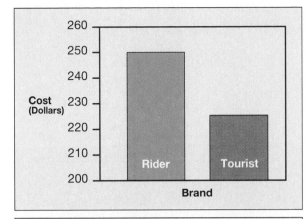

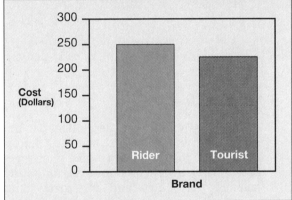

Figure 10. Graphs with the Same Information but Different Points of View

were sold instead of two times as many. But if only the unshaded portion of the Tasty Flakes box were shown, the boxes would be of equal width. Then the visual image would be consistent with the information the graph is meant to convey.

In other situations, the information presented may be correct, but the graph may highlight a particular point of view. For example, both bar charts in Figure 10 present the same information about the relative cost of two different brands of bicycle, but the graph on the top makes the difference in cost seem much greater. If you look carefully at the scale on the vertical, or cost, axis, you will see that the scale in the graph on the top begins at 200, whereas the scale in the graph on the bottom begins at 0. Although both graphs are technically correct, the top one certainly emphasizes a point of view more favorable to the manufacturers of Tourist bicycles. When you are presented with a graph, therefore, it is important for you to know who produced it and

USING TECHNOLOGY

Drawing graphs by hand can be a challenging yet enjoyable experience. If the data or the method of presentation is very complicated, however, it is easier and more efficient to use modern technology. Today many students learn how to use graphing calculators and computer-graphics software programs in school. People working in universities, in science, in the media, and in business generally use these electronic tools to produce the graphs they need.

JIM O'KEEFE
Assistant Professor of Mathematics
Lesley College

See also STATISTICS.

The Pampa, a great sea of grass in Argentina, stretches for miles.

GRASSES

One way or another, most land-dwelling creatures live on grasses. Grasses furnish more food than any other family of green plants. They furnish food for man, for grazing animals, for birds, and for many other animals. Even if animals do not themselves eat grasses, they often depend on the flesh of animals that do.

The grasses make up the most widespread plant family in the world. There are about 7,000 different kinds. Most grasses grow on land, but some kinds grow in water.

All the grains and cereals are grasses. So are most pasture plants. The grass family also includes the sweet grasses, such as sugarcane and sorghum. Lemon grass and citronella are scented grasses. The tallest of all the grasses is bamboo.

Great "seas" of grass cover natural fields, sometimes for thousands of square miles. These are called prairies or plains in the United States and downs in England. In Australia and sometimes in the United States they are called ranges. The pampas of South America, the Russian steppes, the South African veld, and the savannas of the tropics are all "seas" of grass.

▶ GRASSES AND CIVILIZATION

When man first learned to cultivate grain grasses, his way of life changed. Before then he was mainly a wanderer. When there was no more food to be found in one place, he moved on to another place. But once he knew how to plant grain, he was more certain of his food supply. He did not have to hunt for food. He could grow it himself.

Grain was especially useful as food, because it did not spoil for a long time if it was kept dry. Man was able to store some of his grain for the winter. Now instead of wandering in search of food, many tribes settled down. Their people became farmers.

A new way of life began when man lived in farming settlements. He had time for other things besides finding food. He began to make new and better tools. And he started to become civilized. You might say cultivation of the grain grasses helped bring about civilization.

Some grasses are especially tough and can grow even in sandy areas.

Cattle and goats graze on the veld in Uganda.

Grass-covered hills surround a fertile African valley.

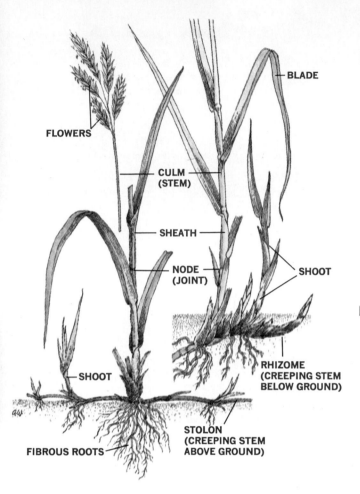

FLOWERS

BLADE

CULM (STEM)

SHEATH

NODE (JOINT)

SHOOT

SHOOT

RHIZOME (CREEPING STEM BELOW GROUND)

FIBROUS ROOTS

STOLON (CREEPING STEM ABOVE GROUND)

▶ ARE ALL GRASSES ALIKE?

All grasses are alike in these ways:

The stems are smooth, shiny, and mostly hollow. At regular spaces the stems have joints. The leaves are usually long and narrow. The veins in the leaves all run in the same direction—that is, they are parallel.

One leaf grows at each joint. Each leaf consists of two parts, a sheath and a blade. The sheath is the lower part of the leaf. It fits closely around the stem. The blade is long and slender. No other plant family has exactly this kind of stem and leaf.

The flowers are at the top of the grass stem. They are usually small, and not showy. They produce the seeds of the grass plant.

▶ HOW GRASSES REPRODUCE

Some grasses reproduce by sending out underground stems. The stem grows sideways. As it grows it puts down new roots a short distance from the parent plant. The underground stem can produce new plants at places where the new roots have grown. If the main stem is broken, the underground stem continues to grow sideways. This makes grass a sturdy plant. It survives a lot of cropping and trampling.

Most grasses reproduce by means of seeds.

When grass is mowed and dried, it becomes hay and is used as food for cattle.

The seeds are scattered in many ways. Some grass seeds are covered with long hairs. They are carried by the wind. Others are blown along the ground. Birds spread seeds by picking the seeds up in their beaks for food. As they fly away they may drop some of them.

The seeds of some water grasses, like the water-pink, have tiny "sails." When the seeds float, wind blowing against the sails may take the seeds a great distance. The seeds of some other water grasses are spread by rain washing over the mud in which the grasses grow. Sometimes these seeds are carried about by water birds.

Some grass seeds have sharp spines. These seeds are spread by animals or by people who pass by the plant and carry away the seeds that stick to their fur or clothing.

Many kinds of grass seeds have been carried, often by accident, along trade routes to distant parts of the world. For instance, ships brought seeds of molasses grass to the New World from Africa. The stalks of the plant were used as bedding for slaves. When the bedding was thrown away on the ground, the seeds took root. In this way the grass spread from Africa to North America.

Once a Year and Through the Years

Some of the grasses live for a season and then die. All the cultivated grain grasses, for example, live for only one season. They must be planted again each year. Such grasses are called annual grasses. ("Annual" comes from the Latin word for "year.") Other grasses come up each year. The roots of pasture grasses and most lawn grasses, for example, live through the winter. New blades come up in the spring. Such grasses are called perennial grasses. ("Perennial" comes from a Latin word meaning "through the years.")

▶ KINDS OF GRASSES

Among the 7,000 kinds of grasses, four large groups are most used by man and grazing animals. These are the pasture grasses, the cereals, the bamboos, and the sweet grasses.

Pasture Grasses

The plains, the prairies, and other seas of grass make natural grazing country for cattle, sheep, and goats. Among the chief pasture grasses are bluegrass, buffalo grass, Bermuda grass, and bent grasses. When they are dried, some pasture grasses keep through the winter without spoiling. For this reason, farmers cut these grasses and let them dry in the fields. When grass dries it becomes hay and is then stored as winter feed for the grazing animals.

Cereal Grasses

The grain grasses—those with seeds that can be eaten—are called cereal grasses. They were named for Ceres, the Roman goddess of grain and of the harvest. The cereal grasses are wheat, rice, corn, oats, barley, rye, and millet.

Wheat was man's earliest grain food. It probably grew first in Mesopotamia about 6,000 years ago, and was spread to China, Egypt, and Europe. In the last 100 years or so, many kinds have been developed to grow in different climates.

More wheat is grown than any other grain. Foods made from wheat, such as bread and spaghetti, are eaten by millions of people in many parts of the world. Wheat can be stored for years if it is kept dry.

Wheat straw, which is the stem of the plant, has many uses in farming. Some of these uses are as feed and bedding for livestock and as fertilizer. Research scientists are looking for still other ways to use wheat straw.

Rice is the second most important grain in the world. It grows best in warm, humid regions. Most kinds of rice plants grow in about 5 inches of water for much of the growing season. For this reason, rice fields are flooded when the plants are about 6 inches high. The fields are drained at harvest time.

Glue, sugar, starch, and wine are made from rice in many parts of Asia. And paper is made from rice straw in China and Japan.

Corn—or maize—is a third very important grain. It was first grown by Indians in North and South America. Corn was unknown in Europe until early explorers brought some back with them from America.

Corn has many uses. Corn oil, corn syrup, and a sugar called dextrose are all made from corn seed. So is laundry starch. And many uses for ground-up corncobs have been found in agriculture and industry.

Other common grains are oats, rye, and barley. **Oats** grow best in cool, moist climates.

The grain is made into oatmeal, a popular cereal food. But in most parts of the world where oats are grown, the stalk and grain are used as food for livestock.

Rye is grown mostly in northern Europe and Russia. Most rye is used for livestock feed. Some of it is ground into flour for bread. Most of the rye grown in Europe is ground into flour.

Most **barley** is grown for food and for cattle feed. Some of it is grown to be made into malt for brewing beer and for making whiskey.

The name **millet** includes several cereal grasses, grown in different parts of the world. Millet supplies about one third of the world's population with cereal food. In the United States, millet is grown mostly as grass for livestock and as feed for poultry. It is also used for birdseed.

Bamboo

Bamboo grows mostly in the Orient and in warm places such as Central America and parts of South America. Bamboo is the giant of all grasses. There are many varieties that grow as tall as trees. One type grows 120 feet tall, with a stem 3 feet in circumference.

Bamboo is one of the fastest-growing plants. Some kinds reach a height of about 70 feet in 6 to 8 weeks. One kind has been known to grow 3 feet in 24 hours. Although most bamboos are tall, there are some kinds that grow only a few inches high.

Tiny bamboo shoots are used as food. But the most important use for bamboo is in making furniture and in building houses. Bamboo can be used for furniture and houses because bamboo stems are very hard. As a bamboo grows it absorbs the mineral silica from the soil. The silica is stored in the hollow, jointed stem and makes it hard.

Bamboo is used to make many other things. Fence posts, bridges, fishing poles, water pipes, and parts of musical instruments are only a few of them. When the stem is split into strips, it can be woven into rugs, mats, fishing nets, cloth, baskets, and bedding. The stems can also be used as plant stakes.

Bamboo was probably the wood used by the Chinese when they first made paper from wood pulp about 2,000 years ago. Today bamboo is used in Burma and India to make paper. Some plant scientists think more

There are more than 700 species, or kinds, of bamboo (*above*). The towering woody grass is found growing in tropical climates and the warm regions of temperate climates. The sturdy stalks of the sugarcane plant (*below*), which grows in tropical and semitropical climates, produce most of the sugar we eat, as well as fiber used in producing fuel and plastic products.

bamboo forests should be grown as a source for wood pulp.

Sweet Grasses

The juices of certain grasses are sweet. Sorghum is such a grass. It grows throughout Africa and in parts of Asia. Small amounts grow in the United States and in some European countries. In Africa the grain is ground into meal and made into bread. People like to chew the stems for the sugar in them. Sorghum is also used in livestock feed. The stem of one kind of sorghum is used for brooms.

The most important sweet grass is sugarcane. Sugarcane grows best in sunny, moist, semitropical places. The stalks of the sugarcane are cut into pieces and crushed to take out the sweet juice. The juice is then strained and the water boiled out of it. The juice is used to make molasses and sugar. The crushed stalks, called **bagasse**, are used for fuel or pressed into boards for building purposes. Bagasse is also used to make the paper for newspaper.

▶**GRASSES AND SOIL**

Grasses are important in keeping farmlands fertile. Every 2 or 3 years most farmers allow a field to "lie fallow," or idle—that is, they do not plant a crop in that field. They allow grass to grow instead. When the grass dies, it decays and fertilizes the field. Many farmers also plant certain grasses in the fields after the harvest in the fall. In the spring they plow the grass into the soil to help fertilize the land.

Grass also helps save the soil. The roots hold down the soil and prevent it from being blown or washed away. Some grasses have root systems that are several miles long. Grass roots mat the soil and make it porous. When it rains heavily, the water soaks into the ground instead of running off to swell streams and cause floods.

Some types of grass, such as cordgrass, help build land out of mud flats. The runners of cordgrass grow through land exposed at low tide along a shore. Stems and blades grow from the runners. When waves hit the grass, they drop sand against the grass. More grass grows on top of this sand. Again waves drop sand against the grass. In this way, little by little, land is built along the shoreline.

Cordgrasses have built land along much of the Atlantic coast of the United States and

The grazing of farm animals has stripped the protective layer of grasses from this hillside, leaving it open to the destructive effects of wind and water.

Canada, as well as along the southern coast of England, near Southampton. The first time cordgrass was seen near Southampton was in 1870. Since then the grass has built solid land for many miles along the coast.

▶**BETTER GRASSES FOR THE FUTURE**

Because grasses are so important to people, plant scientists are working to improve all the useful grasses. In this way they hope to develop new products and to improve the world's food supply.

Reviewed by WALTER SINGER
The New York Botanical Garden

See also PLANTS; WEEDS.

GRASSLANDS. See BIOMES; PLANTS.

GRAVITY AND GRAVITATION

If you throw a ball into the air, it rises then falls to the Earth. If you throw it straight ahead, it begins curving toward the Earth and finally falls. If you hold the ball in your hand and drop it, it falls again. In every case, the ball falls to the ground. The reason the ball always falls is gravity.

Gravity is a force—a push or a pull. Every time you drop a ball from your hand or throw it upward or straight ahead, it is pulled back to the Earth. When an event in nature occurs repeatedly in the same way, we say that it takes place according to natural law. Since the ball or any object is always pulled to the Earth by gravity, the force of gravity acts according to a natural law that is called the law of gravity.

▶ THE DISCOVERY OF GRAVITY

The first person to work out the law of gravity was English scientist and mathematician Isaac Newton (1642–1727), during his studies of the motions of objects. Newton was puzzled about the motion of the moon and wondered why the moon did not just fly off into space;

what force kept it in its orbit, or curved path, around the Earth.

It is said that Newton's study of motion was influenced by his observation of an apple falling from a tree. This and similar events helped him determine that the Earth appeared to be pulling all objects to itself and that the force that pulled the apple to the ground must have been the same one that kept the moon in its orbit around the Earth. Newton went on to discover that this force was indeed universal.

Using mathematics, Newton determined that the moon's orbit is the result of two different motions. One is its movement along a straight line in space. This, according to Newton, is the motion an object will follow if it is not acted upon by any forces other than the one that put it in motion. The other is **acceleration**, a change in the direction or speed of a moving object. In the case of the moon, its movement in a straight line is being constantly changed to a movement that curves toward the Earth. The combination of the two motions, which are happening at the same time, causes the moon to move in a curved path around the Earth. Newton concluded that gravity is what pulls the moon out of a straight path and keeps it in orbit around the Earth.

Newton also determined that every body in the universe must have gravity and that every body pulls on every other body. ("Body" is the word scientists use for an object in space.) His idea that every body possesses gravity is known as the theory of **universal gravitation**.

From his perch on a space shuttle far above the Earth, astronaut William Fisher can maneuver the Syncon IV-3 satellite before it is sent back into orbit. On Earth the stronger pull of gravity on the large mass of the satellite would make it too heavy for Fisher to work with in the same way.

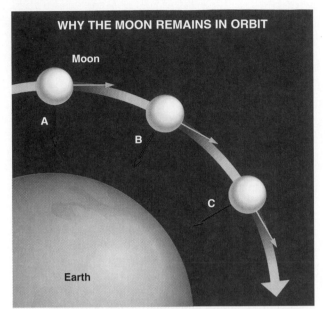

WHY THE MOON REMAINS IN ORBIT

Moon

A

B

C

Earth

The moon's orbit is the result of two motions—its movement in a straight line and its movement toward the Earth caused by the pull of the Earth's gravity.

The words "gravity" and "gravitation" are both used by scientists to describe the pull of one object upon another. They usually use "gravitation" to refer to the idea that every object in the universe attracts every other object. They use "gravity" when speaking of this attraction at the surface of bodies such as the Earth.

Newton used the idea of gravitation to explain how the planets stay in orbit around the sun. All the planets orbiting the sun would fly off into space if some force did not pull them toward the sun. Newton reasoned that the planets are held in their orbits by the same force that holds the moon in its orbit—the force of gravitation.

▶THE STRENGTH OF GRAVITATION

Newton found that the strength of gravitation depends on two things. First, it depends on the **mass**, or amount of matter, that a body contains. A body with a large amount of mass has a stronger gravitational force than a body with a small amount of mass. Because the Earth's mass is greater than the moon's mass, its gravitational pull on us is greater than the moon's gravitational pull would be on us if we stood on the moon. For this reason we weigh more on Earth than we would on the moon.

Second, the strength of gravitation depends on the distance between the bodies. The force of gravitation is strong between bodies that are close together, and it is weak between bodies that are far apart.

Newton worked out a mathematical equation to determine the force of gravitation between two bodies.

The equation is

$$F = \frac{G \times m_1 \times m_2}{r^2}$$

The force of gravity between two objects depends on the mass of each object and the distance between the two objects.

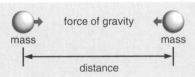

force of gravity

mass   mass

distance

1 If you double the mass of one object, the force of gravity between the two objects doubles.

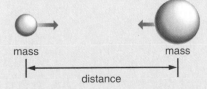

mass   mass

distance

2 If you double the masses of both objects, the force of gravity between them is four times greater.

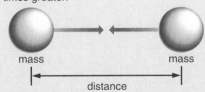

mass   mass

distance

3 If the masses of both objects remain equal but you reduce the distance between them by one-half, the force of gravity between the two objects becomes four times greater.

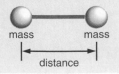

mass   mass

distance

4 If the masses of both objects remain equal but you double the distance between them, you reduce the force of gravity between the two objects to one-fourth its previous strength.

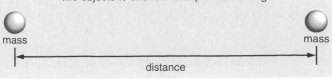

mass   mass

distance

In this equation, *f* stands for the force of gravitation. The mass of the first body is m_1, the mass of the second body is m_2, and *r* stands for the distance between the two bodies. The quantity G stands for Newton's constant of gravitation, a number that is needed to determine the exact force between the two bodies. This equation shows that the amount of mass in each body and the length of the distance between them determine the strength of the gravitational force they exert on one another. When the distance between the two bodies is increased, the force of gravitation between them lessens. If the two bodies are pulled closer together by gravity, the force of gravitation between them increases.

▶ **FALLING BODIES**

How does Newton's law of gravitation apply to an object, such as a ball, that is dropped near the Earth's surface? Because of the Earth's size, the change in the gravitational force experienced by a ball falling a few hundred yards, or even a mile, is hardly noticeable. Thus, the force of gravity can be considered as constant.

This constant force, however, causes the ball to accelerate, or to fall faster and faster. The acceleration near the surface of the Earth is 32 feet (9.8 meters) per second per second. This means that the ball's speed increases by 32 feet (9.8 meters) per second each second that it falls. Just before the ball begins its fall, its speed is zero. One second later it is falling at a speed of 32 feet (9.8 meters) per second. After two seconds of falling, the ball's speed is 32 plus 32, or 64 feet (19.6 meters) per second. Thus, a body that falls from a great height accelerates to a great speed and strikes the Earth with great force. That is why an object is more likely to break if it falls from a great height than if it falls from only a low height. Any object falling in a vacuum, whether it is heavy or light, accelerates at the same rate—32 feet (9.8 meters) per second per second—and will keep on accelerating. A body falling in air, however, is slowed down by air resistance. The amount that it slows down depends on its size and shape. Thus, in a vacuum, a feather and a marble fall with the same acceleration. When falling in air, however, the large surface of the feather will produce more friction, causing it to fall more slowly than the marble. As the speed of a falling body increases, air resistance also increases. If the force of air resistance becomes equal to the force on the body caused by gravity, the body will no longer increase its speed

Speed (Feet per Second)	Falling Body	Speed (Meters per Second)	Time (Seconds)
0		0	:00
32		9.8	:01
64		19.6	:02
96		29.4	:03
128		39.2	:04

Falling objects are pulled by the Earth's gravity with a constant force that causes them to fall faster and faster as they near the Earth (*left*). In a vacuum, falling objects as different as a marble and a feather will reach the ground at the same time (*below, left*). Outside a vacuum, air resistance slows objects down, so the larger surface of the feather will create more friction and cause it to fall more slowly than the marble (*below, right*).

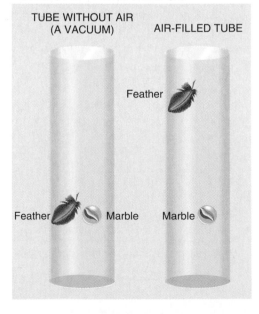

TUBE WITHOUT AIR (A VACUUM)

AIR-FILLED TUBE

Feather

Feather Marble

Marble

Passengers on this amusement park ride are getting quite a thrill because its motions mimic the centrifugal effect and the pull of gravity on the spinning Earth. As the motor in the center of the ride spins their swings into motion, they fly outward in a straight line. But the chains connecting the swings to the ride pull them out of that straight line and into a dizzying motion that goes around and around in a circle.

as it continues to fall. It will have reached its maximum speed, which is called its **terminal velocity**.

MEASURING GRAVITY

Gravity can be measured by using a device known as a **gravimeter**, in which a metal ball is suspended from a very sensitive spring coil. Wherever gravity is stronger, it pulls more on the ball, thus stretching the spring. A pointer attached to the spring shows the increase in gravity.

Scientists measure gravity because many things depend on it. For example, when launching satellites into space, scientists must know the strength of the Earth's gravity so they can determine how fast a satellite must travel to escape the planet's gravity or to remain in orbit around the planet.

THE EARTH'S GRAVITY

The strength of gravity is not the same at all places on the Earth. Three things determine the strength of gravity at any given place: (1) the distance from the center of the Earth, (2) the spin of the Earth, and (3) the nearby sources of gravity variations, such as mountains or underground caverns.

Consider the distance from the center of the Earth. A house at the seashore is at a lower elevation than one in the mountains, which means that it is closer to the center of the Earth. The strength of gravity is stronger at

the seaside house than the strength of gravity is at the mountain house.

The Earth's spin also produces an effect that can appear to reduce the strength of gravity. Known as the **centrifugal effect**, it is caused by the tendency of a body to move in a straight line unless acted upon by a force trying to change its path. The tendency of a body at the surface of the spinning Earth is to move outward in a straight line. At the same time, the Earth's gravitational force is pulling the body toward the center of the planet. Part of the Earth's gravitational force is reduced in changing the body's path from a straight line in space into the circle it actually follows as the Earth rotates, and this serves to lessen the body's weight.

An example is a body at the Earth's equator, where the centrifugal effect is greater than anywhere else on the surface of the planet. A body at the equator must travel nearly 24,000 miles (39,000 kilometers) during one rotation of the planet, but this distance and the centrifugal effect decrease as you move away from the equator and toward the poles. The result is that the weight of a body on the Earth's surface increases slightly as it moves away from the equator and toward the poles. This is because the Earth's gravitational force is slightly less at the equator than at the poles. A bag of sugar at the equator would weigh about $^1/_{1,000}$ less than it would in Honolulu, Hawaii, which is closer to the North Pole.

Variations in gravity may also be caused by nearby concentrations of mass such as mountain ranges or underground deposits of materials. The pull of gravity is greater near large or dense concentrations of mass or deposits of dense materials, and it is weaker near underground caverns or deposits of light materials, such as oil. Looking for gravity variations with a gravimeter is an important way of searching for deposits of oil or minerals.

▶MASS AND WEIGHT

It is important to distinguish between mass and weight. Remember that mass is the amount of matter in a body. The mass of a body remains the same wherever the body may be. For example, the mass of an astronaut is the same whether the astronaut is on the Earth, the moon, or any other place in the universe. **Weight** is a measure of the pull of gravity on a body. Therefore, the weight of a body can vary depending upon the pull of gravity on it. For example, if the Earth's gravity pulls on an astronaut with a force of 154 pounds (70 kilograms), the astronaut's weight is 154 pounds. Suppose, however, that this same astronaut visits the moon. The moon has less mass than the Earth, so its pull of gravity is less. On the moon, the astronaut's weight would only be about 26 pounds (12 kilograms). Although weight may change from place to place, mass remains the same.

Weightlessness and Acceleration

Suppose a person and a scale are falling freely somewhere within the Earth's gravitational field. If the person is standing on the scale, the arrow on the scale will point to zero, indicating that the person weighs nothing. This is because both the person and the scale are experiencing the same acceleration. This effect takes place within a spacecraft. Inside a freely falling spacecraft, all objects are experiencing the same acceleration. The result is that to the people in the spacecraft, gravity appears to have disappeared, and all of the

Astronaut Mae Jemison has no trouble clicking her heels in midair in the science module of the space shuttle *Endeavour* as it orbits the Earth. Because the shuttle and everything in it are falling freely through space at the same acceleration, gravity appears to have disappeared. To the astronaut, the shuttle and all the objects in it, including herself, appear to be weightless.

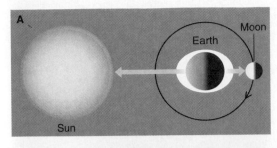

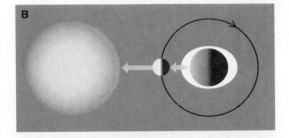

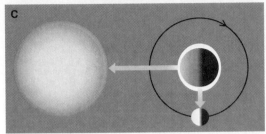

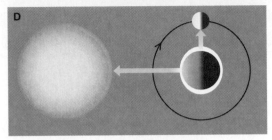

The force of gravitation between the Earth and the moon, and to a lesser degree between the Earth and the sun, causes the tides in our planet's oceans. High tides form on the two sides of the Earth most strongly attracted by the moon's pull — the side nearest the moon and the side farthest away. Low tides form on the other two sides, where ocean waters flow toward the two high tide locations. When the sun, moon, and Earth are aligned (A and B), the sun's gravitational pull added to the moon's causes spring tides, the highest and lowest tides. When the moon and the sun are each at right angles to the Earth (C and D), the tides produced by the sun partially cancel those produced by the moon, causing neap tides, in which there is much less difference between high and low tides.

objects in the spacecraft, including themselves, seem to be weightless.

Now imagine a spacecraft in empty space far from the gravitational pull of any planet or star. If the spacecraft's rockets began to blast, the astronauts inside would feel a force pressing them toward the floor, and they would be unable to distinguish this from the force of gravity. The scientist Albert Einstein (1879–1955) was the first person to point out that the effects of gravitation and acceleration are the same. He called this idea the **principle of equivalence**.

In his general theory of relativity, Einstein also proposed that gravity was not a force that pulled bodies in a straight line toward one another but instead was the result of a curving or warping of space and time. A body that moves in the vicinity of another body such as the sun bends to follow the curves in space and time created by the gravitational influence of the sun. This, according to Einstein, produces the orbits of planets, not a force acting between the sun and the planets as Newton believed. Building upon this idea, Einstein developed a mathematical theory of gravity that made some remarkable predictions.

One of Einstein's predictions was that rays of light should be bent by the curved space around a massive body such as the sun as the light rays come near it. This prediction has been verified by scientists. Another prediction was the existence of **black holes**. In black holes, the warping of space and time is so strong that anything unlucky enough to fall inside one can never escape, not even light itself. Although astronomers cannot "see" black holes, there is increasing evidence that they exist. Einstein's theory also predicts that gravitational waves should be produced when two massive bodies such as stars orbit one another. Some evidence for gravitational waves has been discovered by scientists studying a binary pulsar, a swiftly rotating neutron star orbiting a companion star.

COLIN A. RONAN
Fellow of the Royal Astronomical Society

Revised and updated by CLIFFORD M. WILL
Professor of Physics, Washington University

See also EARTH; MOTION; RELATIVITY; SOLAR SYSTEM; SPACE EXPLORATION AND TRAVEL; STARS.

The Sault Sainte Marie (Soo) Canals, on the St. Marys River between Ontario and Michigan, link lakes Superior and Huron.

GREAT LAKES

The Great Lakes of North America are part of an inland superwaterway. The size and depth of these five lakes permit oceangoing vessels to reach the heartland of the continent. The Great Lakes touch eight states in the United States and the Canadian province of Ontario. Four of the five lakes are under the joint control of the United States and Canada. Only Lake Michigan lies entirely within the United States.

The Great Lakes were formed when the ice sheets, or glaciers, disappeared from North America many thousands of years ago. Tongues or lobes of ice filled large river valleys and lowlands. When the ice sheets retreated, lakes were formed in these lower lands. Former shorelines and old outlets show that the lakes were once much larger than they are now. The five Great Lakes of today are reminders of the glacial period.

Because of a series of rapids, the Great Lakes were once largely landlocked (shut in by land). Ships could navigate only in limited waters. Canals now link the five lakes with one another, and the St. Lawrence Seaway links the lakes with the Atlantic Ocean. Except during the winter freeze-up, ships can travel between ports on the lakes and ports all over the world.

There are two other ways for ships to reach the sea from the Great Lakes. A system of waterways called the New York Barge Canal links Lake Erie to the Hudson River and the Atlantic Ocean. The Illinois Waterway links Lake Michigan to the Mississippi River and the Gulf of Mexico. To reach the Mississippi, ships use canals in the Chicago area and the Des Plaines and Illinois rivers.

The Great Lakes have been of great value to the two countries that share their shores. In early times, furs and logs were the chief products transported on the lakes. Today, huge barges carry pulpwood and lumber from northern forests; grain from the prairies of the United States and western Canada; iron ore from Michigan, Minnesota, Quebec, and Labrador; coal from Illinois; and copper from the southern and western shores of Lake Superior. From the great industrial cities along shores of the lakes come petrochemicals, automobiles, steel, processed foods, and many other products.

Commercial fishing has long been important on the Great Lakes, and many parks and resort areas border their shores. Both fishing and tourism have been harmed by the waste materials that people and industries have poured into the waters. Local, state, and federal governments are now working together to control pollution and repair the damage.

Lake Superior

Lake Superior is the largest freshwater lake in the world and one of the deepest. At some points the water is as much as 400 meters (1,300 feet) deep. At its easternmost tip, Lake Superior flows into Lake Huron by way of the St. Marys River. The five locks of the Sault Sainte Marie (Soo) Canals allow ships to bypass rapids on the river.

THE GREAT LAKES

As long ago as 1672, a map of *"le lac supérieur"* was published in France. Early in the 1600's, the explorer Samuel de Champlain sent Étienne Brulé, a French interpreter, to study the languages and customs of the Indians. Brulé sent word by missionaries about "another very great lake" above Lake Huron. He is credited with being the first European to sail on Lake Superior. When the early French explorers called this lake *supérieur*, they meant "upper," because it was above Lake Huron. British explorers changed the French word *supérieur* into the English word "superior."

Missionaries, fur traders, French Canadian and British explorers, and Indians traveling in birchbark canoes investigated the open waters of this vast lake from the 1600's to the early 1800's. Hiawatha, the hero of Longfellow's poem *The Song of Hiawatha*, lived on the shores of Gitche Gumee, "the shining Big-Sea-Water," or Lake Superior.

Lake Huron

There are no large cities or huge industries on the scenic shores of Lake Huron. It is fringed with more islands than the other Great Lakes. And it has the largest and longest freshwater island in the world—Manitoulin. The St. Clair River, Lake St. Clair, and the Detroit River are the connecting waters between Lake Huron and Lake Erie. The two rivers and Lake St. Clair were dredged to provide a channel wide enough and deep enough for ships and cargo carriers. Because it lacks large harbors, Lake Huron is more of a waterway for ships carrying important cargo than the other Great Lakes. Detroit, Michigan, and Windsor, Ontario, are major ports on the Detroit River.

Lake Huron was the first of the Great Lakes to be sighted by European explorers. Brulé may have been the first European to see Georgian Bay, an arm of the lake, about 1612. In 1615, Champlain sailed on the lake. He

GREAT LAKES—FACTS AND FIGURES

NAME	AREA		BORDERS	MAJOR PORTS
	Square kilometers	Square miles		
Lake Superior	82,414	31,820	Minnesota, Wisconsin, Michigan (United States); Ontario (Canada)	Duluth, Superior, Sault Sainte Marie (United States); Sault Sainte Marie, Thunder Bay (Canada)
Lake Huron	59,596	23,010	Michigan (United States); Ontario (Canada)	Port Huron (United States); Sarnia (Canada)
Lake Michigan	58,016	22,400	Illinois, Indiana, Michigan, Wisconsin (United States)	Milwaukee, Racine, Kenosha, Chicago, Gary, Muskegon (United States)
Lake Erie	25,745	9,940	Michigan, New York, Ohio, Pennsylvania (United States); Ontario (Canada)	Toledo, Sandusky, Lorain, Cleveland, Erie, Buffalo (United States)
Lake Ontario	19,529	7,540	New York (United States); Ontario (Canada)	Rochester, Oswego (United States); Toronto, Hamilton (Canada)
Total Area	245,300	94,710		

A body of water called the Straits of Mackinac connects lakes Michigan and Huron. The Mackinac Bridge spans the straits.

called it *La Mer Douce,* the sweet, or fresh-water, sea. Later it was named for the Huron Indians, who lived nearby.

Lake Michigan

Lake Michigan has a more regular shoreline and fewer islands than the other Great Lakes. The Straits of Mackinac connect Lake Michigan with Lake Huron. This body of water is wide and deep enough for ships to pass safely from one lake to the other.

The name for Lake Michigan was taken from an Indian word meaning "large lake" or "big water." Champlain and other people of his day had heard of a great body of water to the west. They thought that it was the Pacific Ocean and that Cathay (China) was on the far shore. Jean Nicolet, a French explorer living in Quebec, set out in 1634 with Indian companions to find this "western sea." He was sure that he would find China, too, and would meet important Chinese leaders. In his canoe he took special clothing to wear. It was recorded that he went ashore wearing "a grand robe of China damask, all strewn with flowers and birds of many colors." But Nicolet did not find what he expected. He found Indians—and what is now the Wisconsin side of Lake Michigan.

Lake Erie

There are several large industrial cities along the southern shores of Lake Erie. The Canadian side of the lake has no large cities and few manufacturing plants. Fishing villages, small towns, summer resorts, and beaches dot the northern shores.

The earliest reported sighting of the lake by Europeans was made by Louis Jolliet in 1669, although Étienne Brulé may have seen it in 1615. On his way to the Lake Superior country, Jolliet found Lake Erie instead of the copper he was seeking. Jolliet, a trained mapmaker, made a careful sketch of the lake.

Lake Erie was named for the Erie Indians who lived south of the lake more than 300 years ago. During the War of 1812, the Great Lakes were a major battlefront. On September 10, 1813, the American naval hero Oliver Hazard Perry and his small force defeated the British in a battle on Lake Erie.

Lake Ontario

Lake Ontario is the smallest and easternmost of the Great Lakes. It is fed by Erie's waters, which leap over Niagara Falls. The locks of the Welland Ship Canal lift or lower ships 99 meters (326 feet) to bypass the falls. The smallest of the Great Lakes receives most of the drainage of the entire lake system, which flows to the Atlantic Ocean by way of the St. Lawrence River.

"Ontario" is an Indian name meaning "Land of Beautiful Waters." Samuel de Champlain sighted Lake Ontario in 1615, and Étienne Brulé may have seen it a short time earlier.

During the 1600's, the French and the English were at war almost constantly for control of the Iroquois country around Lake Ontario. In 1760 the British took control of all the Great Lakes. Their rule lasted until the end of the Revolutionary War, in 1781. Several battles of that war were fought on the waters of Lake Ontario.

Reviewed by JOHN F. LOUNSBURY
Arizona State University

See also ERIE CANAL; NIAGARA FALLS; SAINT LAWRENCE RIVER AND SEAWAY.

GREAT SEAL OF THE UNITED STATES

Many countries stamp official government papers with a seal. This is a metal disk with a design, such as the country's coat of arms, engraved on it. The Great Seal of the United States stands for the power and authority of the United States Government. It is also known as the Seal of the United States of America. It is affixed to official documents, or papers, after they have been signed by the president and secretary of state. Among these papers are presidential proclamations, documents ratifying (approving) treaties, and commissions of officials, such as cabinet members.

On July 4, 1776, the Continental Congress chose a committee to work out a design for an official seal. Not until June 20, 1782, was a design finally accepted. It was the work of William Barton, a private citizen with a knowledge of art and heraldry, and Charles Thomson, secretary of the Continental Congress. In 1789 the secretary of state was named keeper of the seal.

There have been several dies—metal forms used in producing the seal. Only the front, or face, side is used on documents or as the coat of arms of the United States. The only place where the back, or reverse, side appears is on the back of the United States one-dollar bill.

The Front.   Shown here is the American, or bald, eagle with outstretched wings. On its breast is a shield. It stands alone, showing that the United States can do the same. The solid blue bar at the top of the shield stands for the

Congress. There are 13 vertical stripes (7 white and 6 red) for the 13 original colonies. In its right claw the eagle holds an olive branch with 13 leaves and 13 olives. The olive branch is used to symbolize, or stand for, peace. The 13 arrows in its left claw symbolize protection by war. The eagle is looking toward the olive branch, signifying that the United States wants to live in peace. The design shows, too, that the power of peace and war is held by the Congress.

The Latin motto *E Pluribus Unum,* which appears on a ribbon the eagle holds in its beak, means "Out of many [colonies], one [nation]." Over the eagle's head is the constellation—13 stars in a "glory," or sunburst, shining through a cloud. It is a sign that the United States has taken its place among the other nations of the world.

The Back.   The unfinished pyramid with 13 rows of stones portrays the Union being watched over by the all-seeing eye of God, which is contained within a triangle. In Roman numerals at the base is the date the Union was begun—1776. The motto *Annuit Coeptis* above the pyramid means "He [God] has favored our undertakings." On a ribbon below the pyramid is the motto *Novus Ordo Seclorum,* "[A] new order of the ages."

The Great Seal, with its die and mold, is kept in a mahogany case. It can be seen in the exhibition hall of the Department of State building in Washington, D.C.

Reviewed by C. Jane Mossellem
Chief, Presidential Appointments Staff
United States Department of State

The front of the Great Seal.

The back of the Great Seal.

329

The Adoration of the Shepherds (1603–07) by El Greco. Prado, Madrid.

GRECO, EL (1541–1614)

El Greco was an artist of Greek origin who spent most of his life in Spain. His real name was Kyriakos (Domenikos) Theotokopoulos. He is known by his Spanish name, which means simply "the Greek." El Greco is recognized as one of the great geniuses of Western art. He is most famous for his religious paintings, but he also painted portraits of his patrons and friends.

El Greco was born on the island of Crete, off the coast of Greece. Little is known about his childhood, but he apparently studied painting from an early age. As a young man, he went to the city of Venice to learn about Italian art. He studied the work of such masters as Titian and Tintoretto.

By 1570, El Greco had moved to Rome for additional training. Once settled there, he joined a circle of artists and scholars. But in spite of these connections, he never managed to obtain an important commission. For this reason, he left Rome for Spain in 1577, probably to help with the decoration of a family chapel in Toledo.

Toledo was then a prosperous manufacturing city and the center of the Catholic Church in Spain. It was in this city that El Greco produced his greatest masterpieces. He found the patrons he could not find in Rome. Within a few years, he had set up a workshop that produced numerous altarpieces and other paintings for Toledo's churches and monasteries. He also sold paintings in other cities.

Surprisingly, El Greco never managed to obtain the patronage of the Spanish king, who ruled from Madrid. He remained in Toledo, his adopted home, until his death in 1614.

El Greco's artistic style contains traces of his native Greece. But he was influenced mainly by the Italian mannerist school. Members of this school believed that artists had the right to interpret nature in their individual styles. Such ideas led El Greco to lengthen and distort most of his figures. He believed that they were more spiritual and more expressive than ordinary figures. He tried other techniques to express emotion and portray passion in his work. He used bright, vivid colors and painted his subjects in a special, almost heavenly, light.

El Greco was successful in Toledo, but his art was not fully appreciated until long after his death. He was called a madman and a mystic. Some critics falsely believed that poor eyesight caused him to distort the figures in his paintings. The myths and mysteries surrounding him began to disappear when Manuel Cossío, an important critic, published a biography of El Greco in 1908. Since then, El Greco has taken his rightful place among the world's greatest painters.

The Adoration of the Shepherds, which celebrates the birth of the Christ Child, is one of El Greco's well-known religious paintings. A reproduction of another famous work, *View of Toledo,* is included in the article PAINTING in Volume P.

RICHARD L. KAGAN
Johns Hopkins University

GREECE

Greece is a small nation in southeastern Europe where one of the world's great civilizations flourished more than 2,000 years ago. At a time when most of Europe was in cultural darkness, Greek dramatists were writing plays that are still performed today. Greek sculptors and builders were creating statues and temples of unsurpassed beauty. Greek thinkers were laying the foundations of modern science and philosophy. And it was in ancient Greece that the idea of democracy, or government by the people, was born.

Although Greece was conquered by stronger powers, Greek civilization spread across Europe and to parts of Asia. Modern Greece emerged as an independent nation in the 1800's, after a long struggle against foreign rule. The Greeks today are justifiably proud of their heritage, evidence of which they still can see in the land around them.

▶ THE PEOPLE

At one time most Greeks lived in the countryside, usually in small villages. About 60 percent of the people now live in urban areas. Almost one third of the total population lives in the greater metropolitan area of Athens, Greece's capital and largest city, which includes Piraeus, the port of Athens.

Athens is the heart of Greece. It was the most renowned of the cities of classical Greece, and it is now the center of the country's government, industry, culture, and trade. Some government officials believe that Athens dominates Greece too strongly. They feel that Athenians have such a higher standard of living and live so differently than Greeks in the rural areas that Greece sometimes seems to be two nations—one of city people and one of country people.

Greece has few other cities to compare with Greater Athens in size. Salonika, a seaport in the north, is the country's second largest city. Patras, in the northern Peloponnesus, is an important commercial city and port.

Language and Education

Modern Greek grew out of the classical Greek of ancient times. There are two forms of the modern language. The pure form, called *katharevousa*, is used mostly in writing. For their spoken language, Greeks use an everyday form of Greek called *demotic*. The alphabets of most European languages were strongly influenced by the classical Greek alphabet. For more information on the Greek alphabet, see the article ALPHABET in Volume A.

Greek children must attend at least nine years of school beginning at age 6. Greece has a number of universities and colleges. The largest is in Athens.

A ruined temple near Corinth dating from the 500's B.C. is a reminder of the glory of ancient Greece.

Religion

Almost all Greeks belong to the Greek Orthodox Church, which separated from the Roman Catholic Church in the 1000's. The government supports the church, but the constitution gives toleration to all faiths. The colorful religious holidays, with processions and music and rituals, enliven the Greek scene. The Orthodox priest is a striking figure—long-haired and bearded, dressed in flowing black robes. Unlike the Roman Catholic priest, he may marry and have a family.

Greece has many monasteries and nunneries, although today fewer people live in them than formerly. Mount Athos on Chalcidice peninsula is a tiny religious state by itself. It has 20 monasteries, and no women may ever enter this area.

Muslims make up about 2 percent of the population, a reminder of the time when Turkish Muslims ruled Greece. Before World War II more than 70,000 Jews lived in Greece, mostly in Salonika. Less than 10 percent of the Jews survived the Nazi occupation of Greece.

Way of Life

Most Greeks, especially those living in rural areas, have lower incomes and simpler ways of life than people living in countries of western Europe. Country people, even children, spend long hours tending livestock and working in the fields. One of the chief aims of recent Greek governments has been to improve the standard of living.

Greeks are an especially sociable people and enjoy such pleasures as eating, singing, and dancing together. The family plays an important role in Greek life. Family ties are strong and extend from the immediate family to include more distant relations. Traditionally, one's first loyalty was to the family household. A business or farm often was operated as a family enterprise, permitting the pooling of resources. Greeks have a strict sense of honor and the achievements or failures of one family member reflected on the entire family.

Because of the generally warm climate, Greeks spend much of the year out-of-doors. The local coffee house is the traditional meeting place for Greek men, who gather to discuss politics and play backgammon as well as to sip coffee. Greek women spend much of their leisure time with other women.

The Greek diet includes such staple foods as bread, cheeses, lamb, olives, fruits, and a variety of vegetables. Typical dishes are spit-roasted lamb; *mousáká* (ground lamb, eggplant, and cheese); *souvlakia*, or *shish kabab* (roast lamb on skewers); *dolmádhes* (grape leaves stuffed with meat and rice); and chicken soup flavored with lemon. Greek feta cheese is made from goat's or sheep's milk. Greeks generally take wine with their meals; a favorite is the resin-flavored *retsína*. *Oúzo*, an anise-flavored liquor, is often drunk before meals. Sweet, flaky pastries, usually made with honey, are popular desserts. Coffee is thick and strong and served in small cups.

▶THE LAND

Greece is located on a rugged peninsula in the southeastern corner of Europe. It occupies a strip of mainland on the north shore of the Aegean Sea and the southern part of the Balkan Peninsula, between the Aegean Sea and the Ionian Sea. Deep bays give Greece a long, jagged coastline. Greece's four neighbors are Albania, the former Yugoslav republic of Macedonia, Bulgaria, and Turkey. Southern Greece, called the Peloponnesus, is

---

FACTS AND FIGURES

HELLENIC REPUBLIC is the official name of the country.

THE PEOPLE are known as Greeks.

LOCATION: Southeastern Europe.

AREA: 51,000 sq mi (131,990 km^2).

POPULATION: 10,000,000 (estimate).

CAPITAL AND LARGEST CITY: Athens.

MAJOR LANGUAGE: Greek.

MAJOR RELIGION: Greek Orthodox.

GOVERNMENT: republic. **Head of state**—president. **Head of government**—prime minister. **Legislature**—parliament.

CHIEF PRODUCTS: Agricultural—wheat, corn, barley, and other grains, tobacco, sugar beets, cotton, olives, grapes, livestock. **Manufactured**—processed foods and beverages, metals and metal products, textiles, clothing, chemicals, tobacco products, refined petroleum products (including fuels). **Mineral**—bauxite (aluminum ore), petroleum, nickel, lignite (brown coal), iron, magnesium.

MONETARY UNIT: Drachma (1 drachma = 100 lepta).

NATIONAL ANTHEM: "Hymn to Liberty" (First line begins: "I shall always recognize you by the dreadful sword you hold").

GREECE

shaped somewhat like a human hand with peninsulas for fingers. At the top of the hand, the Gulf of Corinth and other bodies of water cut in so deeply that they almost pinch the Peloponnesus off into an island.

Landforms

Greece is a land of mountains, peninsulas, and islands. Nearly one fifth of its area is islands. The greatest number of islands dot the Aegean Sea. They include the Northern Sporades, Cyclades, and Dodecanese groups, with big islands like Rhodes, Lesbos, Euboea, Chios, Samos, Lemnos, and Thasos. To the south lies Crete, the largest of the Greek islands. The Ionian Islands, including Corfu, are to the west.

Three fourths of Greece is hilly. The rugged Pindus range in western Greece is the country's mountain backbone. It includes some peaks that are over 7,000 feet (2,100 meters) high. Mountain spurs run eastward, with fertile valleys between them, such as the plain of Thessaly in east central Greece. In Greek Macedonia and in Thrace the plains are hemmed in by the Rhodope Mountains. Olympus, in northern Greece, is the country's tallest mountain. It rises to 9,570 feet (2,917 me-

ters). Ancient Greeks believed it was the home of their gods.

Lakes and Rivers

No large rivers start within Greece. Most streams are short, swift torrents. They may flood in winter and dry up in summer. This is because Greece has little rainfall, and the rains come all at once in winter. Streams are short because no part of Greece is more than about 90 miles (150 kilometers) from the sea. Rivers inside Greece include the Aliakmon, Peneus, and Achelous. The large permanent rivers in northern Greece start outside the country. Among these are the Vardar, Struma, and Maritsa rivers.

The plains of Greece were once dotted with lakes and marshes. Now most have been drained for farmland. Fairly large lakes are Trichonis, Ioannina, and Prespa, which lies along the northern border. Other lakes are Voiveis in Thessaly, and Vegoritis, Koroneia, and Volve in Macedonia.

Climate

Greece has a typical Mediterranean climate, with hot, dry summers and mild, rainy winters. In general the temperatures decrease from south to north, and the rainfall lessens from west to east. Except for the interior mountain regions, all Greece is near the sea. The sea keeps temperatures even. Northern Greece has more extremes of temperature because of continental influences.

January is usually the coldest month, but below-freezing temperatures are common only in the mountains. In the lowlands, January temperatures average about 45°F (7°C), with occasional freezing spells. Snow is rare in Greece, except in the mountains. But winter rains may bring 20 inches (500 millimeters) or more of precipitation to the plains. Temperatures in the lowlands usually average about 80°F (27°C) during July. Except for a few thunderstorms, almost no rain falls during the summer months.

Natural Resources

Greece has limited natural resources, including land that can be used for agriculture. Only about one fifth of its land is suitable for farming. The rest is too mountainous or too rocky to be farmed. In addition, much of the usable land has poor soil or is too dry for crops to be grown without irrigation. Some of the fertile soil has been washed away by erosion, caused by the runoff of winter rains from the mountains.

Forests, once widespread, now cover only about one fifth of the land. In recent years the government has undertaken a massive reforestation program. Millions of new trees are being planted in order to increase the supply of timber and to protect the land against further erosion of the soil.

The seas surrounding the Greek mainland and numerous islands traditionally have been an important source of fish, both for domestic use and for export.

Greece has a variety of mineral resources, although many are found in relatively small amounts. The chief minerals are bauxite (aluminum ore), petroleum, nickel, lignite (low-grade brown coal), iron, and magnesium. Other minerals of commercial importance include antimony, sulfur, gypsum, marble, and limestone.

One of Greece's most valuable natural resources is its generally mild, sunny climate. The climate, together with the country's many historical and cultural sites, has made tourism a major industry.

Plant Life

Dryness limits plant growth, but plants with roots long enough to reach underground water can grow all year. Others live only for a season. Most flowers bloom only in spring or fall. The lowlands have typically Mediterranean plants, with little grass except tough annual grasses. Bulbs and tubers flourish, including anemones, asphodels, crocuses, irises, and hyacinths. In spring these blaze into a gay carpet of color.

Except for scattered pines and cypresses, lowland Greece has few trees. Willows, poplars, and planes grow along streams. The lower slopes of mountains are dotted with dry evergreen brush. Aleppo pines and oaks cling here and there between bare rocky slopes. Higher up, the hills have thin stands of oak, chestnut, and beech. Pines and firs grow in the high mountains.

▶ THE ECONOMY

The Greek economy was long based on agriculture, and Greece remains a land of many small farms. But industry, particularly manufacturing, has grown greatly in importance.

Agriculture

Agriculture supports a little more than one quarter of the working population. Most farms are worked by their owners. Often the farms are cut up into numerous, scattered plots. The richest soils are found in the plains of Thessaly and Macedonia. Since level land is scarce, farmers often work narrow, terraced strips on hillsides or thin, stony soil on steep slopes. But the mild climate favors a wide range of crops. Short winters and early warm springs permit early harvests.

Wheat is the main crop, especially in Thessaly and Macedonia. It is grown on about half the farmland. Other grains are corn, barley, oats, and rye. Tobacco, grown mainly in Macedonia and Thrace, is one of Greece's chief agricultural exports. In central Greece, cotton is important. Other crops are potatoes, beans, sugar beets, peas, and melons.

Greece is famous for its olive trees and grapevines. Grapes supply wine, desserts, and raisins. Olives grow well in central and southern Greece. They are used to make olive oil and are also exported whole. Citrus fruits, peaches, figs, apples, pears, and nuts are also grown.

A waterfront café on the island of Hydra, the home of an international art colony.

The ancient Parthenon on the Acropolis contrasts with the modern buildings and neon lights of downtown Athens.

Greek tragedies are still performed at the ancient theater of Epidaurus.

Repairing nets at Aegina, one of the many fishing ports of Greece.

Dancers dressed in costumes of Evzones
(Presidential Guards) perform a folk dance.

On the Greek islands many people still spin wool by hand.

Livestock raising is an important part of Greek agriculture. Large numbers of sheep and goats are kept, since they can be grazed on thin, stony soils. Some cattle are raised in the northern plains. Donkeys, horses, and mules are the chief work animals. Although livestock production has increased in recent years, Greece must still import considerable quantities of meat and dairy products.

Industry

Manufacturing now ranks ahead of agriculture as a source of income for Greece. Most Greek factories are small and are clustered around Athens and Salonika, the major industrial regions. Athens and its port of Piraeus alone account for about two thirds of the country's industrial sites. The chief manufactured goods are processed foods and beverages (including wines), metals and metal products, textiles, clothing, chemicals, tobacco products, and refined petroleum products, including fuels.

Mining is of growing importance. Petroleum was discovered in the northern Aegean Sea, off the island of Thasos, in the early 1980's. Before this, Greece's only mineral fuel was lignite, and its lignite deposits are expected to be exhausted in the near future. Greece's petroleum deposits are relatively small, however, and it must still import fuels to meet its energy needs.

Greece has a busy fishing industry. Most ports have independent fishing fleets of small boats. Sponge-fishing fleets sail out from the islands of Kalymnos and Lemnos in the Aegean Sea.

Transportation

Because Greece is mountainous, there are still parts of the interior that can be reached only by donkey or mule. But all major towns are linked by highways. Airplane service connects mainland Greece and the larger islands. Olympic Airways, the state airline, provides domestic and international air service.

Greeks have been famed as sailors since ancient times. Greece is still a leading shipping nation, with one of the world's largest merchant fleets.

▶ GOVERNMENT

For most of its modern history, Greece was a monarchy. The last king went into exile fol-

lowing a military takeover of the government in 1967. The monarchy was abolished in 1973. When a civilian government was restored in 1974, Greeks rejected a return of the king in a referendum (vote by the people). A republic was officially established under a new constitution, which went into effect in 1975.

The legislature is a parliament elected for four years. Parliament elects the president, who is head of state, for a 5-year term. The president appoints a prime minister to head the government. The prime minister is usually the leader of the political party that wins a majority (more than half) of seats in parliament in an election.

▶ HISTORY

For an account of the history of early Greece, see GREECE, ANCIENT, which follows this article.

Byzantium to Turkish Rule. In A.D. 330 the Emperor Constantine, the first Christian Roman emperor, made the Greek city of Byzantium the capital of the Roman Empire. He named it New Rome. Later the rebuilt city was renamed Constantinople in his honor. (The city is now called Istanbul.) In A.D. 395 the empire broke into eastern and western halves. By the 400's, the western empire had fallen to barbarian invaders. But the eastern half, usually referred to as the Byzantine Empire, lived on as a Greek-speaking state which preserved Greek culture and traditions.

The new empire was different from the old Greek city-states. It was a Christian theocracy, led by priests according to religious laws. To defend itself against invaders, the empire raised great armies.

In the A.D. 500's the Byzantine Emperor Justinian I went to war to get back lost lands. But attempts to reunite the two halves of the old Roman Empire ended in A.D. 800, when Charlemagne was crowned Roman emperor in the West. After that, Byzantium went its own way. A religious split in 1054 separated the Orthodox Church from the Roman Catholic Church.

In 1204 Constantinople was captured by Crusaders from western Europe. The crusading knights divided Greece into small states. Byzantine rulers won back Constantinople in 1261, but they had only a shaky hold over their shrunken lands. In 1453 the Turks took Constantinople, ending the 1,000-year rule of the Byzantine Empire, heir to Greece and Rome.

The Turkish Ottoman Empire ruled most of old Greece, or Byzantium. Crete and the Ionian Islands, held by Venice, escaped Turkish rule for several more centuries. The Christian Greeks suffered under the rule of the Muslim Turks. Most became landless peasants working for Turkish masters. The Turks allowed the Greek Church only limited freedom, yet Greek traditions stayed alive. In time the Turks relaxed their grip. After 1600, Greeks could own land and engage in trade.

Independence. As the Ottoman Empire began to weaken in the 1700's, the Greeks saw their chance to win their freedom. The first major revolt took place in 1770 in the Peloponnesus, but it failed. There were other unsuccessful rebellions, but in 1821—with support from Russia, France, and Britain—an uprising led to the establishment of an independent Greek state in 1830. The new Greece consisted only of the Peloponnesus and south central Greece with some islands. Otto, a German prince, became the first king of modern Greece in 1832. The early years of independence were marked by struggles to recover Greek lands. The Ionian Islands were restored to Greece in 1863. In 1881, Thessaly and part of Epirus were regained. As a result of the Balkan Wars (1912–13), Greece acquired part of Macedonia. Crete was also united with Greece in 1913.

World War I. When World War I began in 1914, Prime Minister Eleutherios Venizelos supported the Allies, led by Britain and France. The king, Constantine I, who favored Germany, sought to keep Greece neutral. In 1917 the king was forced to abdicate (give up the throne) and Greece entered the war on the side of the Allies. Under the peace treaties signed after the war ended in 1918, Greece received West Thrace from Bulgaria and East Thrace from Turkey.

Constantine I regained the throne in 1920, and in 1921, Greece renewed its war with Turkey. The Greek forces were crushingly defeated in 1922. King Constantine abdicated in favor of his son, George II, and Greece was forced to return East Thrace to Turkey. A Greek republic was established in 1924, but in 1935 the monarchy was restored. From 1936 to 1941 the government was led by General Joannes Metaxas, who ruled as a dictator.

World War II and Civil War. Greece was neutral when World War II broke out in 1939, but in 1940 it was invaded by Italy. When the small Greek Army routed the Italians, Germany came to the aid of its ally and overran Greece in 1941. At the war's end in 1945, Greek Communists attempted to seize power. They were resisted by the legal government, backed first by Britain and then the United States. Civil war raged from 1946 to 1949, when the Communists were defeated. Massive U.S. economic aid to Greece in the 1950's helped rebuild the war-torn country.

Recent History. Constantine Karamanlis served as prime minister from 1955 to 1963. He was succeeded by George Papandreou. In 1964 the young Constantine II became king. Constantine quarreled with Papandreou over the role of the king in Greek politics and dismissed him from office in 1965. In 1967, Greek army officers, led by Colonel George Papadopoulos, took over the government. King Constantine attempted to overthrow the military regime. He failed and fled with his family into exile. In 1973, Papadopoulos abolished the monarchy and was named president. Soon after, Papadopoulos himself was removed from power in a new military coup.

The downfall of the military government came in 1974. Greece and Turkey had long been at odds over Cyprus. An attempt by the Greek military leaders to overthrow the Cyprus government led to a Turkish invasion and the partition of the island nation.

In 1974 elections, Karamanlis, as leader of the New Democracy party (ND), was returned as prime minister, holding office until 1980, when he was elected president. In 1981, Andreas Papandreou, son of the former prime minister and head of the Panhellenic Socialist Movement (PASOK), became prime minister. That same year Greece joined the European Community (Union). In 1990 the ND, now led by Constantine Mitsotakis, won a bare one seat majority, but in 1993 elections, Papandreou and PASOK were returned to power. Papandreou resigned in 1996 due to illness and died soon after. He was succeeded as party leader and prime minister by Costas Simitis. PASOK kept its majority in 1996 elections.

KENNETH THOMPSON
University of California—Davis

See also BYZANTINE EMPIRE; CYPRUS; GREECE, ANCIENT; OTTOMAN EMPIRE.

GREECE, ANCIENT

The civilization of ancient Greece centered in the islands of the Aegean Sea and the lands bordering both sides of the Aegean, a region that includes most of present-day Greece and the western coast of Turkey. The people who inhabited these areas never numbered more than 1½ to 2 million, yet they produced a culture that is generally considered to be the foundation of Western civilization. The accomplishments of the Greeks (or Hellenes, as they called themselves) in architecture, sculpture, literature, philosophy, science, and politics were often imitated by later cultures, and they continue to dazzle us today. Few peoples have made such lasting contributions to human thought and art.

The Land and People: An Overview. The land that gave rise to Greek civilization is a rugged one, with few natural resources. Largely mountainous, only about one fifth of the land is able to support farming or the pasturing of livestock. The climate of the coastal areas, where most of the people live, is warm, sunny, and dry for most of the year. Winter rains make cultivation of the soil possible.

Most places in Greece are close to the sea, and the irregular coastline provides many fine harbors. The sea, traditionally, has played an important role in the lives of Greeks. The ancient Greeks were skilled sailors, equally at home on ships of war or on merchant vessels trading goods across the Mediterranean Sea.

Aside from malaria, which was a serious disease for the very young or the very old, the ancient Greeks were a healthy people. The basic food crops, including olives, cereal grains, and fruits and vegetables, provided a simple but nutritious diet. (Olive oil was also used as fuel for lamps.) Goats were a source of milk, and sheep yielded wool and, occasionally, meat. The surrounding waters teemed with fish. Wine was enjoyed, but usually in moderation.

In general, the Greeks of ancient times, even in their cities, lived close to the land and to nature. This may help explain the richness of their art and architecture, which depended so much on the use of natural materials and an appreciation of color and light.

Early Greece: The Mycenaeans. The definition of a "Greek," according to the Greeks themselves, was a person whose native language was Greek. Archaeologists and language scholars believe that sometime after about 1900 B.C. there was a movement of peoples speaking an Indo-European language into the Greek peninsula. Their interaction with the peoples already living there produced the Greek language.

These early Greeks eventually founded a number of small kingdoms, which were inde-

The Lion Gate at Mycenae and gold burial mask date from the Mycenaean Greek period, which reached its height about 1250 B.C. The mask is sometimes called the Mask of Agamemnon, after the legendary king of Mycenae.

the Minoans. The Minoans (named after their legendary king, Minos) were a non-Greek people who had created a wealthy and advanced civilization. The Minoans eventually came into conflict with the more warlike Mycenaeans. The Mycenaeans conquered Crete but, in doing so, adopted many aspects of Minoan art, architecture, and writing.

See the article TROJAN WAR in Volume T. For more information on the Minoans, see ANCIENT CIVILIZATIONS (Cretan Civilization) in Volume A.

A Dark Age. Mycenaean civilization collapsed in a violent upheaval in about 1050 B.C. It was once thought that the Mycenaeans had been overrun by a new group of Greek-speaking invaders, the Dorians. But now most archaeologists and historians believe that the Mycenaean kingdoms fell to internal rebellion and disorder. By about 1000 B.C., Greece had been plunged into a Dark Age, which lasted for more than two centuries.

The Polis, or City-State. By about 750 B.C., a new type of Greek community, the *polis*, or city-state, was beginning to take shape. The city-state consisted of a town surrounded by the territory needed to support it. The town and its lands formed an independent state. There were perhaps as many as a thousand different city-states. Most had only a few thousand inhabitants.

City-states were also established as colonies of older cities. They were founded along the coastal areas of the Black Sea, southern Italy, the island of Sicily, and what are today France and Spain. These colonies were, like their mother-cities, independent states. They were settled for agricultural and commercial reasons and as a relief from overpopulation at home.

The colonies also spread Greek culture throughout the Mediterranean world. The Greeks believed themselves superior to non-Greek-speaking peoples. A non-Greek man, for example, was called a *barbaros*, because to a Greek his language sounded like *bar-bar*, or nonsense. This is the origin of the English word "barbarian," meaning "uncivilized."

pendent of each other, while sharing a common culture. This culture is called Mycenaean, after one of the leading kingdoms of the time, Mycenae. A typical Mycenaean settlement consisted of a large fortified palace and administrative center, surrounded by villages and farmland. During times of war and disorder, the palace was a place of refuge for the local people, most of whom were farmers.

The king's scribes kept records of taxes paid, written on clay tablets. From the surviving tablets we know that the language of the Mycenaeans was an early form of Greek.

The power of the Mycenaean kings grew, and by about 1250 B.C., they were involved in military expeditions overseas. The famous Trojan War may have been just such an expedition, an attempt by the Mycenaeans to conquer the Asian coastal city of Troy.

The Minoans. To the south of Mycenaean Greece lay the large island of Crete, home of

One of the virtues of the polis system was also one of its failings. The Greeks' fierce love of independence made it impossible for the city-states to unite. They were highly competitive and often at war with one another. This lack of unity also made the Greek cities vulnerable to foreign invasion.

Life in the Polis: Athens. With a total population of about 250,000, Athens was one of the largest of the city-states. The city itself was surrounded by heavily fortified walls. Outside the walls lay the countryside, with its olive orchards, farmland, and grazing areas. More than three quarters of all Athenians lived in such rural areas. Those who lived close enough would visit the city often, to buy and sell goods, take part in major religious festivals, and participate in politics.

Inside the walls, whose gates were locked at night, Athens was a town of winding streets and low one-story buildings. Private homes were modest, since the home was not the central part of an Athenian citizen's life. Socially, Athenian men (only men could be citizens) preferred the company of other men. Wives, who had no public life, raised the children and managed the household affairs.

Dominating the center of Athens was the Acropolis ("high city"), a fortified rocky hill on which the city's major temples were built. Just below was the *agora*, the public marketplace, which also served as a political arena. The *agora* hummed with activity, as both farmers and townspeople mixed to argue over the price of goods or debate politics.

Slavery. Slavery was a feature of life in most Greek cities and was considered a part of the natural order of things. Most slaves had been captured in war. Domestic slaves assisted in household tasks. Those with special skills worked as metalsmiths, pottery makers, or in other crafts. Domestic slaves were relatively well-treated and some managed to save enough money to buy their freedom. This was not the case for those who worked in the silver mines of Athens or at similar labors. Their lives were harsh and short.

Forms of Government. The ancient Greeks had various forms of government, whose names are often familiar to us today. Some city-states were oligarchies—that is, governed by a relatively few wealthy and powerful individuals. Some were ruled by tyrants, who had seized power by force. And some were governed by large groups of citizens. The Greek word for people is *demos*. Thus, a city-state that was governed by the people was called a democracy.

Athens was the most famous of the democratic city-states. No more than 30,000 to 40,000 of its inhabitants, however, were entitled to full rights as citizens, including the right to vote and hold office. Athenian women, children, slaves, and resident foreigners had no political rights.

When an Athenian boy reached age 18, he received military training and eventually assumed the rights of citizenship. He became a member of an assembly, made up of all Athenian citizens, that elected officials, passed

An artist's depiction of the *agora*, or public marketplace, of ancient Athens. In the background is the Acropolis ("high city"), on which the city's chief temples were built.

The religion of the ancient Greeks included the worship of numerous gods and goddesses, among them Poseidon, the god of the seas.

laws, set taxes, and supervised foreign policy, including matters of peace and war.

For more information on the development of democracy in Athens, see the article on Solon, the lawgiver, in Volume S.

Sparta: City of Soldiers. The Greeks of the city-state of Sparta developed an altogether different way of life. Always suspicious of outsiders and constantly fearful of invasion, the Spartans had one single goal—the creation of the finest type of soldier. Only native Spartans could qualify for citizenship. Spartan boys spent only their first six years at home, after which they were enrolled in military training schools. They received training until they were in their 20's and served on active military duty until they were 30. Only then were they permitted to marry, establish homes, and raise families.

Spartan girls were given extensive physical training, so that they could produce strong, healthy babies who would one day take their fathers' places in the army. The result was a superb Spartan army that was widely admired (and often feared) throughout ancient Greece.

Religion. The ancient Greeks believed in numerous gods and goddesses who controlled the world. The gods resembled the Greeks themselves, even including some of their faults. But they were more powerful as well as immortal (able to live forever). These beliefs most likely originated with the first Greek-speaking peoples, who also adopted some of the religious ideas of the earlier, non-Greek inhabitants. Although the Greeks were very religious, religion never interfered with their need to experiment, explore, and think freely for themselves. For the story of the Greek gods and goddesses, see the article GREEK MYTHOLOGY in this volume.

The Persian Wars. The city-states faced a serious threat to their freedom in the early 400's B.C. from the huge Persian Empire. The

At the battle of Plataea in 479 B.C., a combined force of Athenian and Spartan infantry (on the left) crushed a Persian army that had invaded European Greece. The victory ended the Persian Wars and allowed the Greek city-states the freedom to seek their own destinies.

Greek cities in Asia Minor (modern Turkey) had earlier fallen to the Persians, who then turned to the cities of European Greece. In 490 B.C. an army sent by the Persian king Darius attacked Athens. The Persians were met at Marathon by the outnumbered Athenian citizen-soldiers, who won a stunning victory.

Ten years later, in 480 B.C., King Xerxes led an enormous Persian army in a full-scale invasion of Greece. In the face of this danger, most of the city-states abandoned their traditional independence to form an alliance. At the pass of Thermopylae, the Spartan king Leonidas sacrificed himself and three hundred fellow Spartans to delay the Persian march on Athens and permit the other Greeks to complete their military preparations. That same year, in a great battle off the island of Salamis, near Athens, the Athenian navy defeated a larger Persian fleet. In 479 B.C. a combined force of Athenians and Spartans crushed the Persian army at Plataea. The Persians retreated from Europe, leaving the city-states free to seek their own destinies.

The Golden Age. The years from about 500 to 323 B.C. are considered the Golden Age (or Classical Age) of Greek civilization. One of the Greeks' greatest achievements was the invention of philosophy, meaning "love of wisdom." The Greeks were the first people to attempt to explain the origin and composition of the universe in scientific terms. They believed that, since there were laws regulating the physical universe, there must also be laws to govern human relations. Great schools of philosophy were established in Athens, led by Plato and his student Aristotle. Plato had been inspired by his own teacher, Socrates, who taught his students to ask "What is good?" "How can one live well?" and "How can I find out the answer to these questions?"

Greek philosophy continued to grow over the next few centuries. It had enormous influence on Western thought and the development of Christianity. The Greeks also advanced the study of mathematics. The rules and proofs of geometry (meaning "to measure the earth") were first compiled by Euclid in the 300's B.C.

The Greeks were especially creative in literature. Greek is a rich language and the Greeks used it to describe how they felt about themselves and their gods. Their ability to express human emotions and to relate the facts of their history resulted in a heritage of drama and

Pericles (495?–429 B.C.) led Athens during its great age of democracy and cultural achievement. But his successful defensive strategy in the Peloponnesian War against Sparta was dropped after his death, eventually bringing about Athens' defeat.

poetry among the greatest ever written. The Greeks also invented the writing of history. Herodotus has left us an account of the Persian wars, and Thucydides a retelling of the Peloponnesian War.

The Greeks built marble monuments of enduring beauty. Temples like the Parthenon (dedicated to the goddess Athena Parthenos) in Athens remind us of the grandeur of ancient Greece. Sculptors created statues of such grace and vitality that artists still study and imitate them.

See GREECE, ART AND ARCHITECTURE OF and GREECE, LANGUAGE AND LITERATURE OF in this volume. Also see the separate articles on Aristotle, Plato, and Socrates in the appropriate volumes.

Athletics. The ancient Greeks strove for physical as well as intellectual excellence. Several panhellenic ("all-Greek") festivals provided them with the opportunity to compete peacefully in athletics, both for their cities and for individual glory. The most famous of these was the Olympic Games, from which our modern Olympics are derived. Originating as a religious festival in honor of Zeus, the king of the gods, they were held every four years. Truces were declared in times of war, so that the athletes could travel safely. See also OLYMPIC GAMES (Origin and History) in Volume O.

The Peloponnesian War. Athens had emerged from the Persian Wars as the most formidable naval power in Greece. Still fearful of the Persians, nearly two hundred city-states formed a defensive league under Athenian leadership. But by the 450's B.C. the Athenians had converted this voluntary league into an Athenian empire. The Spartans were suspicious of this growth of Athenian power. The unity that had developed against the Persian threat was replaced by two hostile alliances, led by Athens and Sparta.

In 431 B.C. war broke out between Athens and Sparta. It was called the Peloponnesian War because Sparta and most of its allies were located in the southern part of Greece, or Peloponnesus. The war lasted on and off until 404 B.C. For part of this period Athens was led by its great statesman Pericles. Although the Spartan army was usually supreme on land, the Athenians were protected by their navy and strong walls. The defeat of an Athenian expedition against the Greek city of Syracuse, in Sicily, in 413 B.C was a turning point in the war. Eventually, the Spartans defeated the Athenian fleet, which had protected the shipments of food into Athens from overseas colonies. With the failure of their navy, the Athenians were starved into submission.

See the article PERICLES in Volume P.

The Rise of Macedon. North of the Greek cities lay the kingdom of Macedon, which had played only a minor role in Greek history. In 360 B.C., however, Philip II came to the Macedonian throne. Philip's aim was to attack the Persian Empire and seize the riches of Asia. However, he could not risk leaving an unsettled Greece behind him. When the Greeks, led by the brilliant Athenian orator (public speaker) Demosthenes, rejected Philip's offer of an alliance under Macedon, Philip went to war against them.

The matter was settled at the battle of Chaeronea in 338 B.C., during which Philip's young son Alexander distinguished himself. The Greeks were defeated and forced to accept Philip's terms. He returned to Macedon to prepare for the invasion of Asia, but was assassinated by one of his own bodyguards. The 20-year-old Alexander was hailed as king.

Alexander the Great. The career of Alexander III, called the Great, was one of the most extraordinary in history. Before his death at age 32, he had conquered the Persian Empire and founded his own empire, stretching from Macedon and Greece to Egypt and across Asia to the borders of India. His conquests permitted the spread of Greek culture into western Asia, where it remained an important cultural force until the rise of the Arabs and the Islamic religion some 900 years later. See the article ALEXANDER THE GREAT in Volume A.

The Hellenistic age. The centuries following Alexander's death are known as the Hellenistic Age. His empire, now divided into several independent kingdoms, was ruled by his former generals and their descendants. In Egypt, Ptolemy I founded a dynasty, or royal family, that lasted for three centuries. In Syria the Seleucid kingdom, named after Seleucus I, controlled much of what we now call the Middle East. And in Macedon itself, a new dynasty, the Antigonids, replaced the family of Philip and Alexander.

Greek culture was dominant among the Macedonians and Greeks who ruled the Hellenistic kingdoms, but it did not penetrate deeply into the native traditions of these lands. Thus two cultures, Greek and native, existed side by side, but with little influence on one another.

Rome and Later Greek Culture. The rising power of Rome marked the end of the Hellenistic kingdoms, which fell to Roman armies in a series of wars. The last to succumb was Egypt, led by its queen Cleopatra VII, who killed herself in 30 B.C., rather than become a captive of Rome. See the article CLEOPATRA in Volume C.

Roman conquest did not mean the end of Greek civilization. Many educated Romans spoke and wrote the Greek language, imitated Greek authors, admired Greek philosophy, and collected Greek art. In A.D. 330, the Roman emperor Constantine I, the Great, rebuilt the old Greek city of Byzantium, which was renamed Constantinople (that is, the city, or *polis,* of Constantine). After the collapse of the Western Roman Empire in the A.D. 400's, Constantinople remained the capital of the Eastern Roman, or Byzantine, Empire. The surviving part of the Roman Empire thus was the Greek part. Centered in Constantinople (modern Istanbul), it lasted, with a few interruptions, for another thousand years.

See BYZANTINE ART AND ARCHITECTURE and BYZANTINE EMPIRE in Volume B.

EUGENE N. BORZA
The Pennsylvania State University
Author, *The Classical Tradition*

The ruins of the Temple of Apollo, which was built about 540 B.C., still stand at Corinth. The designs of Greek temples influenced much later architecture.

GREECE, ART AND ARCHITECTURE OF

The ancient Greeks helped shape the world of today. Many accepted traditions of Western culture—in philosophy, education, and government as well as in art and architecture—were first defined in Greece centuries ago. The Greek concept of beauty was based on a pleasing balance and proportion of form. The design of graceful columned Greek temples has influenced architecture from the Renaissance to modern times. Greek sculpture established an ideal standard for the human form that served as a model for artists in ages to come.

▶EARLY GREEK ART: THE MYCENAEAN AGE

The earliest development of Greek art took place during the period from 1600 to 1100 B.C. This is known as the Mycenaean Age, because its most famous center was the town of Mycenae. The Mycenaeans found much to admire in the arts and skills of older civilizations, such as Assyria and Egypt. The art of the island of Crete had an especially strong influence on early Greek artists. It is not surprising, then, that Greek art of the Mycenaean period is similar to the art of these other countries. The Greeks appreciated beautiful things and quickly learned from the experience of others. They soon developed skills of their own and then wholly new styles.

Archeologists have dug up great palaces at Mycenae, Pylos, Tiryns, and Gla. These well planned, luxurious buildings were heavily fortified against invaders. The ruins of these palaces closely match the descriptions of royal houses by the Greek poet Homer. The ground floor of a palace was built of large, carefully shaped stones. The second story was made of wood. The plaster-covered walls were bright with lively paintings of birds, animals, flowers, and geometrical designs. The main room was the **megaron**. It was square and had a round hearth in the center. The middle of the megaron was open to the sky. The rest of the room was covered by a slanting roof supported by columns. Around the megaron were rooms of different sizes, fully roofed and gaily painted. Ordinary houses were, of course, less splendid, but they were well designed and solidly built.

The royal tombs of the 1300's B.C. were impressive. Large round holes were dug into the hillside, and the tombs were built inside them. The tombs had high domes shaped like beehives, built up by layer upon layer of huge stones. The tomb of Atreus (known as the Treasury of Atreus), built about 1330 at Mycenae, was the greatest of these tombs. The dome was more than 45 feet (14 meters) across and 44 feet (13 meters) high. Across the top of the entrance was a single huge, flat stone slab.

Homer called Mycenae "rich in gold," and he often described the beautiful art works of the period. Among the most remarkable objects found anywhere in the ancient world were the bronze daggers from the royal tombs of the Mycenaean kings. The daggers are decorated with designs in gold and silver fitted into the cutout bronze. One of these daggers has a scene of an exciting moment in a lion hunt. With great skill the artist captured the motion, fear, and courage of the dangerous battle. The king of Mycenae who owned this dagger must have been proud of it, for he had it buried with him.

Two gold cups found in a tomb in Vaphio near Sparta were of the same period. The design was raised from the surface by beating the gold on a carved wooden mold. The design on one cup shows men capturing wild bulls. The other shows cattle peacefully grazing on the farm. The work was done in great detail and with such skill that the figures almost seem real.

Parts of wall paintings from Mycenaean palaces have survived. There are bullfights, processions, hunting scenes, and geometrical designs in bright colors. Although the paintings are similar to those found in earlier Cretan wall paintings, they also indicate that Greek taste was different from Cretan.

Cup decorated with pecking bird (1300's or 1200's B.C.), from the Mycenaean Age. British Museum, London.

***Standing Maiden*, carved from marble and painted about 520 B.C. Acropolis Museum, Athens.**

Gold cup found in a tomb in Vaphio, near Sparta (1400's B.C.). Athens Museum.

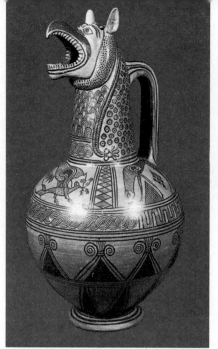

Red-figure vase, Attic style (465? B.C.). Museum of Fine Arts, Boston.

Wine pitcher (600's B.C.) with griffin head. British Museum.

Black-figure vase, Attic style (520? B.C.). Metropolitan Museum, New York.

A great variety of Mycenaean vases have been found—large storage urns for water, wine, and oil, and small jugs for drinking or table use. Usually the clay is tan, and the designs are in brown, black, or a glossy orange-red. Most of the designs are flower-like patterns or imaginative combinations of broad lines, spirals, zigzags, and circles. Some have scenes of birds or animals. One cup is decorated with a long-beaked bird picking at the bugs on a friendly bull. The drawing is amusing and imaginative. It shows not the real world, but a private world that the artist invented. His starry-eyed bull has ridiculously scrawny legs, and the bird's tail is absurdly tiny. Wall painting influenced pottery, and

Mosaic of Dionysus riding a panther. It was created in the 1st century B.C. on a wall in the House of Masks, Delos.

occasionally a vase shows hunters or warriors in chariots.

The Mycenaean Age came to a violent end about 1050 B.C., perhaps due to an internal rebellion. The great palaces were burned down. Trade and business were ruined. For several centuries afterward no large works of art were produced, but statuettes and pottery were made.

▶GREEK VASES

Pottery was the one art form that flourished during the long period of change from the Mycenaean to the Classical era. More than 100,000 Greek vases have survived, complete or in part, from the period between 1000 and 300 B.C. They form an important record of the development of Greek art.

Vases in the 900's, 800's and 700's were most frequently decorated in geometrical designs—circles, triangles, diamonds, and sharply turning lines. The design was painted in black or dark brown on the light brown clay. Many of these vases were large storage urns, although there are also many examples of small tableware. In the 700's, animal and human figures became common subjects. People were usually shown in silhouette. The men had triangular chests and very narrow waists and hips.

In the 600's, Greek vasemakers were influenced by Egyptian and Assyrian styles. Scenes of human or animal life became more important than geometric patterns. Sometimes a vase was in the shape of an animal, such as a wine pitcher with a spout like a snarling griffin's head. (The griffin is an imaginary animal said to have the body of a lion and the head and wings of an eagle.)

Vases made in different areas of the Greek world differed in style, color, shape, and decoration. Vases from Ionia and the island of Rhodes often had graceful figures of long-horned goats and cattle. Flowers and small circular or square designs were scattered among the animals to fill up the background. The forms were painted on white in black, red, or brown. Potters in the city of Corinth used a special purple-red color as well as black, brown, and yellow for the figures, which were often owls or roaring lions. The backgrounds were covered with rosettes—designs taken from the shape of a rose—and other flower shapes.

The most important vases were **Attic**, which were produced in and around Athens. Styles of the 600's featured large figures of men and animals in black, brown, and red on a tan background. They also had some geometric decoration. Many were painted with scenes from the *Iliad* and the *Odyssey*.

The style common in the 600's and 500's was called **black-figure**. Figures were painted in a special glaze that turned a glossy black when the vase was baked. The rest of the vase became light red. Details of faces and clothes were made on the figures by scratching lines through the black glaze to the red clay. Often other details were emphasized by white and red paint.

About 530 B.C. a different technique was introduced. The backgrounds were painted in black. The figures were left in the red of the clay—just the opposite of the black-figure style. This **red-figure** style gave the artists much more freedom. Figures were shown in a greater variety of actions. As in the sculpture and wall painting of the time, the figures appeared more natural and lifelike. Scenes of human life were the most popular. Backgrounds were no longer filled with flowers and geometric shapes.

On more expensive vases, the whole background was sometimes painted an ivory white. The figures stood out more strikingly on this white background. Details were highlighted by the use of red, blue, yellow, or brown. These **white-ground** vases are rarer than black- or red-figured ones.

The beautiful shapes of their vases and the way the designs fit these shapes show the Greeks' wonderful sense of proportion.

▶PAINTING

Very little painting has survived from ancient Greece except for the drawings on vases. Paintings on wood, plaster, or cloth disappeared long ago. We know about Greek painting from literary descriptions and from Roman paintings and mosaics that copied Greek works. Some drawings from the late 500's on marble, **terra-cotta** (baked reddish clay), and pieces of wood have been found.

A painter named Cimon of Cleonae was a great experimenter. Before, faces had been painted only in profile. Cimon is thought to be the first painter to show human faces from different angles.

This Roman copy of Myron's *Discus-Thrower* shows the sculptor's skill at portraying the human form in motion. The original sculpture was made about 450 B.C.

In the 400's B.C., one of the first Greek artists to paint large pictures was Polygnotus. His paintings covered whole walls of public buildings. Polygnotus was famous for the human feeling expressed in his style. He was also the first to paint lifelike portraits. A later master in the same century was Apollodorus (called the "shadow-painter"). He achieved lifelike effects by skillful use of color, shading, and **perspective** (the way distance is shown on the flat surface of a painting).

At the end of the century, Zeuxis further perfected the methods of showing light and shade. He was able to make his figures seem almost real. There is a legend that he once painted grapes so realistically that birds flew down and pecked at his picture.

Apelles, who lived in the 300's, was the court painter for Alexander the Great. Apelles was considered the best Greek painter of his time. He had great technical skill, and he was famous for his delicate style. The painter Pausias invented a way of mixing colors with hot wax. This method is called **encaustic**.

▶MOSAICS

One special, and very difficult, art form is **mosaic**. Mosaics are pictures made by setting small colored stones, pieces of marble, or glass in cement. As early as the 400's B.C. some fine mosaics were made in Greece. Black and white pebbles were set in a cement floor to depict animals, flowers, and mythological stories. Sometimes these floors had complicated border designs. The mosaics served as decorative floor coverings in important rooms of the house.

In the 200's and 100's an improved method was developed. Small, brightly colored cubes of marble, glass, or tile were used instead of pebbles. Many of these mosaics have survived to our own time.

▶SCULPTURE

Very little sculpture was made in Greece during the Mycenaean Age or the following three centuries. The earliest statues of gods were stiff and lifeless wood carvings. Many of the early small bronze statuettes, however, were more graceful. Gradually a change took place. The Greeks wanted large statues of their gods. Because there was no Greek tradition of large sculpture, sculptors of the 600's turned to Egypt and the East for models. Thousands of statues—often life-size or bigger—were created in marble, stone, or bronze. Many typical statues remain. As with Greek painting, much of what we know about Greek sculpture comes from old descriptions and from copies made by the Romans.

Archaic Period

The early statues of the Archaic Period, from the 600's to the 400's B.C., were rather formal and heavy-looking. The figures stood stiffly, their arms close to their sides—with hands clenched or flat against the legs. The left foot was placed slightly forward. The figures had narrow waists and broad shoulders. The heads were oval with firm mouths and almond-shaped eyes. Hair was elaborately arranged in rhythmic rows and curls. Women's clothing fell in carefully planned folds. In all periods of Greek sculpture, statues were painted with many colors to make the eyes, lips, hair, jewelry, and clothing seem natural.

The *Charioteer*, a bronze statue made about 470 B.C., portrays the winner of a chariot race. It is an example of Greek sculpture from the early Classical Age.

Greek sculptors rapidly mastered the techniques of sculpture. They began to break away from foreign influence, developing styles that were more natural. Many beautiful pieces of later sculpture show this new Greek spirit. A statue of a maiden, or Kore, from about 520 B.C. that was found on the Acropolis, the central hill in Athens, illustrates the stately pose, drapery, and facial expression characteristic of this period.

The Classical Age

The Classical Age began in the 400's B.C. Some fine large bronze statues dating from the early Classical Period show how rapidly Greek sculpture advanced. A famous example is the *Charioteer* from Delphi. The athlete stands waiting for the race to begin, holding the reins of the four horses that pull his chariot. His face is calm. His eyes are made to look real by the use of colored inlay. He even has eyelashes made of little copper strips.

The Greek interest in human beauty and movement is expressed in Myron's great *Discus-Thrower*. The sculptor has shown an athlete in the middle of a complex movement —the exact moment between the windup for the throw and the release of the discus. The two curves of the arms and body and the two circles of the head and discus balance each other perfectly. The precise carving shows that Myron made careful studies of living men. This exactness became the rule in Greek sculpture.

The full classical style came after the middle of the 400's. The influential classical sculptor Polyclitus was impressed by the beauty of the human body at rest. His statue of the *Spearbearer* (or *Doryphorus*) established the ideal measurements and proportions of the body. Polyclitus wrote a book that described the way to present the body realistically, yet with perfect beauty.

The Greeks considered Phidias their greatest sculptor. Two colossal gold-and-ivory statues of Zeus and Athena, both now known only from descriptions, were considered his masterpieces. The statue of Athena was made for the Parthenon, the temple built in her honor on the Acropolis.

From the 600's B.C., sculpture in **relief** (sculpture carved on a background) was used to decorate temples. The style of these reliefs developed in the same manner as that of free-standing statues. Among the most famous of these sculptural decorations were the statues and reliefs for the Parthenon. Phidias designed and supervised this work. The continuous relief decorating the inner hall of the temple showed a procession of the citizens of Athens bringing gifts to Athena. Young men rode horses, played musical instruments, and led bulls. The skillfulness of the carving represents classical art at its height.

Two outstanding sculptors of the 300's were Scopas and Parxiteles. Scopas emphasized strong emotions in his statues by deep-set eyes, upturned faces, and twisted positions. A new element of softness was introduced by Praxiteles, who worked in marble. A typical example of late classical sculpture is the bronze *Boy* from Marathon, probably by Praxiteles.

Lysippus (last half of the 300's) was the supreme master of bronze sculpture. He is believed to have made more than a thousand stat-

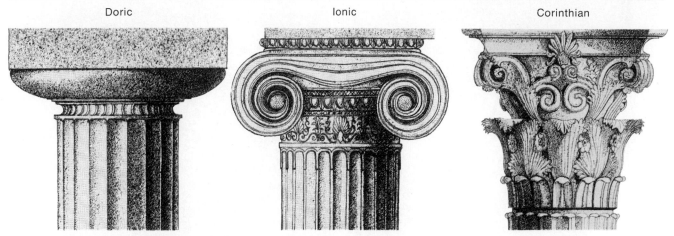

Doric   Ionic   Corinthian

The three Greek architectural orders can be identified by the different designs of their capitals, or column tops.

ues, though none still exists. He especially liked to represent the slim, firm bodies of athletes. Lysippus also did realistic **busts** (head and shoulders), including the official portrait of Alexander the Great.

Hellenistic Period

The period, 323–146 B.C., between the conquests of Alexander the Great and the Roman conquest of Greece is called the Hellenistic Age. During this time many sculptors continued to work in the style of the 300's. Such masterpieces as the *Venus de Milo* and the statue known as the *Winged Victory* of Samothrace date from this period.

But there grew up at this time a new interest in down-to-earth themes. For the first time ordinary people like market women and boxers were portrayed. There was great interest in the individual character of each person. Children were shown as children, rather than little adults, for the first time.

Some Hellenistic works are humorous. There is a delightful small bronze statue of a comic actor playing the role of a saucy slave who refuses to obey his master.

▶ARCHITECTURE

The most famous Greek buildings are temples. Since the temple was built as a home for the statue of a god, primitive temples imitated earlier Greek houses. Later they developed according to the design of the Mycenaean megaron. Most early Greek temples were built of wood. By the late 600's B.C. they were usually built of limestone or marble. A typical temple had a porch and large hall (**cella**) surrounded by a **colonnade** (row of columns).

Greek temples were built in three different styles, or orders—Doric, Ionic, and Corinthian. Today we remember these orders best by their distinctive columns and **capitals** (decorated column tops).

Doric. The Dorian tribes on the Greek mainland developed the Doric order. They were influenced by buildings at Mycenae and Crete. The Doric order is sturdy and dignified. The greatest example of this style is the Parthenon, built between 447 and 432, at the height of the classical age. Made entirely of marble, the building was constructed with great technical skill. All the parts of the building look even and straight. The columns, however, tilt inward slightly, and the base of the temple curves slightly upward in the center. These and several other slight changes were carefully planned by the architect Ictinus because he wished to create a feeling of energy.

Ionic. In contrast to the sturdy Doric, Ionic architecture is more delicate and ornate. It was created by the Ionians, a Greek tribe living along the coast of Asia Minor. The influence of Egypt and Assyria can be recognized. The most elegant example of the Ionic style is the Erechtheum, built about twenty years after the Parthenon on the Athens Acropolis. Its design is unusual because it was built on three ground levels. Another striking feature of the building is the Porch of the Maidens. The six columns that support the roof of the porch are carved in the shape of girls with long locks of hair and flowing garments.

A statue from the Temple of Apollo (100's B.C.), Pompeii, was made during the Hellenistic Age, a period that saw the continued spread of Greek culture.

The bronze *Boy* from Marathon (late 300's B.C.), probably by Praxiteles, is a typical example of late classical Greek sculpture. Athens Museum.

Corinthian. The Olympieum at Athens is an example of the Corinthian style. In many ways it is much like Ionic architecture, but it is sturdier. It also has acanthus-leaf capitals instead of Ionic scrolls. Corinthian is the most elaborate Greek style and the one that the Romans imitated most often.

As well as the usual rectangular form, round temples were constructed. The Tholos at Delphi has Doric columns around a circular marble hall.

There were also important government buildings and outdoor theaters. The Greeks made **stoae**, long roofs supported by colonnades, for protection from rain or the hot sun.

▶**MINOR ARTS**

Greek artists produced fine works in many other fields. We have small clay statuettes of fashionably dressed women, children seated or at play, and men of different occupations. These are mostly from the 200's B.C., and the best examples came from the workshops at Tanagra. The Greeks were also skilled at carving ivory.

In the wealthier homes colored glass containers in graceful shapes were valued possessions. Some artists specialized in carving complicated mythological scenes in cameo technique. Cameos are carved from stones or glass that have layers of different colors. The designs are carved in the top layer. The layer beneath acts as a contrasting background.

The Greeks carved gems on a small scale. Usually less than 1 inch across, the gems were intricately carved with forms of animals or men. Seals were made by pressing the carved gems first into clay or wax and then onto special letters and documents.

Gold jewelry was often decorated with precious stones. Bracelets, earrings, and pins from ancient Greece can be seen in many of the world's museums.

Nothing is more practical than money; yet the Greeks made even that beautiful. The designs on gold and silver coins were made with great care. In spite of modern tools, the coins made today are not as handsome as ancient Greek coins.

RAYMOND V. SCHODER, S.J.
Loyola University (Chicago)

See also ARCHITECTURE; DECORATIVE ARTS; PAINTING; POTTERY; SCULPTURE.

GREECE, LANGUAGE AND LITERATURE OF

The Greek language is part of the Indo-European language family. To this group belong such ancient languages as Latin and Sanskrit, and such modern ones as English, French, German, Russian, Hindi, and Persian. The ancient Greeks in various districts spoke and wrote many different dialects, with slightly different words and sounds. They could usually understand one another, but for many centuries there was no single standard Greek language.

After 500 B.C., when Athens grew into the most powerful single state in Greece, with the richest literature, its dialect became the most important. (This dialect was called Attic, because the region around Athens was named Attica.) Later, after King Philip of Macedonia and his son Alexander the Great had conquered all the independent Greek states, a simple common language (based on Attic) spread over all Greece. It followed Alexander's conquering armies through Egypt and Asia Minor. It is the ancestor of the tongue spoken in Greece today.

Many Greek words have come into English. Some are taken from the Bible: *angel, Christ, devil,* and *Bible* itself, which means "book." Many are scientific words: *amoeba, electric, plastic.* Some are names for branches of

SOME WORDS IN EVERYDAY USE

ENGLISH	CLASSICAL		MODERN (demotic)		
Book	ΒΙΒΛΟΣ	(bíblos)	ΒΙΒΛΙΟ	βιβλίο	(vivlío)
Child (young)	ΠΑΙΔΙΟΝ	(paidíon)	ΠΑΙΔΙ	παιδί	(pedhí)
City	ΠΟΛΙΣ	(pólis)	ΠΟΛΗ	πόλη	(póli)
Father	ΠΑΤΗΡ	(patḗr)	ΠΑΤΕΡΑΣ	πατέρας	(patéras)
Five	ΠΕΝΤΕ	(pénte)	ΠΕΝΤΕ	πέντε	(pénde)
Friend	ΦΙΛΟΣ	(phílos)	ΦΙΛΟΣ	φίλος	(phílos)
Horse	ΙΠΠΟΣ	(híppos)	ΑΛΟΓΟ	ἄλογο	(álogo)
Letter	ΓΡΑΜΜΑ	(grámma)	ΓΡΑΜΜΑ	γράμμα	(grámma)
Man	ΑΝΘΡΩΠΟΣ	(ánthropos)	ΑΝΘΡΩΠΟΣ	ἄνθρωπος	(ánthropos)
Mother	ΜΗΤΗΡ	(mḗtēr)	ΜΗΤΕΡΑ	μητέρα	(mitéra)
People	ΔΗΜΟΣ	(dḗmos)	ΚΟΣΜΟΣ (a large crowd)	κόσμος	(kózmos)
River	ΠΟΤΑΜΟΣ	(potamós)	ΠΟΤΑΜΙ	ποτάμι	(potámi)
Ten	ΔΕΚΑ	(déka)	ΔΕΚΑ	δέκα	(dhéka)
Word	ΛΟΓΟΣ	(lógos)	ΛΟΓΟΣ	λόγος	(lógos)

The words in parentheses are phonetic spellings of the Greek. In classical Greek the accent marks indicate the syllables pronounced on a higher level of tone. In modern Greek the accent marks indicate which syllable is stressed. The ē is pronounced as the "ay" is in "day" and "may." The "dh" sound is like the "th" in "they" and "either."

literature: *comedy, epic, history, poetry*. This is because the Greeks started nearly all the types of literature we read and write today. Some school and college subjects have Greek names: *arithmetic, biology, geography*. This is because the ancient Greeks started and built up most of the fields of modern education. "School" itself comes from the Greek word *scholē*. This word first meant "leisure" and then "discussion."

Sometime between the 1200's and the 800's B.C. the Greeks borrowed the Phoenician alphabet, but the Phoenicians had no signs to show vowels. The Greeks then made the letters A, E, I, O, and U to stand for vowel sounds. This made the alphabet clearer and more useful.

The Romans took over the Greek alphabet, changed it a little, and then passed it on to us.

Early Poetry

Homer. Greek literature begins with Homer. The ancient Greeks themselves did not know much about him, nor do we. The two poems —the *Iliad* and the *Odyssey*—that have come down to us under his name are the earliest complete books in all Western literature.

Both the *Iliad* and the *Odyssey* are epics. (An epic is a long narrative poem, written in a grand style, about the adventures of a hero.) The *Iliad* tells how the Greeks besieging Troy about 1185 B.C. were nearly beaten because they quarreled among themselves and because their best champion, Achilles, refused to fight. The *Odyssey* shows how, after Troy was finally captured, Odysseus returned home through many dangers, found his house taken over by intruders, and, helped by his son Telemachus, killed them all.

Homer lived long after the time of the Trojan War. Many short poems about the war and the exploits of the chief warriors were made up soon after it ended. They were repeated and added to for hundreds of years. Then, perhaps about 750 B.C., Homer selected some of these short poems, wove them together, and put in much of his own, so as to make two long epics. We do not know for certain whether he could read and write. In early times most poetry was not written down to be read, but carried in the poet's head and recited. Perhaps Homer dictated his work to pupils who wrote it down. Nor do we know whether the same man composed both the *Iliad* and the *Odyssey*. Some experts believe the *Iliad* came first and then later someone who knew and admired the *Iliad* made the *Odyssey,* as a sort of sequel.

Hesiod and Other Poets. The second Greek poet was Hesiod, who lived during the 700's B.C. His chief poems are *Works and Days* and *The Theogony*. The first advises farmers, rather as Benjamin Franklin's *Poor Richard's Almanack* does. The second has stories of the origin of the world and the birth of the Greek gods.

From this early period, also, we have a set of poems called *Homeric Hymns*. These were not written by Homer, but by later poets who looked up to him and copied his style. They are songs of praise to the Greek gods, telling of their miracles and their various adventures. Much gayer and less reverent than the hymns sung in our churches, they are delightful poetry.

Most of the poetry written in the two following centuries, from about 700 to 500 B.C., has been lost. It was written in a new style, much shorter and more personal than the long works of Homer and Hesiod. It told of the joys and sorrows of the poets themselves. Many of these poems were songs, called lyrics because they were meant to be sung to the lyre. The most important lyric poets were Alcaeus and Sappho. Sappho was one of the few famous women writers in all history, and her poems are tender and haunting.

There was also Anacreon (582?–488? B.C.), who wrote merry drinking songs, and Archilochus, who wrote the earliest satirical poems, bitterly attacking his personal enemies. Patriotism was the theme of Tyrtaeus, who composed fine war songs for the Spartans. Then there was Solon (638?–559? B.C.), the Athenian lawgiver, whose poetry is full of deep political wisdom. Somewhat later, Pindar (522?–443 B.C.) wrote fine triumphal odes honoring victors in the Olympic Games and other such contests.

Early Prose

Herodotus and Thucydides. So far Greek literature was all poetry. Prose writing started with an author almost as important as Homer.

This was Herodotus, "the father of history." He was born sometime between the two Persian invasions of Greece (490 and 480 B.C.). When he grew up, he gathered much information about the invasions by traveling widely and talking with people who had witnessed them. Then he built it all into a great story of the Persian power and the Greek resistance, adding many strange tales about other parts of the world, such as Egypt and Babylonia. He was really writing a prose epic, not to copy Homer but to rival him in another field.

The Athenian Thucydides (455?–400 B.C.) was a general in the war waged against Athens by Sparta and her allies (431–404 B.C.). He lost an important outpost and was banished by the angry Athenians. He spent the rest of his life observing the war as a reporter and analyst, and writing its history. His *History of the Peloponnesian War* was unfinished at his death. It is more careful than that of Herodotus and much more difficult to read. Still, it is a great mine of wisdom for those who want to understand politics and warfare.

Tragedy

Meanwhile, in Athens a new kind of literature was being built up. This literature was made up of plays, not recited, but acted before a big audience, and all in poetry, with music and dancing. There had been dramatic sketches in many districts of Greece, but it was in Athens that the two great types of drama, tragedy and comedy, were perfected.

Tragedy was started about 540 B.C. by the Athenian writer Thespis and improved by many playwrights who followed him. A Greek tragedy shows how great men and women, although they may have fine ideals, sometimes end in failure and misery. A tragedy is usually a sad play, yet always noble and thoughtful, and sometimes quite simple in staging. Greek tragedies were performed at festivals honoring the god Dionysus, whose altar stood in the middle of the theater. In most plays only three actors appeared on the stage at one time. A space between the actors and the audience was called the *orchestra,* Greek for "dancing place." A chorus occupied the orchestra. They danced, sang, and spoke in harmony, commenting on the events of the play. Only 33 of

the many hundreds of tragedies written in the 400's B.C. have survived through the Dark Ages. All but one are about the heroes and heroines of Greek mythology, whose stories were well-known. The audience therefore did not expect brand-new plots, as modern audiences do.

The three great writers of Greek tragedy were Aeschylus (525–456 B.C.), Sophocles (496?–406 B.C.), and Euripides (485?–406? B.C.).

Aeschylus. Aeschylus wrote on grand and terrifying subjects. *Prometheus Bound,* for instance, is about the damnation and torture of the Titan Prometheus, who rebelled against Zeus. Another theme is the working out through murder and madness of the curse on the family of Agamemnon. Aeschylus told the story of the curse in three tragedies linked together as a trilogy: *Agamemnon, Choephori* (or *The Mourners*), and *Eumenides* (or *The Furies*). This trilogy, called the *Oresteia* ("Story of Orestes"), is the only complete one that survives, but we know that Aeschylus wrote many others. He also wrote the only surviving historical play, *The Persians*.

Sophocles. Sophocles was a master at drawing character. He is most famous for his three plays (not, however, a trilogy) on the story of Oedipus and his family. In *King Oedipus* he tells how Oedipus, King of Thebes, investigates a curse that has fallen on the state. He discovers that he has brought it on his citizens and himself by having murdered his father and married his own mother. In *Oedipus at Colonus,* Sophocles shows us the same man approaching death, old and purified by suffering. In *Antigone,* Oedipus' daughter decides to bury her brother, who was killed in a civil war against Thebes, even though Creon, its ruler, has forbidden the rebels burial. As punishment Antigone is buried alive in a tomb, where she hangs herself. Creon's son, who was in love with her, commits suicide. This is the tragedy caused by the conflict between conscience and the law of the state.

Sophocles' *Electra* (on the same theme as Aeschylus' *Mourners*) shows Prince Orestes returning from exile and being welcomed by his sister Electra. She encourages him to avenge their murdered father, Agamemnon, by killing their mother. *Philoctetes* is about

A scene from a recent production of *Oedipus Rex* (*King Oedipus*) at Delphi.

the wily Odysseus and Neoptolemus, who visit a Greek hero on a desert island and persuade him to return and fight against Troy. *Ajax* concerns the madness and suicide of Ajax after he lost a contest to Odysseus. *The Women of Trachis* shows the tragic death of Heracles.

Euripides. Euripides was less noble, more bitter, and more puzzling than the other two tragedians. Lonely and unpopular while he lived, he achieved fame only after his death. Among his famous plays are *Medea,* in which Medea murders her children, and *Alcestis,* in which Alcestis agrees to die for her husband and is then rescued by Heracles. Hippolytus,

in the play of the same name, is falsely accused of evil by his stepmother, Phaedra, and so cursed by his father, Theseus. Hippolytus' story was also treated by the French playwright Racine. *The Trojan Women* is against all war. In *Bacchantes,* a mother under the influence of religious frenzy kills her son. Euripides' *Electra* covers the same story as Sophocles' *Electra* and Aeschylus' *Mourners.*

Several of Euripides' plays are officially tragedies, but they are actually much closer to romantic comedy. One of these is *Helen,* in which Helen is supposed to have spent the Trojan War in Egypt, where she is later found by her husband. Euripides, although considered the most tragic of the dramatists, is also called the father of New Comedy.

Comedy

Greek comedy began about 500 B.C. Until about 400 it was written in a special style, which is now called Old Comedy. Its playwrights put real people on the stage—politicians, poets, philosophers like Socrates—and poked fun at their mannerisms and their ideas. The humor is often very dirty, but often clean and bright and fanciful. The comedies are not straight plays, but "musicals" or comic operas, with many songs and dances by single actors and by the chorus. In modern times George Gershwin's *Of Thee I Sing,* which kids a presidential election, and Gilbert and Sullivan's *H.M.S. Pinafore,* which spoofs the British Navy, are very much like the plays of the Greek Old Comedy.

Aristophanes. Many fragments and quotations have survived, but we have only eleven complete comedies, all by Aristophanes (448?–380 B.C.), who started writing in 427 B.C. He made fun of everything and was particularly hard on extremist politicians and such difficult poets as Euripides. In *The Clouds* he attacked Socrates and modern education. In *The Birds* he invented an imaginary state in the air ruled by birds, because he thought they could govern better than people. *Lysistrata* showed the women of Athens and Sparta going on strike against their husbands to make them give up the war and declare peace. In *The Frogs* he made Dionysus go to the underworld and run a contest between Aeschylus and Euripides to see which of them ought to be brought back to life. In spite of his rough jokes and crazy notions, Aristophanes was really a great poet who saw the world as a comedy, not as a tragedy.

Middle Comedy and New Comedy. All the plays of the Middle Comedy period (about 400–330 B.C.) have been lost. We know little about Middle Comedy except that it specialized in drawing eccentric characters who were types rather than real people: chefs, doctors, funny foreigners.

The New Comedy plays came to the stage about 330 B.C., after Alexander had conquered Athens and taken the spirit out of its people. The plays were much quieter and less gay than earlier comedies, with no choruses and scarcely any singing and dancing. Mostly they are straight romantic dramas about love affairs and domestic squabbles, especially between fathers and sons. The plots are very complicated, and the characters carefully drawn from real life.

The most famous writer of New Comedy was Menander (342–291 B.C.), whose play *The Curmudgeon* (or *The Grouch*) was discovered in Egypt only a few years ago. The Roman authors Plautus (254?–184 B.C.) and Terence (185–159 B.C.) greatly admired Menander and the other playwrights of New Comedy, and copied their clever plots. Shakespeare and other dramatists copied Plautus and Terence—so that Menander is really one of the ancestors of modern drama.

Philosophy

Socrates and Plato. Philosophy, the search for truth, also flourished in the 400's. Before Socrates (470?–399 B.C.), philosophy was closely related to what we now call science. The philosophers of that time asked questions about such matters as the basic element of the universe. We have only fragments of their writings. Socrates was interested in man and his behavior. He tried to find definitions for concepts such as virtue, wisdom, and courage. Socrates himself never wrote anything. Instead, he talked with young men, so that together they might discover truth. We still use this Socratic, or dialectical, method in teaching. We hear about Socrates mainly through Plato.

The Sophists also appeared during the time of Socrates. They promised to teach a man how to win any argument. One of them, Protagoras, said that "man is the measure of all things," which shocked the more religious Athenians.

Plato (427?–347 B.C.) was a pupil of Socrates. He wrote dialogues in which Socrates explained his ideas. In *Apology* (or *Defense*) Socrates defends himself against charges of corrupting the young and introducing new gods. In *Crito* he is in prison and refuses to escape, because he is a good citizen. In *Phaedo* we see Socrates just before his execution. He talks with his friends about the immortality of the soul.

Many of the ideas may belong more to Plato than to Socrates. The *Republic* presents

Rembrandt's *Aristotle Contemplating the Bust of Homer*. Metropolitan Museum.

a very interesting discussion of the nature of justice, and what education should be like. Plato wants to set up an ideal form of government, which he thinks of as the very opposite of democratic Athens. However, Plato himself feared that it would be impos-sible to create a state in which the rulers would be philosopher-kings.

Xenophon and Aristotle. Xenophon (434?–355? B.C.) in his *Memorabilia* (or *Memoirs*) recounts his experiences with his teacher, Socrates. He wrote essays on horsemanship, the education of a Persian prince, and the Spartan system. Xenophon also wrote history, starting where Thucydides left off. He is most famous for his exciting *Anabasis* (or *March Up Country*). This tells how 10,000 Greek soldiers under Cyrus the Younger invaded Persia and were stranded when Cyrus was killed. Xenophon took command and led them hundreds of miles to the Black Sea and back to Greece.

Plato's chief disciple was Aristotle (384–322 B.C.). Aristotle's range of interests is amazing. His chief influence has been in the natural sciences, particularly the classification of animals. Alexander the Great, who was a pupil of Aristotle, sent exotic specimens to his teacher from many parts of the world.

In *Nicomachean Ethics,* Aristotle searches for the meaning of human happiness. He calls virtue the mean, or middle way, between the two extremes of excess and defect, both of which are bad. For instance, courage is the mean between rashness and cowardice. Aristotle's *Politics* has exerted enormous influence on political science. His *Poetics* is the first work of pure literary criticism to come down to us. *Rhetoric* shows how to become an effective orator.

Oratory

The art of writing and delivering speeches was developed in Greece during the 400's. In Athens everybody had to be his own lawyer, but not everybody knew how to write a good speech. So orators, who were really ghost-writers, were employed. The best-known orator of the early period is Lysias (450?–380? B.C.).

In the 300's the trend was toward political oratory. Isocrates (436–338 B.C.) pleaded for Greek unity against Persia in *Panegyricus*. Demosthenes (384–322 B.C.), the greatest of all Greek orators, tried to unite Greece to resist Philip II of Macedon, the father of Alexander the Great. In *On the Crown*, Demosthenes surveys his political life. It is a defense of his policy, against charges made by his chief opponent, Aeschines.

Hellenistic Period

The Hellenistic period covers the years 323–146 B.C. It was the time when Greece and Egypt and Asia Minor were ruled by fighting kings, who carved up Alexander the Great's empire. Athens and the other Greek cities now lost their energy, but Greek culture spread outside Greece and helped to produce new kinds of literature.

Alexandria in Egypt became the center of Greek literature. Callimachus, a librarian there, said that a big book was a big evil. So most writers, including Callimachus himself, wrote short pieces of poetry. Among longer works was the epic poem *Argonautica,* by Apollonius of Rhodes. It tells about Jason's search for the Golden Fleece and about Medea's love for the hero.

The most original poet was Theocritus, who lived during the 200's B.C. He was the first Greek to write pastoral poetry, in which shepherds sing about their feelings. Theocritus called these poems *Idylls*.

Herodas wrote little dramatic character sketches. Theophrastus wrote similar works, but in prose, called *Characters*. In these he describes typical people, such as the stupid or the tactless.

Greco-Roman Period

Some writers from the Greco-Roman period, starting in 146 B.C., deserve mention. Polybius (205?–125? B.C.), a Greek prisoner of war in Rome, learned to admire the Romans and explained their history and government. Josephus (37?–100?) was Jewish, and translated his *History of the Jewish War* from Hebrew into Greek. Strabo (63? B.C.–A.D. 24?) was a geographer. Pausanias, who lived during the 100's A.D., was a traveler. His *Tour of Greece* provides a wealth of information about the customs and art of the Greeks of his time.

Better known to most readers today is Plutarch (46?–120?). In *Parallel Lives* he contrasts famous Greeks and Romans. Shakespeare borrowed much from him. The Roman emperor Marcus Aurelius (121–180) tells his inmost feelings in *Meditations* (or *To Himself*). Lucian wrote fiction and was very witty. Satire appears in all his works, including *Dialogues of the Dead* and *True History,* in which some people make a trip to the moon.

URSULA SCHOENHEIM
Queens College
Reviewed by GILBERT HIGHET
Formerly, Columbia University

GREEK MYTHOLOGY

"Greek mythology" refers to the myths and hero legends of the ancient Greeks. Myths are stories about gods or other supernatural beings. They usually explain the origins of the world or how human customs came to be. Myths are typically set in the distant past, during the early history of the world, before or soon after the first appearance of human beings. Hero legends are stories about remarkable human beings. They are set in the recent past, after the familiar world has been formed, and recount the lives and adventures of remarkable men and women.

Greek mythology contains much of what the ancient Greeks accepted about the early history of the world and early human life. Although individual Greeks did not believe every detail of every story, nearly everyone thought that the myths and legends were mainly true.

The civilization that eventually would be called Greece had its origins some 4,000 years ago, about 2000 B.C. At this time there was a movement of people into the Greek peninsula. They brought many of their own myths and legends with them, but later they also became acquainted with the mythologies of peoples of neighboring regions, including Crete, Egypt, and Phoenicia. All these ancient peoples borrowed myths and legends from one another, adding them to their own mythologies and substituting the names of their own gods for the names of foreign gods.

▶ SOURCES

For many years, Greek mythology was passed along orally, from one generation to the next, through storytelling, song, and the recitation of poetry. But most of our knowledge about the myths comes from later written versions. Among the best sources are **epics**, long narrative poems recounting the great deeds of heroes. Two well-known epics are the *Iliad* and the *Odyssey*, by the Greek poet Homer. The *Iliad* focuses on the hero Achilles, the foremost hero of the Trojan War, while the *Odyssey* tells of the adventures of the hero Odysseus (Ulysses). Other good sources are Hesiod's *Theogony*, which describes the origins of the world and the gods; the *Homeric Hymns*, a collection of poems addressed to different gods; Apollodoros' *Library*, an ancient hand-

Clockwise from bottom left: Poseidon, Hestia, Demeter, Ares, Hephaestus, Apollo, Dionysus, Aphrodite, Artemis, Hermes, Hera, Zeus, Athena.

book of mythology; and the Greek tragedies, which concern famous heroes and heroines.

We can also learn about Greek mythology from the literature of the ancient Romans, who borrowed much from the Greeks. Two important works are Vergil's *Aeneid*, an epic poem about the Trojan hero Aeneas, and Ovid's *Metamorphoses*, a collection of mythological stories about people and animals who change into something else.

Because the Romans adopted so much Greek mythology, the myths and legends of the Greeks

and Romans are often considered together, as **classical mythology**. The most important sources of classical mythology date from about 750 B.C. until about A.D. 200, but in most cases the myths themselves are much older than the written works in which they appear.

▶ **THE ORIGINS OF THE UNIVERSE**

According to a Greek myth about the origins of the universe (**cosmos**), Chaos, a huge space, came into being first. It was followed by Earth, Tartarus, and Love. Tartarus was a great prison for gods and other immortal beings, who could not be killed; it was located far beneath the earth.

Thus the universe began with an immense space for everything to fit in (Chaos), a world for gods and humans (Earth), an underworld for defeated immortals (Tartarus), and a force of attraction (Love) that caused living beings to be drawn together and to mate with one another, producing nearly everything in the world. In this myth, most elements in the cosmos are living beings who belong to a single great family. Nonhuman elements are treated as though they have human qualities. Scholars refer to this practice as **anthropomorphism**.

Succession Myth

One myth about the beginnings of the world is called the succession myth, because it tells how the universe was ruled by a succession, or series, of kings.

According to this myth, among the beings who mated with each other in the early days of the world were Earth and Sky. The children of mother Earth and father Sky included the gods called **Titans**. Sky became the first ruler of the world, but he was a cruel king and jealous father. He prevented some of his children from being born from their mother. As a result,

Earth plotted against Sky with one of her children, Cronus, who overthrew his father.

Cronus replaced Sky as ruler, and soon he and his mate Rhea had children of their own, gods called **Olympians**. But Cronus proved to be just as bad as his father had been, for whenever Rhea gave birth to a child, Cronus swallowed it alive. He feared that one of his children would overthrow him, just as he had overthrown his own father. Finally, Rhea gave birth to Zeus, whom she concealed. When Zeus grew up, he forced Cronus to vomit up his other children. Then Zeus led the Olympian gods in a great battle against Cronus and the other Titans to decide who would rule the universe. After ten years, the Olympians won and imprisoned the Titans in Tartarus. Then Zeus defeated Typhon, a huge, violent monster with snaky heads, and became the third and final ruler of the cosmos. He nurtured his children and ruled justly.

Atlas

▶ **THE MYTHOLOGICAL WORLD**

In Greek mythology, the earth was shaped like a flat disk and was surrounded by a river named Oceanus. The sky was a great dome, like a roof over the earth. It was held up by one of the Titans, Atlas, who supported it on his shoulders.

The souls of the dead resided in Erebus, a land located beneath the earth or far to the west beyond the place where the sun sets. It was ruled by a king and queen, Hades and Persephone, and was also called the House of Hades, or simply Hades. Hades and Persephone had a watchdog named Cerberus, with three fierce heads; instead of keeping people out of the House of Hades, it kept them in.

The Olympian gods were the main gods in the universe. They were members of a single family headed by Zeus and his wife, Hera. The other Olympians were brothers, sisters, sons, or daughters of Zeus and Hera. The Olympians were named for their dwelling

The Romans had their own names for the Olympian gods described below. These are given in parentheses following the Greek names.

Zeus (Jupiter) was ruler of the cosmos. Zeus's favorite weapon was the thunderbolt, the supreme weapon in the universe. His special bird was the eagle, the king of birds. As god of the sky, Zeus sent rains down upon the earth. He was also the god of justice, because he could look down from the heavens and see everything that people did.

Hera (Juno), queen of the gods, was Zeus's sister and wife. Just as Zeus was the patron of kings on earth, Hera was the patron of queens. She was the goddess of women in the three main stages of life: maiden (unmarried girl), matron (married woman), and widow. In myths she often angrily punished women to whom her husband Zeus was attracted

or the children he fathered by them. Her special bird was the peacock, which drew her chariot through the air.

Athena (Minerva), often called Pallas Athena, was born from the head of Zeus as a fully grown maiden. For women, she was the goddess of female arts, which meant especially weaving, for in ancient times girls and women were in charge of making clothing for the family. For men, she was a goddess of war. In general, Athena was the goddess of wisdom, and her special bird was the owl. She was also the patron of the city of Athens.

Ares (Mars) was a son of Zeus and Hera. A god of war, he loved battle, but sometimes he himself was a coward. In the Trojan War, Ares sided with Troy. He is often depicted carrying a spear.

Hermes (Mercury) was among the cleverest of the gods. When this son of

Zeus was only a baby, he crawled out of his cradle without being noticed and stole cattle belonging to his older brother Apollo. (A clever and deceitful character such as Hermes is called a **trickster** .) Serving as the gods' herald, or messenger, Hermes possessed winged sandals, which enabled him to fly through the air with great speed. He carried a magic wand, which had the power to make one fall asleep.

Poseidon (Neptune), a brother of Zeus, was god of the waters, especially the seas, in which he made his home. He could be recognized by the trident he carried, a three-pronged spear such as fishermen used to spear fish. He was also the god of horses and earthquakes.

Hephaestus (Vulcan), a son of Hera, was a blacksmith whose feet were crippled but whose arms were powerful. As the craftsman of the gods, Hephaestus

place, Mount Olympus, a great mountain range in northern Greece. Often they were thought to live in the sky rather than on a mountain, but their home in the sky was also called Olympus. Descriptions of the 13 Olympian gods are given in the feature below.

In addition to the gods, there were beings called demigods, or half gods, because they were greater than humans but less great than gods. The demigods lived very long lives but were not immortal. They dwelled in the mountains and countryside away from human communities.

Centaurs were part human and part horse. They had the upper body of a man (from head to waist), which was connected to the body and four legs of a horse. **Satyrs**, like centaurs, were a mixture of man and animal. They had the upper body of a man (from head to waist) and the lower body of a horse or goat, but with only two legs. (Although not a demigod, the god Pan was likewise a mix-

Centaur

ture of man and animal in his appearance. Like a satyr, he was goat-legged. Sometimes he was represented as having the horns and beard, or "goatee," of a goat.)

Nymphs were female nature spirits, who had entirely human form. Some nymphs spent their time frolicking with satyrs, while others avoided males. Some followed the goddess Artemis as she roamed the wilds.

▶ **THE ORIGIN OF HUMANS**

One Greek myth says that the god Prometheus created the first man and woman out of earth and water, modeling them after the gods. But according to a different myth, when the Olympian gods created the first human beings, they made only men. At that time the world was a wonderful place to live in, for a man had to work only one day a year for his food, and the gods lived nearby as neighbors.

fashioned wonderful weapons and utensils for the gods. He was the god of human smiths and potters, whose crafts require working with fire.

Aphrodite (Venus), the beautiful goddess of love, had the power to make people become attracted to one another and fall in love. In some accounts she is called a daughter of Zeus, while in others she is said to have sprung from the foam of the sea. Her son **Eros (Cupid)** was a winged, mischievous boy. An arrow from his bow made a human or god fall in love.

Apollo, also called Phoebus Apollo, was the son of Zeus and the goddess Leto (Latona). An archer, Apollo was also god of music, prophecy, and healing. He had a famous **oracle** in Delphi. It was a place where people could ask Apollo questions. A priestess of Apollo answered on behalf of the god.

Artemis (Diana), Apollo's sister, was a huntress who roamed the hills as the leader of a band of maidens called nymphs. She loved living free in the wilds, away from men. The guardian of wild animals, Artemis also protected the young of all creatures.

Dionysus (Bacchus) was son of Zeus and a human mother named Semele. He was god of vines, including grapevines, and so was the patron of wine and drinking. Several myths told how he toured the earth introducing his cult to different human communities. Since his worship involved drinking, dancing, and wild music, some people rejected it, regarding it as a threat to public order. In Athens, an important part of his festival was the presentation of plays in his honor, both tragedies and comedies.

Demeter (Ceres), a sister of Zeus and Hera, was goddess of agriculture. She

once traveled all over the earth teaching humans how to grow crops. Demeter had a daughter **Persephone (Proserpina)**. One day, Hades, god of the dead, suddenly came up from the land of death, seized Persephone, and took her down to his kingdom to be his bride. Demeter was so unhappy at the disappearance of her daughter that she brought agriculture to a halt. All plants stopped growing. Finally, Zeus arranged a compromise between Demeter and Hades. Henceforth Persephone would spend part of the year with her mother among the living and part of it with her husband among the dead.

Hestia (Vesta), another sister of Zeus and Hera, was goddess of the hearth, or fireplace. She represented the security and hospitality of the home but was the subject of few myths and legends. In ancient Rome, the priestesses who served her were called **vestal virgins**.

MYTHOLOGICAL MONSTERS

What makes monsters look monstrous? Nearly all monsters in mythology have certain characteristics in common, such as large size and multiple body parts. Some of the most horrible monsters are those that combine two or more kinds of creatures. Descriptions of several memorable monsters of Greek mythology follow.

The **Chimera** was a fire-breathing monster with the head of a lion, the body of a goat, and the tail of a serpent. It was killed by Bellerophon, the son of Sisyphus of Corinth.

The **Gorgons** were three sisters who had writhing snakes for hair and tusks like those of a boar. Anyone who looked at them was instantly turned to stone. One of the Gorgons, Medusa, was killed by the hero Perseus.

Griffins combined two of nature's fiercest creatures. The front part of a griffin's body was like an eagle's, with wings, a beaked head, and clawed legs, while the hindquarters and tail were those of a lion. Griffins were the guardians of valuable golden treasures.

Harpies were foul, winged creatures with the heads of women and the bodies of vultures. In one myth, three harpies were sent by Zeus to plague Phineus, the king of Thrace, by snatching his food away whenever he tried to eat.

The **Minotaur** was a creature that was half man and half bull. It was imprisoned in the labyrinth at the palace of King Minos of Crete. Many youths and maidens were sacrificed to the Minotaur until it was finally killed by Theseus of Athens.

The **Sphinx**, in Greek mythology, was a winged monster with the head of a woman and the body of a lion. In the legend of Oedipus, the Sphinx stood on a rock outside the gates of Thebes and devoured everyone who failed to solve her riddle. When Oedipus answered it correctly, the Sphinx hurled herself to her death. Oedipus, hailed as a hero, was made king of Thebes. (The riddle of the Sphinx and its answer can be found in JOKES AND RIDDLES in Volume J-K.)

Griffin

Things started to go wrong when men and gods held a meeting to decide how to divide food between them. Prometheus, who always sided with men, tricked the gods into taking the worse portion. In revenge, Zeus made the earth stop producing food on its own, forcing men to work in order to eat. He also hid fire so that men would have no fire with which to cook their food and warm themselves. But Prometheus stole fire back from the Olympian gods. Now Zeus became really angry. First he punished Prometheus by tying him to a mountain, where every day an eagle came and nibbled at his liver. Next he punished mankind by arranging for the creation of Pandora, the first woman. Many miseries came from her. As for the Olympians, they eventually withdrew from earth and made their home in the sky.

The Great Flood

After the behavior of human beings had become terrible, Zeus decided to destroy them by sending a great flood. He made the sky send down endless rain, and Poseidon made the seas rise. Soon the entire earth was covered with water, and most living creatures perished. But one man, Deucalion, and one woman, Pyrrha, survived the flood in a boat. Deucalion and Pyrrha were good and pious persons, unlike other people of their time. Prometheus had secretly warned them of the flood.

As the waters receded, their boat came to land at the top of Mount Parnassus, where they disembarked and prayed to the gods. Deucalion and Pyrrha were unhappy to be the only humans left on earth. The goddess Themis, taking pity on them, told them to throw stones over their shoulders. The stones that Deucalion threw turned magically into men, and those that Pyrrha threw turned into women.

▶ **THE HEROIC AGE**

After the gods withdrew to Olympus, they visited human beings only occasionally. Sometimes they mated with mortal men and women, producing extraordinary offspring: the heroes and heroines of old. Some heroes, however, had mortal parents. Heroes went on difficult quests for unusual objects, faced terrifying monsters, and fought in great wars. Among the greatest Greek heroes were Perseus, Heracles (Hercules), Jason, Theseus, and the heroes of the Trojan War.

Perseus

Acrisius, king of Argos, heard a prophecy that his daughter Danaë would give birth to a son who would someday kill him. Acrisius therefore confined his daughter to an underground room. But Zeus came to Danaë as a shower of gold, and she gave birth to a son, Perseus. When Acrisius discovered Perseus, he placed mother and son in a chest and cast it into the sea. The chest was found by a fisherman from a little island, who cared for Danaë and Perseus. When Perseus grew up, the king of the island, Polydectes, wanted to get rid of Perseus and marry Danaë. So he told Perseus to bring him the head of Medusa, expecting him to die in the attempt.

Medusa was one of three horrible Gorgon sisters who lived in a distant part of the world. Gorgons had snakes for hair and tusks for teeth. Worst of all, if a person merely glanced at a Gorgon, he or she turned to stone, like a statue. With the help of the gods, Perseus located the sleeping Gorgons and, using his shield as a mirror, cut off Medusa's head without looking directly at her.

On his way home, Perseus noticed a beautiful African maiden, Andromeda, who was being sacrificed to a sea monster. He fought the monster, rescuing Andromeda and winning her as his wife. When Perseus returned to evil King Polydectes, he showed him the head of Medusa, so that the king turned to stone. Finally, Perseus went back to Argos to see his grandfather, Acrisius. There he killed the old king in an accident. Thus Acrisius died at the hands of Danaë's son, just as the oracle had predicted.

The Labors of Heracles

Zeus fell in love with a married woman, Alcmene, who was a granddaughter of Perseus and Andromeda. Zeus visited Alcmene in the form of her husband, and she gave birth to a son, Heracles. Even as an infant the hero was brave and strong. Zeus's wife Hera, jealous of Heracles, placed two large snakes in his cradle to kill him, but the baby strangled them with his bare hands.

Heracles' strength was unsurpassed and his courage unmatched. But in a period of madness, he killed his own wife and children. As punishment for this terrible deed, the gods commanded him to perform twelve difficult tasks, or labors, which were set by King Eurystheus of Mycenae.

Perseus rescuing Andromeda

First, Heracles had to kill the **Nemean lion**, a beast whose skin could not be pierced by any weapon. Heracles strangled it and made clothes for himself from the lion's skin. His second labor was to kill the **hydra of Lerna**, a nine-headed water snake. This was particularly difficult because whenever a head was cut off, two would grow back in its place. As Heracles cut off each head, a helper seared the hydra's neck with fire, so that new heads could not emerge.

The third labor was to capture the **stag of Ceryneia**, a deer with golden horns that belonged to Artemis. Heracles chased it for a year before capturing it and handing it over to King Eurystheus. For his fourth labor, the hero had to capture another animal, the dangerous **Erymanthian boar**. His fifth labor was to clean in one day the **Augean stables**, which held thousands of cattle but had not been cleaned in many years. Once again Heracles was able to do the impossible, by changing the direction of two rivers so that they ran through the stalls and left them clean.

Heracles' next task was driving away the **Stymphalian birds**, which were plaguing the people of that land; he frightened them away by making a loud sound with a rattle. For his seventh labor, Heracles captured alive the fierce **bull of Minos**. His eighth labor was to

Myth of Icarus

The following characters figure in some of the best-known Greek myths and legends. Some of their stories provide a moral lesson or mark the triumph of good over evil. Others illustrate the power of love or the error of human failings such as arrogance and greed. All offer the timeless pleasures of a good tale.

Castor and Pollux were twin sons of Zeus and the mortal woman Leda. Their sisters were Helen of Troy and Clytemnestra. The mortal Castor, a skilled horseman, was killed in battle. Pollux, who was immortal, asked to share his immortality with Castor. His wish was granted. Eventually they became two stars, Alpha and Beta, in the constellation Gemini, worshiped as patrons of travelers and athletes.

Daedalus was an architect and inventor. He designed the labyrinth for King Minos that was used to house the Minotaur. Later imprisoned by the king with his son

Icarus, Daedalus made wings of wax and feathers with which father and son escaped. But when Icarus flew too close to the sun, the wax holding his wings together melted, and he fell into the sea and perished.

Damon and Pythias were two noblemen who lived in the ancient city of Syracuse. Pythias was condemned to death but was given permission to leave and settle his affairs if Damon took his place in prison as a pledge against his return. Pythias was delayed and returned just as Damon was to be killed. The king was so impressed with their loyalty to one another that he pardoned Pythias. Today they are remembered as models of devoted friendship.

Daphne was a mountain nymph who was loved by Apollo. When he tried to woo her, Daphne fled and prayed to her father, the river god Peneus, to protect her. He turned her into a laurel tree,

which Apollo took as his symbol. Today, as in ancient times, a wreath of laurel leaves symbolizes victory.

Hero and Leander were a famous pair of lovers. Hero, a priestess of Aphrodite, lived in Sestos. Leander lived in Abydos, on the other side of the Hellespont (the strait of the Dardanelles). Each night, Leander swam across the strait to be with Hero. One stormy night, Hero's guiding torch was extinguished, and Leander was drowned. When Hero found his body, she cast herself into the sea.

Midas was king of Phrygia. In return for a kindness, Dionysus granted Midas' request that all he touched would turn to gold. After a brief period, when his food, drink, and even his daughter were all turned to gold, Midas implored Dionysus to release him from his wish. He was directed to wash his hands in the Pactolus River, and, ever after, the sands of that river were golden.

capture the man-eating **horses of Diomedes**. Heracles killed their monstrous owner, fed him to his own horses, and drove them away.

As his ninth labor, Heracles had to obtain the **belt of Hippolyte**, queen of the Amazons, for Eurystheus' daughter. The tenth labor was to capture the **cattle of Geryon**. Heracles had to fight and kill the three-headed monster Geryon to get them.

The hero's eleventh labor was to obtain the **golden apples of the Hesperides**. Since the apples belonged to the gods, they were later returned to the Hesperides, the nymphs who guarded them. As his twelfth and final labor, Heracles had to descend into the House of Hades and fetch the three-headed dog **Cerberus**. Not surprisingly, Eurystheus hid in fear when he saw this monstrous and terrifying creature.

Jason and the Argonauts

Jason's father ruled Iolkos, but Jason's uncle Pelias drove the king from his throne and took it for himself. When Jason grew up and informed Pelias that he wanted to be king, Pelias told him that he must first show his heroism by going on a quest for the fleece of a golden ram. It hung on a tree in a distant land. Of course, Pelias hoped that Jason would fail and never return.

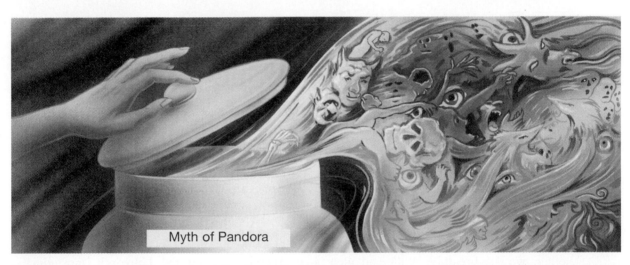

Myth of Pandora

Narcissus was a beautiful youth who scorned all of his many admirers. One maiden prayed that he, too, might suffer as a rejected lover. Nemesis, goddess of just revenge, caused Narcissus to fall in love with his own reflection in a pool. Gazing at his image, he withered away and was transformed into the flower that bears his name. Today the term "narcissism" means excessive self-love. Among those who loved Narcissus was the mountain nymph **Echo**. She helped Zeus distract his wife, Hera, from his love affairs by detaining her with lengthy conversation. In punishment, Hera deprived Echo of normal speech; she could only repeat the last words of each utterance she heard. Spurned by Narcissus, Echo pined away until only the sound of her voice remained.

Orpheus was the son of Apollo and Calliope, the muse of poetry. He was known for his ability to charm wild beasts with the music of his lyre. He was one of the Argonauts who sailed with Jason. When his wife, Eurydice, died of a snakebite, Orpheus played on his lyre and charmed Hades, god of the underworld, into releasing her. The one condition was that Orpheus not look back as they left the underworld. Orpheus did look back—and lost Eurydice forever.

Pandora was the first woman, according to one Greek myth. Zeus, who wished to punish mankind for accepting fire stolen by Prometheus, arranged for Pandora's creation. The gods bestowed on her beauty, charm, and other gifts but also made her deceptive. Pandora opened a large storage jar, releasing all the evil, troubles, and diseases that now plague the world. But she managed to seal the opening in time to save the one good thing the jar held—hope.

Pygmalion was a sculptor who carved an ivory statue of a beautiful maiden, with which he then fell in love. In answer to his request, Aphrodite gave life to the statue, and Pygmalion married her.

Sisyphus, the king of Corinth, was called by Homer the "slyest of all men." Sisyphus incurred the wrath of the gods and was punished in the underworld by having to roll a huge stone uphill eternally. As he neared the top of the hill, the stone always slipped from his grasp, and he had to start again.

Tantalus, a son of Zeus, was king of Lydia. He was punished for serving his son Pelops as food to the gods and for stealing nectar and ambrosia, the food of the gods, to give to his friends. For his crimes, he was condemned to suffer eternal hunger and thirst. He was made to stand in a pool of water up to his chin beneath a fruit-laden tree, unable to partake of either fruit or water. Today the word "tantalize" means to tempt someone with something by keeping it out of his or her reach.

The Trojan Horse

Jason had a shipbuilder construct a marvelous ship, the *Argo*, and he gathered together a large crew of other heroes to sail with him. They were called Argonauts, meaning "Argo sailors." After many adventures, Jason and the Argonauts reached the land whose inhabitants possessed the Golden Fleece. The local king, Aietes, promised to give Jason the fleece if he could yoke together two fire-breathing bulls and plow a field full of snakes. Next, Jason was to sow the field with dragon's teeth, which would immediately grow into an army of warriors that Jason would have to fight. Fortunately, Medea, the king's daughter and also a witch, fell in love with him and helped him complete the tasks by means of her magic. Then Jason and Medea took the Golden Fleece from the sacred grove where it was kept, and they all sailed back to Greece.

Theseus

King Aigeus of Athens had a son, Theseus, who grew up with his mother Aithra in another town. When the boy came to his father in Athens, he found trouble. The Athenians had lost a war to the Cretans and every nine years had to send to King Minos of Crete seven youths and seven maidens to be eaten by the Minotaur, a monster with the head of a bull and the body of a man. The creature lived in the palace at Crete in a maze called the Labyrinth. The year had come when the Athenians had to send victims to the Minotaur, and Theseus courageously volunteered to be one of them. The young people sailed to Crete, where Minos' daughter Ariadne fell in love with Theseus and decided to help him. She gave him a sword and a spool of thread. Theseus entered the Labyrinth, unwinding the thread as he went into the maze. After killing the Minotaur with the sword, he retraced his steps by means of the thread and found his way out again.

The Trojan War

The most beautiful woman in the world was Helen, daughter of Zeus and a mortal woman, Leda. She married Menelaus, the king of Sparta. But the goddess Aphrodite caused Helen to fall in love with the handsome Paris, a son of the Trojan king Priam, and she ran off with him to Troy. Menelaus gathered together a great army and sailed to Troy to demand Helen's return, but the Trojans refused to give her back. Thus began the Trojan War.

Agamemnon. The man chosen to lead the Greeks was Menelaus' brother, Agamemnon. It took him two years to make plans and pre-

pare the great fleet. When the fleet finally set sail, the wind suddenly died. The Greeks prayed in desperation to the gods and learned that, to ensure favorable winds, Agamemnon's daughter Iphigenia had to be sacrificed to Artemis. But just as Iphigenia was about to be killed, Artemis snatched her away and put a deer in her place. Soon a fresh wind filled the sails, and the fleet was able to sail to Troy.

Achilles was the greatest of the Greek heroes who fought at Troy. According to one legend, when Achilles was a baby, his mother dipped him in the river Styx to make his body safe from wounds. Because she held him by one heel, it was not covered by the water. It was therefore the only unprotected part of his body. Achilles was killed in a battle at the gates of Troy when an arrow shot by Paris struck him in the heel. (Today, the term "Achilles' heel" means anything about a person that is weak or open to attack.)

Hector was the bravest and noblest son of King Priam of Troy. Hector did not think it right that so much blood should be spilled over Helen, but he fought loyally to defend his city. It was Achilles who finally killed him.

Odysseus. The king of the island of Ithaca was Odysseus (Ulysses), a very clever ruler who was not eager to fight a war over Helen's unfaithfulness. He was married to Penelope and had a fine son called Telemachus. With the help of the goddess Athena, Odysseus devised the clever plan that finally brought victory to the Greeks after ten years of fighting.

The Greeks built a huge, hollow horse out of wood and left it outside the gates of Troy. Then they pretended to sail back to Greece, as though they had given up. In reality, their best fighters were concealed inside the horse. The Trojans took the horse into Troy, convinced that its presence would protect the city. During the night, the Greeks slipped out of the horse and opened the city gates for their companions, who in the meantime had returned. Once inside Troy, the Greeks destroyed the city and got Helen back.

Odysseus' adventures did not end with the fall of Troy. He had a long and eventful trip back to his faithful wife, Penelope. So many years had passed since Odysseus left for the Trojan War that most people believed he was dead. Other heroes wanted to marry Penelope. Finally she agreed to choose a new husband when she finished the cloth she was weaving. However, she fooled them by undoing at night all the work she had done during the day. So when Odysseus finally returned, he found her still waiting for him. The story of what happened to him on his return voyage is found in Homer's *Odyssey*.

Aeneas. One of the greatest Trojan heroes was Aeneas. After the fall of Troy, he and a few other surviving Trojans sailed to Latium, Italy, where they settled down with the local inhabitants. The ancient Romans believed that they were the descendants of these Trojans and Latins.

The conclusion of the Trojan War marks the end of the Heroic Age. Today we live in an age when important events and the deeds of remarkable men and women are chronicled by historians and journalists more often than by poets and storytellers. Yet the spirit of Greek mythology lives on in many aspects of modern culture.

WILLIAM HANSEN
Classical Studies and Folklore Institute
Indiana University

See also AENEID; ILIAD; MYTHOLOGY; ODYSSEY; TROJAN WAR.

GREELEY, HORACE. See NEW HAMPSHIRE (Famous People).

GREENAWAY, KATE (1846–1901)

Beautiful children dressed in the charming style of the early 1800's, with long flowing dresses, ribbons and bows, pinafores and hats, buttoned trousers and ruffled shirts—these are the boys and girls drawn by the author and illustrator Kate Greenaway.

Catherine Greenaway was born in London, England, on March 17, 1846. Her mother was a shopkeeper, her father a well-known wood engraver. Kate showed a talent for drawing, and at age 12 she began formal art training.

Greenaway began her career designing greeting cards and illustrating the works of other writers. For her first book, *Under the Window* (1878), she wrote verses to accompany a collection of her drawings. It was an immediate success. Later books for which she supplied both text and illustrations include *Language of Flowers* (1884), *Marigold Garden* (1885), and *A—Apple Pie* (1886). She also illustrated *The Queen of the Pirate Isle* (1880), by American author Bret Harte, and *The Pied Piper of Hamelin* (1888), by English poet Robert Browning.

The charm of Greenaway's children caught the fancy of the public. Her style influenced the fashion world of her day, and her illustrations were used on such items as greeting cards, china, buttons, embroidery patterns, dolls, and even wallpaper. Her work was exhibited at the Fine Art Society in London, and she was elected to the Royal Institute of Painters in Watercolors in 1898.

Kate Greenaway died on November 6, 1901. Her quaint illustrations helped change the appearance of children's books, making them more entertaining and enjoyable.

SUSAN RUTH THOMSON
Author, *A Catalogue of the Kate Greenaway Collection, Rare Book Room, Detroit Public Library*

GREENE, GRAHAM (1904–1991)

The English writer Graham Greene was a leading figure of 20th-century literature. The fictional world he created, often referred to as Greeneland, is shabby and dangerous, inhabited by outwardly ordinary characters who struggle with moral and spiritual issues. In addition to his serious novels, Greene also wrote lighter works, such as detective novels and thrillers, which he called entertainments.

Henry Graham Greene was born on October 2, 1904, in Berkhamsted, England, one of six children of the headmaster of Berkhamsted School. Happy at home, young Graham detested school and ran away; as a result, he underwent psychoanalysis in his teens. Greene attended Oxford University, graduating in 1925. The next year he converted to Catholicism and in 1927 married Vivien Dayrell Browning, a Catholic.

Greene had begun writing at the age of 14; at 21 he published a volume of poems. During his 50-year literary career, he produced 24 novels, several volumes of short stories, plays, film scripts, travel writings, two autobiographical works, and much literary and film criticism. Greene's many travels in Europe, Africa, Asia, and South America contributed memorable settings, characters, and plots to his fiction.

Perhaps his most remarkable literary achievement is the sequence of four "Catholic" novels: *Brighton Rock* (1938), *The Power and the Glory* (1940), *The Heart of the Matter* (1948), and *The End of the Affair* (1951). While Greene's theme in these works is nothing less than human salvation or damnation, it is his sensitive and accurate portrayal of human nature that makes the novels memorable. Later books, such as *The Quiet American* (1955), *A Burnt-Out Case* (1961), *The Comedians* (1966), and *The Honorary Consul* (1973), have political rather than religious themes. Greene died in Vevey, Switzerland, on April 3, 1991.

DORIS L. EDER
Freelance Writer

GREENFIELD, ELOISE. See CHILDREN'S LITERATURE (Profiles).

Shrimp boats, shown in the harbor at Christianshaab, fish the waters off Disko Island.

GREENLAND

The huge island of Greenland lies off the northeast coast of Canada. Greenland is a county of Denmark. Yet it is about 2,100 kilometers (1,300 miles) away from Denmark and is more than 50 times as large.

▶ **THE PEOPLE**

Large as it is, Greenland has only about 50,000 inhabitants. Most Greenlanders live in the ice-free districts of the southwest coast. A few thousand people live in eastern Greenland, and fewer than a hundred in the north. But several thousand American troops are stationed at the large air base and radar station at Thule in the far northwest.

The Greenlanders are a people of mixed Eskimo and Scandinavian blood. Their language is an Eskimo dialect, but Danish is also taught in the schools. Many Greenlanders belong to the Lutheran Church.

Originally the Greenlanders lived in small scattered outposts and settlements. Each outpost centered around a Royal Greenland Trading Company store and perhaps a church. Today more and more Greenlanders are moving into towns. To be sure, these are small towns, but they provide a variety of goods and services not found in the more isolated places.

Besides stores, churches, and schools, the towns have hospitals, recreation centers, and modern houses.

Many Greenlanders who were born in sod huts and whose families earned their livings by hunting seals today find themselves living in apartments and working in offices or factories. Electric lights have replaced oil lamps for lighting. And in at least one town, five-story "skyscrapers" now rise where a summer encampment of Eskimo tents once stood.

The largest of Greenland's towns is Godthaab, known as *Nuk* ("The Point") in the Eskimo language. Godthaab, the island's administrative center, has about 7,000 inhabitants. It has a newspaper, a radio station, a movie theater, several schools, and the island's largest hospital. Godthaab's houses and buildings are scattered, and there is no orderly layout of streets. But Danish officials are working out plans for all the larger towns of Greenland so that their growth will not be haphazard.

To help in the building of a new Greenland, the young Greenlanders themselves are being educated. The Danes have greatly enlarged and improved the school system. After seven

Above: Greenland's only community playground is at Holsteinsborg, a fishing port on Davis Strait. Below: Pupils in an elementary school at Godthaab.

years in the primary (elementary) school, girls and boys in the towns may go on to secondary school. This lasts from four to six years, depending on the course of study. The six-year course is then followed by three years in the "gymnasium," or high school. Qualified students may continue their studies in a Danish university. In addition to the usual subjects, schools in the northern areas of Greenland also give courses in hunting and the preparation of animal skins.

▶ THE LAND

No one is sure whether Greenland is one island or several. This is because most of Greenland is covered by an ice cap more than 3,000 meters (10,000 feet) thick in some places. Greenland is like a great ice-filled bowl. Its center is being pushed below sea level by the crushing weight of the ice. Around the rim, mountains rise to about 3,700 meters (12,000 feet). The ice cap covers about seven eighths of Greenland's total land area of 2,175,600 square kilometers (840,000 square miles). Most of the ice-free land lies along the coast. The remainder is on offshore islands.

Greenland reaches closer to the North Pole than any other land area in the world. About five sixths of the island lies north of the Arctic Circle. Because of Greenland's high latitude

Below, left: The hospital at Umanak Fjord nestles at the foot of a glacier. Right: Modern five-story apartment buildings at Sukkertoppen.

location, the midnight sun shines continuously in the northern part of the island from early April until early September. During early September the sun slowly disappears below the horizon. The sun does not rise in the most northerly part of Greenland from the middle of October until the end of February. From the end of February until early April the sun rises slowly over the horizon again.

Only the hardiest plants and animals can survive the rigorous tundra climate at the edges of the Greenland ice cap. Winters are bitter cold in Greenland. Summers are short and cool. Grasses, heather, crowberries, low, flowering plants, and clumps of dwarf birch carpet the areas where there are thin patches of soil. Much of the ice-free surface is barren rock, thinly covered by mosses and lichens.

Among the few wild animals able to live in Greenland are lemmings, field mice, white and blue foxes, and wild reindeer. Greenland's coastal waters are rich in fish, and there are numerous seabirds, seals, walruses, and whales. The polar bear, which preys chiefly on fish and seals, is still found in eastern Greenland.

▶ **THE ECONOMY**

Great schools of codfish swarm off the west coast of Greenland, and fishing is now the island's most important industry. Herds of tame reindeer have been imported from Lapland, and flocks of sheep are increasing. Hardy seedlings of spruce and pine have been planted to provide a supply of wood. Greenland is the world's only major source of cryolite, a mineral used in making aluminum. Lead and zinc mines have been producing since 1973. The first oil well was drilled in 1976. Exploration for minerals continues.

▶ **HISTORY**

Archeologists have found relics of early inhabitants in Greenland. About 2000 B.C., tribes of Eskimo hunters began wandering into northern Greenland from the nearby western islands of the Canadian archipelago. These early people probably never traveled beyond the northern ice cap into the ice-free areas of western and eastern Greenland. They lived mainly on musk oxen and reindeer.

A second wave of hunting people came to northern Greenland about 1000 B.C. Although

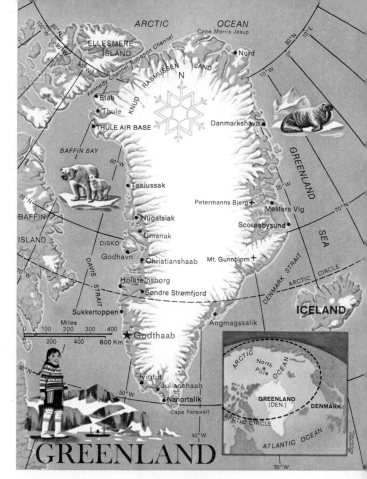

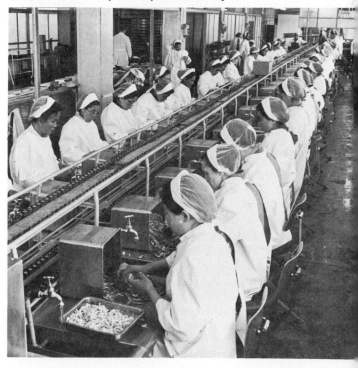

In this shrimp-packing plant at Christianshaab about 1,500,000 tins of shrimp can be processed each year.

Godthaab, on the southwestern coast, is the capital and largest town of Greenland.

they hunted the walrus and the seal, they did not get beyond the northern part of the island, either.

About the same time, however, a third group of Eskimo slowly spread south along the west coast of Greenland and then north again along the east coast. These people also hunted but depended more on fishing.

The last prehistoric people to reach the island arrived about the time of the birth of Christ. They were chiefly hunters of walrus and seal. During the winter they lived in snow houses, or igloos. They resembled the Indians of the Canadian mainland more than they did the Eskimo of the far north.

In the year A.D. 982 an Icelander named Eric Thorvaldsson came to southwestern Greenland. This rugged man, better known as Eric the Red, had been exiled from Iceland for three years for killing a man. Eric spent his exile exploring the western land described by Icelandic sailors. Three years later he returned to Iceland and told the people

about his explorations. He named the island Greenland to attract settlers.

In the summer of 985 or 986, 25 boatloads of people with all their livestock and possessions left Iceland for the new land. Storms battered and scattered the little fleet. At last 14 ships reached the southwestern·coast of the island. The people settled chiefly in two areas. One was near present-day Julianehaab, which they called the Eastern District. The other was near present-day Godthaab, which they called the Western District. From this small beginning the Icelandic settlement of Greenland grew. At its peak the settlement probably numbered between 3,000 and 4,000 people.

When the Icelanders arrived in Greenland, the climate was much milder than it is today. They were able to raise livestock and grow crops just as they had done in Iceland. But after the year 1200, the climate grew colder. The Icelanders' crops failed to ripen. Their herds of livestock began to die. At the same time a new wave of Eskimo hunters reached northwestern Greenland and started moving southward along the coast. In 1261, after nearly three centuries of independence, the Greenland settlers swore their allegiance to the king of Norway in return for his promise to send them supplies each year. About the same time, much to the surprise of both groups, the Icelanders and the Eskimo each discovered that they were not the only people living in Greenland.

As the climate became steadily colder, Eskimo hunters started moving into the Western District. By about 1350 all farming in that area was given up. All the Icelandic settlers either had been killed or absorbed by the people from the north. Within 30 years the Eskimo were attacking the Eastern District. Shortly after 1400 almost all traces of the Icelandic farming settlement and its people disappeared from the pages of history. In the meantime the royal family of Norway had died out. All possessions of the Norwegian king, including Greenland, became colonies of Denmark.

In the centuries that followed, expeditions from many countries moved along Greenland's coasts, searching for the Northwest Passage and hunting for whales. In 1776 the Danish king established the Royal Greenland Trading Company to carry on trade with the island.

Icebergs loom behind Greenlanders paddling kayaks.

Commercial planes now stop at Greenland air bases.

Greenland's contact with Denmark was interrupted during the Napoleonic Wars in Europe (1796–1815). And there were many epidemics. In spite of this, trade and population grew. The Danish government tried to keep outsiders from upsetting the Greenlanders' way of life. More attention was paid to Greenland as scientific expeditions crossed its ice cap and charted its coasts.

The importance of Greenland on major world air routes was proved in 1924 when two planes from the United States landed there on the first around-the-world flight. In World War II, Denmark was occupied by the Germans. But the Danish ambassador in Washington gave the United States permission to build air bases in Greenland to protect ships crossing the North Atlantic. After the war, as a member of NATO (North Atlantic Treaty Organization), Denmark has allowed the United States to maintain and expand some of these bases. Greenland is now a stop on some commercial air routes.

The early 1970's were marked by increasing resentment of Danish influence in the economy and education. In 1978 the Danish parliament voted to offer Greenland a system of home rule, with its own separate parliament and executive. The first elections under home rule were held in 1979.

VINCENT H. MALMSTROM
Dartmouth College
Reviewed by C. H. W. HASSELRIIS
Danish Information Office, New York

GREENSBORO. See NORTH CAROLINA (Cities).

GREENWICH OBSERVATORY

The Royal Greenwich Observatory was originally located in Greenwich, England, a suburb of London. King Charles II ordered the establishment of the observatory in 1675. Under the original orders of the King, the observatory was founded for the purpose of studying the heavenly bodies to help in navigation. Later Greenwich became famous when it was selected as the location of an imaginary line called the zero, or prime, meridian. France and Spain wanted their capital cities named as the site of the prime meridian. But Greenwich was finally accepted by all countries.

The prime meridian is the beginning point for the measurement of longitude. By using this imaginary line, we can find the east-west location for any place on the globe. The 180th meridian is a continuation of the prime meridian on the opposite side of the globe. Together they divide the world into eastern and western hemispheres.

During its long history the Royal Observatory had added to its activities. Several telescopes—including a large 2.5-meter (98-inch) telescope and a number of smaller ones—are used to study and photograph the stars and other heavenly bodies. Photographs of sunspots are taken whenever the weather permits and are kept on file for further study.

The prime meridian, sometimes called the Greenwich meridian, also serves as a basis for setting standard time. Every day the correct time is flashed around the world from the Greenwich Observatory. Ships use this information to find their east-west position. In addition, the observatory broadcasts important events and weather information to ships at sea.

After World War II the Royal Greenwich Observatory was moved not far from London to Herstmonceux Castle in Sussex, where the atmosphere was clearer. However, the original observatory still maintains its position on the prime meridian.

JAMES MATTHAI
Murray State University (Kentucky)

GREETING CARDS

Sending greeting cards is a popular custom in every English-speaking country in the world, and the custom is growing in a number of European, Asian, and South American countries. Nowhere, however, are as many greeting cards exchanged as in the United States.

The cards are usually illustrated messages that express—either seriously or humorously—friendship, love, goodwill, gratitude, sympathy, and other sentiments. They are most often sent by mail to observe a special day or event.

Generally, greeting cards can be divided into two types: "seasonal" and "everyday" cards. Seasonal cards are sent at Christmas, New Year's Day, Valentine's Day, Saint Patrick's Day, Easter, Mother's Day and Father's Day, Halloween, Thanksgiving, and holy days of many faiths.

Everyday cards include birthday greetings; "get well" wishes; anniversary, graduation, wedding, and birth congratulations; birth announcements; "thank you" cards; sympathy and condolence cards; and "bon voyage" cards for people taking trips.

In the United States there are several hundred greeting card publishers, and they produce billions of cards a year. Christmas cards make up about half of the total. Of the remainder—other seasonal cards and cards for everyday occasions—birthday cards are among the most popular.

Most greeting cards are made of paper or cardboard. Others are made of cloth, leather, plastic, and even cork. The size of a card is usually limited to that of an average letter enclosed in an envelope. Among the famous exceptions were an inscribed grain of rice presented in 1929 as a Christmas card to Britain's Prince of Wales, and a Christmas card to President Calvin Coolidge in 1924 that measured 53 by 84 centimeters (21 by 33 inches). The imprinted messages on cards vary in length from a brief word or two to 100 words in verse or prose.

HISTORY OF GREETING CARDS

The custom of sending greeting cards may be traced back 4,000 years. In Egypt the New Year was celebrated by exchanging symbolic good-luck presents such as scarabs, which were precious gems in the form of beetles. A few of the stones were inscribed with the words *oudja ib k,* which means "all good luck."

Romans exchanged seasonal symbols of goodwill or good health. These included dried fruits and honey and sometimes figures made of baked clay that carried the Latin message: *Anno novo faustum felix tibi sit,* which means "May the New Year be happy and lucky for you." These new-year greetings and messages of goodwill spread through Europe in the early days of Christianity. A 15th-century wood engraving shows the Christ Child holding a scroll that reads, in German, "A good and happy New Year."

EARLY VALENTINES

The valentine is also considered a forerunner of the greeting card. Its history is traced to the early days in Rome, where the Lupercalia was celebrated on the 15th of February. It became the custom for boys to draw the names of girls from a huge urn or vase. Each young man then became a girl's partner during the festival.

In order to give the pagan custom a Christian meaning, the Church transferred the celebration to February 14, the day on which a priest named Valentine had been martyred.

The first paper valentines probably date from the 16th century. These early ones contained love poems and illustrations of Cupid, the god of love, with his bow and arrows. Valentines became especially popular and very flowery in the middle of the 19th century, when penny postage and envelopes were introduced to the public.

CHRISTMAS CARDS

The very first Christmas card was of that same period. It was designed for Sir Henry Cole by John Calcott Horsley (1817–1903), a noted London artist. The card was divided into three panels. The center panel shows a family at Christmas dinner. The smaller panels on either side show people practicing the Christian virtues of feeding the hungry and clothing the needy. Across the bottom of the card was printed what is now the very familiar greeting: "A Merry Christmas and a Happy New Year to You."

Great quantities of greeting cards first began to be published in 1880. They were mostly valentines and rather plain-looking Christmas cards with holly or mistletoe around the edges. Then lace-paper cards, which were really valentines, were used for Christmas, New Year's, and even birthdays, with the same designs but different messages printed on them.

Louis Prang of Boston is called the father of the American greeting card. He was a refugee from Germany who opened the first shop to print advertising cards and announcements. He designed and sold his first colored Christmas card in 1874. His cards became popular in the United States and in England.

MODERN TIMES

From about 1900 until World War I, the greeting-card business declined due to the popularity of penny postcards. But the separation of families during the war brought a great demand for more personal greetings. The custom of exchanging cards has been growing ever since.

In 1945 humorous greeting cards were introduced. The messages are short and sometimes funny, and the illustrations usually show comical-looking people. These cards represent an important development in the greeting card business, for they have become increasingly popular.

The use of quotations from the writings of

First Christmas card was made by John Horsley in 1843.

GREETING CARDS ARE FUN TO MAKE

The greeting card you make yourself always means a great deal to the person who receives it. You may paint or draw your design or use cutouts from fancy wrapping papers, printed fabrics, or felt. Make your cards of paper that is stiff enough to stand upright when folded. Colored construction paper will do for most cards. For pen drawings use paper that has a smooth, hard surface. Use rubber cement or paper cement for pasting, as it will not wrinkle the paper. Before designing your card check the size of the envelope you will use. The card may be a little smaller, but **never** larger, than the envelope. Cards may be either a single sheet bearing your name and message or a folded sheet with the greeting and your name on the inside page. Here are a few cards that can start you thinking about your own designs:

NEW YEAR CARD
Card of colored paper. Paste paper in contrasting color over front, leaving a large border. Paste circles of fancy gift-wrapping paper into a balloon design. Use a coin—penny or dime—to trace the circles. Draw balloon strings with pen.

CHRISTMAS CARD
Card of folded green construction paper. Paste paper of contrasting color over front, leaving small border. Cut tree triangle from green paper, blotter, or felt. Decorate with sequins and border cut from gold, silver, or white paper in colored ink.

CHRISTMAS CARD
Snowman drawn with white ink on colored paper. Earmuffs cut from paper of contrasting color. Top hat brushed with glue and sprinkled with black or colored glitter.

EASTER CARD
Card of colored paper. Paste white paper over front, leaving border. Draw Easter egg with pen, and paste your picture in center. Paste a few sequins on egg.

MOTHER'S DAY CARD
Card of folded colored paper. Paste lighter shade of same color over front, leaving border. Cut circles of different-colored papers, and arrange with leaves cut from green paper.

BIRTHDAY CARD
Cut petal, stem, and leaf shapes from white and green felt or blotting paper. Paste on bright-colored construction paper to make some pretty birthday daisies for someone you love.

famous authors and full-color reproductions of the paintings of great artists is becoming very popular on greeting cards, especially Christmas cards. The more traditional cards still lead in popularity, however, and serious messages outsell the funny ones.

The United States is producing an ever increasing number of greeting cards in all languages. These cards are sold both in the United States and abroad.

JEANNETTE LEE
Hallmark Cards, Inc.

GREGORY VII, POPE (1020?–1085)

Hildebrand, one of the greatest of the popes, was born between 1020 and 1025 in Tuscany, in central Italy. He was educated in Rome, where he became a monk and attracted the attention of John Gratian. When Gratian became Pope Gregory VI in 1045, he brought Hildebrand into the papal household.

Rome was then in such a state of lawlessness that the new pope was exiled in 1046. Hildebrand accompanied him to Germany. Gregory VI died in 1047. In 1049 Hildebrand returned to Rome with the newly elected Pope Leo IX. He was made a cardinal and placed in charge of the Patrimony of St. Peter. He became the strong man in the papal government under the five popes who preceded him. On April 22, 1073, he was elected pope and took the name Gregory VII.

The 11th century was a stormy one for the church, mainly because of the interference of political leaders in the appointment of the higher clergy. This interference was motivated largely by a desire to control the property of the church. It led to many unfortunate and even scandalous appointments. These in turn affected the lower clergy, the religious orders, and the religious life of the people. Reform was impossible until the church could reassert its independence, curb interference by the nobles, and improve the moral character of the bishops and clergy. Gregory VII had the strength of character needed to push such a program against apparently overwhelming odds. He was the first pope elected under the law restricting the voting to the cardinals. And he was the last whose election was ratified by the Holy Roman Emperor.

The most famous episode in his life took place in 1077, at Canossa. There the Holy Roman Emperor, Henry IV (1050–1106), did public penance for having appointed high churchmen without papal approval. But Henry soon renewed his quarrel with the Pope. Gregory was driven from Rome and died in exile in Salerno on May 25, 1085. His cause triumphed after his death.

Gregory VII was canonized in 1728. His feast is celebrated on May 25th.

Msgr. Florence D. Cohalan
Cathedral College

GREGORY XIII, POPE (1502–1585)

Ugo Buoncompagni was born in Bologna, Italy, on January 2, 1502. He was the son of a prosperous merchant. After studying law at the University of Bologna, Buoncompagni taught law there for many years and became known as a fine scholar. In 1539 he went to Rome, where Pope Paul III employed him in legal work for the church. He twice attended the Council of Trent, as legal advisor to the papal legates (representatives) and as deputy of Pope Pius IV. He also served on brief diplomatic missions to Brussels, Paris, and Madrid.

Buoncompagni became a priest in 1558. That same year he was made bishop of Vieste. In 1564 he was created cardinal by Pope Pius IV. On May 13, 1572, Buoncompagni was elected pope and took the name Gregory XIII. His election, which took only one day, was popular in Rome.

Gregory XIII was a tireless worker. He was a good judge of men, a capable organizer, and was devoted to the interests of the church. His chief task was to enforce the reform decrees of the Council of Trent. He began at the top by selecting new cardinals and bishops with extreme care. He founded seminaries in many parts of the world. In Rome he built the vast Roman College and the Quirinal Palace. Gregory was a generous patron of the foreign missions, especially in the Far East. He encouraged the work of the Jesuits everywhere and helped Saint Charles Borromeo, Saint Teresa of Avila, and Saint Philip Neri.

Gregory corrected the Julian calendar and introduced our modern calendar, which bears his name, in 1582.

As a temporal ruler Gregory was less successful because he was too busy to concentrate on the Papal States.

Gregory died on April 10, 1585. He is buried in St. Peter's Basilica.

Msgr. Florence D. Cohalan
Cathedral College

GRENADA

Grenada is a small island nation located in the Caribbean Sea, off the northern coast of South America. A former British colony, Grenada gained its independence in 1974. The country's green, yellow, and red flag shows a nutmeg. It is an appropriate symbol, for the fragrant nutmeg is the country's single most important product and Grenada was long known as "the isle of spice."

▶THE PEOPLE

Little trace remains of the original inhabitants of Grenada, Arawak, and Carib Indians. Today most Grenadians are descendants of African slaves, brought to Grenada between the 17th and 19th centuries to work on sugar plantations. There are also a few Grenadians of Asian and European background. The official language is English. A French dialect, handed down by early French settlers, is spoken in some villages but is dying out. Over half the people are Roman Catholic. Most of the others are Protestant. About one third of the population lives in the area around the town of St. George's.

▶THE LAND

The most southerly of the Windward Islands, Grenada lies on the eastern rim of the Caribbean Sea. The country is made up of the main island of Grenada and a number of smaller islands of the Grenadine chain, including Carriacou. Grenada has a striking landscape. On Grenada island a central ridge of green mountains rises to the peak of Mount St. Catherine—838 meters (2,749 feet) above sea level. High in the hills, in the crater of an extinct volcano, lies Grand Etang Lake. Sparkling streams, tall palm trees, and vividly colored flowers add to the beauty of the land.

Grenada has a pleasant tropical climate, with an average year-round temperature of 27°C (80°F). There are two seasons—wet and dry. The rains during the wet season seldom last more than an hour or two a day.

Grenada's capital and largest town is St. George's on the island of Grenada. It has a magnificent, natural, deep harbor and a sheltered inner lagoon. Houses with red tile roofs are nestled into the hills around the harbor.

▶THE ECONOMY

Grenada's economy is based largely on agriculture. A variety of vegetables are grown for food. But spices, particularly nutmeg and mace (which comes from the nutmeg); cacao (used in making cocoa and chocolate); and bananas are the most important exports. Since

St. George's—the capital, largest town, and chief port of Grenada—was founded by the French in 1650. The town is built on hills surrounding a deep, natural harbor, which is considered to be one of the most beautiful in the Caribbean.

the price of these crops rise and fall on world markets, the country's economy is subject to sudden changes.

Tourism once ranked second in economic importance. The islands' white beaches and transparent blue waters attracted many visitors. But tourism dropped sharply because of political unrest in the early 1980's.

▶ HISTORY AND GOVERNMENT

Christopher Columbus visited Grenada on his third voyage to America in 1498. In 1609, English planters attempted to establish a colony but were driven off by the Carib Indians. The French later succeeded in establishing a settlement by killing off most of the Caribs. The islands changed hands several times until 1763, when France ceded Grenada to Great Britain. African slaves were brought to the islands to cultivate sugar, cotton, and tobacco. The slaves were freed in the 1830's. Around 1843, nutmeg trees were brought to Grenada to replace crops that had become unprofitable. The nutmegs thrived and became the basis of Grenada's spice industry.

Grenadians gradually gained control over their own government. In 1967, Grenada was granted internal self-government. Grenada won independence in 1974 and established a government based on the British model. The British monarch, represented by a governor-general, is head of state. The legislature consists of an appointed Senate and a House of Representatives whose members are elected.

The leader of the majority party in the House of Representatives becomes prime minister.

Grenada's first prime minister, Eric Gairy, accused by some Grenadians of being a dictator, was overthrown in 1979 in a military coup. The legislature was dissolved, and a new, leftist government was established under Maurice Bishop, who developed close ties with the Soviet Union, Cuba, and other Communist countries. Bishop was killed in another coup in 1983, led by more radical leftists. The U.S. Government announced its belief that Cuba was planning to set up a military base on Grenada, and that American students there were in danger. Soon after the coup, U.S. troops and forces from several Caribbean nations landed in Grenada. After some fighting they took control of the island. U.S. combat forces were withdrawn at the end of 1983, and the last troops left the island in 1985.

New elections, held in 1984, resulted in a victory for the middle-of-the-road New National Party (NNP), led by Herbert A. Blaize. Blaize served as Grenada's prime minister until 1989, dying later that year. In 1990 elections the NNP won the largest number of seats in the parliament, but failed to gain a majority.

Reviewed by THOMAS G. MATHEWS
Author, *Politics and Economics
of the Caribbean*

GRENADINES. See ST. VINCENT AND THE GRENADINES.

FACTS AND FIGURES

GRENADA is the official name of the country.

THE PEOPLE are known as Grenadians.

LOCATION: Caribbean Sea.

AREA: 133 sq mi (344 km^2).

POPULATION: 100,000 (estimate).

CAPITAL AND LARGEST CITY: St. George's.

MAJOR LANGUAGE: English (official).

MAJOR RELIGION: Christian (Roman Catholic, Protestant).

GOVERNMENT: Constitutional monarchy. **Head of state**— British monarch, represented by a governor-general. **Head of government**—prime minister. **Legislature**— parliament (composed of a Senate and a House of Representatives).

CHIEF PRODUCTS: Agricultural—nutmeg, mace, cacao, bananas, various vegetables for local consumption.

MONETARY UNIT: East Caribbean dollar (1 EC dollar = 100 cents).

NATIONAL ANTHEM: "Hail, Grenada, land of ours."

GRIEG, EDVARD (1843–1907)

Edvard Hagerup Grieg, Norway's most famous composer, was born June 15, 1843, in Bergen, Norway. His mother, a talented amateur musician, gave Edvard his first piano lessons when he was 6 years old. At 9 he was already composing little pieces of his own. Ole Bull, a famous violinist, heard Edvard play some of his compositions on the piano and persuaded the boy's parents to send him to the music conservatory in Leipzig, Germany. Edvard studied there from 1858 to 1862 and graduated with honors. During this time, he suffered from a lung illness that injured his health for the rest of his life.

In 1863, Grieg went to Copenhagen, where he studied with Niels Gade, Denmark's foremost composer. On his return to Norway in 1866, Grieg became friendly with a group of patriotic young musicians and artists. In their works they tried to express their love for their beautiful native land and its people. Grieg was caught up in their enthusiasm. He came to love the old Norwegian folk tunes and peasant dance music and to use them—and similar tunes that he made up—in his compositions.

In 1867, Grieg opened the Norwegian Academy of Music, which featured concerts of his country's music. That same year, he married his cousin Nina Hagerup, who was a fine singer. Grieg often accompanied her at the piano in songs he had written especially for her.

The first performance of Grieg's well-known Piano Concerto in A minor took place on April 3, 1869, in Copenhagen. The composer himself played the solo piano part. Grieg's music became so popular in Norway that the government gave him enough money to allow him more composing time. Grieg made several concert tours through Europe and met many of the best-known musicians of his time.

In 1874, Henrik Ibsen, Norway's greatest dramatist, asked Grieg to write music for his play *Peer Gynt*. Today the two orchestral suites arranged from the music for *Peer Gynt* are among Grieg's most frequently performed works. His *Lyric Pieces* for piano and many of his songs are still very popular, too.

Grieg went on composing during his later years, when he lived quietly at his home near Bergen. When he died of a heart ailment on September 4, 1907, in Bergen, all of Norway mourned his death.

Reviewed by SYLVAN SUSKIN
Oberlin College Conservatory of Music

GRIFFITH, D. W.   See MOTION PICTURES (Profiles: Directors).

GRIMM, JACOB (1785–1863) and WILHELM (1786–1859)

The Grimm brothers were German scholars who became known for their collection of fairy tales. They were born in Hanau, near Frankfurt. Jacob was born on January 4, 1785, and Wilhelm on February 24, 1786. They went to school in Kassel and studied law at the University of Marburg. While they were at the university they became interested in studying the German language and in collecting old folktales.

The brothers then worked together in the library at Kassel. They spent their spare time studying language and collecting fairy tales and legends. Jacob made the first scientific study of German grammar. It was also the first study of any language that considered language as something closely linked to the life of the people who speak it.

In 1830 the Grimms moved to the University of Göttingen in the kingdom of Hanover. But in 1837 they were banished from Hanover for signing a protest against the king. They were invited to teach in Berlin and spent their last seven years working on a great German dictionary. Wilhelm died on December 16, 1859, and Jacob on September 20, 1863.

The first volume of the Grimms' fairy tales appeared in 1812, the second in 1815, and the third in 1822. They were collected over a period of about 13 years. The tales were popular because the brothers wrote them down just as they heard them, so that they caught the spirit of the German people. Many were told to them by Frau Viehmännin, a peasant woman who lived near Kassel, and by Wilhelm's wife. Hans Christian Andersen became a friend of the Grimms when he visited Berlin. Some of Andersen's fairy tales follow his biography and the article on fairy tales. Three favorite Grimms' tales follow here.

▶ THE SHOEMAKER AND THE ELVES

There was once a shoemaker who made shoes and made them well. Yet luck was against him for, although he worked hard every day, he became poorer and poorer until he had nothing left but enough leather for one pair of shoes.

That evening he cut out the leather for the last pair of shoes, and then after laying the pieces in a neat row on his workbench, he said his prayers and went peacefully to bed.

"I'll get up early in the morning," he thought. "Then I can finish the shoes and perhaps sell them."

But when he arose the next morning, the pieces of cut leather were nowhere to be seen, and in their stead stood a pair of beautiful shoes, all finished to the last seam, and sewn so neatly, too, that there was not a flaw nor a false stitch in them. The shoemaker was amazed and did not know what to make of it, but he picked up the shoes and set them out for sale. Soon a man came and bought them, and because he was so pleased with their fine workmanship, he paid more than the usual price for them. With this money the shoemaker was able to buy enough leather for two pairs of shoes.

As before, he cut the leather for the next day's sewing, laid it out on his workbench and went to bed. In the morning, there again were the shoes—two pairs this time—all ready to wear. The hammer, the knife, the awl, the wax and twine, the needles and pegs, still lay about on the bench as though someone had been working there, yet no one could be seen. The shoemaker didn't know how such a thing could

happen but he was glad it happened, all the same. Again he was lucky enough to sell the shoes for more than the usual price, and this time he was able to buy enough leather for four pairs of shoes.

Well, so it went on. Night after night he cut out the leather and laid it on his workbench; morning after morning, there stood a row of handsome shoes, ready to sell, ready to wear. And day after day buyers came and paid such a good price for the shoes that the shoemaker was able to buy more and more leather, and sell more and more shoes until at last he was poor no longer and even became a well-to-do man.

Then one evening—it was not long before Christmas—the shoemaker, after laying out the leather for many pairs of shoes, went to his wife and said, "How would it be now, if we stayed awake tonight and watched for a while? I would like to see who it is, or what it can be, that is so good to us."

"Yes," said his wife, "that I would like to know too."

They lit a candle and set it on the table, then hid in a corner behind some clothes which were hanging there. Here they waited until at last, just at midnight, there came two pretty little elves without a stitch of clothing to cover them. Quickly the little creatures sprang upon the workbench and began making shoes. Swiftly and nimbly they worked—piercing and punching and sewing, pegging and pounding away with such skill that the man and his wife could scarcely believe their eyes.

And so the little elves worked on with tiny

flying fingers, and didn't stop for a moment until all the shoes were finished down to the last stitch and peg. Then, in a twinkling, they leaped up and ran away. Next morning the woman said, "Husband, what I was going to say, those little elves have made us so rich—to show our thanks would be no more than right. There they run around, poor little wights, all bare and must surely freeze. Do you know what? I will make them some clothes and knit them each a pair of stockings. You can make them each a pair of little shoes, yes?"

Oh yes, the shoemaker would gladly do that. And so one evening, when everything was ready, they laid out their presents instead of the cut-out leather, then hid once more behind the clothes in the corner and waited to see what the little creatures would do.

At midnight, there came the two little elves, skipping along, ready to sit down and work as usual. They looked, but saw no leather anywhere. They looked again and spied the row of little garments lying on the workbench: two little shirts and jerkins, two pairs of breeches, two peaked hats, four little stockings and four tiny shoes with pointed toes. At first they seemed puzzled, as though wondering what these things were for, but then, when they understood that the clothes were meant for them, they were filled with joy. Quickly they picked up one little garment after another, dressing themselves with lightning speed; and all the time they laughed with delight, and sang:

> Now we are jaunty gentlemen,
> Why should we ever work again?

When they were fully dressed, from peaky hats to pointy toes, they began to skip and run around like wild, so glad and gleeful were they. There seemed to be no end to their capers as they leaped over the chairs, and delved among the shelves and benches, but at last, after spinning round and round like tiny tops, they clasped hands and went dancing out of the door.

They never came back, but the shoemaker and his wife were always lucky after that, and they never forgot the two little elves who had helped them in their time of need.

▶RAPUNZEL

Once upon a time a man and his wife were very unhappy because they had no children. These good people had a little window at the back of their house, which looked into the most lovely garden, full of all manner of beautiful flowers and vegetables; but the garden was surrounded by a high wall, and no one dared to enter it, for it belonged to a witch of great power, who was feared by the whole world. One day the woman stood at the window overlooking the garden and saw there a bed full of the finest rampion. The leaves looked so fresh and green that she longed to eat them. The desire grew day by day, and just because she knew she couldn't possibly get any, she pined away and became pale and wretched. Then her husband grew alarmed and said:

'What ails you, dear wife?'

'Oh,' she answered, 'if I don't get some rampion to eat out of the garden behind the house, I know I shall die.'

The man, who loved her dearly, said to himself, 'Come! Rather than let your wife die you shall fetch her some rampion, no matter the cost.' So at dusk he climbed over the wall into the witch's garden and, hastily gathering a handful of rampion leaves, he returned with them to his wife. She made them into a salad, which tasted so good that her longing for the forbidden food was greater than ever. If she were to know any peace of mind, there was nothing for it but that her husband should climb over the garden wall again and fetch her some more. So at dusk over he went, but when he reached the other side he drew back in terror, for there, standing before him, was the old witch.

'How dare you,' she said, with a wrathful glance, 'climb into my garden and steal my rampion like a common thief? You shall suffer for your foolhardiness.'

'Oh,' he implored, 'pardon my presumption; necessity alone drove me to the deed. My wife saw your rampion from her window and had such a desire for it that she would certainly have died if her wish had not been gratified.'

Then the witch's anger was a little appeased, and she said,

'If it's as you say, you may take as much rampion away with you as you like, but on one condition only—that you give me the child your wife will shortly bring into the world. All shall go well with it and I will look after it like a mother.'

The man in his terror agreed to everything she asked. As soon as the child was born the witch appeared and, having given it the name of Rapunzel, which is the same as rampion, she carried it off with her.

Rapunzel was the most beautiful child under the sun. When she was twelve years old the witch shut her up in a tower, in the middle of a great wood, and the tower had neither stairs nor doors, only high up at the very top a small window. When the old witch wanted to get in she stood underneath and called out:

'Rapunzel, Rapunzel,
Let down your golden hair.'

For Rapunzel had wonderful long hair, and it was as fine as spun gold. Whenever she heard the witch's voice she unloosed her plaits, and let her hair fall down out of the window, and the old witch climbed up by it.

After they had lived like this for a few years, it happened one day that a prince was riding through the wood and passed by the tower. As he drew near it he heard someone singing so sweetly that he stood still spellbound, and listened. It was Rapunzel in her loneliness trying to while away the time by letting her sweet voice ring out into the wood. The prince longed to see the owner of the voice, but he sought in vain for a door in the tower. He rode home, but he was so haunted by the song he had heard

that he returned every day to the wood and listened. One day, when he was standing thus behind a tree, he saw the old witch approach and heard her call out:

'Rapunzel, Rapunzel,
Let down your golden hair.'

Then Rapunzel let down her plaits and the witch climbed up by them.

'So that's the staircase, is it?' said the prince. 'Then I too will climb it and try my luck.'

So on the following day, at dusk, he went to the foot of the tower and cried:

'Rapunzel, Rapunzel,
Let down your golden hair.'

And as soon as she had let it down the prince climbed up.

At first Rapunzel was terribly frightened when a man came in, for she had never seen one before. But the prince spoke to her kindly and told her at once that his heart had been so touched by her singing he felt he should know no peace of mind till he had seen her. Very soon Rapunzel forgot her fear, and when he asked her to marry him she consented at once.

For, she thought, he is young and handsome, and I'll certainly be happier with him than with the old witch. So she put her hand in his and said:

'Yes, I will gladly go with you, only how am I to get down out of the tower? Every time you

come to see me you must bring a skein of silk with you, and I will make a ladder of them, and when it is finished I will climb down by it, and you will take me away on your horse.'

They arranged that, till the ladder was ready, he was to come to her every evening, because the old woman was with her during the day. The old witch, of course, knew nothing of what was going on, till one day Rapunzel, not thinking of what she was about, turned to the witch and said:

'How is it, good mother, that you are so much harder to pull up than the young prince? He is always with me in a moment.'

'Oh, you wicked child,' cried the witch. 'What is this I hear? I thought I had hidden you safely from the whole world and in spite of it you have managed to deceive me.'

In her wrath she seized Rapunzel's beautiful hair, wound it round and round her left hand, and then grasping a pair of scissors in her right, snip snap, off it came, and the beautiful plaits lay on the ground. And, worse than this, she was so hardhearted that she took Rapunzel to a lonely desert place and there left her to live in loneliness and misery.

But on the evening of the day in which she had driven poor Rapunzel away, the witch fastened the plaits on to a hook in the window, and when the prince came and called out:

> 'Rapunzel, Rapunzel,
> Let down your golden hair.'

she let them down, and the prince climbed up as usual. But instead of his beloved Rapunzel he found the old witch, who fixed her evil, glittering eyes on him, and cried mockingly:

'Ah, ah! You thought to find your lady love, but the pretty bird has flown and its song is dumb. The cat caught it and will scratch out your eyes too. Rapunzel is lost to you forever— you will never see her more.'

The prince was beside himself with grief, and in his despair he jumped right down from the tower and, though he escaped with his life, the thorns among which he fell pierced his eyes. Then he wandered, blind and miserable, through the wood, eating nothing but roots and berries and weeping and lamenting the loss of his lovely bride.

So he wandered about for some years, as wretched and unhappy as he could well be, and at last he came to the desert place where Rapunzel was living. Of a sudden he heard a voice which seemed strangely familiar to him. He walked eagerly in the direction of the sound, and when he was quite close, Rapunzel recognized him and fell on his neck and wept. Two of her tears touched his eyes, and in a moment they became quite clear again, and he saw as well as ever he had. Then he led her to his kingdom, where they were received and welcomed with great joy, and they lived happily ever after.

▶HANSEL AND GRETEL

In a little hut near the edge of a deep, deep forest lived a poor woodchopper with his wife and his two children, Hansel and Gretel.

Times were hard. Work was scarce and the price of food was high. Many people were starving, and our poor woodchopper and his little brood fared as badly as all the rest.

One evening after they had gone to bed, the man said to his wife, "I don't know what will become of us. All the potatoes are gone, every head of cabbage is eaten, and there is only enough rye meal left for a few loaves of bread."

"You are right," said his wife, who was not the children's real mother, "and there is nothing for us to do but take Hansel and Gretel into the woods and let them shift for themselves."

She was a hard-hearted woman and did not much care what became of the children. But the father loved them dearly and said, "Wife, what are you saying? I would never have the heart to do such a thing!"

"Oh well then," snapped the stepmother, "if you won't listen to reason, we'll all have to starve." And she nagged and scolded until the poor man, not knowing what else to say, consented to do it. "May heaven keep them from harm," he sighed.

Hunger had kept the children awake that night, and, lying in their trundle-beds on the other side of the room, they had heard every word their parents had said. Gretel began to cry softly but her brother Hansel whispered, "Don't worry, little sister; I'll take care of you."

He waited until the father and mother were sleeping soundly. Then he put on his little jacket, unbarred the back door and slipped out. The moon was shining brightly, and the white pebbles which lay in front of the house glistened like silver coins. Hansel bent down and gathered as many of the shiny pebbles as his pockets would hold. Then he tiptoed back to bed and told Gretel he had thought of a very good plan for the morrow.

At break of day the mother came to wake the children. "Get up, you lazy things," she said, "we're off to the forest to gather wood. Here is a piece of bread for each of you. Don't eat it until noon; it's all you'll get today."

Gretel carried both pieces of bread in her apron because, of course, Hansel's pockets were so full of pebbles. They were soon on their way to the forest: the mother first with a jug of water, the father next with an ax over his shoulder, Gretel with the bread and Hansel bringing up the rear, his pockets bulging with pebbles. But Hansel walked very slowly. Often he would stand still and look back at the house.

"Come, come, Hansel!" said the father. "Why do you lag behind?"

"I'm looking at my little white kitten, papa. She's sitting on the roof and wants to say good-by."

"Fool!" said the mother. "That's not your kitten. That's only the morning sun shining on the chimney."

But Hansel lingered on and dropped the pebbles behind him, one at a time, all along the way.

It was a long walk, and Hansel and Gretel became very tired. At last the mother called a halt and said, "Sit down, children, and rest

yourselves while we go off to gather some wood. If you feel sleepy you can take a little nap."

Hansel and Gretel sat down and munched their bread. They thought their father and mother were nearby, because they seemed to hear the sound of an ax. But what they heard was not an ax at all, only a dry branch which was bumping against a dead tree in the wind.

By and by the two little children became so drowsy they lay down on the moss and dropped off to sleep. When they awoke it was night and they were all alone.

"Oh Hansel, it's so dark! Now we'll never find our way home," said Gretel, and began to cry.

But Hansel said, "Don't cry, little sister. Just wait until the moon is out; I'll find the way home."

The moon did come out, full and round and bright, and it shone on the white pebbles which Hansel had strewn along the way. With the glistening pebbles to guide them, they found their way back easily enough.

Dawn was stealing over the mountains when they reached their home, and with happy faces they burst in at the door. When their mother saw them standing before her, she was taken aback. But then she said, "Why, you naughty children! Where have you been so long? I began to think you didn't want to come back home."

She wasn't much pleased but the father welcomed them joyfully. He had lain awake all night worrying over them.

Luckily, things now took a turn for the better, and for several weeks the woodchopper was able to earn enough money to keep his family from starving. But it did not last, and one evening the children, still awake in their trundle-beds, heard the mother say to the father: "I suppose you know there's only one loaf of bread left in the house, and after that's eaten, there's an end to the song. We must try once more to get rid of the children, and this time we'll take them still deeper into the woods, so our sly Hansel can't find his way back."

As before, the father tried to talk her out of it, but the hard-hearted stepmother wouldn't listen to him. He who says A must also say B, and because the father had given in the first time, he had to give in this time as well.

Hansel saw that he would have to get up and gather pebbles again, and as soon as his parents were asleep, he crept out of bed. But alas! the door was locked now and he had to go back to bed and think of a different plan.

The next day everything happened as it had the first time. Hansel and Gretel were each given a crust of bread and then they all went forth into the forest. Hansel brought up the

rear as before, and kept straggling behind the rest.

"Come, come, Hansel!" said the father. "Why do you lag behind?"

"I see my pet dove, papa. It is sitting on the roof and wants to say good-by to me."

"Fool!" said the mother. "That's not your dove. That's only the morning sun shining on the chimney."

But Hansel kept on loitering because he was again busy making a trail to guide them back home. And what do you think he did this time? He had broken his bread-crust into tiny pieces and now he was carefully scattering the crumbs, one by one, behind him on the path.

They had to walk even farther than before, and again the parents went to gather wood, leaving Hansel and Gretel behind. At noon Gretel shared her bread with Hansel, and then they both fell asleep.

When they awoke, it was dark and they were all alone. This time Gretel did not cry because she knew Hansel had scattered crumbs to show them the way back. When the moon rose, Hansel took her hand and said, "Come, little sister, now it's time to go home."

But alas! when they looked for the crumbs they found none. Little twittering birds which fly about in the woods and glades, had eaten them all, all up.

The two unhappy children walked all that night and the next day too, but the more they looked for the way, the more they lost it. They found nothing to eat but a few sour berries; and at last, weak and hungry, they sank down on a cushion of moss and fell asleep.

It was now the third morning since they had left their home. They started to walk again, but they only got deeper and deeper into the wood.

They felt small and strange in the large, silent forest. The trees were so tall and the shade was so dense. Flowers could not grow in that dim, gloomy place—not even ferns. Only pale waxy mushrooms glowed faintly among the shadows, and weird lichens clung to the treetrunks. Suddenly, into the vast green silence fell a ripple of sound so sweet, so gay, so silvery, that the children looked up in breathless wonder. A little white bird sat there in a tree; and when its beautiful song was ended, it spread its wings and fluttered away with anxious little chirps as though it wished to say, "Follow me! Follow me!"

Hansel and Gretel followed gladly enough, and all at once they found themselves in a fair flowery clearing, at the edge of which stood a tiny cottage.

The children stood hand in hand and gazed at it in wonder. "It's the loveliest house I ever saw," gasped Gretel, "and it looks good enough to eat."

They hurried on, and as they reached the little house, Hansel touched it and cried, "Gretel! It *is* good enough to eat."

And, if you can believe it, that's just what it was. Its walls were made of gingerbread, its roof was made of cake. It was trimmed with cookies and candy, and its window-panes were of pure transparent sugar. Nothing could have suited the children better and they began eating right away, they were so hungry! Hansel plucked a cookie from the roof and took a big bite out of it. Gretel munched big slabs of sugar-pane which she had broken from the window.

Suddenly a honeyed voice came floating from the house. It said:

    Nibble, nibble, nottage
    Who's nibbling at my cottage?

To which the children said mischievously:

    It's only a breeze,
    Blowing down from the trees.

At this, the door burst open, and out slithered a bent old woman, waggling her head and leaning on a knotted stick. Hansel stopped munching his cookie and Gretel stopped crunching her sugar-pane. They were frightened—and no wonder! The Old One was far from beautiful. Her sharp nose bent down to meet her bristly chin. Her face, all folds and wrinkles, looked like an old shriveled pear; and she had only three teeth, two above and one below, all very long and yellow.

When the Old One saw that the children were turning to run away, she said in sugary tones, "Ei, ei! my little darlings, what has brought you here? Come right in and stay with me. I'll take good care of you."

She led them inside, and there in the middle of the room was a table neatly spread with toothsome dainties: milk, pancakes and honey, nuts, apples and pears.

While the children were eating their fill, the Old One made up two little beds which stood at one end of the room. She fluffed up the feather bed and puffed up the pillows, she turned

back the lily-white linen, and then she said: "There, my little rabbits—a downy nest for each of you. Tumble in and slumber sweetly."

As soon as Hansel and Gretel were sound asleep, the Old One walked over and looked at them.

"Mm! Mm! Mm!" she said. "They're mine for certain!"

Now why should she do that? Well, I must tell you the real truth about the Old One. She wasn't as good and friendly as she pretended to be. She was a bad, bad witch who had built that sweet and sugary house on purpose to attract little children. Witches have ruby-red eyes and can hardly see at all, but oh! how they can smell with those long sharp noses of theirs! What they can smell is human beings; and that morning, as Hansel and Gretel were wandering around in the forest, the Old One knew it well enough. Sniff! sniff! sniff! went her nose—she had been sniffing and waiting for them all day.

The next morning while the two little innocents were still sleeping peacefully, the Old One looked greedily at their round arms and rosy cheeks. "Mm! Mm! Mm!" she mumbled. "Juicy morsels!"

She yanked Hansel out of bed, dragged him into the back yard, and locked him up in the goose-coop. Hansel screamed and cried but it did him no good.

Then the Old One went into the house, gave Gretel a rough shake and cried, "Up with you, lazy bones. Make haste and cook some food for your brother. He's out in the goose-coop and if we feed him well, ei! ei! what a tasty boy he'll make!"

When Gretel heard this she burst into tears, but the Old One gave her a cuff on the ears and said, "Stop howling, you fool. Pick up your legs and do as I tell you."

Each day Gretel had to cook big pots full of fattening food for Hansel, and each morning the Old One hobbled out to the goose-coop and cried, "Hansel, let me see your finger so I can tell how fat you're getting."

But Hansel never showed her his finger. He

always poked out a dry old bone, and the Old One, because of her red eyes, never knew the difference. She thought it really was his finger, and wondered why it was that he did not, did not get fat.

When four weeks had passed and Hansel seemed to stay thin, the Old One became impatient and said to Gretel, "Hey there, girl! Heat up a big kettle of water. I'm tired of waiting and, be he fat or lean, I'm going to have Hansel for my supper tonight."

Gretel cried and pleaded with her. But the Old One said, "All that howling won't do you a bit or a whit of good. You might as well spare your breath."

She built a roaring fire in the stove and said to Gretel, "First we'll do some baking. I've mixed and kneaded the dough, and the loaves are all ready for the oven." Then she opened the oven door and added in a sweet voice, "Do you think it's hot enough for the bread, Gretel dear? Just stick your head in the oven and see, there's a good girl!"

Gretel was about to obey, when a bird (the same white bird which had led them out of the forest) began to sing a song. It seemed to Gretel he was singing:

> Beware, beware,
> Don't look in there.

So Gretel didn't look into the oven. Instead she said to the Old One, "Well, I really don't know how to go about it. Couldn't you first show me how?"

"Stupid!" cried the Old One. "It's easy enough. Just stick your head way in and give a good look around. See? Like this!"

As the Old One poked her horrid old head into the oven, Gretel gave her a push and a shove, closed the oven door, bolted it swiftly and ran away. The Old One called and cried, and frizzled and fried, but no one heard. That was the end of her, and who cares?

Gretel was already in the back yard. "Hansel!" she cried. "We are free!" She opened the door of the goose-coop and out popped Hansel. The children threw their arms about each other and hopped and skipped around wildly.

But now there came a soft whirr in the air. The children stopped dancing and looked up. The good white bird and many others—all the twittering birds from the fields and glades— were flying through the air and settling on the cake-roof of the gingerbread house.

On the roof was a nest full of pearls and sparkling gems. Each little forest-bird took out a pearl or a gem and carried it down to the children. Hansel held out his hands, and Gretel held up her apron to catch all these treasures, while the little white bird sat on the roof and sang:

> Thank you for the crumbs of bread,
> Here are gems for you instead.

Now Hansel and Gretel understood that these were the very same birds who had eaten up their crumbs in the forest, and that this was how they wished to show their thanks.

As the birds fluttered away, Hansel said, "And now, little sister, we must make haste and get out of this witchy wood. As for me, I got very homesick sitting in that goose-coop week after week."

"And I," said Gretel. "Yes, I've been homesick too. But, Hansel, here we are so far from home, and how can we ever find our way back?"

Ho, what luck! There was the little white bird fluttering ahead of them once more. It led them away and soon they were in a green meadow. In front of them lay a big, big pond. How to get over it! As Hansel and Gretel stood on the shore wondering what to do, a large swan came floating by, and the children said:

Float, swan, float!
Be our little boat.

The swan dipped its graceful head, raised it

and dipped it again—that meant yes. When the swan had taken the children, one by one, to the other shore, they thanked it prettily and patted its long curved neck. Near the water's edge ran a neat little path. Hansel and Gretel followed it, and now the trees and the fields began to look familiar. Soon they saw their father's house gleaming through the trees and they ran home as fast as they could. The father, who had been grieving and looking for his lost children all this time, was sitting in front of the hearth gazing sadly into the fire. As the door burst open and his two little ones ran in with shouts and laughter, his eyes filled with tears of joy. He hugged them and kissed them, and all he could say was: "My treasures, my little treasures!"

"Oh, as to treasures, papa," said Hansel, putting his hands into his pockets, "we'll show you some! See, now we will never have to starve again." At this, Gretel poured a shower of jewels from her apron, while Hansel added handful after handful from his pockets.

And the hard-hearted stepmother, where was she? Well, I'll tell you. When Hansel and Gretel seemed to be gone for good, the woman saw that her husband could think of nothing but his lost children. This made her so angry that she packed up her things in a large red handkerchief and ran away. She never came back, and Hansel and Gretel and their good father lived happily ever after.

GRINDING AND POLISHING

Grinding is a way of shaping an object by wearing away some of the material of which it is made. There are two chief reasons for grinding something into a desired shape rather than simply cutting or stamping it out. Grinding is the cheapest and fastest way of shaping very hard, tough materials. Grinding wheels are used to cut long bars of steel into shorter lengths. These wheels can cut through a 2-inch-square steel bar in less than 3 seconds. That is much faster than the fastest metal-cutting saw can cut. Grinding is also used when the measurements of a piece must be very exact. The piece is usually first cut or cast, but it is made slightly larger than the finished piece must be. This piece is then ground down to within $\frac{3}{1000}$ of an inch of the exact measurement. Many automobile parts are made in this way.

Rough or uneven surfaces are made smooth by grinding down the high spots of the surface.

A dull surface may seem smooth, but if you look at it under a microscope you can see that it is quite rough. **Polishing**—a very fine kind of grinding—is used to make a dull surface shiny. Both grinding and polishing are done by means of materials called **abrasives**.

▶ **ABRASIVES**

Abrasives are very hard materials that are crushed to form a powder that is used for grinding and polishing. This powder is made up of small bits, or particles, of material having sharp, jagged edges. Usually the abrasive powder is either cemented together to form a solid wheel, or else used to coat a piece of cloth or paper. Sandpaper is an example of a **coated abrasive**. As an abrasive wheel, cloth, or paper is rubbed against an object, the sharp edges of the tiny abrasive pieces act like tiny knives and cut away very small chips of the material. Bit by bit this wears the material away. If you look through a microscope at a surface that has been ground or polished with an abrasive, you will see that it is full of tiny scratches. But to the naked eye the same surface looks bright and shiny. That is because the scratches are so small. The smaller the little bits of abrasive are, the smaller the scratches will be, and the smoother the surface

of the object will be. The larger the particles are, the more material the abrasive will wear away. Larger particles work faster, but leave a rough surface. The particles or grains of some grinding abrasives are as big as barley grains, while particles of fine polishing abrasives can only be seen with a microscope.

Because the effect of the abrasive depends upon the size of the individual grains, the abrasive manufacturer must sort the grains according to size. After crushing the abrasive material, he passes it through screens. First he uses a screen with large holes, then one with holes that are a little smaller, then one still smaller, and so on. An abrasive grain that will pass through a screen having 20 holes per inch, but will not pass through a screen having 24 holes per inch (the next smaller size), is called 20 **grit**. A 20-grit grain is roughly twice the size of the period at the end of this sentence. The higher the grit number, the smaller the size of the grain.

Abrasive Materials

Many different materials are used as abrasives. Many of these materials are found in nature, but the most important ones are manufactured. The most important natural abrasives are diamonds (which are also manufactured), corundum, emery, quartz, flint, and garnet. All these materials are very hard. Except for diamond, they all contain one or both of the very hard materials silica and alumina.

Diamond, a form of carbon, is the hardest material known. Therefore it makes a very good abrasive for cutting very hard materials such as hard steel. Diamonds themselves must be cut and polished by means of diamond abrasives. **Corundum**, though not as hard as diamond, is one of the hardest materials known. It is a form of alumina. Rubies and sapphires are precious forms of corundum. As an abrasive, corundum is especially useful for grinding and polishing glass to make lenses. **Emery** is an impure form of corundum. Because of the impurities, it is not as hard as corundum. One kind of grinding for which emery is used is filing fingernails. An emery board is a kind of nail file made of cardboard covered with emery abrasive. Nail boards are also made with quartz and garnet.

Quartz is a form of silica. Sand and sandstone are usually almost pure quartz. They are

Grinding wheels cut very hard materials, such as this slab of stainless steel.

the forms of quartz that are usually used as abrasives. Ordinary sandpaper used to be made from quartz sand, although most sandpaper now is made with crushed garnet or aluminum oxide. Quartz is not as hard as corundum or emery. **Flint** is a black, impure form of quartz, but it has about the same hardness. **Garnet** contains silica, alumina, and other compounds. Garnet is usually not as

Grinding a steel part of exact measurements. Running water carries away heat and dust produced by grinding.

hard as quartz, though some kinds are harder. Emery, quartz, flint, and garnet are very common abrasives. They are used to make different kinds of sandpapers that are used for many purposes, including sanding wood and removing rust from iron and steel. These abrasives are also used to make many different grinding and polishing tools.

In 1891 an American scientist named Edward Acheson (1856–1931) discovered a new material, which he called **carborundum**. The chemical name for carborundum is silicon carbide. Acheson made it by heating a mixture of clay and powdered coke to a very high temperature by means of electricity. Today carborundum is made by an improvement on Acheson's method. Sand, coke, and sawdust are heated in an electric furnace. Carborundum was the first man-made abrasive, and it is now one of the two most important abrasives.

The other, **aluminum oxide,** or **alumina**, is also man-made. It is chemically the same as the natural abrasive corundum. Like carborundum, aluminum oxide is made in an electric furnace, but from a mixture of bauxite (aluminum ore), coke, and iron.

Carborundum is harder and sharper than aluminum oxide, but it is brittle; that is, its grains break easily. Aluminum oxide is softer but tougher; that is, its grains do not break as easily. Because of this, aluminum oxide is used to grind materials that are hard and tough, such as steel and stainless steel. Carborundum is used for grinding and polishing materials that are brittle and hard, such as glass and plastics. Carborundum is also a common household abrasive. It is used as a block or wheel to sharpen knives, scissors, axes, and other tools.

Most of the abrasive materials used today are made of either carborundum or aluminum oxide. The advantage manufactured abrasives have over natural abrasives is that they are uniform. That is, the person who uses a particular abrasive can always be sure that the abrasive from one shipment will be exactly as hard and as sharp as the abrasive from another shipment. Also, by adding certain other substances an abrasive manufacturer can change the properties of the abrasive to make it more suitable for a particular job.

Abrasive Tools

While there are other forms, the most common forms into which abrasives are made are grinding wheels and sandpaper. For most uses, grinding wheels or sandpaper belts are turned at fast speeds that may be from about ¼ mile to more than 2 miles per minute. Some grinding wheels turn at speeds of 16,000 feet per minute, or about 3 miles a minute. For most grinding and polishing uses, a speed of about 6,000 feet per minute (slightly more than 1 mile a minute) has been found to work best.

Grinding wheels are made in many sizes. Tiny wheels the size of a pinhead are used for grinding and polishing very small machine parts. Great wheels over 5 feet in diameter are used to grind logs into pulp for making paper. Whatever the size, all grinding wheels are made in more or less the same way. The abrasive powder of the proper grit is mixed with a **binder** (the material that will hold the abrasive grains together). The mixture is then put into a mold and compressed. Finally it is baked in a hot oven. Sometimes sawdust is added to the mixture. The sawdust burns away, leaving small holes that help make the wheel cut faster.

Grinding wheels are very good cutting tools not only because they are fast and accurate, but also because they do not need sharpening. They sharpen themselves. As the wheel is used the cutting edges of the abrasive grains become dull. Dull grains cannot cut as easily as sharp ones. As the dull grains are forced against the material being ground, they either break, making new sharp edges, or they are torn off the wheel. Thus dull grains are removed from the wheel, leaving the sharp grains underneath. For this reason it is important that the wheel be made with a binder that is suited to the purpose. If the binder is too weak, the grains will be torn off before they are too dull and the wheel will wear out too soon. If the binder is too strong, the dull grains will not be torn off and the wheel will get dull.

In making coated abrasives, such as sandpaper, a backing such as paper or cloth is covered with glue or other adhesive. Then the abrasive is placed on the adhesive. When the adhesive is partly dry, another coat of adhesive is placed over the abrasive to make sure it will hold to the backing.

Coated abrasives are cut to many sizes for different uses. Small abrasive belts the size of a lady's watchband are used for sharpening the knife blades used for cutting stacks of cloth in clothing factories. Belts up to 7 feet wide are used for grinding and polishing metal sheets used for covering jet airplanes and rockets. Small squares of sandpaper are used for smoothing and finishing furniture and other woodwork.

Other Abrasives

Carborundum, aluminum oxide, and the important natural abrasives are used for many different jobs. They are used for heavy industrial jobs such as cutting and polishing steel. They are also used for very fine, delicate jobs such as grinding and polishing lenses for telescopes and microscopes. Besides these useful hard abrasives, many softer materials are used for special tasks.

Pumice (a volcanic rock) and the mineral feldspar are used in scouring powders and abrasive soaps for cleaning especially dirty hands. Pumice is also used as a metal polish. Steel wool is a very important abrasive that is used for many industrial jobs as well as for finishing furniture, cleaning floors, and scrubbing pots and pans. Abrasives are even used to help polish teeth. A form of the chemical calcium carbonate is used as a gentle abrasive in toothpaste.

WARREN K. SEWARD
The Carborundum Company

See also DIAMONDS.

GUATEMALA

Guatemala is the most populous country in Central America. Its people generally follow three distinct ways of life—modern, colonial, and Indian. In the capital, Guatemala City, people live as they do in other modern cities. In the countryside are the large estates of the wealthy, who live much as wealthy people did in Spanish colonial times. The Indians, who make up the majority of the population, follow their traditional ways of life, as they have for ages past.

▶THE PEOPLE

Guatemala has more Indians than any other Central American country. They are descendants of the ancient Maya, who developed a great civilization in the region. About 40 percent of the people are mestizos, who are of mixed European and Indian ancestry. Mestizos or Indians who follow a modern way of life are called Ladinos. The rest of the population is mainly of Spanish descent. A few blacks live in the city of Puerto Barrios. The official language is Spanish, although numerous Indian languages and dialects are spoken. Most of the people are Roman Catholics.

Indian Way of Life. Many Guatemalan Indians live in small villages in the uplands. Their way of life has not changed much in over 400 years. Many speak or understand Spanish, but so far they have resisted most Spanish customs. The strongest Spanish influence on the Indians is Roman Catholicism. By adding their own ancient rites to the Catholic service, the Indians have made it their own.

Each Indian region has its own dialect and its own customs. In every Indian village in Guatemala, people have their own special way of dressing. A person who knows the Indians can always tell to what group they belong by the color and design of the clothes they wear.

In all Indian villages the most important place is the central plaza. Here, once or twice every week, there is an open market. Indians come from the surrounding countryside to trade with one another. If they are too poor to own pack animals, they come on foot, loaded with their own goods.

In their villages, the Indians live in thatch-roofed adobe (sun-dried brick) houses with earthen floors. They are a hardworking people who spend most of their time trying to grow enough food to feed their families. A basic food is tortillas—flat pancakes made from corn, baked on top of a hot oven. Beans or vegetables are wrapped inside the tortillas. Meat or chicken is eaten on special occasions. Most Indian children begin to work when they are very young.

The most important event in an Indian village is the celebration of its patron saint. On this day the people have a great fiesta, or festival, including a religious procession, dances, games, and a big display of fireworks. Communities compete to see which one can have the finest fiesta. The Indians dress in their best clothes and perform Indian dances to music played on ancient instruments. These include wind instruments like the *chirimía*

FACTS and figures

REPUBLIC OF GUATEMALA (República de Guatemala) is the official name of the country.

LOCATION: Central America.

AREA: 42,042 sq mi (108,889 km²).

POPULATION: 10,300,000 (estimate).

CAPITAL AND LARGEST CITY: Guatemala City.

MAJOR LANGUAGES: Spanish (official), Indian languages.

MAJOR RELIGIOUS GROUP: Christian (Roman Catholic).

GOVERNMENT: Republic. **Head of state and government**—president. **Legislature**—National Congress.

CHIEF PRODUCTS: Agricultural—coffee, sugarcane, bananas, cardamom, corn, beans, rice, livestock. **Manufactured**—processed foods, textiles, pharmaceuticals, chemicals, forestry products. **Mineral**—petroleum, antimony, lead, iron ore, tungsten.

MONETARY UNIT: Quetzal (1 quetzal = 100 centavos).

(clarinet) and the *xul* (flute); drums and rattles; and the marimba, a wooden instrument resembling the xylophone. Guatemalan Indians are fine artisans, and during the fiesta they sell bright handwoven blankets, embroidered cloth, and handmade pottery.

Culture. Guatemalan culture is strongly Indian in character. The ancient Maya built great cities and produced two great books— *Popol-Vuh*, a collection of myths, and *Chílan Bálam*, which described ancient Indian religious beliefs. Mayan carvings can be seen in museums in Guatemala City. The place of the Indian in Guatemalan life has been set forth vividly by such well-known artists as the painter Carlos Mérida, the composer José Castañeda, and the novelist Miguel Ángel Asturias, who was awarded the 1967 Nobel Prize for literature.

The Spanish Tradition. Centuries-old Spanish traditions are proudly maintained by middle-class Ladinos and by wealthy Guatemalans of European descent. They take great pride in their social position and their families. Children are taught to respect and obey their parents. Homes are attractive and comfortable, built, as in colonial times, with thick walls, latticed doors, and wooden balconies.

Education. Primary education is free and compulsory in urban areas for children between the ages of 7 and 14. But in the rural areas, schools are rare. A little more than 55 percent of the adult population is literate, or able to read and write. There are a number of universities for those students who complete their secondary education. The largest, as well as the oldest, is San Carlos University of Guatemala, founded in 1676.

▶**THE LAND**

Guatemala can be divided into four land regions: the Pacific coastal plain, the highlands, the Caribbean lowland, and the Petén.

The **Pacific coastal plain** is hot, humid, and swampy. As in all of Guatemala, the difference in temperature from month to month is small. The rainy season (May to October) is called *invierno* ("winter"). The dry season (November to April) is called *verano* ("summer"). The natural vegetation of the coastal plain is grass. But forests border the many short rivers that plunge from the high mountains to the coastal plain. The government is trying to encourage the settlement of this region.

GUATEMALA

The second land region, the **highlands**, covers over a third of the country. It is an area of rugged mountains, high, grassy plateaus, and steep-walled valleys. A striking feature is a line of 33 high, cone-shaped volcanoes overlooking the Pacific coastal plain. One, Tajumulco, rises 13,816 feet (4,211 meters) and is the highest mountain in Central America. A few volcanoes are still active. Volcanic ash has made some of the soils very fertile. The highlands are cooler than the lowlands. Because the soils and the climate are good, it is the most densely populated region.

Trees cover much of the highlands. Hardwoods such as rosewood, cedar, mahogany, and cypress grow in the mountain forests. Orchids grow wild, and parrots and macaws are common. The brilliantly feathered quetzal bird, Guatemala's national symbol, can still be seen in these forests. Two highland lakes —Atitlán and Amatitlán—are famous for their breathtaking location amid volcanic peaks.

The third region is the **Caribbean lowland**. Like the Pacific coastal plain, it is hot, humid, and swampy. Because it is exposed to trade winds, the Caribbean lowland has heavy rainfall and only a short dry season. The dense tropical rain forest is the home of varied wildlife—sloths, monkeys, jaguars, lizards, and hundreds of kinds of insects. Poisonous snakes such as the coral snake and fer-de-lance are common. Few people live in this forbidding region.

The fourth region is the limestone plain of **Petén**, which covers the entire northern third of the country. This was once a part of the great Mayan Empire. Its climate is warm and humid, too, and the soils are very poor. The relatively few people who live here are employed mainly in lumbering or gathering the sap of the sapodilla tree. This sap is called chicle and is used in making chewing gum. A highway has opened this sparsely populated region to new settlement.

▶THE ECONOMY

Agriculture is the mainstay of the country's economy. However, manufacturing has increased greatly in recent years and Guatemala is the most industralized of the Central American nations.

Agriculture. Agriculture employs nearly 60 percent of the workforce. The major commercial crop is coffee, which provides nearly 25 percent of the country's export income. Sugar cane, bananas, cardamom (a spice), and cotton are also leading cash crops. They are traditionally grown on large plantations. Basic food crops are cultivated on small plots of land and include corn, beans, and rice. Cattle are raised for beef and sheep mainly for their wool.

Manufacturing. Manufacturing engages about 14 percent of the labor force. Most of the country's industries are located in Guatemala City. The chief manufactured products, measured by value of output, are processed foods, textiles, pharmaceuticals (medical drugs), and chemicals for industry.

Mining, Fishing, Forestry. Guatemala has important mineral deposits, but much of its mineral resources remain to be fully developed. The most valuable mineral export is petroleum. Antimony, lead, iron ore, and tungsten are also mined, but on a smaller scale.

Guatemala's surrounding waters abound in fish and shellfish, particularly shrimp, which are a significant export. The forests, which cover about 40 percent of the land, are an import natural resource, supplying valuable hardwoods, timber, and chicle.

▶CITIES

Guatemala City, the capital, is by far the largest city in the country and the largest city in Central America. It is linked to Puerto Barrios on the Caribbean coast and San José on the Pacific coast by railroad. The Inter-American Highway runs through Guatemala City. Antigua, a former capital, is famous for its Spanish colonial architecture. Puerto Barrios is the nation's leading port.

▶GOVERNMENT

Guatemala's government is based on a 1986 constitution, revised in 1994. The legislative body is the National Congress, elected for four years. A president, also elected for a 4-year term, serves as head of state and government. The president is assisted by an elected vice president and an appointed cabinet.

▶HISTORY

Early History. Guatemala had an important Indian civilization long before the Spanish arrived in the 1500's. From A.D. 300 to 900 the Petén was part of the first Mayan Empire. Today Mayan ruins at Piedras Negras, on the Usumacinta River, and the marvels at Tikal are much visited and studied.

After Pedro de Alvarado defeated the Indians in 1523, the first Spanish town was established in 1524. By 1543, Guatemala's authority stretched from the Yucatán Peninsula to Panama. The Spaniards who chose to settle in Guatemala were given large estates by the Spanish king. They raised cattle and harvested crops by using Indians for forced labor. In 1773, Antigua was destroyed by an earthquake and the capital was moved to Guatemala City in 1776.

Independence. On September 15, 1821, Guatemala declared itself independent from Spain in a bloodless revolt. The country joined Agustín de Iturbide's Mexican Empire. In 1824, Guatemala broke with Mexico and joined in a federation called the United Provinces of Central America, but the union fell apart in 1839. Much of Guatemala's subsequent history was marked by dictatorships. Rafael Carrera ruled from 1839 to 1865; Justo Rufino Barrios from 1871 to 1885; Manuel Estrada Cabrera from 1898 to 1920; and Jorge Ubico from 1931 to 1944.

In 1944 a revolution overthrew the dictator Jorge Ubico. Juan José Arévalo was elected

Boys play soccer on a hilltop overlooking Guatemala City.

Left: In front of La Merced in Antigua, devout Catholic Indians perform the Stations of the Cross. Right: An inactive volcano near Lake Atitlán.

Left: Machete in hand, a worker severs the stem from a banana plant. Bananas are one of Guatemala's most important export crops. Above: The modern Social Security Building in Guatemala City. Below: Coffee beans, Guatemala's major export, are spread out to dry.

president and began a program of social reform. His successor, Colonel Jacobo Arbenz Guzmán, turned many large plantations over to landless peasants. This land program was opposed by Guatemalan landowners, the U.S. companies that owned many of the plantations, and the army. The United States feared the growth of Communist influence in the Arbenz government. In 1954, forces led by Colonel Carlos Castillo Armas, with U.S. assistance, overthrew Arbenz. Castillo became president but was assassinated in 1957.

Recent History. The years that followed were marked by political unrest and periods of military rule. Almost all of Guatemala's presidents during this time were army officers or were kept in power by the support of the army. Meanwhile, leftists were waging a guerrilla war in the countryside against the government, and the country was torn by violence.

In 1983, General Oscar Humberto Mejía Victores took over the government and promised a return to civilian control. A new constitution was adopted, and in 1986, Marco Vinicio Cerezo Arévalo became Guatemala's first civilian president in a generation. He was succeeded, in 1991, by Jorge Serrano Elias.

In 1993, however, Serrano suspended the constitution and instituted rule by decree. Increasing protests soon forced the army, which had originally supported Serrano, to remove him. He was replaced as president by Ramiro de León Carpio. Álvaro Arzú Irigoyen won the presidency in 1996. That same year, the government and the main rebel group, the Guatemalan National Revolutionary Union (UNRG), signed peace accords formally ending Latin America's longest civil war.

MORTON D. WINSBERG
Florida State University

GUERRILLA WARFARE

Guerrilla warfare is fought by irregular troops—soldiers who are not sponsored by a recognized government. Guerrillas may be fighting the armies of a foreign enemy or they may be rebels in a civil war against the army of their own government. The tactics used in guerrilla warfare are as varied as the people who invent them and are usually determined by the local geography and available resources. Generally the guerrilla seeks to disrupt the enemy by attacking without warning and then withdrawing quickly before the enemy's regular army can react.

Because they are usually lacking in numbers, guerrillas rely on slyness, cunning, and the advantages of surprise. They try to attack an enemy's weak points and spread their own forces out over a large area to engage as many enemy troops as possible, usually on difficult terrain that only the guerrillas know well. It is also important for guerrillas to have allies within the local population, on whom they can depend to supply food, shelter, supplies, and, most important, information about the enemy's movements.

Weapon selection is also crucial for guerrillas. Because rapid strikes and withdrawals are the keys to success, they rarely carry heavy weapons such as large machine guns or use tanks. They rely more on light weapons, explosives such as dynamite, hand grenades, and light mortars. Also, because supply lines can be so easily interrupted or cut, guerrillas cannot rely on outside sources for weapons and ammunition, so their ability to capture weapons from the enemy is basic to their success.

▶ HISTORY

Although guerrilla warfare is as old as warfare itself, the term originated in Spain in the early 1800's, when Spanish patriots used hit-and-run tactics against the invading forces of the French emperor Napoleon rather than engaging the enemy in full-scale battle. In Spanish, *guerrilla* means "little war."

In North America, Native Americans, who did not have the advantage of superior weapons, successfully employed guerrilla tactics for centuries against Spanish, English, French, and later American and Canadian opponents. In the 1700's, English colonists used both a conventional army (commanded by George Washington) and guerrillas (often working with Native American allies) in their successful struggle for independence from England. During the United States Civil War, guerrilla bands operated on both the Union and Confederate sides. Of these, William Quantrill's Confederate band, which included Frank and Jesse James, was the most famous.

Guerrilla warfare became more commonplace in the 1900's. Emiliano Zapata and Francisco "Pancho" Villa were two popular guerrilla leaders of the Mexican Revolution (1910–20). During World War I (1914–18), the British soldier T. E. Lawrence, better known as Lawrence of Arabia, made a major contribution to guerrilla strategy. Lawrence's army

Since 1994, the Zapatista National Liberation Army has made guerrilla war against the government of Mexico, demanding help for the Native Americans in the impoverished southeastern state of Chiapas.

of irregular Arab soldiers actually defeated the Turks by attacking not their men but their supplies—weapons, ammunition, food, and communication and transportation networks. Lawrence argued that it was far more important to destroy a key bridge or a supply depot than it was to engage the Turkish army in battle.

One of the best-known and most gifted guerrilla masterminds was Mao Zedong

Above: In the 1980's, the contra rebels of Nicaragua fired on the Sandinistas, a Soviet-backed guerrilla group that had overthrown the Somoza dictatorship in 1979. *Right:* In the 1960's, Che Guevara's guerrilla tactics and theories spread throughout Central and South America.

(Mao Tse-tung), leader (1949–76) of the Communist People's Republic of China, who used guerrilla tactics against the Japanese in World War II and also against the Nationalist Chinese led by Chiang Kai-shek. Mao emphasized the importance of the small guerrilla unit, which could move quickly and strike rapidly at various points at the same time, giving the impression that the force was much larger than it actually was. Mao also argued that natural geographical obstacles, such as mountains and deserts, and extreme weather conditions could and should be used to the guerrilla's advantage. Above all, guerrillas had to be able to react instantly to new or changing conditions in a way that large conventional armies could not. "In guerrilla warfare," Mao said, "select the tactic of seeming to come from the east and attacking from the west; avoid the solid, attack the hollow; attack; withdraw; deliver a lightning blow, seek a lightning decision."

In Indochina, the Vietnamese general Vo Nguyen Giap used Mao's theories first in his struggle against the Japanese during World War II and later against the French and Americans in Vietnam. To Mao's theory, Giap added the concept of a "people's war," that would frustrate and gradually wear down the enemy forces. Giap's guerrilla tactics worked well against the United States, which failed to gain the advantage in the war against Vietnam in the 1960's and 1970's.

Another famous champion of guerrilla warfare was Ernesto "Che" Guevara. In 1959, Guevara led guerrillas in Cuba to help Fidel Castro bring down the government of Fulgencio Batista. Later guerrilla movements in the Central and South American countries of Guatemala, El Salvador, Nicaragua, Colombia, Venezuela, Peru, Bolivia, Uruguay, Brazil, and Argentina all recognized Che Guevara as their intellectual and political inspiration. Likewise, the United States viewed Che Guevara, his political associates, and his military-political tactics as a real threat to the non-Communist countries in the Western Hemisphere. Fearing that Che's guerrillas would spread Communism throughout Central and South America, American president John F. Kennedy and his administration (1961–63) developed elaborate new political, economic, and military policies. Kennedy's economic and social plan was called the Alliance for Progress. The military plans were based on the idea of **counterinsurgency**, meaning "against the insurgents" (rebels)—in this case, the guerrillas. Kennedy's counterinsurgency programs were continued and expanded by his successors as president.

In some rare cases, the United States has supported guerrilla fighters. In 1979 the United States supported the Muslim guerrillas in Afghanistan, known as the *mujahidin* ("holy warriors"), who were resisting an invasion by the Soviet Union. Later, in the 1980's, the United States supported the contras, or counterrevolutionaries, in Nicaragua. The contras were fighting the Soviet-backed government of the Sandinistas, who themselves had used guerrilla warfare to overthrow the Somoza regime in 1979.

THOMAS M. DAVIES, JR.
Director, Center for Latin American Studies
San Diego State University

GUIANA(S). See FRENCH GUIANA; GUYANA; SURINAME.

GUIDANCE COUNSELING

Guidance counselors are school professionals who specialize in helping students make decisions about their personal, vocational, and educational needs and concerns. Guidance counselors actually do many things in their work. They counsel students individually or in small groups; they lead classroom discussions about issues that affect young people; they meet with students, parents, teachers, and other members of the school staff to discuss such issues; they administer certain tests and inventories; they help students arrange their classroom schedules; and they participate in a variety of school activities.

We live in a very complex world that presents problems of real concern to students that they often need help in solving. It is the role of the guidance counselor to help students deal with these problems and to alert them to the opportunities for personal development that are available to them in their schools and communities.

▶ THE WORK OF THE GUIDANCE COUNSELOR

A guidance counselor's main goal is to help young people understand themselves in order to develop into adults who are capable of living productive and fulfilling lives. How guidance counselors work toward this goal varies according to the ages of the students.

In elementary schools, guidance counselors try to anticipate problems that may occur in students' lives and prevent these problems from arising. Some elementary school counselors also work with students such as gifted learners or young people with learning disabilities, who have special needs. Sometimes counselors work with a team that may include the school principal, a psychologist, a testing specialist or evaluator, a social worker, special-education teachers, and parents. At all times elementary school counselors work closely with parents, teachers, and school administrators and their staffs.

In middle and junior high schools, guidance counselors work with other school professionals to identify the developmental and learning needs of students in this age group. Adolescents at these grade levels experience many physical and emotional changes that can affect how they view themselves and how they perform in school.

In high schools, counselors are more concerned with educational and career guidance and with the general personal development of students. High school counselors help students choose school courses and activities that relate to their interests and prepare them for life after high school. In addition, they show students how to apply for college or for job-training programs. To help students make informed choices, counselors can provide information on almost any topic and then help the students put this information to use.

For students who want to continue their formal education, counselors provide information about colleges or training programs, including information about entrance requirements, financial-aid plans, and entry-level job opportunities in areas where they will be going to school. In some high schools, counselors coordinate programs in which students can work part-time. Other counselors work in drug and alcohol abuse programs as well as in programs for high school dropouts or for teenage parents.

Taking the time to discuss school-year goals with a guidance counselor will help a student identify what needs to be done to achieve them successfully.

Guidance Methods

Guidance counselors use a variety of methods in their work. Each method requires special training.

Individual Interviews. Because every person is unique, counselors try to work with students on an individual basis as often as possible. It is important for students and counselors to get to know one another so that students will feel free to discuss their concerns and feelings and to ask questions they might find awkward or embarrassing.

Young people worry about how well liked they are, how they look, how well they are expected to do in school or in meeting family responsibilities, and how to deal with peer pressure that may involve them in activities that are risky or wrong. During individual counseling a guidance counselor can help a student reach an understanding of how to cope with these situations.

One outcome of counseling is clarification of a student's values and goals. A related outcome might be a student's decision about how to help a friend, which courses to take in school, or what to do after high school graduation. Often the understanding of a sympathetic counselor can help young people face their difficulties realistically and learn to cope more readily with the problems of their daily lives.

Group Discussions. Sometimes it is appropriate to discuss problems or issues with a large or a small group of students. In group discussions, attitudes, values, and feelings are emphasized. A large group discussion might take place in a classroom where a specially trained counselor helps students discuss their feelings about such things as the death of a classmate or peer pressure, or with drug-related problems.

Depending upon the topic and student needs, counselors also conduct small group discussions of seven to ten students. Some students are more comfortable speaking and discussing problems in small groups, and there is also more opportunity for each participant to speak.

The value of group discussions is that young people of the same age often have similar concerns, but sometimes they view these concerns quite differently. By discussing their concerns in a group, students soon learn that they are not alone. Listening to other students share similar problems can lessen the burden students feel, and listening to the views of other students can be informative.

Information Service. An important part of a counselor's work is to provide information about educational, job, and career opportunities. To make the information readily available, counselors maintain files of printed, filmed, taped, and computerized materials. Providing this information can be useful, but the job is complete only after the counselor, the student, and perhaps the student's parents have discussed what this information means to the student.

▶ HOW TO BECOME A GUIDANCE COUNSELOR

Each state has educational requirements for guidance counselors. Most states require a college degree plus one to two years of special study in guidance counseling. Some states also require teaching experience.

The personal characteristics of people who want to be guidance counselors are as important as the educational requirements. The capacity to be caring, patient, cheerful, and open-minded, and to believe that everyone can change and develop is essential.

▶ THE FUTURE OF GUIDANCE COUNSELING

Although no one can predict with certainty the future of guidance counseling, various trends can be identified. Nearly one hundred years ago, talented, caring teachers helped students plan their futures. By the early 1900's, students had many more occupational and educational options than students of the late 1800's, and guidance counseling became a profession that included many specialists, each of whom focused on different areas of career guidance.

Today opportunities for students are even more varied, but so are the problems and concerns of our society. In addition, changes in society seem to occur rapidly and the amount of new information people are expected to absorb seems to be growing just as quickly. All of these factors emphasize the need for trained guidance counselors to help young people learn to lead meaningful and satisfying lives.

PROFESSOR RICHARD E. ELLIS
Department of Applied Psychology
New York University

See also TESTS AND TEST TAKING.

GUIDED MISSILES. See MISSILES.

Guildhalls built hundreds of years ago can still be seen in Ghent, Belgium.

GUILDS

Guilds were societies or associations formed during the Middle Ages in Europe by people in the same line of work. There were merchant guilds and craft guilds. Each guild protected the common interests of its members. Each guild had a patron saint.

There were guilds as early as the 11th century A.D. Between the 12th and 15th centuries guilds sprang up in towns all over England and Europe.

▶ MERCHANT GUILDS

In the early Middle Ages traders traveling from town to town needed protection from robbers. Even nobles sometimes turned highwaymen and robbed passing merchants. Nobles often collected tolls from traders who journeyed across their land. So merchants banded together to protect lives and goods.

The merchants of a town also wanted protection against competition from other traders. A guild's main purpose was to hold a monopoly of trade. Only guild members were allowed to do business in a town. Each guild received a charter from the local king or lord.

The charter gave the guild this right of monopoly. A visiting trader could do business only after he had received permission from the guild of the town and had paid a high fee.

Guilds had their own courts and settled quarrels between members. They fixed prices and set standards of weights, measures, and quality. Guilds were social clubs, too, with guildhalls where merchants met for grand feasts and other celebrations. Each guild held parades in honor of its patron saint.

A guild looked after its members. When a member died, the guild might pay for his funeral. It helped his widow and fatherless children. If a member was thrown into jail in another town, the guild worked to free him.

A guild included all the merchants in a town. Since the guild had a monopoly on trade, it often grew rich and powerful.

▶ CRAFT GUILDS

Skilled craftsmen made by hand everything medieval people used—saddles, woolen cloth, shoes, furniture. Like the merchants, they were free men living in towns. At first craftsmen produced goods mainly for the nobles. As market towns grew they produced more

Each craft had its own guild. From the Middle Ages through the 18th century, shoes were handmade by members of the cobbler's, or shoemaker's, guild.

and more for the general trade. Increased trade demanded more craftsmen. Soon the craftsmen organized guilds of their own.

Each craft guild had a charter granted by the king or noble. Unlike the members of the merchant guilds, the craft guild members made one particular product. Only guild members in a town had the right to make certain articles. Each craft—the goldsmith's, arrowsmith's, weaver's, cobbler's—had a separate guild. In fact, a guild might specialize in making a single kind of hat, as the peacock-hatters did.

The guild controlled hours, wages, and standards of workmanship. Members took pride in their fine craftsmanship. Like the merchant guild, the craft guild fixed prices and conditions of sales.

Occasionally, however, a workman might fold cloth to hide a worn spot. Or a customer would complain that a pot was made of bad metal that melted on the fire. If a guild caught a member doing such things, it fined him. A member who continued might be banished from the town, which meant that he could no longer sell his goods there.

FACTS ABOUT GUILDS

Apprentice—Person who is learning a craft or trade by practical experience under the guidance of a skilled craftsman.

Charter—Official paper giving certain rights and privileges.

Commerce—Buying and selling of goods on a large scale.

Craft—Trade or occupation that requires manual (hand) skill.

Guild—Association or society for the mutual aid and protection of people engaged in the same trade or occupation.

Guildhall—Meeting place of members of a guild.

Journeyman—One who works for another by the day (from the French word *journée*, meaning "day").

Livery—Special uniform worn by members of certain groups or associations.

Master craftsman—Expert or skilled workman.

Masterpiece—Piece of work presented to a guild as proof of qualification to the rank of master craftsman.

Medieval—Refers to the Middle Ages in Europe, a period from about A.D. 500 to 1400.

Merchant—Person who buys and sells goods for profit.

Monopoly—Anything that is controlled or possessed by one person or one group.

Privilege—Special right or favor given to one person or group of persons.

To trade—To buy and sell goods for money.

   A trade—An occupation.

Craft guilds also had guildhalls, festivals, patron saints, and parades. A guild was the center of social life for its members and their main safeguard against need and disaster. Some guilds set up schools and hospitals. Some helped with street paving, water systems, and other town projects. At their peak, guilds controlled all a town's trade and industry.

▶ TRAINING FOR THE CRAFT GUILDS

Apprentice. The craft guild had three ranks: apprentice, journeyman, and master. A boy in his teens became apprenticed to a master. He served for 3 to 12 years, depending on how much skill he needed for his craft. Seven years was usual in England. The apprentice lived like a son in his master's house and worked in his master's shop. His master gave him clothing, room, board, and training. The boy received no money, except sometimes during the last years of his service. If he ran away, he was brought back and punished. But the guild also punished masters who were cruel to apprentices. When an apprentice finished his service, he received a sum of money and "graduated" to journeyman.

Journeyman. The journeyman (the French word *journée* means "day") hired out his services by the day to master craftsmen for wages. He improved his skill and saved money to buy his own tools and hoped to set up his own shop. Sometimes he chose to work for an aging master. When the master died, he might inherit the shop. Usually he had to produce a "masterpiece" as proof of his skill and pay a sum of money. Only then would the guild promote him to master rank and admit him to membership.

Master. A journeyman was usually in his early 20's when he became a master. A master craftsman directed the work in his own workshop and owned the materials and tools used there. On festival days he was entitled to wear a special uniform called livery. Master craftsmen ran the guilds and elected their officers. They also inspected the workshops of guild members.

▶ THE GUILDS WEAKEN

As time passed the guilds became less democratic. A father handed down his membership to his son. Outsiders found it harder and harder to join. Some of them set up their own shops and competed with the guilds. Masters controlled the guilds and made journeymen work many years before promoting them to master rank. Many never became masters. They remained journeymen all their lives. After a while journeymen broke away and formed their own associations. These were the forerunners, or ancestors, of the labor unions of today.

By the 16th century, guilds began to lose their monopolies. Central governments became stronger, and towns were no longer so independent. Independent businessmen hired people living outside the towns to do piecework in their homes. These home, or domestic, workers were not under guild regulations. The introduction of machines during the 18th century further weakened the guilds' control over production. Many of the special rights were taken away from the guilds.

Home workshops and then factories took over the production of goods, but the guild lingered on as a social club. Guild members still wore their bright costumes for special parades on traditional feast days.

Reviewed by KENNETH S. COOPER
George Peabody College

See also MIDDLE AGES.

GUINEA

Guinea is a nation of West Africa, one of several situated on the great western bulge of the continent. It is bordered by the nations of Guinea-Bissau, Senegal, and Mali in the north; the Ivory Coast in the east; and Sierra Leone and Liberia in the south. The western edge of Guinea lies on the coast of the Atlantic Ocean. Guinea was formerly a colony of France, part of the territory of French West Africa, before gaining its independence in 1958.

▶THE PEOPLE

Ethnic Groups. The people of Guinea belong to a variety of ethnic groups. The largest group is the Fulani, who live mainly in the northeast. A proud and independent people, the Fulani are descended from desert dwellers of northern Africa who came to Guinea as conquerors centuries ago. The Fulani traditionally are nomadic herders of cattle and other livestock, although some have turned to settled farming. Fulani women are noted for the baskets and fans they weave from grass. Fulani homes are round structures with the roof extended to form the sides.

The Malinke (or Mandingo) are mostly farmers who live in houses grouped into compounds within a village. The Sousou (Susu) inhabit the coastal region, around the capital city of Conakry. They moved to this area in earlier times, fleeing the invading Fulani.

The dense forests of southeastern Guinea are the home of several smaller ethnic groups, including the Kissi and Toma. Because they were long isolated by the difficult terrain, they have tended to keep their traditional customs and religious beliefs.

Language and Religion. French is the official language of the country, but many African languages, including Fulani, Malinke, and Sousou, are spoken. The great majority of Guinea's people are Muslims. Some Guineans continue to practice traditional African religions. A relatively small percentage of the population is Christian, mainly Roman Catholic.

▶THE LAND

Guinea has four distinct geographic regions. They are the coastal region, or Lower Guinea; the Fouta Djallon, or Middle Guinea; the savanna region, or Upper Guinea; and the highland region in the southeast. Each region is marked by differences in vegetation, climate, and terrain.

Along the coast are flat swamplands where palm and mangrove trees grow. The climate here is hot with heavy rainfall. The Fouta Djallon plateau rises from the narrow coastal strip. This is an area of prairies and scattered clumps of trees, crossed by rivers, waterfalls, and gorges. The climate is cooler and drier than along the coast. To the northeast of the plateau is a broad region of savanna, or grasslands, with little rainfall. To the southeast are the dense tropical rain forests of the highland region.

Three of West Africa's major rivers—the Niger, Senegal, and Gambia—originate in the Fouta Djallon region of Guinea.

▶THE ECONOMY

Guinea's economy is based largely on agriculture. Most of the people earn their living from farming or livestock raising. The chief food crops are rice, corn, millet, yams, and

---

FACTS and figures

REPUBLIC OF GUINEA (République de Guinée) is the official name of the country.

LOCATION: West Africa.

AREA: 94,926 sq mi (245,857 km²).

POPULATION: 6,300,000 (estimate).

CAPITAL AND LARGEST CITY: Conakry.

MAJOR LANGUAGES: French (official); Fulani, Malinke, Sousou, and other African languages.

MAJOR RELIGIOUS GROUP: Muslim.

GOVERNMENT: Republic. **Head of state and government**—president. **Legislature**—National Assembly.

CHIEF PRODUCTS: Rice, millet, yams, cassava, bananas, pineapples, palm nuts and oil, kola nuts, livestock, bauxite (aluminum ore), diamonds.

MONETARY UNIT: Guinean franc (1 franc = 100 centimes).

cassava. Bananas are becoming one of Guinea's chief exports. Pineapple is another important fruit. Other agricultural exports are palm nuts and oil, and kola nuts, which are used in making soft drinks. Coffee and tobacco, grown in the forest regions, are becoming more important in the Guinean economy. Small factories process palm oil, rice, coffee, and other agricultural products.

The plateau of the Fouta Djallon and the savanna grasslands of upper Guinea are ideal for raising animals. Cattle, sheep, and goats provide the main source of income for these regions.

Beneath the soil of Guinea are many valuable minerals. Diamonds are mined in the Macenta region in the southeast. Iron ore is mined near Conakry. Most important, however, are Guinea's bauxite deposits, estimated to form one fourth of the world's reserves. The bauxite—located in central, northern, and eastern Guinea—is the chief export. It is used in making aluminum. Guinea's swift-flowing rivers also give it great potential for hydroelectric power.

Guinea has a network of roads, which

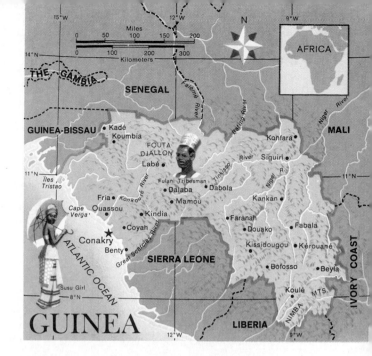

connects all of its regions. A railroad runs from Conakry to Kankan. The port of Conakry serves oceangoing ships. It has special equipment for loading bananas and iron ore. Airports are located at Conakry and Kankan.

Conakry, the capital, is the country's largest

The modern city of Conakry is the capital and chief port of Guinea.

Children study the Koran, the holy book of Islam.

city and chief port. It has a population of over 500,000 in its metropolitan area. Guinea's second largest city is Kankan, which is located in the interior.

▶ HISTORY AND GOVERNMENT

Guinea was first visited by Europeans in the 14th century. The Portuguese came first, followed by French and British explorers and traders. The French gradually extended their control along the coast until they controlled the entire region between British Sierre Leone and Portuguese Guinea (now Guinea-Bissau). The colony of Guinea was established in 1891. In 1895, Guinea was joined to the newly created federation of French West Africa.

Samoury Touré, a Guinean hero, fought against the control of the French. He led the Malinke people from 1882 until he was captured by the French in 1898.

The history of French Guinea up until the late 1950's is very much like that of other French colonies in Africa. At first these territories were governed as if they were to become part of France. Later, France granted them a certain degree of self-government.

In 1958 the French colonies in Africa were given the choice of remaining tied to France or becoming completely independent. Guinea voted for independence, with Sékou Touré as its first president.

At independence, Guinea's economy was in chaos. Touré accused various nations of trying to overthrow his government, and he isolated Guinea from much of the world. The economy was placed under government control, and thousands of people suspected of being against the government were arrested. Many others left the country.

After Touré's death in 1984, the military, led by Colonel Lansana Conté, took power. Conté assumed the presidency and, in 1988, began to establish a democratic government. A new constitution was approved in 1990, providing for a multiparty political system and an elected president and National Assembly. The first presidential elections under the new constitution were held in 1993 and resulted in a victory for Conté. Elections for the National Assembly were held in 1995.

SANFORD GRIFFITH
New York University

GUINEA-BISSAU

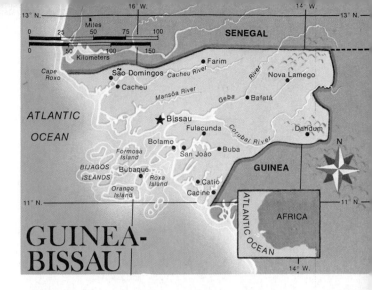

GUINEA-BISSAU

Guinea-Bissau is a small nation of West Africa. It is bordered by the Atlantic Ocean on the west and by the nations of Senegal on the north and Guinea on the east and south. In addition to its territory on the African mainland, Guinea-Bissau also includes the Bijagós chain of islands and other offshore islands. Guinea-Bissau was long governed by Portugal and was formerly known as Portuguese Guinea. Its independence was recognized by Portugal in 1974, following years of bitter guerrilla war.

▶THE PEOPLE

Guinea-Bissau's people include many different ethnic groups, with varied languages, customs, and religious beliefs.

Ethnic Groups. The country's major ethnic groups are the Balante, the Fulani, the Mandyako, and the Malinke (or Mandingo). The largest group is the Balante, who make up about 30 percent of the population. The Balante live in the Atlantic coastal region, where they are mainly rice farmers. The Fulani, who make up about 20 percent of the population, live in the interior. They are traditionally

herders of cattle and other livestock. Some Fulani have become settled farmers, growing millet, cotton, and peanuts.

The Mandyako, like the Balante, live mainly in the coastal area. Making up about 14 percent of the population, the Mandyako cultivate palm trees, from which they obtain palm oil and coconuts. The Malinke, who make up about 13 percent of the population, live in the northeast. They are craft workers and traders as well as farmers.

Language and Religion. Portuguese is the official language of Guinea-Bissau, but most of the people speak one of the many African languages. The most widely used language is Criolo, which combines a Portuguese dialect with African languages.

The majority of the people practice traditional African religions. About 30 percent of the population, mostly among the Fulani and Malinke, are Muslims. A small minority of Guinea-Bissauans are Christians, mainly Roman Catholics.

Way of Life. Most of the people live in villages of varying size and earn their livelihood as farmers. Only about 20 percent of the population live in towns or cities.

The long war of independence strongly affected the traditional way of life. During the fighting, many people fled their homes or were moved into special settlements by the Portuguese. When the war ended in 1974, many of the people were moved again by the new government of Guinea-Bissau. In all, about 100,000 people—or more than 10 percent of the total population—had to be resettled. Guinea-Bissau's economy still has not recovered from the effect of the war.

FACTS AND FIGURES

REPUBLIC OF GUINEA-BISSAU (República da Guiné-Bissau) is the official name of the country.

THE PEOPLE are known as Guinea-Bissauans.

LOCATION: West Africa.

AREA: 13,943 sq mi (36,125 km²).

POPULATION: 900,000 (estimate).

CAPITAL AND LARGEST CITY: Bissau.

MAJOR LANGUAGES: Portuguese (official), Criolo, various African languages.

GOVERNMENT: Republic. **Head of state and government—** president of the Council of State. **Legislature**—National People's Assembly.

CHIEF PRODUCTS: Agricultural—rice, peanuts, palm kernels (palm oil), coconuts, cotton, corn, beans, cassava, sweet potatoes, livestock. **Manufactured**— processed agricultural products.

MONETARY UNIT: Guinea-Bissau peso (1 peso = 100 centavos).

NATIONAL ANTHEM: *Esta é a Nossa Pátria Bem Amada* ("This is Our Well-Beloved Land").

Bissau is the capital, largest city, and chief port of Guinea-Bissau. Founded by the Portuguese in the 17th century, it retains the look of a Portuguese town.

▶THE LAND

Guinea-Bissau has a mostly low-lying, flat landscape. Only in the southeast does the land rise to any height, reaching about 800 feet (240 meters) above sea level. The Atlantic coastline is deeply indented by the sea, forming numerous estuaries, or inlets. Much of the coastal region is swampy and thickly forested. The interior of the country is primarily grassland. Guinea-Bissau's chief rivers include the Geba, Cacheu, and Corubal. The capital and the largest city, Bissau, is situated near the mouth of the Geba River. It is the country's main seaport.

The climate is tropical, with generally high temperatures and humidity. There are two distinct seasons—wet and dry. Rainfall is extremely heavy along the coast during the wet season but decreases inland.

▶THE ECONOMY

Guinea-Bissau's economy is based almost entirely on agriculture. About 75 percent of the people practice subsistence farming, growing food only for their own use. Rice, cultivated mainly in the coastal region, is the chief food crop. Millet, corn, beans, sweet potatoes, and cassava are also grown for food.

Cashew nuts, frozen shrimp, peanuts, and palm oil are the leading exports. Cattle, raised on the grassland of the interior, are increasing in economic importance.

Manufacturing is limited largely to the processing of agricultural products. Guinea-Bissau is known to have offshore deposits of petroleum, as well as bauxite (aluminum ore), but lacks the finances to develop them.

▶HISTORY AND GOVERNMENT

Early History. The earliest known inhabitants of what is now Guinea-Bissau were nomadic hunters. They were displaced by agricultural peoples who migrated from neighboring regions. The first Portuguese arrived in the area in the mid-15th century, establishing trading posts on the coast. Between the 17th and 19th centuries the region was a main source of slaves for the Americas.

The territory was governed by Portugal from the Cape Verde Islands until 1876, when Portuguese Guinea became a separate colony. Portuguese Guinea was made an overseas province of Portugal in 1951.

Struggle for Independence. The struggle for independence in both Portuguese Guinea and Cape Verde began in 1956 with the founding of the African Party for the Liberation of Guinea and Cape Verde (PAIGC). Large-scale guerrilla war against the Portuguese began in 1963. By 1973 the PAIGC forces had gained control of most of the countryside and declared the independence of Guinea-Bissau. Portugal officially recognized its independence in 1974. Cape Verde gained independence in 1975.

Recent Events. Guinea-Bissau's first president, Luis de Almeida Cabral, was overthrown in a military coup in 1980. Plans for a possible union with Cape Verde ended with Cabral's fall from power. The country remained under military rule until 1984.

The 1984 constitution was revised in 1991 to end one-party rule and allow a free-market economy. After many delays, the country's first multiparty elections were held in 1993. A president, who is elected directly by the people for a 5-year term, governs with the help of an appointed prime minister. Members of the elected legislature serve for four years.

Reviewed by HUGH C. BROOKS
Director, Center for African Studies
St. John's University (New York)

If you want a small, gentle pet that is easy to care for and fun to watch, consider a hamster. Hamsters are quite tame and can be handled easily. Keep in mind that they are active animals, especially at night, and need lots of exercise.

GUINEA PIGS, HAMSTERS, AND GERBILS

Soft to touch and easy to hold, guinea pigs, hamsters, and gerbils make fine pets. They are gentle, inquisitive animals, easy and inexpensive to raise. If you put your pet on a tabletop and tempt it with a lettuce leaf, the little creature will nibble the lettuce while you gently stroke its back. With careful handling, it will soon be tame.

▶THE GUINEA PIG

The guinea pig is not a pig, and it is not from Guinea. It is a cavy, a South American rodent that was raised for food by the ancient Incas of Peru. From Guiana, not Guinea, Dutch and English traders brought the animal to Europe. It was called a pig because it grunts when it is hungry. It is about 25 centimeters (10 inches) long and weighs almost 0.5 kilogram (about 1 pound).

One variety of guinea pig has short, straight hair. Another has long, silky hair, and a third has coarse hair that grows in whorls. The guinea pig's hair varies in shades and patterns of black, brown, orange, and white.

Its food is grass, other green plants, and roots. When not in captivity, it can manage without water if it gets enough greenery. As a pet, it must have water, particularly if it is eating prepared animal food pellets. Water,

vegetables, and rock salt will keep a guinea pig in good health.

A mother guinea pig usually has one to four young in a litter, five or six times a year. On their first day, the young can move around and eat soft foods, although they nurse for two to three weeks. Males and females should be separated at the age of one month because they should not breed until they are full-grown, at the age of about four months.

▶THE HAMSTER

The golden hamster is about 15 centimeters (6 inches) long and weighs about 140 grams (5 ounces). It is a native of Europe and Asia. Its name comes from the German word *hamstern,* meaning "to hoard." In the wild, the hamster stuffs its large cheek pouches with food, which it then hoards in burrows or holes. The pouches can carry up to half the animal's weight in food. To empty its cheeks, the hamster presses on them with its forefeet and blows. Hamsters have plump bodies and short limbs. The thick, soft fur of golden hamsters is most often reddish gold on the back and grayish white on the belly. Other color varieties have also been bred.

Hamsters are mostly plant eaters, but when they are free, they will eat insects, lizards, and the young of other animals. As pets, they will eat prepared animal pellets, leafy vegetables, grains, fruit, nuts, and even milk.

The guinea pig is a South American animal.

Tiny gerbils are desert animals.

The hamster is one of the fastest-reproducing mammals. It has four or five litters a year. Sometimes there are more than a dozen babies in each litter. The mother nurses the young for about three weeks. During this time she and her litter should be separated from the others. Once the young are weaned, the sexes should be kept apart to prevent fighting and to keep them from breeding at too early an age.

▶ THE GERBIL

This popular, pocket-sized pet originated in the dry, sandy regions of Africa and southwestern Asia. Gerbils measure from 8 to 12 centimeters (about 3 to 5 inches), not counting their tails, which are usually as long as their bodies. The Mongolian gerbil is the most popular breed in the United States. It is a gentle, playful pet that adapts well to captivity.

Gerbils may live from one to five years—sometimes longer. They live in mated pairs

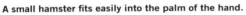

A small hamster fits easily into the palm of the hand.

and may produce litters of up to eight babies as often as once a month. Both mother and father share in caring for the young.

Because of their desert background, gerbils need very little water. Their preferred diet includes sunflower seeds, apples, and carrots—and maybe an occasional dog biscuit.

▶ CARE OF GUINEA PIGS, HAMSTERS, AND GERBILS

All three of these animals should be kept in cages. The size of the cage depends on the size of the animal. A guinea-pig cage should measure about 1 meter on each side. A gerbil can make do with much smaller quarters. A hamster needs a cage about half the size of a guinea-pig cage, and it should have an exercise wheel. If no wheel is available, the hamster should be allowed to run outside the cage because it needs a great deal of exercise to prevent a form of paralysis.

Metal cages with removable, tray-type floors are easy to keep clean. A glass aquarium with a wire-mesh top can also be used to house your pet. A water bottle with a bent tube reaching into the cage should be provided. The tube releases a drop of water at a time, which the animal can lick when it is thirsty. A hamster also needs a block of wood to gnaw on, to keep its teeth in good condition.

Cages should be cleaned regularly by washing with soap and hot water and putting down fresh bedding. Hay or wood shavings make equally good floor coverings.

Reviewed by ALVIN SILVERSTEIN
VIRGINIA SILVERSTEIN
Co-authors, *Gerbils; Guinea Pigs; Hamsters*

GUITAR

The guitar is a stringed instrument made of wood. Its six strings are traditionally tuned E A D G B E from the low sixth string to the high first string. Other tunings are sometimes used, especially in blues and folk music.

Guitars come in many shapes and sizes, but all have certain features in common: a body made of wood; a neck with metal strips called frets; strings made of nylon or steel; and a head with tuning keys that fasten the strings at the end of the neck.

The guitar is played in either a sitting or standing position. The strings are plucked and strummed with the fingers or with a plectrum, commonly called a pick. The pitch of the strings is changed by pressing them behind the frets with the fingers of the other hand.

The guitar originated in Persia and reached Spain by the 1100's. It later appeared throughout Europe under different names and in various forms. Early guitars had four or five **courses**, or pairs of strings. The transition to six single strings occurred during the late 1700's. The model for the modern guitar was created by Spanish guitar maker Antonio de Torres Jurado in the mid-1800's.

Most modern styles of guitar playing have roots in American blues and folk music. From these early guitarists came a generation of popular, jazz, and rock-and-roll musicians. The electric guitar, developed in the 1930's, became the dominant instrument of popular and rock music.

Because it is portable and can provide simple accompaniment to singing, the guitar is widely popular. Beginners find it relatively easy to learn chords, while dedicated musicians find nearly endless depth and challenge in an instrument well suited to many styles of music. Guitars fall into two broad categories: acoustic and electric. There is also a guitar that combines elements of the two basic types: the acoustic-electric guitar.

▶ ACOUSTIC GUITARS

The acoustic guitar produces sound from the vibrations of the strings. The sound resonates in the body, or sound box, of the guitar and is amplified (made louder).

Even beginners can experience the pleasures of playing the guitar. It is relatively easy to learn chords that can provide simple accompaniment to singing.

An acoustic guitar may have either nylon or steel strings depending on its design and purpose. A hardwood, such as rosewood, is used for the back and sides of the instrument. The top of the acoustic guitar is most commonly made of cedar or spruce, each wood giving the instrument a distinctive tone. The neck is joined to the body and is often made of a wood such as mahogany. The fingerboard is usually rosewood or ebony.

Nylon-string acoustics are used in classical and flamenco music. These classical, or Spanish, guitars may also be used in other styles and are prized for their rich, warm sound. The basic design of these guitars has remained almost unchanged from the design of Torres Jurado.

The Spanish guitarist Andrés Segovia is generally considered to be responsible for the re-emergence of classical guitar in the 1900's. He established the guitar as a legitimate concert instrument. One of his innovations was the use of the fingernails in plucking the strings to enhance clarity and tone.

Steel-string acoustics are used in virtually all kinds of music except classical. There are two main forms of steel-string acoustics: flat-top and arch-top guitars. Both were developed in the United States during the late 1800's.

The flat-top or folk guitar resembles its classical ances-

Classical guitar

tor but has a slightly larger body and a narrower neck. Compared with the classical guitar, it produces greater volume and has a bright, ringing tone favored by folk singers. While there are many flat-top virtuosos, such as Tony Rice and Leo Kottke, the emphasis for this instrument tends to be on simple accompaniment to singing.

The second type of steel-string acoustic is the arch-top guitar. Its top, thicker than those of the classical and flat-top guitars, curves outward and has f-shaped sound holes. Arch-top guitars reached their peak of popularity in the jazz and big band music of the 1920's and 1930's. They were loud enough to project a clear, warm tone in ensembles. Freddie Greene, of the Count Basie Band, was considered by many to be the master of orchestral rhythm-section guitar playing.

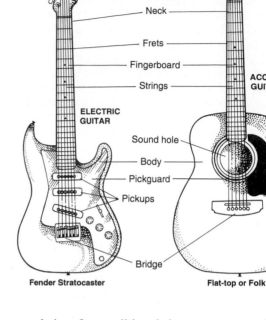

ELECTRIC GUITAR

ACOUSTIC GUITAR

Head
Tuning keys
Neck
Frets
Fingerboard
Strings
Sound hole
Body
Pickguard
Pickups
Bridge

Fender Stratocaster

Flat-top or Folk

Arch-top acoustic

Les Paul-style electric

▶ELECTRIC GUITARS

The electric guitar was also developed in the United States, during the 1930's. It uses a pickup to amplify the sound instead of a hollow sound box. The pickup works like a microphone. It converts the sound of the string into an electrical impulse and sends it to an amplifier. There the signal is strengthened and sent to the speaker, which emits the signal as sound.

Early electric guitars were simply acoustic guitars with pickups attached. This created amplification but also problems of unwanted vibrations and noise. These problems were solved by making the body of the guitar from one or more solid pieces of wood, usually around 1½ to 2½ inches (3.8 to 6.4 centimeters) thick.

Because the body is solid, it can be formed to any shape or size for purposes of comfort or visual appeal. Solid-body guitars have been made in a few traditional shapes, most notably the Les Paul shape, developed by recording artist Les Paul for the Gibson company, and the Stratocaster shape designed by Leo Fender.

Acoustic-electric guitars are still made today and have evolved into an instrument that brings the qualities of both types together. Some emphasize the acoustic characteristics while others favor the electrical qualities.

The electric guitar has great appeal due to its range of expressiveness and ease of playing. It is effective as a solo instrument as well as for accompaniment. Lighter gauge strings used on these instruments make them softer to the touch. Their slim body design also makes them comfortable to hold.

The electric guitar dominates the pop- and rock-music industry and has produced virtuosos comparable to those in the world of other styles of music. Early electric guitar pioneers in the field of rock music include Chuck Berry, Jimi Hendrix, and Eric Clapton.

Electric guitars can also draw on a vast array of electronic devices, such as wa-wa and distortion pedals, to create effects impossible to achieve on acoustic instruments.

MICHAEL VAHILA
Author, *How to Master Any Musical Instrument*
See also ELECTRONIC MUSIC.

GULF STREAM

The Gulf Stream is a large current of tropical water that flows northward along the east coast of North America. It is one of the most conspicuous ocean currents in the world, with its warm temperatures, blue color, and rapid motion. This current brings warmer temperatures and moisture to the eastern coast of North America and especially to the countries of northern Europe.

The Gulf Stream is part of a vast circular swirl of water, called a **gyre**, that encircles the North Atlantic. Easterly trade winds set a large volume of westward-flowing water in motion just south of the Tropic of Cancer. This is known as the North Equatorial Current. As this current nears the Americas, it bends northward and separates into two branches. One branch, flowing into the Caribbean Sea and the Gulf of Mexico, is called the Florida Current. The other branch flows just east of the Caribbean Islands and is known as the Antilles Current. These two currents reunite just north of the Bahamas where they merge to become the Gulf Stream.

The Gulf Stream flows northward along eastern North America to about 45° N. There it turns eastward and flows toward Europe. At this stage the stream is known as the North Atlantic Drift. As it approaches the coast of Europe, some of this water flows southward as the Canaries Current to join with the North Equatorial Current and continue as part of this vast water circulation.

The average width of this broad ocean current is 60 to 100 miles (95 to 160 kilometers). The stream is a combination of small currents and eddies, with a volume of water perhaps 1,000 times greater than that of the Mississippi River. It flows at about 3 to 6 miles (5 to 10 kilometers) an hour and often changes direction. It sometimes forms huge loops. At times these loops are cut off from the major current and remain as warm cores of water in the colder Atlantic.

Early explorers observed and charted the Gulf Stream and its branches. Columbus was probably speeded in his journey to the New World by the North Equatorial Current. Ponce de León was one of the first to record correctly the movements of the Florida Current. In 1770, Benjamin Franklin prepared the first accurate chart of the Gulf Stream and North Atlantic Drift to help speed mail packets (ships) sailing for Europe.

As the Gulf Stream turns eastward off the coast of North America, it meets the cold Labrador Current flowing southward out of the Arctic Ocean. The mixing of water along the margins of these currents stirs up the sediments of the ocean floor and enriches the mineral content of the water. This provides food for tiny plant and animal life, which serve as food for great numbers of fish. The meeting place of these two great currents has always provided important fishing grounds for the people of Europe and North America.

JOHN F. LOUNSBURY
Eastern Michigan University

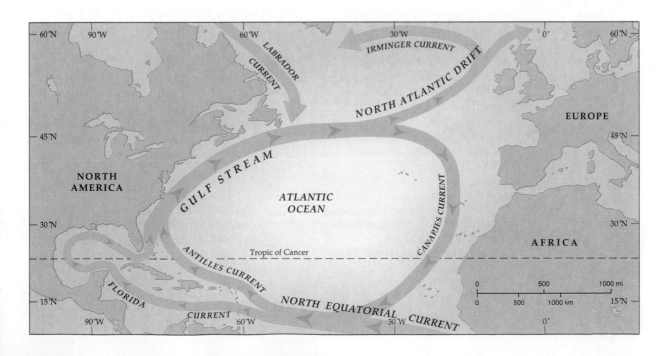

GUNS AND AMMUNITION

Guns have done as much to change history as any other single invention. Guns spelled the end of feudalism by making it possible to destroy the stout stone walls of castles. Guns changed the whole art of warfare because it was easier to train a soldier to fire a gun than to use a bow. Guns made life easier for the hunter and gave people a new advantage over large and dangerous animals. Guns were important in opening North and South American frontiers for European settlement.

Guns come in different sizes. A pistol is a short-barreled gun that is held in one hand. Rifles and shotguns are called shoulder arms. They have long barrels, and wooden stocks that are held against the shoulder. Very large guns are called cannons. They are often mounted on wheels.

The earliest known guns date from the beginning of the 14th century. These were clumsy cannons used for battering down enemy walls. Around the middle of the 14th century, smaller guns that could be carried were developed. These hand cannons were nothing more than a metal tube on the end of a wooden pole. They were set off by a red-hot iron or a glowing coal. Sometimes they did not go off at all; sometimes they blew up, wounding or killing the shooter.

Guns have come a long way since these crude and unreliable weapons. But the basic principle is still the same. A gun is a machine for shooting bullets. The bullet is propelled by the force of an explosive going off. The barrel of the gun is a tube that contains the explosion and gives the bullet its direction. A gun also must have some kind of device for setting off the explosive. And as guns were made better, sights were added to help the shooter take better aim.

For hundreds of years bullets were propelled by black powder. This explosive, which may have been invented by the Chinese about A.D. 1000, is a mixture of three chemicals: saltpeter, sulfur, and charcoal (carbon). Black powder gave a powerful explosion, but it also produced a mess of soot, ashes, and smoke. In fact, one of the surest signs of a battle was the dense, gray cloud of smoke from the firing of the guns. Sometimes the gunsmoke became so thick that the soldiers could not see what they were firing at.

Not until about 1885 was a good smokeless powder invented. Today there are many kinds of smokeless gunpowder. Some are used for pistols, some for shotguns, and some for rifles. A special type of powder is used to blast the nose cone away from the rest of a space rocket.

These new types of gunpowder are too powerful to be used in guns that were made to use black powder. The old guns usually had iron barrels. Even if they had steel barrels, the metal was not as strong as today's steel. If the newer kinds of gunpowder were set off in one of these guns, the barrel would explode. Today gun barrels are made of strong steel. They can stand the great force of the smokeless powder explosions.

The inside of a gun barrel is called the bore. Before the 16th century all gun bores were smooth, like an ordinary piece of pipe. Smoothbore guns used by soldiers were called

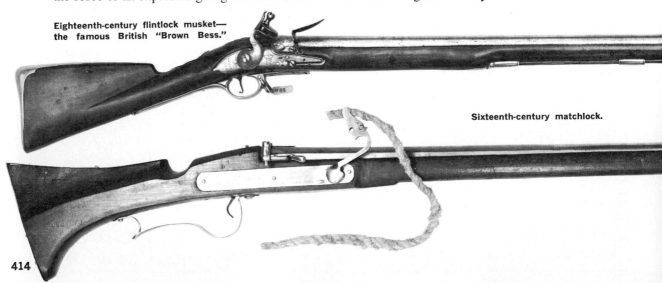

Eighteenth-century flintlock musket—
the famous British "Brown Bess."

Sixteenth-century matchlock.

A replica of Mons Meg, famous 14th-century Scottish cannon.

muskets; those used for hunting were called fowling pieces.

The soot and ashes from the black powder, known as fouling, used to clog up gun barrels. It is thought that early in the 16th century gunsmiths tried to take care of this problem by cutting grooves inside the barrels. The soot and ashes would be blown into the grooves and not block up the barrel. This feature was the forerunner of rifling—spiral grooves in the barrel to help guns shoot more accurately. Rifling causes a bullet to spin like a well-thrown football as it travels through the air.

Although rifles were much more accurate than smoothbores, they were also much more expensive to make and harder to load. For these reasons rifles did not become common until the 19th century, when production techniques were improved.

▶FROM MATCHLOCKS TO BREECH-LOADERS

For centuries the main problem with guns was finding a reliable way to set off the gun-

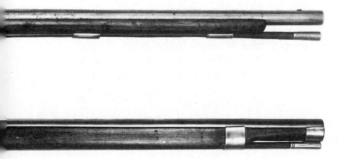

powder. In order for a gun to be any good at all, it had to work properly every time it was fired.

The earliest guns were fired by lighting the powder with a slow-burning wick called a match. Finely ground gunpowder was poured into a small hole near the breech, or rear end, of the barrel. This hole was called a touch hole. When this powder (called priming powder) was lit, it set off the main charge of powder in the barrel. It was almost impossible to shoot straight with these guns because the shooter had to hold the gun with one hand and at the same time insert the match into the touch hole with the other hand. Large cannons, which were fired in the same way, were more accurate because they sat on the ground. They could be aimed and then fired without being moved.

Matchlocks, Wheel Locks, and Flintlocks

Before long, better ways of setting off the gunpowder were found. The matchlock, the first gun with a trigger, had a small spoon-shaped pan next to the touch hole. Priming powder was poured into the pan. When the trigger was pulled, a lever pushed the burning wick, or match, into the pan, setting off the powder. The flame from the burning powder entered the touch hole and set off the main charge of powder in the barrel.

The matchlock was simple to work and was used for a long time. It had drawbacks, however. In rainy weather the priming powder got wet or the match would go out. At night the glowing match gave away the shooter's position.

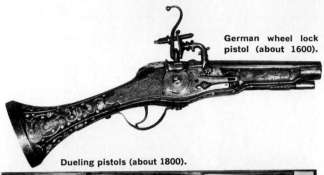

German wheel lock pistol (about 1600).

Dueling pistols (about 1800).

These problems were partly solved by wheel lock and flintlock guns. Both of these guns used sparks instead of a glowing match. The sparks fell into the pan, setting off the powder. Both guns had pan covers to keep the priming powder from getting wet or falling out.

The wheel lock struck sparks in the way a cigarette lighter does—with a scratching steel wheel turning against a piece of flint. The wheel was turned by a wind-up spring. The wheel lock worked well when it was working, but the mechanism often broke down or got clogged with fouling.

The flintlock was a sturdier mechanism. It had a hammer that held a piece of flint. When the trigger was pulled, the hammer snapped forward. The flint struck a piece of steel that was located over the pan. The flint and steel hitting together made sparks that dropped into the pan and lit the powder.

The flintlock was used, as both a hand gun and a shoulder weapon, for over 200 years. Some of the most famous battles in history were fought with flintlocks. Napoleon's armies

used them, and so did the armies of England, Russia, and Austria-Hungary that fought against Napoleon. The wars on the American frontier, as well as the American Revolutionary War, were fought with flintlock weapons.

Special kinds of flintlock pistols were designed for use in the many duels that took place in the 18th and 19th centuries. These expensive dueling pistols were made for quick firing. Taking careful aim in a duel was not considered fair in some places, and a quick shot was important, so the triggers were made to fire at a light touch. These triggers are known as hair triggers. The metal of the guns was dulled so that no glare would interfere with the duelist's aim.

The flintlock was a good gun, but it was not perfect. It took the gun a few moments to fire after the trigger was pulled. This made it difficult for the shooter to keep a good aim. Despite the cover over the pan, the priming powder could get wet and make it impossible to fire the gun. (This was also true of the wheel lock gun.) But until a better way was found to set off gunpowder, the flintlock was the best gun available.

Percussion Caps

A new gun was made possible by a chemical discovery. The salts of some metals were found to be highly explosive when they were struck. These salts are called fulminates. Early in the 19th century a Scottish minister named Alexander Forsyth (1769–1843) worked out a way to use fulminates for firing a gun. He replaced the touch hole, used on older guns, with a hollow metal tube that extended into the gun barrel. A bit of fulminate was placed in the tube and was struck with a firing pin. The firing pin, in turn, was driven down by the gun's hammer. The fulminate exploded, sending flame through the hollow tube and setting off the main charge.

Fulminates were used as gun primers in several forms. The most popular form was a

Kentucky percussion rifle from the mid-19th century.

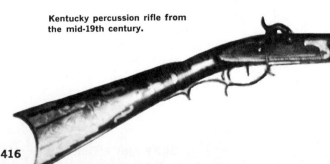

small hat-shaped piece of metal called a percussion cap. The fulminate was sealed inside the cap by a thin piece of metal foil. The percussion cap was the ancestor of the modern cartridge, which has the bullet, the primer, and the main charge of powder in a single cartridge case. Fulminates were also used in the form of small discs and in rolls like the caps used in toy cap pistols today. These caps were placed on nipple tubes and exploded by the blow of the hammer.

▶ MUZZLE-LOADERS

Modern guns are loaded at the breech, or rear end, of the barrel. This is the easiest and most convenient way of loading. Early guns, however, were loaded at the muzzle, or front end, of the barrel. The reason was that early gunsmiths were not able to make a safe and reliable breech-loading mechanism.

Loading a muzzle-loader was a long and complicated process. To load a smoothbore, the shooter had to stand the gun on the ground, pour black powder down the barrel, and then push the bullet down with his long ramrod. The bullet was made a little smaller than the inside of the barrel so that it would go down easily. After seating the bullet down on the powder, the shooter topped off the load with a wad of paper or rags. The wad held the bullet and powder firmly in place and kept them from falling out if the gun was pointed downward. To save time in loading, some armies supplied their soldiers with paper cartridges that held the bullet and the proper load of powder. The soldier tore open the cartridge with his teeth, poured the powder down the barrel, and then rammed down the bullet. The empty paper container served as wadding.

Under these conditions the smoothbore could not shoot accurately. As the loosely fitting ball traveled down the barrel, it struck back and forth along the sides. The direction the bullet took when it left the gun depended on the last contact.

This did not matter in battle. Instead of each soldier's picking a target and firing at it, a whole rank of soldiers simply blazed away straight ahead. The massed fire of all the bullets at once was like a wall of lead. Although no one soldier could be certain of hitting anyone, the chances were that some of the enemy would be hit by the hail of bullets.

Loading a rifle was even more difficult than loading a smoothbore, because the bullet had to fit the barrel tightly. This made it difficult to push the bullet down. In fact, some early rifles had to be loaded by driving the bullet down with a mallet. This was no great problem for target shooting, but it was not practical for battle. The problem was finally solved by using a bullet that was slightly smaller than the barrel. The bullet was wrapped in a greased patch. The patch made the bullet fit snugly and gave the rifling a grip. And the bullet in its greased patch slid down the barrel easily.

The famous American frontier riflemen of the 18th and early 19th centuries used these greased patches on their bullets. Besides making loading easier, the patch kept gases from the exploding powder from escaping forward past the bullet and being wasted. The bullets flew straight and fast. This helped give the frontier riflemen their reputations as sharpshooters.

The complicated process of loading a gun was not only difficult and slow—it could also be dangerous. During a battle the rifleman would have to stand up or at least kneel to get his rifle loaded. This made him a good target for the enemy. Excitement and fear might make the rifleman do things all wrong. He might forget to take the ramrod out of his rifle. When he fired, the ramrod would go sailing across toward the enemy line. If this happened, the soldier was unable to shoot again until he got another ramrod to push the bullets down the barrel of his gun. The soldier might also put the bullet in first and then the powder. This would leave him with a useless rifle because he could not blast the bullet out with the powder in front, and the bullet usually fit too tightly to roll out by itself.

Thousands of muzzle-loaders that were loaded wrong or had more than one load in them were found on Civil War battlefields. Some of the guns had as many as 5 or even 10 loads of bullet and powder in them. In the heat of battle a soldier might not know whether his gun had gone off properly or not. He might be so anxious to reload that he would put in more powder and bullets without realizing that his first shot had not gone off.

The slowness of muzzle-loading was a special problem during the wars against the Indians in the American West. Sometimes shrewd Indian leaders would get the soldiers to fire a volley at a few Indian warriors. While the soldiers were trying to reload, the main force of Indians would swoop down on the soldiers and massacre them.

Breech-Loaders

At a very early stage gunsmiths realized that a gun that could be loaded from the breech was much more convenient than one that had to be loaded from the muzzle. Over the years many inventors experimented with various designs for breech-loaders. But their breech-loaders were not safe to use. Gas leaked out at the joint where the breech opened and closed. Sometimes the burning-hot gases would be blasted right into the shooter's face. It was no wonder that people were afraid of breech-loaders.

Another bad effect of gas leakage was that the force of the shot was cut down. A weakly propelled bullet would not fly as straight as one that was propelled forcefully, let alone hit as hard.

The problem of gas leakage was finally solved by the development of the metal cartridge around the middle of the 19th century. The metal cartridge expanded slightly when the powder exploded. It sealed the rear end of the barrel tightly and prevented gas from escaping to the rear. All the force of the expanding gases went forward out the shooting end of the barrel. After the explosion the cartridge case shrank back to its normal size and could easily be extracted.

Some breech-loading guns were manufactured before metal cartridges came into use. By the end of the 18th century, better tools enabled gunsmiths to make breeches that fitted quite closely and reduced gas leakage. One of the most famous early breech-loaders was the Hall rifle, patented in 1811 and used in the first half of the 19th century. The Hall rifle had a pivoted chamber at the breech. For loading, the chamber flipped up. Powder and bullet were put in, and then the chamber was pressed down and the gun was ready.

The development of the metal cartridge brought a flood of new breech-loader designs. Some guns had breechblocks that tilted up like trapdoors. Other breechblocks tilted down, swung out to the side, or rolled back like a rocker. Some guns simply broke open at the breech, with the barrel tilting down. This system is still used for shotguns and for the heavy double-barreled rifles used by big-game hunters. But the simple, sturdy bolt action soon displaced most other designs, particularly for military rifles.

A bolt-action gun has a cylindrical piece of metal called a bolt that slides back and forth in a channel behind the breech end of the barrel. The bolt has a handle so that the shooter can work it. When the bolt is pushed all the way forward, it closes the breech. Turning the bolt by pushing down the handle locks it closed. This is an important safety feature. Inside the bolt is a firing pin. When the trigger is pulled, a powerful spring slams the firing pin forward. After firing, the shooter unlocks the bolt and pulls it back. This opens

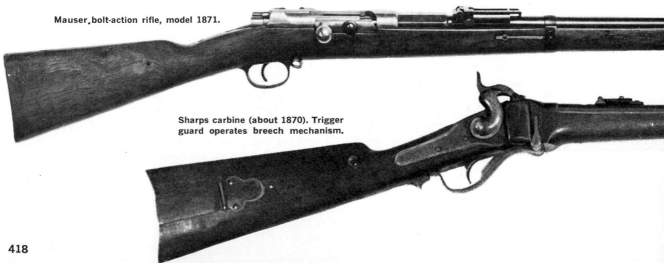

Mauser, bolt-action rifle, model 1871.

Sharps carbine (about 1870). Trigger guard operates breech mechanism.

the breech and at the same time ejects the empty cartridge. Some bolts are made so that they turn themselves when they are pulled back.

The bolt-action idea goes back to a German inventor named Johann Nickolaus von Dreyse (1787–1867). In 1837 Dreyse brought out a strange gun called a needle gun. The needle gun was a breech-loader with a bolt action. It fired an unusual kind of cartridge that Dreyse had patented about 10 years earlier for use in a muzzle-loader. The cartridge had its own percussion primer in a little hollow at the back end of the bullet. A long needle, or firing pin, passed through the base of the cartridge and the powder charge to strike the primer and set it off.

Von Dreyse's needle gun was adopted by the Prussian Army in 1842. With it the Prussians defeated the Danes in 1864 and the Austrians in 1866. An improved version of the needle gun was designed for the French Army in 1866 by Antoine Alphonse Chassepot (1833–1905). This gun performed so well in the Franco-Prussian War of 1870–71 that the Germans afterward adopted Chassepot's design.

The most efficient bolt-action rifle was designed in the late 1860's by a German gunsmith named Peter Paul Mauser. All bolt-action rifles made since his time have used Mauser's basic design. The American model 1903 Springfield rifle was almost an exact copy of Mauser's gun. In fact, the United States Government had to pay royalties to Mauser's company for using the design.

▶ DEVELOPMENTS IN AMMUNITION

The paper cartridge, containing a measured charge of powder, was first used in the late

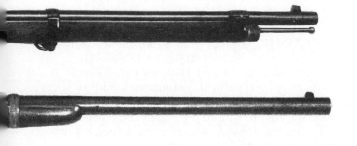

16th century. King Gustavus Adolphus of Sweden (1594–1632) introduced a cartridge that held a bullet as well. With minor changes, the paper cartridge was used through the middle of the 19th century.

Meanwhile, new developments were taking place. The ancestor of the modern self-sealing metal cartridge was developed in 1812 by a Swiss inventor named Samuel Pauly. Pauly's cartridge was designed for use in a breech-loader that he had also invented. Besides powder and bullet it contained a small percussion charge in a tiny pan at the rear of the cartridge. A firing pin struck this percussion charge to set the cartridge off. Pauly made different kinds of cartridges. Some were paper with metal bases, like modern shotgun shells. Others were all metal and could be reloaded. Pauly's system worked well, but his ideas were too advanced for his time. He was unable to sell his gun to any government.

The next step forward was the cartridge used in Dreyse's needle gun. (Dreyse had worked for Pauly as a young man and probably got the idea for the needle gun from Pauly's design.) The self-contained cartridge, carrying its own primer, caught on quickly in Europe. It was slower to catch on in the United States. The first metal cartridge in the United States was simply a brass case with a hole in the bottom. Through this hole the blast from a percussion cap could reach the powder and set it off.

The Rimfire Cartridge. Shortly before the Civil War two American gunsmiths, Horace Smith (1808–93) and Daniel B. Wesson (1825–1906), developed a metal cartridge that had a percussion primer inside the hollow rim of the base. When a firing pin struck the soft metal of the cartridge, it set off the primer. The rimfire cartridge was very popular for a while. However, it was safe for use only with weak loads and was soon replaced by the stronger center-fire cartridge except in small-caliber arms. ("Caliber" means the inside diameter of the bore of a gun. In the United States, caliber is measured in hundredths of an inch. A .45-caliber gun has an inside diameter of 45/100 inch. A .22-caliber gun has an inside diameter of 22/100 inch. In countries that use the metric system of measurement, caliber is measured in millimeters.)

The center-fire cartridge has its primer in

the center of the base of the cartridge. This was one great advance in ammunition.

Smokeless Powder. Another advance was smokeless powder, perfected by the French in 1884. Smokeless powder produces less smoke and dirt in the barrel than black powder. It is also a more powerful explosive.

Black-powder guns were generally of large caliber, from ½ inch to ¾ inch. Black powder propelled bullets relatively slowly, and the bullets usually were big and heavy.

Smokeless powder's greater force made it possible to use smaller, lighter bullets. The saving in size and weight was much appreciated by soldiers and others who had to lug around heavy cartridge belts. At the time of the Civil War, when black powder was still being used, the average caliber of military rifles was between .50 and .60. By the end of the 19th century, they had come down to about .30 caliber. This is still the most common caliber for military rifles.

The shape of bullets, too, changed during the 19th century. Experiments showed that a long, thin bullet flew straighter than a round one. By the time of the Civil War, the old round lead ball was on its way out. The bullet most commonly used in the Civil War was the so-called minie ball. The minie ball was a cylinder with a rounded end and a hollow base. It was made a trifle smaller than the bore of the rifle so that it would slide easily down the bore of a muzzle-loader. When the bullet was fired, its hollow base would expand and grip the rifling tightly. The minie ball was invented in 1849 by a French officer named Claude Étienne Minié (1814–79). Minié's original bullet had an iron cup in its hollow base. When the gun was fired, the cup was driven up into the bullet and forced it to expand. The only trouble was that the iron cup sometimes separated from the bullet and could hit soldiers nearby instead of the enemy. An American gunsmith named James Henry Burton solved this problem by leaving the cup out. The force of the exploding powder was enough to expand the bullet. But Minié's name still stuck to the invention, and "minie ball" it remained.

The changeover in the 1880's to smokeless powder and smaller calibers meant that bullets had to be long in order to be heavy enough to knock down an enemy. The change in bullet shape meant in turn that the bullet had to spin more rapidly in flight. Otherwise it would wobble like a slowing top and go wide of the target. So rifling was made to twist more sharply. Plain lead bullets were apt to have their sides stripped off by the sharply twisting rifling. This soon fouled the barrel badly. So copper- and steel-jacketed bullets came into use. Modern bullets, except in such small calibers as .22, have jackets over the lead cores.

▶REPEATING ARMS

People soon realized the usefulness of a gun that could fire more than one shot without being reloaded. Gunsmiths set to work on the problem.

As early as the 16th century there were guns with two barrels. Each barrel had its own charge of powder and bullet. Most two-barreled guns were pistols. Muskets or rifles with more than one barrel were too heavy to be very practical. Double-barreled shotguns did not become popular until the 19th century.

Pepperboxes

Pistols with three barrels or more were common during the mid-19th century. These guns, called pepperboxes, sometimes had as many as 12 or 18 barrels. Most pepperboxes, however, had from 3 to 8 barrels. The barrels were loaded separately and were turned so that each barrel came into line with the firing mechanism. The barrels were turned by hand. On later models of pepperboxes, the barrels turned each time the hammer was cocked back. A few early pepperboxes were flint-locks, but most of them were fired by percussion caps.

People carried pepperboxes for many reasons. Gold miners carried them to protect their holdings. Westward-traveling pioneers carried them for use in close fighting with Indians and outlaws. Riverboat gamblers carried them in case an argument over a card game came to a violent showdown.

Derringers

Pepperboxes were small enough to be carried secretly. An even more famous pocket gun, however, was the derringer. This was a small percussion pistol of large caliber, originally with one barrel, later with two barrels. The gun was first made by Henry Deringer, Jr. (1786–1868), a Philadelphia gunsmith. Many gunmakers imitated the weapon. All the makes became popularly known as derringers, with two *r*'s.

Derringers were made in many sizes and shapes by dozens of gunmakers. Most der-ringers had short barrels, sometimes only a little over 3 inches long. The large caliber of the derringer made it a deadly weapon at short range. Because many derringers held only one shot, they were sold in pairs. If a man missed with his first shot, he had another gun ready for the second one.

Surprise gave the derringer user a big advantage. He could tuck a pair of derringers into his vest or coat pockets and no one would know he had them—until he was ready to draw and start shooting.

The derringer was a favorite gun for use in towns, especially such wild towns as the gold-rush settlements in California during the early 1850's. On the Barbary Coast (San Francisco's tough section) men carried der-

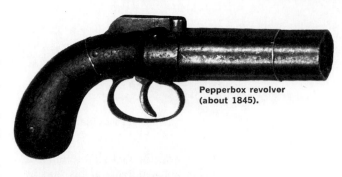

Pepperbox revolver (about 1845).

Derringer pistol—ladies' model.

ringers just as naturally as they wore a shirt or tie.

The Colt Revolver

If a man went into wilder country, away from the towns, he usually preferred to have another kind of gun—the Colt revolver. With a Colt he could fire six shots without reload-ing—hence the name six-shooter. The gun was not harmed by being dropped in sand or on rocks. It was rugged enough to stand being stepped on by a horse.

The Colt revolver was a natural step from the pepperbox pistol. Instead of having re-volving barrels, the revolver has a cylinder with six firing chambers in it. The cylinder revolves, putting a fresh cartridge at the barrel each time the hammer is cocked or the trigger is pulled.

The maker of this famous revolver was a New England inventor named Samuel Colt (1814–62). Other men had made revolvers

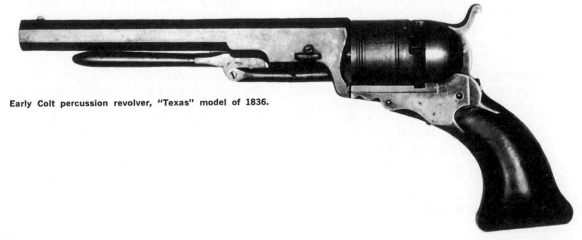

Early Colt percussion revolver, "Texas" model of 1836.

Winchester model '73.

before Colt, but he was the first man to make a practical one. He got a patent on his gun in 1836. Colt revolvers were used in the Mexican War and the Civil War. The Colt became most popular during the late 1860's and the 1870's. Many settlers pushed westward during those years. The simple, rugged Colt was one of the best weapons for defense against Indians, animals, and outlaws. Almost everyone in the West who needed a gun and could afford a revolver carried a Colt.

Until 1872, Colt revolvers were percussion guns. This was because the Smith and Wesson Company held the patent on cartridge revolvers until 1869. Production difficulties kept Colt from getting cartridge revolvers on the market before 1872.

The most popular Colt was the 1872 model, often called the Peacemaker or Frontier model. It was a .45-caliber, six-shot revolver. And it was a single-action gun—that is, the hammer had to be cocked back before each shot. The gun could fire the .44-40 cartridge that was used in the Winchester rifle. So a westerner would need only one type of ammunition for both his rifle and his revolver.

An unusual model of Colt revolver was the Buntline Special. It was an 1872-model Colt with an extra-long barrel. Some of these guns had barrels as long as 16 inches. The gun was made popular by Ned Buntline (1823–86), a writer of western stories and a publicity man for Buffalo Bill Cody. Buntline, whose real name was Edward Judson, gave the revolvers as presents to famous western lawmen such as Wyatt Earp, Bat Masterson, and Bill Hickok. Earp used his Buntline Colt in his job as marshal and made the gun famous.

Repeating Rifles

The Colt revolver was one of the guns that helped win the West. The other famous gun was the Winchester rifle. The Winchester offered the same advantage that the Colt revolver did—it would fire more than one shot

without reloading. The Winchester fired 15 bullets, which were contained in a tube-shaped ammunition holder, or magazine. It was a lever-action rifle and used metal cartridges. A lever that served as a trigger guard was pulled after each shot, ejecting the old cartridge case and putting a fresh cartridge into the firing chamber. Doing this also cocked the gun.

The Winchester was made by the Winchester Repeating Arms Company. The owner of the company, Oliver F. Winchester (1810–80), had been a shirt manufacturer. Winchester made Benjamin Tyler Henry, an expert mechanic, manager of his arms plant. Henry had previously developed the idea of the lever-action rifle. The first lever-action gun made by him, called the Henry rifle, was patented in 1860.

In 1866 the first Winchester model appeared. It was a .44-caliber gun holding 15 shots, or rounds. The cartridges were the rim-fired type (the firing pin struck the lower rim of the cartridge to set it off). The famous Winchester 1873 model used a center-fire cartridge. Since the center-fire cartridge could safely take a bigger load of powder than the rimfire cartridge, the newer model was a more powerful weapon.

The lever-action rifle was a popular gun, but the bolt-action rifle was a sturdier repeating weapon. The bolt-action gun was also easier to operate for a soldier lying flat on the ground. This gun has been the most-used military rifle since late in the 19th century.

One of the final steps in the development of the modern repeating rifle was the invention of the cartridge clip, a metal container that holds a number of cartridges. The clip and its cartridges are loaded into the rifle in one simple operation. A clip is really like a disposable magazine. The idea was developed in 1885 by Ferdinand Ritter von Mannlicher (1848–1904), an Austrian. It made for quick loading and allowed a number of shots before the gun had to be reloaded.

AUTOMATIC WEAPONS

After the quick-loading and rapid-firing modern rifle was developed, there was only one more step to take—to make an automatic gun. This is a gun that fires without the shooter having to do anything but pull the trigger. Fully automatic guns fire shot after shot as long as the trigger is held down. The trigger of a semi-automatic gun has to be pulled for each separate shot. Many so-called automatic pistols are really semi-automatic weapons.

Automatic and semi-automatic guns make use of the power of the gases from the exploding gunpowder. These gases drive the bolt back and forth, ejecting used cartridges and loading fresh ones. The best-known modern example of this kind of gun is the M-1 rifle, which was adopted by the United States Army in 1936. The M-1 was the standard rifle for United States forces in World War II.

The original M-1 was a semi-automatic weapon. Some new military rifles, such as the M-14, are made so that they can be fired as either a semi-automatic or an automatic weapon. An automatic gun delivers a lot of firepower, but it also uses up ammunition at a fast rate. A soldier might not easily be able to carry enough ammunition around with him.

During World War II an M-1 carbine was made. It was a light, compact, semi-automatic gun. The carbine is not a new invention. It was being used by cavalrymen as long ago as the 17th century (in non-automatic form, of course). Artillerymen also carried carbines, just as machine-gun and mortar crews did in World War II. Carbines are usually built like rifles, except that they are shorter, lighter, and less powerful.

Machine Guns

The machine gun is another well-known modern weapon that has a long history. Multi-barreled guns were being made in the 16th century. The first close relative of the modern machine gun, however, was the invention of James Puckle (1667?–1724), an English author. Puckle's gun, patented in 1718, had from six to nine firing chambers, each with a flintlock firing device. The gun was mounted on a tripod. A crank turned each chamber to the barrel. When that shot was fired, the next chamber was turned to the barrel. An odd feature of Puckle's gun was the kind of ammunition he suggested for it— round bullets for use against Christians, and square bullets for "Turks," as Muslims were called.

One of the most famous of the early machine guns was the Gatling gun, invented in 1862 by Dr. Richard J. Gatling (1818–1903) of North Carolina. The gun had from four to ten barrels, which were rotated by a crank. Bullets were fed continuously from a trough as long as the handle was turned. Each barrel was fired in turn to prevent overheating of any one barrel. A five-barreled, .45-caliber Gatling gun was able to fire 700 shots a minute. The Gatling gun was used in the American Civil War and by other armies throughout the world.

In 1884 Hiram S. Maxim (1869–1936), an American-born inventor who lived in England, made a truly automatic machine gun. Instead of being operated by hand, the Maxim gun used the energy of its recoil, or kick, to reload itself. The gun was mounted on a tripod, and ammunition was fed into it on a belt. The gun barrel could be either water-cooled or air-cooled. The Maxim machine gun

U.S. Army M-1 rifle.

U.S. Army M-14 rifle equipped with flash suppressor.

Gatling gun.

was a familiar sight on the battlefields of World War I. It continued to be used until more modern machine guns were developed during World War II. The new guns still used Maxim's basic idea, however.

A smaller version of the machine gun is the Thompson submachine gun, a lightweight, portable, automatic weapon. It became well-known as the tommy gun and was used by gangsters as well as by the military.

Shotguns

The modern shotgun is the descendant of the old smoothbore muskets and fowling pieces. For hunting small game and birds, gunners discovered that they had better luck when they loaded their guns with small pellets instead of a single, heavy ball. The pellets spread out when they left the gun and so increased the chance of hitting the target. Today's shotguns are, first and foremost, pellet-firing guns. The size of the pellets varies according to the game the hunter is after—small for birds and larger for animals. For big game there are also special shotgun slugs. These slugs have rifling cut on them so that they spin like a rifle bullet.

In the United States the pump-action repeating shotgun is widely used. After each shot the gunner pulls on the sliding pump shaft under the barrel. This slides a fresh cartridge into the chamber. European shooters prefer the double-barreled shotgun, which holds two shots. The gun opens at the breech for reloading. It can be safely carried in the field because when it is opened it cannot go off accidentally.

Air Guns

Not all guns have to have gunpowder to fire. Air guns shoot bullets or pellets with compressed air or gas.

The oldest kind of air gun is the blowgun, which is still used by primitive tribes in many parts of the world. Blowguns are much like peashooters, but they are usually larger and are used for hunting and warfare. The blowgun shoots a poisoned dart.

Air guns were known as early as the 15th and 16th centuries. The famous Italian artist and inventor Leonardo da Vinci (1452–1519) mentioned air guns in his writings.

One type of air gun uses a spring-driven piston to compress air for shooting. This gun must be cocked after each shot. The well-known BB gun, or air rifle, is a gun of this kind.

Other air guns have containers into which compressed air is pumped. A valve releases just enough air for each shot. Some repeating air guns are able to shoot 20 to 30 times before needing refilling.

Guns that use high-pressure carbon dioxide gas for their shooting power were invented in the 19th century. Like the air rifle, these guns are still used for target shooting and for hunting small game.

▶ARTILLERY

Cannons, mortars, and other weapons too heavy to be carried by hand are called artillery. The name "artillery" comes from an old French word meaning to equip or fortify.

The first guns of all were cannons. Many of the early cannons would look strange to

U.S. Army M-60 machine gun.

modern eyes. Some were shaped like over-grown, bulbous flower vases. Others were simply tubes of various lengths. Because of the difficulty of casting large masses of metal, many cannons, especially the large ones, were built up from long bars of wrought iron instead. The iron bars, heated red-hot, were placed around a wooden core, and then welded together edge-to-edge by hammering. To strengthen the gun, iron hoops were forced down over the bars. The completed tube looked very much like a barrel, with the iron bars for staves. In fact, some historians believe that the gun barrel got its name from this resemblance.

At first, cannons were relatively small. But by the middle of the 14th century, very large cannons were being made. One famous cannon called Dulle Griete (Dutch for "Mad Margaret") had a bore of 33 inches and fired a 600-pound stone ball. (In comparison, the largest cannon in the United States in the 20th century has a 16-inch bore. The atomic cannon developed after World War II has a bore of a little over 11 inches.)

Another famous gun was the Scottish cannon called Mons Meg, which had a barrel 13 feet 4 inches long and a 20-inch bore. An even larger gun was made in 1453 for the Sultan of Turkey, who used it against the walls of Constantinople. This monster was 17 feet long and weighed over 17 tons. It is said to have been able to shoot a half-ton ball nearly a mile.

These monster cannons, designed to destroy fortifications, were transported on heavy wooden sledges. Huge teams of horses or oxen painfully dragged them along. In wet weather the big guns mired down and could not be moved. They were of little use against troops in the field because it took so long to load and aim them. Gradually, smaller and more maneuverable cannons took the place of the monsters. Around the middle of the 15th century, wheeled gun carriages came into use. These made artillery much more maneuverable.

Aiming was almost as difficult as transportation. The muzzles of the cannons had to be propped up on a mound of dirt or on wooden supports to give them the proper elevation, or tilt. A 15th-century invention, the trunnion, solved this problem. Trunnions were a pair of short axlelike projections that stuck out from the sides of the gun barrel and carried the weight of the gun. Swinging on its trunnions, the gun barrel could easily be given the proper tilt.

During the next 3 centuries, basic cannon design changed little. However, cannons were steadily made lighter and more maneuverable. Better workmanship made them more accurate.

The great changes in artillery came in the 19th century as a result of the Industrial Revolution. Advances in chemistry made possible the large-scale production of iron and steel. The quality of the metal was vastly improved. Better metalworking tools made it possible to drill truly accurate bores and precision parts for aiming. Standardized gunpowder made it possible for the gunner to calculate how far a shot would carry. The first steel cannon was produced in the mid-19th century, though cast iron and bronze were still used until the 1870's.

The American Civil War saw the first large-scale use of breech-loading, rifled cannons. Actually these two ideas had been used in some cannons as early as the 15th century. But with the crude gunmaking techniques of that time, they did not work well and were abandoned. It took the knowledge gained in the Industrial Revolution to make them practical for big guns. Today all cannons are rifled and load at the breech.

One of the most important developments in the history of artillery was the invention of the recoil mechanism late in the 19th century. Before this invention, every time a cannon was fired the recoil would knock it out of position. Then the cannon had to be brought back to its position and re-aimed for the next shot. The recoil mechanism took up the force of the recoil so that the cannon's position was not disturbed.

World War I brought rapid-firing cannons and improved aiming devices. The French Army's rapid-firing 75-millimeter cannon, popularly called the French 75, became the best-known gun of the war. Another famous gun of World War I was the German Big Bertha, a giant cannon that fired a shell nearly 17 inches in diameter and 1,980 pounds in weight. It was used by the Germans to bombard the Belgian city of Liège in 1914.

Army gun crew prepares to fire a howitzer.

Another giant gun was used by the Germans in 1918 to shell Paris from a position 76 miles away. This gun fired an 8-inch shell, and its barrel was 110 feet long. The shells were made in a series of slightly larger sizes for each shot to make up for the wearing away of the bore. However, this gun did relatively little damage and failed to frighten the French into begging for peace, as the Germans had hoped it would.

In World War II, anti-aircraft guns came into wide use. These rapid-firing guns were often aimed automatically. Today, computers have taken over the job of aiming anti-aircraft and naval guns.

Modern Artillery. Modern artillery is divided into three basic classes. **Guns** are long-range weapons with long barrels. They fire directly at the target, with a low trajectory. ("Trajectory" means the path the shell takes in flight. A low trajectory is like a line drive in baseball. A high trajectory is like a high fly.) **Mortars** have short barrels. They fire indirectly at the target, with a high trajectory. **Howitzers** have relatively short barrels and can fire either high or low—that is, they can be used as either a gun or a mortar. The names of these classes differ from country to country. Guns and howitzers have rifled

barrels and load at the breech. Mortars are usually smoothbored and load from the muzzle. Mortar shells are designed to fire themselves when they are dropped down the barrel of the mortar.

Modern shells are of several kinds: armor-piercing, high explosive, gas, antipersonnel. Explosive shells are set off by three different types of fuses. The contact fuse explodes the shell when it hits the target. Contact fuses are used against buildings, tanks, and other large objects. The time fuse is set to explode the shell after a certain number of seconds in flight. The time fuse is used for antipersonnel shells, which are designed to mow down enemy soldiers with many bits of metal. The proximity fuse is used against fast-moving targets, such as planes and missiles. Electronic devices inside the fuse explode the shell within a certain distance of the target.

In recent years rockets have taken the place of cannons for many uses, particularly for defense against aircraft and missiles. Such rockets are considered artillery.

ELDON G. WOLFF
Curator, History Department
Milwaukee Public Museum

See also EXPLOSIVES; HUNTING.

GUPPIES.   See FISH AS PETS.

Johann Gutenberg perfected the printing press in the 1400's. This artist's interpretation shows Gutenberg examining the first page printed from movable type.

GUTENBERG, JOHANN (1398?–1468)

Until Johann Gutenberg invented a way to print from movable type, books had to be written out by hand. As a result they were scarce and expensive. Gutenberg's invention made books available to everyone.

Very little is known about Gutenberg's life. His full name was Johann Gensfleisch zum Gutenberg. He was born about 1398 in the free city of Mainz, Germany, where his father was a tax collector. As a young man, Johann learned the art of goldsmithing. Working in the Mainz mint, he learned to make coins.

In 1428, Gutenberg left Mainz because of a dispute between the workers' guilds and the patrician (aristocratic) families like his own. He went to Strasbourg, where he developed the idea of casting (forming) letters in metal. He invented a special mold for making movable type—letters that could be moved around and reused.

In 1444, Gutenberg returned to Mainz, where he perfected his invention for "artificial writing," as it was then called. He received a commission from the Bishop of Strasbourg to print the Bible. But he needed a great deal of money to pay for this work. It was lent to him by Johann Fust, a wealthy lawyer.

Gutenberg redesigned a wine press to serve as a printing press. He used paper, vellum (treated calfskin), and an oil-based ink. He experimented with molds to form the letters and with frames to hold the letters in the press. He mixed different metals together to find one hard enough to stand repeated use.

But Gutenberg spent all his time and most of Fust's money on his experiments. Fust sued him, but Gutenberg was unable to pay off the loan and was forced out of business. Later he found another backer.

Fust and his son-in-law, Peter Schoeffer, carried on Gutenberg's work, and the Bible was completed in 1455. But it was Johann Gutenberg who had perfected the process for printing this landmark work. After his death on February 3, 1468, his discovery spread rapidly when many printers left Mainz to establish printing shops in other countries.

Gutenberg's invention was one of the most important milestones in the development of Western culture. It was the beginning of today's technological revolution in the storage and spread of information.

PAUL A. WINCKLER
Palmer School of Library
and Information Science

See also PRINTING.

GUTIÉRREZ, JOSÉ A. See TEXAS (Famous People).

GUYANA

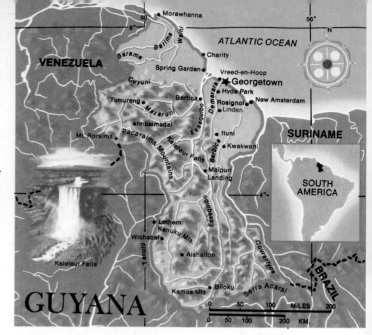

GUYANA

The Republic of Guyana occupies a part of the northeastern coast of South America just north of the equator. It shares the region with Suriname (formerly Dutch Guiana) and French Guiana. Because the three territories have similarities in land formation and climate, and in some aspects of their history, they are often called the Guianas. Guyana, the largest of the three, was formerly known as British Guiana. It gained its independence from Great Britain in 1966.

▶THE PEOPLE

Most of Guyana's people live on a coastal plain bordering on the Atlantic Ocean. They live either in cities or towns or in the many small villages near the rivers. The country has a varied population. Slightly over half the Guyanese are descendants of people from India (East Indians), who came to Guyana to work on plantations. About a third are descended from African slaves. There are people of mixed ethnic background and small groups of Portuguese and Chinese. The original inhabitants, South American Indians, now make up a small part of the population. Most of them live in the sparsely populated interior, where their ancestors fled to escape forced labor under European settlers.

About half the population is Christian. The East Indians are mainly Hindus or, to a lesser extent, Muslims. Some South American Indians observe their traditional religions. English is the official and most commonly used language. But Hindi and Urdu (two languages of India), Portuguese, Chinese, and South American Indian languages are also spoken. A local patois, or mixed language, is used by some Guyanese. Guyana has a high literacy rate: most of its people can read and write.

▶THE LAND

Like the larger region in which it is located, Guyana takes its name from the South American Indian word *guiana,* meaning "land of waters." The name describes the country well, for many rivers and steams flow within

its borders. The three largest rivers are the Berbice, the Demerara, and the Essequibo.

Beyond the narrow coastal plain, the land rises to rolling hills and a central plateau. The western part of the country is mountainous. Mount Roraima, at 2,810 meters (9,219 feet), is the highest point. There are many waterfalls in the mountains. Kaieteur Falls is known for the rainbow mists that rise from its waters, which plunge from a height of 226 meters (741 feet). In the southwest is the savanna, a region of grassland. Dense rain forests cover about three quarters of the country.

Guyana's climate is tropical. Temperatures are high all year along the coast. The mountains of the interior are somewhat cooler. Rainfall is abundant.

Guyana's capital, largest city, and chief port is Georgetown. It lies on the Atlantic coast at the mouth of the Demerara River. The two other largest towns are Linden (formerly Mackenzie), the center of Guyana's mining industry, and New Amsterdam.

▶THE ECONOMY

Guyana's economy is based chiefly on agriculture and mining. Sugarcane, the main export crop, is raised on large plantations. Many of the plantations are owned by a government corporation. Rice, another important export, is cultivated by East Indians. Coconuts, vegetables, and citrus fruits are grown for food. Cattle, sheep, pigs, and poultry are also raised for food.

Guyana is an important producer and exporter of bauxite, the main ore of aluminum. Gold exports now provide more income than bauxite. There are also deposits of diamonds and other minerals.

Valuable hardwoods grow in Guyana's dense forests. The sturdy greenheart tree is harvested in large numbers and is an important source of timber for export.

▶ HISTORY AND GOVERNMENT

The first inhabitants of what is now Guyana were Carib, Arawak, and Warrau Indians. The Dutch set up trading posts in the 17th century. Later the British established a number of settlements. For many years the British and Dutch struggled for control of the region. In 1814 the colonies of Essequibo, Berbice, and Demerara were ceded to Great Britain. In 1831 the three colonies were merged and became known as British Guiana. Slaves from Africa had been brought to the area as laborers. When slavery was abolished in the 1830's, workers were brought from India.

British Guiana began to move toward independence in 1945. It became fully independent as the nation of Guyana in 1966. Guyana's last ties with the British monarchy were cut in 1970, when the country became a republic. A new constitution came into effect in 1980 and established the present form of government. It consists of a president and cabinet and an elected legislature called the National Assembly. The candidate of the political party receiving the most votes in elections for the National Assembly becomes president.

Guyana Today. Guyana today faces deep economic, social, and political problems. These include a declining economy, high foreign debt, and widespread unemployment. Guyana's difficulties also include a long-standing border dispute with the neighboring country of Venezuela.

From 1964 until his death in 1985, Forbes Burnham, leader of the People's National Congress (supported mainly by black Guyanese), was prime minister and then president. He was succeeded by his associate Desmond Hoyte. In 1992 the People's Progressive Party of Cheddi Jagan, an early leader of the independence movement, came to power. After his death in 1997, his American-born wife, Janet Jagan, was elected president.

Reviewed by ROBERT H. MANLEY
Author, *Guyana Emergent*

See also GUIANA.

FACTS and figures

COOPERATIVE REPUBLIC OF GUYANA is the official name of the country.

LOCATION: Northeastern coast of South America.

AREA: 83,000 sq mi (214,970 km²).

POPULATION: 800,000 (estimate).

CAPITAL AND LARGEST CITY: Georgetown.

MAJOR LANGUAGE: English (official).

MAJOR RELIGIOUS GROUPS: Christian, Hindu, Muslim.

GOVERNMENT: Republic. **Head of state and government**—president. **Legislature**—National Assembly.

CHIEF PRODUCTS: Agricultural—sugarcane, rice, timber, coconuts, fruits. **Mineral**—gold, bauxite (aluminum ore).

MONETARY UNIT: Guyana dollar (1 G dollar = 100 cents).

The City Hall in Georgetown, the capital, is a reminder of the time when Britain governed Guyana. Most Guyanese are descendants of people from India and Africa.

To perform successfully, gymnasts must reach a high level of physical fitness. Strength, flexibility, good coordination, and endurance are needed to execute the demanding routines precisely and confidently with fluid, graceful, daring movements and split-second timing.

GYMNASTICS

Gymnastics is a sport that develops physical fitness, physical and mental coordination and endurance, and flexibility, balance, and beauty of movement in its athletes. In most countries of the world, including the United States, gymnastics is a competitive sport.

Gymnastics as a sport can be traced back to ancient Greece. Present-day gymnastics began in the early 1800's in Sweden. At about the same time, gymnastic apparatus was also developed in Germany and Czechoslovakia, and gymnastics became a popular sport throughout northern and middle Europe.

Gymnastic competition became part of the modern Olympic Games in 1896. Since then, gymnasts from all over the world have met in countless competitions. Athletes from Eastern Europe, Russia, and Japan have at one time or another been preeminent in the sport. In the 1980's, Mary Lou Retton, Bart Connor, and Kurt Thomas put the United States on the gymnastics' world map. Retton was the first American gymnast to receive a perfect 10 in international competition. Competitive events include routines for floor exercises; vaulting; the pommel horse; the horizontal, parallel, and uneven parallel bars; the balance beam; the still rings; and the all-around.

Gymnastic elements can be divided into four basic categories referred to as hanging, swinging, supporting, and release elements. In **hanging elements**—used in the uneven parallel bars for women and the horizontal bar, still rings, and parallel bars for men—the weight of the body is suspended from the wrists. The **swinging element** is used in routines for all of the women's and men's events. In the **support element**, the shoulders are usually higher than the wrists. Gymnasts performing in the women's uneven parallel bars and the men's still rings, pommel horse, and parallel bars must

Floor Exercises

show support elements during their routines. Today's gymnasts use **release elements** in the women's uneven bars and in the men's horizontal bar, parallel bars, and in some routines on the still rings. The release element is very exciting and also very dangerous, and it usually takes the longest time to learn. In a release element, the athlete actually "flies" through the air from bar to bar. Leaping movements also fall into the release category and are used by both men and women.

In planning a practice or workout session, it is necessary to work on all four basic elements to obtain perfection. A practice session plan should be based on the body type and skill level of the athlete.

▶**HOW TO BEGIN**

It is desirable for the beginner to start with floor exercises or tumbling. Before any practice begins, a gymnast needs to warm up with slow stretching exercises. These exercises loosen the body as well as warm up the muscles that will be used. Some beginners are limited by their lack of flexibility, which can be developed by performing floor exercises and by stretching. Any size area can be used for stretching and warm-up exercises. Tumbling can be done on a straight mat that is 40 by 6 feet (12 by 1.8 meters) and

A handspring (*right*) is included in the men's floor exercise. The routine's demanding movements call for flexibility, strength, balance, and a good sense of timing.

A women's floor exercise routine (*far right*) includes dance, leaping, and tumbling movements. The gymnast is evaluated on form, flexibility, body control, and timing.

Floor exercise routines are made up of leaps, handsprings, and other tumbling skills. The men's routine includes some balancing pauses between movements and lasts from 50 to 70 seconds. The women's routine, performed to music, includes various poses in addition to dance and tumbling movements. It lasts from 60 to 90 seconds.

2 inches (5 centimeters) thick, or it can be done on an area that is 40 by 40 feet (12 by 12 meters). The normal floor exercise mat is 42 by 42 feet (13 by 13 meters) and it is covered with foam and carpet.

Practice mats should always be used. The mats should be at least 5 by 12 feet (1.5 by 3.6 meters) and 2 to 4 inches (5 to 10 centimeters) thick. Today's mats are usually made of foam. Safety should always be the first consideration in choosing a mat.

Routines

Many varieties of movements and combinations can be included in floor exercises. First you should learn the skills, then choose which ones you wish to put into a routine.

Floor exercises often begin with tumbling and may include handstand, balance, and leaping movements. For a final impression of good form and body control, the routine should end with a perfect landing, often called a "stuck" landing.

There should be definite harmony and connection between the movements, so that they all fit smoothly into the exercise. Variety, called originality, is also needed, and movements can also be combined in unusual ways so that the entire routine is interesting and exciting. Another important consideration is where each movement will be performed. The gymnast should use the entire floor area, moving diagonally as well as forward and backward. Diagonal patterns should be reserved for routines demonstrating the highest level of skill. Advanced gymnasts are expected to demonstrate more difficult skills than are beginning gymnasts.

Side Horse Vault

In the women's vault, the gymnast goes across the width of the horse, performing a handspring, somersault, or cartwheel (*far left*) that begins as she leaps onto and pushes herself off the horse with her hands.

Long Horse Vault

The men's long horse vault is similar to the women's vaulting event, but the male gymnast must leap across the entire length of the horse (*left*).

strength movements. It is also good to show some form of flexibility in a routine. Most routines finish with a tumbling pass. The women's routine is set to music and needs to include some form of dance. This is usually ballet, but it can be modern dance. In both men's and women's floor routines, the gymnast's timing, flexibility, and form are very important, as are the heights of the tumbling

A Word of Caution to Young Gymnasts

Floor exercises are the basis for gymnastics development, and they prepare you for the events on gymnastic apparatus. You may safely practice many floor exercises, but take care to choose the proper ones. Never attempt a skill that you are not ready to perform. When you practice, take safety precautions. Do not force yourself beyond your abilities.

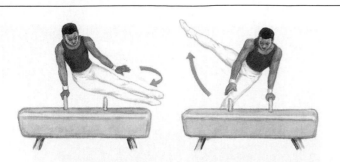

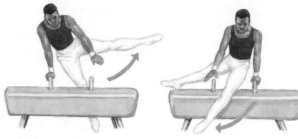

Pommel Horse

The gymnast continuously swings his body around the pommel horse, supporting himself by placing one or both hands on the wooden pommels, or handles, or on the padded horse itself. He may swing his legs over the horse separately or together and may also perform scissor movements with his legs. The difficulty for the gymnast is to keep his weight centered over his hands while his body is constantly moving.

The pommel horse demands fine balance and control as well as strength in the arms, hands, and abdominal muscles.

Still Rings

On the still rings, a gymnast performs a series of strength and swinging movements, keeping the rings almost motionless. A routine for competition includes complete circles and two handstands, one based on strength and the other on the momentum of the swing.

A gymnast supports himself on the still rings with his arms extended sideways. This movement requires tremendous strength in the arms, chest, and back.

At all times exercises should be performed only when an adult is present to lend assistance, to help eliminate mistakes or repetition in a routine, and to guard or "spot" (catch or break the fall of) the performer. Many falls are caused by perspiration, which makes the hands slip on the apparatus. Veteran gymnasts find that their hands begin to perspire even before they mount the apparatus. To prevent slipping, gymnasts use hand guards, or grips, or they may rub their palms with bicarbonate of magnesia, or chalk.

▶ COMPETITION IN GYMNASTICS

There are seven championship events for men: floor exercise, long horse vault, pommel horse, still rings, parallel bars, horizontal bar, and the all-around (the combined score of the first six events). For women, there are five championship events: floor exercise, balance beam, side horse vault, uneven parallel bars, and the all-around.

In top-level international competitions, some events include compulsory and optional routines. Compulsory routines are a set of pre-written routines that all gymnasts perform. These routines are rated by the ease with which they are done as well as by how they are performed for form or execution. They are judged for mechanics, grace and rhythm, and how well they are performed within the overall routine.

Optional routines are put together by each individual performer. The gymnast selects the skills for the event that he or she can perform well. These routines are judged for originality, correctness, form, and daring or risk. If a performer demonstrates too much strain while performing a skill, his or her score will be lower. Today many com-

Balance Beam

On the balance beam, the gymnast must demonstrate dancing ability, grace, and perfect balance (*above left*).

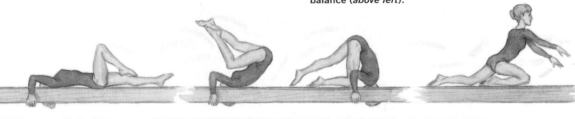

Leaps, turns, running and walking steps, lying and sitting positions, and the graceful roll shown above are among the required elements in a routine on the balance beam. The gymnast tries to use the entire beam during the exercise, which lasts from 80 to 105 seconds.

Uneven Parallel Bars

The women's uneven parallel bars routine (*left*) requires daring, coordination, and strength. The gymnast swings from bar to bar, changing her grip and direction frequently.

petitions use only the optional routine. It is the most difficult routine for the gymnast to do but the most exciting routine for the spectators to watch.

From two to four officials judge the routines. At times a fifth judge, called a superior judge, is used. The superior's job is to keep the other four officials within the judging guidelines. When two judges are used, the scores are averaged; when four judges are used, the highest score and the lowest score are discarded, and the remaining two scores are averaged.

The International Gymnastics Federation conducts the world competitions every year and the Olympic competition every four years. It controls the rules and policies manual, as well as the judging code of points, so that

Horizontal Bar

The men's horizontal bar routine requires strength, split-second timing, and courage. It consists of continuous swinging, release, and regrasping movements that change direction several times and are performed without stops. In some, the gymnast vaults high above the steel bar.

Parallel Bars

A performance on the parallel bars includes high swings and movements that require strength and balance. The gymnast supports himself with his hands but may not touch the bars with any other part of his body.

there is only one basis for judging. This means that the same rules are used to value the routines, regardless of where gymnasts may be performing. Competition within each country is run by a member of the International Gymnastics Federation. In the United States, the gymnastics programs for all levels are directed by U.S.A. Gymnastics. Other organizations that conduct championships are the Amateur Athletic Union (A.A.U.), the National Collegiate Athletic Association (N.C.A.A.), the YMCA's, the American Sokol Educational and Physical Culture Organization, and the Jewish League of America.

In addition to being a competitive sport, gymnastics is also used as physical therapy. Remedial, or corrective, gymnastics uses certain aspects of gymnastic conditioning to help rebuild muscles that have been damaged by injuries or illness.

STANLEY ATKINSON
Chairman, A.A.U.
Gymnastics Committee

Gypsies take to the road in various vehicles—from flower-festooned carts to campers.

GYPSIES

Gypsies are a people who first appeared in Europe several centuries ago. They are nomads—wanderers who travel from one place to another. They have a proud history, their own language, and their own customs and traditions that they have passed on from generation to generation.

▶ ORIGINS AND HISTORY

Gypsies are so named because it was first believed that they traveled to Europe from Egypt. Actually they originated in India. For unknown reasons, they left their homeland about A.D. 1000. They first went to Afghanistan and then to Persia (now Iran). From there, some groups went to Syria and North Africa. Others went to Greek-speaking countries and crossed the Balkan Peninsula. There were Gypsies in the western part of Europe by the 15th century.

For the most part, the Gypsies were dark-skinned, with black hair. They traveled in long caravans. The men went on horse or on foot. The women and children, with their folded tents and their few belongings, traveled in colorfully painted horse-drawn wagons and carts. Wherever they went in Eastern or Western Europe, they were greeted with curiosity and suspicion. This attitude often turned to hostility because, in their customs and physical appearance, the Gypsies differed greatly from the citizens of their host countries. From their earliest years in Europe, the Gypsies insisted on maintaining their own way of life. For this reason, the history of this nomadic people has largely been one of repression and persecution. This has been the case even in the 20th century, when an estimated 500,000 Gypsies were killed in Nazi concentration camps during World War II.

▶ LANGUAGE, CUSTOMS, AND TRADITIONS

That the Gypsies have survived so long in spite of hostility is due to their pride in their language, customs, and traditions. The language spoken by many Gypsies is called Romany. This language has changed over the years—as all languages do. It has been influenced by other languages with which the Gypsies have come into contact during their wanderings, but it is basically a language of India. Its grammar is in many ways similar to that of Sanskrit, the classical language of ancient India, and more than half of its words are related to languages of northern India.

Gypsy life, because it is largely an outdoor life, has always been regulated by the seasons. The people begin their travels in the spring. They settle temporarily in one location during the winter, when traveling is difficult. Gypsies travel in communities—groups that might number as few as ten families or as many as several hundred families. The family is a very close unit.

One man—chosen for his age, experience, and wisdom—rules each community, at times with the aid of a specially chosen court. He acts as judge in all disputes and sees to it that the standards by which the community must live are maintained. He makes sure that all members of the group respect the laws, customs, and traditions of the Gypsies. Gypsies have a great many superstitions, but they also have very well-defined rules concerning social behavior, eating habits, and cleanliness. Some of the rules are quite rigid. For example, dishes cannot be washed in the same sink that is used for the washing of one's hands or personal clothing. Birth, marriage, and death are marked by strictly observed rituals.

The traditional occupations of the Gypsies are determined by their nomadic ways. They have long excelled in occupations that do not require them to remain in one place for a long time. Gypsy men have been expert metalworkers (tinsmiths, coppersmiths, or silversmiths), horse dealers, and artisans. They have been known as talented circus performers, working with bears and horses. Gypsy women often sell the objects the men produce, and they have won fame as fortune-tellers. (It is interesting to note that Gypsies never tell fortunes to one another.) Both men and women are known as excellent musicians and dancers. Gypsy violinists and orchestras have been popular for centuries, and Gypsy dancers have been equally successful.

Gypsy women shop at a market in Rumania.

▶ GYPSIES TODAY

Gypsies are found in almost every part of the world, but today the majority of them live in Europe, with the largest numbers in Spain, Hungary, and France. Because the Gypsies move from place to place, it is difficult to know exactly how many there are.

Gypsies have adjusted to the 20th century by changing some of their ways. Instead of traveling in carts or wagons, many Gypsies use cars, campers, and trailers. Their skills as artisans and metalworkers are no longer so valuable as in the past. Instead, many Gypsy men have become expert at automobile repair. But fortune-telling has remained a popular occupation among Gypsy women.

Many Gypsies have settled in large cities. Some have adjusted to city life, but in most cases their stays have been temporary. When

Gypsy guitar players draw a crowd in Spain.

spring comes, there comes with it an urge to pack up and take to the road.

In April, 1978, a world congress of Gypsies was held in Geneva, Switzerland. Its purpose was to call for an end to discrimination against Gypsies throughout the world. Many Gypsies in the 20th century have successfully become part of the societies of the countries in which they have found themselves. But at the same time, they hope to retain their heritage.

HOWARD GREENFELD
Author, *Gypsies*

GYROSCOPE

A gyroscope, or gyro, is a simple instrument made up of a wheel and an axle mounted in a frame. There are many sizes and types of gyroscopes, and they have many important scientific uses. For example, gyroscopes can aim and guide rockets, missiles, and spacecraft, and they are often used to navigate airplanes, ships, and submarines.

Small gyroscopes make very interesting toys. When the wheel of a toy gyroscope is spinning, it can be balanced on the rim of a drinking glass, on a tight string, or on a pencil point. As long as it is spinning fast, the gyroscope will not fall. It seems to defy gravity.

▶ PROPERTIES OF A GYROSCOPE

Spinning objects, such as a bicycle wheel, a toy top, and a gyroscope, share two unusual properties—gyroscopic inertia and precession. These properties can be demonstrated by performing several simple experiments. If you have a toy gyroscope or can purchase one, you can demonstrate these properties for yourself.

Gyroscopic Inertia. The first property of a gyroscope, gyroscopic inertia, can be described in this way: The axle of a spinning gyro always tends to point in the direction in which it is set. To make your toy gyroscope spin, you will need a piece of string, which should be about 30 inches (75 centimeters) long. The string and instructions usually come with a toy gyroscope.

Wrap the string snugly around the gyro's axle. Then hold the gyro firmly in one hand without touching the wheel. Unwind the string by pulling it quickly with your other hand. This will set the wheel spinning. Once it is spinning, try to make the gyro point in directions other than the one you started it in by gently pushing it. You will see that it remains stable but it also continues to point in the direction you started it in.

When the gyro has stopped spinning, wrap the string around its axle again, and set the gyro so that it points in a different direction. Pull the string quickly. Then gently push the gyro to try to make it point in another direction. Notice that once again the gyro keeps pointing in the direction you set it in when you started it spinning.

Another example of gyroscopic inertia is planet Earth itself. The Earth spins on its axis like a gyroscope, and it has the first property of a gyroscope. One end of the Earth's axis, the North Pole, always points in the same direction—the direction of our North Star, Polaris.

Precession. The second property of a gyroscope, precession, can be described in this way: If a force tends to change the direction of a spinning gyro's axle, the axle will not move in the direction of the force. Instead, it moves at right angles to the direction of the force.

The special properties of gyroscopes make it possible to create this spectacular effect with three toy gyros.

Spin your toy gyro in front of you with its axle straight up and down. With your finger, push straight ahead on the frame, just above the spinning axle. The axle will not move in the direction in which you push it. Instead, the top of the axle moves to the right or to the left, and then in a circle.

Precession is what keeps the top of the gyro axle moving in a circle after it has been tipped away from the straight up-and-down position. Once the axle has been tipped, the force of gravity tends to tip it farther down. But the axle precesses sideways, at a right angle to the downward pull of gravity.

The spinning Earth also shows precession. A strong force—the gravity of the moon and the sun—acts on the axis of the Earth. This force causes the Earth's axis to precess, which means that the direction in space toward which our planet's axis is pointing is continually changing. At present the axis is pointing close to the position of Polaris in the sky. Therefore, for now, Polaris serves as our North Star. But gradually, due to precession, this will change, and in about 12,000 years the bright star Vega will serve as our North Star.

You experience the two properties of a gyroscope when you ride a bicycle. You point the bicycle in a certain direction, and as long as you keep the wheels turning, by pedaling, the bicycle moves along and does not fall over. What keeps a bicycle upright as long as the wheels are turning? The answer is gyroscopic inertia. When you lean to one side, the bicycle does not fall over. Instead, the front wheel turns, or precesses, to the side. So the bicycle changes direction, but it does not fall over.

▶ USES OF A GYROSCOPE

Commercial gyroscopes spin very fast and electric motors are used to keep them spinning. These gyroscopes are widely used as compasses, automatic pilots, and stabilizers in airplanes, ships, and spacecraft.

Gyrocompass. Because a spinning gyroscope points steadily in a given direction, it can be used as a compass. It is then called a gyrocompass. Gyrocompasses keep ships and aircraft on course. The axle of the gyroscope is pointed at true north. As long as its wheel is spinning, the gyroscope's axle always points to true north. The Earth has two "north" poles. One is the geographic north pole, called true north, which is known as the North Pole. The other is the north magnetic pole, which is located near Bathurst Island in northern Canada.

The gyrocompass is often used in navigation because magnetic compasses are affected by the steel in the ships and aircraft. For this reason the magnetic compass is not very accurate. Since gyrocompasses are not affected by steel, they are more accurate than magnetic compasses.

Automatic Pilot. Automatic pilots are used to keep airplanes on course. An automatic pilot has three gyroscope axles, or axes. ("Axes" is the plural of "axis.") One keeps the airplane headed in the desired direction. If the plane wanders off course, the gyro sends a signal to a special motor, which moves the rudder at the tail of the plane. The rudder moves just enough to correct the drift. The other gyro axes are used to keep the plane from pitching up and down or from rolling to one side or the other. With an automatic pilot, the plane's human pilot is free to watch the instruments and can even go into the main cabin and talk to the passengers.

Stabilizers. Automatic pilots are also used in ships. In addition, gyroscopes and special motors are used to control the stabilizers on each side of a ship. A ship's stabilizers, which are large fins on its underside, keep it from rolling with each big wave.

Missiles and Spacecraft. Gyroscopes are used in missiles and spacecraft to keep them headed toward their targets. Some missiles and spacecraft can be controlled by radio signals that adjust their gyroscopes while in flight. The *Viking* and *Voyager* space probes that were sent to study the outer planets in our solar system were guided in this way.

The Properties of a Gyroscope

When a gyroscope is spinning, it always points in the direction it is set (*right*). If you push forward on the frame of a gyroscope spinning straight up and down, the axle will tilt to the right or left; (*middle and far right*) not in the direction you pushed it.

Axle

Outer gimbal
Inner gimbal] Frame

Wheel

A laser gyro (*above*) is made of a glasslike material and is shaped like a triangle. It is made to exacting specifications.

A laser gyro has no wheel or axle. Instead, a laser beam is split into two parts that move in opposite directions around the gyro's triangle shape (*right*). A detector notes the difference if one beam travels farther than the other, which happens, for example, when a ship or airplane using the gyro for navigation goes off course.

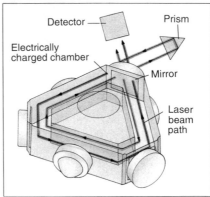

Detector
Prism
Electrically charged chamber
Mirror
Laser beam path

Like an automatic pilot, the laser gyro corrects the course of the airplane or ship.

Laser gyros will probably replace wheel-and-axle gyroscopes in guiding airplanes, ships, spacecraft, and missiles. The laser gyro is simpler and more reliable than a mechanical gyro. It is also cheaper for uses that require a high degree of accuracy.

Scientists have also developed another type of gyroscope—the fiber-optic gyro, which is very similar to the laser gyro. It also uses laser beams, but the beams move through a fine glass fiber.

▶ HISTORY

The word "gyroscope" comes from Greek words meaning "to view the rotation of the Earth." The name was chosen by the French physicist Léon Foucault. In the early 1850's he made a simple gyroscope and used it to prove that the Earth rotates on its axis. At that time there were still people who believed that the Earth stands still and the sun, moon, and stars move around it. A short time before, Foucault had used a pendulum in an experiment that convinced people that the Earth rotates on its axis.

Foucault predicted that the gyroscope would one day be used as a compass. But this did not happen until the invention of the electric motor, which could keep the gyro wheel spinning for long periods of time. Ball bearings also were needed to keep a heavy gyroscope that was running continuously at a high speed from wearing out quickly from friction. By 1911, Elmer A. Sperry, an American electrical engineer, had marketed a successful gyrocompass. Thereafter, inventors in the United States and other countries worked to produce the many kinds of gyroscopic devices that we know today, all of which work according to the laws of motion that Sir Isaac Newton thought out some three hundred years ago.

Reviewed by WILLIAM A. GUTSCH, JR.
Chairman, American Museum-
Hayden Planetarium

▶ OTHER TYPES OF GYROSCOPES

Some jet airliners and surface ships use laser gyroscopes. These gyroscopes are quite different from ordinary gyroscopes. They have no wheel and no axle. In fact, they have no moving parts. But laser gyroscopes can be used to detect rotation, just as mechanical gyroscopes can.

A typical laser gyro is made of a glasslike material and is shaped like a triangle. A laser beam is generated and split into two parts that move in opposite directions around the triangle. If the aircraft or ship moves off course, the movement to one side will make one laser beam travel farther than the other. This difference in travel is noticed by a special detector.

Index

HOW TO USE THE DICTIONARY INDEX

See the beginning of the blue pages in Volume 1.

García Márquez, José Gabriel (Colombian writer)   **C:**403; **L:**72; **N:**363
  picture(s) **N:**362
García Pérez, Alan (Peruvian president)   **P:**165
Garcilaso de la Vega (Spanish poet)   **S:**390
  history of the Incas   **L:**68
Garden City Association   **U:**236
"Gardener, The" (poem by Robert Louis Stevenson)   **S:**451
Garden of Gethsemane *see* Gethsemane, Garden of
Garden of the Gods (Colorado Springs, Colorado)
  picture(s) **C:**438
Garden of the Gulf (nickname for Prince Edward Island)   **P:**460
Gardens and gardening   **G:**26–52 *see also* Flowers; Lawns;
      Soils
  botanical gardens   **B:**342–43
  childhood gardens in Kenya   **K:**229
  experiments with plants   **E:**383
  fertilizer   **F:**96–98
  flowers and their animal pollinators   **F:**286
  garden fruits   **G:**297–301
  how to sprout apple seeds   **A:**332
  lawns   **L:**89
  parks   **P:**76
  plant pests   **P:**286–91
  South Carolina gardens of interest   **S:**304
  terrariums   **T:**102–4
  vegetables   **V:**286–94
  weeds   **W:**104–6
  picture(s)
      Bellingrath Gardens (Alabama)   **A:**138
      Japanese rock garden   **J:**28
      Royal Botanical Gardens (Hamilton, Ontario)   **B:**343
Garden spiders   **S:**403–4, 405
  picture(s) **S:**406
Garden State (nickname for New Jersey)   **N:**164
Gardner, Howard (American psychologist)   **I:**253
Garfield (comic strip)   **C:**129
Garfield, James A. (20th president of the United
      States)   **G:**52–55
  Ohio home   **O:**68
  Pendleton Act passed as a result of his
      assassination   **C:**331
  quoted on Mark Hopkins   **H:**226
  picture(s) **P:**450
Garfield, Lucretia Rudolph (wife of James A.
      Garfield)   **F:**173–74; **G:**53
Gargantua and Pantagruel (book by Rabelais)   **F:**437
  scene from   **G:**203
Gargling (to soothe a sore throat)   **D:**208
Gargoyles (sculptures)   **G:**268
Garibaldi (fish)   **F:**196
Garibaldi, Giuseppe (Italian patriot)   **G:**56; **I:**389
Garland, Hamlin (American writer)   **A:**206; **W:**206
Garland, Judy (American entertainer)   **M:**488
  picture(s) **M:**338
Garlic (plant of onion family)   **O:**123
  bulbs   **P:**305
  supposed medicinal powers   **F:**333
Garment industry *see* Clothing industry
Garmisch-Partenkirchen (Germany)
  Olympic Games (1936)   **O:**110
Garneau, Marc (Canadian astronaut)   **S:**351
  picture(s) **S:**351
Garner, John Nance (American statesman)   **V:**329
  picture(s) **V:**329
Garnerin, André (French aeronaut)   **B:**35
Garnet, Henry Highland (American abolitionist)   **A:**6a
Garnets (gemstones)   **G:**71
  abrasive for grinding and polishing   **G:**392
  picture(s) **G:**73; **M:**316
      South African mine   **M:**317
Garnier, Marie Joseph François (French explorer)   **E:**415
Garonne River (France)   **F:**409; **R:**242
Garrett, Pat (Patrick Floyd) (American sheriff)   **N:**192
Garrett, Robert (American athlete)   **O:**108

Garrett, Thomas (American abolitionist)   **U:**15, 16
Garrison, William Lloyd (American abolitionist)   **A:**6, 79g;
      M:148; **S:**196
  American literature   **A:**203
  Boston   **B:**341
  picture(s) **A:**6a
Garrison Dam (North Dakota)   **N:**335
  picture(s) **N:**327
Garry, Chief (Spokane Indian chief)   **W:**23
Garter snakes   **S:**209, 218
  picture(s) **L:**201
Garter stitch (in knitting)   **K:**281
Garvey, Marcus (African American nationalist)   **A:**79j
  picture(s) **A:**79k
Gary (Indiana)   **I:**153–54
Gary, Romain (French novelist)   **F:**443
Gas, fuel   **P:**522
  natural gas   **N:**58–60
Gaseous diffusion process (for separation of uranium
      isotopes)   **U:**229–30
Gases   **G:**56–61
  air pollution   **A:**122–25
  atmosphere   **A:**479, 482
  balloons and ballooning   **B:**34–38
  Boyle's law   **B:**354
  burping and intestinal gases   **B:**301
  chemical terms   **C:**204
  coal gasification   **C:**390
  Earth's history   **E:**23
  electronics, use in   **E:**158
  Faraday's work   **F:**47
  fires, dangers of   **F:**148
  floating and buoyancy   **F:**250
  fuels   **F:**487–88
  helium   **H:**106
  how heat changes matter   **H:**91
  hydrogen   **H:**316
  kinetic theory   **B:**153
  lasers   **L:**46c
  lighting, use in   **L:**233–34, 236
  liquid gases   **L:**253
  and liquids   **L:**254
  lubricants   **L:**335
  matter, states of   **M:**172, 174, 175–76
  mining dangers   **M:**322
  natural gas   **N:**58–60
  noble gases   **G:**61; **N:**105–6
  ocean water, dissolved gases in   **O:**17
  oxygen   **O:**286–88
  physics, history of   **P:**234
  pneumatic systems   **H:**314
  poison gas in World War I   **W:**277
  public utility   **P:**522
  rocket fuels   **R:**258
  sun   **S:**490, 494, 495
  thermometers   **T:**164
  volcanoes   **V:**379–80, 385
  water, forms of   **W:**48
  What makes a stomach growl?   **S:**461
Gas giant planets
  Jupiter   **J:**159
  Neptune   **N:**111–12
  Saturn   **S:**53
  Uranus   **U:**231–32
Gas lasers (devices projecting light beams)   **L:**46c
Gas masks   **C:**106
Gas meters   **P:**522
Gasoline   **G:**62
  automobile fuel   **A:**540, 542
  coal as source of   **C:**390
  environmental protection   **P:**176
  ethanol as a supplement   **F:**489
  fuel economy of automobiles   **A:**544
  fuels   **F:**487

Gasoline (cont.)
how the gasoline engine works **I:**264–67
lead is a component of **L:**92
petroleum refining **P:**172
picture(s)
gas pump **F:**487
Gasoline engines **E:**230
Gaspée (ship)
Rhode Island residents in rebellion against the Stamp
Act **R:**196, 225
Gaspé Peninsula (Quebec) **C:**52; **Q:**8
picture(s) **Q:**10
Gaspra (asteroid) **S:**361
picture(s) **C:**451
Gaster (part of ant's abdomen) **A:**319
Gastric juice **B:**109; **S:**461
Gastric ulcers (disease of the stomach) **S:**461
Gastrin (hormone) **S:**461
Gastro-intestinal examination (of the body) **M:**208h
Gastropods (mollusks) **M:**406; **O:**294
Gastrula (stage in cell division) **E:**102
Gas turbines **T:**342–43
engines, types of **E:**230–31
internal-combustion engines **I:**268
jet engines **J:**90–92
Gas welding **W:**118
Gatehouse (of a castle) **C:**131
picture(s) **C:**132
Gates (points from which passengers board
airplanes) **A:**127–28
Gates, Horatio (American military leader) **R:**204, 207
rival of Washington **W:**40
special medal awarded to **D:**65
Gates of Paradise (doors by Ghiberti) **R:**164
picture(s) **R:**165
Gates of the Arctic National Park and Preserve (Alaska) **A:**148
Gates of the Mountains (Montana) **M:**436
Gate valves **V:**270
diagram(s) **V:**270
Gateway Arch (Saint Louis, Missouri) **M:**366, 370; **S:**16
picture(s) **M:**367; **S:**16
Gateway National Recreation Area (New Jersey–New
York) **N:**164, 172, 214
Gather (of glass) **G:**229, 233
Gathering (in bookbinding) **B:**332
Gatineau (Quebec) **Q:**11
Gatineau Park (Hull, Quebec) **O:**253
Gatling guns (early machine guns) **G:**423
picture(s) **C:**342; **G:**424
GATT (General Agreement on Tariffs and Trade) *see* World Trade
Organization
Gattamelata (equestrian statue by Donatello)
picture(s) **I:**395
Gatun Lake (Panama) **P:**49
Gauchos (cowboys of the Pampa) **R:**103
Argentina **A:**390, 391
Brazil **B:**376
dances **F:**302; **L:**69
in Latin-American literature **L:**70
Uruguay **U:**238
picture(s) **S:**284
barbeque **L:**55
herding sheep **S:**274
Gaudí, Antonio (Spanish architect)
Barcelona **B:**60a
Gaugamela, Battle of (331 B.C.) **A:**178; **B:**103e; **P:**155
picture(s) **B:**103d
Gauge (width of railroad tracks) **R:**78, 89
Why does the standard gauge measure 4 feet 8 1/2 inches
(1.4 meters)? **R:**78
Gauguin, Paul (French painter) **G:**63
modern art **M:**388
postimpressionism in France **F:**431
reaction against impressionism **P:**29

picture(s)
The White Horse (painting) **G:**63
Gaul (Roman name for France and parts of bordering
countries) **F:**412
Caesar's conquest of **C:**6
Celts **C:**163
early migrations of Gauls to England **E:**235
Gaultier de Varennes, Louis and François (French
explorers) **S:**324
Gauss (unit of measure of a magnetic field) **M:**30
Gauss, Carl Friedrich (German mathematician and
astronomer) **G:64**
algebra **A:**184
non-Euclidean geometries **G:**127; **M:**168
statistics, history of **S:**443
way to find sum of first 100 counting numbers **N:**387
picture(s) **G:**64
Gautama Buddha, Prince Siddhartha *see* Buddha
Gautier, Théophile (French poet)
Giselle (ballet) **B:**27
Gavarnie Falls (France) **W:**62, 63
Gavials (reptiles) **C:**582, 583; **R:**180
picture(s) **C:**584
Gaviria Trujillo, César (Colombian political leader) **C:**408
Gavotte (dance) **D:**29
Gawain (knight of King Arthur's court) **A:**440
Arthurian legends in English literature **E:**269
Gay, John (English playwright) **E:**277, 293; **M:**556
writer of fables **F:**4
picture(s)
scene from *The Beggar's Opera* painted by
Hogarth **E:**277
Gay Divorce (musical by Porter) **M:**558
Gay Head Cliffs (Massachusetts)
picture(s) **M:**138
Gay-Lussac, Joseph Louis (French chemist and physicist) **G:**58
Gayoom, Maumoon Abdul (Maldivian president) **M:**60
Gaza (city in the Gaza Strip) **P:**42
Gaza Strip (land along the Mediterranean Sea) **I:**376
Egypt **E:**109
Palestinian problem **P:**42, 43
Palestinian self-rule **J:**132
· **Gazelles** (hoofed mammals) **H:**220
picture(s) **H:**218
Gazpacho (soup) **F:**337
G clef (in musical notation) *see* Treble clef
Gdańsk (formerly **Danzig**) (Poland) **P:**359, 361
World War II **W:**286
Gdynia (Poland) **P:**361
Ge (Native American language family) **I:**197
Geared locomotives **L:**288
Gear ratios (of transmissions) **A:**548–49; **G:**65
Gears (toothed wheels that pass along motion and
power) **G:65–66**
clocks **C:**369, 370, 371
drive train **A:**550
planetary gears **T:**280
rotary pumps **P:**541
transmissions **A:**548–49; **T:**279–80
trucks **T:**319
watches **W:**45, 46
wheels **W:**160
Gebal *see* Byblos
Gebel-Williams, Gunther (wild-animal trainer) **C:**310
Geber *see* Jābir ibn-Hayyān
Geckos (lizards) **L:**275–76
picture(s) **E:**55
Geddes, Norman Bel (American designer and architect) **I:**215
Geddes, Sir Patrick (Scottish social scientist) **U:**236
Geertgen tot Sint Jans (Dutch painter) **D:**354
picture(s)
Saint John the Baptist in the Wilderness
(painting) **D:**356

Genoa (Italy) **I:**387, 388
  aquarium **A:**337
Genoa (Nevada) **N:**135
Genocide (attempt to destroy an entire people because of their race or religion)
  Armenians **A:**432; **H:**284
  Holocaust **H:**159c–159d
  Nazi policy to murder Jews **N:**81
  racism **R:**34, 34a
Genre art
  American art **P:**30
  Bruegel, Pieter, the Elder **B:**414
  Dutch and Flemish art **D:**354, 359; **P:**23
Genres (categories of motion pictures) **M:**491
Gentamicin (antibiotic) **A:**308
Gentian violet (purple dye used as medicine) **D:**368
Gentile da Fabriano (Italian artist)
  picture(s)
    Adoration of the Magi (painting) **U:**3
    The Nativity (painting) **J:**85
Gentleman (man of noble birth) **K:**276, 277
Gentleman's agreement
  restrictions on immigration **I:**91
Gentleman's Magazine, The **M:**19
Genus (division of biological classification) *see* Genera
Geochemistry (chemistry of Earth's crust) **C:**205; **E:**8
  ore location method **M:**320
Geodesic dome (rounded structure)
  Fuller, R. Buckminster **A:**368, 386a
Geodesy (branch of mathematics that determines the position of geographical points)
  surveying, use in **S:**519
Geodetic surveying **S:**519
Geoffrey of Monmouth (Welsh historian) **A:**443
  claimed that Merlin built Stonehenge by magic **S:**462
  source of the Arthurian legends **E:**269
Geography **G:**97–106
  climate **C:**361–64
  continents **C:**529–30
  deserts **D:**123–31
  dinosaurs' extinction is possibly the result of changes in **D:**175
  earth science **E:**8
  equator **E:**304
  exploration and discovery **E:**400–420
  food habits depend on where you live **F:**330
  geographical human races **R:**28–31
  glaciers **G:**221–25
  Greenwich Observatory's prime meridian **G:**374b
  islands and island groups **I:**360–68
  lakes **L:**24–34
  latitude and longitude **L:**79–80
  maps and globes **M:**92–99
  mountains **M:**501–7
  oceans and seas of the world **O:**43–47
  rivers **R:**235–47
  seasons **S:**109–11
  social studies **S:**227
  surveying **S:**519–20
  tropics **T:**317
  waterfalls **W:**62–63
  world **W:**254–69
Geok-Tepe, Battle of (1879) **T:**352
Geological engineers **E:**226
Geological Survey, United States
  maps, history of **M:**99
Geologic timescale (of geologic eras) **G:**110
  fossil story of past time **F:**383–88
  prehistoric animals **P:**432–34
  table(s) **E:**25; **F:**384
Geology **G:**107–19
  archaeological studies **A:**359
  caves and caverns **C:**155–58
  climatic changes, sources of **C:**364

coal formation **C:**388
earthquakes **E:**33–41
earth science **E:**8
Earth's history **E:**22–29
Earth's interior **E:**10–11
ever-changing earth **E:**11–16
experiments in life sciences **E:**391–92
fossil studies reveal the Earth's history **F:**383–88
geological oceanography **O:**37, 38
geologic analysis in search for minerals **M:**319–20
geysers and hot springs **G:**192–93
glaciers **G:**221–25
How do geologists learn about the history of planet Earth? **E:**28
ice ages **I:**8–16
mountains **M:**501–7
natural gas, location of **N:**59
ocean floor **E:**17–18; **O:**20–21, 23
oceans, origin of the **O:**16
petroleum geology **P:**167–69
radioactive dating **R:**64–66
rocks **R:**263–69
salt beds and salt domes **S:**22
satellites used to study the Earth **S:**367
soils **S:**234–38
sonar used in searching for oil **R:**40
tektites **C:**451
tunnel building **T:**337
ultrasound, uses of **E:**49
underwater research by aquanauts **U:**25
volcanoes **V:**379–86
water shapes the land **W:**51
What is geomythology? **G:**107
table(s)
  geological time scale **E:**25
Geometry **G:**120–28; **M:**157 *see also* Trigonometry
  coordinate geometry **A:**183–84
  Descartes' analytic geometry **D:**123
  fractal geometry **M:**159, 170
  mathematics, history of **M:**163, 169
  non-Euclidean geometries **M:**168–69
  number sequences **N:**383–84
  proportion **R:**107
  Pythagoras **P:**558
  surveying **S:**519–20
  topology **T:**236–39
  What is pi? **G:**128
Geomorphology (study of landforms) **G:**106
Geomythology **G:**107
Geophones (instruments that receive reflected shock waves) **M:**319; **P:**169
Geophysics *see* Geology
George, Jean Craighead (American author and illustrator of children's books) **C:**231
George, Saint **S:**18d
George I (king of Great Britain) **E:**248, 249; **G:**129
  parliamentary government by cabinet **P:**83
  Walpole, Sir Robert **W:**5
  picture(s)
    Handel presenting his *Water Music* **B:**72
George II (king of Great Britain) **E:**248, 249; **G:**129
  gave Georgia to Oglethorpe **T:**178
  William Pitt opposes the king **P:**265
George III (king of Great Britain) **E:**248–49; **G:**129–30
  American Revolutionary War **R:**196, 198
  Declaration of Independence **D:**57, 59, 61
  Pitt, William, the Younger **P:**265
  picture(s)
    political cartoon about Embargo of 1807 **J:**70
George IV (king of Great Britain) **G:**130
George V (king of Great Britain) **E:**253; **G:**130
  picture(s) **G:**131; **W:**270
    visit to India **E:**251

George VI (king of Great Britain)   E:192, 254; G:130–31
  picture(s)   G:131
George I (king of Greece)   G:131
George II (king of Greece)   G:131, 338
George Cross (British award for heroism)   M:64
Georges Pompidou National Center for Art and Culture (Paris) *see*
      Pompidou Center
Georgetown (capital of Guyana)   G:428
  picture(s)   G:428a
Georgetown (area of Washington, D.C.)
  picture(s)   W:36
Georgetown Loop Railroad (Colorado)   C:438
Georgetown University (Washington, D.C.)   W:32
George Tupou I (king of Tonga)   T:224
George Washington Bridge (New York–New Jersey)   N:233
  picture(s)   N:165
Georgia   G:132–46; U:174
  Andersonville National Cemetery   N:30
  Atlanta   A:477
  Civil War   C:343
  Oglethorpe, James, founded state   O:59
  thirteen American colonies   T:178
  picture(s)
      Atlanta   A:477; G:133
      Blue Ridge Mountains   G:133
      Georgia State University   G:136
      Kennesaw Mountain National Battlefield   G:136
      Martin Luther King, Jr., National Historic Site   N:53
      Okefenokee Swamp   U:82
Georgia, Republic of   G:147–48
  Commonwealth of Independent States   C:460
  languages of the USSR   U:34
  Tbilisi   U:43
  picture(s)
      flag   F:231
Georgia, University of   G:132, 137
Georgian Bay (arm of Lake Huron)   G:327
Georgian language   G:147
Georgian Orthodox Church   U:35
Georgian period (England)
  music   E:292–93
Georgian style (in art and architecture)   E:260
  furniture design   A:315
Georgia State University (Atlanta, Georgia)
  picture(s)   G:136
"Georgie Porgie" (nursery rhyme)   N:411
Geostationary operation environmental satellites (GOES)   S:367
  picture(s)   S:366
Geosynchronous orbit (one synchronized with the rotation of the
      Earth)
  communications satellites   T:67
  space satellites   S:365, 367
  telecommunications   T:51
Geothermal energy   E:217, 221–22
  volcanoes   V:384
Geotropism (movement of plants)
  picture(s)   P:314
Gerald R. Ford Museum (Grand Rapids, Michigan)   M:265
Geraniums (flowers)
  picture(s)   G:38, 48
Gerbil (rodent)   G:410
  pets   P:178
Geriatrics (branch of medicine dealing with diseases of old
      age)   O:98
  geriatric nursing   N:418
  hospitals   H:248
Géricault, Théodore (French painter)   F:429; P:29
German Americans (ethnic group)   I:89
German Democratic Republic (East Germany)
      (1949–1990)   G:165–66
  Berlin   B:146
  Communism   C:474
German East Africa Company   T:19

Germanic (Teutonic) languages   L:39
  days of the week   D:46
  English language   E:265–67
  Europe   E:352
Germanic mythology *see* Norse mythology
Germanic (Teutonic) tribes
  days of the week   D:46
  German literature   G:176
  Germany, history of   G:157–58
  invasion of Roman Empire at beginning of the Middle
      Ages   M:289–90
  Viking invasions may have been part of Germanic
      migrations   V:339
Germanium (element)   E:173
  conductor for electricity   C:211
  semiconductors   T:274
German measles (rubella) (disease)   D:192
  deafness caused by   D:48
  mental retardation caused by   R:190
German shepherd (dog)   D:241, 242, 244
German shorthaired pointer (dog)   D:249
German silver *see* Nickel silver
Germans in America   T:176
Germantown, Battle of (1777)   P:139; R:203
Germany   G:149–66
  automobile industry   A:555
  Berlin   B:146–49
  Christmas customs   C:297, 300
  doll making   D:266, 267
  drug industry   D:334
  education, history of   E:80
  emigration to the United States   I:89
  favorite foods   F:335
  Helgoland   I:365
  history *see* Germany, history of
  hosteling movement   H:254–55
  Latvia, history of   L:83
  motion pictures   M:490
  national anthem   N:20
  national dances   D:30
  New Year customs   N:209
  racism   R:34a
  synthetic dyes   D:372
  theater   T:161
  toy making   T:251
  universities   U:226
  watches, history of   W:45, 46
  picture(s)
      costumes, traditional   C:373
      flag   F:236
      Rhine River at Oberwesel   R:244
Germany, art and architecture of   G:167–73
  dollhouses   D:261
  Dresden porcelain   P:412
  furniture   F:513, 516
  modern art   M:391
  painting in the Renaissance   R:171
  romanticism   R:303
  16th-century painting   P:23
Germany, Democratic Republic of *see* German Democratic
      Republic
Germany, East *see* German Democratic Republic
Germany, Federal Republic of (West Germany)
      (1949–1990)   G:165
  Berlin   B:146
  Oktoberfest   H:158
  peace movements   P:106
  states, list of   G:159
Germany, history of   G:157–66
  Bismarck, Otto von   B:250
  Cameroon   C:41
  Charlemagne   C:188
  communism   C:474
  Estonia   E:325

Wovoka **N:**135
picture(s) **I:**182
Ghosts (play by Henrik Ibsen) **I:**2
Ghosts (spirits of dead persons) **G:**199–200
Ghosts (word game) **W:**238
Ghost shrimps (crustaceans) **S:**167
Ghost towns (abandoned towns)
Montana **M:**436
Nevada **N:**126
Ghostwriting (writing for someone else who gets credit as author) **B:**190
G.I. Joe (doll) **D:**271
Giacometti, Alberto (Swiss sculptor and painter)
modern sculpture **M:**394; **S:**104
picture(s)
Chariot (sculpture) **M:**395
Giant anteater (mammal) **A:**296
Giant Canada goose (bird) **D:**343
Giant longhorn beetle
picture(s) **B:**126
Giant pandas **A:**452; **M:**73; **P:**52
picture(s) **E:**211; **P:**52; **Z:**384
Giants (in folklore) **G:**201–3
geomythology **G:**107
Norse mythology **N:**280
Giants (of nature)
giraffes **G:**211–12
Ice Age animals **I:**11–12
largest animals **A:**271
Giant's Causeway (natural wonder, Northern Ireland) **U:**62
picture(s) **R:**263; **U:**61
Giant squids (mollusks) **M:**408
Giant stars **S:**430
Giap, Vo Nguyen *see* Vo Nguyen Giap
Gibberellins (plant hormones) **P:**312
Gibbons (small apes) **A:**325, 326, 327
picture(s) **A:**325, 326; **P:**456
Gibbons, Grinling (Netherlands-born English wood carver) **W:**228
decorative wood pieces for Charles II **E:**259
Gibbons, Orlando (English composer) **C:**184
Gibbous moon **M:**447, 448
picture(s) **M:**448, 449
Gibbs, Josiah Willard (American mathematician) **M:**169
Gibraltar **G:**204
Barbary apes **M:**421
Gibran, Kahlil (Lebanese-American poet and artist) **A:**342
Gibson, Althea (American tennis champion) **A:**79c; **G:**205
Gibson, Bob (American baseball player)
picture(s) **B:**93
Gibson, Josh (American baseball player)
picture(s) **B:**92
Gibson, Robert L. (American astronaut)
picture(s) **S:**350
Gide, André (French author) **F:**115, 442
Gideon (in the Old Testament) **B:**167
Gideon v. *Wainwright* (1963) **S:**509
Giessbach waterfall (Switzerland) **W:**63
Giffard, Henri (French engineer and inventor) **A:**558
Gift, The (sculpture by Man Ray) *see* Cadeau, Le
"Gift of the Magi, The" (story by O. Henry) **C:**299
excerpt from **S:**164
Gifts
Christmas **C:**297, 300–301
gift wrapping **G:**206–7
New Year customs **N:**208–9
thank-you notes **E:**339
Gift wrapping **G:**206–7
Gigabytes (of computer-stored information) **C:**489, 490
Gila monsters (lizards) **L:**276, 277
picture(s) **R:**180
Gila River (United States)
Arizona **A:**405
New Mexico **N:**183
Gila Trail **O:**275

Gilbert, Cass (American architect) **U:**133; **W:**30
picture(s)
Supreme Court Building **S:**507
Gilbert, Sir Humphrey (English soldier and navigator)
early exploration of America **C:**70; **T:**165
Gilbert, William (English physicist) **S:**67
theory of Earth's magnetic field **M:**30
Gilbert, Sir William S. (English playwright and librettist) **G:**208–9
Gilbert and Ellice Islands (former British colony) **K:**266
Gilbert and Sullivan operettas **G:**208–9
English music **E:**293
musical theater **M:**557
Gilbert Islands *see* Kiribati
Gilded Age (in American literature) **A:**206
Gilded Man *see* El Dorado
Gilding (in art) **F:**511
Gillespie, Dizzy (jazz musician, composer, and arranger) **J:**62
picture(s) **J:**61
Gillette Castle (Hadlyme, Connecticut) **C:**508
Gill nets (for fishing) **F:**218
picture(s) **F:**219
Gills (of animals)
fish **F:**191
horseshoe crab **H:**245
insects **I:**240
sharks, skates, and rays **S:**140, 142
picture(s)
fish **F:**191
Gills (of mushrooms) **F:**499; **M:**533
Gilman, Daniel Coit (American educator) **M:**132
Gilmore, Patrick S. (Irish-American band leader) **B:**44
Gilpin, Joshua and Thomas (Delaware paper manufacturers) **D:**95
Gilt bronze **J:**48
Gimbals (of rockets) **R:**258; **S:**340d
Gin (distilled beverage) **G:**285; **W:**161
Gin, cotton *see* Cotton gin
Ginastera, Alberto Evaristo (Argentine composer) **A:**390
Ginevra de' Benci (painting by Leonardo da Vinci)
only painting outside Europe generally acknowledged to be by Leonardo **N:**38, 40
picture(s) **R:**168
Ginger (spice) **H:**114
rhizome **P:**305
picture(s) **H:**115
Ginkakuji Temple (Kyoto, Japan) **K:**310
Ginkgo (tree) **E:**379; **P:**301
picture(s) **T:**301
fossil **F:**382
Ginnie Mae *see* Government National Mortgage Association
Ginnungagap (space between realms in Norse mythology) **N:**279
Ginsburg, Ruth Bader (American jurist) **S:**508; **W:**214
picture(s) **U:**171
Ginza (street in Tokyo, Japan) **T:**218–19
picture(s) **C:**311; **J:**26
Ginzberg, Asher *see* Ahad Ha-am
Ginzburg, Natalia (Italian author) **I:**409
Giono, Jean (French writer) **F:**442
Giordano, Umberto (Italian composer)
Andrea Chénier (opera) **O:**150
Giorgione (Italian painter) **I:**398; **R:**169; **T:**210
picture(s)
The Tempest (painting) **I:**399
Giotto (space probe) **S:**360, 361
radar astronomy **R:**76
Giotto di Bondone (Italian painter) **G:**210; **I:**394
Madonna della Costa damaged by car bomb **U:**3
Renaissance art **R:**164
tempera painting **P:**18
picture(s)
The Descent from the Cross (painting) **P:**19
The Lamentation (fresco) **G:**210

Giotto di Bondone (cont.)
   Madonna Enthroned (painting)   **G:**210
   Meeting at the Golden Gate (painting)   **R:**163
Giraffes   **G:**211–12
   adaptation   **A:**268, 270; **L:**198
   hoofed mammals   **H:**217
   Lamarck's theory of long necks   **E:**376
   picture(s)   **A:**281, 287; **L:**198; **M:**67
Girardelli, Marc (Luxembourg skier)
   picture(s)   **S:**184e
Girardon, François (French sculptor)   **F:**427
Giraudoux, Jean (French playwright, novelist, and
      diplomat)   **F:**442
Girl Before a Mirror (painting by Picasso)
   picture(s)   **A:**438e
Girl Guides of Canada   **G:**218
Girls' camps   *see* Camping, organized
Girls Clubs   **G:**213
Girl Scout National Center West (Wyoming)   **G:**217–18
Girl Scouts   **G:**214–19
   picture(s)   **G:**214, 215, 217
      badges and patches   **G:**218, 219
      camping   **G:**216
Girls' Day (Festival of Dolls) (Japan)   **H:**159a; **J:**31
Girl with a Mandolin (painting by Picasso)
   picture(s)   **D:**136
Girl with a Watering Can, A (painting by Renoir)
   picture(s)   **N:**39
Girne (Cyprus)   *see* Kyrenia
Gironde estuary (Garonne River, France)   **R:**242
Girondists (French revolutionaries)   **F:**471
Gironella, José María (Spanish writer)   **S:**392b
Girtin, Thomas (English painter)   **E:**262
Giscard d'Estaing, Valéry (president of France)   **F:**420
Giselle (ballet)   **B:**27–28
GI series   *see* Gastrointestinal examination
Gish, Dorothy (American actress)   **M:**488
Gish, Lillian (American actress)   **M:**488
Gist, Christopher (American explorer)   **K:**225
   overland trails   **O:**271
Gist, George   *see* Sequoya
Gist's Trace (overland trail)   **O:**271
Gitega (Burundi)   **B:**463
Gitlow v. *New York* (1925)   **S:**510
"Give me liberty, or give me death!" (said by Patrick
      Henry)   **H:**109; **R:**198
Given names   **N:**7
   boys'   **N:**6
   girls'   **N:**6
Giza (Egypt)   **E:**107
   pyramids   **C:**8; **E:**111; **W:**216–17
   Sphinx   **E:**112
   picture(s)
      pyramids   **A:**47
Gizzard (part of some animals' stomachs)
   birds   **B:**219
   fish   **F:**191
Gjoa (first boat to sail Northwest Passage)   **N:**339
Glacial epochs   *see* Ice Ages
Glacial soil   **N:**291
Glacial till   **G:**225; **I:**8; **S:**238
   Nebraska   **N:**82
   picture(s)   **I:**9
Glacier Bay National Park and Preserve (Alaska)   **A:**148
   picture(s)   **E:**13; **W:**51
Glacier bears   **B:**105
Glacier National Park (Montana)   **G:**220; **N:**44
   Going-to-the-Sun Road   **M:**435
   picture(s)   **G:**220; **M:**429
Glaciers   **G:**221–25; **I:**4–6 *see also* Ice Ages
   Agassiz, Jean Louis Rodolphe   **A:**81
   Alps   **A:**194b
   Antarctica   **A:**292
   Cascade Range   **W:**16

caves   **C:**157
Denmark's landform   **D:**110
Earth, history of   **E:**27
erosion   **E:**314–15
Finland   **F:**136
fossils found in   **F:**380
geology   **G:**116–17
Glacier National Park in Montana   **G:**220
Grasshopper Glacier (Montana)   **M:**436
Greenland ice cap   **G:**372
ice ages   **I:**8–9, 14
icebergs   **I:**17–18
Iceland   **I:**34–35
lake basins, formation of   **L:**25, 26, 30–31
Michigan   **M:**260
water shapes the land   **W:**51
picture(s)
   Alaska   **E:**13; **N:**287; **W:**51
   Andes   **S:**277
   calving   **I:**7
   Himalayas   **H:**126
   moraines are glacial deposits   **I:**9
Glacis (of a fort)   **F:**379
Gladiator (in ancient Rome)   **S:**193
Gladioli (flowers)   **G:**40–41, 49; **P:**305
Gladstone, William Ewart (English statesman)   **G:**225; **V:**332a
   supported home rule for Ireland   **E:**252
   picture(s)   **P:**459
Glagolitic alphabet   **A:**194a
Glands   **B:**287–88; **G:**226–28
   adolescence, changes during   **A:**23
   animals, medicines produced from   **M:**198
   cystic fibrosis   **D:**191
   mumps affect   **D:**197
   scent glands of skunks   **O:**256
Glandular fever   *see* Infectious mononucleosis
Glare (in lighting)   **L:**238
Glasgow (Scotland)   **S:**88; **U:**67
Glasgow, Ellen (American novelist)   **A:**212; **V:**358–59
   picture(s)   **V:**358
Glashtins (fairies)   **F:**10
Glasnost (Soviet policy)   **G:**263; **U:**52
Glass   **G:**229–37
   antique   **A:**316
   bottles   **B:**346–47
   electric charges in   **E:**136
   enameling, use of powdered glass in   **E:**202
   fiberglass   **F:**105; **N:**437
   fiber optics   **F:**106–7
   fire makes glass   **F:**142–43
   glassmaking in West Virginia   **W:**126, 132
   lenses   **L:**141–51
   obsidian (natural glass)   **G:**229; **R:**264; **V:**383
   optical glass   **O:**185
   quartz lenses   **Q:**5
   recent steel and glass buildings   **A:**386a
   stained-glass windows   **S:**417–18
   Toledo (Ohio)   **T:**220
   picture(s)
      Corning Museum of Glass   **M:**523
      fire, uses of   **F:**142
      glassmaking in West Virginia   **W:**133
Glass, Philip (American composer)   **M:**548; **U:**210
Glass eels   *see* Elvers
Glasses for the eyes   *see* Eyeglasses
Glass fibers   *see* Fiberglass
Glaucoma (eye condition)   **B:**252; **E:**431
Glaucus (in Greek legend)   **I:**61
Glaze (freezing rain)   **R:**95–96
Glazes (glass coating, or finish)
   ceramics   **C:**177
   pottery   **A:**316–16a; **P:**407
Glazing (of furs)   **F:**503
GLCM (ground-launched cruise missiles)   **M:**349
Glee (musical form)   **E:**292

Glen Canyon Dam (Arizona)   **A:**405; **D:**16
Glendale (Arizona)   **A:**411
Glendower, Owen (Welsh chief)   **W:**4
Glen More (Scotland)   **S:**86
Glenn, John H., Jr. (American astronaut and U.S. senator)   **A:**469; **E:**419; **G:**237; **S:**346
  first American to orbit the Earth   **S:**338, 347
  picture(s)   **G:**237; **S:**347
Glickel of Hameln (Yiddish writer)   **Y:**350
Glidden, Carlos (American inventor)   **T:**374
Gliders (engineless aircraft)   **G:**238–40; **I:**284 *see also* Hang gliders
  aerodynamics, principles of   **A:**41
  airplane models   **A:**105
  aviation history   **A:**558–59
  Wright brothers' early experiments   **W:**318
Gliding (animal locomotion)   **A:**279; **B:**215
  lizards   **L:**277
  mammals   **M:**72
Gliding joints (in the skeleton)   **S:**184b
Gliding possum (marsupial)   **M:**115
Glière, Reinhold (Russian composer)   **R:**382
Glinka, Mikhail (Russian composer)   **R:**381
Glissando (in music)   **M:**540
GLM (graduated length method) (of learning to ski)   **S:**184c
Global Surveyor (spacecraft) *see* Mars Global Surveyor
Global warming *see* Greenhouse effect
Globe and Mail, The (Canadian newspaper)   **O:**130
Globes (round representations of the Earth) *see* Maps and globes
Globe Theater (Elizabethan theater in London)   **E:**272
  Shakespeare, William   **S:**131
Globe valves   **V:**270
  diagram(s)   **V:**270
Globular clusters (of stars)   **U:**212
  picture(s)   **U:**215
Globulins (proteins)
  use in immunization   **M:**210
Glockenspiel (musical instrument)   **M:**555; **P:**149
  picture(s)   **M:**555
Glomach Falls (Scotland)   **W:**63
Glomeruli (of the kidneys)   **D:**197; **K:**243
  picture(s)   **K:**243
Glomerulonephritis (kidney disease)   **K:**244
Glorieta, Battle of (1862)   **N:**193
Glorious Flight, The (book by Alice and Martin Provensen)   **C:**240
  picture(s)   **C:**247
Glorious Revolution (1688, in England)   **E:**246
Glory holes (furnaces)   **G:**233
Glossary (list of terms relating to a subject)
  computers   **C:**490
  sailing   **S:**12
  textiles   **T:**144
Gloss paints   **P:**33
Gloves   **G:**240–41
  baseball players   **B:**78, 80
  boxing   **B:**351
  glove or hand puppets   **P:**545
  ice hockey goalies   **I:**25
  picture(s)
    baseball players   **B:**79
Glowworms   **B:**203
Glucagon (hormone)   **B:**256; **G:**228
Gluck, Christoph Willibald (German composer)   **G:**185–86, **241**
  classical age, operas of   **C:**351
  French opera   **F:**446
  opera   **O:**143–44
  Orfeo ed Euridice (opera)   **O:**159
  theatrical dance   **D:**36
Gluconeogenesis (formation of glucose by the liver)   **L:**268
Glucose (dextrose) (kind of sugar)   **L:**199; **S:**483
  body sugar   **B:**292
  liver converts to glycogen   **L:**268
  photosynthesis   **L:**116; **P:**220

Glue   **G:**242–43
  experiment testing the strength of   **E:**398
  how wood furniture is made   **F:**515
Glue prints (art)   **G:**308
Gluons (subatomic particles)   **A:**489; **F:**366b
Gluten (in wheat)   **W:**156
  bread   **B:**386, 387
  flour and flour milling   **F:**276
Glycerol (glycerin)   **O:**76, 79
Glycogen (form in which carbohydrate is stored in animal tissue)   **B:**292, 299
  human body   **B:**277–78
  liver converts glucose into   **L:**268
  muscular system   **M:**519
  nutrition   **N:**424
Glyndebourne Festival (England)   **M:**559
G-men (Federal Bureau of Investigation agents)   **F:**77
Gnadenhutten massacre (Ohio, 1782)   **O:**72
Gnats (insects)   **H:**261
Gneiss (metamorphic rock)   **G:**118; **R:**269
  oldest known rock ever found   **R:**266
  picture(s)   **R:**267
Gnomons (L-shaped figures)   **N:**387
Gnossus *see* Knossos
GNP *see* Gross national product
Gnu (wildebeest) (hoofed mammal)   **M:**74
  picture(s)   **A:**280, 286; **B:**204; **H:**218
Go (an ancient Asian board game)   **G:**13
Goa (India)   **I:**132
Goalies (goalkeepers in sports)
  ice hockey   **I:**24, 25
  soccer   **S:**219, 221
Goat (constellation) *see* Capricorn
Goat cheese   **C:**195
Goatfish   **F:**194
Goats   **G:**244
  cloven-hoofed   **F:**82
  distinguished from sheep   **S:**145
  hoofed mammals   **H:**220
  livestock   **L:**271, 272
  milk   **F:**330; **M:**307
  picture(s)
    Rocky Mountain goat   **H:**219; **M:**431
    wild goats and sheep   **H:**219
Go-Bang (game) *see* Go
Gobbler (male turkey)   **T:**350
Gobelins tapestries   **T:**22
  carpet and tapestry workshops   **R:**353
  picture(s)   **T:**21
Gobi Desert (central Asia)   **M:**417
  pastoral nomads   **D:**128
  picture(s)
    pastoral nomads   **D:**129
Goblet cells (exocrine glands)   **G:**226
Goblets (drinking glasses)
  picture(s)   **G:**232
"Goblin Market" (poem by Christina Rossetti)
  picture(s)   **F:**12
Goby fish   **A:**271; **F:**186
God *see* Philosophy; Religions; the names of religions, denominations, and sects
God, Kingdom of *see* Kingdom of God
Godard, Jean-Luc (French film director)   **M:**494
"God Bless America" (song by Irving Berlin)   **B:**150; **N:**25
Goddard, Robert Hutchings (American physicist)   **G:**244–46; **I:**284; **N:**192
  liquid-propellant rockets   **R:**255
  picture(s)   **N:**193; **R:**255
Goddard Space Flight Center (Greenbelt, Maryland)   **G:**246
  picture(s)   **M:**127
"Goddess of Liberty" (statue, Beijing, China)
  picture(s)   **C:**474
Godey's Lady's Book (magazine)   **M:**19

Godfather, The (motion picture, 1972)
    picture(s) M:495
Godfrey, Sir Daniel (English bandmaster) B:43
Godfrey, Thomas (American inventor) N:76
Godoy, Lucila (Chilean poet) see Mistral, Gabriela
Godparents (in Latin America) L:52
"God Rest Ye Merry, Gentlemen" (carol) C:118
Gods and goddesses (in mythology) M:566–75
    Greek and Roman mythology G:360–69
    Hawaii, ancient H:48, 54
    Hinduism H:128, 129
    Norse N:277–81
"God Save the Queen" (national anthem of the United
    Kingdom) N:20, 22
Godspeed (ship) see Goodspeed
Godthaab (capital of Greenland) G:371, 374
Godwin, Linda M. (American astronaut) S:350
Godwin, Mary Wollstonecraft (English writer) W:214
Godwin Austen, Mount (Pakistan) see K2
Goelet House (dollhouse)
    picture(s) D:260
Goeppert-Mayer, Maria (American physicist) P:232, 236–37
    picture(s) P:236
Goering, Hermann Wilhelm (German Nazi political
    leader) G:164
    plan for air attack on England W:290
GOES (space satellites) see Geostationary operation
    environmental satellites
Goes, Hugo van der (Flemish painter) D:353; R:171
Goethals, George Washington (American engineer)
    Panama Canal, history of P:51
Goethe, Johann Wolfgang von (German writer) G:178, **246**
    Faust F:72–73
    German romantic drama D:300
Go Fish (card game) C:109–10
Gog and Magog (in Old Testament)
    British legend G:201
Goggles (for the eyes) E:432
    first underwater goggles U:17
Gogh, Vincent van see Van Gogh, Vincent
Gogol, Nikolai (Russian author) R:377–78
    drama, history of D:301
    novels N:360
    short stories S:162
Goh Chok Tong (Singapore prime minister) S:181
Going-to-the-Sun Road (Montana) G:220; M:435
Goiter (mineral-deficiency disease) N:429
Go-karts see Karting
Gokstad ship (Viking ship) V:339
Golan Heights (Syria) I:376; P:42; S:552
Golconda (India) D:145
Gold G:247–49
    Africa A:49
    Africa, art of A:72, 74
    Alaska A:152
    alchemy C:207
    Archimedes and the golden crown A:367
    art works of ancient Greece G:346
    California C:26
    coins and coin collecting C:399
    decorative arts, uses in D:70, 73, 76
    dolls made of D:268
    El Dorado legend of the New World C:406
    elements E:173
    furniture decoration F:511
    jewelry J:94
    Korean metalworking K:298
    luster M:315
    metals and metallurgy M:233, 236
    mining, chief centers for M:318
    needlecraft, use in N:97
    Nevada mines N:131
    silver found with gold ores S:177
    South Africa's production S:271

South Dakota leading producer S:312, 317, 321
What is fool's gold? G:249
world distribution W:261
    map(s)
        world distribution W:264
    picture(s)
        African art I:418
        crystals M:314; O:217
        Fort Knox (Kentucky) depository K:220
        gold bars S:319
        grain structure of pure gold and copper-gold
           alloy A:191
        Inca mask E:411
        Korean metalworking K:299
        ornament of the early Indian people of
           Colombia C:407
        panning for gold B:406b
        Scythian stag statue A:360
        South African mine S:271
        Tutankhamen's coffin A:351
    table(s) M:235, 315
Gold, discoveries of G:250–52
    Alaskan strikes A:157–58
    Australia A:509–10, 513
    Brazil's gold rush B:378
    British Columbia B:407
    California C:18, 30
    Canadian gold rush in 1896 Y:364–65
    Colorado gold rush C:430, 434, 442–43
    Georgia G:145
    Idaho I:58
    mines and mining M:324
    Montana M:432, 439
    Nevada N:135
    San Francisco and the gold rush of 1848 S:32
    South Africa S:273
    South Dakota S:325
    picture(s)
        California U:185
Goldbach, Christian (German mathematician) N:385–86
"Gold Bug" (story by Poe)
    picture(s) F:116
Gold Coast (area of West Africa) G:194, 197–98
Gold Coast (city, Queensland, Australia) A:512
    picture(s) A:512
Gold Cup race (boating) B:265
Gold dust G:251
Golden Age (of Greek civilization) see Classical Age
Golden Age (of Spanish culture) S:386, 390–91
Golden Age of television T:70–71
Golden apples of the Hesperides (in Greek mythology) G:367
Golden Bull (charter in Hungarian history) H:297
Golden Calf (in the Old Testament) M:469
Golden eagles E:2
    picture(s)
        feet B:216
Goldeneyes (waterbirds)
    picture(s)
        feet B:216
Golden Fleece (in Greek mythology) G:367–68
    Colchis (republic of Georgia) G:147
    primitive mining device M:324
Golden Gate Bridge (San Francisco, California)
    picture(s) B:398; C:19; S:32
Golden Gate Park (San Francisco, California) S:32
Golden Gloves Association B:352
Golden Hind (ship of Sir Francis Drake) D:293
Golden Horn (inlet of Bosporus, Turkey) I:377; T:347
    picture(s) M:302; T:348
Golden Mean (in philosophy)
    Aristotle's middle way A:397; G:359
Golden plovers (birds) H:187
Golden poppy (flower)

economics **E:**59
energy supply, effect on **E:**220
food regulations and laws **F:**345–47
hazardous wastes, cleanup and control of **H:**73
laws to protect labor **L:**5–7
public health **H:**77
public utilities **P:**520, 523
radio, control of **R:**57
transportation industry **T:**290
trucking industry **T:**321
Governor (machine control device) **A:**529
Governor-general (in Canadian government) **C:**77
Governors (of states) **S:**437–38
forms of address **A:**22
list of **S:**437
terms of *see* individual state articles
Gowda, H. D. Deve (prime minister of India) **I:**134
Gower, John (English poet) **E:**269
"Go west, young man" (Horace Greeley's advice) **N:**162
Gowon, Colonel Yakubu (Nigerian political leader) **N:**258
Goya, Francisco (Spanish painter) **G:**277
art of the artist **A:**438e
drawing, history of **D:**316
impressionism, influence on **I:**105
leading graphic artist of 19th century **G:**307–8
place in Spanish art **P:**27; **S:**387
Por que fue sensible (aquatint) **G:**307
Prado **P:**424
romanticism **R:**303
picture(s)
Blind Man's Buff (painting) **G:**277
portrait of a young aristocrat **S:**386
Self Portrait (painting) **P:**27
The Sleep of Reason Produces Monsters
(engraving) **E:**326
The Third of May, 1808 (painting) **A:**438d; **S:**380
Goyathlay (Native American leader) *see* Geronimo
Goytisolo, Juan (Spanish writer) **S:**392b
Gozo (island, Malta) **M:**63
GPO *see* Government Printing Office
Grab dredges **D:**320
Grabe, Ronald J. (American astronaut) **S:**350
picture(s) **S:**351
Gracchus, Gaius (Roman political leader) **R:**315
Gracchus, Tiberius (Roman political leader) **R:**315
Grace (sharing in the divine life through Christ) **R:**294
Grace, Princess (Grace Kelly) (princess of Monaco and movie
actress) **M:**410
Graceland (home of Elvis Presley, Memphis,
Tennessee) **M:**219; **T:**82
picture(s) **T:**82
Grace note (in music) **M:**540
Gracián, Baltasar (Spanish poet) **S:**391
Grade (degree of slope, of railroad tracks) **R:**79–80
Grade, Chaim (Yiddish poet) **Y:**351
Grade A (milk label) **D:**9
Graders (earth-moving machinery) **E:**32
Grades (dairy cattle of mixed breeds) **D:**5
Grading (of foods) **F:**348
meat and meat packing **M:**198
Graduate, The (motion picture, 1967) **M:**495
Graduated circles (of optical instruments) **O:**183
Graduated (progressive) income tax **I:**111
Graduated length method (of learning to ski) *see* GLM
Graduate schools **U:**221
Grady, Henry W. (American editor) **G:**144
Graf, Steffi (German tennis player)
picture(s) **T:**92, 95
Grafting (of plants)
apple trees **A:**333
nut trees **N:**432
rubber trees **R:**345
Grafting (of skin)
hair transplants **H:**6

Graham, Billy (American evangelist) **C:**294; **N:**320
picture(s) **N:**320
Graham, Martha (American dancer and choreographer) **D:**33;
P:140
picture(s) **P:**141
Seraphic Dialogue (ballet) **D:**32
Graham, Otto (American football player) **F:**362
picture(s) **F:**362
Grahame, Kenneth (English author) **G:**278–79
fantasy in children's literature **C:**239
quoted on boats **B:**265
The Wind in the Willows, excerpt from **G:**278–79
Grain (measure of weight) **W:**114
Grain (of wood)
picture(s) **W:**223–24
Grain (solid-propellant rocket fuel) **R:**257
Grain alcohol **G:**285
Grain (cereal) and grain products **G:**280–87
barley **B:**60b
beer and brewing **B:**114
Canada **C:**61–62
cereal grasses **G:**317–18
cooking **C:**536
corn **C:**550
dairy cattle feed **D:**6
early income tax paid in grain **A:**225; **I:**111
flour and flour milling **F:**276–77
food from plants **P:**296
Green Revolution **F:**351
harvested by combines **F:**57–58
important agricultural products **A:**89
nutrition **N:**424
oats **O:**3–4
processing and storage **F:**52
rice **R:**228–29
rye **R:**386
what you eat depends on where you live **F:**330
wheat **W:**156–58
Grain boundary (defect in a crystal) **M:**153
Grain drills (farm machines) **F:**56
Grain elevators **G:**285–86
wheat storage **W:**158
picture(s) **F:**52; **G:**287; **N:**83; **S:**48
Grain exchange (place where wheat is bought and
sold) **W:**158
Grainger, Percy Aldridge (Australian-American pianist and
composer)
picture(s) **A:**501
Graininess (of photographic film) **P:**204–5
Grains (atomic planes) *see* Crystallites
Grains (in alloy structures) **A:**190–91
Gram (unit of weight) **W:**114
Grammar **G:**288–90
anthropological linguists study **A:**304–5
English language **E:**267
learning rules **P:**508
parts of speech **P:**92–94
punctuation **P:**541–44
"Grammar in a Nutshell" (poem) **G:**290
Grammar schools **E:**76–77
Gramme, Zénobe (Belgian inventor) **I:**278
developed electric generator **E:**154
Gramophone *see* Phonograph
Grampian Mountains (Scotland) **S:**86
Granada (Nicaragua) **N:**246, 247
Granada (Spain) **F:**88; **S:**379
Alhambra **S:**383
picture(s)
Alhambra **I:**356
Granados, Enrique (Spanish composer) **S:**392d
Gran Chaco (South America) **I:**197; **S:**277, 282
Gran Colombia (Greater Colombia) (former republic of Colombia,
Ecuador, and Venezuela) **B:**305; **C:**408; **E:**58; **V:**299
Grand Bahama Island **B:**17

Grand Banks (off Newfoundland) C:52, 60, 70
   fishing industry F:216
   meeting of Labrador Current and Gulf Stream G:413
   Newfoundland N:140
Grand Canal (China) C:87
Grand Canal (Venice) V:301
   picture(s) V:300
Grand Canyon (gorge cut by Colorado River) W:51
   Arizona A:402, 404
   created by erosion E:314
   Earth's fossil record F:382–83
   picture(s) A:403; F:383; W:50, 216
      grooved rock R:263
Grand Canyon National Park (Arizona) A:410; G:290–92
   picture(s) A:410; G:291, 292; N:45
Grand Canyon of the Yellowstone River (Wyoming) W:345
Grand Canyon State (nickname for Arizona) A:403
Grand Central Station (New York City) N:233
Grand Coulee Dam (Washington) D:16, 19; W:17, 20
   picture(s) G:102; I:340
Grande Comore Island (Indian Ocean) C:475
Grande Dixence Dam (Switzerland) D:20
Grande Peur (Great Fear) (in French history) F:467–68
Grande Rivière (Quebec) Q:8
Grand Falls (Labrador) W:62, 63
Grandfather clause (in constitutions of some southern
    states) A:79i
Grandfather clock
   picture(s) C:369
Grand Forks (North Dakota) N:330
Grand Illusion (motion picture, 1937) M:493
Grand Island (Nebraska) N:89
Grand Isle (Louisiana) L:322
Grand jury J:163
   courts C:567
Grand Lake (Colorado) C:433
Grand Lake (New Brunswick) N:138a
Grand mal (type of epilepsy) D:192
Grandma Moses *see* Moses, Grandma
Grand master keys L:283
Grand Mesa (Colorado) C:432
Grand Mesa, Uncompahgre, and Gunnison National Forest
    (Colorado)
   picture(s) N:32
Grandmother (collage by Arthur Dove)
   picture(s) D:137
Grand National Steeplechase (horserace, Aintree,
    England) H:231
Grand Ole Opry (Nashville, Tennessee) C:563–64; N:18; T:80
Grand opera O:145–65
   Italian I:412
Grand Palace (Bangkok, Thailand) B:47
Grandparents' Day, National *see* National Grandparents' Day
Grand piano
   picture(s) K:239; M:552; P:240
Grand Portage National Monument (Minnesota) M:334
Grand Pré National Historic Park (Nova Scotia) N:356
Grand Prix (international auto racing) A:536–37
   picture(s) A:539
Grand Rapids (Michigan) M:265, 268
   picture(s) M:268
Grands Ballets Canadiens, Les B:32
Grand slam (in baseball) B:83
Grand Slam (of tennis) T:99
Grand staff (in music) M:540
Grandstand (at an agricultural fair) F:14
Grand Sultan Mosque (Singapore)
   picture(s) I:350
Grand Teton National Park (Wyoming) W:334
   picture(s) N:45
Grand Trunk Railway (Canada) C:74
Grand Turk (island capital of Turks and Caicos Islands) T:353
Grandview State Park (West Virginia) W:135
   picture(s) W:128

Grange, Harold "Red" (American football player) F:362, 364
   picture(s) F:362
Grange, National (rural fraternal organization) U:188
Granite (rock) R:264
   Barre (Vermont) has world's largest quarries V:314
   building stone Q:5
   Earth's crust E:10
   geology G:113, 117
   volcanic rocks V:383
   picture(s)
      quarry R:269
Granite mosses (plants) M:472–73
Granite Peak (Montana) M:429
Granite Railway Company R:87
Granite State (nickname for New Hampshire) N:150, 151
Granny knots
   picture(s) K:287
Granny Smith (variety of apple) A:330–31
Gran Quivira (legendary land) C:551
Grant, Cary (American film actor) M:489
   picture(s) M:492
Grant, James (British explorer) U:6
Grant, Julia Dent (wife of Ulysses S. Grant) F:173; G:294
   picture(s) F:172; G:295
Grant, Ulysses S. (18th president of the United
    States) G:293–96
   birthplace in Ohio O:68
   Civil War C:338, 342–43, 347, 497
   General Grant National Memorial (New York City) N:214
   Lee and Grant L:126
   Lincoln promoted L:246
   Mexican War M:239b
   Ulysses S. Grant Home State Historic Site (Galena,
     Illinois) I:70
   picture(s) C:343; P:447
      Civil War C:346
Grants (of foundations) F:391
Grant's gazelle
   picture(s) A:297
Grant's Tomb (New York City)
   picture(s) G:296
Granulated sugar S:483
Granulation (appearance of solar surface) S:492
Granville-Barker, Harley (English critic and playwright) S:144
Grapefruit O:189
   picture(s) F:484; O:186
Grapes G:297–98 *see also* Vineyards
   garden fruits G:51
   tendrils P:305
   wine W:188–89
   picture(s) G:299
      California C:26
      Chile C:252
      French harvest A:90
      Portugal P:393
Grapes of Wrath, The (novel by John Steinbeck) A:212; N:362;
    S:446
   migrants from Oklahoma O:94
   picture(s) N:361
Grape sugar S:483
Graphic arts G:302–8 *see also* Painting
   computer graphics C:480–82
   drawing D:306–12
   engraving E:294
   etching E:326–27
   linoleum-block printing L:251
   newspaper design N:201
   printing P:468–79
   Rosenwald collection in National Gallery of Art N:40
   silk-screen printing S:176
   type faces T:369–70
   woodcut printing W:229
Graphic design *see* Commercial art
Graphic (bar) scale (of maps) M:95
Graphics tablets (computer input devices) C:480

Greasewood *see* Creosote bush
Great apes **A:**325
Great Barrier Reef (Australia)   **A:**504; **P:**5
   national parks **N:**56
   picture(s) **A:**504; **J:**75
Great Basin region (United States)   **N:**124; **U:**244–45
   Indians of North America **I:**186
Great Bear (constellation) *see* Ursa Major
Great Bear Lake (northwest Canada)   **N:**340
Great blue heron **A:**268
   picture(s)
     nest **B:**224
Great blue whale **A:**271
Great Bombardment (of meteorites)   **M:**229
Great Britain (largest island of the British Isles and part of the
   United Kingdom)   **U:**54, 60, 66
Great Britain and Northern Ireland, United Kingdom of *see* United
   Kingdom
Great Central Plain (North America)   **N:**285–86, 291
Great-circle route **G:**100
Great circles (on maps)   **M:**95–96
Great Compromise (for the Constitution) *see* Connecticut
   Compromise
Great Compromiser, The *see* Clay, Henry
Great Dane (dog)   **D:**245, 253
Great Dark Spot (on Neptune)   **N:**112; **P:**282
Great Depression *see* Depression of the 1930's
Great Design (plan for peace)   **P:**105
Great Dictator, The (motion picture, 1940)   **C:**185–86
Great Dismal Swamp (Virginia–North Carolina)   **V:**346, 348,
   349
Great Dismal Swamp National Wildlife Refuge   **N:**308
Great Dissenter, The (nickname for Oliver Wendell Holmes,
   Jr.)   **H:**159b
Great Divide *see* Continental Divide
Great Dividing Range (mountains, Australia)   **M:**506
Great Dying (in geology)   **E:**27–28
Great Eastern (steamship)   **O:**33
Great Emancipator, The (Abraham Lincoln)   **E:**200
Greater Antilles (Caribbean island group)   **C:**112–13
   Cuba **C:**596–600
   Hispaniola **D:**280–83; **H:**9–12
   Jamaica **J:**15–19
   Puerto Rico **P:**526–32
Greater Colombia *see* Gran Colombia
Greater Sunda Islands (Indonesia)   **I:**208–9
Greater Swiss mountain dog   **D:**251
Great Expectations (novel by Dickens)   **D:**150
Great Falls (Montana)   **M:**431, 435, 437
Great Gatsby, The (novel by F. Scott Fitzgerald)   **A:**211; **F:**224
Great Geysir (hot spring, Iceland)   **I:**34
Great gray owl
   picture(s) **B:**222
   provincial bird of Manitoba **M:**80
Great Hall of the People (Beijing, China)   **B:**127c
Great hornbill (bird)   **B:**241
Great horned owl
   picture(s)
     provincial bird of Alberta **A:**164
Great Karroo (plateau area, South Africa)   **S:**270
Great Lakes (North America)   **G:**326–28
   Canada **C:**71
   fisheries of the world **F:**216
   industry in Cleveland (Ohio) **C:**356
   lamprey invasion **F:**184
   Michigan **M:**258, 260, 267
   Saint Lawrence River and Seaway **S:**14–15
   War of 1812 **W:**9
   water pollution **W:**66
Great Lakes Plain (Erie-Ontario Lowland) (North
   America)   **N:**213; **O:**62; **P:**128
Great Lakes-Saint Lawrence Lowlands (landform region of
   Canada)   **C:**52–53, 67; **O:**124
Great Lakes-Saint Lawrence waterways   **G:**326; **O:**130; **S:**14–15
Great Lakes State (nickname for Michigan)   **M:**258, 259

Great Land (nickname for Alaska)   **A:**144, 145
Great London Fire (1666)   **L:**298
Great Migration, The (book by Walter Dean Myers)
   picture(s) **C:**247
Great Mogul (diamond)
   picture(s) **D:**146
Great Mosque (Córdoba, Spain)   **S:**382–83
   picture(s) **I:**351; **S:**382
Great Mosque (Damascus, Syria)   **I:**356
Great Mosque (temple that encloses the Kaaba in
   Mecca)   **M:**199
   picture(s) **I:**352
Great Northern War (1699–1721)   **F:**460
Great Observatories   **O:**10–11; **T:**61
Great October Socialist Revolution, Day of the   **H:**156
Great Palace (Moscow, Russia)   **M:**466
Great Plains (North America)   **U:**81
   agriculture **N:**300
   Canada **C:**54
   Colorado **C:**430, 432
   Kansas **K:**178
   Montana **M:**428
   Nebraska **N:**82, 84
   New Mexico **N:**182
   overland trails **O:**267–83
   pioneer life **P:**254
   prairies **P:**426
   South Dakota **S:**312, 314–15
   Texas **T:**126
   westward movement **W:**143–44
   picture(s) **N:**284, 288
Great Pocomoke Swamp (Delaware)   **D:**91
Great Proletarian Cultural Revolution *see* Cultural Revolution
   (1966–1969, China)
Great Pyramid of Cheops (Giza, Egypt)   **A:**222; **E:**111, 227;
   W:216–17
   picture(s) **B:**394
Great Quillow, The (by James Thurber)
   excerpt from **T:**188
Great Railroad Strike (1877)
   picture(s) **L:**13
Great Red Spot (on Jupiter)   **J:**160, 161; **P:**279
Great Rift Valley (Africa)   **A:**48
   Ethiopia **E:**298
   Kenya **K:**230–31
   lakes of the world **L:**33
   Malawi **M:**52
   mountain formation **M:**505
   Tanzania **T:**17
   Uganda **U:**5
   volcanoes **V:**386
Great Saint Bernard Pass (Swiss Alps)   **A:**194b
   Hospice of Saint Bernard (early inn) **H:**258–59
Great Salt Flats (Colombia)
   picture(s) **G:**102; **S:**22
Great Salt Lake (Utah)   **L:**24, 28; **U:**247, 248
   brine shrimp live in the lake **C:**591
   picture(s) **L:**26
Great Salt Lake Desert (Utah)   **U:**244
Great Sand Dunes National Monument (Colorado)   **C:**438
Great Schism (division of the Christian Church)   **E:**45
   Hus, Jan **H:**306
   Patriarch of Constantinople excommunicated **R:**285
Great Seal of the United States   **G:**329
Great Serpent Mound (Ohio)   **O:**68
   picture(s) **O:**61
Great Slave Lake (northwest Canada)   **N:**340
   Mackenzie's explorations **M:**5
Great Slave Railway (Alberta)   **A:**170
Great Smoky Mountains (eastern United States)   **T:**74
   picture(s) **N:**286, 309; **T:**75, 77
Great Smoky Mountains National Park   **N:**314; **T:**82
   picture(s) **N:**49; **T:**82
Great Society (program of President Johnson)   **J:**123; **U:**200
Great Spiral Galaxy (in Andromeda)   **U:**214, 217

Greece, literature of (cont.)
    oratory **O:**190
    poets and playwrights in ancient Greece **A:**230
Greek Catholic (Uniate) Church B:128; **U:**8
Greek fire (Byzantine weapon) **B:**495
Greek language *see* Greece, language of
Greek literature *see* Greece, literature of
Greek mythology G:360–69
    giants **G:**201
    Iliad (by Homer) **I:**61
    Odyssey **O:**51–52
    Olympic Games **O:**102
    Theogony **M:**568–69
    Trojan War **T:**316
    picture(s)
        Athena **M:**567
        Poseidon **M:**566
Greek Orthodox Church G:332
    hymns **H:**321
    picture(s)
        clergyman carrying cross **P:**40d
        dignitary **M:**299
Greek philosophy P:189–90
Greek Revival (in American architecture) **U:**129
Greeks in America
    picture(s) **M:**263
Greeley (Colorado) **C:**439–40
Greeley, Horace (American editor) **N:**162
Green (color) **C:**424–25, 429
Green (of a golf course) **G:**253, 255
Green, Andy (American automobile racer) **A:**538
Green, Hetty (American financier) **N:**178
Green Acres program (for land conservation) **N:**168
Green algae A:180; **P:**299, 300
    picture(s) **A:**180
Green almond *see* Pistachio
Greenaway, Kate (English illustrator and watercolorist) **G:**370; **I:**82
    illustration of children's books **C:**233
    Kate Greenaway Medal **C:**240
    picture(s)
        illustration **G:**370; **I:**81
Greenback-Labor Party (in the United States) **H:**70–71
    Cooper, Peter **C:**543
    history of the labor movement **L:**17
Green Bay (Wisconsin) **W:**205
Greenbelt (Maryland)
    picture(s)
        Goddard Space Flight Center **M:**127
Green Berets (members of United States Army Special Forces) **U:**107
Greenberg, Hank (American baseball player) **B:**88–89
    picture(s) **B:**89
Greenbottle fly
    picture(s) **I:**248
Green card *see* Identification card
Green Coca-Cola Bottles (painting by Warhol)
    picture(s) **P:**31
Greene, Freddie (American guitarist) **G:**412
Greene, Graham (English writer) **G:**370
    English literature, history of **E:**290; **N:**363
    picture(s) **E:**290
Greene, Nathanael (American Revolutionary War officer) **R:**199, 207
    Greensboro (North Carolina) named for him **N:**315
Greene, Robert (English writer) **E:**273
Greeneville (Tennessee, home of Andrew Johnson) **J:**116–17
Greenfield, Eloise (American poet) **C:**231
Greenfield Village (Dearborn, Michigan) **M:**262, 265
    museums **M:**525
Green Gables (house, Prince Edward Island)
    picture(s) **P:**465
Greenhouse (glass or plastic structure)
    botanical gardens **B:**342

Greenhouse effect (in the atmosphere) **C:**364; **E:**219–20
    changing biomes **B:**210
    fire and the environment **F:**144
    Ice Age return might be prevented **I:**16
    ice sheets could melt **G:**225
    Is the earth's atmosphere warming? **A:**482
    leaves help determine global climate patterns **L:**118
    rain forest destruction **E:**300–301
Greenland G:371–74a
    Arctic region **A:**386c
    Danish overseas region **D:**110, 111, 113
    Ericson, Leif **E:**307–8
    Eric the Red **E:**308; **V:**342
    Eskimos (Inuit) **E:**316–21
    glaciers **G:**223–24
    icebergs **I:**17, 18
    ice sheet depths **I:**5
    Peary, Robert E. **P:**117
Greenland Current I:18, 35
Green manure F:97; **S:**236
Green Mountain Boys (local militia in colonial times) **V:**318
    Allen, Ethan, was leader **A:**189
    Revolutionary War **R:**199
Green Mountain National Forest (Vermont)
    ski area **V:**316
Green Mountains (Vermont) **N:**285; **V:**309
Green Mountain State (nickname for Vermont) **V:**307
Green olives O:101
Greenough, Horatio (American sculptor)
    picture(s)
        statue of George Washington **U:**128
Green revolution (development of high-yielding cereal grains) **F:**351; **W:**157–58
Green River (North America) **W:**327
    picture(s) **N:**283
Greens (German peace party) **P:**106
Greensboro (North Carolina) **N:**315, 321
    African American civil rights **A:**79n
Green Still Life (painting by Picasso)
    picture(s) **P:**31
Green tea T:35
Green turtles T:357, 358
Greenville (Mississippi) **M:**359
Greenville (South Carolina) **S:**301, 306
Greenville, Treaty of (1795) **O:**73
Greenwich meridian *see* Prime meridian
Greenwich Observatory (England) **G:**374b
    prime meridian **L:**80
Greeting cards G:374b–376
    Christmas **C:**298
    New Year good wishes **N:**209
    valentines **V:**266–68
    picture(s)
        commercial art **C:**458
Greetings (in etiquette) **E:**337
Gregg, John Robert (Irish-American inventor of Gregg shorthand system) **S:**160
Gregorian calendar C:15, 16
    Gregory XIII **G:**377
    religious holidays **R:**153
Gregorian chants
    hymns **H:**321–22
    Middle Ages **M:**296
Gregory (antipope) **R:**290
Gregory, Lady Augusta (Irish playwright) **D:**302; **I:**326–27
    Yeats and Lady Gregory **Y:**344
Gregory VIII (antipope) **R:**290
Gregory I, Saint (pope, "Gregory the Great") **C:**289; **R:**290
    Middle Ages, music of **M:**296
Gregory II, Saint (pope) **R:**290
Gregory III, Saint (pope) **R:**290
Gregory IV (pope) **R:**290
Gregory V (pope) **R:**290
Gregory VI (pope) **R:**290

Gregory VII, Saint (pope, real name Hildebrand) G:377; R:290
  church reforms R:285
  Holy Roman Empire H:162
Gregory VIII (pope) R:291
Gregory IX (pope) R:291
  Jewish persecution J:107
Gregory X (pope) R:291
Gregory XI (pope) R:291
Gregory XII (pope) R:291
Gregory XIII (pope) G:377; R:291
  calendar C:15
Gregory XIV (pope) R:291
Gregory XV (pope) R:291
Gregory XVI (pope) R:291
Gregory of Nazianzus, Saint C:289
Gregory of Nyssa, Saint C:289
Gregory the Great (pope) see Gregory I, Saint
Greiner, Ludwig (German-born American doll maker) D:267
Grenada G:378–79; L:50
  Caribbean Sea and islands C:114, 115
  picture(s)
    flag F:240
    Saint George's C:113
Grenadines (group of islands in the Caribbean)
  Grenada G:378
  Saint Vincent and the Grenadines S:19–20
Grendel (monster in Beowulf) B:144b; E:268; F:12
Grenoble (France)
  Olympic Games (1968) O:113
Grenville (Greynnville), Sir Richard (English naval officer)
  Virginia colony T:165
Grethel, Gammer (Grimm brothers' storyteller) F:21
Gretzky, Wayne (Canadian hockey player) I:31–32
Grevy's zebra H:244
Grey, Lady Jane (queen of England for 9 days)
  England, history of E:243
Grey Cup (Canadian football championship) C:69
Greyhound (dog) D:246, 247
  dog racing R:33
  picture(s) D:244
Greylag geese (ancestors of domesticated geese) P:417
Greylock, Mount (Massachusetts) M:138
Gridiron (name for a football field) F:353
Gridley, Charles V. (American naval captain) S:393
Grids, geographic (on maps and globes) M:92, 94
Griebling, Otto (German-born American clown) C:310
Grieg, Edvard (Norwegian composer) G:380
Grievance procedure (in labor-management relations) L:8
Griffey, Ken, Jr. (American baseball player)
  picture(s) B:94
Griffin, Donald R. (American scientist) B:103
Griffin, Walter Burley (American architect) C:89
Griffins (monsters in Greek mythology) G:364
  picture(s) G:364
Griffith, D. W. (American motion picture director and
    producer) M:488, 494
Griffith, Emily (American teacher) C:442–43
Griffith Joyner, Florence (American track star) O:118; T:263
Griffiths, Martha (American politician) W:213
Grille (for sending secret messages) C:395
Grilling (method of cooking) C:533
Grillparzer, Franz (Austrian dramatist) A:522; G:179
Grimaldi, Joey (British comic singer and mime) C:386
Grimaldi family (rulers of Monaco) M:409–10
Grimké, Sarah and Angelina (American abolitionists and
    women's rights advocates) W:214
Grimm, Jacob and Wilhelm (German scholars and collectors of
    fairy tales) G:380–90
  children's literature C:232
  folklore collections F:312
  German literature G:179
  "Hansel and Gretel" G:384–90
  history of the fairy tale F:20, 113
  "Rapunzel" G:382–84

"The Shoemaker and the Elves" G:381–82
  short stories S:161
  storytelling S:463–64
Grimmelshausen, Hans von (German writer) G:177
Grinch, the (fictional character)
  picture(s) S:128
Grinding and polishing G:391–93
  diamonds and diamond dust D:145
  optical glass O:185
  tools T:232
Grinkov, Sergei (Russian figure skater) O:119
  picture(s) I:41
Grinnell, George Bird (American conservationist) G:220
Griots (African performers) F:320–21
Grippe see Influenza
Grisi, Carlotta (Italian ballerina) B:27; D:25
Grissom, Gus (Virgil Ivan Grissom) (American astronaut) S:346
  picture(s) S:347
Griswold v. Connecticut (1965) D:288; W:213
Grit numbers (of sandpaper) G:391
Grizzly bears B:106–7; M:70
  Yellowstone National Park Y:345
Grocery shopping see Food shopping
Groined vault (in architecture) A:374
Groningen (the Netherlands) N:120c
Grooming (care of a horse) H:228
Gropius, Walter (American architect)
  architecture, history of A:382, 383
  Bauhaus founded by G:173
  picture(s)
    Fagus shoe factory G:173
Groseillers, Médart Chouart, Sieur de (French explorer) F:520,
    522; S:14
Gros Morne National Park (Newfoundland) N:145
Gros Piton (volcano, Saint Lucia) S:17
Gross, Michael (German swimmer) S:538
  picture(s) S:538
Grossglockner (highest mountain in Austria) A:520
  picture(s) A:518
Gross income B:471
Gross national product (GNP) E:62; G:100
  depressions and recessions D:121
Grossularite (gem mineral) G:75
Gros Ventres (Indians of North America) I:180
Grotesque clown C:387
Grotesquerie (Italian Renaissance furniture designs) D:77
Grotius, Hugo (Dutch scholar) P:105
Groton (Massachusetts)
  picture(s)
    Congregational church P:492
Ground (acid-resisting substance used in etching) E:326,
    327; G:305
Ground beetle
  picture(s) B:126
Ground-controlled approach (GCA) (radar technique in
    aviation) A:39
Groundfish (bottomfish) F:217
Groundhog Day F:74; H:158
Groundhogs (woodchucks) (rodents) R:273–74
  body changes in hibernation H:118
  table(s)
    body changes in hibernation H:119
Grounding (in electricity) T:187
Ground-launched cruise missiles (GLCM) M:349
Ground nuts see Peanuts
Grounds (for divorce) D:230
Ground speed (of an airplane) A:118
Ground squirrels R:273
  hibernation H:118
  table(s)
    hibernation H:119
Ground stroke (in tennis) T:88, 91
Groundwater W:54, 56–57
  drought D:328

Groundwater (cont.)
  lake basins, formation of **L:**25
  mines require constant pumping **M:**322
  Nebraska **N:**86, 95
  pollution of **H:**72; **W:**65, 69
  wells **W:**121, 122
Groundwood papers **P:**56
Ground zero (target area for a nuclear weapon) **N:**375
Group (Air Force unit) **U:**112
Group counseling **G:**402
Groupers (fish) **F:**186, 200, 219
Group homes (for foster care of children) **F:**390
Group life insurance see Insurance, group life
Group of seven (Canadian painters) **C:**83
Group therapy (for the mentally ill) **M:**228
Grouse (game birds)
  ruffed grouse **A:**286; **B:**238
  picture(s)
    ruffed grouse is state bird of Pennsylvania **P:**127
    sage grouse **B:**223, 224
    sharp-tailed grouse is provincial bird of
      Saskatchewan **S:**42
Grove, Robert Moses "Lefty" (American baseball player) **B:**89
  picture(s) **B:**89
Growing seasons
  forest growth **F:**373
  length of summer days offsets short growing season in
    Alaska **A:**147
  vegetables **V:**286–94
Growling (of dogs) **D:**247
Growth **L:**196
  bones usually stop growing during the teen years **S:**184a
  child development **C:**223–26
  human growth hormone produced by gene splicing **G:**91
  organisms grow and develop **B:**194
  plant growth patterns **K:**256; **P:**312–13
Growth hormone see Human growth hormone
Growth rings (of trees) **W:**225
Gruber, Edmund L. (American officer) **N:**25
Gruber, Franz (Austrian organist, composer of "Silent Night,
  Holy Night") **C:**118
Grubs (larvae)
  plant pests **P:**286, 287
Grundtvig, Nikolai F. S. (Danish educator and poet) **S:**58g
Grünewald, Matthias (German painter) **G:**170
  picture(s)
    Isenheim altarpiece (painting) **G:**170
Grunion (fish) **F:**195
Gryphius, Andreas (German dramatist) **G:**177
Guadalajara (Mexico) **M:**247
Guadalcanal (Pacific island) **P:**9; **S:**252, 253
  battle of (1942) **W:**295
Guadalquivir River (Spain) **R:**242; **S:**375
Guadalupe, Basilica of the Virgin of (shrine near Mexico City,
  Mexico) **M:**244; **R:**155
Guadalupe, Day of Our Lady of see Our Lady of Guadalupe, Day
  of
Guadalupe fur seals **F:**518
Guadalupe Hidalgo, Treaty of (1848) **M:**239b; **U:**184
  Arizona **A:**412
  Mexican cession of territory to United States **T:**111
  New Mexico **N:**193
  Polk, James K. **P:**377
Guadalupe Mountains (New Mexico–Texas) **T:**126, 132
  Carlsbad Caverns **C:**155
Guadarrama, Sierra de (Spain) **S:**375
Guadeloupe (Caribbean islands) **C:**114; **L:**50
Guaíra Falls (Brazil–Paraguay) **W:**62, 63
Guam **P:**9; **T:**113, 115; **U:**93
Guanabara Bay (Rio de Janeiro, Brazil)
  picture(s) **B:**379
Guanacos (hoofed mammals) **H:**212; **S:**283
  picture(s) **H:**213
Guangzhou (China) see Canton

Guano (fertilizer) **P:**163
  found in caves **C:**158
  pelicans **P:**120
Guano Act (United States, 1856) **T:**114–15
Guantánamo (Cuba)
  United States Naval Base **C:**599; **T:**113
Guaraní (Indians of South America) **I:**197–98
  language **S:**288
  Paraguay **P:**62, 65
Guaranty Building (Buffalo, New York) **A:**381
Guard cells (of leaves) **L:**113, 116; **P:**306
Guard dogs **D:**241
Guard hair (of furs) **F:**501
Guardi, Francesco (Italian painter) **I:**402
Guardia, Tomás (Costa Rican dictator) **C:**559
Guards (in basketball) **B:**95b
Guarino of Verona (Italian scholar) **H:**283
Guarneri family (violin-makers) **B:**71; **V:**344
Guast, Pierre du see Monts, Pierre du Guast
Guatemala **G:**394–98
  Belize boundary dispute **B:**138
  Central America **C:**172–75
  folk dance **D:**30
  Indians, American **I:**194–95
  lakes **L:**29
  Latin America **L:**48, 49, 50, 56
  Maya, attacks on **M:**187
  slavery in recent times **S:**197
  picture(s)
    Antigua **G:**397
    banana harvesting **G:**398
    boys playing soccer **G:**397
    coffee beans drying **G:**398
    flag **F:**241
    Guatemala City **G:**398
    inactive volcano **G:**397
    religious procession **L:**51
    special stamp **S:**421
    weaving **W:**96
Guatemala City (capital of Guatemala) **G:**395, 396
  picture(s) **C:**172; **G:**398
Guava (tropical fruit) **M:**78
Guayana Highlands (South America) see Guiana Highlands
Guayaquil (Ecuador) **E:**64, 67
Guayas (river system in Ecuador) **E:**66
Guaymí Indians (of Panama) **P:**44
Guayule (wild bush that produces rubber) **R:**345
Gubarev, Aleksei (Soviet cosmonaut) **S:**348
Gudea (king of Sumer) **A:**235
  picture(s)
    statue **A:**234
Guelphs and Ghibellines (Italian political parties) **P:**369
  Holy Roman Empire **H:**162
Guenons (monkeys) **M:**422
Guericke, Otto von (German physicist) **S:**71; **V:**265
Guéridon, Le (The Pedestal Table) (painting by Braque)
  picture(s) **B:**371
Guernica (mural by Picasso) **A:**438e; **P:**243–44; **S:**387
  picture(s) **S:**387
Guernsey (breed of dairy cattle) **C:**154
  picture(s) **C:**153; **D:**5
Guernsey (one of the Channel Islands, Great Britain) **I:**363
Guerrero, Vicente (Mexican patriot) **M:**249
Guerrière (British naval vessel) **W:**10
  picture(s) **W:**9
Guerrilla warfare (fought by irregular troops) **G:**399–400
  American tactics during Revolutionary War **R:**207
  Colombia **C:**408
  Indochina War **V:**335
  underground movements **U:**13
  Vietnam War **V:**336
Guess, George see Sequoya
Guessing games
  charades **C:**186–87
Guess Who's Coming to Dinner? (motion picture, 1967) **M:**495

PHOTO CREDITS

The following list credits the sources of photos used in THE NEW BOOK OF KNOWLEDGE. Credits are listed, by page, photo by photo—left to right, top to bottom. Wherever appropriate, the name of the photographer has been listed with the source, the two being separated by a dash. When two or more photos by different photographers appear on one page, their credits are separated by semicolons.